Classic Papers in Natural Resource Economics Revisited

Classic Papers in Natural Resource Economics Revisited is the first attempt to bring together a selection of classic papers in natural resource economics, alongside reflections by highly regarded professionals about how these papers have impacted the field. The seven papers included in this volume are grouped into five sections, representing the five core areas in natural resource economics: the intertemporal problem; externalities and market failure; property rights, institutions and public choice; the economics of exhaustible resources; and renewable resources. The seven papers are written by distinguished economists, five of them Nobelists. The papers, originally published between 1960 and 2000, addressed key issues in resource production, pricing, consumption, planning, management and policy. The original insights, fresh perspectives and bold vision embodied in these papers had a profound influence on the readership and they became classics in the field. This is the first attempt to publish original commentaries from a diverse group of scholars to identify, probe and analyse the ways in which these papers have impacted and shaped the discourse in natural resource economics. Although directed primarily at an academic audience, this book should also be of great appeal to researchers, policy analysts and natural resource professionals, in general.

This book was published as a series of symposia in the *Journal of Natural Resources Policy Research*.

Chennat Gopalakrishnan is Professor (Emeritus) of Natural Resource Economics at the University of Hawaii, USA. He has published eight books and approximately 120 journal articles and technical papers on current and emerging issues in natural resource economics and policy. He is the Editor-In-Chief of the *Journal of Natural Resources Policy Research*.

Classic Papers in Natural Resource Economics Revisited

Edited by
Chennat Gopalakrishnan

Routledge
Taylor & Francis Group

LONDON AND NEW YORK

First published 2016
by Routledge

2 Park Square, Milton Park, Abingdon, Oxfordshire OX14 4RN
711 Third Avenue, New York, NY 10017

Routledge is an imprint of the Taylor & Francis Group, an informa business

First issued in paperback 2017

British Library Cataloguing in Publication Data
A catalogue record for this book is available from the British Library

ISBN 13: 978-1-138-90579-5 (hbk)
ISBN 13: 978-1-138-50245-1 (pbk)

Typeset in Times New Roman
by RefineCatch Limited, Bungay, Suffolk

Publisher's Note
The publisher accepts responsibility for any inconsistencies that may have
arisen during the conversion of this book from journal articles to book chapters,
namely the possible inclusion of journal terminology.

Disclaimer
Every effort has been made to contact copyright holders for their permission to
reprint material in this book. The publishers would be grateful to hear from any
copyright holder who is not here acknowledged and will undertake to rectify
any errors or omissions in future editions of this book.

Contents

CONTENTS

Part II: Externalities and Market Failure – Ronald H. Coase

Part III: Property Rights, Institutions and Public Choice – Garrett J. Hardin and Elinor Ostrom

CONTENTS

Part IV: The Economics of Exhaustible Resources – William Nordhaus and Robert Solow

CONTENTS

Section V: Renewable Resources – Paul A. Samuelson

Citation Information

The following chapters, except chapter 1, were originally published in the *Journal of Natural Resources Policy Research*, volume 6, issue 1 (January 2014). When citing this material, please use the original page numbering for each article, as follows:

Chapter 1
Uncertainty and the Evaluation of Public Investment Decisions
Kenneth J. Arrow and Robert C. Lind
Originally published in: *American Economic Review*, 60: 364–378. Appearing in: *Journal of Natural Resources Policy Research*, volume 6, issue 1 (January 2014)
pp. 29–44

Chapter 2
The relevance and the limits of the Arrow-Lind Theorem
Luc Baumstark and Christian Gollier
Journal of Natural Resources Policy Research, volume 6, issue 1 (January 2014)
pp. 45–49

Chapter 3
A reconsideration of Arrow-Lind: risk aversion, risk sharing, and agent choice
Eric Fesselmeyer, Leonard J. Mirman and Marc Santugini
Journal of Natural Resources Policy Research, volume 6, issue 1 (January 2014)
pp. 51–56

Chapter 4
Evaluating uncertain public projects with rival and non-rival benefits
Bram Gallagher and Arthur Snow
Journal of Natural Resources Policy Research, volume 6, issue 1 (January 2014)
pp. 57–63

Chapter 5
Probing the limits of risk-neutral government
Alan Randall
Journal of Natural Resources Policy Research, volume 6, issue 1 (January 2014)
pp 64–69

Chapter 6
Are we in this together? Risk bearing and collective action
Carlisle Ford Runge and Justin Andrew Johnson
Journal of Natural Resources Policy Research, volume 6, issue 1 (January 2014)
pp 71–76

Chapter 7
Evaluation of public investments and individual discounting
Mario Tirelli
Journal of Natural Resources Policy Research, volume 6, issue 1 (January 2014)
pp 77–84

Chapter 8
Rebutting Arrow and Lind: why governments should use market rates for discounting
Deborah Lucas
Journal of Natural Resources Policy Research, volume 6, issue 1 (January 2014)
pp. 85–91

Chapter 9
Revisiting Arrow-Lind: Managing Sovereign Disaster Risk
Reinhard Mechler and Stefan Hochrainer-Stigler
Journal of Natural Resources Policy Research, volume 6, issue 1 (January 2014)
pp. 93–100

Chapter 10
Size matters: capital market size and risk-return profiles
Keiran Sharpe and Massimiliano Tani
Journal of Natural Resources Policy Research, volume 6, issue 1 (January 2014)
pp. 101–107

Chapter 11
Microeconomic foundations of bailouts
Marian Moszoro
Journal of Natural Resources Policy Research, volume 6, issue 1 (January 2014)
pp. 109–112

The following chapters, except chapter 12, were originally published in the *Journal of Natural Resources Policy Research*, volume 5, issue 4 (October 2013). When citing this material, please use the original page numbering for each article, as follows:

Chapter 12
The Problem of Social Cost
Ronald H. Coase
For full text, see: *Journal of Law and Economics*, 3 (1960), pp. 1–44.

Chapter 13

Battles lost and wars won: reflections on 'The Problem of Social Cost'
Mary M. Shirley
Journal of Natural Resources Policy Research, volume 5, issue 4 (October 2013)
pp. 243–247

Chapter 14

The importance of being misunderstood: the Coase theorem and the legacy of 'The Problem of Social Cost'
Steven G. Medema
Journal of Natural Resources Policy Research, volume 5, issue 4 (October 2013)
pp. 249–253

Chapter 15

Infringement as nuisance: intellectual property rights and The Problem of Social Cost
Paul J. Heald
Journal of Natural Resources Policy Research, volume 5, issue 4 (October 2013)
pp. 255–260

Chapter 16

About some distortions in the interpretation of 'the problem of social cost'
Claude Ménard
Journal of Natural Resources Policy Research, volume 5, issue 4 (October 2013)
pp. 261–265

Chapter 17

The successes and failures of Professor Coase
Ning Wang
Journal of Natural Resources Policy Research, volume 5, issue 4 (October 2013)
pp. 267–271

The following chapters, except chapter 18, were originally published in the *Journal of Natural Resources Policy Research*, volume 1, issue 3 (July 2009). When citing this material, please use the original page numbering for each article, as follows:

Chapter 18

The Tragedy of the Commons
Garrett Hardin
Originally published in: *Science*, volume 162, No. 3859 (13 December 1968), pp. 1243–1248. Appearing in: *Journal of Natural Resources Policy Research*, volume 1, issue 3 (July 2009) pp. 243–253

Chapter 19

The Core Challenges of Moving Beyond Garrett Hardin
Xavier Basurto & Elinor Ostrom
Journal of Natural Resources Policy Research, volume 1, issue 3 (July 2009)
pp. 255–259

Chapter 20

Revising the Commons Paradigm
Fikret Berkes
Journal of Natural Resources Policy Research, volume 1, issue 3 (July 2009)
pp. 261–264

Chapter 21

Hardin's Brilliant Tragedy and a Non-Sequitur Response
Thráinn Eggertsson
Journal of Natural Resources Policy Research, volume 1, issue 3 (July 2009)
pp. 265–268

Chapter 22

Free Parking at Christmas Is Not a Tragedy of the Commons
William A. Fischel
Journal of Natural Resources Policy Research, volume 1, issue 3 (July 2009)
pp. 269–273

Chapter 23

Guarding the Guardians: Enforcement in the Commons
C. Ford Runge
Journal of Natural Resources Policy Research, volume 1, issue 3 (July 2009)
pp. 275–281

Chapter 24

From 'Tragedy' to Commons: How Hardin's Mistake Might Save the World
Peter A. Walker
Journal of Natural Resources Policy Research, volume 1, issue 3 (July 2009)
pp. 283–286

The following chapters, except chapter 25, were originally published in the *Journal of Natural Resources Policy Research*, volume 6, issue 4 (October 2014). When citing this material, please use the original page numbering for each article, as follows:

Chapter 25

Collective action and the evolution of social norms
Elinor Ostrom
Originally published in: *Journal of Economic Perspectives*, 14 (3) (Summer 2000)
pp. 137–158. Appearing in: *Journal of Natural Resources Policy Research*, volume 6, issue 4 (October 2014) pp. 235–252

Chapter 26

The collective action theory path to contextual analysis
Paul Dragos Aligica and Filippo Sabetti
Journal of Natural Resources Policy Research, volume 6, issue 4 (October 2014)
pp. 253–258

Chapter 27
Contextualizing the influence of social norms, collective action on social-ecological systems
Tom P. Evans and Daniel H. Cole
Journal of Natural Resources Policy Research, volume 6, issue 4 (October 2014)
pp. 259–264

Chapter 28
Collective Action and the Evolution of Social Norms: the principled optimism of Elinor Ostrom
Matthew R. Auer
Journal of Natural Resources Policy Research, volume 6, issue 4 (October 2014)
pp. 265–271

Chapter 29
Crossing disciplinary boundaries
L. Schroeder
Journal of Natural Resources Policy Research, volume 6, issue 4 (October 2014)
pp. 273–277

Chapter 30
Elinor Ostrom's challenge for laboratory experiments
Rick K. Wilson
Journal of Natural Resources Policy Research, volume 6, issue 4 (October 2014)
pp. 279–283

Chapter 31
The evolution of social norms in conflict resolution
Lisa Blomgren Amsler
Journal of Natural Resources Policy Research, volume 6, issue 4 (October 2014)
pp. 285–290

Chapter 32
The evolution of elite and societal norms pertaining to the emergence of federal-tribal co-management of natural resources
Shane Day
Journal of Natural Resources Policy Research, volume 6, issue 4 (October 2014)
pp. 291–296

The following chapters, except chapter 33, were originally published in the *Journal of Natural Resources Policy Research*, volume 7, issues 2–3 (April–July 2015). When citing this material, please use the original page numbering for each article, as follows:

Chapter 33
The Allocation of Energy Resources
William Nordhaus
For full text, see: *Brookings Papers*, 3 (1973, pp. 529–576)

The following chapters, except chapter 42, were originally published in the *Journal of Natural Resources Policy Research*, volume 1, issue 1 (January 2009). When citing this material, please use the original page numbering for each article, as follows:

Chapter 42

The Economics of Resources or the Resources of Economics
Robert M. Solow
Originally published in: *The American Economic Review*, volume 64, no. 2, Papers and Proceedings of the Eighty-sixth Annual Meeting of the American Economic Association (May, 1974), pp. 1–14. Appearing in: *Journal of Natural Resources Policy Research*, volume 1, issue 1 (January 2009) pp. 69–82

Chapter 43

Reflections on Solow's The Economics of Resources or the Resources of Economics
Peter Berck
Journal of Natural Resources Policy Research, volume 1, issue 1 (January 2009) pp. 83–86

Chapter 44

What Does the Empirical Work Inspired by Solow's The Economics of Resources or the Resources of Economics *Tell Us?*
Robert Halvorsen
Journal of Natural Resources Policy Research, volume 1, issue 1 (January 2009) pp. 87–90

Chapter 45

What Would Solow Say?
John M. Hartwick
Journal of Natural Resources Policy Research, volume 1, issue 1 (January 2009) pp. 91–96

Chapter 46

Reflections on Solow's 1974 Richard T. Ely Address
Alan Randall
Journal of Natural Resources Policy Research, volume 1, issue 1 (January 2009) pp. 97–101

Chapter 47

The Economics of Resources and the Economics of Climate
R. David Simpson
Journal of Natural Resources Policy Research, Vol. 1, issue 1 (January 2009) pp 103–106

Chapter 48

Celebrating Solow: Lessons from Natural Resource Economics for Environmental Policy
V. Kerry Smith
Journal of Natural Resources Policy Research, volume 1, issue 1 (January 2009) pp. 107–113

CITATION INFORMATION

The following chapters, except chapter 49, were originally published in the *Journal of Natural Resources Policy Research*, volume 4, issues 3 (July 2012). When citing this material, please use the original page numbering for each article, as follows:

Chapter 49

Economics of Forestry in an Evolving Society
Paul A. Samuelson
Originally published in: *Economic Inquiry,* 14: 466–492. Appearing in: *Journal of Natural Resources Policy Research*, volume 4, issues 3 (July 2012) pp. 173–195

Chapter 50

Samuelson's Economics of Forestry in an Evolving Society: *Still an Important and Relevant Article Thirty Six Years Later*
Gregory S. Amacher
Journal of Natural Resources Policy Research, volume 4, issues 3 (July 2012) pp. 197–201

Chapter 51

Reflections on Samuelson's Economics of Forestry in an Evolving Society
Peter Berck & Lunyu Xie
Journal of Natural Resources Policy Research, volume 4, issues 3 (July 2012) pp 203–207

Chapter 52

Samuelson and 21st Century Tropical Forest Economics
Elizabeth J. Z. Robinson & Heidi J. Albers
Journal of Natural Resources Policy Research, volume 4, issues 3 (July 2012) pp. 209–213

Chapter 53

Putting Samuelson's Economics of Forestry *into Context: The Limits of Forest Economics in Policy Debates*
David H. Newman & John E. Wagner
Journal of Natural Resources Policy Research, volume 4, issues 3 (July 2012) pp. 215–218

Chapter 54

Samuelson on Forest Economics: An Inadvertent Tribute to Faustmann, and a Few Others
Colin Price
Journal of Natural Resources Policy Research, volume 4, issues 3 (July 2012) pp. 219–222

Chapter 55

Thoughts on Paul Samuelson's Classic, Economics of Forestry in an Evolving Society
Roger A. Sedjo
Journal of Natural Resources Policy Research, volume 4, issues 3 (July 2012) pp. 223–225

For any permission-related enquiries please visit:
http://www.tandfonline.com/page/help/permissions

List of Contributors

Frank Ackerman, Synapse Energy Economics Inc., & Massachusetts Institute of Technology, USA

Heidi Albers, Oregon State University, USA & Environment for Development Tanzania, USA & Tanzania

Paul D. Aligica, George Mason University, USA

Gregory Amacher, Virginia Tech, USA

Lisa B. Amsler, Indiana University Bloomington, USA

Kenneth J. Arrow, Stanford University, USA

Matthew R. Auer, Bates College, USA

Xavier Basurto, Duke University, USA

Luc Baumstark, Universite Lumiere, France

Peter Berck, University of California Berkeley, USA

Fikret Berkes, University of Manitoba, Canada

Ronald H. Coase (deceased), (formerly with) University of Chicago, USA

Daniel H. Cole, Indiana University Bloomington, USA

Shane Day, University of New Mexico, USA

Thráinn Eggertsson, New York University, USA

Tom P. Evans, Indiana University Bloomington, USA

John Feddersen, Aurora Energy Research, UK

Eric Fesselmeyer, National University of Singapore, Singapore

William A. Fischel, Dartmouth College, USA

Roger Fouquet, Grantham Research Institute on Climate Change and the Environment, London School of Economics and Political Science (LSE), UK

Isabel Galiana, McGill University, Canada

Bram Gallagher, Middle Tennessee University, USA

Christian Gollier, University of Toulouse, France

Chennat Gopalakrishnan (Emeritus Professor), University of Hawaii at Manoa, USA

Florian Habermacher, Aurora Energy Research, UK

Robert Halvorsen, University of Washington, USA

Garrett J. Hardin (deceased), (formerly with) University of California – Santa Barbara, USA

John M. Hartwick, Queens University, Canada

Paul J. Heald, University of Illinois, USA; Bournemouth University & Cambridge University, UK

Stefan Hochrainer-Stigler, Vienna University of Economics and Business, Austria

Jan Imhof, Aurora Energy Research, UK

Justin A. Johnson, University of Minnesota, USA

Phoebe Koundouri, Athens University of Economics and Business & International Centre for Research on the Environment and the Economy, Greece

Robert C. Lind, (formerly with) Cornell University, USA

Deborah Lucas, Massachusetts Institute of Technology, USA

Reinhard Mechler, International Institute of Applied Systems Analysis (IIAS), Austria

Steven G. Medema, University of Colorado – Denver, USA

Claude Ménard, University of Paris, France

Leonard J. Mirman, University of Virginia, USA

Marian Moszoro, IESE Business School & Kozminski University, Poland

Gregory F. Nemet, University of Wisconsin – Madison, USA

David H. Newman, Syracuse University, USA

William Nordhaus, Yale University, USA

Elinor Ostrom (deceased), (formerly with) Indiana University – Bloomington, USA

Colin Price, UK

Alan Randall, University of Sydney, Australia

Dimitrios Reppas, International Centre for Research on the Environment and the Economy, Greece

Elizabeth J. Z. Robinson, University of Reading, UK

C. Ford Runge, University of Minnesota, USA

Filippo Sabetti, McGill University, Canada

Paul A. Samuelson, (deceased) (formerly with) Massachusetts Institute of Technology, USA

Marc Santugini, Institute of Applied Economics & CIRPEE, Canada

LIST OF CONTRIBUTORS

Larry Schroeder (Emeritus Professor), Syracuse University, USA

Roger A. Sedjo, Resources for the Future, USA

Keiran Sharpe, University of New South Wales, Australia

Mary M. Shirley, Ronald Coase Institute, USA

R. David Simpson, National Centre for Environmental Economics, USEPA, USA

V. Kerry Smith (Emeritus Professor), Arizona State University, USA

Arthur Snow, University of Georgia, USA

Robert M. Solow (Emeritus Professor), Massachusetts Institute of Technology, USA

Ioannis Souliotis, Athens University of Economics and Business, Greece & International Centre for Research on the Environment and the Economy, Greece

Massimiliano Tani, University of New South Wales, Australia

Mario Tirelli, University of Rome, Italy

Rick van der Ploeg, University of Oxford, UK & Aurora Energy Research, UK

Aviel Verbruggen, University of Antwerp, Belgium

John E. Wagner, Syracuse University, USA

Peter A. Walker, University of Oregon, USA

Ning Wang, Ronald Coase Institute, USA & Zhejiang University, China

Rick K. Wilson, Rice University, USA

Franz Wirl, University of Vienna, Austria

Lunyu Xie, University of California Berkeley, USA

Introduction: classic papers in natural resource economics revisited

Chennat Gopalakrishnan

Department of Natural Resources and Environmental Management, University of Hawaii, Honolulu, HI, USA

Natural resource economics has been a subject of serious academic inquiry for approximately a century. Arguably, Harold Hotelling's path-breaking paper titled "The Economics of Exhaustible Resources", published in 1931, in the *Journal of Political Economy* marks the beginning of natural resource economics as an academic discipline. And the last 85 years (1930–2015) have witnessed a rapid growth in the field of natural resource economics.

Classic Papers in Natural Resource Economics Revisited makes a unique contribution to the field of natural resource economics. The seven classic papers – Arrow-Lind, Coase, Hardin, Ostrom, Nordhaus, Solow and Samuelson – included in this volume attempt to capture the essence of discourse in the field in a representative fashion. These papers are written by distinguished economists, five of them Nobelists. The papers, originally published between 1960 and 2000, addressed key issues in resource production, pricing, consumption, planning, management and policy. The original insights, fresh perspectives and bold vision embodied in these papers had a profound influence on the readership and they became classics in the field.

This book represents the culmination of a 7-year effort. A total of 71 scholars from 11 countries, in 48 papers, examine, analyze, evaluate and probe the 7 classic papers included in this book in an attempt to understand why these papers have become classics in the field. In addition to economics, the contributors are drawn from other disciplines such as sociology, political science, geography, anthropology, public policy, law and more. This is the first attempt to publish original commentaries from a diverse group of scholars that explain the ways in which these papers have impacted and shaped the intellectual content of the field of natural resource economics. Although directed primarily at an academic audience, this book should also be of great appeal to researchers, policy analysts and natural resource professionals, in general.

A clear measure of the impact of these papers can be found in the number of times each paper has been cited: Hardin (1968): 24,680; Coase (1960): 24,147; Arrow & Lind (1970): 13,132; Ostrom (2000): 1,914; Solow (1974): 1,636; Nordhaus (1973): 583; and Samuelson (1976): 577[1]. In addition, the papers, over the years, have generated considerable discussion and debate in the scholarly community, profoundly influencing the discourse in the field.

The papers are grouped into five parts representing the five core areas in natural resource economics: the intertemporal problem; externalities and market failure; property rights, institutions and public choice; the economics of exhaustible resources; and the economics of renewable resources. A brief discussion of each of the seven papers included in this volume follows (for perspective, a brief review of each core area and an overview of the corresponding invited commentaries are also included in each part).

Part 1: The Intertemporal Problem

It is becoming increasingly clear that actions by the current generation in the exploitation of natural resources could result in deleterious impacts on the welfare of future generations. Examples include the rapid depletion of exhaustible natural resources leading to resource scarcity and limits to growth and a sharp decline in environmental quality due to a steep increase in carbon emissions and the discharge of environmental pollutants. Designing policies to ensure the well-being of future generations through ensuring intertemporal efficiency and intergenerational equity is thus a core area of concern in natural resource economics.

Kenneth Arrow and Robert Lind (1970) examine the issues involved in the incorporation of risk and uncertainty in public investment decisions. They argue that public projects, whose benefits are widely distributed, should be discounted at a risk-free rate, instead of at market rates, since the risks tend to be negligible when spread among a large group of stakeholders. The authors hold the view that "individual preferences are not of normative significance for government decisions and suggest that time and risk preferences relevant for government decisions should be developed as a matter of national policy", (Gopalakrishnan, 2000, p. 3). It is to be noted, however, that the focus of the paper is on traditional government spending on infrastructure projects such as roads, dams, etc., as opposed to natural and financial disasters. The paper has influenced the evaluation and the selection of interest rates for a number of major government projects globally.

Seventeen scholars in ten papers offer their thoughts and insights on the Arrow-Lind paper, taking into account the many changes that have occurred in the discourse in economics, public policy and the social sciences, since the paper's original publication. Aspects examined include the relevance and the limits of the Arrow-Lind theorem (Baumstark & Gollier); risk aversion, risk sharing and agent choice (Fesselmeyer, Mirman & Santiguini); evaluation of uncertain public projects with rival and non-rival benefits (Gallagher & Snow); the limits of risk-neutral government (Randall); risk bearing and collective actions (Runge & Johnson); evaluation of public investments and individual discounting (Tirelli); the case for governments using market rates for discounting (Lucas); managing sovereign disaster risk (Mechler & Hochrainer-Stigler); capital market size and risk-return profiles (Sharpe & Tani); and the micro-economic foundations of bailouts (Moszoro).

Part 2: Externalities and Market Failure

There is a growing body of literature in natural resource economics that points to the divergence between private costs and social costs and its impacts and implications for natural resource allocation and policy. The concept has its beginnings in early economic thought (e.g. Marshall & Pigou), followed by considerable discussion over the years, among them, Baumol, Turvey and Buchanan. The broad classifications of externalities are pecuniary, technological (production), and political externalities. Recent years have seen a remarkable increase in the exploitation of natural resources globally causing significant adverse impacts to the environment and this has led to a heightened interest in the discussion of externalities.

Ronald Coase (1960) in his paper on "The Problem of Social Cost" proposes a framework for optimal resource allocation, in the presence of externalities, without market intervention or government regulation. This involves the idea of voluntary negotiated agreements among the parties involved in a conflict or a bargaining solution. Coase argues that efficient resource allocation would result from such agreements, provided property rights are well-defined, transaction costs are negligible, parties involved are few and perfect competition prevails. This important new insight into the regulation of pollution without government control or intervention constitutes the essence of the Coase theorem and this has exerted a profound influence on conflict resolution policy in the context of natural resources.

Five scholars have examined in five papers the impact and implications of the Coase paper from multiple perspectives: the core argument, the controversies and the transformative power of the paper (Shirley); the Coase theorem and the legacy of the Coase paper (Medema); infringement as nuisance: a study of intellectual property rights as viewed by Coase (Heald); distortions in the interpretation of 'the problem of social cost' (Ménard); and an assessment of the 'successes and failures of Coase' (Wang).

Part 3: Property Rights, Institutions and Public Choice

Property rights, institutions and public choice are central to the discussion on the ownership, allocation and use of natural resources. A well-defined property right should possess four characteristics: universality, exclusivity, transferability and enforceability. Institutions and public choice are also equally important in the allocation and management of natural resources. The term "institutions" has been variously defined. Ruttan and Hayami (1984) regard "institutions (as) the rules of a society or of organizations that facilitate coordination among people by helping them form expectations which each person can reasonably hold in dealing with others". Public choice refers to the application of economics to political decision-making.

A rather dramatic exposition of the "perils" of common ownership, as exemplified by the English grazing commons, is contained in Garrett Hardin's (1968) paper, "The Tragedy of the Commons". The tragedy he alludes to in the title would manifest itself in the form of resource degradation, congestion externalities, environmental pollution and rent dissipation on account of unbridled overgrazing of the pastures. Hardin's analysis has some major limitations. The assertion that a herdsman would increase the size of his herd without limit doesn't square with the facts. Private costs associated with each addition would clearly set the limit to such expansion. Furthermore, his assumption that common land was subject to open access – unlimited entry – is also historically inaccurate. Nevertheless, Hardin's essay conveys a powerful message for resource conservation.

Original commentaries by seven scholars, in six papers, on the legacy of the Hardin paper are included. The issues examined are: the core challenges of moving beyond Garrett Hardin (Basurto & Ostrom); revising the commons paradigm (Berkes); the underpinnings of the Hardin paper (Eggertsson); an elaboration and clarification of the concept of 'tragedy of the commons' (Fischel); enforcement in the commons (Runge); and a critical look at the reasons for the prominence and popularity of the Hardin paper (Walker).

Elinor Ostrom's (2000) paper titled "Collective Action and the Evolution of Social Norms" presents an insightful analysis of the conditions for collective management of natural resources such as common pool resources (e.g. forest and fisheries). Drawing on theoretical/experimental and empirical evidence, Ostrom challenges the "zero contribution thesis" held by Olson and others, questioning the viability of self-organized collective action. She also draws on eight key design principles that have played a central role in the "long-term survival and comparative effectiveness" of resource regimes. Furthermore, the author brings together insights from many disciplines, among them, economics, political science, sociology and anthropology, to illustrate and illuminate the evolution, development and sustainability of collective action. An important contribution of this paper is

Ostrom's analysis of the crucial role of social norms (e.g. trust, fairness and reciprocity) in the growth and sustainability of collective action.

Nine scholars in seven papers have offered their thoughts and insights on the Ostrom paper. Aspects examined are: collective action theory path to contextual analysis (Aligica & Sabetti); contextualizing the influence of social norms, collective action social-ecological systems (Evans & Cole); collective action and the evolution of social norms (Auer); the crossing of disciplinary boundaries by Ostrom in her paper (Schroeder); Ostrom's challenge for laboratory experiments (Wilson); the evaluation of social norms in conflict resolution (Amsler); and the evolution of norms pertaining to federal-tribal co-management of natural resources (Day).

Part 4: The Economics of Exhaustible Resources

An inherent characteristic of many natural resources such as oil, natural gas, minerals and ground water is that their supplies have an absolute limit which cannot be extended or augmented in a reasonable timeframe. Given this constraint, the major issue to be tackled has to do with the determination of an optimal rate of depletion of exhaustible or nonrenewable resources. From the perspectives of both current and future generations, it is crucial to determine such a rate.

William Nordhaus (1973) in his paper, examines the use of markets for the allocation of scarce resources over time, followed by an "explicit" empirical estimation of the efficient allocation of energy resources. Toward this end, he uses an economic-engineering model spanning a 200-year period. Based on empirical analysis the paper concludes that the calculated prices do not differ much from the actual market prices, except in the case of petroleum products and coal. It is noteworthy that Nordhaus espouses free trade and supports fuel imports. The paper predicts a positive energy future through technological advances. Nordhaus omits climate change and environmental constraints and pays little attention to the role of alternative energy sources such as solar and wind. A unique contribution of this paper is the introduction of the concept of "backstop technology".

Thirteen scholars offer their thoughts and insights on the Nordhaus paper in eight commentaries. Aspects covered include: modeling long-term energy futures after Nordhaus (1973) (Nemet); the allocation of energy resources in the very long run (Fouquet); the world before climate change – a look at Nordhaus' 1973 projections of long-term world energy futures (Ackerman); energy modeling post 1973 (Feddersen, Habermacher, Imhof & van der Ploeg); the allocation of energy conservation (Wirl); a retrospective on Nordhaus' paper (Koundori, Reppas & Souliotis); a review and analysis of Nordhaus' concept of "backstop technology" (Verbruggen); and caveats for climate policy from the Nordhaus paper (Galiana).

Robert Solow (1974) in his paper examines the economic theory of exhaustible resources as a partial equilibrium market theory with interest rate and demand as given. He discusses the problem from the perspectives of efficiency and intergenerational equity. The paper starts out with the premise that Hotelling's rule, the fundamental principle of natural resource economics, is a necessary condition for efficiency and, hence, for social optimality. Market price can decrease or remain constant if extraction costs are falling. Empirical studies suggest that low-cost resources will be exploited first and that backstop technology will set a ceiling for the market price of the natural resource. "Solow points out that technical progress and substitutability between exhaustible resources and reproducible capital and labor will greatly affect the gravity of the resource exhaustion problem. Solow has made a significant contribution to the conceptualization of the problem of exploitation of exhaustible resources." (Gopalakrishnan, 2000, p. 8) An important contribution of the paper is the concept of sustainable consumption.

Commentaries by six scholars on the impact and implications of Solow's paper are included: reflections on the core ideas explored by Solow (Berck); a survey and synthesis of the empirical work inspired by Solow's paper (Halvorsen); a speculative essay about what Solow would say if he were to revisit his paper today (Hartwick); another set of reflections on Solow's paper (Randall); thoughts on how Solow might have approached the economics of climate as gleaned from his 1973 paper (Simpson); and ruminations on lessons from natural resource economics for environmental policy a la Solow (Smith).

Part 5: The Economics of Renewable Resources

Renewable resources differ from exhaustible resources in a fundamental way viz they can regenerate in a meaningful timeframe that lends itself to human exploitation. Examples of renewable resources include forest, fisheries and an array of energy sources such as solar, wind and waves. Advances in technology could make these energy sources cost-effective and affordable to large segments of people. Furthermore, these are also relatively pollution free.

Samuelson (1976) in his paper revisits the forester's concept of maximum sustainable yield (MSY), points out its limitations and suggests a modified theory for optimal forest management. Samuelson shows that it is economically inefficient to wait until the time of MSY to start harvesting. "Previous studies in forestry economics, with the possible exception of Faustmann's 1849 paper, seriously failed to accommodate land rent, labor input, wage rate, output price, etc., all subject to change, in determining the optimal rotation period in forestry." (Gopalakrishnan, 2000, p. 8). To correct these deficiencies, he proposes a new model that includes a host of variables such as time, interest rate, propensity to save, labor, wage, output price, land rent and the growth function of forest. This leads to an optimal rotation period in Samuelson's model shorter than MSY, but longer than in the other theoretical models. This paper, incorporating the essential features of real world forestry, is a major contribution to forestry economics.

Nine scholars, in six papers, have contributed original insights on the impact of Samuelson's paper on the discourse on the economics of forestry. These consist of an overall assessment of the enduring legacy of the paper (Amacher); reflections on the paper (Berck & Xie); Samuelson's paper in relation to 21st century tropical forest economics (Robinson & Albers); the limits of forest economics in policy debates vis-à-vis Samuelson's paper (Newman & Wagner); a review of the historical roots of the paper (Price); and some thoughts on the paper (Sedjo).

Notes

1. The citation information presented here was collected separately for each individual author through Google Search. No single website with the citation information for all authors could be located.

References

Gopalakrishnan, C. (2000). "Classic Papers in Natural Resource Economics: An Overview" in: *Classic Papers in Natural Resource Economics*. London and New York: Macmillan Press Ltd. and St. Martin's Press Inc., pp. 1–10.

Ruttan, V.M., Hayami, Y. (1984). Towards a theory of induced institutional innovation. *Journal of Development Studies*, 20: 203–223.

Uncertainty and the Evaluation of Public Investment Decisions

Kenneth J. Arrow and Robert C. Lind

The implications of uncertainty for public investment decisions remain controversial. The essence of the controversy is as follows. It is widely accepted that individuals are not indifferent to uncertainty and will not, in general, value assets with uncertain returns at their expected values. Depending upon an individual's initial asset holdings and utility function, he will value an asset at more or less than its expected value. Therefore, in private capital markets, investors do not choose investments to maximize the present value of expected returns, but to maximize the present value of returns properly adjusted for risk. The issue is whether it is appropriate to discount public investments in the same way as private investments.

There are several positions on this issue. The first is that risk should be discounted in the same way for public investments as it is for private investments. It is argued that to treat risk differently in the public sector will result in overinvestment in this sector at the expense of private investments yielding higher returns. The leading proponent of this point of view is Jack Hirshleifer.[1] He argues that in perfect capital markets, investments are discounted with respect to both time and risk and that the discount rates obtaining in these markets should be used to evaluate public investment opportunities.

A second position is that the government can better cope with uncertainty than private investors and, therefore, government investments should not be evaluated by the same criterion used in private markets. More specifically, it is argued that the government should ignore uncertainty and behave as if indifferent to risk. The government should then evaluate investment opportunities according to their present value computed by discounting the expected value of net returns, using a rate of discount equal to the private rate appropriate for investments with certain returns. In support of this position it is argued that the government invests in a greater number of diverse projects and is able to pool risks to a much greater extent than private investors.[2] Another supporting line of argument is that many of the uncertainties which arise in private capital markets are related to what may be termed moral hazards. Individuals involved in a given transaction may hedge against the possibility of fraudulent behavior on the part of their associates. Many such risks are not present in the case of public investments and, therefore, it can be argued that it is not appropriate for the government to take these risks into account when choosing among public investments.

There is, in addition, a third position on the government's response to uncertainty. This position rejects the notion that individual preferences as revealed by market behavior are of normative significance for government investment decisions, and asserts that time and risk preferences relevant for government action should be established as a matter of

Originally published in the American Economic Review, Vol. 60, No. 3 (Jun., 1970), pp. 364–378. Reproduced with kind permission of the American Economic Association.

national policy. In this case the correct rules for action would be those established by the appropriate authorities in accordance with their concept of national policy. The rate of discount and attitude toward risk would be specified by the appropriate authorities and the procedures for evaluation would incorporate these time and risk preferences. Two alternative lines of argument lead to this position. First, if one accepts the proposition that the state is more than a collection of individuals and has an existence and interests apart from those of its individual members, then it follows that government policy need not reflect individual preferences. A second position is that markets are so imperfect that the behavior observed in these markets yields no relevant information about the time and risk preferences of individuals. It follows that some policy as to time and risk preference must be established in accordance with other evidence of social objectives. One such procedure would be to set national objectives concerning the desired rate of growth and to infer from this the appropriate rate of discount.[3] If this rate were applied to the expected returns from all alternative investments, the government would in effect be behaving as if indifferent to risk.

The approach taken in this paper closely parallels the approach taken by Hirshleifer, although the results differ from his. By using the state-preference approach to market behavior under uncertainty, Hirshleifer demonstrates that investments will not, in general, be valued at the sum of the expected returns discounted at a rate appropriate for investments with certain returns.[4] He then demonstrates that using this discount rate for public investments may lead to non-optimal results, for two reasons. First, pooling itself may not be desirable.[5] If the government has the opportunity to undertake only investments which pay off in states where the payoff is highly valued, to combine such investments with ones that pay off in other states may reduce the value of the total investment package. Hirshleifer argues that where investments can be undertaken separately they should be evaluated separately, and that returns should be discounted at rates determined in the market. Second, even if pooling were possible and desirable, Hirshleifer argues correctly that the use of a rate of discount for the public sector which is lower than rates in the private sector can lead to the displacement of private investments by public investments yielding lower expected returns.[6]

For the case where government pooling is effective and desirable, he argues that rather than evaluate public investments differently from private ones, the government should subsidize the more productive private investments. From this it follows that to treat risk differently for public as opposed to private investments would only be justified if it were impossible to transfer the advantages of government pooling to private investors. Therefore, at most, the argument for treating public risks differently than private ones in evaluating investments is an argument for the "second best."[7]

The first section of this paper addresses the problem of uncertainty, using the state-preference approach to market behavior. It demonstrates that if the returns from any particular investment are independent of other components of national income, then the present value of this investment equals the sum of expected returns discounted by a rate appropriate for investments yielding certain returns. This result holds for both private and public investments. Therefore, by adding one plausible assumption to Hirshleifer's formulation, the conclusion can be drawn that the government should behave as an expected-value decision maker and use a discount rate appropriate for investments with certain returns. This conclusion needs to be appropriately modified when one considers the case where there is a corporate income tax.

While this result is of theoretical interest, as a policy recommendation it suffers from a defect common to the conclusions drawn by Hirshleifer. The model of the economy upon which these recommendations are based presupposes the existence of perfect markets for claims contingent on states of the world. Put differently, it is assumed that there are perfect insurance markets through which individuals may individually pool risks. Given such markets, the distribution of risks among individuals will be Pareto optimal. The difficulty is that many of these markets for insurance do not exist, so even if the markets which do exist are perfect, the resulting equilibrium will be sub-optimal. In addition, given the strong evidence that the existing capital markets are not perfect, it is unlikely that the pattern of investment will be Pareto optimal. At the margin, different individuals will have different rates of time and risk preference, depending on their opportunities to borrow or to invest, including their opportunities to insure.

There are two reasons why markets for many types of insurance do not exist. The first is the existence of certain moral hazards.[8] In particular, the fact that someone has insurance may alter his behavior so that the observed outcome is adverse to the insurer. The second is that such markets would require complicated and specialized contracts which are costly. It may be that the cost of insuring in some cases is so high that individuals choose to bear risks rather than pay the transaction costs associated with insurance.

Given the absence of some markets for insurance and the resulting sub-optimal allocation of risks, the question remains: How should the government treat uncertainty in evaluating public investment decisions? The approach taken in this paper is that individual preferences are relevant for public investment decisions, and government decisions should reflect individual valuations of costs and benefits. It is demonstrated in the second section of this paper that when the risks associated with a public investment are publicly borne, the total cost of risk-bearing is insignificant and, therefore, the government should ignore uncertainty in evaluating public investments. Similarly, the choice of the rate of discount should in this case be independent of considerations of risk. This result is obtained not because the government is able to pool investments but because the government distributes the risk associated with any investment among a large number of people. It is the risk-spreading aspect of government investment that is essential to this result.

There remains the problem that private investments may be displaced by public ones yielding a lower return if this rule is followed, although given the absence of insurance markets this will represent a Hicks-Kaldor improvement over the initial situation. Again the question must be asked whether the superior position of the government with respect to risk can be made to serve private investors. This leads to a discussion of the government's role as a supplier of insurance, and of Hirshleifer's recommendation that private investment be subsidized in some cases.

Finally, the results obtained above apply to risks actually borne by the government. Many of the risks associated with public investments are borne by private individuals, and in such cases it is appropriate to discount for risk as would these individuals. This problem is discussed in the final section of the paper. In addition, a method of evaluating public investment decisions is developed that calls for different rates of discount applied to different classes of benefits and costs.

I. Markets for Contingent Claims and Time-Risk Preference[9]

For simplicity, consider an economy where there is one commodity and there are I individuals, S possible states of the world, and time is divided into Q periods of equal length. Further suppose that each individual acts on the basis of his subjective probability as to the states of nature; let π_{is} denote the subjective probability assigned to state s by individual i. Now suppose that each individual in the absence of trading owns claims for varying amounts of the one commodity at different points in time, given different states of the world. Let $\bar{x}_{isq}$ denote the initial claim to the commodity in period $q + 1$ if state s occurs which is owned by individual i. Suppose further that all trading in these claims takes place at the beginning of the first period, and claims are bought and sold on dated commodity units contingent on a state of the world. All claims can be constructed from basic claims which pay one commodity unit in period $q + 1$, given state s, and nothing in other states or at other times; there will be a corresponding price for this claim, $p_{sq}(s = 1, \ldots, S; q = 0, \ldots, Q - 1)$. After the trading, the individual will own claims x_{isq}, which he will exercise when the time comes to provide for his consumption. Let $V_i(x_{i1,0}, \ldots, x_{i1,Q-1}, x_{i2,0}, \ldots, x_{iS,Q-1})$ be the utility of individual i if he receives claims $x_{isq}(s = 1, \ldots, S; q = 0, \ldots, Q - 1)$. The standard assumptions are made that V_i is strictly quasi-concave $(i = 1, \ldots, I)$.

Therefore each individual will attempt to maximize,

$$V_i(x_{i1,0} \cdots, x_{i1,Q-1}, x_{i2,0} \cdots, x_{iS,Q-1}) \tag{1}$$

subject to the constraint

$$\sum_{q=0}^{Q-1}\sum_{s=1}^{S} p_{sq} x_{isq} = \sum_{q=0}^{Q-1}\sum_{s=1}^{S} p_{sq}\bar{x}_{isq}$$

Using the von Neumann-Morgenstern theorem and an extension by Hirshleifer,[10] functions $U_{is}(s = 1, \ldots, S)$ can be found such that

$$V_i(x_{i1,0} \cdots, x_{iS,Q-1}) = \sum_{s=1}^{S} \pi_{is} U_{is}(x_{is0}, x_{is1}, \ldots, x_{iS,Q-1}) \tag{2}$$

In equation (2) an individual's utility, given any state of the world, is a function of his consumption at each point in time. The subscript s attached to the function U_{is} is in recognition of the fact that the value of a given stream of consumption may depend on the state of the world.

The conditions for equilibrium require that

$$\pi_{is}\frac{\partial U_{is}}{\partial x_{isq}} = \lambda_i p_{sq} \; (i - 1, \ldots, I; s = 1, \ldots, S; q = 0, \ldots, Q - 1) \tag{3}$$

where λ_i is a Lagrangian multiplier.

From (3) it follows that

$$\frac{p_{sq}}{p_{rm}} = \frac{\pi_{is}\frac{\partial U_{is}}{\partial x_{isq}}}{\pi_{rm}\frac{\partial U_{ir}}{\partial x_{irm}}} \; (i = 1, \ldots, I; r, s = 1, \ldots S; m, q = 0, \ldots, Q - 1) \tag{4}$$

Insight can be gained by analyzing the meaning of the prices in such an economy. Since trading takes place at time zero, p_{sq} represents the present value of a claim to one commodity unit at time q, given state s. Clearly,

$$\sum_{s=1}^{S} p_{s0} = 1$$

since someone holding one commodity unit at time zero has a claim on one commodity unit, given any state of the world. It follows that p_{sq} is the present value of one commodity at time q, given state s, in terms of a certain claim on one commodity unit at time zero. Therefore, the implicit rate of discount to time zero on returns at time q, given state s, is defined by $p_{sq} = 1/1 + r_{sq}$.

Now suppose one considers a certain claim to one commodity unit at time q; clearly, its value is

$$p_q = \sum_{s=1}^{S} p_{sq}$$

and the rate of discount appropriate for a certain return at time q is defined by

$$\frac{1}{1 + r_q} = \sum_{s=1}^{S} \frac{1}{1 + r_{sq}} = \sum_{s=1}^{S} p_{sq} \tag{5}$$

Given these observations, we can now analyze the appropriate procedure for evaluating government investments where there are perfect markets for claims contingent on states of the world.[11] Consider an investment where the overall effect on market prices can be assumed to be negligible, and suppose the net return from this investment for a given time and state is $h_{sq}(s = 1, ..., S; q = 0, ..., Q - 1)$. Then the investment should be undertaken if

$$\sum_{q=0}^{Q-1} \sum_{s=1}^{S} h_{sq} p_{sq} > 0, \tag{6}$$

and the sum on the left is an exact expression for the present value of the investment. Expressed differently, the investment should be adopted if

$$\sum_{q=0}^{Q-1} \sum_{s=1}^{S} \frac{h_{sq}}{1 + r_{sq}} > 0 \tag{7}$$

The payoff in each time-state is discounted by the associated rate of discount. This is the essential result upon which Hirshleifer bases his policy conclusions.[12]

Now suppose that the net returns of the investment were (a) independent of the returns from previous investment, (b) independent of the individual utility functions, and (c) had an objective probability distribution, i.e., one agreed upon by everyone. More specifically, we assume that the set of all possible states of the world can be partitioned into a class of mutually exclusive and collectively exhaustive sets, E_t, indexed by the subscript t such that, for all s in any given E_t, all utility functions U_{is} are the same for any individual i $(i = 1,..., I)$, and such that all production conditions are the same. Put differently, for all s in E_t, U_{is} is the same for a given individual, but not necessarily for all individuals. At the same time there is another partition of the states of the world into sets, F_u, such that the return, h_{sq}, is the same for s in F_u. Finally, we assume that the probability distribution of F_u is independent of E_t and is the same for all individuals.

Let E_{tu} be the set of all states of the world which lie in both E_t and F_u. For any given t and u, all states of the world in E_{tu} are indistinguishable for all purposes, so we may regard it as containing a single state. Equations (3) and (5) and the intervening discussion still hold if we then replace s everywhere by tu. However, $U_{is} = U_{itu}$ actually depends only on the subscript, t, and can be written U_{it}. From the assumptions it is obvious and can be proved rigorously that the allocation x_{isq} also depends only on t, i.e., is the same for all states in E_t for any given t, so it may be written x_{itq}. Finally, let π_{it} be the probability of E_t according to individual i, and let π_u be the probability of F_u, assumed the same for all individuals. Then the assumption of statistical independence is written:

$$\pi_{itu} = \pi_{it}\pi_u \tag{8}$$

Then (3) can be written

$$\pi_{it}\pi_u \frac{\partial U_{it}}{\partial x_{itq}} = \lambda_i p_{tuq} \tag{9}$$

Since p_{tuq} and π_u are independent of i, so must be

$$\left(\pi_{it}\frac{\partial U_{it}}{\partial U_{itq}}\right)/\lambda_i;$$

on the other hand, this expression is also independent of u and so can be written μ_{tq}. Therefore,

$$P_{tuq} = \mu_{tq}\pi_u \tag{10}$$

Since the new investment has the same return for all states s in F_u, the returns can be written h_{uq}. Then the left-hand side of (6) can, with the aid of (10), be written

$$\sum_{Q=0}^{Q-1}\sum_{s=1}^{S} h_{sq}p_{sq} = \sum_{q=0}^{Q-1}\sum_{t}\sum_{u} h_{uq}p_{tuq}$$

$$= \sum_{q=0}^{Q-1}\left(\sum_{t}\mu_{tq}\right)\sum_{u}\pi_u h_{uq} \tag{11}$$

But from (10)

$$P_q = \sum_{s=1}^{S} P_{sq} = \sum_{t}\sum_{u} P_{tuq} = \left(\sum_{t}\mu_{tq}\right)\left(\sum_{u}\pi_u\right) = \sum_{t}\mu_{tq}, \tag{12}$$

since of course the sum of the probabilities of the F_u's must be 1. From (11),

$$\sum_{q=0}^{Q-1}\sum_{s=1}^{S} h_{sq}p_{sq} = \sum_{Q=0}^{Q-1}\frac{1}{1+r_q}\sum_{u}\pi_u h_{uq} \tag{13}$$

Equation (13) gives the rather startling result that the present value of any investment which meets the independence and objectivity conditions, equals the expected value of returns in each time period, discounted by the factor appropriate for a certain return at that time. This is true even though individuals may have had different probabilities for the events that governed the returns on earlier investments. It is also interesting to note that each individual will behave in this manner so that there will be no discrepancy between public and private procedures for choosing among investments.

The independence assumption applied to utility functions was required because the functions U_{is} are conditional on the states of the world. This assumption appears reasonable, and in the case where U_{is} is the same for all values of s, it is automatically satisfied. Then the independence condition is simply that the net returns from an investment be independent of the returns from previous investments.

The difficulty that arises if one bases policy conclusions on these results is that some markets do not exist, and individuals do not value assets at the expected value of returns discounted by a factor appropriate for certain returns. It is tempting to argue that while individuals do not behave as expected-value decision makers because of the nonexistence of certain markets for insurance, there is no reason why the government's behavior should not be consistent with the results derived above where the allocation of resources was Pareto optimal. There are two difficulties with this line of argument. First, if we are to measure benefits and costs in terms of individuals' willingness to pay, then we must treat risk in accordance with these individual valuations. Since individuals do not have the opportunities for insuring assumed in the state-preference model, they will not value uncertainty as they would if these markets did exist. Second, the theory of the second best demonstrates that if resources are not allocated in a Pareto optimal manner, the appropriate public policies may not be those consistent with Pareto efficiency in perfect markets. Therefore, some other approach must be found for ascertaining the appropriate government policy toward risk. In particular, such an approach must be valid, given the nonexistence of certain markets for insurance and imperfections in existing markets.

II. The Public Cost of Risk-Bearing

The critical question is: What is the cost of uncertainty in terms of costs to individuals? If one adopts the position that costs and benefits should be computed on the basis of individual willingness to pay, consistency demands that the public costs of risk-bearing be computed in this way too. This is the approach taken here.

In the discussion that follows it is assumed that an individual's utility is dependent only upon his consumption and not upon the state of nature in which that consumption takes place. This assumption simplifies the presentation of the major theorem, but it is not essential. Again the expected utility theorem is assumed to hold. The presentation to follow analyzes the cost of risk-bearing by comparing the expected value of returns with the certainty equivalent of these returns. In this way the analysis of time and risk preference can be separated, so we need only consider one time period.

Suppose that the government were to undertake an investment with a certain outcome; then the benefits and costs are measured in terms of willingness to pay for this outcome. If, however, the outcome is uncertain, then the benefits and costs actually realized depend on which outcome in fact occurs. If an individual is risk-averse, he will value the investment with the uncertain outcome at less than the expected value of its net return (benefit minus cost) to him. Therefore, in general the expected value of net benefits overstates willingness to pay by an amount equal to the cost of risk-bearing. It is clear that the social cost of risk-bearing will depend both upon which individuals receive the benefits and pay the costs and upon how large is each individual's share of these benefits and costs.

As a first step, suppose that the government were to undertake an investment and capture all benefits and pay all costs, i.e., the beneficiaries pay to the government an amount equal to the benefits received and the government pays all costs. Individuals who incur costs and those who receive benefits are therefore left indifferent to their pre-investment state. This assumption simply transfers all benefits and costs to the government, and the outcome of the investment will affect government disbursements and receipts. Given that the general taxpayer finances government expenditures, a public investment can be considered an investment in which each individual taxpayer has a very small share.

For precision, suppose that the government undertook an investment and that returns accrue to the government as previously described. In addition, suppose that in a given year the government were to have a balanced budget (or a planned deficit or surplus) and that taxes would be reduced by the amount of the net benefits if the returns are positive, and raised if returns are negative. Therefore, when the government undertakes an investment, each taxpayer has a small share of that investment with the returns being paid through changes in the level of taxes. By undertaking an investment the government adds to each individual's disposable income a random variable which is some fraction of the random variable representing the total net returns. The expected return to all taxpayers as a group equals expected net benefits.

Each taxpayer holds a small share of an asset with a random payoff, and the value of this asset to the individual is less than its expected return, assuming risk aversion. Stated differently, there is a cost of risk-bearing that must be subtracted from the expected return in order to compute the value of the investment to the individual taxpayer. Since each taxpayer will bear some of the cost of the risk associated with the investment, these costs must be summed over all taxpayers in order to arrive at the total cost of risk-bearing associated with a particular investment. These costs must be subtracted from the value of expected net benefits in order to obtain the correct measure for net benefits. The task is to assess these costs.

Suppose, as in the previous section, that there is one commodity, and that each individual's utility in a given year is a function of his income defined in terms of this commodity and is given by $U(Y)$. Further, suppose that U is bounded, continuous, strictly increasing, and differentiable. The assumptions that U is continuous and strictly increasing imply that U has a right and left derivative at every point and this is sufficient to prove the desired results; differentiability is assumed only to simplify presentation. Further suppose that U satisfies the conditions of the expected utility theorem.

Consider, for the moment, the case where all individuals are identical in that they have the same preferences, and their disposable incomes are identically distributed random variables represented by A. Suppose that the government were to undertake an investment with returns represented by B, which are statistically independent of A. Now divide the effect of this investment into two parts: a certain part equal to expected returns and a random part, with mean zero, which incorporates risk. Let $\bar{B} = E[B]$, and define the random variable X by $X = B - \bar{B}$. Clearly, X is independent of A and $E[X] = 0$. The effect of this investment is to add an amount $\bar{B}$ to government receipts along with a random component represented by X. The income of each taxpayer will be affected through taxes and it is the level of these taxes that determines the fraction of the investment he effectively holds.

Consider a specific taxpayer and denote his fraction of this investment by $s, 0 \leq s \leq 1$. This individual's disposable income, given the public investment, is equal to $A + sB = A + s\bar{B} + sX$. The addition of sB to his disposable income is valued by the individual at its expected value less the cost of bearing the risk associated with the random component sX. If we suppose that each taxpayer has the same tax rate and that there are n taxpayers, then $s = 1/n$, and the value of the investment taken over all individuals is simply $\bar{B}$ minus n times the cost of risk-bearing associated with the random variable $(1/n)X$. The central result of this section of the paper is that this total of the costs of risk-bearing goes to zero as n becomes large. Therefore, for large values of n the value of a public investment almost equals the expected value of that investment.

To demonstrate this, we introduce the function

$$W(s) = E[U(A + s\bar{B} + sX], \ 0 \leq s \leq 1 \tag{14}$$

In other words, given the random variables A and B representing his individual income before the investment and the income from the investment, respectively, his expected utility is a function of s which represents his share of B. From (14) and the assumption that U' exists, it follows that

$$W'(s) = E\left[U'\left(A + s\bar{B} + sX\right)\left(\bar{B} + X\right)\right] \tag{15}$$

Since X is independent of A, it follows that $U'(A)$ and X are independent; therefore,

$$E[U'(A)X] = E[U'(A)]E[X] = 0$$

so that

$$\begin{aligned} W'(0) &= E[U'(A)(\bar{B} + X)] \\ &= \bar{B}E[U'(A)] \end{aligned} \tag{16}$$

Equation (16) is equivalent to the statement

$$\lim_{s \to 0} \frac{E[U(A + s\bar{B} + sX) - U(A)]}{s} = \bar{B}E[U'(A)] \tag{17}$$

Now let $s = 1/n$, so that equation (17) becomes

$$\lim_{n \to \infty} nE\left[U\left(A + \frac{\bar{B} + X}{n}\right) - U(A)\right] = \bar{B}E[U'(A)] \tag{18}$$

If we assume that an individual whose preferences are represented by U is a risk averter, then it is easily shown that there exists a unique number, $k(n) > 0$, for each value of n such that

15

$$E\left[U\left(A + \frac{\overline{B}+X}{n}\right)\right] = E\left[U\left(A + \frac{\overline{B}}{n} - k(n)\right)\right], \tag{19}$$

or, in other words, an individual would be indifferent between paying an amount equal to $k(n)$ and accepting the risk represented by $(1/n)X$. Therefore, $k(n)$ can be said to be the cost of risk-bearing associated with the asset B. It can easily be demonstrated that $\lim_{n\to\infty} k(n) = 0$, i.e., the cost of holding the risky asset goes to zero as the amount of this asset held by the individual goes to zero. It should be noted that the assumption of risk aversion is not essential to the argument but simply one of convenience. If U represented the utility function of a risk preferrer, then all the above statements would hold except $k(n) < 0$, i.e., an individual would be indifferent between being paid $-k(n)$ and accepting the risk $(1/n)X$ (net of the benefit $(1/n)\overline{B}$).

We wish to prove not merely that the risk-premium of the representative individual, $k(n)$, vanishes, but more strongly that the total of the risk-premiums for all individuals, $nk(n)$, approaches zero as n becomes large.

From (18) and (19) it follows that

$$\lim_{n\to\infty} nE\left[U\left(A + \frac{\overline{B}}{n} - k(n)\right) - U(A)\right] = \overline{B}E[U'(A)] \tag{20}$$

In addition, $\overline{B}/n - k(n) \to 0$, when $n \to \infty$. It follows from the definition of a derivative that

$$\lim_{n\to\infty} \frac{E\left[U\left(A + \frac{\overline{B}}{n} - k(n)\right) - U(A)\right]}{\frac{\overline{B}}{n} - k(n)} = E[U'(A)] > 0 \tag{21}$$

Dividing (20) by (21) yields

$$\lim_{n\to\infty} \left[\overline{B} - nk(n)\right] = \overline{B} \tag{22}$$

or

$$\lim_{n\to\infty} nk(n) = 0 \tag{23}$$

The argument in (21) implies that $\overline{B}/n - k(n) \neq 0$. Suppose instead the equality held for infinitely many n. Substitution into the left-hand side of (20) shows that $\overline{B}$ must equal zero, so that $k(n) = 0$ for all such n, and hence $nk(n) = 0$ on that sequence, confirming (23).

Equation (23) states that the total of the costs of risk-bearing goes to zero as the population of taxpayers becomes large. At the same time the monetary value of the investment to each taxpayer, neglecting the cost of risk, is $(1/n)\overline{B}$, and the total, summed over all individuals, is $\overline{B}$, the expected value of net benefits. Therefore, if n is large, the expected value of net benefits dosely approximates the correct measure of net benefits defined in terms of willingness to pay for an asset with an uncertain return.

In the preceding analysis, it was assumed that all taxpayers were identical in that they had the same utility function, their incomes were represented by identically distributed variables, and they were subject to the same tax rates. These assumptions greatly simplify the presentation; however, they are not essential to the argument. Different individuals may have different preferences, incomes, and tax rates; and the basic theorem still holds, provided that as n becomes larger the share of the public investment borne by any individual becomes arbitrarily smaller.

The question necessarily arises as to how large n must be to justify proceeding as if the cost of publicly-borne risk is negligible. This question can be given no precise answer; however, there are circumstances under which it appears likely that the cost of risk-bearing will be small. If the size of the share borne by each taxpayer is a negligible component of his income, the cost of risk-bearing associated with holding it will be small. It appears reasonable to assume, under these conditions, that the total cost of risk-bearing is also small. This situation will exist where the investment is small with respect to the total wealth of the taxpayers. In the case of a federally sponsored investment, n is not only large but the investment is generally a very small fraction of national income even though the investment itself may be large in some absolute sense.

The results derived here and in the previous section depend on returns from a given public investment being independent of other components of national income. The government undertakes a wide range of public investments and it appears reasonable to assume that their returns are independent. Clearly, there are some government investments which are interdependent; however, where investments are interrelated they should be evaluated as a package. Even after such groupings are established, there will be a large number of essentially independent projects. It is sometimes argued that the returns from public investments are highly correlated with other components of national income through the business cycle. However, if we assume that stabilization policies are success-ful, then this difficulty does not arise. It should be noted that in most benefit-cost studies it is assumed that full employment will be maintained so that market prices can be used to measure benefits and costs. Consistency requires that this assumption be retained when considering risk as well. Further, if there is some positive correlation between the returns of an investment and other components of national income, the question remains as to whether this correlation is so high as to invalidate the previous result.

The main result is more general than the specific application to public investments. It has been demonstrated that if an individual or group holds an asset which is statistically independent of other assets, and if there is one or more individuals who do not share ownership, then the existing situation is not Pareto-efficient. By selling some share of the asset to one of the individuals not originally possessing a share, the cost of risk-bearing can be reduced while the expected returns remain unchanged. The reduction in the cost of risk-bearing can then be redistributed to bring about a Pareto improvement. This result is similar to a result derived by Karl Borch. He proved that a condition for Pareto optimality in reinsurance markets requires that every individual hold a share of every independent risk.

When the government undertakes an investment it, in effect, spreads the risk among all taxpayers. Even if one were to accept that the initial distribution of risk was Pareto-efficient, the new distribution of risk will not be efficient as the government does not discriminate among the taxpayers according to their risk preferences. What has been shown is that in the limit the situation where the risk of the investment is spread over all taxpayers is such that there is only a small deviation from optimality with regard to the distribution of that particular risk. The overall distribution of risk may be sub-optimal because of market imperfections and the absence of certain insurance markets. The great advantage of the results of this section is that they are not dependent on the existence of perfect markets for contingent claims.

This leads to an example which runs counter to the policy conclusions generally offered by economists. Suppose that an individual in the private sector of the economy were to undertake a given investment and, calculated on the basis of expected returns, the investment had a rate of return of 10 per cent. Because of the absence of perfect insurance markets, the investor subtracted from the expected return in each period a risk premium and, on the basis of returns adjusted for risk, his rate of return is 5 percent. Now suppose that the government could invest the same amount of money in an investment which, on the basis of expected returns, would yield 6 percent. Since the risk would be spread over all taxpayers, the cost of risk-bearing would be negligible, and the true rate of return would be 6 percent. Further, suppose that if the public investment were adopted it would displace the private investment. The question is: Should the public investment be undertaken? On the basis of the previous analysis, the answer is yes. The private investor is indifferent between the investment with the expected return of 10 percent, and certain rate of return of 5 percent. When the public investment is undertaken, it is equivalent to an investment with a certain rate of return of 6 percent. Therefore, by undertaking the public investment, the government could more than pay the opportunity cost to the private investor of 5 percent associated with the diversion of funds from private investment.

The previous example illustrates Hirshleifer's point that the case for evaluating public investments differently from private ones is an argument for the second best. Clearly, if the advantages of the more efficient distribution of risk could be achieved in connection with the private investment alternative, this would be superior to the public investment. The question then arises as to how the government can provide insurance for private investors and thereby transfer the risks from the private sector to the public at large. The same difficulties arise as before, moral hazards and transaction costs. It may not be possible for the government to provide such insurance, and in such cases second-best solutions are in order. Note that if the government could undertake any investment, then this difficulty would not arise. Perhaps one of the strongest criticisms of a system of freely competitive markets is that the inherent difficulty in establishing certain markets for insurance brings about a sub-optimal allocation of resources. If we consider an investment, as does Hirshleifer, as an exchange of certain present income for uncertain future income, then the misallocation will take the form of under-investment.

Now consider Hirshleifer's recommendation that, in cases such as the one above, a direct subsidy be used to induce more private investment rather than increase public investment. Suppose that a particular private investment were such that the benefits would be a marginal increase in the future supply of an existing commodity, i.e., this investment would neither introduce a new commodity nor affect future prices. Therefore, benefits can be measured at each point in time by the market value of this output, and can be fully captured through the sale of the commodity. Let $\bar{V}$ be the present value of expected net returns, and let V be the present value of net returns adjusted for risk where the certainty rate is used to discount both streams. Further, suppose there were a public investment, where the risks were publicly borne, for which the present value of expected net benefits was P. Since the risk is publicly borne, from the previous discussion it follows that P is the present value of net benefits adjusted for risk. Now suppose that $\bar{V} > P > V$. According to Hirshleifer, we should undertake the private investment rather than the public one, and pay a subsidy if necessary to induce private entrepreneurs to undertake this investment. Clearly, if there is a choice between one investment or the other, given the existing distribution of risk, the public investment is superior. The implication is that if a risky investment in the private sector is displaced by a public investment with a lower expected return but with a higher return when appropriate adjustments are made for risks, this represents a Hicks-Kaldor improvement. This is simply a restatement of the previous point that the government could more than pay the opportunity cost to the private entrepreneur.

Now consider the case for a direct subsidy to increase the level of private investment. One can only argue for direct subsidy of the private investment if $V < 0 < \overline{V}$. The minimum subsidy required is $|V|$.

Suppose the taxpayers were to pay this subsidy, which is a transfer of income from the public at large to the private investor, in order to cover the loss from the investment. The net benefits, including the cost of risk-bearing, remain negative because while the subsidy has partially offset the cost of risk-bearing to the individual investor, it has not reduced this cost. Therefore, a direct public subsidy in this case results in a less efficient allocation of resources.

We can summarize as follows: It is implied by Hirshleifer that it is better to undertake an investment with a higher expected return than one with a lower expected return. (See 1965, p. 270.) This proposition is not in general valid, as the distribution of risk-bearing is critical. This statement is true, however, when the costs of risk-bearing associated with both investments are the same. What has been shown is that when risks are publicly borne, the costs of risk-bearing are negligible; therefore, a public investment with an expected return which is less than that of a given private investment may nevertheless be superior to the private alternative. Therefore, the fact that public investments with lower expected return may replace private investment is not necessarily cause for concern. Furthermore, a program of providing direct subsidies to encourage more private investment does not alter the costs of risk-bearing and, therefore, will encourage investments which are inefficient when the costs of risk are considered. The program which produces the desired result is one to insure private investments.

One might raise the question as to whether risk-spreading is not associated with large corporations so that the same result would apply, and it is easily seen that the same reasoning does apply. This can be made more precise by assuming there were n stockholders who were identical in the sense that their utility functions were identical, their incomes were represented by identically distributed random variables, and they had the same share in the company. When the corporation undertakes an investment with a return in a given year represented by B, each stockholder's income is represented by $A + (1/n)B$. This assumes, of course, that a change in earnings was reflected in dividends, and that there were no business taxes. Clearly, this is identical to the situation previously described, and if n is large, the total cost of risk-bearing to the stockholders will be negligible. If the income or wealth of the stockholders were large with respect to the size of the investment, this result would be likely to hold. Note that whether or not the investment is a large one, with respect to the assets of the firm, is not relevant. While an investment may constitute a major part of a firm's assets if each stockholder's share in the firm is a small component of his income, the cost of risk-bearing to him will be very small. It then follows that if managers were acting in the interest of the firm's shareholders, they would essentially ignore risks and choose investments with the highest expected returns.

There are two important reasons why large corporations may behave as risk averters. First, in order to control the firm, some shareholder may hold a large block of stock which is a significant component of his wealth. If this were true, then, from his point of view, the costs of risk-bearing would not be negligible, and the firm should behave as a risk averter. Note in this case that the previous result does not hold because the cost of risk-bearing to each stockholder is not small, even though the number of stockholders is very large. Investment behavior in this case is essentially the same as the case of a single investor.

The second case is when, even though from the stockholder's point of view, risk should be ignored, it may not be in the interest of the corporate managers to neglect risk. Their careers and income are intimately related to the firm's performance. From their point of view, variations in the outcome of some corporate action impose very real costs. In this case, given a degree of autonomy, the corporate managers, in considering prospective investments, may discount for risk when it is not in the interest of the stockholders to do so.

Suppose that this were the case and also suppose that the marginal rate of time preference for each individual in the economy was 5 percent. From the point of view of the stockholders, risk can be ignored and any investment with an expected return which is greater than 5 percent should be undertaken. However, suppose that corporate managers discount for risk so that only investments with expected rates of return that exceed 10 percent are undertaken. From the point of view of the stockholders, the rate of return on these investments, taking risk into account, is over 10 percent. Given a marginal rate of time preference of 5 percent, it follows that from the point of view of the individual stockholder there is too little investment. Now suppose further that the government were considering an investment with an expected rate of return of 6 percent. Since the cost of risk-bearing is negligible, this investment should be undertaken since the marginal rate of time preference is less than 6 percent. However, in this case, if the financing were such that a private investment with a 10 percent expected rate of return is displaced by the public investment, there is a loss because in both cases the risk is distributed so as to make the total cost of risk-bearing negligible. The public investment should be undertaken, but only at the expense of consumption.

III. The Actual Allocation of Risk

In the idealized public investment considered in the last section, all benefits and costs accrued to the government and were distributed among the taxpayers. In this sense, all uncertainty was borne collectively. Suppose instead that some benefits and costs of sizeable magnitudes accrued directly to individuals so that these individuals incurred the attendant costs of risk-bearing. In this case it is appropriate to discount for the risk, as would these individuals. Such a situation would arise in the case of a government irrigation project where the benefits accrued to farmers as increased income. The changes in farm income would be uncertain and, therefore, should be valued at more or less than their expected value, depending on the states in which they occur. If these increases were independent of other components of farm income, and if we assume that the farmer's utility were only a function of his income and not the state in which he receives that income, then he would value the investment project at less than the expected increase in his income, provided he is risk averse. If, however, the irrigation project paid out in periods of drought so that total farm income was not only increased but also stabilized, then the farmers would value the project at more than the expected increase in their incomes.

In general, some benefits and costs will accrue to the government and the uncertainties involved will be publicly borne; other benefits and costs will accrue to individuals and the attendant uncertainties will be borne privately. In the first case the cost of risk-bearing will be negligible; in the second case these costs may be significant. Therefore, in calculating the present value of returns from a public investment a distinction must be made between private and public benefits and costs. The present value of public benefits and costs should be evaluated by estimating the expected net benefits in each period and discounting them, using a discount factor appropriate for investments with certain returns. On the other hand, private benefits and costs must be discounted with respect to both time and risk in accordance with the preferences of the individuals to whom they accrue.

From the foregoing discussion it follows that different streams of benefits and costs should be treated in different ways with respect to uncertainty. One way to do this is to discount these streams of returns at different rates of discount ranging from the certainty rate for benefits and costs accruing to the government and using higher rates that reflect discounting for risk for returns accruing directly to individuals. Such a procedure raises some difficulties of identification, but this problem does not appear to be insurmountable. In general, costs are paid by the government, which receives some revenue, and the net stream should be discounted at a rate appropriate for certain returns. Benefits accruing directly to individuals should be discounted according to individual time and risk preferences. As a practical matter, Hirshleifer's suggestion of finding the marginal rate of return on assets with similar payoffs in the private sector, and using this as the rate of discount, appears reasonable for discounting those benefits and costs which accrue privately.

One problem arises with this latter procedure which has received little attention. In considering public investments, benefits and costs are aggregated and the discussion of uncertainty is carried out in terms of these aggregates. This obscures many of the uncertainties because benefits and costs do not in general accrue to the same individuals, and the attendant uncertainties should not be netted out when considering the totals. To make this clear, consider an investment where the benefits and costs varied greatly, depending on the state of nature, but where the difference between total benefits and total costs was constant for every state. Further, suppose that the benefits and costs accrued to different groups. While the investment is certain from a social point of view, there is considerable risk from a private point of view.

In the case of perfect markets for contingent claims, each individual will discount the stream of costs and benefits accruing to him at the appropriate rate for each time and state. However, suppose that such markets do not exist. Then risk-averse individuals will value the net benefits accruing to them at less than their expected value. Therefore, if net benefits accruing to this individual are positive, this requires discounting expected returns at a higher rate than that appropriate for certain returns. On the other hand, if net benefits to an individual are negative, this requires discounting expected returns at a rate lower than the certainty rate. Raising the rate of discount only reduces the present value of net benefits when they are positive. Therefore, the distinction must be made not only between benefits and costs which accrue to the public and those which accrue directly to individuals, but also between individuals whose net benefits are negative and those whose benefits are positive. If all benefits and costs accrued privately, and different individuals received the benefits and paid the costs, the appropriate procedure would be to discount the stream of expected benefits at a rate higher than the certainty rate, and costs at a rate lower than the certainty rate. This would hold even if the social totals were certain.

Fortunately, as a practical matter this may not be of great importance as most costs are borne publicly and, therefore, should be discounted using the certainty rate. Benefits often accrue to individuals, and where there are attendant uncertainties it is appropriate to discount the expected value of these benefits at higher rates, depending on the nature of the uncertainty and time-risk preferences of the individuals who receive these benefits. It is somewhat ironic that the practical implication of this analysis is that for the typical case where costs are borne publicly and benefits accrue privately, this procedure will qualify fewer projects than the procedure of using a higher rate to discount both benefits and costs.

Notes

1. J. Hirshleifer (1965, 1966) and Hirshleifer, J. C. De Haven, and J. W. Milliman (pp. 139–50).
2. For this point of view, see P. A. Samuelson and W. Vickrey.
3. For this point of view, see O. Eckstein and S. Marglin.
4. Hirshleifer (1965, pp. 523–34); (1966, pp. 268–75).
5. Hirshleifer (1966, pp. 270–75).
6. Hirshlelfer (1966, pp. 270–75).
7. Hirshielfer (1966, p. 270).
8. For a discussion of this problem see M. V. Pauly and Arrow (1968).
9. For a basic statement of the state-preference approach, see Arrow (1964) and G. Debreu.
10. J. von Neumann and O. Morgenstern, and Hirshleifer (1965, pp. 534–36).
11. The following argument was sketched in Arrow (1966, pp. 28–30).
12. Hirshleifer (1965, pp. 523–34).

References

K. J. Arrow, "The Role of Securities in the Optimal Allocation of Risk-Bearing," *Rev. Econ. Stud.,* Apr. 1964, *31,* 91–96.

——, "Discounting and Public Investment Criteria," in A. V. Kneese and S. C. Smith, eds., *Water Research.* Baltimore 1966.

——, "The Economics of Moral Hazard: Further Comment," *Amer. Econ. Rev.,* June 1968, *58,* 537–38.

K. Borch, "The Safety Loading of Reinsurance," *Skandinavisk Aktuarietid-skrift,* 1960, 163–84.

G. Debreu, *Theory of Value.* New York 1959.

O. Eckstein, "A Survey of the Theory of Public Expenditure," and "Reply," *Public Finances: Needs, Sources, and Utilization,* Nat. Bur. Econ. Res., Princeton 1961, 493–504.

J. Hirshleifer, "Investment Decision under Uncertainty: Choice-Theoretic Approaches," *Quart. J. Econ.,* Nov. 1965, *79,* 509–36.

——, "Investment Decision under Uncertainty: Applications of the State-Preference Approach," *Quart. J. Econ.,* May 1966, *80,* 252–77.

——, J. C. De Haven, and J. W. Milliman, *Water Supply: Economics, Technology, and Policy,* Chicago 1960.

S. Marglin, "The Social Rate of Discount and the Optimal Rate of Investment," *Quart. J. Econ.,* Feb. 1963, *77,* 95–111.

M. V. Pauly, "The Economics of Moral Hazard: Comment," *Amer. Econ. Rev.,* June 1968, *58,* 531–37.

P. A. Samuelson and W. Vickrey, "Discussion," *Amer. Econ. Rev. Proc.,* May 1964, *59,* 88–96.

J. von Neumann and O. Morgenstern, *Theory of Games and Economic Behavior,* 2d ed., New York 1964.

The relevance and the limits of the Arrow-Lind Theorem

Luc Baumstark[a] and Christian Gollier[b]

[a]Faculté de Sciences Economiques et de Gestion Université Lumière Lyon, Bernard, France;
[b]Toulouse School of Economics, University of Toulouse, allée de Brienne, France

1. Introduction

When an investment project yields socio-economic net benefits that are uncertain but independent of the systematic risk of the economy, these benefits should be discounted at the risk free rate if they are disseminated among a large population of stakeholders. This may be the case of a public project whose benefits are distributed within the large population of taxpayers. This is the essence of the Arrow-Lind Theorem, which played a crucial role in the evaluation of public policies around the world since its publication in 1970. Because of the differentiated treatment of investments evaluation that this result supports, it has also been extremely controversial. By reducing the discount rate to evaluate risky projects in the public sphere, it has certainly contributed to the expansion of the public sector in several western countries over the last four decades. We hereafter explain why this has been a mistake due to a fallacious interpretation of the Theorem.

2. The fundamental argument: second-order risk aversion

In an economy of von Neumann-Morgenstern consumers with identical risk aversion and riskless income levels, it is optimal to maximize the dissemination of a given collective risk by a fair sharing of its burden in the population. The intuition of this result is based on the Arrow-Pratt approximation which states that the cost of risk is approximately proportional to its variance, or equivalently to the *square* of its size. This means that risk aversion is a second-order phenomenon (Segal & Spivak, 1990).[1] This implies that if each of the n agents bears $1/n$ of the collective risk, each of them bears a cost of risk proportional to $1/n^2$, yielding a collective cost of risk proportional to $n/n^2 = 1/n$. When n tends to infinity, this risk dissemination washes out the collective cost of risk. This can be better understood in Figure 1, where we represented the quadratic relation between the size of individual risk and the individual cost of risk. When the collective risk is better disseminated, as when moving from A to B, the marginal cost of risk tends to zero, so that at the limit when $B \rightarrow 0$, this cost vanishes completely.

This result is robust to the introduction of a 'background risk' on the initial wealth levels of the stakeholders, as long as the risk involved in the collective project is independent of these background risks (Gollier & Pratt, 1996). The only effect of this background uncertainty is to raise the induced risk aversion to be used in the Arrow-Pratt approximation to evaluate the individual costs of risk.

The publication of Arrow-Lind's paper was concomitant with the golden age of the Capital Asset Pricing Model (CAPM), and its improved version, the Consumption-based CAPM (CCAPM, Lucas, 1978). In the CCAPM as in the Arrow-Lind Theorem, idiosyncratic risks should not be priced in efficient financial markets. More generally, let us consider an investment project whose flow of net benefits $(F_0, F_1, F_2, ...)$ is statistically linked to the flow of aggregate consumption $(c_0, c_1, c_2, ...)$ in the economy through the following log-linear relation:

$$\ln F_t = \alpha + \beta \ln c_t + \varepsilon_t, \tag{1}$$

for all $t > 0$, where $(\varepsilon_1, \varepsilon_2, ...)$ are independent and identically normally distributed. If the stochastic process for aggregate consumption is a geometric Brownian motion and if relative risk aversion is constant, then it is socially desirable to implement this project if and only if the Net Present Value (NPV) of its flow of expected net benefits is positive, with a discount rate being equal to

$$r = r_f + \beta\pi. \tag{2}$$

In this fundamental CCAPM formula, r_f is the risk free rate, π is the systematic risk premium, and β is the so-called beta of the project. This formula generalizes the Arrow-Lind Theorem by showing that when the project is not correlated to the systematic risk in the economy ($\beta = 0$), then the project should be discounted at the risk free rate. However, when the correlation between F_t and c_t is positive ($\beta > 0$), then the discount rate to be used to evaluate this project should be larger than the risk free rate. The intuition of this result is also based on the Arrow-Pratt approximation: When the risk of the project has a statistical component aligned on the systematic risk of consumption, this means that the representative agent in the economy already bears some positive component of it. In other words, contrary to lying at the origin of the axes in Figure 1 as assumed in the Arrow-Lind Theorem, the representative agent is positioned at some point A originally. Said differently, the second-order risk aversion argument underlying the Arrow-Lind Theorem does not apply here, because the risk is not marginal even after its dissemination. In this context, a perfect dissemination of the risk of the project does not eliminate the collective cost of risk, because the individual marginal cost of risk is not zero at point A. So, this increase in the collective risk that the project generates should be recognized in the evaluation process. This should be done by raising the discount rate. By how much depends upon the size of the systematic risk premium π and the projects' beta. Because

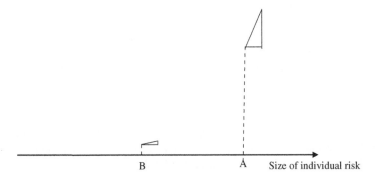

Figure 1.   The individual cost curve of risk.

the systematic risk premium on markets has been somewhere between $\pi = 3\%$ and $\pi = 6\%$ over the last century (see for example Gollier, 2012), to be compared to a risk free rate around $r_f = 0.5\%$, the effect of risk on the discount rate should be a crucial element of the evaluation process.

3. Critiques to the Arrow-Lind Theorem

Although, Arrow and Lind recognize in their paper that their result holds technically only for idiosyncratic risks, they support the idea that it has a much broader domain of applications. They first claim that 'the government undertakes a wide range of public investments and it appears reasonable to assume that their returns are independent'. In other words, they suggest that the average project in the economy should have a zero beta. This cannot be true. Because the economy can be represented as a portfolio of projects, the mean beta should be 1, and there is no reason to believe that the public sector has a portfolio of projects whose betas are systematically downward biased. Quite to the contrary, many public projects have large betas. Let me illustrate this with two examples. The infrastructure of highways is often justified on the basis of the time gained by their users, and by the number of lives saved. But the elasticity of the value of time and of the value of life with respect to changes in GDP are often assumed to be large. This implies a large beta for highway projects. In the case of the construction of a new high voltage line of electricity transportation justified by the anticipated increase in demand for electricity in a specific isolated region, the value of the project is positive only if the regional economy will indeed be growing in the future. This also yields a large beta. The same argument applies for fast train lines.

Arrow and Lind (1970) also justify the recommendation to discount public projects at the risk free rate r_f by suggesting that the systematic risk premium should be close to zero: 'It is sometimes argued that the returns from public investments are highly correlated with [...] the business cycle. However, if we assume that stabilization policies are successful, then this difficulty does not arise.[...]' (p. 373). The facts have clearly contradicted this claim over the last four decades, and the systematic risk premium remained large on financial markets.

The bottom line has however been that the Arrow-Lind Theorem has often been interpreted in its broader, fallacious, sense. It is hard to evaluate the consequence of this wrong interpretation, but our own experience in France and elsewhere tells us that it has been sizeable. In the 1980s and 1990s, many French public firms have justified their investments on the basis of a low discount rate on the basis of the Arrow-Lind Theorem. For example, it is likely that the French nuclear industry could not have attained its full scale (75% of French electricity is produced using the nuclear technology) without the Theorem, before the privatization of Electricité de France 10 years ago (which indeed radically transformed the way in which EDF evaluated its investment projects). We also believe that many public-private partnerships exist just because of the discrepancies in the way the two sectors evaluate the cost of risk. This potentially generated a massive transfer of risk from the private sector to the public one.

In the academic world, the influence of the Arrow-Lind Theorem remains strong, but is somewhat more implicit. For example, in the context of climate change, most of the debate on the climate discount rate and on the social cost of carbon that followed the publication of the Stern Report (2007) relied on the Ramsey rule, which characterizes the socially efficient discount rate r_f to be applied to *safe* projects (see Gollier, 2012 for a survey). This approach is correct only if we believe that the benefits of fighting climate change for future generations are not correlated with the level of development that they will achieve. This is quite unrealistic. In particular, a large growth of consumption will generate more emissions and therefore larger marginal climate damages. Thus, it is likely that the climate beta is positive, so that the Arrow-Lind Theorem cannot be applied for climate change.

Arrow and Lind convincingly argue that the dissemination of risk and the risk sharing are not efficiently organized by financial markets, so that their result cannot be applied to the private sector. Some insurance markets are missing, whereas others are plagued with adverse selection and moral hazard problems. This implies that the CCAPM formula (2), which relies on efficient risk sharing in the economy, can only be interpreted as a rule-of-thumb for the evaluation of private projects. Investors and firms should take into account the fact that some of the risks generated by the project are retained by a limited number of stakeholders, which implies a positive collective cost of risk even when it has a zero beta. But it should also be noticed that the public sector also face frictions and inefficiencies from the same diseases. Various principal-agent problems force States to limit the dissemination of risk in the economy, as shown for example by Laffont and Tirole (1993). The goals of public servants are rarely aligned with the general interest, so that some risky rent should be allocated to them in order to provide better incentives. There is no reason *a priori* to believe that the public sector is more efficient than the private sector to disseminate risk in the population. In fact, there are some reasons to believe that the opposite is true. For example, financial markets are in a better position than states to disseminate country-specific risks around the planet.

4. Concluding remarks

In spite of its limited domain of applicability, the Arrow-Lind Theorem has probably played a crucial role in the development of the public sector in many countries over the last 40 years. Relying on a wrong interpretation of the Theorem, some lobbies have used this result to support their investment projects whose expected rate of return was not large enough to compensate for the increased systematic risk that they imposed on their stakeholders. Many countries have reacted to this behavior by imposing a large discount rate in the public sector. This is a second-best strategy, which implies not enough public investments in safe projects, and too many investments in risky projects. The first-best solution is to use risk-sensitive discount rates following the CCAPM rule (2), as has been done in Norway and in France over the last few years (see Gollier, 2011). Because of the well-known puzzles in finance, there is no global agreement about the levels of the risk-free rate r_f and of the systematic risk premium π to calibrate this formula. For long maturities, we believe that $r_f = 2\%$ and $\pi = 3\%$, so that socially efficient discount rates r should be set around $(2 + 3\beta)\%$, where β is the beta of the project under consideration.

Note

1. In many models alternative to expected utility, as the rank-dependent expected utility model (Quiggin, 1982), risk aversion is a first-order phenomenon and the Arrow-Lind Theorem does not hold in these contexts. But the expected utility theory and its associated independence axiom have a very strong normative appeal, so we do not attach much weight to this potential critique.

References

Arrow, K. J., & Lind, R. C. (1970). Uncertainty and the evaluation of public investment decision. *American Economic Review, 60,* 364–378.

Gollier, C. (2011). *Le calcul du risque dans les investissements publics,* Centre d'Analyse Stratégique, Rapports & Documents n°36, La Documentation Française.

Gollier, C. (2012, October). *Pricing the planet's future: The economics of discounting in an uncertain world.* Princeton, NJ: Princeton University Press.

Gollier, C., & Pratt, J. W. (1996). Risk vulnerability and the tempering effect of background risk. *Econometrica, 64,* 1109–1124.

Laffont, J.-J., & Tirole, J. (1993). *The theory of incentives in procurement and regulation.* Cambridge: The MIT Press.

Lucas, R. (1978). Asset prices in an exchange economy. *Econometrica, 46,* 1429–1446.

Quiggin, J. (1982). A theory of anticipated utility. *Journal of Economic Behavior and Organization, 3,* 323–343.

Segal, U., & Spivak, A. (1990). First order versus second order risk aversion. *Journal of Economic Theory, 51,* 111–125.

Stern, N. (2007). *The economics of climate change: The stern review.* Cambridge: Cambridge University Press.

A reconsideration of Arrow-Lind: risk aversion, risk sharing, and agent choice

Eric Fesselmeyer[a], Leonard J. Mirman[b] and Marc Santugini[c]

[a]Department of Economics, National University of Singapore, Singapore; [b]Department of Economics, University of Virginia, Charlottesville, USA; [c]Institute of Applied Economics and CIRPEE, HEC Montreal, Montreal, Canada

1. Introduction

Virtually all projects in an economy yield uncertain benefits. Uncertainty is present in both public investment undertaken by governments, as well as in market activities in the private sector. In each situation, agents must share the risk and therefore must decide how much of the risk to share. Moreover, due to risk aversion, each participant faces a cost of bearing risk. Thus, each participant must choose whether and how much they are willing to contribute to these risky projects (i.e., to share the risk). It is important to understand the basis for evaluating, and thus allocating, these risky projects.

Arrow and Lind (1970) provides an early analysis of evaluating risky projects in the context of a large population of participants sharing the risk of a public investment. The Arrow-Lind theorem states that as the population of participants tends to infinity, social risk becomes negligible. More specifically, as the number of participants grows, the risk premium of a risk-averse participant (corresponding to a share of the public risky project) decreases, and, in the limit, goes to zero. Moreover, the social risk premium also goes to zero. Hence, with a large population, it is argued that projects can be evaluated on the basis of expected (net) benefits alone without any concern for risk.

The reasoning in Arrow and Lind (1970) is not based on a model in which the link between a zero risk premium and risk-neutral behavior interact, but depends on risk-averse agents who are not engaged explicitly in trading and decision making. In this paper, we investigate the effect of letting the number of participants get infinitely large by modeling the decision mechanism of these participants. Indeed, there are choices to be modeled and decisions to be made, as well as an equilibrium that must be taken into account, before understanding the effect of the number of agents getting large as well as in the limit. In particular, in a free-market economy, the interaction of the choice of risk and the decisions by risk-averse agents determines the amount and the allocation of risk in the economy.

We first consider the original Arrow-Lind framework in which a government undertakes a risky project to be shared among many taxpayers. In our model, the taxpayers decide the level of participation in the risky project. Moreover, the amount of taxes collected by the government fully finances the public project. In this case, we show that projects cannot be evaluated only on the basis of expected benefits since the resulting tax determined by the model is incompatible with any risk sharing. That is, if the effect of the cost of bearing risk is excluded, then taxpayers refuse to contribute any amount to finance public investment. Thus, no equilibrium would ensue. Because the Arrow-Lind theorem has had a profound impact beyond the sphere of public investment under uncertainty, we then discuss the issue of risk sharing in a more market oriented setting, with trading.

2. Choosing and sharing a public investment

In this section, we extend the Arrow-Lind framework by allowing the taxpayers to choose their levels of contribution to the public investment and by endogenizing the total tax such that the project is fully funded. The inclusion of decision making in the Arrow-Lind framework has a profound effect on the interpretation of limiting cases. Specifically, we show that perfect risk spreading (due to the population of taxpayers tending to infinity) does not imply that social risk is negligible. In other words, if the public investment is evaluated on the basis of expected benefit, then risk-averse taxpayers are unwilling to contribute. We first present the model and characterize the equilibrium for any finite number of taxpayers. We then discuss the limiting case. This model is in the spirit of the model used in Arrow and Lind (1970). It does not consider the free rider problem, that is, the revelation of truthful valuations for the taxpayers. Prices are uniform and the government's budget is balanced. This model is used primarily to study the effect of risk aversion and risk sharing.

Consider an economy with a government and $n > 0$ taxpayers. The government undertakes a public investment. The random benefit for the project is represented by $\tilde{B} = \bar{B} + \tilde{\varepsilon}$ where $\bar{B}$ is the expected social benefit and $\tilde{\varepsilon}$ is a random shock.[1] Taxpayer i's disposable income is

$$\tilde{Y}_i = A_i + \tilde{B}s_i - ps_i,$$ (1)

where A_i is income excluding the benefits emanating from the public investment,[2] and $(\tilde{B} - p)s_i$ is taxpayer i's random return for the public investment. Here, $s_i \in [0, 1]$ is taxpayer i's level of participation in the public investment. Hence, given s_i, $\tilde{B}s_i$ is the random benefit accruing to taxpayer i whereas ps_i is the contribution toward the total tax raised by the government, $p > 0$.[3] At the aggregate level, taxpayers must fully contribute to the public investment, that is, $\sum_{i=1}^{n} s_i = 1$. Unlike Arrow and Lind (1970), the disposable income is explicitly written as the difference between income $A_i + \tilde{B}s_i$ and taxes ps_i.[4]

To simplify the analysis, we assume that the taxpayers exhibit constant absolute risk aversion over disposable income and the random benefits of the public investment are normally distributed. That is, the public project is potentially harmful. However, this does not detract from the results since all decisions variables are positive.

Assumption 2.1. *The coefficient of absolute risk aversion is $a > 0$ for any taxpayer. In other words, the utility function for wealth Y_i is exponential: $u(Y_i) = -e^{-aY_i}$.*

Assumption 2.2. $\tilde{\varepsilon} \sim N(0, \sigma^2)$.

Assumptions 2.1 and 2.2 yield a closed-form solution of the certainty equivalent. Given the choice s_i and the total tax p, taxpayer i's certainty equivalent is[5]

$$CE(s_i, p) = A_i + (\bar{B} - p)s_i - a\sigma^2 s_i^2/2 \tag{2}$$

where $A_i + (\bar{B} - p)s_i$ is the expected disposable income and $a\sigma^2 s_i^2/2$ is the risk premium. Following the notation in Arrow and Lind (1970), let

$$k(s_i) \equiv a\sigma^2 s_i^2/2 \tag{3}$$

be the risk premium so that $\sum_{i=1}^{n} k(s_i)$ is the social risk premium.

Having presented the setup, we now define the equilibrium. In equilibrium, given the total tax raised by the government, each taxpayer chooses an optimal level of contribution. Moreover, the value of the total tax induces full participation on the part of the taxpayers. In other words, p^* clears the market so that the public investment undertaken by the government is desired by the taxpayers. These two aspects, not present in Arrow and Lind (1970), reflect the idea that in a functioning democracy, public investment is not imposed by the government, but requires the agreement of voting taxpayers. Specifically, in our model, the taxpayers express their willingness to take part in the project by choosing their level of contribution whereas in Arrow and Lind (1970), the level of contribution is set *ex ante*, that is, $s_i = 1/n$. Moreover, in our model, the total tax is endogenous, which reflects the market value of the project. In the analysis, the equilibrium value of the total tax forms the basis for evaluating a public investment.

Definition 2.3 The tuple $\left\{ \{s_i^*(p^*)\}_{i=1}^{n}, p^* \right\}$ is an equilibrium if

(1) Using Equation (2), given $p^* > 0$, for $i = 1, \ldots, n$,

$$s_i^*(p^*) = \underset{s_i}{argmax} \quad \{A_i + (\bar{B} - p^*)s_i - a\sigma^2 s_i^2/2\}. \tag{4}$$

(2) Given $\{s_i^*(p^*)\}_{i=1}^{n}$, p^* satisfies $\sum_{i=1}^{n} s_i^*(p^*) = 1$.

Proposition 2.4 characterizes the unique equilibrium for a finite number of taxpayers. For any finite number of taxpayers, the project is fully funded and always desired by the taxpayers.

Proposition 2.4. *For $n < \infty$, there exists a unique equilibrium. In equilibrium, each taxpayer contributes a fraction*

$$s_i^*(p^*) = 1/n \tag{5}$$

to the public project and the tax raised by the government is

$$p^* = \bar{B} - \frac{a\sigma^2}{n}. \tag{6}$$

Proof. The first-order condition corresponding to Equation (4) is $\bar{B} - p - a\sigma^2 s_i = 0$ which yields $s_i^*(p) = \frac{\bar{B}-p}{a\sigma^2}$. Plugging $s_i^*(p)$ into $\sum_{i=1}^{n} s_i^*(p^*) = 1$ and solving for p^* yields Equation (6). Plugging Equation (6) back into $s_i^*(p) = \frac{\bar{B}-p}{a\sigma^2}$ yields Equation (5).

From Proposition 2.4, for any finite number of taxpayers, $s_i^*(p^*) = 1/n$ as in Arrow and Lind (1970). Moreover, in this case, both the risk premium and the social risk premium tend to zero as the population of taxpayers tends to infinity. That is, plugging $s_i^*(p^*) = 1/n$ into Equation (3) yields the equilibrium risk premium

$$k^*(s_i^*(p^*)) = \frac{a\sigma^2}{2n^2}. \tag{7}$$

Using Equation (7), $\lim_{n\to\infty} k(s_i^*(p^*)) = \lim_{n\to\infty} n \cdot k(s_i^*(p^*)) = 0$. The reason is that given the demand schedule of the taxpayer derived under a finite number of taxpayers, the gamble disappears in the limit. Consequently, the value of the public investment (in terms of the total tax) tends to the expected benefit, that is, from Equation (6), $\lim_{n\to\infty} p^* = \overline{B}$.

Note that a vanishing (social) risk premium does not imply that projects can be evaluated on the basis of expected benefit alone. The issue here is that any evaluation that disregards risk implies a profound change in the optimal behavior of risk-averse taxpayers, that is, there is a discontinuity in the equilibrium in the limit. To see this, suppose that a vanishing social risk premium is interpreted as making social cost negligible so that the value of the project depends only on the expected benefit. Hence, the total tax is set equal to the expected benefit as in the limiting case, that is, $p^* = \overline{B}$, which removes any consideration for uncertainty and risk aversion in evaluating the risky public project. Now, regardless of the number of taxpayers, each taxpayer makes an optimal decision on whether and how much to contribute to the project by taking account of the total tax. In this case, each taxpayer receives a zero expected return, that is, $\overline{B} - p^* = 0$. With zero expected return, no risk-averse taxpayer has an incentive to contribute to the risky project. Formally, from Equation (2), for $s_i \in [0, 1]$,

$$\left.\frac{\partial CE(s_i, p^*)}{\partial s_i}\right|_{p^*=\overline{B}} < 0. \tag{8}$$

That is, there is no gain from contributing on the part of the taxpayers, which induces each taxpayer to opt out of the public investment. There is thus a discontinuity in the sense that as long as the project is not evaluated on the basis of expected return, the taxpayers are willing to fully contribute to the project, but as soon as it is evaluated on the basis of expected return, the taxpayers are unwilling to participate. This discontinuity implies that the expected value of benefits does not closely approximate the correct measure of benefits defined in terms of willingness to pay for an asset with an uncertain return when n is large since the limiting case is not an equilibrium itself. Formally,

Proposition 2.5. *Suppose that the project is evaluated on the basis of expected payoff, that is, $p^* = \overline{B}$. Then, there is no equilibrium since for all i, $s_i^*(p^*)|_{p^*=\overline{B}} = 0$.*

3. Risk sharing in markets

The previous discussion focuses on the evaluation of public investment under uncertainty. We now discuss a more general framework in which several agents share risky projects via the financial sector. This is relevant since the financial sector of an economy plays an increasingly important role in a growing and more complex economy that generates more savings and investments. The financial sector influences not only the various types of risk undertaken in the economy, but also how these risks are shared among agents.

One standard approach to study the financial sector is to assume that agents are risk averse. Thus, the Arrow-Lind argument can be exported to the private financial sector. That is, with a very large number of risk-averse investors, risk spreading implies that the risk premium goes to zero eliminating any exposure to, and concern for risk. In other words, while the shareholders are risk averse, there is no need to account for their risk aversion, that is, they act as if they are risk neutral. The implication that a zero risk premium in the limit implies risk neutrality leads falsely to the conclusion that it is equivalent to assume that agents are risk neutral and not risk averse. However, no matter what the conclusion of agents' behavior in a model in which the number of agents is large (so that the exposure to risk is very small), the results depend on the assumption that agents are risk averse. Indeed, agents acting as if they are risk neutral in the limit is a conclusion of the model in which agents are risk averse and all risk disappears. However, the conclusion of the model with respect to behavior should not lead to a change in the assumptions of the model, that is, that agents are not risk averse.

To see this, consider several risk-averse investors who must decide whether to invest in a risky firm owned by a risk-averse entrepreneur. Specifically, consider an economy with one entrepreneur and several investors whose objective is to maximize the expected utility of wealth over a portfolio of a risky asset and a risk-free asset. The entrepreneur, the founder and initial owner of the firm, issues equity shares that are claims on the profit generated by the firm. Investors do not have entrepreneurial prospects. However, they do have initial wealth that they use to purchase shares of the risky and the risk-free asset.

As in the case of sharing risk of a public investment, it can be shown that there is no equilibrium with perfect risk spreading (i.e., when the number of investors goes to infinity) because no risk-averse agent wishes to trade. While risk-neutral investors have no concern for risk and are indifferent to sharing risk, risk-averse agents in an economy with perfect risk spreading do not want to share risk. To understand this result, consider a group of risk-averse investors deciding whether to buy shares from a risk-averse entrepreneur. The market price of the risky asset is endogenous and is affected by the number of agents. On the one hand, when the number of investors grows, risk spreading increases the price of the risky asset and, in the limit, is equal to the expected payoff of the asset, so that the investors, who are risk averse, get no risk premium and, thus, do not want to hold any of the random asset. In other words, perfect risk spreading implies a price equal to the expected payoff so that there is no gain in engaging in risk sharing, and, in addition, holding even a tiny share of the risky asset makes it costly in terms of risk. On the other hand, with the price of the asset equal to its expected value, the entrepreneur would like to push the entire investment off on the investors. This is not viable since the risk-averse agents refuse to accept the trade, and, thus, no trading is possible.

This result is in stark contrast to the outcome derived from assuming risk-neutral investors. If investors are risk neutral, the risk-averse entrepreneur passes all the risk to the investors. Hence, the assumption of risk aversion and the explicit modeling of trade have a powerful effect on the conclusion of the model. Indeed, the limiting price of the asset is such that expected return is zero and any risk-averse investor still cares about risk and incurs a cost. The reason for this difference is due solely to whether trading is modeled. It should be pointed out that, in the limit, even when trading is not modeled, the agent does not become risk neutral, but the risk premium goes to zero.[6] On the other hand, when trading is modeled, in the limit, risk-averse investors instead of behaving in a risk-neutral way, do not, in fact, share risk.

Notes

1. A tilde distinguishes a random variable from its realization.
2. Unlike Arrow and Lind (1970), we assume that private income is nonstochastic. This simplification has no bearing on the analysis.
3. Foldes and Rees (1977) consider the role of the fiscal system and public expenditures in the Arrow-Lind framework.
4. We implicitly assume that A_i includes transfers from the government which are unrelated to agent i's tax contributions.
5. The certainty equivalent is implicitly defined by $Eu(A_i + (\tilde{B} - p)s_i) = u(CE(s_i, p))$.
6. This is true since the gamble disappears and so does the risk. Consider N agents who are forced to share a risk. Dividing a given risk more and more finely causes the risk premium to vanish not because the agents become risk neutral but because the gamble disappears.

References

Arrow, K. J., & Lind, R. C. (1970). Uncertainty and the evaluation of public investment decisions. *American Economic Review, 60*(3), 364–378.

Foldes, L. P., & Rees, R. (1977). A note on the arrow-lind theorem. *American Economic Review, 67*(2), 188–193.

Evaluating uncertain public projects with rival and non-rival benefits

Bram Gallagher[a] and Arthur Snow[b]

[a]Department of Economics and Finance, Middle Tennessee State University, Murfreesboro, USA;
[b]Department of Economics, University of Georgia, Athens, USA

1. Introduction

Governments must often make decisions about the allocation of public funds among competing projects of uncertain value. With the benefits and costs of public projects evaluated in terms of consumers' willingness to pay, consistent accounting requires that the social cost of a project's risk be assessed according to the same metric. In an influential paper, Arrow and Lind (1970) argue that, when this approach to evaluating public projects is adopted, the social cost of project risk in a large economy is negligible, and projects should be evaluated solely on the basis of their expected values. The argument is that, as the number of consumers becomes large, the private risk borne by any one consumer becomes small and, more decisively, the aggregate (social) cost of risk becomes small as well – a result known as the Arrow-Lind Theorem.

A serious limitation of the Theorem, however, pointed out by Fisher (1973) and by Foldes and Rees (1977), is that the result does not apply to public projects that produce goods whose benefits are consumed collectively. For these Samuelson (1954) public goods, the cost of risk borne by an individual consumer associated with project benefits is unaffected by the size of the population, and hence the social cost of risk for these projects is positive. By contrast, for the Arrow-Lind Theorem to hold, the public project must, in the limit, have no effect on any consumer; that is, not only must the taxes paid to finance the project approach zero for each consumer as the population grows, but the benefit enjoyed by each consumer must also approach zero. Therefore, the project must have not only a fixed cost, but also a fixed aggregate expected benefit. Hence, a public project for which the Arrow-Lind Theorem is applicable must produce benefits by providing the services of a private good, and then the project is simply a private investment undertaken by government on behalf of taxpayers.

Thus, at one extreme public projects provide the services of a private good and consumers' risk preferences have no bearing on project evaluation in a large economy, while at the other extreme projects provide the services of a public good and consumers' risk preferences are paramount in project evaluation, whatever the size of the economy. Often, however, public expenditures provide both private (rival) and public (non-rival) consumption benefits. Public expenditures on education offer a classic example, enhancing the production of human capital by individuals – a private good – while also cultivating an ethic of civic responsibility and respect for the rule of law – a public good. Likewise, national defense expenditures protect private property as well as the economy's infrastructure, and the construction and maintenance of dams provide both hydroelectric power and pollution abatement when used as a substitute for fossil fuels.

In this paper we focus on public projects that provide a mixture of rival and non-rival consumption benefits. We adopt the basic elements of the Arrow-Lind model, but elaborate by assuming that a proportion α of the project's benefits are rival in consumption while the proportion $1 - \alpha$ of the project's benefits are non-rival in consumption. When $\alpha = 1$ the Arrow-Lind Theorem applies and the social cost of the project's risk is negligible in a large economy; when $\alpha = 0$ the Theorem does not apply and the social cost of the project's risk is positive regardless of the size of the economy. It follows that, the social cost of risk must decline in an overall sense as the degree of rivalry increases from $\alpha = 0$ to $\alpha = 1$, and as the size of the population increases, at least when benefits are perfectly rival.

Our analysis shows that, while expected project benefit for each consumer declines as α increases, the private and social costs of project risk also decline uniformly as α increases if consumers are risk averse and exhibit constant or increasing absolute risk aversion (CARA or IARA). Although the social cost of risk bearing increases with greater rivalry if decreasing absolute risk aversion (DARA) is sufficiently strong, the social cost of risk declines with greater rivalry if relative risk aversion is less than one and relative prudence is less than two. Regardless of its effects on the cost of risk, greater rivalry increases the social value of a public project, suggesting that projects with largely rival consumption benefits should prevail over projects with similar cost, but largely collective consumption benefits.

We also show that the private cost of risk bearing is lower with a larger population if all benefits are non-rival and consumers exhibit DARA, or if benefits are at least partially rival, consumers exhibit CARA or DARA, and the social cost of risk declines with greater rivalry. We conclude that intuitive predictions regarding the influence of rivalry and population size on the cost of bearing the risk associated with public projects of uncertain value are confirmed when relative risk aversion is less than one and relative prudence is less than two.

2. A model of public projects with collective and private benefits

The economy is comprised of $n > 1$ identical consumers who derive utility from consumption of a single good. Each consumer is endowed with a sure income A plus a random, zero-mean component ε. The public project produces an output with expected benefit $\bar{\theta}$ at a total cost of c. Each consumer pays a lump-sum tax of c/n to finance the project and enjoys the consumption benefits of both its private good and public good services. We assume that these benefits are random. For example, public expenditures on national defense are more valuable in a state of war than in peace, but which state shall obtain is uncertain; public expenditures on education have an uncertain effectiveness in generating both rival and non-rival benefits; hydroelectric power generation depends on river flow, which in turn depends on uncertain rainfall.

Following Arrow and Lind, we assume that the random benefits of the public project are independent of the endowed income risk and abstract from temporal considerations. For simplicity, we assume that the random rival and non-rival benefits are perfectly positively correlated. Thus, in consumption, the project yields a random, positive flow of services θ, with a portion α of these services providing benefits that are rival in consumption. The remaining portion provides benefits that are non-rival in consumption. The net benefit of the project to each consumer is measured by net willingness to pay, which in state θ is equal to

$$B(\theta, \alpha, n) \equiv \theta(1 - \alpha) + \frac{\theta\alpha - c}{n}$$
$$\equiv \omega\theta - \frac{c}{n}, \tag{1}$$

so that all consumers receive the project's non-rival benefit $\theta(1 - \alpha)$ along with an equal share of the project's rival benefit $\theta\alpha$, and pay the lump-sum tax. The second line, serves to define the coefficient $\omega = 1 - \alpha(n - 1)/n$, which depends on the degree of rivalry and the size of the population.

The expected utility of the representative consumer is given by

$$E_\theta E_\varepsilon[U(A + \varepsilon + B(\theta, \alpha, n))] = E_\theta[V(A + B(\theta, \alpha, n))], \tag{2}$$

where E_θ and E_ε denote the expectation operators for the independent random variables θ and ε, and U is the consumer's von Neumann-Morgenstern utility function, assumed to be strictly concave, reflecting risk aversion. From a consumer's perspective, the endowed income risk ε represents an independent background risk when evaluating the net benefits of the project, and therefore the relevant criterion is the derived utility function for the project's net benefits,

$$V(A + B(\theta, \alpha, n)) \equiv E_\varepsilon[U(A + \varepsilon + B(\theta, \alpha, n))], \tag{3}$$

which accounts indirectly for the endowed background risk ε.[1] The cost to each consumer of bearing the project's risk is measured by the risk premium for V, denoted $\pi(\omega, W)$ and defined implicitly by

$$E_\theta[V(W + \omega\theta)] = V(W + \omega\bar{\theta} - \pi(\omega, W)), \tag{4}$$

where $W = A - c/n$.

For the two polar cases we have

$$E_\theta[V(W + (\theta - c)/n)] = V(W + [\bar{\theta} - c]/n) - \pi(1/n, W)) \tag{5}$$

when all benefits are rival, and

$$E_\theta[V(W + \theta - c/n)] = V(W + [\bar{\theta} - c/n] - \pi(1, W)) \tag{5'}$$

when all benefits are non-rival. Although expected net benefits are greater when all benefits are non-rival, deviation about the mean is lower when all benefits are rival. With CARA, the difference in expected net benefit has no bearing on the magnitude of the risk premiums, and thus with less risk the project having only rival benefits has the smaller risk premium, and $\pi(1/n, W) < \pi(1, W)$.

3. Changes in the collective-private benefit mix

Many public projects provide both collective and private benefits. In these instances, α lies between the extremes of zero and one. From the two polar cases, we would expect the risk premium, and thus the social cost of risk, to be lower for projects providing relatively more private consumption benefits. However, we find that this intuitive prediction is not universally valid. Nonetheless, the social value of the project increases as α increases, *ceteris paribus*. We first investigate the effect of rivalry on the risk premium.

3.1. Risk-bearing cost and greater rivalry

Since an increase in α, representing an increase in rivalry, reduces the coefficient ω while leaving wealth unaffected, an increase in rivalry reduces the social cost of project risk if and only if π increases as ω increases. Differentiating Equation (4) with respect to ω yields $E_\theta[V'(W + \omega\theta) \cdot \theta] = V'(W + \omega\bar{\theta} - \pi(\omega, W)) \cdot (\bar{\theta} - \pi_\omega)$, which implies

$$\pi_\omega = \bar{\theta} - E_\theta[V'(W + \omega\theta) \cdot \theta]/V'(W + \omega\bar{\theta} - \pi). \tag{6}$$

The social cost of risk declines as the degree of project rivalry increases if and only if

$$d\pi/d\alpha = \pi_\omega \omega_\alpha = -\frac{n-1}{n}\pi_\omega \tag{7}$$

is negative. The following is an immediate consequence of Equations (6) and (7).[2]

Proposition 1 π_ω is positive, and $d\pi/d\alpha$ is negative, if and only if

$$V'(W + \omega\bar{\theta} - \pi) \cdot \bar{\theta} > E_\theta[V'(W + \omega\theta) \cdot \theta]. \tag{8}$$

Applying the covariance rule to the random variables on the right-hand side of inequality Equation (8), while recognizing that V is risk averse, we obtain

$$0 > \text{cov}(V'(W + \omega\theta), \theta) = E_\theta[V' \cdot \theta] - E_\theta[V'] \cdot \bar{\theta}. \tag{9}$$

It follows that inequality Equation (8) holds if $V'(W + \omega\bar{\theta} - \pi) \geq E_\theta[V'(W + \omega\theta)]$, or equivalently, if

$$V'(W + \omega\bar{\theta} - \pi) \geq V'(W + \omega\bar{\theta} - \psi), \tag{10}$$

where ψ is the prudence premium for V introduced by Kimball (1990). Given risk aversion, inequality Equation (10) holds if and only if $\pi \geq \psi$, which requires that V exhibit constant or increasing absolute risk aversion (CARA or IARA).[3]

Corollary 1 π_ω is positive and $d\pi/d\alpha$ is negative if V exhibits CARA or IARA.

We next establish the existence of environments in which the social cost of project risk increases as the degree of rivalry increases. To this end, we introduce the random variable $\eta = \theta - \bar{\theta}$ and conclude that inequality Equation (8) fails to hold if and only if

$$E_\theta[V'(W + \omega\theta)\eta] \geq [V'(W + \omega\bar{\theta} - \pi) - E_\theta V'(W + \omega\theta)]\bar{\theta}$$
$$= [V'(W + \omega\bar{\theta} - \pi) - V'(W + \omega\bar{\theta} - \psi)]\bar{\theta}. \tag{11}$$

The left-hand side of inequality Equation (11) is negative and the inequality holds if ψ exceeds π by a sufficiently wide margin. Since $\psi - \pi$ is directly related to the strength of DARA, we have the following result.

Proposition 2 π_ω is negative, and $d\pi/d\alpha$ is positive, if DARA is sufficiently strong.

Nonetheless, we can establish that greater rivalry reduces the social cost of risk for an important class of environments with DARA by introducing the function

$$H(\theta) \equiv V'(W + \omega\theta) \cdot \theta. \tag{12}$$

Since $V'(W + \omega\bar{\theta} - \pi) \cdot \bar{\theta} > V'(W + \omega\bar{\theta}) \cdot \bar{\theta}$, the following is a sufficient condition for inequality Equation (8),

$$H(\bar{\theta}) \geq E_\theta[H(\theta)]. \tag{13}$$

This sufficient condition holds if and only if H is concave. For the derivatives of H, we obtain $H' = V''\omega\theta + V'$ and

$$\begin{aligned} H'' &= [V'''\omega\theta + 2V'']\omega \\ &= V''\omega[2 - \hat{P}], \end{aligned} \tag{14}$$

where $\hat{P} = -\omega\theta V'''(W + \omega\theta)/V''(W + \omega\theta)$ is the index of partial relative prudence. For $\hat{P} = -bV''(a + b)$ to be less than or equal to two for all $b \geq 0$ and $a + b > 0$, it is necessary and sufficient that the index of relative prudence $P = -bV'''(b)/V''(b)$ be less than or equal to two for all $b > 0$. Hence, H is concave if $P \leq 2$.

Corollary 2 π_ω is positive, and $d\pi/d\alpha$ is negative, if $P \leq 2$.

Eeckhoudt, Etner, and Schroyen (2009) show that preference for 'harm disaggregation', or combining bad with good, is necessary and sufficient for $P \geq 2$, while their proof also shows that the opposite preference is necessary and sufficient for $P \leq 2$. The latter is consistent with DARA provided the index of relative risk aversion is less than P. Analyzing the portfolio problem, Choi, Kim, and Snow (2001) show that investment in the risky asset increases with first-order stochastic dominance improvement in the random rate of return if and only if relative risk aversion is less than or equal to one, and that investment declines with an increase in risk if and only if relative prudence is less than or equal to two. Thus, under conditions necessary and sufficient for the validity of intuitive predictions regarding investor responses to changes in the random rate of return, the social cost of risk declines with greater rivalry and preferences exhibiting DARA.

3.2. Social value and greater rivalry

Differentiating the certainty equivalent wealth argument on the right-hand side of Equation (4) with respect to α yields

$$\partial[W + \omega\bar{\theta} - \pi(\omega, W)]/\partial\alpha = -\frac{n-1}{n}(\bar{\theta} - \pi_\omega) \tag{15}$$

as the effect of greater rivalry on individual net benefits. Substituting for π_ω from Equation (6), we obtain

$$-\frac{n-1}{n}(\bar{\theta} - \pi_\omega) = \frac{n-1}{n} \cdot \frac{E_\theta[V' \cdot \theta]}{\bar{V}'}, \tag{16}$$

which is positive since θ is positive. Multiplying by n yields the change in the project's social value as a result of greater rivalry.

Proposition 3 The social value of a public project of uncertain value increases as the degree of rivalry increases.

4. Changes in population

With a larger population, the coefficient ω is smaller, but the value of W is greater, resulting in potentially opposing effects on the private cost of risk bearing. Differentiating the individual risk premium with respect to n yields

$$d\pi/dn = [-\alpha\pi_\omega + c\pi_W]/n^2 \tag{17}$$

since $\omega_n = -\alpha/n^2$ and $W_n = c/n^2$. Differentiating Equation (4), which defines the risk premium, with respect to W yields $E_\theta[V'(W + \omega\theta) \cdot \theta] = V'(W + \omega\bar{\theta} - \pi) \cdot (1 - \pi_W)$, which implies

$$\pi_W = 1 - E_\theta[V'(W + \omega\theta) \cdot \theta]/V'(W + \omega\bar{\theta} - \pi). \tag{18}$$

Substituting from Equations (6) and (18) into Equation (17) yields

$$n^2 d\pi/dn = -\alpha\left[\bar{\theta} - \frac{E_\theta[V'\theta]}{\bar{V}'}\right] + c\left[1 - \frac{E_\theta[V']}{\bar{V}'}\right], \tag{19}$$

where $\bar{V}' = V'(W + \omega\bar{\theta} - \pi)$. It follows that

$$c\left[1 - \frac{E_\theta[V']}{\bar{V}'}\right] < \alpha\left[\bar{\theta} - \frac{E_\theta[V'\theta]}{\bar{V}'}\right] = \alpha\bar{\theta}\left[1 - \frac{E_\theta[V'\theta]}{\bar{V}'\bar{\theta}}\right] \tag{20}$$

is necessary and sufficient for the private cost of risk bearing to decline as the population increases.

Equation (17) reveals that, when all project benefits are non-rival and α equals zero, the sign of $d\pi/dn$ is the same as the sign of π_W, which is negative if and only if consumers exhibit decreasing absolute risk aversion. Inequality Equation (8), which is necessary and sufficient for $d\pi/d\alpha$ to be negative, implies that the final term multiplying $\alpha\bar{\theta}$ in Equation (20) is positive, while the term multiplying c is non-positive with CARA or DARA. In that event, $d\pi/dn$ is again negative.

Proposition 4 $d\pi/dn$ is negative, and the private cost of risk is lower with a larger population, if all benefits are non-rival and consumers exhibit DARA, or if some portion of benefits is rival, preferences exhibit CARA or DARA, and the cost of risk bearing declines with greater rivalry.

5. Conclusions

In the spirit of Arrow and Lind's analysis, we have reexamined the private and social costs of bearing the risks associated with public expenditure on projects of uncertain value. Beginning with the observation that the Arrow-Lind Theorem applies to projects whose benefits are provided by services that are wholly rival in consumption, we analyze the cost of risk for projects that provide a mix of rival and non-rival consumption benefits. Intuition suggests that both private and social costs of risk bearing decline as the degree of rivalry increases and as the size of the population increases, since these costs both vanish in the limit case with perfect rivalry and an infinite population. We confirm these intuitive predictions for selected economic environments, but show that if DARA is sufficiently strong these predictions fail to hold.

Despite these conflicting results, we show that the social cost of risk declines with greater rivalry when relative risk aversion is less than one and relative prudence is less than two, conditions that are necessary and sufficient for intuitive predictions regarding the effects of changes in risk in the portfolio problem. Additionally, we find that the social value of a public project increases for any finite population as the degree of rivalry increases.

Notes

1. Gollier and Pratt (1996) show that, in the presence of a zero-mean, independent background risk ε, V is more risk averse than U if U exhibits decreasing absolute risk aversion and decreasing absolute prudence.
2. Throughout, primes on univariate functions denote derivatives, and subscripts on multivariate functions denote partial derivatives.
3. See, for example, Gollier (2001, p. 25). Note that V inherits decreasing absolute risk aversion from U, but may not inherit CARA or IARA. See Gollier (2001, pp. 114ff).

References

Arrow, K. J., & Lind, R. C. (1970). Uncertainty and the evaluation of public investment decisions. *American Economic Review, 60*, 364–378.

Choi, G., Kim, I., & Snow, A. (2001). Comparative statics predictions for changes in uncertainty in the portfolio and saving problems. *Bulletin of Economic Research, 53*, 61–72.

Eeckhoudt, L., Etner, J., & Schroyen, F. (2009). The values of relative risk aversion and prudence: A context-free interpretation. *Mathematical Social Sciences, 58*, 1–7.

Fisher, A. C. (1973). A paradox in the theory of public investment. *Journal of Public Economics, 2*, 405–407.

Foldes, L. P., & Rees, R. (1977). A note on the Arrow-Lind theorem. *American Economic Review, 67*, 188–193.

Gollier, C. (2001). *The economics of risk and time*. Cambridge: MIT Press.

Gollier, C., & Pratt, J. W. (1996). Risk vulnerability and the tempering effect of background risk. *Econometrica, 64*, 1109–1123.

Kimball, M. S. (1990). Precautionary saving in the small and in the large. *Econometrica, 58*, 53–73.

Samuelson, P. A. (1954). The pure theory of public expenditure. *Review of Economics and Statistics, 36*, 387–389.

Probing the limits of risk-neutral government

Alan Randall

Agricultural and Resource Economics, School of Economics, University of Sydney, Australia

Times were different in 1970, when 'Uncertainty and the Evaluation of Public Investment Decisions' was published (Arrow and Lind, 1970). Environmentalism was in the air, but it hardly was mainstream yet. The debate about discounting distant-future prospects had scarcely begun. Most economists were clear about the motivation for discounting: it was all about efficiency in capital markets. From this standpoint, it was self-evident that a government seeking to invest on behalf of the public has an affirmative duty to ensure that the investment will generate a market rate of return (adjusted appropriately). For economists sympathetic to the 'small government' position, in which capital is thought to reside in private hands in the right and proper scheme of things, the list of plausible adjustments was short – there was obvious need to adjust for inflation but other proposed adjustments were viewed skeptically. Those inclined to see government's duty in terms less of mimicking the market and more of restraining its excesses were willing to consider additional adjustments for failures in capital markets.

It was clear that markets adjusted interest rates for uncertainty – a lender would demand to be compensated for foregoing the use of her capital and for the chance that the borrower would fail to repay it. Various plausible arguments were offered that government was a different kind of investor, especially in its capacity to deal with uncertainty, and its investments should be evaluated in ways that reflect that fact. Arrow and Lind (A-L) stepped into what was, at one level, a rather esoteric debate among specialists.

The standard argument for government as a risk-neutral investor in the mid-1960s was that the government's portfolio is large and diversified. Hirshleifer (1965) recognized that government can pool risk over many projects but argued that, since private risk can be hedged, the inherent risk management advantage of government was illusory. To treat risk differently in the public sector would result in excessive public investment at the expense of private investments yielding higher returns. While A-L took time to protest that Hirshleifer was too sanguine about the completeness and accessibility of markets in contingencies, their main thrust was to argue instead that government should be risk-neutral 'not because (it) is able to pool investments but because (it) distributes the risk associated with any investment among a large number of people' (p. 366).[1] Government should be risk-neutral because it has very-many 'shareholders' each of whom is benefitted trivially by each project and taxed trivially for it.

The A-L argument had, and still has, a major impact on the discussion of the efficiency of public investment in general, and the proper discount rate for long-lived public projects in particular. But its influence has spread far beyond this initial focus. It is now a default assumption that government should be in most of its domain an expected-value (EV) maximizer. For example, Zivin and Bridges (2002) discern a default assumption of EV-maximization in health policy, and credit the A-L argument with motivating it. The A-L argument, seen in this light, has become anything but esoteric.

The major caveats to A-L's key proposition that have emerged in the literature in the more than forty subsequent years were foreshadowed by Fisher (1973). Where there is risk of non-negligible environmental damage, the assumption of risk-spreading among the whole population may not hold. There are two distinct ideas here. First, where public goods are involved, risk-spreading breaks down because a true public good is indivisible so that each individual gets to consume it all, an idea elaborated subsequently by, for example, Gallagher (2011). Second, environmental goods and bads have a spatial dimension, in the most extreme cases visiting huge and pervasive impacts in specific places, a concern developed by, for example, Hochrainer and Pflug (2009). These are cases where the crucial A-L assumptions – the benefits and costs are money-equivalent (and therefore rival and fungible), and each of the very-many citizens is benefitted trivially by each project and taxed trivially for it – are violated. On the other hand, A-L risk-neutrality should be an ideal fit for Norway's sovereign wealth fund (a large fund investing on a global scale for benefit of a national population); or more precisely, the fund should be neutral to idiosyncratic risk, but one might expect aversion to systemic risks.

The A-L analysis was developed for the problem of selecting capital projects and programs for the government's portfolio. However, that portfolio is quite diverse with respect to the key dimensions identified above: the degree to which impacts are rivalrous in consumption, and the very wide dispersion of benefits and costs among the citizenry. The national suite of public investment projects includes some for producing truly national public goods such as defense, basic research, and applied research, for example in agriculture and medicine, where benefits are quite diffuse. But even for these the economic and environmental impacts for better or worse are spatially and sectorally uneven. There is also a suite of more targeted public investments whose immediate beneficiaries are obvious while the trickle-down or spin-off benefits to the broader public are more obscure, and an infrastructure portfolio of mostly local and regional investments. In addition, the suite of regulatory initiatives – many of them designed to redirect investment in ways intended to promote the public wellbeing – is national in scope. Nevertheless, many of these initiatives bite with greater force in particular locations, regions, and/or sectors of the economy.

The A-L analysis, which applies so well to investments such as Norway's sovereign wealth fund, may not be so well-aligned with the broader public investment problem for which it was developed. It is important to note that these considerations would not surprise Arrow and Lind. Recognizing that, for many public projects, government pays the public costs with diffuse taxes but the benefits and the private costs are more narrowly focused, they suggested that risk-neutral evaluation of public costs and risk-averse evaluation of private benefits and costs often might be a good fit. The remainder of this essay develops this idea in the context of a particular example.

Risk-neutrality in regulating medical treatments and drugs?

To probe the limits of risk-neutral government, consider the argument that government should be an EV maximizer in regulating drugs and medical treatments. The claim under scrutiny is constructed as follows. Government should maximize a welfarist objective. In a certain world, Benthamite welfare can be maximized by approving proposed initiatives for which the value-sum of benefits from treatment exceeds the value-sum of harm. Where there is uncertainty about benefits and harm, a risk-neutral benefit-cost criterion will maximize expected national net benefits.

Economists have questioned, at least since the late-1960s, the apparent risk-aversion reflected in governmental approaches to regulating drugs and medical treatments. Sunstein (2005) expressed concern that risk-averse regulatory approaches to new drugs and medical treatments simply get risk-risk trade-offs wrong. All else equal, similar risks should be treated similarly, and a patient risks harm from treatment and harm from letting the affliction take its course. Sunstein speculated that approval processes for new drugs and treatments over-provide protection from adverse side-effects while delaying access to life-saving innovations.

It is a stylized fact in some circles that preventable mortality while waiting for the Food and Drug Administration (FDA) to complete its approval process for drugs exceeds mortality prevented by the FDA's vigilance against unsafe drugs (e.g., Gieringer, 1985). This critique persists without much empirical evidence but, to be fair, the counterfactuals would be hard to establish. There is, however, a literature on the 'drug lag' offering cross-jurisdictional comparisons of time to approval, and safety problems (e.g., adverse drug reactions) post-approval, that addresses pieces of the picture. For example, Grabowski and Wang (2008) found that drugs receiving lengthier pre-approval scrutiny in the US had lower counts of serious adverse post-approval drug reactions. Abraham and Davis (2005) conclude that the more stringent drug approval regime in the US took longer than its counterpart in the UK, but protected the US market from drugs that proved unsafe when marketed in the UK. Olson (2013) concludes that there are more post-approval problems with drugs approved first under less strict European procedures than those approved first under US/FDA procedures.

What do we know about public risk preferences in the health arena? Inferring public preferences from political outcomes is always somewhat speculative, but here goes.

First, people want risk-averse regulation of new drugs and medical treatments. All else equal, they want assurances of safety, and they are quick to express their horror when things go badly wrong with approved treatments. FDA requirements were strengthened substantially in reaction to the *Thalidomide* disaster in other countries, even though *Thalidomide* had not been approved in the US.

Second, the 'drug lag' argument has some resonance with people – they do not want excessive regulatory delays. In particular, they want patients with serious afflictions to have the option of promising but still experimental treatments.

Should we interpret these preferences as contradictory and, if so, how can we explain their coexistence? Risk-aversion is likely exacerbated in health matters for two reasons: health is no trivial matter, especially for oneself and those one cares about personally; and the respect and deference demanded by medical professionals comes with a *quid pro quo*. There seems to be a kind of implicit contract at work: we ordinary folk cede some substantial part of our autonomy to certified experts in the health fields in return for an assured reduction in the risks associated with treatment, and the experts had better not mess up!

Most people understand risk as chance of harm, and our aversion to some newly proposed risk is circumstantial in that it depends on the chance of harm in the default, the no-action scenario. If the prospects from letting the affliction take its course are really grim, even very risky alternatives may start to look acceptable. *Thalidomide* was pre-scribed for relief of morning sickness and hastily withdrawn when horrendous side-effects became apparent. Yet *Thalidomide* is now approved for treatment of certain debilitating afflictions including leprosy, under very tightly controlled conditions.

We can expect people to be very risk-averse when it comes to adverse reactions to cosmetics and routine treatments for relief of minor pains and infections but, when faced with really grim afflictions, less so for unproven treatments and treatments known to involve a chance of serious side-effects. Perhaps ordinary people do not perform so badly after all, in sorting-out the risks and rewards.

Is there a reasonable argument that government could provide more welfare for its citizens if it were a little less sensitive to people's risk-attitudes concerning their own health? Not surprisingly, risk-aversion is heightened by the immediacy of one's own health and its centrality to life-prospects. Furthermore, we know a lot about our own condition and our likely prospects under the no-action scenario. Might a 'veil of ignorance' thought experiment lead to different conclusions about the risk attitudes appropriate for government?

At first blush, government might emerge as an EV maximizer in a veil of ignorance process in which hypothetical people are trading-off hypothetical adverse drug reactions for hypothetical drug discoveries. However, concerns about incentives and behavior might undermine this outcome, much as incentives issues undermined a strict egalitarian solution to Rawls' fairness problem. An EV-maximizing government would approve drugs and treatments so long as the EV of so doing exceeds the EV of no-action. At the margin – and the margin would be rather wide in the absence of detailed personal and product-specific information – consumers would be close to indifferent between the prescribed treatment and no-action. We are better-off on average when people are motivated to follow the prescribed regimen, which is unlikely if we sense that there is little expected advantage (Carpenter, Grimmer, & Lomazoff, 2010), and for that reason it is likely that even a veil of ignorance process would choose a risk-averse regulatory stance.

If government as EV maximizer in the health arena seems less than ideal under a veil of ignorance, it is a non-starter in the real world. We have identities, self-awareness and, especially for those with serious afflictions, detailed knowledge of our own health status. Quite rationally, we are very risk-averse when the promised benefits of a drug or treatment are modest, and less averse to treatment risk when our default prospects are grim. The beneficiaries of a pro-innovation EV-maximizing stance are hypothetical future people, including the contingent future selves of some of us. We are not likely to want to submit to bigger risks today on behalf of these people, even if some of us will eventually be among them, and it is not clear that we are morally obligated to do so.

A bottom-line conclusion re risk-neutral government

More than forty years later, it is clear that Arrow and Lind should be credited with two things: first, a big idea – government should be a risk-neutral investor because each of its very-many citizens is benefitted trivially by each project and taxed trivially for it – that is now embedded securely in the corpus of economic principles; and second, the insight (almost hidden in their concluding comments) that for much of what government actually does – collect funds from diffuse sources and focus them on specific kinds of benefits and impacts in specific places – risk-neutral evaluation of public costs and risk-averse evaluation of private benefits and costs often might be a good fit.

The A-L's key result, and the conditions they assumed in order to demonstrate it, are well-suited to Norway's sovereign wealth fund. For much of government's actual investment portfolio, the caveats foreshadowed by Fisher in 1973 tell much of the story. A-L's big idea does not apply well to government investments focused on economic sectors, regions, and localities. We can identify with economic sectors, regions, and localities, and see non-trivial personal benefits and costs in public actions focused upon them. But this kind of personal identification hits nowhere near so close to home as does an individual's risk of an adverse drug reaction, or her treatment for serious and debilitating affliction.

Note

1. They recognize two additional arguments for risk-neutral government – government is able to avoid many of the moral hazards that exacerbate private risk; and government as a matter of policy should choose its risk preferences, not merely infer them by observing private markets – but offer little comment on them.

References

Abraham, J., & Davis, C. (2005). A comparative analysis of drug safety withdrawals in the UK and the US (1971–1992): Implications for current regulatory thinking and policy. *Social Science and Medicine, 61*, 881–892.

Arrow, K. J., & Lind, R. C. (1970). Uncertainty and the evaluation of public investment decisions. *American Economic Review, 60*(3), 364–378.

Carpenter, D., Grimmer, J., & Lomazoff, E. (2010). Approval regulation and endogenous consumer confidence: Theory and analogies to licensing, safety, and financial regulation. *Regulation and Governance, 4*, 383–407.

Fisher, A. C. (1973). Environmental externalities and the Arrow-Lind public investment theorem. *American Economic Review, 63*(4), 722–725.

Gallagher, B. (2011). Optimal Provision of a Public Good with Uncertainty and State-Dependent Preferences. Working Paper. Retrieved from http://www.bramgallaghereconomics.com/PublicGoodswithUncertaintyandStateDependentPrefsv3.3.pdf

Gieringer, D. H. (1985). The safety and efficacy of new drug approval. *Cato Journal, 5*, 177–201.

Grabowski, H., & Wang, Y. (2008). Do faster Food and Drug Administration drug reviews adversely affect patient safety? An analysis of the 1992 prescription drug user fee act. *Journal of Law and Economics, 51*(2), 377–406.

Hirshleifer, J. (1965). Investment decision under uncertainty: choice-theoretic approaches. *Quarterly Journal of Economics, 79*, 509–536.

Hochrainer, S., & Pflug, G. (2009). Natural disaster risk bearing ability of governments: Consequences of kinked utility. *Journal of Natural Disaster Science, 31*(1), 11–21.

Olson, M. K. (2013). Eliminating the US drug lag: Implications for drug safety. *Journal of Risk and Uncertainty, 47*, 1–30.

Sunstein, C. (2005). *Laws of fear: Beyond the precautionary principle*. Cambridge: Cambridge University Press.

Zivin, J. G., & Bridges, J. F. P. (2002). Addressing risk preferences in cost-effectiveness analysis. *Applied Health Economics and Health Policy, 1*, 135–139.

Are we in this together? Risk bearing and collective action

Carlisle Ford Runge and Justin Andrew Johnson

Department of Applied Economics, University of Minnesota, St. Paul, MN, USA

1. Introduction

'How selfish so ever man may be supposed, there are evidently some principles in his nature, which interest him in the fortune of others, and render their happiness necessary to him, though he derives nothing from it, except the pleasure of seeing it' (Smith, 1759).

Since the publication of the Arrow-Lind public investment theorem in 1970, the role of the public sector as a mechanism of risk bearing has changed dramatically. The focus of the Arrow-Lind (A/L) Theorem was on public expenditures such as roads, dams or other infrastructure (see Arrow & Lind, 1970). But in the last 40 years, the most memorable events in which federal government spending has spread risk across the taxpaying public have been natural and financial disasters, notably Hurricane Katrina in 2005 and Sandy in 2012 and the financial meltdown of 2008–2009. In these cases, all taxpayers effectively bore collective responsibility for the plight of those buffeted by nature or financial markets (while infrastructure languished).

Collectivizing responsibility gives rise to many of the same issues faced in any collective action problem or commons dilemma, which we will discuss in terms of a theory of reciprocal interaction. However, it bears mention that the financial magnitude of hurricane relief or financial meltdowns makes the idea of spreading risks across the taxpaying public so as to approach a risk share of zero, as Arrow and Lind argued, much less plausible.

Within 10 days of Hurricane Katrina, the federal government approved $62.3 billion in aid payments (Griffith, 2005). In response to the financial meltdown, the federal government purchased $1.75 trillion worth of mortgage-backed securities, agency debt and long-term Treasury securities (Board of Governors of the Federal Reserve System 2009). When spread across the 146.2 million individual tax returns (Internal Revenue Service (IRS), 2013), each event when apportioned left each tax return burdened with a respective share of about $426 and $11,970 dollars apiece. In such cases taxpayers are being asked to surrender real money to cover these risks, which cannot be discounted by a limit argument as approaching zero.

As the nature of risk bearing has changed, the question raised by the A/L theorem now is whether the public will support interventions that cost taxpayers money to cover natural or financial risk. Arrow and Lind's answer was not to worry due to the risk spreading mechanism they outline. This is less than reassuring today and has become the stuff of intense political rhetoric between those who still believe in government's role and those who seem to think that government spending, by definition, is a waste.

Shortly after the Arrow-Lind article appeared, Fisher (1973) commented on the need to account for negative environmental externalities associated with a public project. At the time, however, the broad theory of collective action commons dilemmas and public support for government intervention in response to natural and financial disaster was enveloped in his generic term 'externality'.

2. Collective responsibility and reciprocity

If United States citizenship confers an implicit obligation to come to the aid of those affected by adversity via the tax mechanism, it requires an operational exercise in what Arrow (1977) termed 'extended sympathy', a form of interpersonal comparison in which one puts oneself in the place of others and operates based not only on narrow self-interest but a form of other-regardedness. Perhaps the most telling example in the current period is the mandate of collective responsibility implicit in the Patient Protection and Affordable Care Act of 2010: 'Obamacare'. The legitimacy of the legislation and indeed of the entire Obama administration rests on the willingness of citizens to be required to seek coverage, pooling risks, even if otherwise they might choose to remain uncovered. This requires some surrender of self-interest in the name of positive other-regardedness. Those who deny the legitimacy of Obamacare as a collec-tivization exercise (such as the Tea Party) may not accept the legitimacy of this other-regardedness, or may actually bear negative attitudes toward those who are uninsured as undeserving of health care. An analogous case is the debate over food stamps benefits, which are federally-mandated entitlements to the poor and hungry. Again, public support for the program (known as SNAP, the Supplemental Nutrition Assistance Program) depends not only on self-interest but on extended sympathy for those who qualify for the benefits. Again, it is easy to find opponents of SNAP benefits who not only reject the role of the federal feeding programs, but regard their recipients nega-tively as undeserving poor (see Runge, 2013).

Recent research in cognitive psychology and economics supports the idea of such behavior, both in terms of positive rewards and negative punishments to others. In a study in *Science* (Ruff, Ugazio, & Fehr, 2013), subjects received money and were asked to share some of it with an anonymous partner. Self-interest dictated that the player keep the money to themselves, but a prevalent fairness norm common in Western culture dictated an even split (see Marwell & Ames, 1981; Runge, 1984). In another experiment, subjects were aware that if they did not share enough, the other player could punish them, reducing their funds. Using an electric device that sends the brain weak and painless currents to the prefrontal cortex, the experimenters found that the strength of the fairness or sharing norm, in both voluntary cases or under threat of punishment, were directly influenced by this 'transcranial stimulation'. After this stimulation, the effect of a threat of punishment enhanced sharing behavior, but voluntary sharing decreased. When neural activity was decreased, voluntary sharing increased, but decreased under threat of punishment. Although neural stimulation influenced behavior, it did not affect the perception of the social norm. There is thus an apparent neurological foundation to the propensity to contribute to collective action and common welfare which would lead some, and perhaps most citizens to support the use of government funds for relief purposes. But the 'weight' given to self versus others varies in the population, helping to define a continuum of norms related to public spending as a form of risk sharing. During the height of Hurricane Katrina, former first lady Barbara Bush's unkind remarks about the thousands made homeless and sleeping in Houston's superdome, may have been controversial precisely because they violated such a norm. As she noted, 'so many people in the arena here, you know, were underprivileged anyway, so this is working very well for them' (New York Times, 2005).

Lieberman (2013) has explored numerous dimensions of the role of such norms in cognitive psychology, noting work on the 'neural signature of norm compliance' (Spitzer, Fischbacher, Herrnberger, Gron, & Fehr, 2007). He reports on one study (Rilling, Sanfey, Aronson, Nystrom, & Cohen, 2004) in which functional magnetic resonance imaging of subjects playing a 2-person Prisoner's Dilemma game were analyzed. Subjects were paired with other players who chose to cooperate rather than defect or 'free ride'. More brain activity (in the ventral striatum) occurred in players when, given cooperation by another player j, player i/self also chose to cooperate rather than defect: 'The ventral stratum seemed to be more sensitive to the total amount earned by both players, rather than to one's personal outcome. Moreover, the lateral prefrontal regions were not engaged in the study when the subjects cooperated, suggesting that cooperating involves a real preference, not a sense of obligation' (Lieberman, 2013, p. 85).

3. Reciprocal utility and conditional commitment

Numerous attempts have been made to include considerations of reciprocity in utility models of voluntary contributions to public welfare (Fehr & Schmidt, 1999; Rabin, 1993; Runge, 1981, 1984; Sugden, 1977). In most of these, reciprocity is introduced exogenously or imposed as an obligation prior to the players' strategy choices. Marchiori (2010) and Dufwenberg and Kirchsteiger (2004) endogenize reciprocity, resulting in lowered levels of defection or free riding relative to cooperation. We present the following model to extend these works and apply them to risk-bearing collective action situations.

Our model is presented in reduced form below. Two players (without loss of generality to n-players) must decide whether to consume privately or support the dedication of some part of their income to a collective good, such as a portion of their taxes that will be used for public policies of hurricane relief or food stamps. Utility is increasing in private consumption but decreasing in dedicated taxes via forgone private consumption. Each player's utility is non-separable from the other's insofar as the level of public support for relief policies results from the level of support from other players.

Define player i's payoff as $u_i^D\left(c_i, a_i, \sum_{j\neq i}^{N} a_j\right)$, where c_i is consumption, a_i is the i-th

player's contribution to the collective good. We use the superscript D to indicate that this is the direct utility an individual receives. Direct utility, in our definition, is self-regarding and assumes a rational preference set and utility that is separable among players. Given these payoff functions, together with prices of consumption and government support for relief, p_c and p_a, and wealth w_i, the i-th individual solves:

$$\max_{c_i,\, a_i} u_i^D\left(c_i, a_i, \sum_{j\neq i}^{N} a_j\right) \tag{1}$$

$$\text{Subject to } p_c c_i + p_a a_i \leq w_i$$

The solution to this traditional collective action problem will result in under-contribution to the collective good due to excessive free-riding. If the price of consumption is normalized to unity and there are two identical players, i and j, we can re-express consumption in terms of wealth and support for public welfare contributions, which reduces the problem to one choice variable:

$$\max_{a_i} u_i^D \left(w_i - P_a a_i, a_i; a_j \right) \tag{2}$$

This type of model has been well-studied (see Varian, 2004), and results in under-provision of effort towards the collective good because each player considers only their own marginal benefit and the resulting allocation in equilibrium has less support for public welfare than the Samuelson condition for a pure public good, $\sum_{i=1}^{N} \frac{\partial u_i^D}{\partial a_i} = p_a$.

We extend the model by augmenting direct utility, $u^D(\cdot)$, with an interpersonal utility component, $u^I(\cdot)$. The interpersonal utility function describes the gain or loss of utility that player i experiences from observing a change in another player's utility. The basic assumption underlying the indirect component of utility is that humans enjoy seeing benefit come to those whom they perceive as deserving and may enjoy seeing harm come to those who are undeserving. Cikara, Botvinick, and Fiske (2011), along with many others in the cognitive psychology literature, explore the evidence for this, noting that 'The failures of an in-group member are painful, whereas those of a rival out-group member may give pleasure – a feeling that may motivate harming rivals'. Our interpersonal utility component seeks to identify and correctly parameterize this type of reciprocity.

To account for the variety of ways in which individuals react to interpersonal exchanges, we define a response function $R_{ij}(\cdot)$ that represents how player j's contributions (a_j) determine if player i will regard player j as deserving or undeserving. We allow this to be determined by the exchanges that take place between pairs of players and their observations of other players' contributions. An important component is the extent to which players believe other players have acted reciprocally in giving a 'fair share' of support for public relief (as in Rabin, 1993). In this case, a higher value of $R_{ij}(\cdot)$ implies that player i believes player j has acted fairly and will want to reward player j with reciprocal behavior. Similarly, a lower value for $R_{ij}(\cdot)$ implies that player i believes player j has not acted fairly and so will want to punish player j. Rewarding supportive behavior and punishing unsupportive behavior is what we refer to as reciprocity. Our model also allows players to have different intensities of reciprocal response, defined by $\beta_i \in (0, 1)$, based on the degree to which player i cares about reciprocity overall.[1] Thus, we define interpersonal utility for player i as:

$$u_i^I(\cdot) = \beta_i R_{ij}\left(a_j\right) u_j^D\left(a_i, a_j\right)$$

In this formulation, if player i views player j as deserving ($R_{ij}(a_j) > 0$), then player i will receive an increase in interpersonal utility when player j receives an increase in direct utility. By separating the interpersonal component of utility from traditional utility and by endogenizing the relationship orientation between players, our model provides a framework that more easily captures norms and institutions than traditional utility functions.

We combine our interpersonal utility expression with the direct utility expression to identify the total utility a player receives as the sum of these components. We label this function as reciprocal utility:

$$u_i^R(a_i, a_j) = \underbrace{u_i^D(a_i, a_j)}_{\substack{\text{Player } i's \\ \text{direct utility}}} + \underbrace{\beta_i R_{ij}(a_j) u_j^D(a_i, a_j)}_{\substack{\text{Player } i's \\ \text{interpersonal utility, } u_i^I}} \qquad (3)$$

In the context of a collective commitment to risk sharing, the term on the left of Equation (3) represents the direct utility player i receives from consumption after disutility from taxation has been subtracted. These damages are a function of total costs of relief for all players. The term on the right, conversely, represents the additional utility that player i receives from reciprocal assessment of player j's behavior. Assuming that player i views public relief policies positively and their recipients as deserving, she will receive more utility when other highly supportive players also receive utility. This term represents the player's utility from their perception of reciprocity, but not the utility they gain from the other players' actual investment in the public good (this portion of utility is expressed in the direct utility term, as a part of the direct effect of the public relief). In this framework, individuals maximize their reciprocal utility by choosing support levels taking into account both impacts from damages from hurricanes or financial losses, but also any potential gains or losses from how other players perceive their supportiveness. The results will differ from the direct-utility framework because support for taxation for public relief affects the best-response functions of each player in both the direct and the interpersonal or reciprocal terms, allowing contributions above those predicted by the free-rider hypothesis.

4. Conclusion

In other work (Johnson & Runge, 2013) we extend and explore the implications of this formulation in a variety of collective action or commons dilemmas. Here we draw attention to three main implications. First, our model is consistent with cognitive psychological studies that suggest positive individual rewards from seeing others benefit from public relief policies, even if they are anonymous. Second, the model allows for a continuum of human types, from those who care deeply about reciprocal relations and the collective responsibility to share in risks, to those who may not give a whit. Third, our model shows that the state of individual utility is conditional on the commitment we perceive by others to accepting a share of the risk via the tax mechanism to pursue such public relief policies (see Petit, 2005; Sen, 1977). This takes us well away from the Arrow-Lind theorem into the behavioral foundations of risk-sharing and public policy.

Note

1. We define β_i as fundamental to the player, derived from their genetic inheritance, which does not change with norms and institutions.

References

Arrow, K. J. (1977, Febraury). Extended sympathy and the possibility of social choice. *American Economic Review, 67*(1), 219–225.

Arrow, K. J., & Lind, R. C. (1970). Uncertainty and the evaluation of public investment decisions. *American Economic Review, 60*(3), 364–378.

Board of Governors of the Federal Reserve System (2009, March 18). Press Release. Accessed online at http://www.federalreserve.gov/newsevents/press/monetary/20090318a.htm

Cikara, M., Botvinick, M. M., & Fiske, S. T. (2011). Us versus them social identity shapes neural responses to intergroup competition and harm. *Psychological Science, 22*(3), 306–313.

Dufwenberg, M., & Kirchsteiger, G. (2004). A theory of sequential reciprocity. *Games and Economic Behavior, 47*(2), 268–298.

Fehr, E., & Schmidt, K. M. (1999). A theory of fairness, competition, and cooperation. *The Quarterly Journal of Economics, 114*(3), 817–868.

Fisher, A. C. (1973). Environmental externalities and the Arrow-Lind public investment theorem. *The American Economic Review, 63*(4), 722–725.

Griffith, S. (2005, September 8). USA: President approves 51.8 billion dollars in Katrina aid. Agence Frence-Presse. Accessed online at http://reliefweb.int

Internal Revenue Service (IRS) (2013). Tax Statistics. Accessed online at http://www.irs.gov/uac/Tax-Stats-2

Johnson & Runge (2013). Rationality and Reciprocity in Commons Dilemmas. Manuscript. University of Minnesota, Department of Applied Economics.

Lieberman, M. D. (2013). *Social: Why Our Brains are Wired to Connect*. New York: Crown Publishers.

Marchiori, C. (2010). Concern for fairness and incentives in water negotiations. *Environmental and Resource Economics, 45*(4), 553–571.

Marwell, G., & Ames, R. E. (1981). Economists free ride, does anyone else? Experiments on the provision of public goods, IV. *Journal of Public Economics, 15*, 295–310.

New York Times. (2005). Barbara Bush Calls Evacuees Better Off, September 7.

Petit, P. (2005). Construing sen on commitment. *Economics and Philosophy, 21*, 15–32.

Rabin, M. (1993, December). Incorporating fairness into game theory and economics. *American Economic Review, 83*(5), 1281–1302.

Rilling, J. K., Sanfey, A. G., Aronson, J. A., Nystrom, L. E., & Cohen, J. D. (2004). Opposing BOLD responses to reciprocated and unreciprocated altruism in putative reward pathways. *NeuroReport, 15*(16), 2539–2543.

Ruff, C. C., Ugazio, G., & Fehr, E. (2013). Changing social norm compliance with noninvasive brain stimulation. *Science, 342*(6157), 482–484.

Runge, C. F. (1981). Common property externalities: isolation,assurance, and resource depletion in a traditional grazing context. *American Journal of Agricultural Economics, 63*(4), 595–606.

Runge, C. F. (1984, Febraury). Institutions and the free rider: the assurance problem in collective action. *Journal of Politics, 46*(1), 154–181.

Runge, C. F. (2013, September/October). All you can eat. *The American Interest, 9*(1), 72–75.

Sen, A. K. (1977, Summer). Rational fools: a critique of the behavioral foundations of economic theory. *Philosophy and Public Affairs, 6*(4), 317–344.

Smith, A. (1759). *The Theory of Moral Sentiments*. Oxford: Clarendon Press.

Spitzer, M., Fischbacher, U., Herrnberger, B., Gron, G., & Fehr, E. (2007, October 4). The neural signature of social norm compliance. *Neuron, 56*(1), 185–196.

Sugden, R. (1977, December). Reciprocity: the supply of public goods through voluntary contributions. *The Economic Journal, 94*, 772–787.

Varian, H. (2004). System reliability and free riding. In L. J. Camp and S. Lewis (Eds.), *Economics of Information Security*, vol. 12, pp. 1–15. Kluwer Academic: Dordrecht, Netherlands.

Evaluation of public investments and individual discounting

Mario Tirelli

Department of Economics, University of Rome III, Rome, Italy

1. Introduction

Arrow and Lind's (1970) theorem postulates that 'when the risks associated with a public investment are publicly borne, the total cost of risk-bearing is insignificant and, therefore, the government should ignore uncertainty in evaluating public investments. Similarly the choice of the rate of discount should in this case be independent of considerations of risk' (p. 366). The theorem holds regardless whether security markets are complete, for any public project that is: (1) statistically independent of individual income, (2) measured according to an objective probability distribution, (3) evaluated considering individual costs and benefits represented by von Neumann-Morgestern, state-independent utilities; moreover, it holds provided (4) the government spreads the project risks among a large population of people.

The independence assumption is necessary to attain that, at the margin, the individual values a public investment as a risk-free claim on future income. Yet, it is a strong one. Arrow and Lind, along with other economists (e.g., Samuelson, 1964; Vickrey, 1964), recognize that many public projects alter individuals' income profiles, either providing new (social) insurance opportunities or representing a further source of risk. They, briefly, address the issue in Section III of their paper and conclude that in such cases 'it is appropriate to discount for risk as would these individuals' (p. 377).

In this note we discuss and elaborate on Arrow and Lind's consideration that public projects should effectively be evaluated from the perspective of individuals. The main issue at stake is that this approach, although theoretically sound, is informationally very demanding, requiring the measurement of individuals' benefits and costs or, equivalently, the observation of their preferences and income profiles. Our main point is to argue that this requirement can be weakened exploiting the information revealed by security market prices. More precisely, we appeal to well known results in the theory of asset prices in economies with incomplete markets, to discuss how a (public) decision maker could use market data on security prices to infer on traders' discount factors and, ultimately, to construct (approximate) measures of the individuals' willingness to pay for a project. These are the cost-benefit measures suggested by Arrow and Lind, that can be utilized to evaluate any investment project, public and private, independently of the fact this is marketable or it gives rise to a risk that is uninsurable. At the end of this note we also mention which are the alternative data, different from those on security prices, that can be exploited to attain information on individual discount factors.

We carry over our discussion by retaining all the assumptions in Arrow and Lind's Section II, except for the one on independence. In particular, we shall keep considering a finite economy where the government is able to distribute the net-benefits from each project to a large number of individuals. We also assume that the economy has financial markets on which all individuals trade competitively.

2. Definitions

2.1. The economy

We consider a two-period economy, with the current and next period, respectively indexed by zero and one. Next-period uncertainty is represented by a finite number S, of states of nature, indexed by s, and by a probability distribution π assigning π_s to every state s. A vector (x_0, x_1) is used to specify a change in the current level of income (or consumption of a single commodity) x_0 and a contingent claim x_1 on date-one income. The space of all contingent claims X is a finite (topological) vector space endowed with the probability inner product, $E[x] := \sum_s \pi_s x_s$. We also assume that contingent claims have finite second moments, $\|x\| := (E[x^2])^{1/2} < +\infty$ (i.e. $X \subseteq L^2$). X is endowed with a natural ordering $\geq$, which defines the positive cone $X_+ = \{x \in X : x \geq 0\}$, and the strictly-positive cone $X_{++} = X_+ \backslash \{0\}$.

There are $0 < J \leq S$ financial markets in which J independent securities are traded. Securities income-payoffs is represented by a matrix V in $\mathbb{R}^{S \times J}$ of full rank. The span of marketed securities is a linear space, $\mathcal{X} = \{x \in X : x = V\theta, \theta \in \mathbb{R}^J\}$. $\mathcal{X}^\perp$ is the π − orthogonal complement of $\mathcal{X}$ in X: $\mathcal{X}^\perp = \{x \in X : E[xz] = 0, z \in \mathcal{X}\}$. We also assume there exists a security portfolio θ_f paying a sure rate of return $r^f > 0$ (i.e. $(1 + r^f)(1, ..., 1)' = V\theta_f$). Then, security prices $q(\mathcal{X}) := (q(x^1), .., q(x^J))$ are strictly positive linear functionals if and only if there is no-arbitrage (i.e., $x \in \mathcal{X} \cap X_{++} \Rightarrow q(x) > 0$).[1]

There is a finite number of individuals/investors I indexed by i. Every individual i has an initial, endowment of income $e^i := (e_0^i, e_1^i)$ in $\mathbb{R}_{++} \times X_{++}$ and tastes which are represented by a complete, reflexive preference ordering on the space of final consumption/income (y_0^i, y_1^i), $\mathbb{R}_+ \times X_{++}$. Preferences are smooth (i.e., indifference surfaces are $C^{p \geq 1}$), strictly increasing in time-zero consumption, convex and they are represented by an expected-utility function $E[U^i(y^i)] = v^i(y_0^i) + \sum_s \pi_s u^i(y_s^i)$. In this context, the (intertemporal) marginal rate of substitution is well defined, $(1, m^i) := (\partial U/\partial x_0)^{-1}(\partial U/\partial x_0, \partial U/\partial x_1, .., \partial U/\partial x_S)$, continuous and strictly positive.

Finally, we assume that investors are rational and trade competitively the marketed securities: at market prices $q = (q^1, .., q^J)$, an individual i optimum is a marketed security portfolio θ^i satisfying $q = E[m^i V]$, where m^i is evaluated at the budget-feasible income,

$$y^i = e^i + \begin{pmatrix} -q \\ V \end{pmatrix} \theta^i$$

Hence, at an individual optimum the pricing functional is linear, implying no-arbitrage. Conversely, if q gives rise to an arbitrage, then an individual optimum does not exist. For these reasons we call any linear functional q a no-arbitrage equilibrium. Finally, we define the set of individual marginal rate of substitutions m satisfying no-arbitrage,

$$\mathcal{M} = \{m \in X : E[mx] > 0 \text{ for all } x \in X_{++}\}$$

2.2. Evaluation measures

For all i, let (y_0^i, y_1^i) be the status-quo income profile attained at a no-arbitrage equilibrium. The individual i willingness to pay for a contingent claim x on date-1 income (where $y_1 + x_1 >> 0)^2$ in terms of date-0 income y_0 is the supremum w^i on $\mathbb{R}$ satisfying,

$$E[U^i(y_0 - w^i, y_1 + x)] \geq E[U^i(y_0, y_1)] \qquad (*)$$

The supremum $w^i = w^i_y(x)$ exists and is a function of x, which is bonded above by y_0, whose argument we shall drop unless necessary. Moreover, if preferences are Inada in date-0 consumption (*i.e.* $y_0 + w^i > 0$), then its value satisfies $(*)$ with equality. In addition, because preferences are convex, if x is in X_{++}, $w^i > 0$.[3]

The timing of 'payment' – out of current consumption, not future – matches the interpretation of the evaluation and preferences as being *ex ante* the realization of uncertainty. *Ex post*, the willingness to pay in the realized state s may be different, if naturally defined, such as with state-separable preferences.

Notice that, by analogy with Arrow and Lind's (1970) Equation (19), the willingness to pay can also be defined just with respect to the *risk* component of a project x, with $(*)$ substituted by the following,

$$E[U^i(y_0 - k^i, y_1 + x)] \geq E[U^i(y_0, y_1 + E[x])]$$

and the supremum being $k^i = k^i_y(x) = w_{y+E[x]}(x)$. It is the willingness to pay associated to x at the status-quo income $(y_0, y_1 + E[x])$ (rather than at (y_0, y_1)).

Next, because preferences are smooth, by the implicit function theorem, the individual i willingness to pay for an arbitrarily small share of the pre-specified change in individual income x is,

$$w^i = E[m^i x]$$

We call w^i the marginal willingness to pay for x; where, it goes by itself that m^i and w^i are functions of the individual i status-quo income y. By an analogous derivation it is immediate to show that the marginal willingness to pay for the risk component of x is,

$$k^i = E[m^i x] - E[m^i]E[x] = E[m^i x] - \frac{E[x]}{1 + r^f} \qquad (k)$$

where, in the latest, $E[m^i] = (1 + r^f)^{-1}$ holds at a no-arbitrage equilibrium.

To complete the illustration, following Arrow and Lind, define the risk component of x as $\xi := x - E[x]$. Then, substituting $x = \xi + E[x]$ in (k) and simplifying, yields $k^i = E[m^i \xi]$ which is exactly the marginal willingness to pay for the risk component of x. Hence, we can decompose w^i as the sum of the willingness to pay for the sure and the risk component of x as,

$$w^i = \frac{E[x]}{1 + r^f} + E[m^i \xi] \qquad (w)$$

3. Projects evaluation

Assume that the public investment project is a claim x in X and, as in Arrow and Lind's, that there is a large number of tax payers, each of whom participates in a 'marginal' share (or infinitesimal unit) of the project. Then, every individual i evaluates a 'unit' participation at her marginal willingness to pay (w), where the discount factors $(m^1, .., m^I)$ are computed at the status-quo equilibrium income $y = (y^1, .., y^I)$.

First, following Arrow and Lind, assume that for every individual i, the status-quo income y_1^i is independent of x. Since, this implies that also m^i is independent of x, from (w), we find

$$w^i = \frac{E[x]}{1 + r^f} + E[m^i]E[\xi] = \frac{E[x]}{1 + r^f}$$

where, by definition, $E[\xi] = 0$. By (k), the willingness to pay k^i for the risk component of x, is equal to zero; and this holds for all i. This yields Arrow and Lind theorem, in their Section II and results in the public project being discounted at the return quoted for the riskless portfolio.

Relaxing the independence assumption makes Arrow and Lind's theorem fail. In Section III of their paper they acknowledge this fact indicating a possible way out to the problem of social discounting. In particular, Arrow and Lind – referring to Hirshleifer (1966) – say that the [..] 'suggestion of finding the marginal rate of return on assets with similar payoffs in the private sector, and using this as the rate of discount, appears reasonable' [..] (p. 377). In the rest of the paper we try to qualify this point further, also providing some practical indications.

3.1. Relaxing the independence assumption

First, we highlight when and why, in Arrow and Lind's framework, relaxing the independence assumption makes social discount an hard problem. To this end, observe that any project x in X can be uniquely decomposed as $\bar{x} + \tilde{x}$, where $\bar{x}$ is in $\mathcal{X}$ and $\tilde{x}$ in $\mathcal{X}^\perp$. The easy case is when $x = \bar{x}$ (e.g., see Sadmo, 1972), that is when x can be replicated by a portfolio $\theta(x)$ of securities V, traded at prices q. Indeed, its value is well defined by $q(x) = q\theta(x)$. This case, known as partial spanning, extends to economies with a complete set of security markets. In other words, under partial spanning, social discounting is achieved exploiting asset prices; and this is so as equilibrium prices fully reveal all the information of individual preferences that is required to achieve a correct project evaluation. As a matter of fact, under no-arbitrage, individuals discount public investments lying in the asset span of marketed securities at the same rate $\bar{m}$; that is preferences 'aggregate' to that of a representative agent with a discount factor $\bar{m}$.[4]

In a more general case, namely if a project x is not in $\mathcal{X}$, but is traded competitively we can still evaluate it at no-arbitrage prices. In our context, one can 'extend' $q : \mathcal{X} \to \mathbb{R}$ to the whole space of contingent claims X. That is, imposing no-arbitrage, an investment that is initially non-marketed can be valued at a continuous linear functional $\hat{q} : X \to \mathbb{R}$ that, when restricted to $\mathcal{X}$, assumes the same values of $q(\cdot)$. This result is known as the 'extension theorem' in the asset pricing literature (see, among others, Clark's, 1993 theorem 5 and 6 or the seminal contribution by Harrison & Kreps, 1979).

The problem of exploiting the logic of the extension theorem to evaluate public projects is that these are typically non-tradable. Therefore, imposing no-arbitrage on a public investment seams absolutely inappropriate. Yet, as we explain next, one can still hope to exploit equilibrium restrictions on asset prices to achieve an approximate computation of the individuals' willingness to pay for it or, equivalently, of individuals' discount factors $(m^1, .., m^I)$.

3.2. Implementation using information revealed by security prices

Consider the case in which x has both a marketed component $\bar{x}$ in $\mathcal{X}$ and a non-marketed one $\tilde{x}$ in $\mathcal{X}^{\perp}$. We can still think at $\bar{x}$ as one that makes anyone agree on its evaluation; the question is how to discount the remaining component $\tilde{x}$, given that this is neither replicable by a marketed portfolio, nor it is tradable.

The difficulty is that, when markets are incomplete, even restricting discount factors to satisfy no-arbitrage on tradable securities, at given market prices, does still lead to a situation in which individuals would disagree on how to value $\tilde{x}$. Indeed, this equilibrium restriction would only limit the disagreement to $\mathcal{X}^{\perp}$, a linear subspace of $\mathbb{R}^S$ of positive dimension: for any two individuals i,j, with m^i, m^j in $\mathcal{M}$, $m^i - m^j$ belongs to $\mathcal{X}^{\perp}$,

$$0 = E[(m^i - m^j)V] = E[(\tilde{m}^i - \tilde{m}^j)V]$$

and $\mathcal{X}^{\perp}$ has dimension $S - J > 0$. Hirshleifer's suggestion seems to go in the direction of ignoring this, by proposing to approximate individuals' evaluation looking at $\bar{m}$ only. But this might really be too rough of an approximation, disregarding exactly the marginal willingness to pay for the non-marketed component of the project, the one that individuals neither can replicate nor can insure for.

A more promising direction is, first, to acknowledge the fact that no-arbitrage is only one possible restriction and that may be others which are plausible. In fact, following the asset pricing literature, no-arbitrage restrictions might still leave attractive investment opportunities, or 'good deals', that investors can trade on the markets at no cost. For example, in an economy with $S = 2$ and $\pi_1 = 1/2$, a claim with zero price that pays $1000 if $s = 1$ and -1 otherwise, is one with a no-arbitrage price that still offers a 'good' investment opportunity.[5] Second, if 'good deals' are valued, the resulting equilibrium restrictions might be effectively tighter than those imposed by no-arbitrage, thereby leading to a situation in which the individual's disagreement on security evaluation are reduced.

These two considerations have been, first, drawn by Hansen and Jagannathan (1991), who identify a 'good deal' with an investment displaying a high Sharp ratio of mean excess return (risk premium) to standard deviation.[6] They also establish a duality link between the restrictions imposed on Sharp ratios, using market data, and the minimum volatility of traders' discount factors. Cochrane and Saa-Requejo (2000) add the important point that this duality link can also be used in the opposite direction, to impose an upperbound on discount factors volatility. Other definitions of 'good deals' have been used in the literature (e.g., see Bernardo & Ledoit, 2000) and still the same considerations hold true (see Černý & Hodges, 2000).

We argue that, whenever such considerations apply, no-good-deal equilibria result in tighter bounds on individuals' discount factors volatility and in sharper predictions on their willingness to pay for any investment project, public ones included.

To illustrate the idea behind the duality approach, following Černý and Hodges (2000), we assume that 'good deals' are identified by claims with a high Sharp ratio and X coincides with L^2. Redefining marketed contingent claims as the excess return r over the riskless portfolio, we recall that the Sharp ratio $S(r)$ associated to r, is defined as,

$$S(r) = \frac{E[r]}{\sigma[r]},$$

where $\sigma[r]$ is the standard deviation of r. This definition extends trivially to a portfolio of securities, or tradable contingent claim. Then, denoting by $\bar{S}$ the 'high' Sharp ratio considered, the set of 'good deals', traded in this economy, is one in which every claim with excess return r has a Sharp ratio $S(r)$ that is at least as high as $\bar{S}$; or, equivalently, r satisfies,

$$\frac{E[r]}{\|r\|} \geq \frac{\bar{S}}{\sqrt{1+\bar{S}^2}}$$

This results in the definition of the set of 'good deal' claims (in terms of excess returns) as,

$$\mathcal{G}(\bar{S}) = \left\{ r \in X : \frac{E[r]}{\|r\|} \geq \frac{\bar{S}}{\sqrt{1+\bar{S}^2}} \right\}$$

Denoting by X^* the dual of (i.e., the space of linear functionals on) X, the set of prices excluding 'good deals' is,[7]

$$\mathcal{Q}(\bar{S}) = \left\{ q \in X^* : q(r) > 0 \text{ for all } r \in \mathcal{G}(\bar{S}) \right\}$$

and defines the space of no-good-deal equilibrium prices. Moreover, we use the fact that any $q(\cdot)$ in $\mathcal{Q}(\bar{S})$ can be uniquely represented by a discount factor m, satisfying $q(r) = E[mr]$ for all r in X. Therefore, we can restrict (no-good-deal) discount factors in,

$$\mathcal{M}(\bar{S}) = \left\{ m \in X : E[mr] > 0 \text{ for all } r \in \mathcal{G}(\bar{S}) \right\}$$

As for no-arbitrage, $q(r) = E[mr]$ is a linear functional for all m in $\mathcal{M}(\bar{S})$.

Finally, to show how $\mathcal{M}(\bar{S})$ can effectively shrink with $\bar{S}$, Černý and Hodges (2000) provide an intuitive geometric representation (see Figure 1). They observe that $\mathcal{G}(\bar{S})$ is a circular cone, AOA' in Figure 1, generated by the axis formed by the claim on the riskless portfolio and with the angle at the vertex α, such that $cos(\alpha) = \frac{\bar{S}}{\sqrt{1+\bar{S}^2}}$ and consequently, $cot(\alpha) = \frac{cos(\frac{\pi}{2}-\alpha)}{cos(\alpha)} = \bar{S}$. $\mathcal{M}(\bar{S})$ is also a cone pointed at O, BOB' in Figure 1, with axis also generated by the riskless claim and with the angle at the vertex $\beta = \pi/2 - \alpha$ (i.e., B, B' are, respectively, perpendicular to A, A'):

$$\mathcal{M}(\bar{S}) = \left\{ m \in X : \frac{E[m]}{\sigma(m)} > cot(\beta) = \frac{1}{cot(\alpha)} = \frac{1}{\bar{S}} \right\}$$

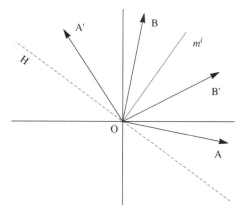

Figure 1.   (Colour online) Good-deal opportunities and equilibrium discount factors.

Therefore, any m in $\mathcal{M}(\bar{S})$ is one preventing trades with a Sharp ratio higher than $\bar{S}$, a restriction,

$$\frac{\sigma[m]}{E[m]} \leq \bar{S}$$

In words, good-deal equilibrium prices with a lower upper-bound $\bar{S}$ entail a lower discount factors variability, as in Cochrane and Saa-Requejo (2000); something, geometrically, corresponding to a sharper (wider) vertex-angle β (respectively, α). In the limit, when $\bar{S}$ approaches zero, the good-deal cone collapses to the hyperplane H (drawn with a dashed line in Figure 1); implying that there is a unique discount factor m^i at which all portfolios and investments can be evaluated (i.e., the no-good-deal cone BOB′ is a line-segment identified by m^i).

3.3.   Implementation using information revealed by other sources

Using market data on Sharp-ratios as a primitive information is not the only way to attain better predictions on individual willingness to pay for an investment. Another, related, way to approach the problem is to collect information on individual preferences, perhaps through survey data or experiments, so as to restrict them to some parametric class (e.g., quadratic, constant relative risk aversion CRRA. etc.) with certain risk-aversion properties. Then, use this information to specify no-good-deal restrictions for that class. Černý (2003), for example, shows that the set of claims which contains neither arbitrage opportunities nor high Sharpe ratios is generated by a truncated quadratic utility function; a utility that is increasing up to its bliss point and is constant for higher levels of income. He has also derived discount factors restrictions (and Generalized Sharp Ratios) for CRRA and constant absolute risk aversion families of von Neumann-Morgestern utilities. Tirelli and Turner (2010), for different purposes, develop an approximation method to compute individual willingness to pay for certain families of von Neumann-Morgestern utilities.

Acknowledgements

I acknowledge financial support from the Italian Ministry of University and Research (PRIN 2010).

Notes

1. See, for example, Clark's theorem 1 (1993).
2. For any $z = (z_1, .., z_S) \in X$, $z \gg 0$ reads $z \in X_{++}$ and $z_s \neq 0$ for all s.
3. See, for example, Tirelli and Turner (2010).
4. To see this, one uniquely decomposes m^i as the sum $\bar{m}^i + \tilde{m}^i$, $\bar{m}^i \in \mathcal{X}, \tilde{m}^i \in \mathcal{X}^\perp$. No arbitrage implies that for every i, m^i satisfies $q\theta = E[m^i V\theta] = E[m^i x]$. Hence, for two individuals i, j, $E[(m^i - m^j)x] = 0$. Using $x = V\theta$, this yields $E[(\bar{m}^i - \bar{m}^j)x] = 0$. Hence, $(\bar{m}^i - \bar{m}^j) \in \mathcal{X}^\perp$. Since, by construction, $(\bar{m}^i - \bar{m}^j) \in \mathcal{X}$ too, we conclude that $(\bar{m}^i - \bar{m}^j) \in \mathcal{X} \cup \mathcal{X}^\perp = 0$, or that $\bar{m}^i = \bar{m}^j$. $\bar{m} := m^i$.
5. This example is by Černý and Hodges (2000).
6. Historically, the idea that investments with high Sharp ratio might be attractive goes back to Ross's (1976) APT – see p. 354.
7. Behind this definition, in analogy with no-arbitrage price theory, there is an extension theorem for no-good-deal claims. See theorems 2.3 and 2.5 in Černý and Hodges (2000).

References

Arrow, K. J., & Lind, R. C. (1970). Uncertainty and the evaluation of public investment decisions. *American Economic Review, LX*(June), 364–378.

Bernardo, A. E., & Ledoit, O. (2000). Gain, loss, and asset pricing. *Journal of Political Economy, 108*(1), 144–172.

Černý, A. (2003). Generalised Sharpe ratios and asset pricing in incomplete markets. *European Finance Review, 7*(2), 191–233.

Černý, A., & Hodges, S. (2000). The theory of good-deal pricing in financial markets. In Geman, M. & Pliska, V. (eds.), *Mathematical finance – Bachelier Congress 2000* (pp. 175–202). Springer Verlag, Berlin Heidelberg, 2002.

Clark, S. A. (1993). The valuation problem in arbitrage price theory. *Journal of Mathematical Economics, 22*(5), 463–478.

Cochrane, J. H., & Saa-Requejo, J. (2000). Beyond arbitrage: Good-deal asset price bounds in incomplete markets. *Journal of Political Economy, 108*(1), 79–119.

Hansen, L. P., & Jagannathan, R. (1991). Implications of security market data for models of dynamic economies. *Journal of Political Economy, 2*, 225–262.

Harrison, J. M., & Kreps, D. M. (1979). Martingales and arbitrage in multiperiod securities markets. *Journal of Economic Theory, 20*(3), 381–408.

Hirschleifer, J. (1966). Investment decision under uncertainty: Applications of the state-preference approach. *Quarterly Journal of Economics, 80*, 252–277.

Ross, S. A. (1976). The arbitrage theory of capital asset pricing. *Journal of Economic Theory, 13*(3), 341–360.

Sadmo, A. (1972). Optimality rules for the provision of collective factors of production. *Journal of Public Economics, 1*, 149–157.

Samuelson, P. A. (1964). Discussion. *American Economic Review, LIV*(May), 93–96.

Tirelli, M., & Turner, S. (2010). Quantifying the cost of risk in consumption. *The BE Journal of Theoretical Economics, 10*(1), Article 31, 1–31.

Vickrey, W. (1964). Discussion. *American Economic Review, LIV*(May), 88–92.

Rebutting Arrow and Lind: why governments should use market rates for discounting

Deborah Lucas

Massachusetts Institute of Technology, Sloan School of Management, Cambridge, USA

1. Historical perspective

The radical proposition of Arrow and Lind (1970) – that governments should use risk-free rates instead of market rates to discount their risky investments – can best be understood by first considering the work in its historical context.[1] During the late 1960s and early 1970s, a debate was raging between the leading economists of the time about the cost of risk to the government, and related, the identification of the social discount rate. Recent advances in general equilibrium theory (notably, Arrow & Debreu, 1954; Debreu, 1959) allowed for more general welfare analyses of policy than had been undertaken previously; underscored the benefits of risk-sharing as well as the aggregate limits on risk-sharing; and clarified the role of market prices in aggregating the risk preferences of society. Such analyses also highlighted the potentially salutary role for governments in improving risk-sharing when markets are incomplete.

On one side of the debate were authors who took the position that governments should rely on market prices in evaluating the cost of investments. Diamond (1967) analyzed an economy with technology risk and a stock market. Perhaps not surprisingly, he concluded that if markets are sufficiently complete for stock prices to reflect the social cost of risk, then those prices are also relevant to the government in evaluating its investment policy. Hirshleifer (1964, 1966) reached similar conclusions and argued forcefully for the use of market prices by governments.

Other leading economists of the time advocated the position that was subsequently formalized in Arrow and Lind. Samuelson and Vickrey (in Jorgenson et al., 1964) argued that because of the large and diversified portfolio held by the government, the marginal return from public investment overall is virtually risk-free, and hence should be evaluated at the risk-free rate rather than the higher market rate demanded by less diversified investors. (The government's own borrowing rate is usually taken as a proxy for the risk-free rate.)

The specialness of the assumptions required to formalize the idea that the cost of market risk is irrelevant to the government – in particular, that there is no aggregate uncertainty affecting the value of government investments – was acknowledged by Arrow and Lind: 'The results...depend on returns from a given public investment being independent of other components of national income' (p. 373). Arrow and Lind defended that assumption with the assertion that correlated risk is likely to be insignificant for many government investments.

The crux of the difference between the two camps was already well-understood at the time. For instance, Sandmo (1972) writes that the Hirshleifer view can be reconciled with Arrow and Lind's conclusions only by recognizing that:

> ...the two sets of arguments are based on entirely different assumptions concerning the relationship between private and public investment with respect to risk. Arrow and Lind assume that the returns on private and public investment are uncorrelated; indeed this assumption is crucial for their main result. The Hirshleifer view, however, is clearly based on the assumption that for each type of public investment it is possible to find a private industry such that the returns are highly correlated (p. 287).

Sandmo goes on to note that for the modern economies of Europe and the US, Hirshleifer's view is likely the more plausible. Importantly, he observes that the contributions of Sharpe (1964), Lintner (1965), and Modigliani and Miller (1958) – a body of work that forms the underpinning of modern financial economics – are highly relevant to this debate but rarely cited in the context of public investment.

The closely related question of whether there is a well-defined social (risk-free) discount rate, and whether it could be gleaned from market prices was also being debated at that time (see Sandmo & Dreze, 1971, and references therein). Proxies for the pure rate of time preference derived from capital market prices (e.g., Treasury rates) also may lead to suboptimal government investment decisions when markets are insufficiently complete. The broad conclusion of those theoretical investigations was that, in the presence of distorting taxes and other sources of market incompleteness, the rate of time preference appropriate for evaluating all public investment projects is not unique. Hence, the same concerns about market incompleteness which cause Arrow and Lind to question the relevance of the market price of risk for the government also bring into question the use of government borrowing rates as proxies for the social discount rate.

2. The economic case for using market discount rates

The conclusions of Arrow and Lind rest on the presumption that government investments are free of aggregate risk. That assumption is clearly violated for many if not most of the investments made by governments around the world. For example, in the United States, the federal government's credit-related investments – which include trillions of dollars of mortgage guarantees, student loans, and pension and deposit guarantees –have close analogs that are priced in competitive markets, and payoffs which are sharply lower during downturns. Most real government investments also have private sector analogs and are subject to aggregate risk; for example, government-owned electricity generation or transmission facilities have a similar exposure to demand shocks as do private utilities.

However, even if Arrow and Lind were to acknowledge that government investments are susceptible to aggregate risk, there remains the question of whether the price of the aggregate risk which is relevant to government investments can be inferred from capital market returns. Specifically, Arrow and Lind conjecture that the observed market risk premium is primarily compensation for diversifiable risks rather than for aggregate risk. If that were true, and if governments were to more effectively diversify such risks than private firms, then using a market discount rate that includes compensation for diversifiable risk would result in systematic undervaluation of government investments.

The question of whether market participants require a significant premium to bear diversifiable risk is an empirical one. There was much less evidence available to resolve the issue when Arrow and Lind were writing, but subsequently, numerous studies have examined whether diversifiable risk is priced in financial markets. The weight of the cross-sectional evidence on asset returns suggests that diversifiable risk does not explain the market risk premium. Tests of the Sharpe and Lintner Capital Asset Pricing Model (CAPM), which decomposes asset returns into a market and idiosyncratic component, show that idiosyncratic risk has little or no explanatory power for the cross-section of stock returns. Tests of more modern asset pricing models also offer little support for the idea that differences in idiosyncratic risk explain the cross-section of returns (e.g., Fama & French, 1992). Such empirical findings are consistent with the observation that wealthy individuals, whose preferences are likely to be the primary determinants of asset market prices, hold diversified portfolios. Further, even small investors can diversify financial risk quite inexpensively using mutual funds. Overall, the evidence seems to weigh against the supposition of Arrow and Lind that market prices overstate the cost of aggregate risk to the government because investors put significant weight on diversifiable risk.

Some observers have also interpreted the inability of parameterized versions of standard neoclassical general equilibrium models to account for the historically high average spreads between risky securities and short-term Treasury rates (the 'equity premium puzzle') as evidence of capital market imperfections. Taking into account individual risk exposure, however, does not appear to explain that puzzle (e.g., Heaton & Lucas, 1996). In fact, the robust predictions of economic theory put very few quantitative restrictions on price levels or returns. Hence, observed market premiums are difficult to interpret as evidence for or against the efficiency of financial markets in spreading risk.

Although the debate over government discount rates has largely moved from academic to policy circles, the view that market rates should be used to discount risky government investments appears to be the predominant one among present-day financial economists. For example, the Financial Economists Roundtable, a group of prominent senior financial economists, endorsed that position in the context of government credit assistance in its 2012 policy statement.

3. The practical case for using market discount rates

A critical assumption implicit in the analysis of Arrow and Lind is that governments behave benevolently, only making worthwhile investments and optimally allocating the associated risks. More nuanced theories of political economy, or a casual look at government investment practices, suggest this assumption is routinely violated. When principal-agent or moral hazard problems significantly impede the efficient functioning of governments, a major consideration in setting the rules for evaluating government investments is aligning the incentives of policymakers with welfare maximization. The case is outlined here for why the use by governments of below-market discount rates creates serious incentive problems that tend to lead to overinvestment and excessive financial risk-taking by governments.

To explore the practical implications of the choice of government discount rates, it is natural to focus on the budget process, which is the mechanism by which policymakers make tradeoffs between competing uses of scarce resources, including the risk-bearing capacity of society. Government accounting rules determine how budgetary costs are calculated, including the selection of discount rates.[2]

Perhaps the most significant hazard of governments using a risk-free rate (or their own borrowing rate) for discounting is that it creates a money machine for politicians. In the extreme, all public spending could be financed on paper by issuing government debt and using the proceeds to finance stock market investments. The apparent gain would be the equity premium times the principal invested, discounted over the assumed life of the investment at a risk-free rate. In general, the more market risk associated with an investment, the larger this potential 'budgetary arbitrage'.

While extreme forms of budgetary arbitrage are rare (but not unheard of),[3] more subtle versions of the same phenomenon occur routinely in the US, where federal credit programs are accounted for as Arrow and Lind would suggest – by projecting future cash flows and discounting them at Treasury rates. Investments in risky loans and loan guarantees look cheap for a government when the price of market risk is neglected.

There are many examples of credit programs that appear profitable or costless to the government because of the use of Treasury rates for discounting. For instance, on mortgages insured by the US Federal Housing Administration, borrowers are able to obtain loans on more favorable terms than what would be offered by competitive private financial institutions. The program nevertheless shows a budgetary profit because the cost of market risk is not recognized in that accounting.

Another example is Title XVII of the Energy Policy Act of 2005 which provides qualifying developers of innovative fuel technologies with federal loan guarantees. The Act requires that the loan guarantees have a zero budgetary cost. To satisfy that requirement, the guarantee recipients pay an upfront fee that covers the estimated government cost. The value of the subsidy to the recipients – many of which are utilities and other large firms that without support would have access to capital markets – is the difference between the market value of the credit guarantee and value calculated using Treasury rates. Growing awareness of this legislative mechanism to create 'free' subsidies has resulted in an increasing number of proposals designed to exploit it.

The overall impact on the budget deficit of discounting credit programs at Treasury rather than market rates is significant. Congressional Budget Office (2012) estimated that government loans and loan guarantees newly issued in 2013 would generate budgetary savings of $45 billion over their lifetime when their costs were calculated using Treasury rates, whereas those same loans and guarantees would have a lifetime cost of $11 billion using a market or fair-value approach to assessing cost.

Relatedly, the use of government rates for discounting encourages the provision of subsidies in the form of credit assistance over what may be a more suitable alternative in a given instance. Governments can provide assistance to target groups of equivalent value to recipients via credit subsidies or in non-credit forms. Neglecting the market price of risk lowers the budgetary cost of credit assistance relative to that of economically equivalent grant or benefit payments, providing policymakers with an incentive to over-rely on credit assistance. For example, the increasing reliance over time on student loans (which also appear to make money for the government) relative to grant aid to students may be an example of that phenomenon.

The use of Treasury rates for discounting also makes it more difficult for the government to disinvest when it is optimal for it to do so. That is, even if an asset can be sold at a fair market price, governments may avoid a sale if it would entail a substantial budgetary cost. That consideration is salient in discussions of privatizing the mortgage giants Fannie Mae and Freddie Mac. The two companies were purchased by the government during the financial crisis of 2008, and most policymakers would like to return them (or successor entities) to private control. Both firms currently appear profitable to the government when the priced risks associated with mortgage guarantees are not included in cost estimates.

Feasibility, transparency, consistent application across programs and auditability are all practical concerns in choosing a rule for selecting discount rates. Some government officials favor using government rates for discounting because it is simple and familiar. However, the simplicity is at least in part illusory. Often the biggest challenge in estimating the net present value of an investment is projecting its future cash flows. Whereas benchmarks do not exist for valuations based on risk-free rates, estimates that employ market-based discount rates allow the reasonableness of the assumed cash flows to be implicitly tested by comparison with market prices. Furthermore, using the same discount rates across different programs favors high-risk programs and therefore does not meet the goal of consistency across programs.

Considerations of transparency, consistency and auditability suggest limiting the discretion of policymakers and government analysts in the selection of discount rates.[4] One way to do that, but at the same time emulate market rates, is to adopt private sector standards for applying a 'fair value' approach to selecting discount rates. The fair value of an investment is defined as the price that would be received if it was sold in an orderly transaction (one that occurs under competitive market conditions between willing participants and does not involve forced liquidation or a distressed sale). In estimating fair values, current private sector accounting standards require firms to use the most accurate approach for cost estimates, and suggest broad approaches that apply to a variety of situations. By adopting the private sector standard, the government would impose on itself the same transparency requirements that it imposes on private sector financial institutions. Aligning federal and private sector guidelines for fair value computations would allow the government to draw on technical assistance from the many private accounting and valuation firms that assist private financial institutions to comply with fair value reporting requirements. The availability of private sector expertise would also make estimates more auditable, and could be used to help to ensure discipline and defensibility, and to standardize practices across agencies.

4. Conclusions

In this essay I have made the case that:

(1) The assumptions underlying the Arrow-Lind theorem were highly controversial from the start, and their conclusions do not represent the mainstream view of financial economists today;

(2) A large body of empirical evidence casts doubt on the critical assumption that markets demand a significant premium for diversifiable risks; and

(3) In practice, the incentives of policymakers are seriously distorted when market prices are ignored when evaluating the cost of government investments.

If these conclusions are correct, a natural question is why Arrow and Lind's paper has had such staying power. I can only offer speculative answers. One is that, with a few notable exceptions, academic economists appear to have lost interest in writing on the topic of government discount rates.[5] Another is that the practice of using government borrowing rates for discounting is in the interest of policymakers, who benefit from being able to show government investments that are popular with constituents as profitable. Many government analysts, who receive little training in finance, do not appear to recognize the physical impossibility of financing risky investments with risk-free government debt, thereby failing to realize that taxpayers are effectively equity holders in risky government investments. Furthermore, under the dominant regime of cash-accounting, interest is a visible cost but risk-bearing by taxpayers is not.

Finally, it must be emphasized that in instances where market incompleteness clearly is of first order importance, it may be possible for economists to identify compelling reasons to use alternatives to market discount rates. For example, for policies whose payoffs extend beyond the time horizons usually covered by financial markets, and whose benefits accrue primarily to unborn generations, the choice of discount rates is far from obvious. However, discounting at the risk-free rate is unlikely to be the answer either. For example, in the current discussion over how to discount the benefits from abating greenhouse gasses, Arrow (1995) argues for using a discount rate of zero based on considerations of intergenerational fairness. Given the growing scope and scale of government investment activities and the high stakes involved, a return by more academic economists to these fundamental questions would appear to a valuable investment for society in itself.

Notes

1. The discussion here draws on Lucas and Phaup (2010).
2. Most governments budget on a cash basis for most investment activities, a practice that makes the choice of discount rates moot. However, in some cases budgeting is done on an accrual basis that requires a choice of discount rates. In the US, most real investments are accounted for on a cash basis but by law, direct government loans and loan guarantees are budgeted for on an accrual basis using Treasury rates for discounting. For a discussion of international government accounting practices for investments and their consequences, see Lucas (2013).
3. Something akin to a money machine appears to be operative in Brazil, where the government has issued large amounts of government debt and channeled it to highly risky investment projects through loans to state-owned banks (Garcia, 2013).
4. Some have suggested seeking a middle ground where the components of the market risk premium that are relevant to governments are identified and the rest discarded (e.g., adjustments for taxes). However, the considerable amount of discretion that would entail, as well as the lack of agreement on which components of the risk premium are relevant, suggest this would be a problematic approach.
5. For example, Bazelon and Smetters (1999) and Elliott (2011); Lucas (2012) provides additional references and surveys the literature on government valuation.

References

Arrow, K. (1995), '*Intergenerational equity and the rate of discount in long-term social investment,*' manuscript, Stanford University

Arrow, K., & Debreu, G. (1954). Existence of an equilibrium for a competitive economy. *Econometrica, 22*(3), 265–290.

Arrow, K., & Lind, R. (1970). Uncertainty and the evaluation of public investment decisions. *American Economic Review, 60*, 364–378.

Bazelon, C., & Smetters, K. (1999). Discounting inside the Washington D.C. Beltway. *Journal of Economic Perspectives, 13*(4), 213–228.

Congressional Budget Office. (2012), 'Fair-Value Estimates of the Cost of Federal Credit Programs in 2013.' Retrieved from http://www.cbo.gov/publication/43352

Debreu, G. (1959), A theory of value: An axiomatic analysis of economic equilibrium. unpublished manuscript.

Diamond, P. (1967). The role of the stock market in a general equilibrium model with technological uncertainty. *American Economic Review, 57*, 759–776.

Elliott, D. (2011). *Uncle sam in pinstripes*. Washington, D.C.: The Brookings Institution Press.

Fama, E. F., & French, K. R. (1992). The cross-section of expected stock returns. *Journal of Finance, 47*, 427–465.

Financial Economists Roundtable. (2012), 'Accounting for the Cost of Government Credit Assistance,' 2012 Statement. Retrieved from http://fic.wharton.upenn.edu/fic/Policy%20page/FER.htm

Garcia, M. (2013), *The gross debt and the fiscal stance,* manuscript, Pontificia Universidade Catolica do Rio de Janeiro.

Heaton, J., & Lucas, D. (1996). Evaluating the effects of incomplete markets on risk sharing and asset pricing. *Journal of Political Economy, 104*(3), 443–487.

Hirshleifer, J. (1966). Investment decisions under uncertainty: Applications of the state preference approach. *Quarterly Journal of Economics, 80*(2) (May, 1966), 252–277.

Hirshleifer, J. (1964). Efficient allocation of capital in an uncertain world. *American Economic Review, 54*, 72–85.

Jorgenson, D. W., Vickrey, W., Koopmans, T. C., & Samuelson, P. A. (1964). Discussion. *American Economic Review, 54*, 93–96.

Lintner, J. (1965). The valuation of risk assets and the selection of risky investments in stock portfolios and capital budgets. *Review of Economics and Statistics, 47*, 13–37.

Lucas, D. (2012). Valuation of Government Policies and Projects. *Annual Review of Financial Economics, 4*, 39–58 (Volume publication date October 2012).

Lucas, D. (2013). "Evaluating the Cost of Government Credit Support: The OECD Context," manuscript, Massachusetts Institute of Technology.

Lucas, D., & Phaup, M. (2010). The cost of risk to the government and its implications for federal budgeting. In D. Lucas (Ed.), *Measuring and managing federal financial risk*. Chicago, IL: University of Chicago Press.

Modigliani, F., & Miller, M. H. (1958). The cost of capital, corporation finance, and the theory of investment. *American Economic Review, 48*, 261–297.

Sandmo, A. (1972). Discount rates for public investment under uncertainty. *International Economic Review, 13*(2), 287–302.

Sandmo, A., & Dreze, J. (1971). Discount rates for public investment in closed and open economies. *Economica, 38*(152), 395–412.

Sharpe, W. F. (1964). Capital asset prices: A theory of market equilibrium under conditions of risk. *Journal of Finance, 19*, 425–442.

Revisiting Arrow-Lind: Managing Sovereign Disaster Risk

Reinhard Mechler[a,b] and Stefan Hochrainer-Stigler[a]

[a]IIASA - International Institute for Applied Systems Analysis, Austria; [b]WU Vienna University of Economics and Business, Austria

1. Introduction: governments and the financing of disaster risk

In their seminal paper of 1970, Kenneth Arrow and Robert Lind investigated how governments should treat uncertainty in the evaluation of public investment decisions. Their main argument was that if risks associated with a public investment are publicly borne (e.g., through taxation), the total cost of risk bearing is insignificant. Besides the risk spreading ability, they also argued that, as governments are able to pool a large number of assets, their risk portfolio is highly diversified. Consequently, Arrow and Lind (AL) suggested that governments can behave risk neutrally and evaluate their investments only through the expected net present (social) value.

AL's analysis has been subject to debate over the years (Anginer et al., 2013; Blake & Burrows, 2001; Fisher, 1973; Foldes & Rees, 1977; Gardner, 1979; Hochrainer, 2006; McKean & Moore, 1972; Mechler, 2004; Mishan, 1972; Nichols, 1972; Priest, 2003; Wellington, 1972). However, only few of these analysts explicitly studied and criticized the details of the theorem for the disaster dimension. On the other hand, one could argue that public policy in this domain used to have been based on AL's findings. Governments indeed used to assume and actually ignore catastrophic risks in their planning, therefore, implicitly or explicitly exhibiting risk neutrality (see Gurenko 2004; Mechler, 2004).

Our analysis shows, that there are important qualifications to be considered, and the last few years have seen a critical re-evaluation of governments' risk neutral approach to managing risks both in theory and practice. Faced with massive losses and reduced capacity to absorb risk, many governments have started to behave disaster risk aversely, incorporated disaster risk into their fiscal planning and even purchased sovereign insurance.

The next section summarizes and critically reflects on the main assumptions and conclusions made by Arrow and Lind. This is followed by empirical analysis and modeling results which suggest there are limits to the risk neutrality assumption. Finally, we summarize our discussion and discuss key implications.

2. Governments and disaster risk: qualifying Arrow-Lind

Generally speaking, preferences of different risk bearers (individuals, households, firms or governments) depend on how much effect a risk is assumed to have on the specific agent over time, such as causing liquidity constraints or leading to budget crises. If this effect is deemed to be large and behavior adjusted so that large risks are avoided or transferred, we one can speak of risk aversion; on the other hand, if the effect is thought to be marginal, risk neutrality may prevail. Generally, individuals and smaller firms are generally assumed to be risk averse as they will value potential losses higher than gains and bearing risk will have a cost for these agents (Dinwiddy & Teal, 1996).

Arrow and Lind (1970) proposed that governments should behave risk neutrally, as they are considered the entity best suited to deal with risk via efficiently pooling and spreading potential losses. More precisely, the argument did not favor completely neglecting uncertainty, rather AL suggested considering expected values only: '[…] the government should behave as an expected-value decision maker' (Arrow & Lind, 1970: 366), without accounting for the volatility around the mean.

Mechler (2004) challenged this view and suggested that in the context of disasters, volatility is of utmost importance and risk pooling and spreading may not be possible. A number of qualifications are listed in Table 1 and suggest risk neutrality will not hold if (1) there is a limited number of public assets at risk, (2) local or regional consequences are massive, (3) the tax base and savings are generally limited (4) distributional impacts matter and (5) there is irreversibility.

Additionally to these qualifications based on economic analysis, from a mathematical point of view starting from the original proof made by AL, Hochrainer and Pflug (2009) challenged the risk neutrality paradigm in the context of catastrophe risk via the introduction of kinked utility functions, which can arise from natural disaster events. They showed that in this situation the collective risk premium is not approaching zero and therefore risk aversion has to be assumed for catastrophe events.

Table 1. Qualifications to non-applicability of risk neutrality – theorem for disaster risk.

Qualifications related to risk pooling	
Existence of few and large government projects	Many times, governments undertake just a few large investment projects, which does not result in a highly diversified portfolio of projects, thus risk pooling is not viable. Also for smaller countries independent risk pooling is not possible.
Large local or regional consequences when assets are lost	Disaster risk is covariate risk, which will usually affect whole regions thus there is loss correlation. The independence assumption of risk is not valid for disasters, which can lead to considerably underestimating the risk.
Qualifications related to risk spreading	
Narrow tax and financing resources base for financing losses of projects	The tax base is often too narrow to spread risk sufficiently. Other potential government financing sources such as domestic credit or private sector lending are generally very limited as well. Reduction of fiscal space may cause important opportunity costs.
Distributional impacts	In some countries large distributional impacts may occur post-disaster when infrastructure projects whose prime goal is poverty reduction (e.g., through road or sanitation projects) are affected. The poor are the group most affected by a loss of infrastructure. Other important ripple effects on all levels can be expected if the systems lacks redundancies
Irreversibility	If additional funds are not available to continue crucial projects or rebuild assets there can be irreversible effects, such as on health service provision.

Source: Based on Mechler (2004).

While both, risk pooling and risk spreading are relevant, especially the second argument on the risk spreading capacity of governments has received interest, on which we build our further discussion. In the next section, we provide empirical and modeling evidence regarding instances where disaster risk spreading is facing limits.

3. Understanding fiscal vulnerability and risk

The qualification of the narrow tax and financing resources base for spreading risk can be illustrated by studying empirical evidence as well as conducting modeling exercises, both by looking at credible worst case scenarios.

Empirical evidence focusing on impacts

We present impacts of recent large disasters in two very different countries – the USA and Haiti (Table 2 and Figure 1). For illustrative purposes, these overall losses are compared with domestic resources for risk spreading. Governments own only part of these losses, yet need to provide support for households and businesses that are not able to absorb losses themselves. This will overstate the potential losses governments face, but shows the entire country risk.

Volatility of disaster risk in the context of general macroeconomic performance and financial vulnerability clearly is of importance. While in the USA, Hurricane Katrina caused

Table 2. Historical disaster losses and availability of resources for spreading risk.

2005 values	USA Hurricane 2005	Haiti Earthquake 2010
GDP (million current USD)	12,564,300	4307
Population (mill.)	296	9.9
GDP per capita	42,516	435
Losses (million current USD)	125,000	7271
Losses/capita	423.0	734.4
Losses/GDP (%)	0.99	168.8
Losses/Tax revenue (%)	8.9	993.0
Losses/Gross Domestic Savings	7.0	445.5

Data sources: NatCatService 2010; World Bank (2013).

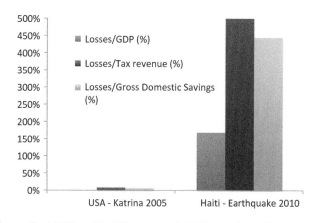

Figure 1. (Colour online) Differential ability to spread risk for two large disasters in the US and Haiti.

colossal losses of about USD 125 billion, this amounted to less than 1% of GDP. In comparison, while the absolute losses for Haiti were smaller, in terms of relative losses they were tremendous at more than 160% of their GDP, and serious negative fiscal and macro-economic effects have to be expected in the medium- to longer-term, although in practice these effects are often not monitored and difficult to isolate from the background noise (see Noy, 2009). By all means, however, comprehensively spreading the losses using tax revenue or savings seems impossible for Haiti. This is also partly due to the smaller population, and small total area of Haiti as well as relative low tax revenues in terms of GDP.

Modelling fiscal and economic disaster risks – the European perspective

While the former analysis was based on observed losses, in the face of risk, it is important to be forward looking. IIASA's (International Institute for Applied Systems Analysis) Catastrophe Simulation (CatSim) model helps to project fiscal and aggregate economic vulnerability and risk as a function of losses and fiscal resilience (see Figure 2).

Fiscal resilience in turn, is defined by a government's portfolio of *ex ante* and *ex post* financial measures available to refinance losses. The model can be used to calculate fiscal vulnerability and risk in terms of disaster-related deficits, fiscal space in the face of disaster risk as well as threshold events (in return periods) beyond which fiscal space would be reduced to zero (called a resource gap) (see Hochrainer, 2006; Mechler, 2004).

As one example, Figure 3 charts out government flood risk liabilities for 100 year flood risk as compared to reported fiscal deficits for a number of flood prone Eastern European countries.

The figure indicates that large disasters could indeed pose serious stress on the fiscal position for these flood-prone countries. As flood risk is not budgeted for the assessed countries, one could argue that this additional risk presents a hidden deficit. The inclusion of contingent risk is therefore a very important consideration to determine the real risk level of government exposed to disasters and to assess whether risk aversion should be assumed and at what level.

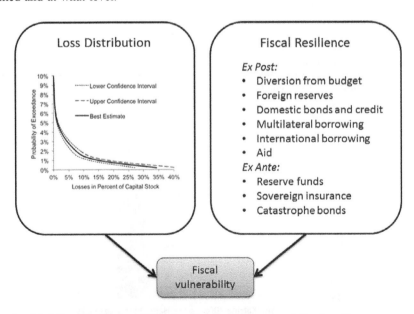

Figure 2. Modeling fiscal vulnerability as a function of losses and fiscal resilience.
Source: Hochrainer-Stigler et al. (2013).

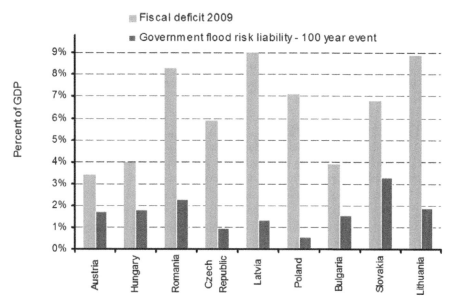

Figure 3. (Colour online) Governments' explicit fiscal deficits and hidden disaster deficits in selected flood-prone European countries.

Source: Mechler, Hochrainer, Aaheim, Salen, and Wreford (2010).

Modeling fiscal and economic disaster risks – the global perspective

For the global level, we show analysis regarding country resource gaps in the face of weather related disaster risk – floods, storms or droughts (Figure 4).

The resource gap year event indicates at what annual probability governments are expected to be unable to finance disaster events. As it can be seen on the chart, larger

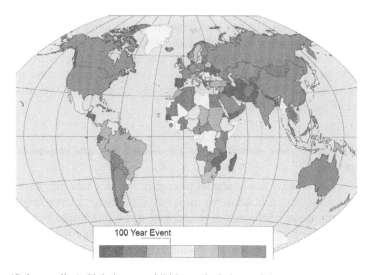

Figure 4. (Colour online) Global map exhibiting calculations of the resource gap year event.

Source: Hochrainer-Stigler et al. (2014) (*forthcoming*).

and/or wealthier countries are more or less able to finance even high-loss disaster events and the Arrow Lind Theorem may seem valid (which does not indicate that there could not be important negative regional or fiscal effects), while for heavily exposed, smaller and less diversified economies, resource gaps would start way below a 100 year event, which would suggest a need to act in line with risk aversion.

4. Conclusions and implications

The Arrow and Lind theorem has been fundamental for suggesting a risk-neutral approach for managing sovereign risk. As already tentatively indicated by Arrow and Lind (1970), yet not picked up by practice and theory, it does however not apply for a number of countries subject to high natural disaster risk and with lesser means at disposal for spreading or pooling the risks. Especially the risk spreading capacity of governments and the resulting individual cost being negligible is debatable. In reality, external aid or loans have often to be sought post-disaster to somewhat continue with business as usual. Crucial about risk preference is that if governments are perceived to be risk neutral and thus risk and potential losses are only included as expected value, there is no incentive for a decision maker to evaluate risk financing mechanisms as the price of risk financing mechanisms is usually higher than the expected loss.

Some countries should exhibit risk aversion and plan for disaster risk

Overall, we discussed that substantial risk (a hidden disaster deficit) coupled with weak fiscal conditions can lead to substantial additional stress on the fiscal position, and lead to reduced space for public finances to fund other public investment projects. In order to reduce fiscal vulnerability, *ex ante* risk management and financing measures can be taken such as implementing risk prevention, offering state sponsored insurance to households or engaging in sovereign risk financing measures. It is interesting to note that, conceptually, this array of measures transforms the contingent disaster liability in a direct liability with certain annual premiums, fund outlays and debt service payments replacing ad-hoc *ex post* disaster expenditure. Thus, such options help to move at least a part of disaster risk liabilities to regular budget practice and improved accountability and possibilities to combine it with risk reduction incentives. Generally, to transform a contingent state of the world into a certain one, a probabilistic approach using an estimate of risk is necessary, however. Schematically, the following simplistic visualization of a government's balance sheet may be a basis for planning and the inclusion of contingent risk is key to determine the real risk level (Table 3).

A number of countries have started to plan for disaster risk and engage in sovereign risk insurance

A number of countries have lately started to engage in risk financing more broadly. In 2006, the Mexican government chose to insure its catastrophe reserve fund, FONDEN, against major earthquakes with a mix of reinsurance and a catastrophe bond, and in 2009 renewed this transaction in conjunction with cover for hurricane risk. Mexico received substantial technical assistance from the World Bank and Inter-American Development Bank over the years, but as a middle-income developing country and member of the OECD, it financed the transaction out of its own means (Cardenas, Hochrainer, Mechler, Pflug, & Linnerooth-Bayer, 2007). The World Food Programme (WFP) with USAID

Table 3. Government liabilities and disaster risk.

Liabilities	Direct	Contingent
	Obligation in any event	Obligation if a particular event occurs
Explicit Government liability recognized by law or Contract	Foreign and domestic sovereign borrowing, expenditures by budget law and budget expenditures	State guarantees for non-sovereign borrowing and public and private sector entities, **reconstruction of public infrastructure**
Implicit A 'moral' obligation of the government	Future recurrent costs of public investment projects, pension and health care expenditure	Default of subnational government or public or private entities, **disaster relief**

Source: Modified after Schick and Polackova Brixi (2004).

funding sponsored an index-based insurance scheme for government relief expenditure in Ethiopia for extreme drought risk (Hess et al., 2006). Caribbean island states in 2007 formed the world's first multi-country and index-based catastrophe insurance pool for providing governments with immediate liquidity in the aftermath of hurricanes or earthquakes, donors and International Financing Institutions (IFI) have provided significant capital to the extent of USD 50 million. This funding helps to back up the pool in its early years when accumulated country contributions are insufficient to render this scheme robust to withstand major events such as hurricanes (Ghesquiere & Mahul, 2007).

Ultimately, risk aversion and large costs of risk are just a necessary condition to motivate the decision to conduct risk transfer. Whether it is desirable for a country's government will depend on the government's fiscal vulnerability and the cost of risk management instruments compared to the cost of other financing options.

References

Anginer, D., de la Torre, A., & Ize, A. (2013) Risk-bearing by the state: When is it good public policy?. *Journal of Financial Stability,* Retrieved from http://dx.doi.org/10.1016/j.jfs.2013.03.006

Arrow, K. J., & Lind, R. C. (1970). Uncertainty and the evaluation of public investment decisions. *The American Economic Review, 60*, 364–378.

Blake, D., & Burrows, W. (2001). Survivor bonds: Helping to hedge mortality risk. *The Journal of Risk and Insurance, 68*, 339–348.

Cardenas, V., Hochrainer, S., Mechler, R., Pflug, G., & Linnerooth-Bayer, J. (2007). Sovereign financial disaster risk management: The case of Mexico. *Environmental Hazards, 7*, 40–53.

Dinwiddy, C. & Teal, F. (1996). Principles of Cost-Benefit Analysis For Developing Countries. Cambridge University Press, Cambridge.

Fisher, A. C. (1973). Environmental externalitites and the arrow-lind public investment theorem. *The American Economic Review, 63*, 722–725.

Foldes, L. P., & Rees, R. (1977). A note on the arrow-lind theorem. *The American Economic Review, 67*, 188–193.

Gardner, R. (1979). The Arrow-Lind theorem in a continuum economy. *The American Economic Review, 69*, 420–422.

Ghesquiere, F., & Mahul, O. (2007). Sovereign natural disaster insurance for developing countries: A paradigm shift in catastrophe risk financing. Policy Research Working Paper 4345. The World Bank, Washington DC.

Gurenko, E. (2004). Introduction. In E. Gurenko (Ed.), *Catastrophe risk and reinsurance: A country risk management perspective* (pp. xxi–xxvi). London: Risk Books.

Hess, U., Wiseman, W., & Robertson, T. (2006). Ethiopia: Integrated Risk Financing to Protect Livelihoods and Foster Development, Discussion Paper, November 2006.

Hochrainer, S. (2006). *Macroeconomic risk management against natural disasters*. Wiesbaden: German University Press (DUV).

Hochrainer, S., & Pflug, G. (2009). Natural disaster risk bearing ability of governments: Consequences of kinked utility. *Journal of Natural Disaster Science, 31*(1), 11–21.

Hochrainer-Stigler, S., Mechler, R., & Pflug, G. (2013). Modeling macro scale disaster risk: The CATSIM model. In A. Amendola, T. Ermolieva, J. Linnerooth-Bayer, & R. Mechler (Eds.), *Integrated catastrophe risk modeling: Supporting policy processes* (pp. 119–144). Dordrecht: Springer.

Hochrainer-Stigler, S., Mechler, R., Pflug, G., & Williges, K. (2014). Financial vulnerability to climate-related natural hazards on the global scale. *Global Environmental Change*, (Forthcoming)

McKean, R. N., & Moore, J. H. (1972). Uncertainty and the evaluation of public investment decisions: Comment. *The American Economic Review, 62*, 165–167.

Mechler, R. (2004). *Natural disaster risk management and financing disaster losses in developing countries*. Karlsruhe: Verlag fuer Versicherungswissenschaft.

Mechler, R., Hochrainer, S., Aaheim, A., Salen, H., & Wreford, A. (2010). Modelling economic impacts and adaptation to extreme events: Insights from European case studies. *Mitigation and Adaptation Strategies for Global Change, 15*(7), 737–762.

Mishan, E. J. (1972). Uncertainty and the evaluation of public investment decisions: Comment. *The American Economic Review, 62*, 161–164.

NatCatService (2010). Munich Re Database on Disaster Losses. Munich Re, Munich.

Nichols, A. (1972). Uncertainty and the evaluation of public investment decisions: Comment. *The American Economic Review, 62*, 168–169.

Noy, I. (2009). The macroeconomic consequences of disasters. *Journal of Development Economics, Elsevier, 88*(2), 221–231.

Priest, G. L. (2003). Government insurance versus market insurance. *The Geneva Papers on Risk and Insurance, 28*, 71–80.

Schick, A., Polackova Brixi, H. (Eds.). (2004). *Government at risk*. Washington, DC: World Bank and Oxford University Press.

Wellington, D. (1972). Uncertainty and the evaluation of public investment decisions: Comment. *The American Economic Review, 62*, 170.

World Bank. (2013). *World bank development indicators*. Washington, DC: The World Bank.

Size matters: capital market size and risk-return profiles

Keiran Sharpe and Massimiliano Tani

School of Business, UNSW, Canberra, Australia

1. Introduction

The Arrow-Lind (1970) proposition on risk sharing is the public sector analogy of the well-known proposition of the theory of finance that, as the membership of an insurance syndicate is increased (where each member of the syndicate is risk averse and where his income is uncorrelated with the payoffs of the syndicate) then the syndicate tends to act in a manner that approaches risk neutrality, and that the syndicate acts in a risk neutral manner as the membership tends to infinity. The logic underlying this proposition is relatively easy to grasp. As the population of a syndicate is increased, two opposing effects occur. The first tends to undercut the incentive to take on risks, as the increase in an insurance syndicate's population dilutes the rewards to each member. The second effect tends to encourage increased risk-taking by the syndicate, as it diminishes the risk faced by each individual and this itself tends to encourage greater risk-taking. Ultimately, as membership rises, the second effect is the stronger because the risk borne by each syndicate member declines at a faster rate than the reduction in each member's mean income. As a result, larger insurance syndicates are generally able to insure larger corporate risks because the risks faced by individuals within the syndicate are smaller than they are for members of smaller syndicates.

This consideration has relevant policy implications: if we think of capital markets as performing a quasi-insurance function for the investors who compose it (by allowing them to share risks), and risk aversion is randomly distributed across the world population, a country with a small (investor) population is predicted to price a given level of risk at a higher level than a country with a large population. As a result, the 'natural advantage' of the large country in funding risky ventures originating from a small country makes it inefficient, for the latter, to attempt developing a domestic venture capital market to fund local start-ups, new ventures, and even research and development (R&D). Is this the case? Will Australian, New Zealand, and Canadian inventors always find it cheaper to fund their ideas in England or the United States?

This note explores this implication. In so doing, it develops a simple theoretical model capturing the various forces at work. We conclude that large capital markets do not always have a better risk-return profile than small capital markets for a given level of risk, as the marginal return for an additional investment in a risky asset is not constant, as implicitly assumed by finance theory models. The rest of this note is organized as follows: Section 2 briefly reviews the relevant literature prior to developing the theoretical framework to derive testable propositions in Section 3. Section 4 concludes.

2. Literature review

A natural point to start discussion about the impact of size on capital market performance is the capital asset pricing model of Sharpe (1964) and Lintner (1965).[1] For that model, Lintner (1970) showed that an increase in the size of the market – whether measured by an increase in the number of stockholders or in the wealth of each – results in greater 'risk tolerance' of the market as a whole. This is to say that, as the market size increases, the degree of risk aversion of the market as a whole falls, and, accordingly, the price of risk also falls.[2] In the limit, as the number of investors goes to infinity, the market acts as if it were risk neutral – that is, the price of risk falls to zero. The reason for this 'risk elimination' is the greater ability of investors to diversify the risks held by any one of them and the concomitant decline in the total risk borne by all the stockholders in the market as the number of investors increases. In the limit, the risk borne by each investor falls to zero. The result is analogous to the 'risk spreading' proposition in the public sector context of Arrow and Lind (1970).

In the same paper Lintner also showed that, under certain conditions, the behavior of a competitive asset market could be modeled 'as if' there were a single 'mutual fund' or 'syndicate' maximizing the aggregate welfare of the market as a whole. This is so regardless of whether there is a riskless asset or not (Lintner, 1969). The conditions that apply are that each stockholder has a constant degree of risk aversion and that all stockholders' judgments as to the distribution of returns are the same. Utilizing this construction allows us to draw out an interesting corollary of the fact that aggregate risk attitude falls as market size increases.

Suppose that there are two syndicates of different size that face the same 'universe of risks' (i.e., the same set of portfolio choices represented on the (μ, σ^2) plane, where the frontier of risks is not upper-bounded, and where the returns are normally distributed). Furthermore, suppose that each member of each syndicate has the same income and preference profile as that of any other member of that syndicate (i.e., each member is a 'representative agent' of his syndicate), and that that each member is attempting to maximize:

$$U = -\exp[-A(\bar{x} - A \operatorname{var}(x)/2] \tag{1}$$

(where $\times$ denotes the agent's end-of-period wealth which is normally distributed with mean, $\bar{x}$, and variance, var(x); and where A measures the constant degree of risk aversion). Finally, suppose that members of the two different syndicates may have different degrees of risk aversion. Then, given the fact that, in the larger syndicate, stakeholders are better able to disperse risk, we can derive the following comparative static propositions by way of revealed preference arguments:

(1) if the larger syndicate chooses a portfolio with a smaller variance than that chosen by the smaller syndicate, then the population of the larger syndicate must be the more risk averse

(2a) if the larger syndicate chooses a portfolio with a larger variance than that chosen by the smaller syndicate, but the ratio of the variance to the mean return faced by each member of the larger syndicate is smaller than that of the smaller syndicate, then the population of the larger syndicate must be more risk averse than the population of the smaller syndicate

(2b) if the larger syndicate chooses a portfolio with a larger variance than that chosen by the smaller syndicate, and the ratio of the variance to the mean return faced by each member of the larger syndicate is larger than that of the smaller syndicate, then the population of the larger syndicate must be less risk averse than the population of the smaller syndicate.

If we denote the larger syndicate as syndicate I and the smaller as syndicate II, then we can re-state the above propositions symbolically:

(1) $\sigma_I^2 < \sigma_{II}^2 \Rightarrow$ syndicate I is more risk averse than syndicate II

(2a) $\sigma_I^2 > \sigma_{II}^2$ & $\frac{\sigma_I^2/n_I^2}{\mu_I/n_I} < \frac{\sigma_{II}^2/n_{II}^2}{\mu_{II}/n_{II}} \Rightarrow$ syndicate I is more risk averse than syndicate II

(2b) $\sigma_I^2 > \sigma_{II}^2$ & $\frac{\sigma_I^2/n_I^2}{\mu_I/n_I} \geq \frac{\sigma_{II}^2/n_{II}^2}{\mu_{II}/n_{II}} \Rightarrow$ syndicate I is less risk averse than syndicate II

(where μ = the mean return for the syndicate as a whole; and σ^2 = the variance of returns for the syndicate as a whole, and we note that $\bar{x} = \mu/n$ and $\mathrm{var}(x) = \sigma^2/n^2$).

Thus, if two economies face the same universe of risk, we have a test for the relative degree of risk aversion of the two sets of investors. Of course, economies of different size do not generally face the same (unconditional) universe of risk. Rather, they face universes that are conditioned on size (among other things). So practical testing of different risk attitudes in different markets utilizing aggregate level data is only possible once the impact of market size on the set of available assets is modeled. In this paper, we concentrate on assessing the impact of market size on the risk-return performance of markets on the assumption that all investors in all markets share the same attitude to risk; and we leave to future study the analysis of the issue of whether some capital markets are manifestly composed of more risk averse investors than others. This is consistent with our immediate objective of ascertaining whether the differential risk-return performance of capital markets of different size can be accounted for even when all agents have similar degrees of risk aversion.

3. A theoretical construct

To begin to understand the way in which capital market size might impact on performance, we propose a highly simplified model, the purpose of which is to allow us to get a handle on the fundamental issues in play. The model supposes the following.

First, we assume that each capital market operates so as to maximize the utility of the agents who compose it. This is to say, we let each nation's capital market effectively operate as a kind of mutual fund for its stakeholders, and the portfolio of assets that is chosen by each market is the one that maximizes welfare given available capital. This supposition is warranted by the earlier discussion; specifically, since competitive asset markets that efficiently allocate capital can be modeled in such an 'as if' fashion, and since it is simplest to proceed on such a basis, it is convenient to do so.

Second, it is assumed that all markets have the same risk attitude as captured by their coefficients of absolute risk aversion. This presupposes that the distribution of degrees of risk aversion across each population is the same. In other words, no country has a disproportionate preponderance of relatively more or less risk averse types vis-à-vis any other country. This may or may not be the case in reality, as noted at the end of the previous section; but there are no *a priori* grounds for thinking that one or another country is, on the whole, more or less risk averse than another, and so we adopt the assumption on the premise of the principle of insufficient reason.[3]

Third, markets are assumed to inhabit the same universe of risk conditioned on size; which is to say, all markets of any given size are assumed to have access to the same sets of assets. The idea underlying this supposition is that no country of equal size to another lacks the ability to access the same range of assets as the other – there are no technical, or educational or other institutional impediments giving rise to some assets being unavailable. This motivation parallels that which underlies the New Trade Theory: the kinds of firms of any two nations of interest are essentially similar (or at least are symmetrical in nature), and this is reflected in their production activity and risk characteristics (see; Krugman, 1979; Lancaster, 1980). Since this assumption cannot expect to hold for developing or emerging economies, adopting it limits our attention to developed countries.

Finally, it is assumed that returns are normally distributed. As with the previous assumption, this restricts attention to developed capital markets.

The problem facing the capital market is as follows:

$$\max_{\mu,\sigma^2} u = \mu - b\sigma^2 \text{ subject to } \mu = F(\sigma^2)$$

where $b = A/2$ = half the coefficient of absolute risk aversion (A); μ = the mean rate of return; σ^2 = the variance of returns; and $F(.)$ represents the range of portfolios that a capital market of size K can afford (where K = the market cap) with $F' > 0$, $F'' \le 0$.

Solving this in the usual manner gives three first order conditions: $\lambda = 1$, $b = F'(\sigma^2) = F_{\sigma^2}$, and $\mu = F(\sigma^2)$, where λ = the Lagrange multiplier.

Given the last condition and the fact that the position of the frontier is determined by the size of the capital market, K, yields: $d\mu/dK = (F_{\sigma^2})d\sigma^2/dK$. Multiplying by $K/(\mu\sigma^2)$ and rearranging gives:

$$\varepsilon_{\mu\sigma^2} = \varepsilon_{\mu K}/\varepsilon_{\sigma^2 K} \tag{2}$$

where $\varepsilon_{\mu\sigma^2}$ = the elasticity of the mean-variance frontier; $\varepsilon_{\mu K}$ = the elasticity of mean return with respect to capital market size; $\varepsilon_{\sigma^2 K}$ = the elasticity of variance with respect to capital market size. This last equation implies that the greater is $\varepsilon_{\mu K}/\varepsilon_{\sigma^2 K}$, that is, the greater is the capacity of the market to generate expected returns as its size increases relative to its capacity to sustain risk as its size increases, then the greater is the elasticity of the mean-variance frontier.

To grasp the comparative static implications of this, recall the second first order condition to obtain:

$$\mu = \left(\frac{b}{\varepsilon_{\mu\sigma^2}}\right)\sigma^2 \tag{3}$$

Hence, if market capitalization rises whilst risk attitudes (given by b) are constant, the mean-variance ratio (μ/σ^2) will be lower at the optimum the greater is $\varepsilon_{\mu\sigma^2} = \varepsilon_{\mu K}/\varepsilon_{\sigma^2 K}$. Hence μ/σ^2 is lower the greater is the market's capacity to generate mean returns relative to its capacity to sustain risk as its size increases. The reason for this is that, as agents pursue the greater returns that are available, they experience declining marginal expected

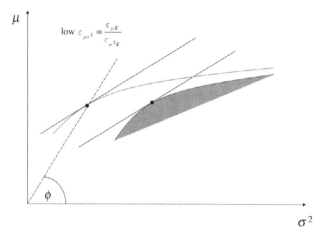

Figure 1.   (Colour online) Relative variance displacement in the universe of risk.

returns as greater risk is absorbed, and this drives down the relative mean-variance ratio (see Figures 1 and 2). The case of low $\varepsilon_{\mu K}/\varepsilon_{\sigma^2 K}$ may be referred to as a 'relative-variance displacement' and the case of a high $\varepsilon_{\mu K}/\varepsilon_{\sigma^2 K}$ as a 'relative-mean displacement'.

The key determinant of $\varepsilon_{\mu\sigma^2}$ with which we are here concerned is the covariance amongst assets held in market portfolios. In particular, we observe that the greater is the change in covariance, *ceteris paribus*, the lower is $\varepsilon_{\mu\sigma^2}$. To see this, it is sufficient to note that

$$\frac{\frac{1^T\boldsymbol{\mu}_j - 1^T\boldsymbol{\mu}_i}{1^T\boldsymbol{\mu}_i}}{\frac{1^T\Sigma_j 1 - 1^T\Sigma_i 1}{1^T\Sigma_i 1}}$$

where $\boldsymbol{\mu}_i$, $\boldsymbol{\mu}_j$ = the vector of returns when $K = K_1$, K_2 respectively; Σ_i, Σ_j = the matrix of variances when $K = K_1$, K_2 respectively; and $\mathbf{1}$ = the unit vector. Evidently, the smaller is the change in the covariance matrix, *ceteris paribus*, the greater is the given ratio.

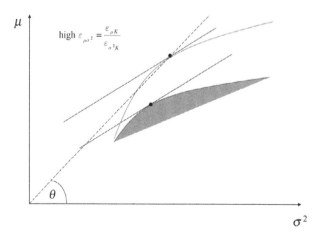

Figure 2.   (Colour online) Relative mean displacement in the universe of risk.

Our initial hypothesis can then be stated as follows. As capital markets increase in size the variance-to-market cap ratio falls (i.e., $\varepsilon_{\sigma^2 K} < 1$). There are four reasons why this might be so:

(1) the industry effect: or, more fully, the inter-industry effect, whereby negative co-variances between different industries rise as the economy and the market cap become larger (Silicon Valley booms as Detroit rusts);
(2) the competition effect: or the intra-industry effect, whereby industry variances decline as competition becomes more intense with larger market size (as competition increases, the ability to generate discretely different profits declines);
(3) the derivative asset effect: derivative assets, which allow firms to preserve mean returns whilst reducing variances, are more widely available in larger than in smaller capital markets;
(4) the asset pricing effect: asset prices of the same classes of assets are more stable the deeper is the capital market, hence markets with a larger cap have a lower volatility of asset prices and, so, lower variances of returns.

This is to say, in brief, that, as market cap rises, a combination of financial market deepening and changing industrial structure tends to lower market variances of returns.[4]

We further hypothesize that, as capital markets increase in size, the mean return-to-market cap ratio falls (i.e., $\varepsilon_{\mu K} \leq 1$). The reason for this is owed to a combination of three factors, namely:

(1) the fact that all markets inhabit the same (conditional) universe of risk;
(2) the capacity of each market to fund the minimum efficient scale of operations for each industry within that universe;
(3) non-increasing returns to capital in any given industry.

Our main prediction is then as follows: as capital markets increase in size, they experience a tendency for variances and mean returns to decline relative to the size of the market; which is to say, we expect them to experience a relative variance displacement. As variances tend to decline, the willingness of the economy to support higher risk investments increases, and, as mean returns tend to decline, the corresponding incentive to find and fund such higher risk investments rises. This increasing tolerance of risk is reinforced by the fact that larger capital markets are able to absorb greater risk in aggregate for the kinds of reasons given in the Lintner/Arrow-Lind argument: for reasons of risk spreading. (This latter phenomenon is captured in our simple model by lower values of b for larger capital markets.) Hence, as market capitalization increases, we expect to see markets subscribe riskier projects than are subscribed by markets of smaller size; and, despite this being the case, the larger market may still have a lower mean return in aggregate than the smaller market.

4. Conclusions

We propose a simple approach to assess the impact of capital market size on the risk/return profile of capital markets. The thought motivating the study is that markets of different size ought to behave differently even when they are composed of agents whose risk attitudes are all alike. Smaller, or shallower, markets are less able to pool and spread risks than are deeper markets and we might expect this to be reflected in the observed risk/

return profiles of capital markets of differing size. However, when the marginal return per additional unit of risk decreases, the larger market is able to absorb a higher level of risk but may also experience a lower mean return in aggregate than the smaller market. Subsidies to foster venture capital funds subscribing risks in new ventures and R&D in small-to-medium sized capital markets such as Australia are not necessarily displaced by lower ability to subscribe risky ventures of a small market.

Notes

1. Although there are well known problems with the empirical validity of the model (Fama & French, 1992), especially in the case of international capital market comparisons (Erb, Harvey, & Viskanta, 1997, p. 9), the model is familiar and sufficiently robust to form the foundation for discussion.
2. Strictly speaking, Lintner showed this for the class of utility functions in which risk tolerance is linearly related to wealth. The discussion in Budd and Litzenberger (1972) and Lintner (1972) clarifies the issue.
3. Keynes (1921, pp. 52–53) referred to the principle of insufficient reason as the principle of indifference, formulating it as: 'if there is no known reason for predicating of our subject one rather than another of several alternatives, then relatively to such knowledge the assertions of each of these alternatives have an equal probability'.
4. Bekaert and Harvey (1997, p.58), in their discussion of emerging market volatility, also give four reasons for differential market volatility. Two of the factors mentioned by them – 'asset concentration' and 'political risk' – are effectively ruled out by our concentrating upon developed, rather than emerging markets. Specifically, they are ruled out by the assumption that firms inhabit the same conditional universe of risk. The two other factors mentioned – 'stock market/economic integration' and 'microstructure effects' – correspond to points (1)–(2) and (3)–(4) above.

References

Arrow, K. J., & Lind, R. (1970). Uncertainty and the evaluation of public investments. *American Economic Review, 60*, 364–378.

Bekaert, G., & Harvey, C. R. (1997). Emerging equity market volatility. *Journal of Financial Economics, 43*, 26–77.

Budd, A. P., & Litzenberger, R. H. (1972). The market price of risk, size of market, and investor's risk aversion: A comment. *Review of Economics and Statistics, LIV*(May), 204–206.

Erb, C. B., Harvey, C. R., & Viskanta, T. E. (1997). *Country risk in global financial management.* Charlottesville, VA: The Research Foundation of the Institute of Chartered Financial Analysts.

Fama, E. F., & French, K. R. (1992). The Cross-section of expected stock returns. *The Journal of Finance, XLVII*(2), 427–465.

Keynes, J. M. (1921). *A treatise on probability.* London: Macmillan.

Krugman, P. R. (1979). Increasing returns, monopolistic competition, and international trade. *Journal of International Economics, 9*, 469–479.

Lancaster, K. (1980). Intra-industry trade under perfect monopolistic competition. *Journal of International Economics, 10*, 151–175.

Lintner, J. (1965). The valuation of risk assets and the selection of risky investments in stock portfolios and capital budgets. *Review of Economics and Statistics, XLVII*(February), 13–37.

Lintner, J. (1969). The aggregation of investor's diverse judgments and preferences in purely competitive security markets. *Journal of Financial and Quantitative Analysis, 4*(4), 347–400.

Lintner, J. (1970). The market price of risk, size of market, and investor's risk aversion. *Review of Economics and Statistics, LII*(February), 87–99.

Lintner, J. (1972). The market price of risk, size of market, and investor's risk aversion: A reply. *Review of Economics and Statistics, LIV*(May), 206–208.

Sharpe, W. (1964). Capital asset prices: A theory of market equilibrium under conditions of risk. *Journal of Finance, XIX*, 425–442.

Microeconomic foundations of bailouts

Marian Moszoro

IESE Business School, Av. Pearson, Barcelona, Spain and Kozminski University, Ul. Jagiellonska, Poland

1. Introduction

Arrow and Lind's classic paper 'Uncertainty and the Evaluation of Public Investment Decisions' (1970; hereafter, often abbreviated as 'A-L') has been a point of reference in the discussion about the efficiency of public vs. private financing and risk bearing (Clark et al. 2002; Grimsey & Lewis, 2004; Grout, 2003; Gurenko & Lester, 2005; Jenkinson, 2003). One of the direct consequences of A-L theorem is that public investments should be discounted at a lower rate than private investments and that catastrophic risks should be borne by the public sector. I revisit the Arrow and Lind's contribution in the light of the 2008–2009 financial crisis, from the perspective of the Troubled Asset Relief Program (TARP) and the American Recovery and Reinvestment Act (ARRA). The question is whether A-L economic theory validates the government's actions involving the use of public funds to bail out near-bankrupt businesses.

Some authors have not spared words of criticism towards the basic assumptions set by A-L, namely, that 'the share of the net benefits of an investment accruing to any person becomes negligible as population tends to infinity' and argue that this assumption does not apply to 'public goods, where the benefit is not "shared" but increases with the population; for projects whose scale must be adjusted roughly in proportion to the size of population [...]; and [to] projects whose benefits accrue wholly or in part to a section of the population which is "small" in the sense of the theorem' (Foldes & Rees, 1977, p. 188). Thus, the independence assumption – meaning that 'the net returns from an investment be independent of the returns from previous investments' (A-L, 369) – cannot refer to too-big-to-fail bailouts since they are strongly correlated with the government's and individuals' income. Agreeing on these criticisms, I would like to point out in this paper some of A-L's valuable remarks that are applicable to the actions undertaken by governments worldwide. Surprisingly, I have found no reference to A-L in the context of the financial crisis and bailouts.

2. A brief description of bailout programs

The Troubled Asset Relief Program (TARP) of October 2008 allowed the Department of Treasury to purchase or insure assets and equity from financial institutions to strengthen the financial sector. The program later expanded to other industries.[1] Firms selling assets to TARP were required to issue equity warrants (i.e., rights to purchase shares at a specific price), or equity or senior debt securities (for non-publicly listed companies) to the Treasury. In the case of warrants, the Treasury only received warrants for non-voting shares, or agreed not to vote the stock. While Congress authorized $700 billion for TARP, Treasury utilized only $420 billion TARP funds. As of 30 June 2013, American taxpayers have recovered almost 95% – or more than $400.5 billion of funds disbursed.[2]

The American Recovery and Reinvestment Act (ARRA) of February 2009, commonly referred to as the Stimulus or The Recovery Act, was an economic stimulus package aimed at saving and creating jobs through investments in infrastructure, education, health, and renewable energy, federal tax incentives, and expansion of unemployment benefits and other social welfare provisions. The approximate cost of the economic stimulus package was estimated to be $787 billion at the time of passage, later revised to $831 billion between 2009 and 2019.[3]

3. Ownership dispersion and risk bearing

The main insight of the A-L theorem that has an application to the 2008–2009 crisis policy debate has to do with the distribution of the cost of risk-bearing at a firm level. Too big to fail? There may be more to it. If bailouts equal ownership dispersion – that is, every taxpayer becomes a shareholder – then it may be not about the size, but about liquidity risk appraisal. According to Holmström and Tirole (2011), the government has an active role to play in improving risk-sharing between consumers with limited commitment power and firms dealing with the high costs of potential liquidity shortages. In this perspective, private risk sharing is always imperfect and may lead to financial crises that can be alleviated through government interventions.

Arrow and Lind would vindicate TARP as a program aimed to reduce risk aversion by shareholder ownership dispersion through public (governmental) ownership. Since every taxpayer has a stake in the state, it implies that the bailed out company should be discounted at a lower risk premium, i.e., valued higher and continue operations in turmoil times, as was the case of AIG. The alternative risk-averse solution, implying a higher discount rate and negative net present value, would implicate the liquidation of the company and the recovery of its residual claims, as in the case of the Lehman Brothers.

4. Discount rate of public investments

At first the issue of the discount rate for public investments should be reviewed. According to A-L, the 'government can better cope with uncertainty than private investors and, there- fore, government investments should not be evaluated by the same criterion used in private markets. Many [...] risks [related to moral hazards] are not present in the case of public investments and, therefore, it can be argued that it is not appropriate for the government to take these risks into account when choosing among public investments' (A-L, p. 364).

Arrow and Lind purposely ignored the principal-agent problem in public investments. Therefore, they stated that 'the government should behave as an expected-value decision maker and use a discount rate appropriate for investments with certain returns' (A-L, p. 366). The undertaking of investment projects – I treat firms as investment projects – by the public sector is justified by the lack of perfect insurance markets through which individuals may individually pool risks.

In the case of projects evaluated as a package, projects borne by the public sector should also be assessed at their expected value. 'This result is obtained not because the government is able to pool investments but because the government distributes the risk associated with any investment among a large number of people. It is the risk-spreading aspect of the government investment that is essential to this result' (A-L, p. 366). That is, in contemporary finance terms, A-L do not refer to portfolio management, but to efficient insurance. What is more, 'in the case of a [government-]sponsored investment, [the number of taxpayers] n is not only large but the investment is generally a very small fraction of national income even though the investment itself may be large in some absolute sense' (A-L, p. 373).

On the one hand, the government values companies at lower risk premium and, on the other hand, managers in companies with government ownership enjoy more discretion (recall the Treasury only received warrants for non-voting shares, or agreed not to vote the stock) and are less risk averse in selecting projects. Therefore, idiosyncratic events have lower impact on portfolios with government ownership. Thus, investors demand lower liquidity premiums for firms with government ownership. Managers who enjoy more discretion behave risk neutral: screen projects at a lower discount rate (invest more and more promptly) in companies without government ownership. By the same token, investors in companies with government ownership know managers behave risk neutral and value them accordingly.

5. Pareto vs. Hicks-Kaldor improvement

From the perspective of public investments in private companies, it is worth considering Jack Hirshleifer's (1966) recommendation to undertake the private investment rather than the public one, and pay a subsidy if necessary to induce private entrepreneurs to undertake the investment. Conversely, A-L commented that 'clearly, if there is a choice between one investment or the other, given the existing distribution of risk, the public investment is superior. The implication is that if a risky investment in the private sector is displaced by a public investment with a lower expected return but with a higher return when appropriate adjustments are made for risks, this represents a Hicks-Kaldor improvement' (A-L, p. 375). Moreover, consider the case of a private investment that becomes partially public. 'By selling some share of the asset to one of the individuals not originally possessing a share, the cost of risk-bearing can be reduced while expected returns remain unchanged. The reduction in the cost of risk-bearing can then be redistributed to bring about a Pareto improvement' (A-L, p. 373).

Finally, 'suppose the taxpayers were to pay this subsidy, which is a transfer of income from the public at large to the private investor, in order to cover the loss from the investment. The net benefits, including the cost of risk-bearing, remain negative because while the subsidy has partially offset the cost of risk-bearing to the individual investor, it has not reduced this cost. Therefore, a direct public subsidy in this case results in a less efficient allocation of resources' (A-L, p. 375). According to A-L, thus, bailouts are more efficient than direct subsidies and tax reliefs to the private sector, which were part of ARRA.

6. Concluding remarks

Are less wealthy economies that cannot afford bailouts condemned to less efficient solutions? A-L seemed to have foreseen the problem and added that the 'program which produces the desired results [i.e., encourages private investments and makes the costs of risk-bearing lower] is one to insure private investments' (A-L, p. 375). The government does not need to finance directly a project spread risks. In the situation of lack of complete markets, guarantees from the government may fairly fulfill this function.

In A-L's general conception, the state is 'more than a collection of individuals' (A-L, p. 365). It is not certain that where individuals are moral hazard-seekers, the bundle of them, acting in a perfectly democratic society, will behave in the interest of the public at large. Political agents may behave in their own interest, or the interest of some group or political party, which brings us into public choice theory and, ironically, to Arrow's (1951) voting paradox and impossibility theorem.

Notes

1. The Automotive Industry Financing Program (AIFP) was launched in December 2008 to prevent the uncontrolled liquidation of Chrysler and General Motors (GM) and the collapse of the US auto industry. The potential for such a disruption at that time posed a significant risk to financial market stability and threatened the overall economy.
2. Information on the date and amount of bailouts by the government is available at the official TARP transaction reports: http://www.financialstability.gov/latest/reportsanddocs.html.
3. Cfr. Congressional Budget Office (2012). Estimated Impact of the American Recovery and Reinvestment Act on Employment and Economic Output from October 2011 Through December 2011, The Congress of the United States, Washington, DC.

References

Arrow, K. (1951). *Social choice and individual values*. New York: Wiley.

Arrow, K., & Lind, R. (1970). Uncertainty and the evaluation of public investment deci- sions. *American Economic Review, 60*, 364–378.

Clark, T., Elsby, M., & Love, S. (2002). Trends in British public investment. *Fiscal Stud- Ies, 23*(3), 305–342.

Foldes, L. P., & Rees, R. (1977). A note on the Arrow-Lind theorem. *American Economic Review, 67*(2), 188–193.

Grimsey, D., & Lewis, M. (2004). Discount debates: Rates, risk, uncertainty and value for money in PPPs. *Public Infrastructure Bulletin, 3*, 4–7.

Grout, P. A. (2003). Public and private sector discount rates in public-private partnerships. *The Economic Journal, 113*, C62–C68.

Gurenko, E., & Lester, R. (2005). *Rapid Onset Natural Disasters: The Role of Financing in Effective Risk Management*. In F.-A. Messy (Ed.), *Catastrophic risks and insurance*. OECD Publishing.

Hirshleifer, J. (1966). Investment decision under uncertainty: Applications of state prefer- ence approach. *Quarterly Journal of Economics, 80*, 270–275.

Holmström, B., & Tirole, J. (2011). *Inside and outside liquidity*. Cambridge, Mass: MIT Press.

Jenkinson, T. (2003). Private finance. *Oxford Review of Economic Policy, 19*(2), 323–334.

In Memoriam

Ronald H. Coase (1910–2013)

The Problem of Social Cost

Ronald H. Coase

For the full text, see: *Journal of Law and Economics*, 3 (1960), pp. 1–44.

Battles lost and wars won: reflections on 'The Problem of Social Cost'

Mary M. Shirley

Ronald Coase Institute

'The Problem of Social Cost' (Coase, 1988B) is one of the most consequential and controversial economic articles ever published. Consequential because it helped 'transform the structure of microeconomics', as indeed Ronald Coase once predicted (Coase, 1991). Controversial because it has been so misinterpreted as to provoke articles just to explain the persistent misunderstandings (Yalcintas, 2010). The most cited article in social science, 'The Problem of Social Cost' has had a profound impact on economics, law, and the social sciences generally.[1] Because of its stormy history, I begin with a brief summary of the article's core argument and the roots of the controversy before I explain how the article is transformative.

'The Problem of Social Cost' analyzes costs that arise when a business activity has harmful effects on others, for instance when the noise from an airport disturbs those occupying neighboring properties. For Coase, in the absence of clear property rights social costs are reciprocal: true, the airport causes noise, but also true, the neighbors choose to locate in a place where they will be irritated by the noise. Coase faults the standard approach of most economists, and in particular A.C. Pigou (1932), for obscuring this reciprocal nature of the problem. Treating airport noise as an external harm imposed by a perpetrator on a victim ignores the interaction between the airport and its neighbors that creates the problem. This approach also ignores the alternative ways to address the problem, depending on the allocation of property rights. On the one hand, regulators could force; government taxes, fees, or subsidies could motivate; or payments or lawsuits by neighbors could induce the airport to reduce the irritations from its noise. (This could be done by changing the flight paths, changing the schedule, reducing the number of planes allowed to land, permitting only quieter planes, etc.) Alternatively, government could require or motivate, or payments by the airport could induce the airport's neighbors to reduce the harmful effects of the noise on themselves. (They could move to another location, soundproof their houses, wear earplugs, etc.) Any solution will have costs, and Coase maintained that it was the job of the economist to evaluate 'patiently' the actual costs of alternative solutions on a case-by-case basis and determine which allocation of rights or liabilities maximized net benefits, including the solution of doing nothing. These assessments should not compare a state of laissez faire with some sort of ideal world; rather they should strive to be as accurate as possible in measuring the ways real governments behave compared to the behavior of real markets.

In proposing this careful, realistic, and case-by-case assessment of all costs and remedies as the appropriate way to choose between alternative policies, Coase was calling for a fundamental change in the standard economic approach. Economists' focus on negative externalities, what Pigou termed the divergence between private and social product, led them to concentrate their attention on 'particular deficiencies in the system, and tends to nourish the belief that any measure which will remove the deficiency is necessarily desirable. It diverts attention from those other changes in the system which are inevitably associated with the corrective measure, changes which may well produce more harm than the original deficiency' (Coase, 1988, p. 153). By proposing another way of assessing social costs, Coase was indeed proposing a transformation of microeconomics.

But this was not the most revolutionary consequence of 'The Problem of Social Cost'. The article also implied that economists should incorporate institutions and transaction costs into their models. And it was this issue of transaction costs that gave rise to a great deal of subsequent controversy and profound consequences for scholarly research.

In 'The Problem of Social Cost' Coase showed that under the standard assumptions of economic theory – perfect competition with zero transaction costs, in other words, perfect information, frictionless bargaining, rational actors, and the like – two parties such as the airport and its neighbors can negotiate a bargain that allocates rights in a way that will maximize production regardless of the initial assignment of those rights. George Stigler, in the third edition of his *Price Theory* textbook, labeled this idea the Coase Theorem: under perfect competition, private and social costs are equal and the assignment of liability does not matter (1966, pp. 113–114). Coase himself, however, viewed the assumption of zero transaction costs as 'very unrealistic' (Coase, 1988, p. 114). In fact, the bulk of 'The Problem of Social Cost' deals with the case of positive transaction costs, where the delineation of legal rights does matter and where the cost of rearranging rights through the market to reach an efficient solution may outweigh the gains.

A strangely large number of economic publications have failed to recognize that 'The Problem of Social Cost' does not advocate addressing externalities by means of the Coase Theorem. A survey of 45 textbooks found that 80% of them misrepresented Coase's arguments (Butler & Garnett, 2003). Another, later survey of 40 of the most cited and most recent articles on the Coase Theorem concluded that 75% of them misrepresented Coase's viewpoint (Yalcintas, 2010). A plethora of publications have been devoted to analyzing, refuting, or extending the Coase Theorem. This was a pursuit that Coase disdained, arguing that the insights gained from studying a world of zero transaction costs are 'without value except as steps on the way to the analysis of the real world of positive transaction costs. We do not do well to devote ourselves to a detailed study of the world of zero transaction costs, like augurs divining the future by the minute inspection of the entrails of a goose' (1981, p. 187).

Such misinterpretations and misguided conclusions notwithstanding, 'The Problem of Social Cost' has been hugely influential, reshaping the way many scholars think about the workings of firms, markets, law, politics, and society. This impact has been profound despite the fact that many economists have not, in fact, followed Coase's advice in their study of social harms. Many still define a social cost as an 'externality' and then look for ways for government to require the actor 'causing' the harm to 'internalize the externality', rather than considering the reciprocal nature of the problem. Few compare the total costs and benefits of alternative remedies or weigh the cost of remedies against the original harm. Assessing all costs and remedies is a very demanding task. But it is a task worth doing. The few studies that attempt a thorough analysis have, despite their limitations, identified woeful policy errors. For example, US ethanol policies and fuel economy standards (CAFE standards) have harmful effects that outweigh their benefits when all costs are taken into account; (see, for example, Hahn & Cecot, 2009; the literature cited in de Gorter & Just, 2010; and Parry, Walls, & Harrington, 2007).

It was not through its treatment of social costs but through its emphasis on transaction costs and institutions that 'The Problem of Social Cost' altered the terms of scholarly debate. The costs of transacting in markets – of finding someone with whom to deal, drawing up the terms of the deal, striking a bargain, and monitoring and enforcing the bargain – had largely been ignored since Coase first articulated their pivotal role in explaining the existence of firms in his 1937 article, 'The Nature of the Firm' (Coase, 1988A). 'The Problem of Social Cost' finally brought transaction costs to the fore. As Barzel and Kochin (1992, p. 22) pointed out (in an article written for the Nobel Committee when it was considering awarding Coase the prize), 'Coase's explicit separation of the zero and positive transaction cost models made economists aware of the need to spell out the transaction cost assumptions under which analysis is conducted . . . [G]iven that transaction is costly, whether it is carried out in the market or by government, Coase pointed out the need to compare outcomes of actions carried out under different institutional settings'.

The powerful implications of Coase's ideas for empirical analysis are well illustrated in Gary Libecap's forthcoming *Journal of Economic Literature* survey of how transaction costs affect global environmental actions. Libecap analyzes international cooperation over global environmental issues as a contractual process that assigns property rights to the costs and benefits of mitigating environmental costs. Transactions costs play a key role in determining the sort of cooperative agreements that can be reached, particularly the costs of measuring, collecting, and analyzing the extent of the environmental harm and the gains from mitigation; the costs of negotiating between a country's politicians and their domestic constituents; the costs of forming a political coalition to set national positions; the international costs of negotiating an agreement among country delegates; and the costs of enforcement. Libecap surveys cases of environmental negotiations with increasing transaction costs, starting with simpler negotiation involving one country, such as national parks to mitigate CO_2 emissions. He moves to more complex international negotiations with a limited number of countries and low transaction costs relative to the Gross Domestic Products of the most interested countries, such as bans on substances that reduce the ozone layer, and finally considers costly and complex negotiations involving many countries and scientific uncertainty about effects, such as reductions in greenhouse gas emissions. The cases illustrate increasingly complex measurement costs, increasingly asymmetric information about costs and benefits, growing numbers of interested constituencies and jurisdictions with widening differences in preferences and perceptions, and greater and greater scientific uncertainties about the environmental harm and its response to mitigation efforts. Libecap shows convincingly how such increasing transaction costs make cooperative agreements increasingly less likely and in doing so illustrates the powerful analytical tools that have evolved from Coase's original ideas.

These tools have been fundamental to the success of the burgeoning field of new institutional economics (NIE). Coasian transaction costs profoundly influenced the work of three Nobel laureates who were crucial in developing NIE: Oliver Williamson, Douglass North, and Elinor Ostrom (see Menard & Shirley, 2012, in press). NIE rests on three core concepts – transaction costs, property rights, and contracts – and follows Coase in studying the real world of positive transaction costs where the assignment of rights matters fundamentally. It also follows Coase in addressing fundamental issues that had been skirted or ignored by standard economic theory. NIE is especially occupied by two questions: (1) whether to make or buy – the choice of firms to organize their activities through the market, the firm, or some hybrid of the two, and (2) why countries are rich or poor – the historical development of institutions that reduce transaction costs and nurture property rights, innovation, and growth.

New institutional economics has been especially influential in development economics and economic history, has fostered new approaches in political science, legal studies, and management studies, and has had a profound impact on regulation, especially antitrust regulation. Through the pioneering work of Elinor Ostrom, institutional analysis has also fundamentally changed ideas about common pool problems and the circumstances under which communities or user groups manage common resources better than state or private alternatives. Coase's ideas have been highly influential among younger scholars. NIE's adherents formed the International Society for New Institutional Economics in 1997, which spread the Coasian concepts widely among younger researchers, while the Ronald Coase Institute, which fosters the study of institutions by assisting young scholars from around the world, numbers over 400 alumni of its workshops in institutional analysis.

It has been 53 years since 'The Problem of Social Cost' was published and Ronald Coase is almost 103 years old. It has taken some time, but the eventual influence of the article has been widespread and profound. Although much of mainstream economics was initially resistant to Coase's transformative ideas, transaction costs have reshaped the standard paradigm to the point where few economists today are comfortable with the institution-free model of zero transaction costs. As Coase said at the conclusion of his speech accepting the Nobel prize, ' . . . a scholar must be content with the knowledge that what is false in what he says will soon be exposed and, as for what is true, he can count on ultimately seeing it accepted, if only he lives long enough' (1992, p. 719). 'The Problem of Social Cost' is not just accepted; together with 'The Nature of the Firm', it has transformed large parts of social science.

Acknowledgements

I am grateful to Lee Benham, Frans Kok, Gary Libecap and Claude Menard for their very helpful suggestions.

Note

1. According to one inclusive source (Publish or Perish), 'The Problem of Social Cost' has been cited more than 20,500 times. Using more exclusive methodologies, Shapiro and Pierce find it the most cited law review article of all time (Shapiro & Pierce, 2012).

References

Barzel, Yoram & Kochin, Levis A. (1992). Ronald Coase on the nature of social cost as a key to the problem of the firm. *Scandinavian Journal of Economics, 94*(1), 19–31.

Butler, Michael R. & Garnett, Robert F. (2003). Teaching the Coase Theorem: Are we getting it right? *American Economic Review, 31*(2, June), 133–145.

Coase, Ronald H. (1981). The Coase Theorem and the empty core. *The Journal of Law and Economics, 24*, 183–187.

Coase, Ronald H. (1988A). The Nature of the Firm. In Ronald H. Coase (Ed.), *The firm, the market, and the law*, Chicago: University of Chicago Press, Chapter 2, pp. 33–55. (This article was originally published in *Economica*, 4(16) [November 1937], 386–405.

Coase, Ronald H. (1988B). The Problem of Social Cost. In Ronald H. Coase (Ed.), *The firm, the market, and the law*, Chicago: University of Chicago Press Chapter Five, pp. 95–185. (This article was originally published in *The Journal of Law and Economics, 3*, 1–44 [October, 1960]).

Coase, Ronald H. (1991). The Nature of the Firm: Influence. In Olilver E. Williamson and Sidney G. Winter (Eds.) *The Nature of the Firm. Origins, Evolution, and Development*, Chapter 5, pp. 61–74.

Coase, Ronald H. (1992). The institutional structure of production. *The American Economic Review, 82*(4), 713–719.

de Gorter, Harry & Just, David R. (2010). The social costs and benefits of biofuels: The intersection of environmental, energy and agricultural policy. *Applied Economic Perspectives and Policy*, *32*(1), 4–32.

Hahn, Rober W. & Cecot, Caroline. (2009). The benefits and costs of ethanol: An evaluation of the government's analysis. *Journal of Regulatory Economics*, *35*(3), 275–295.

Libecap, Gary D. (in press). Addressing global environmental externalities: A transaction cost approach. *Journal of Economic Literature.*

Menard, Claude & Shirley, Mary M. (2012). *New institutional economics: From early intuitions to a new paradigm?* (Ronald Coase Institute Working Paper #8, September 2012). Retrieved from http://www.coase.org/workingpapers/wp-8.pdf

Menard, Claude & Shirley, Mary M. in press). The contribution of Douglass North to new institutional economics. In Sebastian Galiani & Itai Sened (Eds.), *Institutions, property rights and economic growth: The legacy of Douglass North*. Cambridge, MA: Cambridge University Press.

Parry, Ian W. H., Walls, Margaret, & Harrington, Winston. (2007). Automobile externalities and policies. *Journal of Economic Literature*, *45*(2), 373–409.

Pigou, A. C. *The Economics of Welfare*, 4th ed. London: Macmillan & Co., 1932.

Shapiro, Fred R. & Pierce, Michelle. (2012). The most cited law review articles of all times. *Michigan Law Review*, *110*, 1483–1520.

Stigler, George J. *The Theory of Price*, 3rd Edition. New York: Macmillan Co., 1966.

Yalcintas, Altug. (2010). *The 'Coase Theorem' vs. Coase Theorem Proper: How an error emerged and why it remained uncorrected so long* (MPRA Paper #37936). Retrieved from http://mpra.ub.uni-muenchen.de/37936/

The importance of being misunderstood: the Coase theorem and the legacy of 'The Problem of Social Cost'

Steven G. Medema

Department of Economics CB, University of Colorado Denver, Denver, USA

Introduction

The publication of Ronald Coase's article, 'The Problem of Social Cost' (1960), led to a fundamental rethinking of the economic theory of externalities and of market failure generally. While this article is most commonly associated with the 'Coase theorem' – the idea that agents will negotiate efficient and invariant solutions to externality problems in an environment free of transaction costs, assuming some initial definition of legal rights over the relevant resources – the messages contained in it were much more broad than this, even if, as it happened, much more slow to gain traction in the economics profession. These other messages were (1) that the received (Pigovian) approach to externality theory and policy, with its emphasis on the necessity of governmental controls for the efficient resolution of externalities, was fundamentally misguided, (2) that the efficient course of action in situations of externality may be to maintain the status quo, and (3) that a comparative institutional approach was necessary in order to determine the appropriate way to deal with these issues.[1]

While Coase was not attempting to make a contribution to environmental and natural resource economics, the study of which among economists was in its infancy at the time his article was published, his insights emerged relatively quickly within this nascent literature because economists were borrowing heavily from externality theory in the process of working out this new field.[2] The early take on Coase's analysis within this literature was that he was recommending market-based solutions to problems such as pollution, and this recommendation was not warmly received (Medema, 2013a). In time, however, the tide began to turn and those working in these areas came to recognize the possibilities of and to advocate for market/exchange-based mechanisms for dealing with issues of externality. No small amount of credit for this goes to the Coase theorem, though the line running from the theorem to current thinking on this score is not as direct as one might think and would in some ways seem to fly in the face of Coase's quasi-repudiation of the theorem that bears his name.

A careful reading of 'The Problem of Social Cost' suggests that the negotiation result was not its main message but a means to a different end, and Coase has reinforced this perception in several subsequent commentaries. The argument to be made here, however, is that, viewed from the perspective of the history of economics, the Coase theorem *is* the most important message to emerge from Coase's analysis – not because it has been the most remarked upon aspect of Coase's discussion (which is true) but because of the impact that it has had on economic thinking and policy making.

The negotiation result in context

It is important to bear in mind when contemplating 'The Problem of Social Cost' that this was not a work created *de novo*; its basic elements, including the negotiation result, were present in his 1959 *Journal of Law and Economics* article, 'The Federal Communications Commission' (hereinafter, The FCC) (Coase, 1959). This article argued (among other things) that the Commission should consider replacing its fiat-based system of broadcast frequency allocation with a market-based system – one in which rights in the spectrum would be auctioned off or handed out by the Commission, but with the provision that the rights be exchangeable in the marketplace. These rights, Coase noted, are valuable inputs to the production of goods and services, and there was no reason, as he saw it, why the allocation of these rights should not be determined through the pricing system just as are other inputs. The idea, of course, was that these rights would end up in the hands of those who valued them most highly and thus that the inefficient fiat-based system would be supplanted by an efficient allocation based on market principles.

The link to externalities – the subject of 'The Problem of Social Cost' – here is straightforward.[3] The rationale for regulating the frequency spectrum was, at least in part, to ensure that agents did not operate on frequencies sufficiently close to cause interference (the externality) – a significant problem once use of the spectrum became widespread. Coase argued that property rights in the spectrum could also resolve the conflicting use problem, and he employed the negotiation result to demonstrate that, in a world without frictions, each frequency would end up in the hands of the party that valued it most highly if those rights were alienable. The argument in The FCC, though, was not that the Commission should adopt a comprehensive market-based approach to the allocation of frequencies. The problem, said Coase, was that the Commission seemed not even to have given the market option serious consideration for any aspect of frequency allocation. Coase allowed that there may well be justification for employing the regulatory approach in certain instances, but what the decision should ultimately come down to, he argued, was a comparison of the results that would obtain through market allocation with those achieved under the present system – in short, that economists and policy makers needed to move away from the default to the regulatory option and undertake comparative institutional analysis.

'The Problem of Social Cost', which was written only because of the objections raised by some members of the University of Chicago economics faculty to the negotiation result contained in The FCC,[4] can be read as little more than an expansive generalization of these very themes – in essence, a defense of the position taken in his earlier paper and an attempt to correct the 'faulty economic analysis' that he felt grounded the discussion of externality issues (Coase, 1960, p. 19). At the heart of the externality problem, said Coase, is the absence of property rights over relevant resources. The right to impose costs on others or to be free from such costs is valuable, and the negotiation result and the reciprocal view of externalities that underlies it – the subject of the first 15 pages of 'The Problem of Social Cost' – show the possibilities of exchange over these rights in a perfect world. In doing so, they give the lie to Pigovians' theoretical claims that tax, subsidy, or regulatory remedies are *necessary* for the efficient resolution of externality issues. In theory, the one is as good as the other, as Coase pointed out.

When it comes to the analysis of real-world externalities (the subject of the last 30 pages of the article), of course, we confront the problem of imperfect markets – imperfections the source of which Coase grouped under the broad umbrella of transaction costs, a concept whose contents remain rather ill-defined to this day. *But*, Coase argued, if we are to admit of the imperfections that attend markets and exchange, we must do the same for the imperfections that attend state action and recognize that the policies being proffered within the received theory of externalities stand little chance of bringing us to, or even near to, the theoretical optimum. Sound policy, then, becomes an exercise in choosing between imperfect alternatives: allocation via markets/exchange, allocation via state action, or allowing the status quo to persist.[5] Coase argued that there is no remedy that is best in an *a priori* sense, nor will any of these remedies lead us to the optimal solution contemplated by economic theory. Instead, the best attainable outcome, and the means by which to reach it, can only be determined on a case-by-case basis, evaluating the relative efficacy of the various options – though he suspected that the most efficient course of action will often be to leave matters more or less as they are, that the costs associated with market or governmental coordination would likely make such 'cures' worse than the externality disease.

Impact

All of that said, what Coase may have had in mind when writing up his analysis in 'The Problem of Social Cost' is in some sense neither here nor there. What really matters, in the end, is the impact of his work, or, differently put, the uses to which it was put by others.

Interestingly, most of the earliest commentary on Coase's article did emphasize his advocacy of a comparative institutional approach as against the one-sided nature of the Pigovian system.[6] But it was not long before the attention came to focus on the negotiation result, virtually to the exclusion of Coase's larger message.[7] This result, which was christened the 'Coase theorem' by Coase's University of Chicago colleague George Stigler (1966, p. 113), was discussed, probed, mathematized, de-mathematized, experimented with, and debated from virtually every conceivable angle over the next three decades. A legion of scholars claimed to have disproved it only to have their results rebutted by others arguing that Coase was in the right, either because the critics had made slips in their economic logic or because their frameworks for analysis violated one of the theorem's underlying assumptions – usually that regarding the absence of transaction costs. Of course, given the vagueness of the concept of transaction costs, this line of defense was expansive and, in a way, intellectually weak. One comes away from the Coase theorem literature feeling, at times, that the definition of transaction costs is, 'all those things that prevent the Coase theorem from holding true', a position that effectively turns the theorem into a tautology.[8] At the same time, however, a goodly amount of the literature ostensibly disproving the theorem had the effect of drawing attention to the importance and wide-ranging nature of transaction costs, particularly as respects the role of information in the exchange process.

The argument made by Coase some years later, and by others along the way, was that the import of the Coase theorem lay in the focus that it put on transaction costs and property rights – that because transaction costs are positive and property rights are often less than completely specified, to whom rights are assigned *does* impact the allocation of resources. And this is true, but only partially so. Coase's result also brought to the fore the costs associated with state action by saying, in effect, that if you are going to assume a costlessly operating government possessed of the full and perfect information necessary to undertake efficient interventions, you must go all the way and assume that *coordination costs in general* are zero. And within such a system, as Coase demonstrated, exchange processes could accomplish the desired efficient outcome equally well. If one is going to argue transaction costs against market-type solutions, one must also bring into play the costs and other imperfections associated with state action and give up claims for the inevitable efficiency-enhancing power of these moves.

But perhaps the most important legacy of the Coase theorem was its role in effectively forcing economists to confront the possibility of markets or exchange processes as solutions to situations of externality. Contrary to what is sometimes suggested, marketable permit systems for dealing with pollution problems were not developed out of Coase's analysis but instead are due to the work of Thomas Crocker (1966) and J.H. Dales (1968) who, though familiar with Coase's article, developed their ideas independently of it.[9] Indeed, the pollution permits system has far more in common with Coase's analysis of frequency allocation in The FCC than with Coase's two-party negotiation result in 'The Problem of Social Cost'. But a reasonable argument can be made that the attention – both positive and negative – devoted to the Coase theorem put market-like solutions on economists' radar and played a prominent role in their increased willingness to consider, and in the eventual adoption of, market-based systems for dealing with pollution as well as property rights plus exchange-based schemes for dealing with common pool problems and the like. The Coase theorem, then, would seem to have generated its own positive externalities.

Conclusion

Like Adam Smith's reference to 'an invisible hand', Coase's negotiation result very much took on a life of its own in the hands of subsequent commentators. While Smith never had the chance to amplify his remarks or correct the record once the chaos began, Coase did – though it took some time for him to avail himself of the opportunity to do so. Coase's argument – that he had been misunderstood[10] and that devoting attention to the world of zero transaction costs was akin to 'divining the future by the minute inspection of the entrails of a goose' (Coase, 1981, p. 187) – was in a large sense correct. The latter statement, though, ignores the insights and other spillovers that can come from the analysis of fictional worlds, even if fitting in perfectly well with Coase's dismissive attitude toward economists' fixation on what he referred to on numerous occasions as 'blackboard economics'. There can be no question that the whole Coase theorem debate generated more heat than light $(x > y)$ if $x =$ the number of instance of heat and $y =$ the number of instances of light. But if one looks at things from an intensity perspective, the picture changes. It is impossible to know what would have transpired had Coase not penned his negotiation result, or if economists had fixated on his message regarding comparative institutional analysis rather than on the negotiation result. Conjectural history is a dangerous sport, but a good argument can be made that it was the perceived extreme nature of the negotiation result and the heat generated by the controversy over it that led economists and policy makers to contemplate solutions to externality problems that were grounded in property rights and exchange/market processes. Coase wanted economists to think differently, both methodologically and about the possibilities of markets. On the latter score, he clearly succeeded, even if that success came via the violation of his methodological prescription.

Acknowledgements

The financial support of the Institute for New Economic Thinking and the National Endowment for the Humanities is gratefully acknowledged.

Notes

1. See Medema (1996, 2009) for more extensive discussions of Coase's article.
2. See, for example, Kneese (1964).
3. It bears noting that Coase never used the term 'externality', which he felt carried with it the implication that state action was needed.
4. See Stigler (1988) and Kitch (1983). It should be noted that Coase was on the faculty at the University of Virginia at this time. He did not move to the University of Chicago until 1964.
5. Coase suggested a fourth institutional option, the organization of the relevant activities under a single owner, which would also accomplish the internalization of the relevant costs.
6. See the discussion in Medema (2013b).
7. See, for example, Medema (2013c, 2013d).
8. Indeed, several authors, including some sympathetic to Coase's argument, have described the theorem as exactly this. See, for example, Calabresi (1968) and Veljanovski (1977), but also Cooter (1982).
9. See Medema (2013a) for a discussion.
10. See, for example, Coase (1988, p. 174).

References

Calabresi, G. (1968). Transaction costs, resource allocation and liability rules – a comment. *Journal of Law and Economics, 11*(1), 67–73.

Coase, R. H. (1959). The Federal Communications Commission. *Journal of Law and Economics, 2*(1), 1–40.

Coase, R. H. (1960). The problem of social cost. *Journal of Law and Economics, 3*(1), 1–44.

Coase, R. H. (1981). The Coase theorem and the empty core: a comment. *Journal of Law and Economics, 24*(1): 183–87.

Coase, R. H. (1988). *The firm, the market, and the law*. Chicago, IL: University of Chicago Press.

Cooter, R. (1982). The cost of Coase. *Journal of Legal Studies, 11*(1), 1–33.

Crocker, T. D. (1966). The structuring of atmospheric pollution control systems. In: H. Wolozin (Ed.), *The economics of air pollution: A symposium* (pp. 61–86). New York: W.W. Norton.

Dales, J. H. (1968). *Pollution, property & prices: An essay in policy-making and economics*. Toronto: University of Toronto Press.

Kitch, E. W. (1983). The fire of truth: A remembrance of law and economics at Chicago, 1932–1970. *Journal of Law and Economics, 26*(1), 163–234.

Kneese, A. V. (1964). *The economics of regional water quality management*. Baltimore, MD: The Johns Hopkins Press.

Medema, S. G. (1996). Of Pangloss, Pigouvians, and pragmatism: Ronald Coase on social cost analysis. *Journal of the History of Economic Thought, 18*(1), 96–114.

Medema, S. G. (2009). *The hesitant hand: Taming self-interest in the history of economic ideas*. Princeton, NJ: Princeton University Press.

Medema, S. G. (2013a). *The curious treatment of the Coase theorem in environmental economics, 1960–1979* (Working Paper). Denver: University of Colorado.

Medema, S. G. (2013b). *Market failure revisited* (Working Paper). Denver: University of Colorado.

Medema, S. G. (2013c). *Rethinking externalities: Coase's negotiation result before the 'Coase theorem'* (Working Paper). Denver: University of Colorado.

Medema, S. G. (2013d). 1966 and all that: The birth of the Coase theorem controversy. *Journal of the History of Economic Thought* (forthcoming).

Stigler, G. J. (1966). *The theory of price*. New York: Macmillan.

Stigler, G. J. (1988). *Memoirs of an unregulated economist*. New York: Basic Books.

Veljanovski, C. G. (1977). The Coase theorem – the Say's law of welfare economics? *Economic Record, 53*(December), 535–541.

Infringement as nuisance: intellectual property rights and *The Problem of Social Cost*

Paul J. Heald

College of Law, University of Illinois, Champaign, 504 East Pennsylvania Avenue, Champaign, Illinois, USA; Centre for Intellectual Property Policy and Management, Bournemouth University, Bournemouth, UK; and Cambridge University Law Faculty, Cambridge, UK

Ronald Coase was a story-teller and his essay, *The Problem of Social Cost* (1960) contains narrative examples on nearly every page that vividly illustrate his thesis that economic efficiency does not require that those acting in a market should be legally responsible for all the harm they cause. I will proceed in a complementary (and complimentary) manner. My own narrative will consider Firm A, a large car manufacturer that has been working to improve the fuel efficiency of its cars. After several years, its engineers invent a new fuel injection system which promises to be highly successful. After marketing its new cars, however, Firm A is sued by Firm B who claims an enforceable patent on the innovation. This essay explores the usefulness of conceiving of the activity of Firm A, and the activity of other hypothetical intellectual property infringers, as constituting the sort of nuisance considered by Coase (Newman, 2009).

The thought experiment begins with the recognition that Coase himself might think that the infringement/nuisance analogy was useful. At the end of his article, he concluded that '[i]f factors of production are thought of as rights, it becomes easier to understand that the right to do something which has a harmful effect (such as the creation of smoke, noise, smells, etc.) is also a factor of production' (p. 44). In producing and selling its infringing cars, Firm A in my hypothetical may cause harm to the patent owner just as its smokestack or noisy machinery may cause harm to residents situated in the neighborhood of its factory. Any 'factor of production' may cause harm and, of course, the whole point of his essay was to rethink the Pigouvian position that the existence of such harm automatically demands a legal rule or a tax designed to force the one responsible to internalize all the costs it has imposed.

Coase's approach is far more subtle and fine-grained than Pigou's: 'The problem which we face in dealing with actions which have harmful effects is not simply one of restraining those responsible for them. What has to be decided is whether the gain from preventing the harm is greater than the loss which would be suffered elsewhere as a result of stopping the action which produces the harm' (p. 27). This insight both helps explain several doctrines of intellectual property law, offered later as examples of Coase's wisdom, and supports normative arguments for intellectual property reform. But first, we must understand what sorts of costs worried Coase and how they manifest themselves in the intellectual property context.

Private costs and net social costs

Not all private costs represent an equivalent cost imposed on society. I may open a superior Mexican restaurant that results in a competing Mexican restaurant closing down the street. My competitor has surely incurred a cost from my behavior, but it is merely private. Society has come out ahead, as it frequently does from fair competition. In intellectual property infringement cases, one must be especially careful to identify the social costs at issue. In my initial hypothetical, increased sales of Firm A's new fuel efficient cars may impose a private cost on Firm B, but is this a cost that society should care about? If Firm B is out-competed by Firm A, then perhaps the cost of Firm B's lost sales is purely private, and if Firm B is not a competitor, it may be hard to identify a net social loss at all. If we are to find a social cost in the patent infringement context, it will usually be in the dampening of the spirit of inventiveness, a true non-pecuniary externality. This is the social loss at issue in copyright infringement also, but not in trademark infringement, where consumer confusion that raises the cost of searching for goods imposes a distinct social harm.

The usefulness of considering a world with no transaction costs

As Coase famously illustrated, in a world with no transaction costs, a party that creates a nuisance in the course of business and a party that is harmed by the nuisance will contract for a result that is efficient from society's standpoint (he does not consider intentional torts or other opportunistic behavior). He states simply, 'if market transactions were costless, all that matters (questions of equity apart) is that the rights of the various parties should be well-defined and the results of legal actions easy to forecast' (p. 19). The liability rule's target does not matter.

A similarly useful point can be made about the need for legal rights in inventions and artistic creations. In a world with no transaction costs and perfect information,[1] all that is necessary to establish the conditions of optimal innovation is a system of enforceable contracts[2] (Heald, 2008, p. 1165; Merrill & Smith, 2011, p. 78). Those who require inventions or artistic creations will costlessly find and contract with those having inventive or artistic capacity to satisfy perfectly the demand. There is no need for patent law or copyright law in a world with no transaction costs even when the possibility of free riding is considered,[3] because creators incur the cost of creation only when they have adequate contractual commitments from those requiring the creation (often many multiple parties).[4]

The scenario above demonstrates that as regards intellectual property, no initial allocation of property rights in inventions or artistic creations need be made. Coase, of course, in the context of tangibles stated that 'without the establishment of this initial delimitation of [ownership] rights there can be no market transactions to transfer and recombine them' (p. 8). Do inventive and creative activities present a unique case? Perhaps because the parties contract over intangibles? Coase may be technically incorrect about the need for a prior allocation of property rights, but that does not blunt the force of his argument.

Take Coase's own famous example involving sparks flying off a passing train that burn a farmer's crops. He envisions the farmer selling to the rail company the right to damage his property or paying it to cease the damaging activity or to take damage-reducing precautions. Coase assumes that the farmer must have a pre-existing property right in the land itself otherwise the railway will have no incentive to restrain its sparks and therefore no need to negotiate. But this observation is reciprocal. In a world with no pre-allocated property rights, the farmer may tear up the railroad tracks and stop the encroachment of the sparks. The problem inherent in the state of nature is solved both in theory and in practice by the system of enforceable contracts which we think of as the social compact. In an organized society, the farmer implicitly promises to recognize the integrity of the train tracks while the railroad company implicitly promises to recognize the farmer's fee simple ownership of the land. All members of the community make a vast number of reciprocal promises to recognize rights, establishing the web of contracts we conceive of as a functioning society. Coase himself conceives of government as a species of firm, the ultimate web of contracts in the market[5] (p. 17).

So, what is interesting about considering inventions in a world without transaction costs is that it reveals a microcosm of how contracts are used to create property itself. Inventions come into being when their creation is contracted for and the reciprocal promises to make and purchase bring property into being and protect it from the only sort of appropriation society cares about, the sort that dampens the spirit of invention. Coase had no reason to dig so deeply into the theoretical nature of property rights. In fact, his reliance on concepts of property is best seen as prescient recognition that property rights are ultimately a means to reduce transaction costs (Merrill & Smith, 2001). In reality, society reduces the cost of transacting through the creation of property (Heald, 2005). In asserting the need for property, Coase merely let a bit of reality leak into the unreal world of costless transacting that he employs to such spectacular effect.

With transaction costs

For most of his essay, Coase assumes the existence of transaction costs and considers private and public responses[6] (p. 15). The primary private response is the firm; a public response may come in the form of government regulation, either legislative or judicial. He praises any result that mimics the predicted state in a world without transaction costs. To return to the initial hypothetical, if Firm B, the patentee, had the capacity to invent the new fuel injection system more cheaply than Firm A, then in an ideal world, Firm A would license the technology from Firm B and avoid the redundant cost of inventing. Both would have use of the technology with a royalty stream flowing from Firm A to Firm B. This result could be required by a legal rule or, perhaps, be brought about by the merger of Firms A and B. On the other hand, if Firm B knows that Firm A can infringe without penalty and will erode its profits sufficiently, then Firm B may be deterred from incurring the cost of invention in the first place, resulting in no invention at all, a clearly inefficient result.

For Coase, the world without transaction costs constitutes a valuable ruler against which to measure the wisdom of legal intervention in the real world of costly transacting. Two examples are provided immediately below.

Descriptive application

One of the most striking doctrines in intellectual property law is the primary remedy applied in patent infringement cases: the reasonable royalty. Courts are directed to imagine a hypothetical negotiation between a willing licensor of the technology (the patentee) and a willing licensee (the infringer). The damage award from infringement, therefore, typically includes a profit for the infringer, because a willing licensor and licensee typically structure a contract so that both of them will profit. Clearly, any rule that guarantees the infringer a profit is not designed to deter all infringement, and it stands as a bold endorsement of

Coase's insight that not all entities that cause harm should be held liable for the totality of the costs they impose. Moreover, a reasonable royalty typically rewards the patentee with a profit on his invention, virtually guaranteeing that the spirit of invention will not be dampened. And often the public gains a second outlet whereby to access the invention, with the concomitant downward pressure on price through competition.

Where the patentee is the lowest-cost inventor, then the reasonable royalty rule (or perhaps entity merger) should frequently mimic the result that would have been obtained in a world without transaction costs. What is extraordinary about the rule is that the jury instruction on calculation tracks this goal so closely.

A second fruitful example might be found in the trademark law of parody. Imagine a market for Mickey Mouse parodies; the Walt Disney Corporation is unwilling to satisfy it because private damage to its reputation would outweigh any net public benefit to consumers wanting to purchase the parody product. In a world of costless transacting, these private costs and public benefits could be decoupled, allowing consumers in both the wholesome and ribald markets to be satisfied. Trademark parody doctrine accomplishes this efficient decoupling by permitting parodies to be marketed without the permission of the copyright owner under most circumstances, thereby mimicking the result in a world without transaction costs. An overly strong property right granted to Disney would frustrate the efficient result, and so trademark law effectively borrows the parody analysis from copyright's fair use doctrine.

Normative application

Over-protection of intellectual property rights may entail significant social costs: monopoly pricing, lower than optimal production, and diminished incentives for follow-on innovation. In the patent context, one can identify two areas where remedial rules may fail to structure the optimal result. First, the praise above for the reasonable royalty remedy failed to note that in many cases an injunction will be available to the patentee. If the infringer's costs of switching to a comparable non-infringing technology are high enough, then an injunction will give the patentee leverage to extract a post-litigation license from the infringer at a substantially higher rate than a judicially crafted reasonable royalty. This rate may be so high as to force the infringer to operate at a loss (Heald, 2013). In such a case, the rational *ex ante* decision of the infringer would be not to enter the market at all, an inefficient result as regards the hypothetical case of Firm B versus Firm A. Although recent case law following *eBay v. MercExchange*[7] has made it harder to obtain an injunction, the test for relief still does not force judges to expressly account for how an injunction may distort the ideal state of transacting.

In addition, the absence of an independent invention defense may in other circumstances generate sub-optimal results. Imagine that Firm A, an infringer with no knowledge of Firm B's patent, innovates at a significantly lower cost than Firm B. In a world with no transaction costs, Firm B would have licensed to Firm A the right to use the invention, but in the hypothetical, Firm B invented and patented first and is rewarded for its speed and disclosure to the public with the initial property right. Nevertheless, if the costs of finding the invention and contracting with Firm B, the patentee, are high enough,[8] then Firm A should have a partial defense, otherwise the law will sometimes deter efficient independent inventing. For example, if the cost of finding Firm B's patent and negotiating with Firm B are $100,000, and Firm A can invent independently for $50,000, then Firm A should have a defense to infringement. Unless the value of Firm B's early public disclosure of the invention is truly significant, permitting Firm A's 'nuisance' will more closely mimic the result that would be obtained in a world of costless transacting.

A brief consideration of trademark law might also suggest a defense for infringement should be available for those who use a sports team or university logo on promotional goods, like t-shirts, where the goods are of high quality and consumers are not confused. Such a result would increase competition and lower prices while avoiding the potential social costs of imitation (including the potential dampening of inventive activity, since sports teams and universities need no incentive to name themselves).

Conclusion

In a very real sense, *The Problem of Social Cost* is an essay about the danger of overly taxing producers by granting overly broad property rights to the victims of production. Coase's most famous examples involve victims claiming the right to be free from interference, and each one illustrates how in the real world of costly transacting, the recognition of an enforceable property right to stop the interference will sometimes be inefficient. This insight helps both judges in intellectual property cases and legislators crafting innovation policy to ask the proper questions. What sort of transactions involving inventions, art, and brand names would occur in a world without transaction costs? What sort of remedial scheme and constellation of rights will incentivize those transactions in the real world?

Notes

1. Coase does not expressly assume perfect information, but his hypotheticals consistently assume that risks are known and can be easily quantified by the parties when bargaining.
2. Lee and Smith credit Steven Cheung for arguing more broadly that 'in the zero transaction cost world, we would not even need property rights', an idea that Coase had earlier endorsed (Cheung, 1998, pp. 518–520; Coase, 1988a, pp. 14–15). Presumably, the idea behind the assertion is that in a world with zero transaction costs, everyone could simply reach agreements with everyone else about what each person would be allowed to do, and be prohibited from doing, with respect to each aspect of the physical world.
3. In some complex circumstances, the web of contracts might have to include payments made to those who could credibly threaten to misappropriate. Coase did not adjust his model to include the possibility of opportunistic behavior, but discusses the possibility of blackmail in a later article (Coase, 1988b). He suggests that some purely opportunistic wealth transfers should be prohibited as costly sterile transactions (p. 673) and notes intriguingly that 'Harold Demsetz pointed out that if there are many cattle raisers and crop farmers and there is competition among them, since refraining from . . . blackmailing behavior costs nothing, the amount that would have to be paid to obtain an agreement not to engage in it would tend towards zero [in a world with no transaction costs]. Blackmail incidental to a business relationship did not appear normally to be a serious problem" (p. 658).
4. Lee and Smith (2012, p. 148) speak more generally: 'In the zero transaction cost world, the nature and scope of property rights might seem not to matter: any deficiency in the allocation of those rights can be made up for by contracting (or by any other hypothetically costless institutional mechanism)'.
5. 'The government is, in a sense, a super-firm (but of a very special kind)'.
6. '[Assuming no transaction costs] is, of course, a very un-realistic assumption'.
7. 547 U.S. 388 (2006).
8. The cost of finding inventions may be very high indeed and may constitute the primary failure of the patent system (Bessen & Meurer, 2008).

References

Bessen, J. & Meurer, M. (2008). *Patent failure: How judges, bureaucrats, and lawyers put innovators at risk*. Princeton, NJ: Princeton University Press.

Cheung, Stephen. (1998). The transaction costs paradigm. *Economic Inquiry*, *36*, 514–521.

Coase, Ronald H. (1960). The problem of social cost. *Journal of Law & Economics*, *3*, 1–44.

Coase, Ronald H. (1988a). *The firm, the market, and the law*. Chicago, IL: University of Chicago Press.

Coase, Ronald H. (1988b). Blackmail. *Virginia Law Review*, *74*, 655–676.

Heald, Paul J. (2005). A transaction cost theory of patent law. *Ohio State Law Journal*, *66*, 473–509.

Heald, Paul J. (2008). Optimal remedies for patent infringement. *Houston Law Review*, *45*, 1165–1200.

Heald, Paul J. (2013). Permanent injunctions as punitive damages in patent infringement cases. In Shyam Balganesh, (Ed.), *Intellectual property and the common law* (pp. 514–529). Cambridge: Cambridge Univ. Press.

Lee, Brian A. & Smith, Henry E. (2012). The nature of Coasean property. *International Review of Economics*, *59*, 145–155.

Merrill, Thomas W. & Smith, Henry E. (2011). Making Coasean property more Coasean. *Journal of Law & Economics*, *57*, 577–604.

Newman, Christopher. (2009). Patent infringement as nuisance. *Catholic Univ. Law Review*, *59*, 61–123.

About some distortions in the interpretation of 'the problem of social cost'

Claude Ménard

Department of Economics, Maison des Sciences Economiques, University of Paris (Panthéon-Sorbonne), France

> But at least it has made clear that the problem is one of choosing the appropriate social arrangement for dealing with the harmful effects. All solutions have costs [. . .]. Satisfactory views on policy can only come from a patient study of how, in practice, the market, firms and governments handle the problem of harmful effects. (Coase, 1960, p. 18)

Introduction

The extraordinary influence of 'The Problem of Social Cost' is now well acknowledged. Beyond the official recognition coming with the award of the Alfred Nobel Memorial Prize in Economic Sciences, as well as the myriad citations, what may matter most, as emphasized by Mary Shirley (2013) in her paper for this special issue, is that in introducing the concept of 'transaction costs', Coase initiated a revolution in the way economists and social scientists should look at the organization of economic activities in a market economy. Actually, the concept of transaction could well be considered one of the most important in economic theory, together with the concept of the division of labor. As emphasized by Coase (1998), the two concepts complement each other. In order to take advantage of the division of labor, economic actors must specialize their activity; this is sustainable and beneficial if and only if they can organize transactions among them at a cost that is less than the expected benefits.

Paradoxically, this organizational dimension that Coase pinpointed as 'The Institutional Structure of Production' in his Nobel Lecture has been largely neglected in the literature inspired by 'The Problem of Social Cost'. In what follows, I would like to show how this missing dimension is rooted in some misinterpretations of the 1960 paper (Section 1) and what consequences it should have in partially redefining the research agenda sketched by Coase in his paper (Section 2).

Section 1: a black hole rooted in misinterpretations

As is now well known, the first five sections of 'The Problem of Social Cost' focus on different examples – several became famous because of the revolutionary view they introduced on pollution, among other things, in order to establish the key concept of 'transaction'. The issue at stake is not trivial: the economic tradition is built on the very idea that agents are buying or selling physical (or virtual) assets, that is, goods and services, and this trading activity determines what is going to be produced. Coase introduced a radically different perspective: what happens in markets is the transfer of rights. Therefore, a key issue for understanding market economies is to consider the definition and allocation of rights and the mechanism of their transfer.

To make the point, Coase introduced the often cited example of the cattle raiser and the farmer, in which the herd of the former can produce harmful effects on the crop of the latter. One solution would be of course for the farmer to fence his fields, but the cost of doing so and of the maintenance could well exceed the expected benefits from the crop. In a world in which 'the price system works smoothly' (1960, p. 6), that is, at no significant costs, parties would have a strong incentive to reach a mutually satisfactory solution through the bargaining of their rights, ending up in a situation that would be optimal for both of them. In Coase's words, '. . . there is clearly room for a mutually satisfactory bargain . . .' (1960, p. 4) in which each party can use the signals of the price system to balance costs and benefits and reach an ultimate result that is independent of the legal position, that is, independent of the institutional environment. This is the world of zero transaction costs, in which rearrangement of rights will always take place and lead to increase in value of production. It has been encapsulated in what Stigler (1966, p. 113) called the 'Coase theorem'.

There are three important consequences to this representation of a world in which exchanges are costless.

First, this idea of a world with zero transaction costs immediately caught the attention of theoreticians because it greatly facilitates model building. Indeed, this formulation of the Coase theorem, based on the assumption that there is no cost in the running of the price system, allows to establish the existence and stability of a general equilibrium across different markets without having to take into account issues such as the institutions that would be required for the system to work. Notwithstanding numerous warnings by Coase ((the assumption of zero transaction costs is 'a very unrealistic assumption' (1960, p.15). 'My conclusion: let us study the world of positive transaction costs' (1991, p. 9)), as well as by his followers (e.g., North, 1990, chap.4), a considerable part of the literature in economics, particularly the most advanced in terms of modeling, continues to consider a world with transaction costs equaling zero. However, as soon as these costs are introduced into the picture, the representation of economic activities radically changes: institutions, particularly the legal regime defining and implementing rights, matter and the choice among alternative ways of organizing transactions becomes a puzzle.

Second, a representation of the world without transaction costs opens the way to optimal bargaining solutions conditional to well-defined rights, without having to take into account the nature and allocation of those rights. Not long after the publication of 'The Problem of Social Cost', Alchian (1965) published his influential paper on property rights. Maybe due to the interaction of these two approaches, economists building models of optimal transaction mechanisms based on the so-called 'Coase theorem' rapidly associated the definition of rights to the definition of property rights and, progressively, even more restrictively to the definition of private property rights.[1] A sort of reversal of the Coase reasoning progressively prevailed that goes the following way: if (private) property rights are well defined and if the price system runs smoothly, that is: if competition guarantees efficient markets, then transaction costs will be equal to or close to zero and an optimum could be reached. A normative position soon derived from this reasoning, as so well illustrated by the creation of markets of rights to pollute: if rights are well defined and if an efficient market mechanism is implemented, optimal solutions could be reached. Markets would then be *the* solution. This is not the direction Coase wanted to follow. As he repeatedly emphasized, what he was concerned with is a world in which markets do not work that smoothly and in which transaction costs are significant enough to make alternatives to markets plausible solutions that need to be assessed on their own merit.

Third, the discussion of the Pigovian solution to the existence of harmful effects (or 'externalities') occupies a significant place in the 1960 paper; it is used as a sort of benchmark to illustrate the flaws in standard welfare economics. The point Coase wanted to make is quite straightforward, notwithstanding developments that may look here and there a bit over-elaborate for those not familiar with Pigou and not aware of his deep influence on policy makers at the time the 1960 paper was written. Because Pigou developed his arguments in a world with zero transaction costs, there is no logical foundation to the intervention of government that he recommends. In such a world, bargaining among agents would allow reaching the appropriate solution while the Pigovian solution of taxes or subsidies to reduce externalities, for example pollution, could have worse harmful effects than those they intend to circumvent. The conclusion derived by too many economists building on this discussion by Coase of the Pigovian approach is that if rights are well defined, markets always outperform government intervention. Once more, this goes the opposite direction to the one pointed out by Coase: Pigou is wrong and his legitimizing of government intervention is misleading *because* he shares the basic assumption of general equilibrium models, which is that transactions are costless. But if transaction costs are positive, which they are in the real world, the situation is totally different.

Section 2: an ignored dimension to the Coasian research agenda: organizational issues

So, what happens if transaction costs are positive? Let me first emphasize, as Coase did repeatedly, that this is the world in which Coase is interested because this is the one we live in. Section VI of 'The Problem of Social Cost' is central in that respect: it is in this section that Coase shifts the analysis from the hypothetical world of zero transaction costs to a world with costly transactions to organize.

If transaction costs are positive, two major consequences immediately prevail that must be taken systematically into account in economic analysis: (1) 'In these conditions the initial delimitation of legal rights does have an effect on the efficiency with which the economic system operates' (1960, p. 16); (2) 'It is clear that an alternative form of economic organisation which could achieve the same result at less cost than would be incurred by using the market would enable the value of production to be raised' (p. 16). The first consequence has attracted considerable attention among legal scholars, since Coase explicitly emphasized 'the crucial importance of the legal system in this new world' (Coase, 1991, p. 9). Unfortunately, the second consequence did not receive the same attention among economists. So let me turn to the issues at stake.

After having showed that the trade-off developed by Pigou (and the Pigovian tradition) between markets and government as alternative solutions to reduce or eliminate harmful effects such as those coming out of pollution is plainly wrong under the assumption of zero transaction costs, Coase turns to possible solutions when economic agents operate in a world of positive transaction costs. Under this assumption, parties can usually not bargain without costs: the transfer of rights requires mechanisms that are costly. Beside the legal system, which provides the background to all transfer of rights, there are alternative modalities of organization through which the exercise of rights, their possible harmful effects, and their trading can be done. When extensive competitive conditions are present or can be implemented, markets can provide adequate support. However, monitoring rights through market arrangements is not without costs: there are searching, contracting, and implementing costs involved.

When these costs are too high, an alternative solution, initially explored in the famous paper on 'The Nature of the Firm' (1937) is to internalize: firms use 'administrative decision' process to internally allocate rights and organize production and exchange, thus avoiding the costs of going through markets. As noted by Radner (1986) firms can partially be understood as ways to reduce costs in the delivery of 'quasi-public goods'. However, administrative procedures have their own costs: hence the now classical trade-off, explored in depth by Williamson (1975, 1985) between markets and firms (hierarchies). There are situations though, for example when rights are blurred or when harmful effects are difficult to measure, when '. . . the firm is not the only possible answer to this problem' (1960, p. 17).

Coming back to the example of pollution, Coase then considers a third possibility to monitor harmful effects: 'direct government regulation'. Indeed, '. . . it is clear that the government has powers which might enable it to get some things done at lower cost than could a private organization' (1960, p. 18). Government intervention can take different forms, for example the trade-off between taxes or subsidies to reduce pollution. At this point one could wonder: what is the difference from the Pigovian tradition of public intervention? Actually the difference is very fundamental: in the Coasian perspective, government is not a benevolent agent trying to do its best to solve the problem of harmful effects; government has its own agenda, which opens room to a political economy analysis, and above all, its interventions imply transaction costs.

As stated in the title of section X of 'The Problem of Social Cost', the existence of these alternative solutions (and possibly other 'social arrangements') requires 'a change of approach', actually a radical one. Comparing 'laissez-faire' (markets will solve it all) with a 'kind of ideal world' in which government would take care of the harmful effects goes nowhere. There is no optimal solution per se. When confronted with a problem, for example a specific form of pollution, economists should compare 'alternative social arrangements' that could provide (partial) solution and assess their respective costs. Indeed, '. . . the proper procedure is to compare the total social product yielded by these different arrangements' (1960, p. 34) in order to identify the most appropriate solution and/or policy.

To sum up, there is no ideal solution to the harmful effects, either on another party or on an entire community, involved in almost all economic activities. All possible responses involve transfer of rights (e.g., rights to pollute) and, consequently, transaction costs. The appropriate method therefore requires: one, to identify the *alternative arrangements* (markets, firms, government, hybrids . . .) that could be relevant to deal with the problem at stake; second, to assess the *comparative* costs and gains of these alternative solutions. To illustrate, to monitor the 'tragedy of the commons' in the fishing industry one should consider alternative solutions (e.g., laissez-faire, relying on collective action, imposing government regulation, creation of a market for Individual Transferable Quotas, etc.) and assess their comparative costs and benefits. There is a long, long way to go before economists and the policy makers they inspire reach this point.

Conclusion

Reading carefully 'The Problem of Social Cost' over 50 years after its publication, one can measure the relevance of the research agenda it opened . . . and how far we are from having fulfilled this agenda. If we look at the debates surrounding environmental policies, it is astonishing to see how little is done to identify precisely the alternative solutions that could be relevant for dealing with a specific problem and, even worse, how little is done to assess comparatively the costs and benefits of these alternative solutions. The debates remain very much embedded in the Pigovian/welfare tradition, with ideological positions often prevailing as the last resort among those who view market arrangements as the solution and those who consider that only government intervention can discipline parties adequately and provide appropriate answers to the harmful effects resulting from economic actions.

So, much remains to be done to meet the final message from 'The Problem of Social Cost':

> Furthermore we have to take into account the costs involved in operating the various social arrangements (whether it be the working of a market or of a government department), as well as the costs involved in moving to a new system. In devising and choosing between social arrangements we should have regard for the total effect. This, above all, is the change in approach which I am advocating. (1960, p. 44)

Note

1. Interestingly enough, there is not a single explicit reference to property rights in 'The Problem of Social Costs'. Coase seems to be primarily concerned with a very general concept of rights, that is: all rights that can be transferred, thus allowing the organization of economic activities.

References

Alchian, A. A. (1965). Some economics of property rights. *Il Politico, 30*(4), 816–819. Reprint: *Economic Forces at Work*. Indianapolis: Liberty Press.

Coase, R. H. (1937). The nature of the firm. *Economica, 2*(1), 386–405.

Coase, R. H. (1960). The problem of social cost. *The Journal of Law and Economics, 3*(Oct), 1–44.

Coase, R. H. (1991). The Institutional Structure of Production. Alfred Nobel Memorial Prize Lecture in Economic Sciences. *American Economic Review, 82*(4), 713–719.

Coase, R. H. (1998). New institutional economics. *American Economic Review, 88*(2), 72–74.

North, D. C. (1990). *Institutions, institutional change, and economic performance*. Cambridge: Cambridge University Press.

Radner, R. (1986). The internal economy of large firms. *Economic Journal*, 96 (supplement), 1–22.

Shirley, M. (2013) Battles lost and wars won: Reflections on the problem of social cost. *Journal of Natural Resources Policy Research, 5*(4), paper in production.

Stigler, G. (1966). *The theory of price*. New York, NY: Macmillan.

Williamson, O. E. (1975). *Markets and hierarchies: Analysis and antitrust implications*. New York, NY: The Free Press.

Williamson, O. E. (1985). *The economic institutions of capitalism*. New York, NY: The Free Press-Macmillan.

The successes and failures of Professor Coase

Ning Wang[a,b]

[a] *The Ronald Coase Institute, St. Louis, MO, USA;* [b] *Ronald Coase Center for the Study of the Economy, Zhejiang University, Hangzhou, Zhejiang Province, P. R. China*

When 'The Problem of Social Cost' (Coase, 1960) was first published more than half a century ago, it was an instant classic. For the group of Chicago economists who stood as its midwife, the birth of the article made intellectual history (Stigler, 1988).[1] For economists at large, Coase (1960) repudiated the Pigovian analysis of social cost, the fountainhead for modern welfare economics. For legal scholars, Coase (1960) provided an analytical framework to bridge two hitherto separate bodies of law, tort and property, and laid the foundation for the rise of law and economics. For other social scientists, Coase (1960) brought to the front the critical role of rights, including but not limited to legal rights, in structuring social life (Coleman, 1990). The article, or what became known as its main argument, was soon distilled into what George Stigler (1966) called the 'Coase Theorem', which quickly became a household name in the profession, although the phrase has never been endorsed by Coase himself. At the same time, the article has rarely failed to provoke criticism and skepticism (e.g., Cooter, 1982; Demsetz, 2011; Samuelson, 1995). The British economist, Edwin Canan, who was Arnold Plant's teacher, who in turn introduced the young Ronald Coase to economics, once remarked that falsehood may win the day, but in the end truth prevails. Half a century may not be long enough for truth to prevail in the battle of ideas. Still, we cannot help wondering where Professor Coase has triumphed and where he has lost in changing the thinking of his contemporaries and immediate successors. In this short note, we present a progress report, assessing the performance of 'The Problem of Social Cost' in the market for economics ideas over the past half century.

Let us briefly revisit the problem that gave rise to 'The Problem of Social Cost'. A fertilizer plant, while producing fertilizers, pollutes water in a nearby river, and consequently

The title is borrowed from George Stigler (1976). On the 200th anniversary of the *Wealth of Nations*, Stigler (1976) was set to assess 'the successes and failures of Professor Smith'. According to Stigler, 'the triumphs of any scholar are those of his doctrines which he persuades his contemporaries and successors to heed carefully'. One's failures, correspondingly, are 'those theories which his successors ignored or rejected out of hand'. The same criteria is adopted here.

I wish to thank the Ronald Coase Institute for its generous financial support. It was my great luck to have Professor Coase as a mentor, a friend and a collaborator over the past 15 years. After receiving the invitation to contribute to this special issue, I discussed with Professor Coase what I intended to write. He was fond of the article title, doubted he had achieved any success, and wondered what the failures were. I deeply regret that busy travel plans over the summer prevented me from finishing this article earlier. Now I can no longer discuss it with my dear Professor Coase, who left us forever on 2 September 2013 after a month of illness.

harms the operation of a fish farm downstream. In choosing its scale of operation, the fertilizer producer does not consider the damages it imposes on the fish farm, whose existence it may not be aware of at all, creating a gap between what are commonly called private and social cost. Undercounting its cost of operation, the fertilizer plant is inclined to overproduce and fertilizers tend to be underpriced. Egregious resource misallocation follows, or so it seems. To address this seeming inefficiency, the state shall impose a tax on the fertilizer producer, the amount of which is set equal to the harm suffered by the fish farm or the difference between private and social cost. This captures the essence of the Pigovian approach to externalities, which had served as the point of departure for welfare economics. On the surface, its logic appears impeccable. Judicious state intervention helps to equalize private and social cost, restoring efficiency in the economy.

It takes an independent, courageous and imaginative mind to defy, challenge and crack a seemingly solid intellectual consensus. Rather than detecting hiatuses in the chains of the Pigovian reasoning, Coase (1960) proposes an alternative viewpoint, in the light of which the very problem that Pigou sought to resolve emerges anew. The root cause of the problem is not one party (the fertilizer plant) harming the other (the fish farm) and driving a wedge between private and social cost, thus calling for state intervention, but two parties competing for the use of resources (water in the river). When economists abstain themselves from the urge to save the world, what they often view as the villain and victim in a crime scene emerges as rival employers of scarce resource. Not only did Coase recast the problem, but he also opened a new vista in search for a solution. What is called for is no longer state intervention to tax the wrongdoer and equalize private and social cost, but proper institutions that facilitate market transactions. What institutions ease and what hinder market transactions, and how and under what circumstances are too complicated to be stated in any theorem. At least, our current understanding of what Coase (1991) called the 'institutional structure of production' is so limited that any such attempt is bound to fail. One institution Coase singled out in 'The Problem of Social Cost' is property rights. When property rights are well defined, often by law and/or norms, and readily transferable, competition tends to move resources to the highest use as set by the market. This market competition in securing resources may present itself as a conflict among rival employers (the fertilizer plant versus the fish farm); but it is ultimately determined by the relative purchasing power of consumers of respective products (fertilizer versus fish buyers). The 'invisible hand' turns out far more resilient than was understood by Pigou and accepted by his followers.

When comparing economics before and after 'The Problem of Social Cost', we readily recognize the first striking success of Professor Coase, which is definitive and broad-based. Economists have since accepted the critical role of property rights and other market-supporting institutions in facilitating exchange and the division of labor.[2] Built on Coase (1960), the study of property rights has become a fertile subfield of investigation and shed fresh light on many crucial areas of economic inquiry, such as sharecropping (Cheung, 1969), economic history (e.g., North, 1981), economic development (De Soto, 1989), the commons (Ostrom, 1990), corporate governance (Hart, 1995), and economic analysis of law (Posner, 2011). Fifty years ago, property rights would rarely appear in the subject index of any economics textbook; not any more. It is no surprise that when the Nobel Committee awarded the Prize in 1991 to Professor Coase, it singled out 'his discovery and clarification of the significance of transaction costs and property rights for the institutional structure and functioning of the economy'.

It is one thing to recognize the economic significance of property rights; it is quite another to understand how property rights affect the working of the economy and how property rights evolve over time. In this regard, we still have a long way to go and Coase's insight remains as powerful today as it first appeared more than half a century ago. 'The Problem of Social Cost' highlights the delineation of rights as a precondition for market exchange. In the real world, how rights are delineated and exchanged has immediate and far-reaching economic impact. China's recent market transformation offers many illustrative examples (Coase & Wang, 2012). One distinct feature of the Chinese economic reform is that the delineation and exchange of rights are frequently bundled. What rights are defined and in what details are often negotiated by the two transacting parties, one being the government or its local agent in possession of state assets. While this practice has greatly speeded up China's move to a market economy, it has also left the state with enormous discretionary economic power. As a result, how to reign in state power under the rule of law to consolidate and expand China's emerging market order remains a daunting challenge.

The second success is that 'The Problem of Social Cost' has irreversibly established 'Coasean bargaining' as an alternative to Pigovian tax in dealing with externalities. Compared with the first victory, this one is much narrower in focus and far from complete. In economics textbooks, the Pigovian approach is still widely taught, but it is no longer the only solution. Beyond the academic world, the Federal Communication Commission's adoption of auctions since 1994 for the use of electromagnetic spectrums and the acceptance of emission permits in fighting pollution worldwide attest to the triumph of Coase (1960) in the market for ideas.

If not for the limit of space, we can readily expand the list of successes achieved by Coase (1960) in the past 53 years. For example, the reciprocal nature of externalities – that is, for the problem of social cost to arise, it requires the presence of two or more parties competing for certain resources (the fertilizer plant and fish farm in the early example vying for water) – has been widely accepted. It must also be counted as its success that economists have become more accustomed to the view that what is bought and sold in the market is not as much the physical entities (the equipment or land) as the rights to take certain actions with or to those entities. But given its classic status and enormous influences across disciplines, as well as Professor Coase's critical stance toward its popular interpretation, it is certainly more interesting to note its failures. It may strike many as a surprise that we can as readily fill up this side of the evaluation without any head-scratching.

The most ostensible failure must be that Professor Coase's call at the end of 'The Problem of Social Cost' for the 'change of approach' has largely been ignored. Coase (1960, pp. 42–43) put the defects of the prevailing Pigovian approach as follows.

> Analysis in terms of divergences between private and social products concentrate attention on particular deficiencies in the system and tends to nourish the belief that any measure which will remove the deficiency is necessarily desirable. It diverts attention from those other changes in the system which are inevitably associated with the corrective measure, changes which may well produce more harm than the original deficiency.

Accordingly, Coase urged economists to take a systematic approach to examine the full impact of their proposed economic policy.[3] 'When an economist is comparing alternative social arrangements'. Coase reminded us, 'the proper procedure is to compare the total product yielded by these different arrangements. The comparison of private and social product [of any single arrangement] is neither here nor there' (Coase, 1960, p. 34). The same message was emphatically repeated in the concluding sentence: 'In devising and choosing between social arrangements we should have regard for the total effect. This, above all, is the change in approach which I am advocating' (Coase, 1960, p. 44). Were it not for this critical message, 'The Problem of Social Cost' would be merely a correction of Pigou's analysis. This by itself is no small achievement given that the Pigovian approach had been unanimously accepted as the foundation of modern welfare economics. But Professor Coase was more ambitious, not only exposing what is wrong with Pigou's analysis and its flawed methodological approach, but also calling for a fundamental shift in approach. Unfortunately and unmistakably, Professor Coase's call has largely fallen on deaf ears.

As the mainstream economics identifies itself so intimately with marginal analysis that the 'change in approach' that Coase called for amounts to little less than a revolution. The discovery of the marginal (in contrast with the average and the total) and its unique relevance in understanding human choice is no doubt the bedrock of the 'marginal revolution' on which neoclassical economics stands. But our focus on the margin should not blind us to other dimensions in economic calculation. The margin, as Coase (1946, 1960, 1974) has repeatedly shown, is not the only, sometimes even the primary, consideration. An exclusive focus on marginal calculation can easily lead us astray.

As economists in general have not been persuaded by his call for change in approach, which Coase deemed to be the primary message of 'The Problem of Social Cost', they have been instead largely drawn to the 'Coase Theorem'. Despite his repeated measures, Professor Coase has never succeeded in pulling them away from speculations on the imaginary world of zero transaction costs. Will economists in the future take Coase seriously and heed to what Professor Coase meant to say in 'The Problem of Social Cost'?

Notes

1. 'The Problem of Social Cost' would not have been written if not for the fact that a group of Chicago economists, particularly Reuben Kessel, vehemently objected to an argument contained in 'The Federal Communication Commission' (Coase, 1959). The argument was later elaborated into 'The Problem of Social Cost'. Kessel and Coase became close friends after Coase joined Chicago not long after the publication of 'The Problem of Social Cost' to take over from Aaron Director the editorship of the *Journal of Law and Economics*.
2. Armen Alchian has to be recognized as another source of influence. Alchian's impact began as an oral tradition at UCLA and reached wide audience through his textbook, *University Economics* (Alchian & Allen, 1972). Nonetheless, as Steven Cheung (1992), a student of Alchian, admits, it is Coase that offers a penetrating insight and powerful analytical framework that enable economists to study property rights and other institutions.
3. Readers who are familiar with Coase's work will quickly recognize that the same critique can be found in an early article, 'The marginal cost controversy' (Coase, 1946) as well as a later article, 'The lighthouse in economics' (Coase, 1974). Coase pointed out this continuity himself in the introductory chapter of Coase (1988).

References

Alchian, A., & Allen, W. R. (1972). *University economics* (3rd ed.). Belmont, CA: Wadsworth Publishing Company.

Cheung, S. N. S. (1969). *The theory of share tenancy*. Chicago, IL: University of Chicago Press.

Cheung, S. N. S. (1992). The new institutional economics. In L. Werin & H. Wijkander (Eds.), *Contract economics*. Oxford: Blackwell.

Coase, N. (1991). *The Institutional Structure of Production*. The Nobel Prize Lecture.

Coase, R. (1946). The marginal cost controversy. *Economica n.s, 13*, 169–182.

Coase, R. (1959). The federal communication commission. *Journal of Law and Economics, 2*, 1–40.

Coase, R. (1960). The problem of social cost. *Journal of Law and Economics, 3*, 1–44.

Coase, R. (1974). The lighthouse in economics. *Journal of Law and Economics, 17*, 357–376.

Coase, R. (1988). *The firm, the market, and the law*. Chicago, IL: University of Chicago Press.

Coase, R., & Wang, N. (2012). *How China became capitalist*. London: Palgrave Macmillan.

Coleman, J. (1990). *Foundations of social theory*. Cambridge, MA: Harvard University Press.

Cooter, R. (1982). The cost of Coase. *Journal of Legal Studies, 11*, 1.

De Soto, H. (1989). *The other path: The invisible revolution in the third world*. New York, NY: Harper Collins.

Demsetz, H. (2011). The problem of social cost: What problem? *Review of Law and Economics, 7*, 1–13.

Hart, O. (1995). *Firms, contracts, and financial structure*. Oxford: Oxford University Press.

North, D. (1981). *Structure and change in economic history*. New York, NY: Norton.

Ostrom, E. (1990). *Governing the commons*. New York, NY: Cambridge University Press.

Posner, R. (2011). *Economic analysis of law* (8th ed.). New York, NY: Wolters and Kluwer.

Samuelson, P. (1995). Some uneasiness with the Coase theorem. *Japan and the World Economy, 7*, 1–7.

Stigler, G. (1966). *The theory of price* (3rd ed.). New York, NY: Macmillan.

Stigler, G. (1976). The successes and failures of Professor Smith. *Journal of Political Economy, 84*, 1199–1213.

Stigler, G. (1988). *Memoirs of an unregulated economist*. New York, NY: Basic Books.

The Tragedy of the Commons[*]

GARRETT HARDIN

Professor of Biology, University of California, Santa Barbara

**The population problem has no technical solution;
it requires a fundamental extension in morality.**

At the end of a thoughtful article on the future of nuclear war, Wiesner and York (*1*) concluded that: "Both sides in the arms race are . . . confronted by the dilemma of steadily increasing military power and steadily decreasing national security. *It is our considered professional judgment that this dilemma has no technical solution.* If the great powers continue to look for solutions in the area of science and technology only, the result will be to worsen the situation."

I would like to focus your attention not on the subject of the article (national security in a nuclear world) but on the kind of conclusion they reached, namely that there is no technical solution to the problem. An implicit and almost universal assumption of discussions published in professional and semipopular scientific journals is that the problem under discussion has a technical solution. A technical solution may be defined as one that requires a change only in the techniques of the natural sciences, demanding little or nothing in the way of change in human values or ideas of morality.

In our day (though not in earlier times) technical solutions are always welcome. Because of previous failures in prophecy, it takes courage to assert that a desired technical solution is not possible. Wiesner and York exhibited this courage; publishing in a science journal, they insisted that the solution to the problem was not to be found in the natural sciences. They cautiously qualified their statement with the phrase, "It is our considered professional judgment. . . " Whether they were right or not is not the concern of the present article. Rather, the concern here is with the important concept of a class of human problems which can be called "no technical solution problems," and, more specifically, with the identification and discussion of one of these.

It is easy to show that the class is not a null class. Recall the game of tick-tack-toe. Consider the problem, "How can I win the game of tick-tack-toe?" It is well known that I cannot, if I assume (in keeping with the conventions of game theory) that my opponent understands the game perfectly. Put another way, there is no "technical solution" to the problem. I can win only by giving a radical meaning to the word "win." I can hit my opponent

*Originally published in: *Science*, Vol. 162, No. 3859 (13 December 1968), pp. 1243–1248. Reproduced with kind permission of the American Association of the Advancement of Science.

over the head; or I can drug him; or I can falsify the records. Every way in which I "win" involves, in some sense, an abandonment of the game, as we intuitively understand it. (I can also, of course, openly abandon the game—refuse to play it. This is what most adults do.)

The class of "No technical solution problems" has members. My thesis is that the "population problem," as conventionally conceived, is a member of this class. How it is conventionally conceived needs some comment. It is fair to say that most people who anguish over the population problem are trying to find a way to avoid the evils of over-population without relinquishing any of the privileges they now enjoy. They think that farming the seas or developing new strains of wheat will solve the problem—technologically. I try to show here that the solution they seek cannot be found. The population problem cannot be solved in a technical way, any more than can the problem of winning the game of tick-tack-toe.

What Shall We Maximize?

Population, as Malthus said, naturally tends to grow "geometrically," or, as we would now say, exponentially. In a finite world this means that the per capita share of the world's goods must steadily decrease. Is ours a finite world? A fair defense can be put forward for the view that the world is infinite; or that we do not know that it is not. But, in terms of the practical problems that we must face in the next few generations with the foreseeable technology, it is clear that we will greatly increase human misery if we do not, during the immediate future, assume that the world available to the terrestrial human population is finite. "Space" is no escape (2).

A finite world can support only a finite population; therefore, population growth must eventually equal zero. (The case of perpetual wide fluctuations above and below zero is a trivial variant that need not be discussed.) When this condition is met, what will be the situation of mankind? Specifically, can Bentham's goal of "the greatest good for the greatest number" be realized?

No—for two reasons, each sufficient by itself. The first is a theoretical one. It is not mathematically possible to maximize for two (or more) variables at the same time. This was clearly stated by von Neumann and Morgenstern (3), but the principle is implicit in the theory of partial differential equations, dating back at least to D'Alembert (1717–1783).

The second reason springs directly from biological facts. To live, any organism must have a source of energy (for example, food). This energy is utilized for two purposes: mere maintenance and work. For man, maintenance of life requires about 1600 kilocalories a day ("maintenance calories"). Anything that he does over and above merely staying alive will be defined as work, and is supported by "work calories" which he takes in. Work calories are used not only for what we call work in common speech; they are also required for all forms of enjoyment, from swimming and automobile racing to playing music and writing poetry. If our goal is to maximize population it is obvious what we must do: We must make the work calories per person approach as close to zero as possible. No gourmet meals, no vacations, no sports, no music, no literature, no art. . . I think that everyone will grant, without argument or proof, that maximizing population does not maximize goods. Bentham's goal is impossible.

In reaching this conclusion I have made the usual assumption that it is the acquisition of energy that is the problem. The appearance of atomic energy has led some to question this assumption. However, given an infinite source of energy, population growth still produces an inescapable problem. The problem of the acquisition of energy is replaced by the problem of its dissipation, as J. H. Fremlin has so wittily shown (*4*). The arithmetic signs in the analysis are, as it were, reversed; but Bentham's goal is still unobtainable.

The optimum population is, then, less than the maximum. The difficulty of defining the optimum is enormous; so far as I know, no one has seriously tackled this problem. Reaching an acceptable and stable solution will surely require more than one generation of hard analytical work—and much persuasion.

We want the maximum good per person; but what is good? To one person it is wilderness, to another it is ski lodges for thousands. To one it is estuaries to nourish ducks for hunters to shoot; to another it is factory land. Comparing one good with another is, we usually say, impossible because goods are incommensurable. Incommensurables cannot be compared.

Theoretically this may be true; but in real life incommensurables *are* commensurable. Only a criterion of judgment and a system of weighting are needed. In nature the criterion is survival. Is it better for a species to be small and hideable, or large and powerful? Natural selection commensurates the incommensurables. The compromise achieved depends on a natural weighting of the values of the variables.

Man must imitate this process. There is no doubt that in fact he already does, but unconsciously. It is when the hidden decisions are made explicit that the arguments begin. The problem for the years ahead is to work out an acceptable theory of weighting. Synergistic effects, nonlinear variation, and difficulties in discounting the future make the intellectual problem difficult, but not (in principle) insoluble.

Has any cultural group solved this practical problem at the present time, even on an intuitive level? One simple fact proves that none has: there is no prosperous population in the world today that has, and has had for some time, a growth rate of zero. Any people that has intuitively identified its optimum point will soon reach it, after which its growth rate becomes and remains zero.

Of course, a positive growth rate might be taken as evidence that a population is below its optimum. However, by any reasonable standards, the most rapidly growing populations on earth today are (in general) the most miserable. This association (which need not be invariable) casts doubt on the optimistic assumption that the positive growth rate of a population is evidence that it has yet to reach its optimum.

We can make little progress in working toward optimum population size until we explicitly exorcize the spirit of Adam Smith in the field of practical demography. In economic affairs, *The Wealth of Nations* (1776) popularized the "invisible hand," the idea that an individual who "intends only his own gain," is, as it were, "led by an invisible hand to promote . . . the public interest" (*5*). Adam Smith did not assert that this was invariably true, and perhaps neither did any of his followers. But he contributed to a dominant tendency of thought that has ever since interfered with positive action based on rational analysis, namely, the tendency to assume that decisions reached individually will, in fact, be the best decisions for an entire society. If this assumption is correct it justifies the continuance of our present policy of laissez-faire in reproduction. If it is correct we can assume that men will control their individual fecundity so as to produce the optimum population. If the assumption is not correct, we need to reexamine our individual freedoms to see which ones are defensible.

Tragedy of Freedom in a Commons

The rebuttal to the invisible hand in population control is to be found in a scenario first sketched in a little-known pamphlet (6) in 1833 by a mathematical amateur named William Forster Lloyd (1794–1852). We may well call it "the tragedy of the commons," using the word "tragedy" as the philosopher Whitehead used it (7): "The essence of dramatic tragedy is not unhappiness. It resides in the solemnity of the remorseless working of things." He then goes on to say, "This inevitableness of destiny can only be illustrated in terms of human life by incidents which in fact involve unhappiness. For it is only by them that the futility of escape can be made evident in the drama." The tragedy of the commons develops in this way. Picture a pasture open to all. It is to be expected that each herdsman will try to keep as many cattle as possible on the commons. Such an arrangement may work reasonably satisfactorily for centuries because tribal wars, poaching, and disease keep the numbers of both man and beast well below the carrying capacity of the land. Finally, however, comes the day of reckoning, that is, the day when the long-desired goal of social stability becomes a reality. At this point, the inherent logic of the commons remorselessly generates tragedy.

As a rational being, each herdsman seeks to maximize his gain. Explicitly or implicitly, more or less consciously, he asks, "What is the utility *to me* of adding one more animal to my herd?" This utility has one negative and one positive component.

(1) The positive component is a function of the increment of one animal. Since the herdsman receives all the proceeds from the sale of the additional animal, the positive utility is nearly +1.
(2) The negative component is a function of the additional overgrazing created by one more animal. Since, however, the effects of overgrazing are shared by all the herdsmen, the negative utility for any particular decision-making herdsman is only a fraction of –1.

Adding together the component partial utilities, the rational herdsman concludes that the only sensible course for him to pursue is to add another animal to his herd. And another; and another. . . . But this is the conclusion reached by each and every rational herdsman sharing a commons. Therein is the tragedy. Each man is locked into a system that compels him to increase his herd without limit—in a world that is limited. Ruin is the destination toward which all men rush, each pursuing his own best interest in a society that believes in the freedom of the commons. Freedom in a commons brings ruin to all.

Some would say that this is a platitude. Would that it were! In a sense, it was learned thousands of years ago, but natural selection favors the forces of psychological denial (8). The individual benefits as an individual from his ability to deny the truth even though society as a whole, of which he is a part, suffers. Education can counteract the natural tendency to do the wrong thing, but the inexorable succession of generations requires that the basis for this knowledge be constantly refreshed.

A simple incident that occurred a few years ago in Leominster, Massachusetts, shows how perishable the knowledge is. During the Christmas shopping season the parking meters downtown were covered with plastic bags that bore tags reading: "Do not open until after Christmas.

Free parking courtesy of the mayor and city council." In other words, facing the prospect of an increased demand for already scarce space, the city fathers reinstituted the system of the commons. (Cynically, we suspect that they gained more votes than they lost by this retrogressive act.)

In an approximate way, the logic of the commons has been understood for a long time, perhaps since the discovery of agriculture or the invention of private property in real estate. But it is understood mostly only in special cases which are not sufficiently generalized. Even at this late date, cattlemen leasing national land on the western ranges demonstrate no more than an ambivalent understanding, in constantly pressuring federal authorities to increase the head count to the point where overgrazing produces erosion and weed-dominance. Likewise, the oceans of the world continue to suffer from the survival of the philosophy of the commons. Maritime nations still respond automatically to the shibboleth of the "freedom of the seas." Professing to believe in the "inexhaustible resources of the oceans," they bring species after species of fish and whales closer to extinction (9).

The National Parks present another instance of the working out of the tragedy of the commons. At present, they are open to all, without limit. The parks themselves are limited in extent—there is only one Yosemite Valley—whereas population seems to grow without limit. The values that visitors seek in the parks are steadily eroded. Plainly, we must soon cease to treat the parks as commons or they will be of no value to anyone.

What shall we do? We have several options. We might sell them off as private property. We might keep them as public property, but allocate the right to enter them. The allocation might be on the basis of wealth, by the use of an auction system. It might be on the basis of merit, as defined by some agreed-upon standards. It might be by lottery. Or it might be on a first-come, first-served basis, administered to long queues. These, I think, are all the reasonable possibilities. They are all objectionable. But we must choose—or acquiesce in the destruction of the commons that we call our National Parks.

Pollution

In a reverse way, the tragedy of the commons reappears in problems of pollution. Here it is not a question of taking something out of the commons, but of putting something in—sewage, or chemical, radioactive, and heat wastes into water; noxious and dangerous fumes into the air; and distracting and unpleasant advertising signs into the line of sight. The calculations of utility are much the same as before. The rational man finds that his share of the cost of the wastes he discharges into the commons is less than the cost of purifying his wastes before releasing them. Since this is true for everyone, we are locked into a system of "fouling our own nest," so long as we behave only as independent, rational, free-enterprisers.

The tragedy of the commons as a food basket is averted by private property, or something formally like it. But the air and waters surrounding us cannot readily be fenced, and so the tragedy of the commons as a cesspool must be prevented by different means, by coercive laws or taxing devices that make it cheaper for the polluter to treat his pollutants than to discharge them untreated. We have not progressed as far with the solution of this problem as we have with the first. Indeed, our particular concept of private property, which deters us from exhausting the positive resources of the earth, favors pollution. The owner of a factory on the bank of a stream—whose property extends to the middle of the stream—often has difficulty seeing why it is not his natural right to muddy the waters flowing past his door. The law, always behind the times, requires elaborate stitching and fitting to adapt it to this newly perceived aspect of the commons.

The pollution problem is a consequence of population. It did not much matter how a lonely American frontiersman disposed of his waste. "Flowing water purifies itself every 10 miles," my grandfather used to say, and the myth was near enough to the truth when he was a boy, for there were not too many people. But as population became denser, the natural chemical and biological recycling processes became overloaded, calling for a redefinition of property rights.

How to Legislate Temperance?

Analysis of the pollution problem as a function of population density uncovers a not generally recognized principle of morality, namely: *the morality of an act is a function of the state of the system at the time it is performed (10)*. Using the commons as a cesspool does not harm the general public under frontier conditions, because there is no public; the same behavior in a metropolis is unbearable. A hundred and fifty years ago a plainsman could kill an American bison, cut out only the tongue for his dinner, and discard the rest of the animal. He was not in any important sense being wasteful. Today, with only a few thousand bison left, we would be appalled at such behavior.

In passing, it is worth noting that the morality of an act cannot be determined from a photograph. One does not know whether a man killing an elephant or setting fire to the grassland is harming others until one knows the total system in which his act appears. "One picture is worth a thousand words," said an ancient Chinese; but it may take 10,000 words to validate it. It is as tempting to ecologists as it is to reformers in general to try to persuade others by way of the photographic shortcut. But the essence of an argument cannot be photographed: it must be presented rationally—in words.

That morality is system-sensitive escaped the attention of most codifiers of ethics in the past. "Thou shalt not . . ." is the form of traditional ethical directives which make no allowance for particular circumstances. The laws of our society follow the pattern of ancient ethics, and therefore are poorly suited to governing a complex, crowded, changeable world. Our epicyclic solution is to augment statutory law with administrative law. Since it is practically impossible to spell out all the conditions under which it is safe to burn trash in the back yard or to run an automobile without smog-control, by law we delegate the details to bureaus. The result is administrative law, which is rightly feared for an ancient reason—*Quis custodiet ipsos custodes?*—"Who shall watch the watchers themselves?" John Adams said that we must have "a government of laws and not men." Bureau administrators, trying to evaluate the morality of acts in the total system, are singularly liable to corruption, producing a government by men, not laws.

Prohibition is easy to legislate (though not necessarily to enforce); but how do we legislate temperance? Experience indicates that it can be accomplished best through the mediation of administrative law. We limit possibilities unnecessarily if we suppose that the sentiment of *Quis custodiet* denies us the use of administrative law. We should rather retain the phrase as a perpetual reminder of fearful dangers we cannot avoid. The great challenge facing us now is to invent the corrective feedbacks that are needed to keep custodians honest. We must find ways to legitimate the needed authority of both the custodians and the corrective feedbacks.

Freedom to Breed Is Intolerable

The tragedy of the commons is involved in population problems in another way. In a world governed solely by the principle of "dog eat dog"—if indeed there ever was such a world—how many children a family had would not be a matter of public concern. Parents who bred too exuberantly would leave fewer descendants, not more, because they would be unable to care adequately for their children. David Lack and others have found that such a negative feedback demonstrably controls the fecundity of birds (*11*). But men are not birds, and have not acted like them for millenniums, at least.

If each human family were dependent only on its own resources; *if* the children of improvident parents starved to death; *if*, thus, overbreeding brought its own "punishment" to the germ line—*then* there would be no public interest in controlling the breeding of families. But our society is deeply committed to the welfare state (*12*), and hence is confronted with another aspect of the tragedy of the commons.

In a welfare state, how shall we deal with the family, the religion, the race, or the class (or indeed any distinguishable and cohesive group) that adopts overbreeding as a policy to secure its own aggrandizement (*13*)? To couple the concept of freedom to breed with the belief that everyone born has an equal right to the commons is to lock the world into a tragic course of action.

Unfortunately this is just the course of action that is being pursued by the United Nations. In late 1967, some 30 nations agreed to the following (*14*):

> The Universal Declaration of Human Rights describes the family as the natural and fundamental unit of society. It follows that any choice and decision with regard to the size of the family must irrevocably rest with the family itself, and cannot be made by anyone else.

It is painful to have to deny categorically the validity of this right; denying it, one feels as uncomfortable as a resident of Salem, Massachusetts, who denied the reality of witches in the 17th century. At the present time, in liberal quarters, something like a taboo acts to inhibit criticism of the United Nations. There is a feeling that the United Nations is "our last and best hope," that we shouldn't find fault with it; we shouldn't play into the hands of the archconservatives. However, let us not forget what Robert Louis Stevenson said: "The truth that is suppressed by friends is the readiest weapon of the enemy." If we love the truth we must openly deny the validity of the Universal Declaration of Human Rights, even though it is promoted by the United Nations. We should also join with Kingsley Davis (*15*) in attempting to get Planned Parenthood-World Population to see the error of its ways in embracing the same tragic ideal.

Conscience is Self-Eliminating

It is a mistake to think that we can control the breeding of mankind in the long run by an appeal to conscience. Charles Galton Darwin made this point when he spoke on the centennial of the publication of his grandfather's great book. The argument is straightforward and Darwinian. People vary. Confronted with appeals to limit breeding, some people will undoubtedly respond to the plea more than others. Those who have more children will produce a larger fraction of the next generation than those with more susceptible consciences. The difference will be accentuated, generation by generation. In C. G. Darwin's words: "It may well be that it would take hundreds of generations for the progenitive instinct to develop in this way, but if it should do so, nature would have taken her revenge, and the variety *Homo contracipiens* would become extinct and would be replaced by the variety *Homo progenitivus*" (*16*).

The argument assumes that conscience or the desire for children (no matter which) is hereditary—but hereditary only in the most general formal sense. The result will be the same whether the attitude is transmitted through germ cells, or exosomatically, to use A. J. Lotka's term. (If one denies the latter possibility as well as the former, then what's the point of education?) The argument has here been stated in the context of the population problem, but it applies equally well to any instance in which society appeals to an individual exploiting a commons to restrain himself for the general good—by means of his conscience. To make such an appeal is to set up a selective system that works toward the elimination of conscience from the race.

Pathogenic Effects of Conscience

The long-term disadvantage of an appeal to conscience should be enough to condemn it; but has serious short-term disadvantages as well. If we ask a man who is exploiting a commons to desist "in the name of conscience," what are we saying to him? What does he hear?—not only at the moment but also in the wee small hours of the night when, half asleep, he remembers not merely the words we used but also the nonverbal communication cues we gave him unawares? Sooner or later, consciously or subconsciously, he senses that he has received two communications, and that they are contradictory: (i) (intended communication) "If you don't do as we ask, we will openly condemn you for not acting like a responsible citizen"; (ii) (the unintended communication) "If you *do* behave as we ask, we will secretly condemn you for a simpleton who can be shamed into standing aside while the rest of us exploit the commons."

Everyman then is caught in what Bateson has called a "double bind." Bateson and his co-workers have made a plausible case for viewing the double bind as an important causative factor in the genesis of schizophrenia (*17*). The double bind may not always be so damaging, but it always endangers the mental health of anyone to whom it is applied. "A bad conscience," said Nietzsche, "is a kind of illness."

To conjure up a conscience in others is tempting to anyone who wishes to extend his control beyond the legal limits. Leaders at the highest level succumb to this temptation. Has any President during the past generation failed to call on labor unions to moderate voluntarily their demands for higher wages, or to steel companies to honor voluntary guidelines on prices? I can recall none. The rhetoric used on such occasions is designed to produce feelings of guilt in noncooperators.

For centuries it was assumed without proof that guilt was a valuable, perhaps even an indispensable, ingredient of the civilized life. Now, in this post-Freudian world, we doubt it. Paul Goodman speaks from the modern point of view when he says: "No good has ever come from feeling guilty, neither intelligence, policy, nor compassion. The guilty do not pay attention to the object but only to themselves, and not even to their own interests, which might make sense, but to their anxieties" (*18*).

One does not have to be a professional psychiatrist to see the consequences of anxiety. We in the Western world are just emerging from a dreadful two-centuries-long Dark Ages of Eros that was sustained partly by prohibition laws, but perhaps more effectively by the anxiety-generating mechanisms of education. Alex Comfort has told the story well in *The Anxiety Makers* (*19*); it is not a pretty one.

Since proof is difficult, we may even concede that the results of anxiety may sometimes, from certain points of view, be desirable. The larger question we should ask is whether, as a matter of policy, we should ever encourage the use of a technique the tendency (if not the intention) of which is psychologically pathogenic. We hear much talk these days of responsible parenthood; the coupled words are incorporated into the titles of some organizations devoted to birth control. Some people have proposed massive propaganda campaigns to instill responsibility into the nation's (or the world's) breeders. But what is the meaning of the word responsibility in this context? Is it not merely a synonym for the word conscience? When we use the word responsibility in the absence of substantial sanctions are we not trying to browbeat a free man in a commons into acting against his own interest? Responsibility is a verbal counterfeit for a substantial *quid pro quo*. It is an attempt to get something for nothing.

If the word responsibility is to be used at all, I suggest that it be in the sense Charles Frankel uses it (*20*).

"Responsibility," says this philosopher, "is the product of definite social arrangements." Notice that Frankel calls for social arrangements—not propaganda.

Mutual Coercion

Mutually Agreed Upon

The social arrangements that produce responsibility are arrangements that create coercion, of some sort. Consider bank-robbing. The man who takes money from a bank acts as if the bank were a commons. How do we prevent such action? Certainly not by trying to control his behavior solely by a verbal appeal to his sense of responsibility. Rather than rely on propaganda we follow Frankel's lead and insist that a bank is not a commons; we seek the definite social arrangements that will keep it from becoming a commons. That we thereby infringe on the freedom of would-be robbers we neither deny nor regret.

The morality of bank-robbing is particularly easy to understand because we accept complete prohibition of this activity. We are willing to say "Thou shalt not rob banks," without providing for exceptions. But temperance also can be created by coercion. Taxing is a good coercive device. To keep downtown shoppers temperate in their use of parking space we introduce parking meters for short periods, and traffic fines for longer ones. We need not actually forbid a citizen to park as long as he wants to; we need merely make it increasingly expensive for him to do so. Not prohibition, but carefully biased options are what we offer him. A Madison Avenue man might call this persuasion; I prefer the greater candor of the word coercion.

Coercion is a dirty word to most liberals now, but it need not forever be so. As with the four-letter words, its dirtiness can be cleansed away by exposure to the light, by saying it over and over without apology or embarrassment. To many, the word coercion implies arbitrary decisions of distant and irresponsible bureaucrats; but this is not a necessary part of its meaning. The only kind of coercion I recommend is mutual coercion, mutually agreed upon by the majority of the people affected.

To say that we mutually agree to coercion is not to say that we are required to enjoy it, or even to pretend we enjoy it. Who enjoys taxes? We all grumble about them. But we accept compulsory taxes because we recognize that voluntary taxes would favor the conscienceless. We institute and (grumblingly) support taxes and other coercive devices to escape the horror of the commons.

An alternative to the commons need not be perfectly just to be preferable. With real estate and other material goods, the alternative we have chosen is the institution of private property coupled with legal inheritance. Is this system perfectly just? As a genetically trained biologist I deny that it is. It seems to me that, if there are to be differences in individual inheritance, legal possession should be perfectly correlated with biological inheritance—that those who are biologically more fit to be the custodians of property and power should legally inherit more. But genetic recombination continually makes a mockery of the doctrine of "like father, like son" implicit in our laws of legal inheritance. An idiot can inherit millions, and a trust fund can keep his estate intact. We must admit that our legal system of private property plus inheritance is unjust—but we put up with it because we are not convinced, at the moment, that anyone has invented a better system. The alternative of the commons is too horrifying to contemplate. Injustice is preferable to total ruin.

It is one of the peculiarities of the warfare between reform and the status quo that it is thoughtlessly governed by a double standard. Whenever a reform measure is proposed it is often defeated when its opponents triumphantly discover a flaw in it. As Kingsley Davis has pointed out (21), worshippers of the status quo sometimes imply that no reform is possible without unanimous agreement, an implication contrary to historical fact. As nearly as I can make out, automatic rejection of proposed reforms is based on one of two unconscious assumptions: (i) that the status quo is perfect; or (ii) that the choice we face is between reform and no action; if the proposed reform is imperfect, we presumably should take no action at all, while we wait for a perfect proposal.

But we can never do nothing. That which we have done for thousands of years is also action. It also produces evils. Once we are aware that the status quo is action, we can then compare its discoverable advantages and disadvantages with the predicted advantages and disadvantages of the proposed reform, discounting as best we can for our lack of experience. On the basis of such a comparison, we can make a rational decision which will not involve the unworkable assumption that only perfect systems are tolerable.

Recognition of Necessity

Perhaps the simplest summary of this analysis of man's population problems is this: the commons, if justifiable at all, is justifiable only under conditions of low-population density. As the human population has increased, the commons has had to be abandoned in one aspect after another.

First we abandoned the commons in food gathering, enclosing farm land and restricting pastures and hunting and fishing areas. These restrictions are still not complete throughout the world.

Somewhat later we saw that the commons as a place for waste disposal would also have to be abandoned. Restrictions on the disposal of domestic sewage are widely accepted in the Western world; we are still struggling to close the commons to pollution by automobiles, factories, insecticide sprayers, fertilizing operations, and atomic energy installations.

In a still more embryonic state is our recognition of the evils of the commons in matters of pleasure. There is almost no restriction on the propagation of sound waves in the public medium. The shopping public is assaulted with mindless music, without its consent. Our government is paying out billions of dollars to create supersonic transport which will disturb 50,000 people for every one person who is whisked from coast to coast 3 hours faster. Advertisers muddy the airwaves of radio and television and pollute the view of travelers. We are a long way from outlawing the commons in matters of pleasure. Is this because our

Puritan inheritance makes us view pleasure as something of a sin, and pain (that is, the pollution of advertising) as the sign of virtue?

Every new enclosure of the commons involves the infringement of somebody's personal liberty. Infringements made in the distant past are accepted because no contemporary complains of a loss. It is the newly proposed infringements that we vigorously oppose; cries of "rights" and "freedom" fill the air. But what does "freedom" mean? When men mutually agreed to pass laws against robbing, mankind became more free, not less so. Individuals locked into the logic of the commons are free only to bring on universal ruin; once they see the necessity of mutual coercion, they become free to pursue other goals. I believe it was Hegel who said, "Freedom is the recognition of necessity."

The most important aspect of necessity that we must now recognize, is the necessity of abandoning the commons in breeding. No technical solution can rescue us from the misery of overpopulation. Freedom to breed will bring ruin to all. At the moment, to avoid hard decisions many of us are tempted to propagandize for conscience and responsible parenthood. The temptation must be resisted, because an appeal to independently acting consciences selects for the disappearance of all conscience in the long run, and an increase in anxiety in the short.

The only way we can preserve and nurture other and more precious freedoms is by relinquishing the freedom to breed, and that very soon. "Freedom is the recognition of necessity"—and it is the role of education to reveal to all the necessity of abandoning the freedom to breed. Only so, can we put an end to this aspect of the tragedy of the commons.

References

1. J. B. Wiesner and H. F. York, *Sci. Amer.* 211 (No. 4), 27 (1964).
2. G. Hardin, *J. Hered.* 50, 68 (1959); S. von Hoernor, *Science* 137, 18 (1962).
3. J. von Neumann and O. Morgenstern, *Theory of Games and Economic Behavior* (Princeton Univ. Press, Princeton, N.J., 1947), p. 11.
4. J. H. Fremlin, *New Sci.*, No. 415 (1964), p. 285.
5. A. Smith, *The Wealth of Nations* (Modern Library, New York, 1937), p. 423.
6. W. F. Lloyd, *Two Lectures on the Checks to Population* (Oxford Univ. Press, Oxford, England, 1833), reprinted (in part) in *Population, Evolution, and Birth Control*, G. Hardin, Ed. (Freeman, San Francisco, 1964), p. 37.
7. A. N. Whitehead, *Science and the Modern World* (Mentor, New York, 1948), p. 17.
8. G. Hardin, Ed. *Population, Evolution, and Birth Control* (Freeman, San Francisco, 1964), p. 56.
9. S. McVay, *Sci. Amer.* 216 (No. 8>, 13 (1966).
10. J. Fletcher, *Situation Ethics* (Westminster, Philadelphia, 1966).
11. D. Lack, *The Natural Regulation of Animal Numbers* (Clarendon Press, Oxford, 1954).
12. H. Girvetz, *From Wealth to Welfare* (Stanford Univ. Press, Stanford, Calif., 1950).
13. G. Hardin, *Perspec. Biol. Med.* 6, 366 (1963).
14. U. Thant, *Int. Planned Parenthood News*, No. 168 (February 1968), p. 3.
15. K. Davis, *Science* 158, 730 (1967).
16. S. Tax, Ed., *Evolution after Darwin* (Univ. of Chicago Press, Chicago, 1960), vol. 2, p. 469.
17. G. Bateson, D. D. Jackson, J. Haley, J. Weakland, *Behav. Scd.* 1, 251 (1956).
18. P. Goodman, *New York Rev. Books* 10(8), 22 (23 May 1968).
19. A. Comfort, *The Anxiety Makers* (Nelson, London, 1967).
20. C. Frankel, *The Case for Modern Man* (Harper, New York, 1955), p. 203.
21. J. D. Roslansky, *Genetics and the Future of Man* (Appleton-Century-Crofts, New York, 1966), p. 177.

The Core Challenges of Moving Beyond Garrett Hardin

XAVIER BASURTO*,** & ELINOR OSTROM*

*Workshop in Political Theory and Policy Analysis, Indiana University, Bloomington, IN, USA; **Duke Marine Lab, Nicholas School of the Environment, Duke University, Beaufort, NC, USA

Hardin's theory—depicting a set of pastoralists inexorably trapped in the overuse of their common pasture—was thought for many years to be typical for common-pool resources (CPRs) not owned privately or by a government. Since Hardin thought the users would be 'trapped' in their tragic overuse of a resource, he advocated two solutions to prevent future tragedies: state control or individual ownership. We need to move beyond this simplistic approach, but face challenges in doing so.

In efforts to move beyond Hardin, it is important that one does not dismiss his predictions for some CPRs. The major problem of his original analysis was that he presented 'the tragedy' as a *universal* phenomenon. Field settings do exist where Hardin is correct. Overharvesting frequently occurs when resource users are totally anonymous, do not have a foundation of trust and reciprocity, cannot communicate, and have no established rules. In an experimental lab, subjects presented with a common-pool resource problem overharvest when they do not know who is in their group, no feedback is provided on individual actions, and they cannot communicate. They do worse than game theory predicts and fit the behaviour predicted by Hardin (Ostrom *et al.*, 1994).

If the subjects are enabled to sit in a circle talking about the puzzle in a face-to-face group, however, they usually develop trust and reciprocity. Within a few rounds, they reduce overharvesting substantially and do very well (Ostrom *et al.*, 1992). In traditional, non-cooperative game theory, communication is not supposed to improve the outcomes obtained, but many groups solve the problem of overharvesting after engaging in face-to-face communication. Further, many smaller groups that use CPRs—inshore fisheries, forests, irrigation systems, and pastures—have developed a diversity of norms and rules that have enabled them to solve problems of overharvesting (NRC, 1986, 2002; McCay & Acheson, 1987; Berkes, 1989; McKean, 1992; Baland & Platteau, 1996; Dolšak & Ostrom, 2003; Basurto, 2005; Lansing, 2006; van Laerhoven & Ostrom, 2007).

To move beyond Hardin's tragedy of the commons, we need to avoid falling into either of two analytical and policy traps: (1) deriving and recommending policy blueprints or 'panaceas'; or (2) asserting 'my case is unique'. The first trap is caused, to some extent, by the ease with which simple, powerful models can be translated into overarching generalizations, which has led to policy blueprints abounding in the literature. Fisheries, for instance, are rich with examples advocating individual transferable quotas (ITQs), marine protected areas (MPAs), and community-based management (CBM) as cure-alls (Degnbol et al., 2006).

Governing CPRs like fisheries is challenging. CPRs are normally used by multiple individuals generating finite quantities of resource units where one person's use subtracts from the quantity of resource units available to others. Most CPRs are sufficiently large that multiple actors can simultaneously use the resource system, and excluding potential beneficiaries is costly. We need to build a theoretical foundation for explaining why some resource users are able to self-organize and govern the use of a resource over time in a sustainable manner and why others fail or never make the effort. To build theory, it is necessary to move away from both extremes to develop an interdisciplinary diagnostic framework that helps to provide a foundation for further empirical research and learning (Agrawal, 2008; Bardhan & Ray, 2008; Chopra, 2008).

The Panacea Analytical Trap

Historically, the cure-alls that have been recommended most frequently promote government ownership (Ophuls, 1973; Feeny et al., 1996, p. 195) or privatization (Demsetz, 1967; Posner, 1977; Simmons et al., 1996). Panacea-type solutions can be a by-product of approaches that generate highly abstract models and use simple empirical studies to illustrate general patterns of social phenomena (Bouchaud, 2008). For instance, since the important early studies of open-access fisheries by Gordon (1954) and Scott (1955), most theoretical studies by political economists have analyzed simple CPR systems using relatively similar assumptions (Feeny et al., 1996; Ruddle, 2007; Ruddle & Hickey, 2008). In such systems, it is assumed that the resource generates a highly predictable, finite supply of one type of resource unit (one species, for example) in each relevant time period. Resource users are assumed to be homogeneous in terms of their assets, skills, discount rates, and cultural views. Users are also assumed to be short-term, profit-maximizing actors who possess complete information. As a result, this theory universally assumes that anyone can enter the resource and harvest resource units. Users are viewed as able to gain property rights only to what they harvest, which they then sell in an open competitive market. Under this approach, the open-access condition is a given. The users make no effort to change it. Users act independently and do not communicate or coordinate their activities in any way.

This approach emphasizes collecting information on a large number of cases to be able to find the correlation of dependent and independent variables with a statistical degree of significance. This can come at the cost of being able to develop in-depth knowledge of each of the cases under study. Homogenization assumptions about the cases under consideration are often necessary to conduct quantitative analyses. In the process, the analyst risks losing track of the importance of context and history and faces challenges to be able to effectively convey the sense of complexity and diversity that exists in the empirical world.

The basic theory was applied to all CPRs, regardless of the capacity of resource users to communicate and coordinate their activities, until the work of the National Academy of Sciences' Panel on Common Property (NRC, 1986) strongly challenged this approach. The growing evidence from many qualitative studies of CPRs conducted in the field called for a serious rethinking of the theoretical foundations for the analysis of CPRs (Berkes *et al.*, 1989; McCay & Acheson, 1987).

'My-Case-is-Unique' Analytical Trap

The rich case-study literature has played a prominent role in illustrating the wide diversity of settings in which appropriators dependent on CPRs have organized themselves to achieve much higher outcomes than is predicted by the conventional theory (Wade, 1994; Ruddle & Johannes, 1985; Sengupta, 1991). In being able to tap into the rich case-study literature, however, we also need to move beyond the argument that each resource system, and the people who use it, is unique. At one level, that assertion is true. All humans are unique and all human organizations are unique as well. The problem comes from assuming that there are no commonalities across cases that can be the foundation for theoretical analysis, explanations, and diagnosis. Ecologists have long dealt with complex systems that at one level are unique (e.g. individual species), but are also able to move outward to larger systems (e.g. populations or ecosystems) and find commonalities among different species and behaviours. Medical diagnosis of illness and potential remedies is feasible, even though each individual is unique.

Often, the scholarly treatment of social phenomena as unique is the by-product of training scholars in a research strategy that focuses first on understanding the complexity of social phenomena. Qualitative-oriented scholars, such as ethnographers and historians, are usually associated with this approach. Students of this tradition are often interested in understanding how different elements fit together to constitute a case. They examine many parts and attempt to construct a representation from the interconnections among the aspects of each case. In order to be able to do so, it is necessary to acquire in-depth knowledge about the instances under study.

Often, the goal of this research approach is to describe how different aspects constitute the case as a whole, which may then be compared and contrasted with other cases. Given the depth of data that scholars amass about each aspect of their case, qualitative scholars frequently work with one or a few cases at a time. Because of their familiarity with the complexity and in-depth understanding of the particularities of the instances that characterize certain phenomena, qualitative scholars tend to avoid making generalizations about their findings. Sometimes it is precisely the rarity of certain social phenomena, characterized by only one, two, or a handful of instances, that might attract a scholar's attention and curiosity to them in the first place (Ragin, 2000, 2008).

In Closing

To move beyond Hardin's theory, we need to draw on both general theory related to causal processes and learn how to identify key variables present or absent in particular settings, so as to understand successes and failures. We agree that to build a diagnostic theory, it is important to incorporate contextual factors into policy analyses. We also need to avoid falling into the presumption that all individual settings are so different from one another that all we can do is describe the intricate detail of particular settings. Those of us who study institutions and human behaviour, while trying to develop theoretical understanding, do realize that every case, as well as all human beings, is unique. On the other hand, while we have a unique combination of factors affecting our personalities, behaviour, and actions, all humans share some attributes. It is always a challenge to determine which of those attributes are important at any one time. This is what the medical profession has been struggling to do for many eras. The great contribution of medical sciences is the development of *diagnostic theory* that enables medicine to move beyond panaceas. Policy sciences need to work toward the development of a diagnostic theory of the commons.

Acknowledgements

The authors wish to acknowledge essential financial support from the National Science Foundation (Grant # BCS0601320) and from the Workshop in Political Theory and Policy Analysis at Indiana University, as well as the excellent editing of Patty Lezotte. This paper draws in part on a longer invited feature forthcoming in *Economia delle fonti di energia e dell'ambiente*, titled 'Beyond the Tragedy of the Commons'.

References

Agrawal, A. (2008) Sustainable governance of common-pool resources: Context, method and politics, in: P. Bardhan & I. Ray (Eds) *The Contested Commons: Conversations Between Economists and Anthropologists*, pp. 46–65 (Oxford: Blackwell).

Baland, J.-M., & Platteau, J.-P. (1996) *Halting Degradation of Natural Resources: Is There a Role for Rural Communities?* (Oxford: Clarendon Press).

Bardhan, P., & Ray, I. (2008) *The Contested Commons: Conversations Between Economists and Anthropologists* (Oxford: Blackwell).

Basurto, X. (2005) How locally designed access and use controls can prevent the tragedy of the commons in a Mexican small-scale fishing community, *Society and Natural Resources*, 18 (7), pp. 643–659.

Berkes, F. (Ed) (1989) *Common Property Resources: Ecology and Community-Based Sustainable Development* (London: Belhaven Press).

Berkes, F., Feeny, D., McCay, B. J., & Acheson, J. M. (1989) The benefits of the commons, *Nature*, 340 (6229), pp. 91–93.

Bouchaud, J. P. (2008) Economics needs a scientific revolution, *Nature*, 455 (30), p. 1181.

Chopra, K. (2008) Commentary 4: Disciplinary perspectives and policy design for common-pool resources, in: P. Bardhan & I. Ray (Eds) *The Contested Commons: Conversations Between Economists and Anthropologists*, pp. 248–256 (Oxford: Blackwell).

Degnbol, P., Gislason, H., Hanna, S., Jentoft, S., Raakjær Nielsen, J., Sverdrup-Jensen, S., Wilson, D. C.. (2006) Painting the floor with a hammer: technical fixes in fisheries management, *Marine Policy*, 30 (5), pp. 534–543.

Demsetz, H. (1967) Toward a theory of property rights, *American Economic Review*, 57 (2), pp. 347–359.

Dolšak, N., & Ostrom, E. (Eds) (2003) *The Commons in the New Millennium: Challenges and Adaptations* (Cambridge, MA: MIT Press).

Feeny, D., Hanna, S. S., & McEvoy, A.F. (1996) Questioning the assumptions of the 'tragedy of the commons' model of fisheries, *Land Economics*, 72, pp. 187–205.

Gordon, H. S. (1954) The economic theory of a common property resource: The fishery, *Journal of Political Economy*, 62 (2), pp. 124–142.

van Laerhoven, F., & Ostrom, E. (2007) Traditions and trends in the study of the commons, *International Journal of the Commons*, 1 (1), pp. 3–28.

Lansing, J. S. (2006) *Perfect Order: Recognizing Complexity in Bali* (Princeton, NJ: Princeton University Press).

McCay, B. J., & Acheson, J. M. (1987) *The Question of the Commons: The Culture and Ecology of Communal Resources* (Tucson: University of Arizona Press).

McKean, M. A. (1992) Success on the commons: A comparative examination of institutions for common property resource management, *Journal of Theoretical Politics*, 4 (3), pp. 247–281.

NRC (National Research Council) (1986) *Proceedings of the Conference on Common Property Resource Management* (Washington, DC: National Academy Press).

NRC (National Research Council) (2002) *The Drama of the Commons,* E. Ostrom, T. Dietz, N. Dolšak, P. Stern, S. Stonich & E. Weber. (Eds). Committee on the Human Dimensions of Global Change (Washington, DC: National Academy Press).

Ophuls, W. (1973) Leviathan or oblivion, in: H. E. Daly (Ed) *Toward a Steady State Economy,* pp. 215–230 (San Francisco: Freeman).

Ostrom, E., Gardner, R., & Walker, J. (1994) *Rules, Games, and Common-Pool Resources* (Ann Arbor: University of Michigan Press).

Ostrom, E., Walker, J., & Gardner, R. (1992) Covenants with and without a sword: Self-governance is possible, *American Political Science Review*, 86 (2), pp. 404–417.

Posner, R. A. (1977) *Economic Analysis of Law*, 2nd ed. (Boston: Little, Brown).

Ragin, C. C. (2000) *Fuzzy-Sets Social Science* (Chicago: University of Chicago Press).

Ragin, C. C. (2008) *Redesigning Social Inquiry: Fuzzy Sets and Beyond* (Chicago: University of Chicago Press).

Ruddle, K. (2007) Misconceptions, outright prejudice, *Samudra Report*, No. 48, pp. 4–9.

Ruddle, K., & Hickey, F. R. (2008) Accounting for the mismanagement of tropical nearshore fisheries, *Environment, Development, and Sustainability*, 10 (5), pp. 565–589.

Ruddle, K., & Johannes, R. E. (Eds) (1985) *The Traditional Knowledge and Management of Coastal Systems in Asia and the Pacific* (Jakarta: UNESCO).

Scott, A. D. (1955) The fishery: The objectives of sole ownership, *Journal of Political Economy*, 63 (2), pp. 116–124.

Sengupta, N. (1991) *Managing Common Property: Irrigation in India and the Philippines* (New Delhi: Sage).

Simmons, R. T., Smith Jr., F. L., & Georgia, P. (1996) *The Tragedy of the Commons Revisited: Politics Versus Private Property* (Washington, DC: Center for Private Conservation).

Wade, R. (1994) *Village Republics: Economic Conditions for Collective Action in South India* (San Francisco: ICS Press).

Revising the Commons Paradigm

FIKRET BERKES

Natural Resources Institute, University of Manitoba, Winnipeg, Manitoba, Canada

Commons theory has undergone a major transformation since the 1980s. Hardin's 'tragedy of the commons' model, with its negative prognosis, has been replaced by theories based on the idea that resource users are capable of self-organization and self-regulation. A great deal of research in recent decades has focused on institutions for commons use, and on defining the conditions that lead to the solution of the commons dilemma. The purpose of this short article is to reflect on the paradigm change, its cross-disciplinary context, and policy implications. The primary argument is that commons thinking has already experienced a major change, and it continues to evolve, from laboratory-like community-based approaches to those dealing with resource management as complex systems problems in a rapidly changing social-ecological environment.

I started my first study of community-based resource management in the mid-1970s in the Cree Indian village of Chisasibi, James Bay, in eastern subarctic Canada. As a recent science PhD, I had no training to appreciate local resource management institutions. Worse, as a member of a generation of students under the influence of the 'tragedy of the commons' concept, I started with the belief that resources had to be protected from the users by government resource management. This belief was shaken in the course of my studies of the Cree fishery. This was a subsistence fishery, with no commercial component, carried out under no apparent rules or regulations; as an indigenous subsistence fishery, it operated outside the sphere of government regulations. But it turned out there indeed was a management system. Fishers were self-organized and self-managed, contradicting the predictions of the 'tragedy of the commons' (Berkes, 2008; Chapter 7 summarizes some 10 years of this work, published 1977 onwards).

Until the 1980s, the 'tragedy of the commons' was the principal way in which commons were conceptualized. Hardin used the example of an imaginary pasture in Medieval England to which cattle herders had free and open access. Each herder received a direct benefit (say +1) from adding one more animal to graze in the pasture, and the costs of degrading the pasture were shared by all (a fraction of −1). Thus, each herder had the incentive to put as many cattle on the pasture as he could. Adding more animals was the economically rational choice; yet everyone exercising their rational choice led to the degradation of the pasture, hence the 'tragedy'—in the sense of ancient Greek tragedies.

My James Bay Cree fishery did not fit this model at all. These fishers were far from the helpless actors in the Greek tragedy. They decided among themselves on the (unwritten) rules of conduct of the fishery, mutually agreed upon; they communicated and used social sanctions where necessary to get compliance among members. The Cree did not think of these as 'rules' but simply the 'way things were done'. Also of a great deal of interest to me, the locally-designed fishing system was fundamentally different from biological management systems in use in commercial fisheries in subarctic Canada. Commercial fisheries were usually managed by fishing gear and mesh size restrictions, season and area closures (for example, during spawning), and catch quotas. By contrast, Cree subsistence fishers used the most effective gear available, the mix of mesh sizes that gave the highest possible catch per unit of effort by area and by season, and deliberately concentrated their fishing effort on aggregations of the most efficiently exploitable fish.

In short, the Cree fishery violated just about every measure used by government managers. In turn, the Cree fishery used a set of practices seldom seen in conventional management: switching fishing areas according to the declining catch per effort; rotating fishing areas; using a mix of mesh sizes to proportionately thin out populations by size and age; keying harvest levels to needs; having a system of leadership to informally regulate access and effort; and a land use system in which resources were used under principles and ethics agreed upon by all (Berkes, 2008).

The Cree fishery made me reject the 'tragedy of the commons', just as other scholars in various parts of the world were also finding exceptions to the 'tragedy'. A consensus was building among scholars, to the effect that Hardin's model applied to open-access exploitation of the commons but was not valid for community-based resource use systems (NAS, 1986; McCay & Acheson, 1987). In fact, Hardin's own example of the imaginary English pasture was historically incorrect. The medieval English commons were generally used under locally-devised regulations; for example, 'stinting' rules limited the number of heads of animals that each owner was allowed to graze on the village pasture. Medieval English commons operated successfully for many centuries, and several economic historians and other scholars have questioned if a 'tragedy' of the sort described by Hardin ever occurred widely (Feeny et al., 1990).

In his classic *The Structure of Scientific Revolutions*, Kuhn (1962) postulates that in science, a dominant model or way of thinking (paradigm) persists until the accumulation of new evidence forces a re-appraisal and rejection of the old paradigm and the formulation of a new one. This is exactly what happened in the case of commons theory between about 1975 and 1990. Hardin had argued that users of a commons are caught in an inevitable ('remorseless') process that leads to the destruction of the resources on which they depend. But this was simply not so. Exceptions to Hardin's model were coming from all parts of the world, covering various cultures and resource types—fisheries, wildlife, forests, grazing lands, protected areas, irrigation, and ground water. Cases were brought together in several volumes (NAS, 1986; McCay & Acheson, 1987; Ostrom, 1990), necessitating the development of an entirely new theory of the commons.

Constructing a new theory required a clarification of definitions and concepts. Commons (common-pool resources) shared two characteristics: (1) exclusion or the control of access of potential users was difficult; and (2) each user was capable of subtracting from the welfare of all other users (Feeny et al., 1990). The new theory also needed to clarify property-rights relationships and regimes (NAS, 1986; Ostrom, 1990). Commons could be held in one of four basic property rights regimes. Open-access was the absence of well-defined property rights, with free access to all. Private property referred to the situation in which an individual or corporation had the right to exclude others and to regulate use. State property meant that rights to the resource are vested exclusively in government. Common-property or communal-property regimes defined situations in which the resource was held by an identifiable community of users. These four regimes were pure analytical types; in practice, resources were usually held in combinations of property rights regimes.

The evidence accumulating over the last few decades indicates that three of these property-rights regimes (private property, state property, and common property) may, under various circumstances, lead to sustainable resource use. No particular regime is inherently superior to the others, but one may fit a particular circumstance better than the others. No one particular regime guarantees sustainability; there are successes and failures under all three regimes. Regarding the open-access regime, however, there is general consensus that long-term sustainability is not possible (Feeny *et al.,* 1990; Ostrom *et al.,* 2002).

One important conclusion from post-Hardinian work is that common property is not the same as open access, and there is nothing inherent in commons that leads to resource degradation. This has important policy implications, as the 'tragedy' was often used by governments as the justification for centralizing resource management. By contrast, the viability of local management solutions under the new theory opened the way for participatory approaches, co-management, and the devolution of power.

A second conclusion, with policy implications, concerns the recognition of the role of social sciences in resource management. This development follows from a re-conceptualization of commons as involving social relations, for example, in making and enforcing fisheries rules. These social relations often lead to management problem-solving and the formulation of practical rules-in-use or institutions (Ostrom, 1990). Hence, the local rules of Cree fisheries are typical and expected. By contrast, the lack of social relations and communication among Hardin's hypothetical English herders is anomalous and unexpected. Hardin's herders, with free and open access to the pasture, were operating under an open access regime, and not under common property.

What are the implications of these findings for the readers of a policy-oriented, cross-disciplinary, and transnational journal such as the *Journal of Natural Resources Policy Research*? First, commons has evolved into a truly interdisciplinary field, with contributions from political science, economics, anthropology, sociology, geography, applied ecology, and others, addressing multiple resource management domains: forestry, fisheries, wildlife, protected areas, surface and groundwater, and others. The literature base in each of these areas (by resource type and geographic area) is in the thousands (IASC, 2009). Second, commons thinking has been evolving in many ways. One of these ways is that commons research is increasingly seen as dealing with aspects of complex adaptive systems, such as self-organization, non-linearity, uncertainty, and scale (Berkes *et al.,* 2003).

Post-Hardinian research on commons often sought the simplicity of community-based resource management cases to develop theory. One strategy was the use of local-scale commons cases since 'the process of self-organization and self-governance are easier to observe in this type of situation than in many others' (Ostrom, 1990, p. 29). In reality, however, resource boundaries rarely match social boundaries, and resources tend to be used by competing user-groups, even within the same community. As well, drivers originating at other levels of social and political organization have major impacts on what happens at the community level.

We know a great deal about the conditions under which community-based management may or may not work (Dietz *et al.*, 2003; Ostrom, 2005). Commons theory is sufficiently developed to enable prediction at the local level. However, local commons are embedded in a multi-level world. Globalization has a major impact on commons management, for example, through the creation of international markets and speeding up resource exploitation. Can a theory of the commons, originally based on local-level cases, be scaled up to deal with the complexity of communities and institutions at multiple levels? Is the theory of commons applicable to regional and global resources?

The challenges ahead include the need to move to the analysis of complex commons, multi-level in both space and time, and the interplay at various levels (Young *et al.*, 2008). We need to develop a broader approach, moving from management to governance, emphasizing social learning and using a diversity of collaborative, adaptive management experiments (Armitage *et al.*, 2007). Such approaches may be necessary to deal with commons in the context of rapidly changing social-ecological systems in an environment of uncertainty and surprise.

References

Armitage, D., Berkes, F., & Doubleday, N. (Eds) (2007) *Adaptive Co-Management: Collaboration, Learning, and Multi-Level Governance* (Vancouver: University of British Columbia Press).

Berkes, F. (2008) *Sacred Ecology*, 2nd ed. (New York: Routledge).

Berkes, F., Colding, J., & Folke, C. (Eds) (2003) *Navigating Social-Ecological Systems: Building Resilience for Complexity and Change* (Cambridge: Cambridge University Press).

Dietz, T., Ostrom, E., & Stern, P. C. (2003) The struggle to govern the commons, *Science*, 302, pp. 1907–1912.

Feeny, D., Berkes, F., McCay, B. J., & Acheson, J. M. (1990) The tragedy of the commons: Twenty-two years later, *Human Ecology*, 18, pp. 1–19.

International Association for the Study of the Commons (IASC) (2009) Digital resources on the commons. Available at http://www.iascp.org/resources.html (accessed April 2009).

Kuhn, T. (1962) *The Structure of Scientific Revolutions* (Chicago: University of Chicago Press).

McCay, B. J., & Acheson, J. M. (Eds) (1987) *The Question of the Commons: The Culture and Ecology of Communal Resources* (Tucson: University of Arizona Press).

NAS (1986) *Proceedings of the Conference on Common Property Resource Management* (Washington, DC: National Research Council/National Academy Press).

Ostrom, E. (1990) *Governing the Commons. The Evolution of Institutions for Collective Action* (Cambridge: Cambridge University Press).

Ostrom, E. (2005) *Understanding Institutional Diversity* (Princeton, NJ: Princeton University Press).

Ostrom, E., Dietz, T., Dolšak, N., Stern, P. C., Stonich, S., & Weber, E. U. (Eds) (2002) *The Drama of the Commons* (Washington, DC: National Academy Press).

Young, O. R., King, L. A., & Schroeder, H. (Eds) (2008) *Institutions and Environmental Change* (Cambridge, MA: MIT Press).

Hardin's Brilliant Tragedy and a Non-Sequitur Response

THRÁINN EGGERTSSON
Department of Politics, New York University, New York, USA

What Was on Hardin's Mind?

In December 1968, Garrett Hardin, who in his own words was a 'genetically trained biologist' (p. 1247), published a brilliant idiosyncratic essay in *Science*: 'The Tragedy of the Commons'. The essay builds on economics, political economy, evolutionary biology, psychoanalysis, philosophy, and other fields to support two conclusions: (1) 'Freedom to breed will bring ruin to all' (1968, p. 1248); and (2) the authorities must coercively limit reproductive rights because appeal to conscience cannot solve the population problem. Hardin's essay is a classic piece, and is one of the most cited in social science. Below I make four points: (1) Hardin's argument is convincing, if we accept his assumption that the rate of human reproduction is exogenous and relatively constant; (2) in his famous essay on population, Hardin does not rely on modern demography, which weakens his case; (3) the many references I have seen to the 'Tragedy of the Commons' ignore the issues and policies that Hardin discusses in the essay; (4) inadvertently, the essay may have stimulated important work on communal property arrangements for common pool resources, such as forests, fisheries, pastures, and irrigation systems.

Coercive Limits on Reproductive Rights?

In the 1960s, rapid population growth had many people worried—and some made their concerns known. One of those was Paul Ehrlich. Earlier in the year that Hardin published his essay, Erlich turned out a book that received much notice: *The Population Bomb*. To set the stage, Hardin makes the basic observation 'that the world available to the terrestrial human population is finite' (1968, p. 1243). Moreover, he predicts that, with foreseeable technology, the next few generations will face increasing human misery. There is no technical solution, Hardin claims, and 'space is no escape' (1968, p. 1243).

To symbolically illustrate his argument, Hardin makes a fateful comparison between overpopulation and the behaviour of herdsmen on a 'pasture open to all' that eventually destroy the resource (1968, p. 1244). A 'pasture open to all' is an open access arrangement—the rights of exclusion do not exist. Hardin refers to the phenomenon as 'a commons', but he is not talking about a jointly-managed communal property system that excludes outsiders. Someone might object to the comparison and point out that babies are born into a world dominated by exclusive property rights. Our economic systems cannot be characterized as a 'pasture open to all'. Hardin foreshadows this objection: 'Men are not birds', he states (1968, p. 1246). Scientists have observed that among birds negative feedback (starvation) often limits individual reproductive behaviour. In human society people care for each other and share their resources; overbreeding does not swiftly punish individual families (1968, p. 1246). Civilization has made Earth a 'pasture open to all'.

Hardin dismisses attempts to rely on persuasion to limit overpopulation. He uses arguments from game theory, social Darwinism, and Freudian psychology to shoot down the idea that appeals to conscience can be used to defuse the population bomb; massive propaganda campaigns for installing responsibility into human breeders will not work. Coercive limits on reproductive rights are the only practical solution. But that is how we have always solved the problem of scarcity when growing populations put pressure on available resources, says Hardin—with coercion, either through exclusive rights or government regulation. 'First we abandoned the commons in food gathering, enclosed farm land and restricting pastures and hunting and fishing areas' (1968, p. 1248). An urgent next step is 'abandoning the commons in breeding' (1968, p. 1248). And only the state has the coercive power to limit reproductive rights. Hardin, in a fit of forgetfulness, appears to assume that breeders universally live democratic states, which leaves out China: He only recommends 'mutual coercion, mutually agreed upon by the majority of the people affected' (1968, p. 1247). Finally, Hardin does not lay down a plan of action but claims that temperance is best achieved through cautious 'mediation of administrative law' (1968, p. 1246).

Was Hardin Off the Track?

If we exclude revolutionary technical change, a steady increase in population will indeed bring ruin to us all. Hardin is right, although some counteracting forces will delay the moment of truth. The known stock of many natural resources is a positive function of their price. When their price is high, we invest in search for hidden reserves, for instance in finding new oil and natural gas reserves. Also, a very high price of some substance or material creates an incentive to look for or invent substitutes. Yet Hardin is right in concluding that the Earth cannot accommodate an infinite number of individuals. The weak point in his argument is the assumption of exogenous, unswerving birth rates in the absence of state intervention. Hardin makes no reference to the theory of demographic transition, which so far appears to have solid empirical support (Easterlin, 1998, part 2 'Population Growth'). The theory states that rising incomes and urbanization eventually lead to a spontaneous slowdown and even reversal of population growth. The response is lagged, not immediate, and actually, at an early stage, population growth temporarily surges when improved sanitation and higher living standards lower child mortality rates faster than birth rates fall. In their usual cold-hearted manner, economists explain falling birth rates as a rational response by selfish individuals to rising costs of raising children and less use for children in household and farm production and as substitutes for old-age and health insurance. Higher family incomes are also associated with an incentive to invest in raising the quality of children (their human capital) rather than their number.

In his essay, Hardin asks rhetorically whether any nation has solved, even at the intuitive level, the problem of finding the optimum population size (the optimum relationship between population and resources) and responds: 'One simple fact proves that none has: there is no prosperous population in the world today that has, and has had for some time, a growth rate of zero' (1968, p. 1244). In fact, in recent years the population of several European countries is no longer growing but actually shrinking. In the next half century, the European population is expected to fall by as much as 7%, but the rate of growth for the world population, since peaking in 1962–3, has been steadily falling (Wikipedia: World Population; Demographics of Europe). China has followed Hardin's advice (except for his recommendation of 'mutual coercion, mutually agreed upon by the majority of the people affected'). In Europe, the state has not directly enforced zero or negative population growth: the decline reflects spontaneous decisions by individual responding to a changing environment.

Spontaneous demographic transition suggests that population growth is (1) an endogenous phenomenon, and (2) within limits, government can indirectly influence population growth by manipulating material conditions (for instance, by improving job opportunities for women outside the home). We have no reason to conclude, however, that the forces of demographic transition will automatically guide the world population to the optimum level that Hardin discusses. Moreover, a shrinking, aging, and wealthy Europe surrounded by relatively poor and rapidly growing regions is an unstable situation—but that is another story.

Unintended but Beneficial Consequences?

Has 'The Tragedy' changed our views and policies regarding the overpopulation problem? I think not. Overpopulation was already front page news when the essay appeared. The essay's main contribution is an eloquent argument in favour of direct limits on reproductive rights. My informal impression is that Hardin's proposal of 'mutual coercion, mutually agreed upon' has fallen by the wayside, at least in North America and Europe. But the essay may have had consequences unintended by the author.

I did not read the 'Tragedy of the Commons' until about 20 years after its publication and then because I was studying communal property arrangements or regulated commons. I had noticed that nearly all the studies that I consulted cited Hardin's 'Tragedy', usually on the first page, and that the authors followed a common pattern by saying: In his classic study, Hardin got one thing wrong, he failed to recognize that the commons are often well managed. I still remember how surprised I was when I realized the 'Tragedy of the Commons' was a Malthusian essay on overpopulation and moreover the author used the concept of 'a commons open to all' as a metaphor. Hardin was discussing unregulated human breeding and compared the results to overexploitation of natural resources under open access.

Because the classics are known by all and read by few, they sometimes have unexpected functions. In the last decades of the 20th century, the study of regulated commons became an important research programme. Common property regimes play a critical and often beneficial role in the utilization of environmental resources. Yet in the 1960s, 1970s, and even later, many social scientists (and perhaps also Hardin) had partly forgotten this important form of exclusive property rights and often automatically associated a commons with open access. But no longer. The floodgates have opened and a new literature on communal arrangements pours out. Elinor Ostrom's (1990) *Governing the Commons: The*

Evolution of Institutions for Collective Actions, for instance, is a critical contribution to the new literature. In recent years the discussion and analysis of communal property applications extend beyond natural resource management into the realm of the digital revolution and the Internet. I speculate here that Hardin and his 'Tragedy' spontaneously became a focal point for coordinating the new governing-the-commons literature. In the early stages, the literature coalesced around a common theme: No matter what Hardin says, when conditions are right, well-defined local groups are well capable of setting up effective arrangements for communally utilizing, managing, and sustaining common pool natural resources. There need be no tragedy here. Thus, inadvertently, Hardin, like the Good Soldier Svejk, found himself in a war that was not of his making.

You may disagree with these speculations, but at least my story has a happy end.

References

Easterlin, R. A. (1998) *Growth Triumphant. The Twenty-first Century in Historical Perspective* (Ann Arbor: University of Michigan Press).

Ehrlich, P. R. (1968) *The Population Bomb* (New York: Ballantine Books).

Hardin, G. (1968) The tragedy of the commons, *Science*, 162, pp. 1243–1248.

Ostrom, E. (1990) *Governing the Commons: The Evolution of Institutions for Collective Action* (New York: Cambridge University Press).

Wikipedia (n.d.) World Population. Available at http://en.wikipedia.org/wiki/World_population (accessed 19 April 2009).

Wikipedia (n.d.) Demographics of Europe. Available at http://en.wikipedia.org/wiki/Demographics_of_Europe (accessed 19 April 2009).

Free Parking at Christmas Is Not a Tragedy of the Commons

WILLIAM A. FISCHEL

Dartmouth College, Hanover, NH, USA

The late Garrett Hardin's 1968 article, 'The Tragedy of the Commons', is among the most famous statements of the problem of establishing property rights. Without the ability to exclude strangers from grazing their cattle on a meadow, pumping oil from a common pool, or harvesting fish from the sea, unlimited entry will result in wasteful use of the resource and, usually, premature exhaustion of the stock. This is a 'tragedy' in the classical Greek sense because each of the participants in the extraction of resources may foresee the unhappy consequences but none can forebear from his or her actions without some external force.

One reason for the fame of Hardin's article is that, unlike the economists who had earlier analyzed the problem (Gordon, 1954), Hardin adopted an expansive view of the commons. Population growth was his primary target—'freedom to breed is intolerable' was one heading in his 1968 article—but he also included general degradation of environmental assets in which property rights cannot be easily established.

Part of the success of his article was that it used pithy, nontechnical examples. One of Hardin's claims about the source of the 'tragedy' is that there is a natural, populist tendency to undermine solutions to commons problems. He gave an example that surely resonated with many readers who had been frustrated by the scarcity of parking spaces:

> Education can counteract the natural tendency to do the wrong thing, but the inexorable succession of generations requires that the basis for this knowledge be constantly refreshed. A simple incident that occurred a few years ago in Leominster, Massachusetts, shows how perishable the knowledge is. During the Christmas shopping season the parking meters downtown were covered with plastic bags that bore tags reading: 'Do not open until after Christmas. Free parking courtesy of the mayor and city council'. In other words, facing the prospect of an increased demand for already scarce space, the city fathers reinstituted the system of the commons. (Cynically, we suspect that they gained more votes than they lost by this retrogressive act.)

This anecdote reinforces Hardin's pessimism about political attempts to forestall the tragedy of the commons. The mayor and council of Leominster are seen as pandering for populist acclaim by undermining the proper pricing of on-street parking exactly in the season when parking spaces are most scarce. More than one academic has sadly nodded his or her head in agreement. The message is clear. Politicians subject to the popular will, such as those in local governments, cannot be trusted to maintain, let alone adopt, institutional measures to overcome the tragedy of the commons.

The only problem with this story is that it is wrong. Not factually wrong; Leominster did declare a parking meter holiday around Christmas, as hundreds of cities did before and as many continue to do to this day. (More about Leominster at the end of this note.) What is wrong is Hardin's assumption that this policy was a suboptimal use of the resource, scarce street parking.

Parking meters establish hourly prices for downtown spaces. The optimal amount of meter time varies with the use to which the space is expected to be put. (Parking meter technology and pricing are described in Shoup [2003].) If the space is expected to be used by nine-to-five employees, the optimal maximum time is eight hours or so. But for most spaces in a retail business district, the optimal time for the meter is relatively brief, about an hour or less. People drive downtown, go into a pharmacy for a prescription, perhaps get a cup of coffee, and then go on their way. Merchants want these customers to move out of their parking spaces after their business is done. If the customer wants to walk the dog or spend several hours in the library, she should move out of the business district space and let another paying customer use the parking space.

In the month before Christmas, the retail experience changes. Most retailers get at least half of their revenue during this month. The valued customers are not just ducking in to pick up a paint brush. They are doing their Christmas shopping, and that will take longer than an hour. Merchants and the people who depend on them for their prosperity (especially the city government) want to make it easier for such customers to stay longer than an hour in the downtown area.

The technical problem is that the most commonly-used parking meters are not easily recalibrated to reflect seasonal demands: The meter that in July limits parking to one hour or less cannot be easily reprogrammed for a two- or three-hour maximum in December. The parking meter holiday is the answer that many cities have adopted in response to this inflexibility. Their calculation is that the meter revenue foregone will be more than offset by the increased profits from Christmas season sales. Thus the motive for the Christmas parking meter holiday is not populist pandering, but the maximization of the value of business property.

But a meter holiday does bring an obvious problem. How should the city manage the excess demand that free parking will generate? It is this excess demand that economists and Garrett Hardin properly worried about, and their instincts were to condemn the abandonment of the price system. But there are well-developed local institutions that have a stake in the parking situation. Nearly every community has a voluntary institution such as the Chamber of Commerce or Downtown Retailers Association that represent store owners before the city council. They are usually the ones requesting the parking meter holiday.

The store owners want the meter holiday to encourage Christmas shoppers to spend extra time (and dollars) downtown. They know that those free spaces can also be used by non-shoppers, who fall into two categories. One is the employees of the stores themselves. They are tempted to use the newly free and convenient spaces instead having to park at a more remote location. The other group consists of people who want to use downtown parking but have no institutional connection with the retailers.

The first group—employees of the businesses themselves—are more easily dealt with. The problem is not trivial, though. A business owner might tell his own employees not to park on the nearby streets in December and complain to them if he sees their cars out front, but parking in front of other businesses is difficult to detect. Nonetheless, when the stakes are as high as they are in December, businesses have an incentive to submit to collective restraints by the Chamber of Commerce and use various means to assure that their own employees do not upset the plans. A 4 December 1998 editorial from the St. Johnsbury, Vermont, *Caledonian Record* suggests that in a small town, moral suasion may supplement more direct disciplines:

Free To Shop Downtown St. Johnsbury

Credit St. Johnsbury officials for extending their season's greetings in the form of free downtown parking. Beginning Tuesday and lasting until Jan. 4, there will be no need to feed the parking meters. The parking spaces are free. The vast selection of merchandise found in the many shops in downtown St. Johnsbury makes for the perfect one (parking) spot shopping experience. And this holiday season, with the gift of free parking, shoppers can ignore the meters and focus on gift-buying. With the month-long free parking comes a responsibility to not abuse the privilege. The free spots are not for shop owners and employees. The spaces they leave open could be used by several people who just might stop into their store and spend money. The spaces are also not for tenants of downtown apartments. The shoppers themselves also need to realize that as they take advantage of the free parking and array of shops they can patronize without a parking time limit, another shopper also needs a place to park. Take your time, but move along when your shopping is done. So gift-seekers, shop away. The meter isn't running.

The second group whose moral hazard is a problem is not so easily dealt with. Car-parkers without ties to the retail business are unlikely to be told by their boss not to park in the best spaces. A large and diverse downtown may have residents who live in above-store apartments, students who park for daytime classes, employees of non-retail firms, and state-government workers, all of whom are unlikely to be subject to local discipline.

When the latter group is an important component of downtown demand for parking, alternative means of managing excess demand must be adopted. One of the easiest (though obviously less than ideal) is to limit the 'free parking' times to Saturdays and Sundays before Christmas, when non-retail firms, schools, and state offices usually do not operate. Another is to institute the free parking hours later in the morning, after most employees have had to be at work (and parked their cars) but before most Christmas shoppers would arrive. A third way of managing the commons is to have the meter-minders chalk tires instead of collecting meter revenues at the 'bagged' meters and issue overtime tickets only after two or three hours have elapsed.

My online searches indicated that all of these methods have been adopted in one place or another. It is evident, however, that the vast majority of parking meter holidays are conducted in relatively small cities. City council minutes from larger cities that experimented with meter holidays, such as Newark, New Jersey, did mention the problems that come from diversity of purposes in their downtowns, which in Newark's case largely frustrated the merchants' purposes.

The final question concerns the meter revenue foregone by the city when the free parking programme is in effect. One might reasonably ask why, if longer shopping hours in

December are important, the business community does not pay for the meter holiday. The issue does come up, but I found only one instance in which a private merchant group actually paid the city for estimated foregone revenues. The Laguna Beach (California) Visitors & Conference Bureau donated money to the city to 'to provide free parking in the downtown at on-street parking meters from December 17–24, 2004'.

In most other meter holidays, however, the city absorbed the cost. There were sometimes references to the increased sales taxes that the free parking would generate, but sales taxes are not common for most cities. And in one instance where it was mentioned, it was concluded that the additional sales tax revenue would not replace the meter revenues. When cost was discussed by city councils, the free meter programme was most often justified as a means of helping downtown merchants deal with competition from shopping malls in other jurisdictions. In other cases, council members expressed a desire to maintain property values in the downtown area or offer reciprocal benefits to retail firms for their support of community activities at other times of the year.

It is important to understand the role of downtown business districts for the municipalities that have them. For most towns, business districts contribute more in property tax revenues than they pay in services, largely because they do not house school children. They are also an important source of the municipality's identity and its social capital. Local business owners are often the mainstay of volunteer government, but their businesses also indirectly promote the city's interests. Residents who shop or dine or attend meetings in the business district will run into other residents. This promotes the network of acquaintances that makes running a community on a voluntary basis easier (Fischel, 2006). Aside from schools and school events, most residents of a community would have few occasions to casually meet their fellow citizens, since residence and employment are often in different jurisdictions. Subsidizing a parking meter holiday in order to keep downtown businesses viable may be a rational city investment even if the returns are difficult to compute with much precision.

In one sense, though, it does not matter whether the merchants pay the city government for the spaces or not. In either case, the decision-maker (the city council) perceives an opportunity cost (foregone revenues) and decides that having the spaces be free is worth that cost. One could actually agree with Garrett Hardin that this action 'gained more votes' for the city council. But calling this local management decision a 'retrogressive act' does not seem warranted by a closer look into the situation.

As mentioned earlier, the problem that meter holidays deal with was created by the inability to easily recalibrate parking meters to accommodate December shopping habits. Recent parking technology makes this problem obsolete (Shoup, 2003). Electronic meters can be easily reprogrammed to allow longer or shorter maximum stays, and other technologies allow parkers to pay for parking without selecting a time limit in advance. Prices for parking can also be varied. As these new technologies spread, there should be a decline in meter holidays. Cities will not have to balance the lost meter revenues against promoting business prosperity. (Some may still want to use free meters as advertising gimmicks, but that would require them to continue the awkward stratagems to deal with non-shopping parkers.)

Parking meter holidays are declining for another reason. The shopping malls have largely won the retail battle with downtowns. James J. Lanciani, Jr., who served as parking clerk for Leominster, MA, from 1987 to 2004 and has also been a longtime member of city council, told me in a phone interview (22 April 2005) that the demand for on-street parking hardly varies seasonally anymore. Leominster's downtown, like that of many small cities, is now largely given over to offices, banks, restaurants, and other quotidian services for which Christmas sales are not especially important.

Mr. Lanciani said that he discontinued bagging the meters in Leominster a year after assuming his duties in 1987. Instead of an organized programme, he simply stopped imposing overtime fines for the month of December. The few merchants who did depend on Christmas sales could tell customers that they did not have to feed the meters. Most of the non-retail businesses now have off-street parking for their employees, so their inclination to poach on-street parking spaces is not strong. Leominster's foregone revenue from overtime fines was not an issue because the number of metered spaces has dropped as the demand for street parking at all times has declined.

The foregoing remarks demonstrate that the creation of a parking commons during the holiday season is actually not a good example of, in Hardin's phrase, 'how perishable the knowledge is' of the need to ration resources by charging high prices for them. It is clear from almost all the city council deliberations about meter holidays that I located online that city officials knew what they were doing. Leominster was aware of the problems of rationing parking spaces when they were scarce and, like other cities, fine-tuned its programme to deal with those problems. When seasonal parking demand declined over the years, the city rationally cut back on the programme and adopted a low-cost substitute to accommodate the few firms that still cared about parking for Christmas shoppers.

Garrett Hardin (1994) later acknowledged that the general problem he was addressing concerned an 'unmanaged commons', to which no one could be excluded. The historical English commons, in which Hardin set his original parable about grazing animals, was actually reasonably efficient, given the farming and grazing technology of the time and the non-price methods of rationing its use (Dahlman, 1980). As Elinor Ostrom (1990) and others have discovered by painstaking research, traditional commons are often—not always—well managed and can be seen as efficient substitutes for a price system and private property when there are technical or cultural constraints on the operation of a market system. This note has argued that 'free parking at Christmas' appears to fit within this efficient group of commons.

Acknowledgement

I thank without implicating Donald Shoup for his comments, and James Lanciani, Jr., for information about parking in Leominster, Massachussetts.

References

Dahlman, C. J. (1980) *The Open Field System and Beyond: A Property Rights Analysis of an Economic Institution* (Cambridge: Cambridge University Press).

Fischel, W. A. (2006) Why voters veto vouchers: Public schools and community-specific social capital, *Economics of Governance*, 7 (May), pp. 109–132.

Gordon, H. S. (1954) The economic theory of a common property resource: The fishery, *Journal of Political Economy*, 62 (April), pp. 124–142.

Hardin, G. (1968) The tragedy of the commons, *Science*, 162 (December), pp. 1243–1248.

Hardin, G. (1994) The tragedy of the unmanaged commons, *Trends in Ecology and Evolution*, 9, p. 199.

Ostrom, E. (1990) *Governing the Commons: The Evolution of Institutions for Collective Action* (Cambridge: Cambridge University Press).

Shoup, D. C. (2003) Buying time at the curb, in: F. E. Foldvary & D. B. Klein (Eds) *The Half-Life of Policy Rationales: How New Technology Affects Old Policy Issues*, pp. 60–85 (New York: NYU Press).

Guarding the Guardians: Enforcement in the Commons

C. FORD RUNGE

Department of Applied Economics, University of Minnesota, St. Paul, Minnesota, USA

Mechanism Design and the Commons

The classical challenge 'But who will guard the guardians?' was issued by the Roman Juvenal in a warning to a friend not to marry because women cannot be trusted, and even if sequestered and guarded, who will guard their guardians? ('*Sed quis custodiet ipsos custodes?*') Five centuries earlier, Plato put the question in a political and social context, optimistically suggesting that a city-state can be entrusted to leaders who, because of their strength of character, will need no additional guardians. This optimistic view suggested that institutions might be arranged to provide what we today call 'accountability and oversight' in a self-enforcing system.

Juvenal and Plato thus stood, as Leonid Hurwicz noted in his 2007 Nobel economics lecture, on opposite ends of the pessimism/optimism continuum of mechanism design (Hurwicz, 2008, pp. 577–578). The guardian problem is closely related to the incentive and agency issues associated with commons dilemmas and public goods provision outlined by Samuelson (1955), Hardin (1968), Groves and Ledyard (1977), and many others. Many solutions to problems of public goods provision were shown to depend on agents who truthfully revealed their preferences. But agents would always have an incentive to misrepresent these preferences and 'free ride'.

The depiction of commons dilemmas as a form of free rider problem has also been widely discussed as requiring some type of enforcement. In Hardin's words, it required 'mutual coercion, mutually agreed upon' (Hardin, 1968, p. 1247). Yet casual empiricism supports the more optimistic Platonic view that social rules (mechanisms) can be found that achieve objectives (although seldom Pareto-efficiency) and are also self-enforcing, even if incentives to misrepresent preference exist. Mutual coercion, mutually agreed upon, actually seems to occur. Examples include cases in which each guardian is also guarded by others in a logical 'circle', appealing to the sort of social norms found in successful cases of common property or joint resource use (see Ostrom *et al.,* 1992).

In previous work (Runge, 1981, 1984), I have argued that the search for dominant strategies associated with unique Nash-type equilibria in various games including commons dilemmas has overlooked the importance of game forms that involve multiple equilibria and the absence of dominant strategy mechanisms. In such cases, agents must formulate strategies conditional not on a fixed expectation of others' actions, but the realization that what they do will affect what I do and vice-versa. This inherently strategic setting, present in much of Schelling's work (e.g. the *Strategy of Conflict*, 1960) invited recognition of the role of institutions (norms) in regulating and regularizing each individual's expectation of the likely behaviour of others (see Myerson, 2006). The norms can include those of common property (Runge & Defrancesco, 2006).

Let us return to the pessimistic view of Juvenal, in which the problem arises from an incentive to shirk one's duty as a guardian. This takes the form of a classic prisoner's dilemma (PD), in which two guardians (A and B) are faced with a choice: guard faithfully or shirk guarding.

In this case, the payoff to guarding faithfully if both guards do so is clearly Pareto-superior (2,2), and the payoff if both shirk is clearly inferior, since they will face penalties for shirking (1,1). However, if guard A shirks while guard B guards faithfully (0,3), he benefits while the other guard loses out. Since this outcome dominates faithful service (3 > 2), and applies to both guards' incentives $(3 > 2)_A$; $(3 > 2)_B$, both have a dominant strategy to shirk, leading to a Pareto-inferior equilibrium outcome (1,1)*.

The result is a requirement of enforcement 'from above' by a guardian of the guardians. But if this is the continuing structure of incentives, the problem of enforcement simply creates the same dilemma at a higher level, an 'infinite regress of guardians, with the guardian of order k needed to guard the guardian of order k with $k=2,3,....$, *ad infinitum*. Since an infinity of guardians is not usually available, this seems to preclude the possibility of enforcement!' (Hurwicz, 2008, p. 582).

Yet we know of many situations where rules are substantially (even if not perfectly) implemented and/or enforced. Suppose that the guards know that they are part of a community in which infidelity to guard-duty, when known, will lead to what Schelling called the 'pain of conspicuousness'. This sanction may seem mild, but may be sufficient to alter the payoff structure such that the problem becomes a non-symmetrical coordination game, or 'assurance problem' (AP) (Sen, 1967; Runge, 1981; Sandler, 1997).

Here, guarding faithfully is a jointly Pareto-superior strategy for both A and B. The temptation still exists to shirk from guarding if the other guard shirks too $(4,1)_A$ and $(1,4)_B$. However, if both guards follow their temptation, they will be led to an outcome inferior to joint fidelity: (4,4). Hence, if guard A expects guard B to shirk, he will be as

	B Guard faithfully	Shirk guarding
A		
Guard faithfully	(2,2)	(0,3)
Shirk guarding	(3,0)	(1,1)*

Figure 1. Prisoners' Dilemma (PD).

A \ B	Guard faithfully	Shirk guarding
Guard faithfully	*(5,5)	(4,1)
Shirk guarding	(1,4)	*(4,4)

Figure 2. Assurance Problem (AP).

worse off if he shirks too (4,4) and definitely worse off if he does not shirk (1,4). But if he expects guard B to guard faithfully, he is better off if he does so as well (5,5). There is no dominant strategy, and two equilibria: (5,5) and (4,4). One is Pareto-superior: (5,5). Put less formally, it does not predict that the problem of the guardians (or the commons dilemma or free rider problem) *will* be solved; only that they *can* be solved (Sugden, 1984; Runge, 1984). As Schelling described it: 'The force of many rules of etiquette and social restraint . . . seem(s) to depend on their having become 'solutions' to a coordination game: everyone expects everyone to expect observance, so that non-observance carries the pain of conspicuousness' (1960, p. 91).

In the first game (PD), it does not matter what guard A or guard B expects the other to do: they both have a dominant strategy to shirk. But in the second game, (AP) expectations are of the essence; and a degree of uncertainty surrounds the choice of strategy. If the subjective probability defined over the alternatives is complementary, and A expects B to guard faithfully (GF) or shirk guarding (SG) with equal probability, then:

$$\text{Prob}_B \text{ GF} = \text{Prob}_B \text{ SG} = 0.5. \tag{1}$$

Then the expected payoff (assuming Von Neuman–Morgenstern axioms of expected utility) is:

$$0.5 \times 5 + 0.5 \times 4 = 2.5 + 2 = 4.5. \tag{2}$$

By contrast, if the subjective probability attached by A to B's action is weighted in favour of guarding faithfully and vice versa, say 70% to 30%, their expected payoff is:

$$0.7 \times 5 + 0.3 \times 4 = 3.5 + 1.2 = 4.7. \tag{3}$$

Since 4.7 > 4.5, guard A is clearly better off to guard faithfully the greater his expectation is weighted in favour of B guarding faithfully, and vice-versa.

The question, from the point of view of mechanism design, is whether the 'pain of conspicuousness' alone is sufficient to shift both the payoffs and probabilities in favour of fidelity, or whether other institutional norms or mechanisms may be necessary. Consider norms such as right-hand drive. Driving on the right (or left) side of the road is a coordination norm which depends on 'everyone expecting everyone else to expect observance'. Not only does non-observance carry the pain of conspicuousness, it may cause the pain of death. It is thus a norm in which the welfare of drivers is protected by knowing the rule applies both to others and to oneself.

'Nested' Supergames and Historical Examples

Schotter (1981, p. 165, n. 8) makes such enforcement part of a supergame model, in which rather than an infinite regress of incentives to shirk, at some level the circle is closed by the obligations of guardians to those who benefit from their guardianship. As Hurwicz, in an early version of his Nobel address (1998, p. 13) comments:

> [I]n principle, it is conceivable that a second order guardian might be found who could effectively supervise the first order guardian's discharge of his duties and be so beholden to the husband that he would in effect make sure the immediate guardian does discharge his duties. This would close the circle.

If the dominant strategy equilibrium is abandoned in favour of a strategic interaction of the sort described in the AP, strategic behaviour becomes not a barrier but an essential feature of the game. As Gibbard and Satterthwaite proved in a different context (voting schemes), there is no rule that is 'strategy-proof' (Gibbard, 1973; Satterthwaite, 1975).

Consider some historical examples drawn from social behaviour in the Anglo-Saxon world of 1000 AD, some of which take the 'nested' form. In 1000 AD, English King Athelstan maintained his authority using an oath of 'fealty' or loyalty sworn by every boy before the age of 12: "'Even as it behooves a man to be faithful to his lord", the king instructed, "no one shall conceal the breach of it on the part of a brother or family relation, any more than a stranger"' (Lacey & Danziger, 1999, p. 151). This oath went above the question of whether it was advantageous to be disloyal to the king and misrepresent one's own preference, making it one's duty to report the misrepresentations of the preferences of others.

Each became, in effect, their brothers' keeper, or as Lacey and Danziger put it: 'Guardian Angels meet Neighborhood Watch'. The oath, known as the 'frank pledge', allowed England's shires to be subdivided into groupings of hundreds of households—'hundreds'—which in turn were subdivided into groups of 10 or a dozen households. In such relatively small groupings, the 'pain of conspicuousness' would be greater than in an anonymous mass, and the capacity to judge the relative probability of shirking improved by propinquity and better information. The result was to convert incentives to shirk one's loyalty to the king to incentives to be loyal by downloading loyalty oaths from the king's lords to the hundreds, and from them to groups of 10 or so households. By such downloading, public goods were made more local, and the principle-agent problem was converted into one similar to the Assurance Problem discussed above. When the system was scaled up through the levels of authority from below,

> The essence of the frank pledge system was that it transformed obeying the rules from a matter of personal obedience into personal loyalty, which was then extended up the ladder in a series of comprehensible steps to the principal lord, whose authority was endorsed by God. (Lacey & Danziger, 1999, p. 152)

The Case of Common Property

This structure of incentives may also explain why social arrangements of joint use or common property are advantageous in certain choice environments, and by no means a 'tragedy' in all (Runge, 1981). In these cases, the incentives take the 'circular' form described by Hurwicz. A common grazing area or forest with a shirking rule, in which each commoners' cattle or sheep or cutting of wood are observable to others, allows each to monitor all. Because the domain is local, no 'nesting' of authority is required. Again, this assumes a certain familiarity with the village stock and forest, and reduced payoffs or ostracism if violations of the rules are found out. But in historic time, these were not unrealistic conditions. In England, in 1000 AD,

> The average Anglo-Saxon could probably recognise every duck, chicken, and pig in his village and knew whom it belonged to – as he knew everything about his neighbours' lives . . . So just as the village livestock grazed together on communal pasture, the fields created for arable cultivation were also organised on a community basis, with each unit of ploughland taking the form of a long and comparatively narrow strip. (Lacey and Danziger, 1999, pp. 43–44)

A second common pool resource was the village watermill. In the Domesday books recorded by the Normans after their 1066 conquest, England was found to have 5624 watermills, nearly one for every village and hamlet. While each villager might grind their grain in a mortar, a stone mill powered by water or animal draft enjoyed clear economies of scale. Like the plough team, the mill was operated in common by the village (Hoskins, 1970, p. 81). This joint ownership conferred certain rights to bring grain to be ground into flour, and certain obligations by villagers to support the miller in the maintenance of his mill.

Norms Appropriating Divine Guidance

Where the 'pain of conspicuousness' is not enough, norms may appropriate religious or other conventions, raising the stakes of non-compliance by declaring a lack of fealty to be a sin. One of the chronic problems of medieval agriculture was the tendency of grain stocks to be so depleted by poor harvests or post-harvest losses from moisture and pests that there was insufficient grain left to plant for the next year. Depleted seed stock in one year led to less grain the following year, in a downward spiral of scarcity. The survey of the royal manor of Annapes in the 10th century describes the ratio of grain set aside for sowing fresh fields in the spring to the total harvest the previous fall. In one rather poor year, these were 54% of the previous spelt harvest, 60% of the wheat, 62% of the barley and the whole of the rye harvest (Duby, 1974, p. 29).

At the margin, the most crucial time of year was the month or two before the planting moon, when grain needed to be guarded for seed to make the next crop. After one final Bacchanalian feast day now called Fat Tuesday (Mardi Gras), a period of fasting began that was marked by counting backward using the lunar calendar from the planting moon to the beginning of Lent.

Lent is the 40 days prior to Easter, which is set by the first Sunday following the first ecclesiastical full moon that occurs on or after the vernal equinox (21 March) based on

Gregorian rules set by Emperor Constantine in 325 AD. The full moon before Easter is called the Egg Moon, and the Lenten moon the last moon on or before 21 March. Hence the Lenten and Egg moons cover the period from late March to late April, when grain is sown. The Egg Moon, not surprisingly, is known in European folklore as the sprouting grass moon, fish moon, and seed moon. By attaching a Christian duty to the need to fast, and invoking the need to substitute fish protein for bread, the Lenten strictures reinforced the inventory management so critical to survival by promoting the saving of seed from grain stocks.

Information and Institutional Decline

The possibility that social institutions can function effectively by enforcing norms and providing accountability is fraught with the potential for breakdowns in the structures of authority. The information conveyed in the 'message space' of norms and institutions will degrade over time unless effort is expended to maintain it. If the theory developed above is correct, 'tragedy' will result not from dominant strategies to free ride, but from the degradation of this information set. As the capacity of common property or other rules to predict the likely behaviour of others declines, the loss of information can be thought of as entropic (Gray, 2008). Like any system, maintaining the information contained in a norm or institution requires potential work. Thus, a mechanism to guard the guardians, or maintain the commons, will not be free of effort.

References

Duby, G. (1974) *The Early Growth of the European Economy* (Ithaca, NY: Cornell University Press).

Gibbard, A. (1973) Manipulation of voting schemes: A general result, *Econometrica*, 41 (4), pp. 587–601.

Gray, R. M. (2008) *Entropy and Information Theory* (New York: Springer Verlag).

Groves, T., & Ledyard, J. (1977) Optimal allocation of public goods: A solution to the free rider problem, *Econometrica* 45, pp. 783–811.

Hardin, G. (1968) The tragedy of the commons, *Science*, 162, pp. 1243–1248.

Hoskins, W. G. (1970) *The Making of the English Landscape* (London: Pelican).

Hurwicz, L. (1998) But who will guard the guardians? Department of Economics, University of Minnesota, May 13. Working paper.

Hurwicz, L. (2008) 'But who will guard the guardians?' Nobel Prize Lecture, *American Economic Review*, 98 (3), pp. 577–585.

Lacey, R., & Danziger, D. (1999) *The Year 1000 – What Life was Like at the Turn of the First Millennium – An Englishman's World* (Boston: Little, Brown and Company).

Myerson, R. B. (2006) Learning from Schelling's 'Strategy of Conflict'. Paper prepared for a conference in honor of Thomas C. Schelling. University of Maryland, September 29.

Ostrom, E., Walker, J., & Gardner, R. (1992) Covenants with and without the sword: Self-governance is possible, *American Political Science Review*, 86, pp. 404–417.

Runge, C. F. (1981) Common property externalities: Isolation, assurance and resource depletion in a traditional grazing context, *American Journal of Agricultural Economics*, 63 (4), pp. 595–606.

Runge, C. F. (1984) Institutions and the free rider: The assurance problem in collective action, *Journal of Politics*, 46 (1), pp. 154–181.

Runge, C. F., & Defrancesco, E. (2006) Exclusion, inclusion and enclosure: Historical commons and modern intellectual property, *World Development*, 34 (10), pp. 1713–1727.

Samuelson, P. A. (1955) Diagramatic exposition of a theory of public expenditure, *The Review of Economics and Statistics*, 37 (Nov), pp. 350–356.

Sandler, T. (1997) *Global Challenges: An Approach to Environmental, Political and Economic Problems* (Cambridge: Cambridge University Press).

Satterthwaite, M. A. (1975) Strategy-proofness and Arrow's conditions: Existence and correspondence theorems for voting procedures and social welfare functions, *Journal of Economic Theory*, 10 (Apr), pp. 187–217.

Schelling, T. C. (1960) *The Strategy of Conflict* (Cambridge, MA: Harvard University Press).

Schotter, A. (1981) *The Economic Theory of Social* Institutions (Cambridge: Cambridge University Press).

Sen, A. K. (1967) Isolation, assurance and the social rate of discount, *Quarterly*, 81 (1), pp. 112–124.

Sugden, R. (1984) Reciprocity: The supply of public goods through voluntary contributions, *Economic Journal*, 94 (Dec), pp. 772–787.

From 'Tragedy' to Commons: How Hardin's Mistake Might Save the World

PETER A. WALKER

University Geography Department, University of Oregon, Eugene, OR, USA

Each fall term at the University of Oregon, the first reading I assign to 220 or so students in my Introduction to Environmental Studies course is a summary and discussion of Garrett Hardin's classic essay 'The Tragedy of the Commons' (Hardin, 1968). This might not be surprising, since Hardin's essay is often required reading at or near the beginning of many textbooks in environmental studies and related fields. The choice to begin with Hardin's essay might seem more surprising, however, in a course taught by a social scientist such as myself, trained since graduate school in often quite harsh critiques of Hardin's work. I, like many social scientists, consider Hardin's essay deeply flawed as social analysis, and still worse as a prescription for policy. Why, then, does this article continue to hold such a prominent position, even among its critics? The reasons are instructive.

First, without question Hardin's essay is important because, right or wrong, it has been so hugely influential. According to the Web of Science bibliographic reference database, as of April 2009 Hardin's article had been referenced in 3486 scientific articles, which almost certainly greatly under-states the influence of the essay in the scientific as well as popular literature, news media, textbooks, and so on. By any measure, Hardin's 'Tragedy of the Commons' is one of the most influential scientific articles of the 20th century. If for no other reason, students and scholars should read this article because it represents a land-mark of scholarly thought with which anyone engaged in the study of human-environment relations should be familiar.

Second, and more importantly, I assign this reading to my students because it is such a powerful illustration of the force that particular configurations of social relationships can exert on human-environmental interactions. This is no small thing. Those of us in the social sciences (probably excluding economics) forget sometimes how marginal our work is considered by much of the rest of the world. When I first began as a new assistant professor in an environmental studies programme, at a faculty meeting an eminent environmental chemist challenged me by asking what social science has to do with the environment. The chemist asked, with sincere skepticism, 'Where's the beef?' Had I not been so intimidated by my senior colleague, I would have responded by asking whether the chemist was familiar with the idea of the 'tragedy of the commons'—a rare example of social analysis that has been accepted as something akin to scientific 'law' by much of the science community. Much to his credit, considering that he was writing close to the high-water mark of technical-managerial optimism in the 1960s, Hardin argued for the existence of 'a class of human problems which can be called "no technical solution problems"' (Hardin, 1968, p. 1243). The widespread acceptance of Hardin's essay among scientists should be evidence, I would have argued to my senior colleague, that some social analysis is more than self-absorbed, postmodern navel-gazing. Hardin's 'tragedy' is so logically clear and seductively powerful that even people uninitiated in the social analysis can immediately and easily grasp its significance (indeed, that is much of its own shortcoming—but more on this shortly). For new students and senior scientists alike, Hardin's 'tragedy' speaks powerfully to the value of understanding social relationships as critical factors that shape human-environmental interactions. That is an important and useful contribution of Hardin's essay.

Third and finally, Hardin's 'Tragedy of the Commons' merits serious attention because, paradoxically, through its intellectual failings it launched a large body of vibrant and vitally important scholarship and research on the relationships between social organization and human use of the environment. Indeed, it might be fair to say that if human societies manage to escape today's impending human-environmental 'tragedies', this happy outcome may be owed in part to the flaws in Hardin's article that spurred so much good and important research on critically important topics ranging from local land use management to coping with global climate change. Before expanding on this point, however, a brief genealogy of Hardin's essay is in order.

It should be acknowledged (as Hardin himself does) that the 'Tragedy of the Commons' was not Hardin's own idea. Rather, as Hardin puts it,

> With Adam Smith's work as a model, I had assumed that the sum of separate ego-serving decisions would be the best possible one for the population as a whole. But presently I discovered that I agreed much more with William Forster Lloyd's conclusions, as given in his Oxford lectures of 1833. Citing what happened to pasturelands left open to many herds of cattle, Lloyd pointed out that, with a resource available to all, the greediest herdsmen would gain—for a while. But mutual ruin was just around the corner. (Hardin 1998, p. 682).

Readers familiar with Hardin's work will recognize that this is the core concept that Hardin imported into his essay. Hardin also did not coin the term 'tragedy of the commons'—that, too, he borrowed from Lloyd's 1833 lectures (see Lloyd, 1968). Moreover, very similar arguments had been made by Malthus long before (1798).

So, having settled the matter of intellectual paternity, what, exactly, *did* Hardin add that made his essay so influential, whereas Lloyd's lectures had been largely forgotten by history? It is Hardin, and not Lloyd or even Malthus, who is required reading in nearly every introductory environmental studies course today. Why?

For one thing, Hardin's timing was better. Hardin's essay appeared in print in *Science* magazine in December 1968, just as the American environmental movement of the 1960s and 1970s was gaining tremendous momentum, and American culture and politics were primed to receive an authoritative scientific voice in favour of strong policies. Importantly, Hardin's essay was not directly about the environment; rather, it was about the alleged necessity to control human population growth—an idea that reached near-fever pitch in the 1960s and 1970s when global human populations were indeed growing at historically unprecedented rates. The yearly *rate* of increase in the global human population (rather total numbers) peaked at almost the exact date that Hardin's essay was published (and has declined steadily since then). Both Lloyd and Malthus wrote at times when populations in Europe were increasing dramatically, but *global* population growth was relatively modest and mass popular concern about population and environmental issues had not yet emerged.

In addition to writing at a fortuitous time (in terms of publication impact, that is), I submit that Hardin's essay became so influential in no small part because of its simultaneously admirable and problematic simplicity. One of the most striking things about the essay is that it is less than six pages long, and the core argument is presented in nine paragraphs on two pages (1968, pp. 1244–1245). Hardin's writing is succinct, clear, and (to borrow from his own wording) 'remorselessly' seductive in the sense that the reader can immediately grasp the powerful logical argument that Hardin makes, without necessarily carefully examining the many problematic assumptions that Hardin builds quietly into his model. It may be relevant to note that Hardin was a professor of biology (UC Santa Barbara). Many social scientists, frankly, could learn from Hardin's clear and succinct writing. The power of the essay derives in no small measure from this clarity.

Nevertheless, as alluded to earlier, one finds this powerfully seductive logic deeply problematic upon closer examination. For example, Hardin begins his main theoretical argument with the misleadingly benign request to 'Picture a pasture open to all' (1968, p. 1244). Hardin's pasture, however, is mainly hypothetical—presented outside of specific geographic, historical, or social context. As many have noted, to the limited degree that Hardin alludes to any *actual* pasture, his model appears to derive from old English pastures that were in fact *not* 'open to all'; rather, in the real-life circumstances from which Hardin abstracted his largely hypothetical model, communities 'often dealt with conflicts and ecological problems associated with their common lands by creating rules about their use' (McCay & Acheson, 1987, p. 16). Nowhere in Hardin's hypothetical example is there room for the possibility of effective collective management; and Hardin's conclusion that the only 'solutions' are government control or privatization rests precisely on this empirically flawed assumption. Moreover, as many have demonstrated in rebuttal to Hardin, such customary management may be preferred by local users and more effective in conserving resources than privatization or government control (e.g. Peters, 1994).

As any Hollywood scriptwriter might point out, however, facts alone do not tell compelling stories. In contrast, Hardin's 'story', flawed as it is, does indeed seem 'inherently' and 'remorselessly' compelling. Hardin's parable is clear, concise, intuitively sensible, and frightening. Viewed from this perspective, it may not be surprising that in the 40-plus years since the publication of Hardin's essay, the stacks of deeply empirically and theoretically supported research rebutting Hardin's argument do not hold a candle to the influence that Hardin's story still has on much of the scholarly and public imagination.

The fact that Hardin's model may still dominate in the world of introductory environmental studies textbooks, and perhaps in the minds of some scholars, does not, however, mean that his model has trumped more rigorous inquiry. Far from it. In response to Hardin's 'tragedy' has emerged a much deeper understanding of the commons. Hardin's argument helped stimulate a large, vibrant, and important body of scholarship that focuses precisely on the critically important gaps in the 'tragedy' model. Researchers demonstrated that Hardin had failed to distinguish between truly unregulated open-access regimes ('*res nullis*'), and 'common property'—defined as resources where access is shared, but is exclusive to particular social groups who define rules-of-use (Cirancy-Wantrup & Bishop, 1975). As Hardin himself later acknowledged, 'the weightiest mistake in ['The Tragedy of the Commons'] paper was the omission of the modifying adjective "unmanaged"' (Hardin, 1998, p. 683). Thus, the story Hardin told was about an *unmanaged* resource, which he acknowledges is a very different beast than the rich variety of jointly-managed commons revealed in field studies across the world—from lobstering communities in Maine, to grazing communities in Botswana, to complex irrigation-based communities in Asia (McCay & Acheson, 1987; Lansing, 1991; Ostrom, 1992). Moreover, in addition to this rich body of empirical field-based research, rebuttals to Hardin's argument contributed to a highly-developed body of theoretical scholarship (e.g. Ostrom, 1990). This area of study now includes major scholarly institutions such as the International Association for the Study of the Commons, which holds biennial conferences in venues across the globe in which scholars examine precisely the theoretical and empirical gaps that Hardin's essay so clearly (albeit unintentionally) helped to identify.

It something close to an institutional ritual in this emergent scholarly community to begin any work with a critique of Hardin's essay. Yet, it might be equally appropriate to express gratitude. Generations of graduate students (myself included) began their scholarly careers with various exercises in critiquing Hardin. In telling a compelling-but-flawed story, Hardin became the face that launched a thousand scholarly ships. As the world today struggles to cope with urgent and complex challenges to protect resources that by their nature must be managed through collective actions (e.g. global climate, biodiversity, land use decisions, park management), the vibrant scholarship that today explores the many ingenious and effective ways that societies throughout history have overcome the collective-action challenges that Hardin identified may come to play a key role in resolving some of the world's most daunting concerns. Paradoxically, if the world does find ways to overcome the worst effects of (for example) global climate change or biodiversity loss, we may have the *bête noir* of social science graduate studies, the intellectual *agent provocateur* from Santa Barbara, partly to thank.

References

Cirancy-Wantrup, S. V., & Bishop, R. C. (1975) 'Common property' as a concept in natural resources policy, *Natural Resources Journal*, 15(4), pp. 713–728.

Hardin, G. (1998) Extensions of 'The Tragedy of the Commons', *Science*, 280 (5364), pp. 682'683.

Hardin, G. (1968) The tragedy of the commons, *Science*, 162(Dec. 13), pp. 1243–1248.

Lansing, J. S. (1991) *Priests and Programmers: Technologies of Power in the Engineered Landscape of Bali* (Princeton, NJ: Princeton University Press).

Lloyd, W. F. (1968) *Lectures on Population, Value, Poor-Laws, and Rent, Delivered in the University of Oxford During the Years 1832, 1833, 1834, 1835 & 1836, Reprints of Economic Classics* (New York: A. M. Kelley).

Malthus, T. R. (1798) An essay on the principle of population, in: P. Appleman (Ed) *An Essay on the Principle of Population* (New York: W. W. Norton).

McCay, B. J., & Acheson, J. M. (1987) *The Question of the Commons: The Culture and Ecology of Communal Resources* (Tucson: University of Arizona).

Ostrom, E. (1990) *Governing the Commons: The Evolution of Institutions for Collective Action* (Cambridge: Cambridge University Press).

Ostrom, E. (1992) *Crafting Institutions for Self-Governing Irrigation Systems* (San Francisco: ICS Press).

Peters, P. E. (1994) *Dividing the Commons: Politics, Policy, and Culture in Botswana* (Charlottesville: University Press of Virginia).

In memoriam

Elinor Ostrom (1933–2012)

Courtesy of Indiana University

Collective action and the evolution of social norms

Elinor Ostrom

Center for the Study of Institutions, Population, and Environmental Change, Indiana University, Bloomington, IN, USA

With the publication of *The Logic of Collective Action* in 1965, Mancur Olson challenged a cherished foundation of modern democratic thought that groups would tend to form and take collective action whenever members jointly benefitted. Instead, Olson (1965, p. 2) offered the provocative assertion that no self-interested person would contribute to the production of a public good: '[U] nless the number of individuals in a group is quite small, or unless there is coercion or some other special device to make individuals act in their common interest, *rational, self-interested individuals will not act to achieve their common or group interests.'* This argument soon became known as the 'zero contribution thesis.'

The idea that rational agents were not likely to cooperate in certain settings, even when such cooperation would be to their mutual benefit, was also soon shown to have the structure of an n-person prisoner's dilemma game (Hardin, 1971, 1982). Indeed, the prisoner's dilemma game, along with other social dilemmas, has come to be viewed as the canonical representation of collective action problems (Lichbach, 1996). The zero contribution thesis underpins the presumption in policy textbooks (and many contemporary public policies) that individuals cannot overcome collective action problems and need to have externally enforced rules to achieve their own long-term self-interest.

The zero contribution thesis, however, contradicts observations of everyday life. After all, many people vote, do not cheat on their taxes, and contribute effort to voluntary associations. Extensive fieldwork has by now established that individuals in all walks of life and all parts of the world voluntarily organize themselves so as to gain the benefits of trade, to provide mutual protection against risk, and to create and enforce rules that protect

Earlier versions of this paper have been presented at seminars at the Workshop in Political Theory and Policy Analysis, Indiana University; Department of Political Science, Gothenburg University; and the Beijer Institute of Ecological Economics, at the Royal Swedish Academy of Sciences in Stockholm. I appreciate the helpful comments made by Iris Bohnet, Juan-Camilo Cardenas,J Bradford De Long, Bruno Frey, Werner Guth, Roy Gardner, Steffen Huck, Alan Krueger, Fabrice Lehoucq, Frank Maier-Rigaud, Mike McGinnis, Timothy Taylor, Jimmy Walker, and the outstanding editing by Patty Dalecki. Support by the Ford Foundation, the MacArthur Foundation, and the National Science Foundation (Grant #SBR 9521918) is gratefully acknowledged.

Originally published in the "Journal of Economic Perspectives", 14 (3) (Summer 2000): 137-158. Reproduced with kind permission of the American Economic Association.

natural resources.[1] Solid empirical evidence is mounting that governmental policy can frustrate, rather than facilitate, the private provision of public goods (Montgomery & Bean, 1999). Field research also confirms that the temptation to free ride on the provision of collective benefits is a universal problem. In all known self-organized resource governance regimes that have survived for multiple generations, participants invest resources in monitoring and sanctioning the actions of each other so as to reduce the probability of free riding (Ostrom, 1990).

While these empirical studies have posed a severe challenge to the zero contribution theory, these findings have not yet been well integrated into an accepted, revised theory of collective action. A substantial gap exists between the theoretical prediction that self-interested individuals will have extreme difficulty in coordinating collective action and the reality that such cooperative behavior is widespread, although far from inevitable.

Both theorists and empirical researchers are trying to bridge this gap. Recent work in game theory-often in a symbiotic relationship with evidence from experimental studies-has set out to provide an alternative micro theory of individual behavior that begins to explain anomalous findings (Bowles, 1998; Fehr & Schmidt, 1999; McCabe, Rassenti, & Smith, 1996; Rabin, 1993; Selten, 1991). On the empirical side, considerable effort has gone into trying to identify the key factors that affect the likelihood of successful collective action (Baland & Platteau, 1996; Feeny, Berkes, McCay, & Acheson, 1990; Ostrom, forthcoming).

This paper will describe both avenues of research on the underpinnings of collective action, first focusing on the experimental evidence and potential theoretical explanations, and then on the real-world empirical evidence. This two-pronged approach to the problem has been a vibrant area of research that is yielding many insights. A central finding is that the world contains multiple types of individuals, some more willing than others to initiate reciprocity to achieve the benefits of collective action. Thus, a core question is how potential cooperators signal one another and design institutions that reinforce rather than destroy conditional cooperation. While no full-blown theory of collective action yet exists, evolutionary theories appear most able to explain the diverse findings from the lab and the field and to carry the nucleus of an overarching theory.

Laboratory evidence on rational choice in collective action situations

Most studies by political economists assume a standard model of rational individual action-what I will call a rational egoist. A wide range of economic experiments have found that the rational egoist assumption works well in predicting the outcome in auctions and competitive market situations (Kagel & Roth, 1995). While subjects do not arrive at the predicted equilibrium in the first round of market experiments, behavior closely approximates the predicted equilibrium by the end of the first five rounds in these experiments. One of the major successes of experimental economics is to demonstrate the robustness of microeconomic theory for explaining market behavior.

In regard to collective action situations, on the other hand, the results are entirely different. Linear public good experiments are widely used for examining the willingness of individuals to overcome collective action problems. In a linear public good experiment, each individual is endowed with a fixed set of assets and must decide how many of these assets to contribute to a public good. When an individual makes a contribution of, say, 10 units to the public good, each of the participants in the group, including that individual, receive a benefit of, say, five units apiece. In this setting, the optimal outcome for the group of players as a whole is for everyone to contribute all of their endowments to provide the public good (if a group of 10 people, each individual contribution of 10 will have a social payoff of 50!). However, the unique equilibrium for rational egoists in a single-shot game is that everyone contributes zero, since each individual has access to benefits of the public good funded by the contributions of others, without paying any costs.[2]

If the public goods game is played for a finite number of rounds, zero is also the predicted equilibrium for every round. Rational egoists will reason that zero contribution is the equilibrium in the last round, and because they expect everyone to contribute zero in the last round, they also expect everyone to contribute zero in the second-to-last round, and eventually by backward induction they will work their way to the decision not to contribute to the public good in the present. Of course, these predictions are based on the assumptions that all players are fully rational and interested only in their own immediate financial payoff, that all players understand the structure of the game fully and believe that all other players are fully rational, and that no external actor can enforce agreements between the players.

Since the first public good experiments were undertaken by Dawes, McTavish, and Shaklee (1977), a truly huge number of such experiments has been undertaken under various conditions (see Davis & Holt, 1993; Ledyard, 1995; and Offerman, 1997, for an overview). By now seven general findings have been replicated so frequently that these can be considered the core facts that theory needs to explain.

(1) Subjects contribute between 40 and 60% of their endowments to the public good in a one-shot game as well as in the first round of finitely repeated games.

(2) After the first round, contribution levels tend to decay downward, but remain well above zero. A repeated finding is that over 70% of subjects contribute nothing in the announced last round of a finitely repeated sequence.

(3) Those who believe others will cooperate in social dilemmas are more likely to cooperate themselves. A rational egoist in a public good game, however, should not in any way be affected by a belief regarding the contribution levels of others. The dominant strategy is a zero contribution no matter what others do.

(4) In general, learning the game better tends to lead to more cooperation, not less. In a clear test of an earlier speculation that it just took time for subjects to learn the predicted equilibrium strategy in public good games, Isaac, Walker, and Williams (1994) repeated the same game for 10 rounds, 40 rounds, and 60 rounds with experienced subjects who were specifically told the end period of each design. They found that the rate of decay is inversely related to the number of decision rounds. In other words, instead of learning *not* to cooperate, subjects learn how to cooperate at a moderate level for ever-longer periods of time!

(5) Face-to-face communication in a public good game – as well as in other types of social dilemmas – produces substantial increases in cooperation that are sustained across all periods including the last period (Ostrom & Walker, 1997).[3] The strong effect of communication is not consistent with currently accepted theory, because verbal agreements in these experiments are not enforced. Thus, communication is only 'cheap talk' and makes no difference in predicted outcomes in social dilemmas. But instead of using this opportunity to fool others into cooperating, subjects use the time to discuss the optimal joint strategy, to extract promises from one another, and to give verbal tongue-lashings when aggregate contributions fall below promised levels. Interestingly, when communication is implemented by allowing subjects to signal promises to cooperate through their computer

terminals, much less cooperation occurs than in experiments allowing face-to-face communication.

(6) When the structure of the game allows it, subjects will expend personal resources to punish those who make below-average contributions to a collective benefit, including the last period of a finitely repeated game. No rational egoist is predicted to spend anything to punish others, since the positive impact of such an action is shared equally with others whether or not they also spend resources on punishing. Indeed, experiments conducted in the United States, Switzerland, and Japan show that individuals who are initially the least trusting are more willing to contribute to sanctioning systems and are likely to be transformed into strong cooperators by the availability of a sanctioning mechanism (Fehr & Gächter, forthcoming). The finding that face-to-face communication is more efficacious than computerized signaling is probably due to the richer language structure available and the added intrinsic costs involved in hearing the intonation and seeing the body language of those who are genuinely angry at free riders (Ostrom, 1998a).

(7) The rate of contribution to a public good is affected by various contextual factors including the framing of the situation and the rules used for assigning participants, increasing competition among them, allowing communication, authorizing sanctioning mechanisms, or allocating benefits.

These facts are hard to explain using the standard theory that all individuals who face the same objective game structure evaluate decisions in the same way![4] We cannot simply resort to the easy criticism that undergraduate students are erratic. Increasing the size of the payoffs offered in experiments does not appear to change the broad patterns of empirical results obtained.[5] I believe that one is forced by these well-substantiated facts to adopt a more eclectic (and classical) view of human behavior.

Building a theory of collective action with multiple types of players

From the experimental findings, one can begin to put together some of the key assumptions that need to be included in a revised theory of collective action.

Assuming the existence of two types of 'norm-using' players – 'conditional cooperators' and 'willing punishers' – in addition to rational egoists, enables one to start making more coherent sense out of the findings of the laboratory experiments on contributions to public goods.

Conditional cooperators are individuals who are willing to initiate cooperative action when they estimate others will reciprocate and to repeat these actions as long as a sufficient proportion of the others involved reciprocate. Conditional cooperators are the source of the relatively high levels of contributions in one-shot or initial rounds of prisoner's dilemma and public good games. Their initial contributions may encourage some rational egoists to contribute as well, so as to obtain higher returns in the early rounds of the game (Kreps, Milgrom, Roberts, & Wilson, 1982). Conditional cooperators will tend to trust others and be trustworthy in sequential prisoner's dilemma games as long as the proportion of others who return trust is relatively high. Conditional cooperators tend to vary, however, in their tolerance for free riding. Some are easily disappointed if others do not contribute, so they begin to reduce their own contributions. As they reduce their contributions, they discourage other conditional cooperators from further contributions. Without communication or institutional mechanisms to stop the downward cascade, eventually only the most determined conditional cooperators continue to make positive contributions in the final rounds.

The first four findings are consistent with an assumption that conditional cooperators are involved in most collective action situations. Conditional cooperators are apparently a substantial proportion of the population, given the large number of one-shot and finitely repeated experiments with initial cooperation rates ranging from 40 to 60%. Estimating that others are likely to cooperate should increase their willingness to cooperate. Further, knowing the number of repetitions will be relatively long, conditional cooperators can restrain their disappointment with free riders and keep moderate levels of cooperation (and joint payoffs) going for ever-longer periods of time.

The fifth and sixth findings depend on the presence of a third type of player who is willing, if given an opportunity, to punish presumed free riders through verbal rebukes or to use costly material payoffs when available. Willing punishers may also become willing rewarders if the circle of relationships allows them to reward those who have contributed more than the minimal level. Some conditional cooperators may also be willing punishers. Together, conditional cooperators and willing punishers create a more robust opening for collective action and a mechanism for helping it grow. When allowed to communicate on a face-to-face basis, willing punishers convey a considerable level of scorn and anger toward others who have not fully reciprocated their trust and give substantial positive encouragement when cooperation rates are high. Even more important for the long-term sustainability of collective action is the willingness of some to pay a cost to sanction others. The presence of these norm-using types of players is hard to dispute given the empirical evidence. The key question now is: How could these norm-using types of players have emerged and survived in a world of rational egoists?

Emergence and survival of multiple types of players in evolutionary processes

Evolutionary theories provide useful ways of modeling the emergence and survival of multiple types of players in a population. In a strict evolutionary model, individuals inherit strategies and do not change strategies in their lifetime. In this approach, those carrying the more successful strategies for an environment reproduce at a higher rate. After many iterations the more successful strategies come to prominence in the population (Axelrod, 1986). Such models are a useful starting point for thinking about competition and relative survival rates among different strategies.[6]

Human evolution occurred mostly during the long Pleistocene era that lasted for about 3 million years, up to about 10,000 years ago. During this era, humans roamed the earth in small bands of hunter-gatherers who were dependent on each other for mutual protection, sharing food, and providing for the young. Survival was dependent not only on aggressively seeking individual returns but also on solving many day-to-day collective action problems. Those of our ancestors who solved these problems most effectively, and learned how to recognize who was deceitful and who was a trustworthy reciprocator, had a selective advantage over those who did not (Barkow, Cosmides, & Tooby, 1992).

Evolutionary psychologists who study the cognitive structure of the human brain conclude that humans do not develop general analytical skills that are then applied to a variety of specific problems. Humans are not terribly skilled at general logical problem solving (as any scholar who has taught probability theory to undergraduates can attest). Rather, the human brain appears to have evolved a domain-specific, human-reasoning architecture (Clark & Karmiloff-Smith, 1991). For example, humans use a different approach to reasoning about deontic relationships – what is forbidden, obligated, or permitted – as contrasted to reasoning about what is true and false. When reasoning about deontic relationships, humans tend to check for violations, or cheaters (Manktelow & Over, 1991). When reasoning about whether empirical relationships are true, they tend to use a confirmation strategy (Oaksford & Chater, 1994). This deontic effect in human reasoning has repeatedly been detected even in children as young as three years old and is not associated with overall intelligence or educational level of the subject (Cummins, 1996).

Thus, recent developments in evolutionary theory and supporting empirical research provide strong support for the assumption that modern humans have inherited a propensity to learn social norms, similar to our inherited propensity to learn grammatical rules (Pinker, 1994). Social norms are shared understandings about actions that are obligatory, permitted, or forbidden (Crawford & Ostrom, 1995). Which norms are learned, however, varies from one culture to another, across families, and with exposure to diverse social norms expressed within various types of situations. The intrinsic cost or anguish that an individual suffers from failing to use a social norm, such as telling the truth or keeping a promise, is referred to as guilt, if entirely self-inflicted, or as shame, when the knowledge of the failure is known by others (Posner & Rasmusen, 1999).

The indirect evolutionary approach to adaptation through experience

Recent work on an *indirect* evolutionary approach to the study of human behavior offers a rigorous theoretical approach for understanding how preferences – including those associated with social norms – evolve or adapt (Güth & Yaari, 1992; Güth 1995). In an indirect evolutionary model, players receive objective payoffs, but make decisions based on the transformation of these material rewards into intrinsic preferences. Those who value reciprocity, fairness, and being trustworthy add a subjective change parameter to actions (of themselves or others) that are consistent or not consistent with their norms. This approach allows individuals to start with a predisposition to act in a certain way-thus, they are not rational egoists who only look forward – but it also allows those preferences to adapt in a relatively short number of iterations given the objective payoffs they receive and their intrinsic preferences about those payoffs.

Social dilemmas associated with games of trust, like sequential prisoner's dilemma games, are particularly useful games for discussing the indirect evolutionary approach. In such games, if two players trust each other and cooperate, they can both receive a moderately high payoff. However, if one player cooperates and the other does not, then the one who did not cooperate receives an even higher payoff, while the other receives little or nothing. For a rational egoist playing this game, the choice is not to trust, because the expectation is that the other player will not trust, either. As a result, both players will end up with lower payoffs than if they had been able to trust and cooperate. When considering such games, it is useful to remember that most contractual relationships – whether for private or public goods – have at least an element of this basic structure of trying to assure mutual trust. An indirect evolutionary approach explains how a mixture of norm-users and rational egoists would emerge in settings where standard rational choice theory assumes the presence of rational egoists alone.

In this approach, social norms may lead individuals to behave differently in the same objective situation depending on how strongly they value conformance with (or deviance from) a norm. Rational egoists can be thought of as having intrinsic payoffs that are the same as objective payoffs, since they do not value the social norm of reciprocity. Conditional cooperators (to take only one additional type of player for now) would be modeled as being trustworthy types and would have an additional parameter that adds value to the objective payoffs when reciprocating trust with trustworthiness. By their behavior and resulting interaction, however, different types of players are likely to gain differential objective returns. In a game of trust where players are chosen from a population that initially contains some proportion of rational egoists and conditional cooperators, the level of information about player types affects the relative proportion of rational egoists and conditional cooperators over time. With complete information regarding types, conditional cooperators playing a trustworthy strategy will more frequently receive the higher payoff, while rational egoists will consistently receive a lower payoff, since others will not trust them.

Only the trustworthy type would survive in an evolutionary process with complete information (Güth & Kliemt, 1998, p. 386). Viewed as a cultural evolutionary process, new entrants to the population would be more likely to adopt the preference ordering of those who obtained the higher material payoffs in the immediate past (Boyd & Richerson, 1985). Those who were less successful would tend to learn the values of those who had achieved higher material rewards (Börgers & Sarin, 1997).[7] Where a player's type is common knowledge, rational egoists would not survive. Full and accurate information about all players' types, however, is a very strong assumption and unlikely to be met in most real world settings.

If there is no information about player types for a relatively large population, preferences will evolve so that only rational egoists survive.[8] If information about the proportion of a population that is trustworthy is known, and no information is known about the type of a specific player, Güth and Kliemt (1998) show that first players will trust second players as long as the expected return of meeting trustworthy players and receiving the higher payoff exceeds the payoff obtained when neither player trusts the other. In such a setting, however, the share of the population held by the norm-using types is bound to decline. On the other hand, if there is a noisy signal about a player's type that is at least more accurate than random, trustworthy types will survive as a substantial proportion of the population. Noisy signals may result from seeing one another, face-to-face communication, and various mechanisms that humans have designed to monitor each other's behavior.

Evidence testing the indirect evolutionary approach

An indirect evolutionary approach is able to explain how a mixture of contingent cooperators and rational egoists would emerge in settings where traditional game theory predicts that only rational egoists should prevail. The first six of the seven core findings summarized above were in part the stimulus for the development of the indirect evolutionary theory and the seventh is not inconsistent (see below for further discussion of it). Given the recent development of this approach, direct tests of this theory are not extensive. From the viewpoint of an indirect evolutionary process, participants in a collective action problem would start with differential, intrinsic preferences over outcomes due to their predispositions toward norms such as reciprocity and trust. Participants would learn about the likely behavior of others and shift their behavior in light of the experience and the objective payoffs they have received. Several recent experiments provide evidence of these kinds of contingent behaviors and behavioral shifts.[9]

In a one-shot, sequential, double-blind prisoner's dilemma experiment, for example, the players were asked to rank their preferences over the final outcomes after they had made their own choice, but before they knew their partner's decision. Forty percent of a pool of 136 subjects ranked the cooperative outcome (C,C) higher than the outcome if they defect while the other cooperates (D,C), and 27% were indifferent between these outcomes, even though their individual payoff was substantially higher for them in the latter outcome (Ahn, Ostrom, & Walker, 1998).[10] This finding confirms that not all players enter a collective action situation as pure forward-looking rational egoists who make decisions based solely on individual outcomes. Some bring with them a set of norms and values that can support cooperation.

On the other hand, preferences based on these norms can be altered by bad experiences. After 72 subjects had played 12 rounds of a finitely repeated prisoner's dilemma game where partners were randomly matched each round, rates of cooperation were very low and many players had experienced multiple instances where partners had declined to cooperate, only 19% of the respondents ranked (C,C) above (D,C), while 17% were indifferent (Ahn, Ostrom, Schmidt, & Walker, 1999). In this setting, the norms supporting cooperation and reciprocity were diminished, but not eliminated, by experience.

In another version of the prisoner's dilemma game, Cain (1998) first had players participate in a 'dictator game'-in which one player divides a sum of money and the other player must accept the division, whatever it is-and then a prisoner's dilemma game. Stingy players, defined as those who retained at least 70% of their endowment in the earlier dictator game, tended to predict that all players would defect in the prisoner's dilemma game. Nice players, defined as those that gave away at least 30% of their endowment, tended to predict that other nice players would cooperate and stingy players would defect. Before playing the prisoner's dilemma game, players were told whether their opponent had been 'stingy' or 'nice' in the dictator game. Nice players chose cooperation in the prisoner's dilemma game 69% of the time when they were paired with other nice players and 39% of the time when they were paired with stingy players.

Finally, interesting experimental (as well as field) evidence has accumulated that externally imposed rules tend to 'crowd out' endogenous cooperative behavior (Frey, 1994). For example, consider some paradoxical findings of Frohlich and Oppenheimer (1996) from a prisoner's dilemma game. One set of groups played a regular prisoner's dilemma game, some with communication and some without. A second set of groups used an externally imposed, incentive-compatible mechanism designed to enhance cooperative choices. In the first phase of the experiment, the second set gained higher monetary returns than the control groups, as expected. In the second phase of the experiment, both groups played a regular prisoner's dilemma game. To the surprise of the experimenters, a higher level of cooperation occurred in the control groups that played the regular prisoner's dilemma in both phases, especially for those who communicated on a face-to-face basis. The greater cooperation that had occurred clue to the exogenously created incentive-compatible mechanism appeared to be transient. As the authors put it (p. 180), the removal of the external mechanism 'seemed to undermine subsequent cooperation and leave the group worse off than those in the control group who had played a regular ... prisoner's dilemma.'

Several other recent experimental studies have confirmed the notion that external rules and monitoring can crowd out cooperative behavior[11] These studies typically find that a social norm, especially in a setting where there is communication between the parties, can work as well or nearly as well at generating cooperative behavior as an externally imposed set of rules and system of monitoring and sanctioning. Moreover, norms seem to have a certain staying power in encouraging a growth of the desire for cooperative behavior over time, while cooperation enforced by externally imposed rules can disappear very quickly. Finally, the worst of all worlds may be one where external authorities impose rules but are only able to achieve weak monitoring and sanctioning. In a world of strong external monitoring and sanctioning, cooperation is enforced without any need for internal norms to develop. In a world of no external rules or monitoring, norms can evolve to support cooperation. But in an in-between case, the mild degree of external monitoring discourages the formation of social norms, while also making it attractive for some players to deceive and defect and take the relatively low risk of being caught.

The evolution of rules and norms in the field

Field studies of collective action problems are extensive and generally find that cooperation levels vary from extremely high to extremely low across different settings. (As discussed above, the seventh core finding from experimental research is that contextual factors affect the rate of contribution to public goods.) An immense number of contextual variables are also identified by field researchers as conducive or detrimental to endogenous collective action. Among those proposed are: the type of production and allocation functions; the predictability of resource flows; the relative scarcity of the good; the size of the group involved; the heterogeneity of the group; the dependence of the group on the good; common understanding of the group; the size of the total collective benefit; the marginal contribution by one person to the collective good; the size of the temptation to free ride; the loss to cooperators when others do not cooperate; having a choice of participating or not; the presence of leadership; past experience and level of social capital; the autonomy to make binding rules; and a wide diversity of rules that are used to change the structure of the situation (see literature cited in Ostrom, forthcoming).

Some consistent findings are emerging from empirical field research. A frequent finding is that when the users of a common-pool resource organize themselves to devise and enforce some of their own basic rules, they tend to manage local resources more sustainably than when rules are externally imposed on them (for example, Baland & Platteau, 1996; Blomquist, 1992; Tang, 1992; Wade, 1994). Common-pool resources are natural or humanly created systems that generate a finite flow of benefits where it is costly to exclude beneficiaries and one person's consumption subtracts from the amount of benefits available to others (Ostrom, Gardner, & Walker, 1994). The users of a common-pool resource face a first-level dilemma that each individual would prefer that others control their use of the resource while each is able to use the resource freely. An effort to change these rules is a second-level dilemma, since the new rules that they share are a public good. Thus, users face a collective action problem, similar in many respects to the experiments discussed above, of how to cooperate when their immediate best-response strategies lead to suboptimal outcomes for all. A key question now is: How does evolutionary theory help us understand the well-established finding that many groups of individuals overcome both dilemmas? Further, how can we understand how self-organized resource regimes, that rarely rely on external third-party enforcement, frequently outperform government-owned resource regimes that rely on externally enforced, formal rules?

The emergence of self-organized collective action

From evolutionary theory, we should expect some individuals to have an initial propensity to follow a norm of reciprocity and to be willing to restrict their own use of a common pool resource so long as almost everyone reciprocates. If a small core group of users identify each other, they can begin a process of cooperation without having to devise a full-blown organization with all of the rules that they might eventually need to sustain cooperation over time. The presence of a leader or entrepreneur, who articulates different ways of organizing to improve joint outcomes, is frequently an important initial stimulus (Frohlich, Oppenheimer, & Young, 1971; Varughese, 1999).[12]

If a group of users can determine its own membership – including those who agree to use the resource according to their agreed-upon rules and excluding those who do not agree to these rules – the group has made an important first step toward the development of greater trust and reciprocity. Group boundaries are frequently marked by well-understood criteria, like everyone who lives in a particular community or has joined a specific local cooperative. Membership may also be marked by symbolic boundaries and involve complex rituals and beliefs that help solidify individual beliefs about the trustworthiness of others.

Design principles of long-surviving, self-organized resource regimes

Successful self-organized resource regimes can initially draw upon locally evolved norms of reciprocity and trustworthiness and the likely presence of local leaders in most community settings. More important, however, for explaining their long-term survival and comparative effectiveness, resource regimes that have flourished over multiple generations tend to be characterized by a set of design principles. These design principles are extensively discussed in Ostrom (1990) and have been subjected to extensive empirical testing.[13] Evolutionary theory helps to explain how these design principles work to help groups sustain and build their cooperation over long periods of time.

We have already discussed the first design principle – the presence of clear boundary rules. Using this principle enables participants to know who is in and who is out of a defined set of relationships and thus with whom to cooperate. The second design principle is that the local rules-in-use restrict the amount, timing, and technology of harvesting the resource; allocate benefits proportional to required inputs; and are crafted to take local conditions into account. If a group of users is going to harvest from a resource over the long run, they must devise rules related to how much, when, and how different products are to be harvested, and they need to assess the costs on users of operating a system. Well-tailored rules help to account for the perseverance of the resource itself. How to relate user inputs to the benefits they obtain is a crucial element of establishing a fair system (Trawick, 1999). If some users get all the benefits and pay few of the costs, others become unwilling to follow rules over time.

In long-surviving irrigation systems, for example, subtly different rules are used in each system for assessing water fees used to pay for maintenance activities, but water tends to be allocated proportional to fees or other required inputs (Bardhan, 1999). Sometimes water and responsibilities for resource inputs are distributed on a share basis, sometimes on the order in which water is taken, and sometimes strictly on the amount of land irrigated. No single set of rules defined for all irrigation systems in a region would satisfy the particular problems in managing each of these broadly similar, but distinctly different, systems (Lam, 1998; Tang, 1992).

The third design principle is that most of the individuals affected by a resource regime can participate in making and modifying their rules. Resource regimes that use this principle are both able to tailor better rules to local circumstances and to devise rules that are considered fair by participants. The Chisasibi Cree, for example, have devised a complex set of entry and authority rules related to the fish stocks of James Bay as well as the beaver stock located in their defined hunting territory. Berkes (1987, p. 87) explains that these resource systems and the rules used to regulate them have survived and prospered for so long because effective 'social mechanisms ensure adherence to rules which exist by virtue of mutual consent within the community. People who violate these rules suffer not only a loss of favor from the animals (important in the Cree ideology of hunting) but also social disgrace.' Fair rules of distribution help to build trusting relationships, since more individuals are willing to abide by these rules because they participated in their design and also because they meet shared concepts of fairness (Bowles, 1998).

In a study of 48 irrigation systems in India, Bardhan (1999) finds that the quality of maintenance of irrigation canals is significantly lower on those systems where farmers perceive the rules to be made by a local elite. On the other hand, those farmers (of the 480 interviewed) who responded that the rules have been crafted by most of the farmers, as contrasted to the elite or the government, have a more positive attitude about the water allocation rules and the rule compliance of other farmers. Further, in all of the villages where a government agency decides how water is to be allocated and distributed, frequent rule violations are reported and farmers tend to contribute less to the local village fund. Consistent with this is the finding by Ray and Williams (1999) that the deadweight loss from upstream farmers stealing water on government-owned irrigation systems in Maharashtra, India, approaches one-fourth of the revenues that could be earned in an efficient water allocation and pricing regime.

Few long-surviving resource regimes rely only on endogenous levels of trust and reciprocity. The fourth design principle is that most long-surviving resource regimes select their own monitors, who are accountable to the users or are users themselves and who keep an eye on resource conditions as well as on user behavior. Further, the fifth design principle points out that these resource regimes use *graduated sanctions* that depend on the seriousness and context of the offense. By creating official positions for local monitors, a resource regime does not have to rely only on willing punishers to impose personal costs on those who break a rule. The community legitimates a position. In some systems, users rotate into this position so everyone has a chance to be a participant as well as a monitor. In other systems, all participants contribute resources and they hire monitors jointly. With local monitors, conditional cooperators are assured that someone is generally checking on the conformance of others to local rules. Thus, they can continue their own cooperation without constant fear that others are taking advantage of them.

On the other hand, the initial sanctions that are imposed are often so low as to have no impact on an expected benefit-cost ratio of breaking local rules (given the substantial temptations frequently involved). Rather, the initial sanction needs to be considered more as information both to the person who is 'caught' and to others in the community. Everyone can make an error or can face difficult problems leading them to break a rule. Rule infractions, however, can generate a downward cascade of cooperation in a group that relies only on conditional cooperation and has no capacity to sanction (for example, Kikuchi, Fujita, Marciano, & Hayami, 1998). In a regime that uses graduated punishments, however, a person who purposely or by error breaks a rule is notified that others notice the infraction (thereby increasing the individual's confidence that others would also be caught). Further, the individual learns that others basically continue to extend their trust and want only a small token to convey a recognition that the mishap occurred. Self-organized regimes rely more on what Margaret Levi calls 'quasi-voluntary' cooperation than either strictly voluntary or coerced cooperation (Levi, 1988). A real threat to the continuance of self-organized regimes occurs, however, if some participants break rules repeatedly. The capability to escalate sanctions enables such a regime to warn members that if they do not conform they will have to pay ever-higher sanctions and may eventually be forced to leave the community.

Let me summarize my argument to this point. When the users of a resource design their own rules (Design Principle 3) that are enforced by local users or accountable to them (Design Principle 4) using graduated sanctions (Design Principle 5) that define who has rights to withdraw from the resource (Design Principle 1) and that effectively assign costs proportionate to benefits (Design Principle 2), collective action and monitoring problems are solved in a reinforcing manner (Agrawal, 1999).

Individuals who think a set of rules will be effective in producing higher joint benefits and that monitoring (including their own) will protect them against being a sucker are willing to undertake conditional cooperation. Once some users have made contingent self-commitments, they are then motivated to monitor other people's behavior, at least from time to time, to assure themselves that others are following the rules most of the time. Conditional cooperation and mutual monitoring reinforce one another, especially in regimes where the rules are designed to reduce monitoring costs. Over time, further adherence to shared norms evolves and high levels of cooperation are achieved without the need to engage in very close and costly monitoring to enforce rule conformance.

The operation of these principles is then bolstered by the sixth design principle that points to the importance of access to rapid, low-cost, local arenas to resolve conflict among users or between users and officials. Rules, unlike physical constraints, have to be understood to be effective. There are always situations in which participants can interpret a rule that they have jointly made in different ways. By devising simple, local mechanisms to get conflicts aired immediately and resolutions that are generally known in the community, the number of conflicts that reduce trust can be reduced. If individuals are going to follow rules over a long period of time, some mechanism for discussing and resolving what constitutes a rule infraction is necessary to the continuance of rule conformance itself.

The capability of local users to develop an ever-more effective regime over time is affected by whether they have minimal recognition of the right to organize by a national or local government. This is the seventh design principle. While some resource regimes have operated for relatively long times without such rights (Ghate, 2000), participants have had to rely almost entirely on unanimity as the rule used to change rules. (Otherwise, any temporarily disgruntled participant who voted against a rule change could go to the external authorities to threaten the regime itself!) Unanimity as a decision rule for changing rules imposes high transaction costs and prevents a group from searching for better matched rules at relatively lower costs.

Users frequently devise their own rules without creating formal, governmental jurisdictions for this purpose. In many in-shore fisheries, for example, local fishers devise extensive rules defining who can use a fishing ground and what kind of equipment can be used (Acheson, 1988; Schlager, 1994). As long as external governmental officials give at least minimal recognition to the legitimacy of such rules, the fishers themselves may be able to enforce the rules. But if external governmental officials presume that only they can make authoritative rules, then it is difficult for local users to sustain a self-organized regime (Johnson & Libecap, 1982).

When common pool resources are somewhat larger, an eighth design principle tends to characterize successful systems – the presence of governance activities organized in multiple layers of nested enterprises. The rules appropriate for allocating water among major branches of an irrigation system, for example, may not be appropriate for allocating water among farmers along a single distributory channel. Consequently, among long-enduring self-governed regimes, smaller-scale organizations tend to be nested in ever-larger organizations. It is not unusual to find a large, farmer-governed irrigation system, for example, with five layers of organization each with its own distinct set of rules (Yoder, 1992).

Threats to sustained collective action

All economic and political organizations are vulnerable to threats, and selforganized resource-governance regimes are no exception. Both exogenous and endogenous factors challenge their long-term viability. Here we will concentrate on those factors that affect the distribution of types of participants within a regime and the strength of the norms of trust and reciprocity held by participants. Major migration (out of or into an area) is always a threat that may or may not be countered effectively. Out-migration may change the economic viability of a regime due to loss of those who contribute needed resources. In-migration may bring new participants who do not trust others and do not rapidly learn social norms that have been established over a long period of time. Since collective action is largely based on mutual trust, some self-organized resource regimes that are in areas of rapid settlement have disintegrated within relatively short times (Baland & Platteau, 1996).

In addition to rapid shifts in population due to market changes or land distribution policies, several more exogenous and endogenous threats have been identified in the empirical literature (Bates, 1987; Sengupta, 1991; and literature cited in Britt, 2000; Ostrom, 1998b). These include: (1) efforts by national governments to impose a single set of rules on all governance units in a region; (2) rapid changes in technology, in factor availability, and in reliance on monetary transactions; (3) transmission failures from one generation to the next of the operational principles on which self-organized governance is based; (4) turning to external sources of help too frequently; (5) international aid that does not take account of indigenous knowledge and institutions; (6) growth of corruption and other forms of opportunistic behavior; and (7) a lack of large-scale institutional arrangements that provide fair and low-cost resolution mechanisms for conflicts that arise among local regimes, educational and extension facilities, and insurance mechanisms to help when natural disasters strike at a local level.

Contextual variables are thus essential for understanding the initial growth and sustainability of collective action as well as the challenges that long-surviving, self-organized regimes must try to overcome. Simply saying that context matters is not, however, a satisfactory theoretical approach. Adopting an evolutionary approach is the first step toward a more general theoretical synthesis that addresses the question of how context matters. In particular, we need to address how context affects the presence or absence of conditional cooperators and willing punishers and the likelihood that the norms held by these participants are adopted and strengthened by others in a relevant population.

Conclusion

Both laboratory experiments and field studies confirm that a substantial number of collective action situations are resolved successfully, at least in part. The old-style notion, pre-Mancur Olson, that groups would find ways to act in their own collective interest was not entirely misguided. Indeed, recent developments in evolutionary theory – including the study of cultural evolution – have begun to provide genetic and adaptive under-pinnings for the propensity to cooperate based on the development and growth of social norms. Given the frequency and diversity of collective action situations in all modern economies, this represents a more optimistic view than the zero contribution hypothesis. Instead of pure pessimism or pure optimism, however, the picture requires further work to explain why some contextual variables enhance cooperation while others discourage it.

Empirical and theoretical work in the future needs to ask how a large array of contextual variables affects the processes of teaching and evoking social norms; of informing participants about the behavior of others and their adherence to social norms; and of rewarding those who use social norms, such as reciprocity, trust, and fairness. We need to understand how institutional, cultural, and biophysical contexts affect the types of individuals who are recruited into and leave particular types of collective action situations, the kind of information that is made available about past actions, and how individuals can themselves change structural variables so as to enhance the probabilities of norm-using types being involved and growing in strength over time.

Further developments along these lines are essential for the development of public policies that enhance socially beneficial, cooperative behavior based in part on social norms. It is possible that past policy initiatives to encourage collective action that were based primarily on externally changing payoff structures for rational egoists may have been misdirected-and perhaps even crowded out the formation of social norms that might have enhanced cooperative behavior in their own way. Increasing the authority of individuals to devise their own rules may well result in processes that allow social norms to evolve and thereby increase the probability of individuals better solving collective action problems.

Notes

1. See Milgrom, North, and Weingast (1990) and Bromley et al. (1992). An extensive bibliography by Hess (1999) on diverse institutions for dealing with common pool resources can be searched on the web at (http://www.indiana.edu/workshop/wsl/wsl.html) or obtained on a CD-ROM disk.

2. In a linear public good game, utility is a linear function of individual earnings, $U_i = U_i[(E - x_i) + A \cdot P(\Sigma x_i)]$, where E is an individual endowment of asset, x, is the amount of this endowment contributed to provide the good, A is the allocation formula used to distribute the group benefit to individual players, and P is the production function. In a linear public good game, A is specified as $1/N$ and $0 < 1/N < P < 1$ (but both of these functions vary in other types of collective action). So long as $P < 1$, contributing to the collective good is never an optimal strategy for a fully self-interested player.

3. Even more startling, Bohnet and Frey (1999) find that simply allowing subjects to see the other persons with whom they are playing greatly increases cooperation as contrasted to completely anonymous situations. Further, Frank, Gilovich, and Regan (1993) find that allowing subjects to have a face-to-face discussion enables them to predict who will play cooperatively at a rate significantly better than chance.

4. Although the discussion here focuses on collective action and public good games in particular, a broader range of experiments exists in which the rational egoist's prediction pans out badly. These include the ultimatum game, the dictator game, the trust game, and common-pool resources games with communication.

5. Most of these experiments involve ultimatum games but the findings are quite relevant. Cameron (1995), for example, conducted ultimatum experiments in Indonesia and thereby was able to use sums that amounted to three months' wages. In this extremely tempting situation, she still found that 56% of the Proposers allocated between 40 and 50% of this very substantial sum to the Responder.

6. For examples of strict evolutionary models involving collective action, see Nowak and Sigmund (1998); Sethi and Somanathan (1996) and Epstein and Axtell (1996).

7. Eshel, Samuelson, and Shaked (1998) develop a learning model where a population of Altruists who adopt a strategy of providing a local public good interacts in a local neighborhood with a population of Egoists who free ride. In this local interaction setting, Altruists' strategies are imitated sufficiently often in a Markovian learning process to become one of the absorbing states. Altruists interacting with Egoists outside a circular local neighborhood are not so likely to survive.

8. This implies that, in a game where players know only their own payoffs and not the payoffs of others, they are more likely to behave like rational egoists. McCabe and Smith (1999) show that players tend to evolve toward the predicted, subgame perfect outcomes in experiments where they have only private information of their own payoffs and to cooperative outcomes when they have information about payoffs and the moves made by other players (see also McCabe et al., 1996).

9. Further, Kikuchi, Watanabe, and Yamagishi (1997) have found that those who express a high degree of trust are able to predict others' behavior more accurately than those with low levels of trust.

10. To examine the frequency of nonrational egoist preferences, a group of 181 undergraduates was given a questionnaire containing a similar payoff structure on the first day of classes at Indiana University in January 1999. They were a ked to rank their preferences. In this nondecision setting, 52% reflected preferences that were not consistent with being rational egoists; specifically, 27% ranked the outcome (C,C) over (D,C) and 25% were indifferent.

11. Bohnet, Frey, and Huck (1999) set up a sequential prisoner's dilemma, but acid a regulatory regime where a 'litigation process' is initiated if there is a breach of performance. Cardenas, Stranlund, and Willis (2000) describe an experiment based on harvesting from a common-pool resource conducted in three rural villages in Columbia where exogenous but imperfect rule enforcement generated less cooperation than allowing face-to-face communication.

12. Empirical studies of civil rights movements, where contributions can be very costly, find that orga nizers search for ways to assure potential participants of the importance of shared internal norms and that many others will also participate (Chong, 1991). Membership in churches and other groups that jointly commit themselves to protests and other forms of collective action is also an important factor (Opp, Voss, & Gem, 1995).

13. The design principles that characterize long-standing common-pool resource regimes have now been subject to considerable further empirical studies since they were first articulated (Ostrom, 1990). While minor modifications have been offered to express the design principles somewhat differently, no empirical study has challenged their validity, to my knowledge (Asquith, 1999; Bardhan, 1999; Lam, 1998; Morrow, & Hull, 1996).

References

Acheson, J. M. (1988). *The lobster gangs of maine*. Hanover, NH: University Press of New England.

Agrawal, A. (1999). *Greener pastures: Politics, markets, and community among a migrant pastoral people*. Durham, NC: Duke University Press.

Ahn, T. -K., Ostrom, E., Schmidt, D., & Walker, J. (1999). *Dilemma games: Game parameters and matching protocols*. Bloomington: Indiana University, Workshop in Political Theory and Policy Analysis, Working paper.

Ahn, T. -K., Ostrom, E., & Walker, J. (1998). *Trust and reciprocity: Experimental evidence from PD games*. Bloomington: Indiana University, Workshop in Political Theory and Policy Analysis, Working paper.

Asquith, N. M. (1999). *How should the world bank encourage private sector investment in biodiversity conservation? A report prepared for Kathy MacKinnon, Biodiversity Specialist, The World Bank*. Washington, D.C. Durham, North Carolina: Sanford Institute of Public Policy, Duke University.

Axelrod, R. (1986). An evolutionary approach to norms. *American Political Science Review, December 80*(4), 1095–1111. doi:10.2307/1960858

Baland, J. -M., & Platteau, J. -P. (1996). *Halting degradation of natural resources: Is there a role for rural communities?* Oxford: Clarendon Press.

Barkow, J. H.,Cosmides L., & Tooby J. (Eds.). (1992). *The adapted mind: Evolutionary psychology and the generation of culture*. Oxford: Oxford University Press.

Bardhan, P. (1999). *Water community: An empirical analysis of cooperation on irrigation in South India*. Berkeley: University of California, Department of Economics, Working paper.

Bates, R. H. (1987). *Essays on the political economy of rural Africa*. Berkeley: University of California Press.

Berkes, F. (1987). Common property resource management and cree Indian fisheries in Subarctic Canada. In B. McCay, & J. Acheson (Eds.), *The question of the commons: The culture and ecology of communal resources* (pp. 66–91). Tucson: University of Arizona Press.

Blomquist, W. (1992). *Dividing the waters: Governing groundwater in Southern California*. San Francisco, CA: ICS Press.

Bohnet, I., & Frey, B. S. (1999). The sound of silence in prisoner's dilemma and dictator games. *Journal of Economic Behavior & Organization, January, 38*(1), 43–58. doi:10.1016/S0167-2681(98)00121-8

Bohnet, I., Frey, B. S., & Huck, S. 1999. *More order with less law: On contract enforcement, trust, and crowding*. Cambridge, MA: Harvard University, Working paper.

Börgers, T., & Sarin, R. (1997). Learning through reinforcement and replicator dynamics. *Journal of Economic Theory, 77*, 1–14. doi:10.1006/jeth.1997.2319

Bowles, S. (1998). Endogenous preferences: The cultural consequences of markets and other economic institutions. *Journal of Economic Literature, March, 36*, 75–111.

Boyd, R., & Richerson, P. J. (1985). *Cultute and the evolutionmy process*. Chicago, IL: U niversity of Chicago Press.

Bromley, D. W. et al. (Eds.). (1992). *Making the commons work: Theory, practice, and policy*. San Francisco, CA: ICS Press.

Britt, C. 2000. *Forestry and forest policies*. Bloomington: Indiana University, Workshop in Political Theory and Policy Analysis, Working paper.

Cain, M. (1998). An experimental investigation of motives and information in the prisoner's dilemma game. *Advances in Group Processes, 15*, 133–160.

Cameron, L. (1995). *Raising the stakes in the ultimatum game: Experimental evidence from Indonesia*. Princeton, NJ: Plinceton University. Discussion paper.

Cardenas, J. -C., Stranlund, J. K., & Willis, C. E. (2000). Local environmental control and institutional crowding-out. *World Development, Autumn*, forthcoming.

Chong, D. (1991). *Collective action and the civil rights movement*. Chicago, IL: University of Chicago Press.

Clark, A., & Karmiloff-Smith, A. (1991). The cognizer's innards: A psychological and philosophical perspective on the development of thought. *Mind and Language, Winter, 8*(4), 487–519.

Crawford, S. E. S., & Ostrom, E. (1995). A grammar of institutions. *The American Political Science Review, September, 89*(3), 582–600. doi:10.2307/2082975

Cummins, D. D. (1996). Evidence of deontic reasoning in 3- and 4-year-old children. *Memory and Cognition, 24*, 823–829. doi:10.3758/BF03201105

Davis, D. D., & Holt, C. A. (1993). *Experimental economics*. Princeton, NJ: Princeton University Press.

Dawes, R. M., McTavish, J., & Shaklee, H. (1977). Behavior, communication, and assumptions about other people's behavior in a commons dilemma situation. *Journal of Personality and Social Psychology, 35*(1), 1–11. doi:10.1037/0022-3514.35.1.1

Epstein, J. M., & Axtell, R. (1996). *Growing artificial societies: Social science from the bottom up*. Cambridge, MA: MIT Press.

Eshel, I., Samuelson, L., & Shaked, A. (1998). Altruists, egoists, and hooligans in a local interaction model. *American Economic Review, March, 88*(1), 157–179.

Feeny, D., Berkes, F., McCay, B. J., & Acheson, J. M. (1990). The tragedy of the commons: Twenty-two years later. *Human Ecology, 18*(1), 1–19. doi:10.1007/BF00889070

Fehr, E., & Gächter, S. (Forthcoming). Cooperation and punishment in public goods experiments. *Ametican Economic Review, 90*, 1.

Fehr, E., & Schmidt, K. (1999). A theory of fairness, competition, and cooperation. *Quarterly Joumal of Economics, 114*(3), 817–868.

Frank, R. H., Gilovich, T., & Regan, D. T. (1993). The evolution of one-shot cooperation: An experiment. *Ethology and Sociobiology, July, 14*, 247–256. doi:10.1016/0162-3095(93)90020-I

Frey, B. S. (1994). How intrinsic motivation is crowded out and in. *Rationality and Society, 6*, 334–352. doi:10.1177/1043463194006003004

Frohlich, N., & Oppenheimer, J. A. (1996). Experiencing impartiality to invoke fairness in the N-PD: Some experimental results. *Public Choice, 86*, 117–135. doi:10.1007/BF00114878

Frohlich, N., Oppenheimer, J. A., & Young, O. (1971). *Political leadership and collective goods.* Princeton, NJ: Princeton University Press.

Ghate, R. (2000). *The role of autonomy in self-organizing process: A case study of local forest management in India.* Bloomington: Indiana University, Workshop in Political Theory and Policy Analysis, Working paper.

Güth, W. (1995). An evolutionary approach to explaining cooperative behavior by reciprocal incentives. *International Journal of Game Theory, 24*, 323–344. doi:10.1007/BF01243036

Güth, W., & Kliemt, H. (1998). The indirect evolutionary approach: Bridging the gap between rationality and adaptation. *Rationality and Society, August, 10*(3), 377–399. doi:10.1177/104346398010003005

Güth, W., & Yaari, M. (1992). An evolutionary approach to explaining reciprocal behavior in a simple strategic game. In W. Ulrich (Ed.), *Explaining process and change. Approaches to evolutionary economics* (pp. 23–34). Ann Arbor: University of Michigan Press.

Hardin, R. (1971). Collective action as an agreeable n-prisoners' dilemma. *Science, September-October, 16*, 472–481.

Hardin, R. (1982). *Collective action.* Baltimore, MD: Johns Hopkins University Press.

Hess, C. (1999). *A comprehensive bibliogcraphy of common pool resources. CD-ROM.* Bloomington: Indiana University, Workshop in Political Theory and Policy Analysis.

Isaac, R. M., Walker, J., & Williams, A. W. (1994). Group size and the voluntary provision of public goods: Experimental evidence utilizing large groups. *Journal of Public Economics, May, 54*(1), 1–36. doi:10.1016/0047-2727(94)90068-X

Johnson, R. N., & Libecap, G. D. (1982). Contracting problems and regulation: The case of the fishery. *American Economic Review, December, 27*(5), 1005–1023.

Kagel, J., & Roth A. (Eds.). (1995). *The handbook of experimental economics.* Princeton, NJ: Princeton University Press.

Kikuchi, M., Fujita, M., Marciano, E., & Hayami, Y. (1998). *State and community in the deterioration of a national irrigation system.* Paper presented at the World Bank-ED!Conference on "Norms and Evolution in the Grassroots of Asia," Stanford University, February 6–7.

Kikuchi, M., Watanabe, Y., & Yamagishi, T. (1997). Judgment accuracy of other's trustworthiness and general trust: An experimental study. *The Japanese Journal of Experimental Social Psychology, 37*(1), 23–36. doi:10.2130/jjesp.37.23

Kreps, D. M., Milgrom, P., Roberts, J., & Wilson, R. (1982). Rational cooperation in the finitely repeated prisoner's dilemma. *Journal of Economic Theory, 27*, 245–252. doi:10.1016/0022-0531(82)90029-1

Lam, W. F. (1998). *Governing irrigation systems in Nepal: Institutions, infrastructure, and collective action.* Oakland, CA: ICS Press.

Ledyard, J. (1995). Public goods: A survey of experimental research. In J. Kagel, & A. Roth (Eds.), *The handbook of experimental economics* (111–194). Princeton, NJ: Princeton University Press.

Levi, M. (1988). *Of rule and revenue.* Berkeley: University of California Press.

Lichbach, M. I. (1996). *The cooperator's dilemma.* Ann Arbor: University of Michigan Press.

Manktelow, K. I., & Over, D. E. (1991). Social roles and utilities in reasoning with deontic conditionals. *Cognition, 39*, 85–105. doi:10.1016/0010-0277(91)90039-7

McCabe, K. A., Rassenti, S. J., & Smith, V. L. (1996). Game theory and reciprocity in some extensive form experimental games. *Proceedings of the National Academy of Sciences, November, 93*, 13421–13428. doi:10.1073/pnas.93.23.13421

McCabe, K. A., & Smith, V. L. (1999). *Strategic analysis by players in games: What information do they use.* Tucson: University of Arizona, Economic Research Laboratory, Working paper.

Milgrom, P. R., North, D. C., & Weingast, B. R. (1990). The role of institutions in the revival of trade: The law merchant, private judges, and the champagne fairs. *Economics and Politics, March, 2*(1), 1–23. doi:10.1111/j.1468-0343.1990.tb00020.x

Montgomery, M. R., & Bean, R. (1999). Market failure, government failure, and the private supply of public goods: The case of climate-controlled walkway networks. *Public Choice, June, 99*(3/4), 403–437. doi:10.1023/A:1018301628084

Morrow, C. E., & Hull, R. W. (1996). Donor-initiated common pool resource institutions: The case of the yanesha forestry cooperative. *World Development, 24*(10), 1641–1657. doi:10.1016/0305-750X(96)00064-2

Nowak, M. A., & Sigmund, K. (1998). Evolution of indirect reciprocity by image scoring. *Nature, 393*(6685), 573–577. doi:10.1038/31225

Oaksford, M., & Chater, N. (1994). A rational analysis of the selection task as optimal data selection. *Psychological Review, 101*(4), 608–631. doi:10.1037/0033-295X.101.4.608

Offerman, T. (1997). *Beliefs and decision rules in public goods games: Theory and experiments.* Dordrecht, The Netherlands: Kluwer Academic Publishers.

Olson, M. (1965). *The logic of collective action: Public goods and the theory of groups.* Cambridge, MA: Harvard University Press.

Opp, K. -D., Voss, P., & Gem, C. (1995). *Origins of spontaneous revolution.* Ann Arbor: University of Michigan Press.

Ostrom, E. (1990). *Governing the commons: The evolution of institutions for collective action.* New York, NY: Cambridge University Press.

Ostrom, E. (1998a). A behavioral approach to the rational choice theory of collective action: Presidential address, American Political Science Association, 1997. *The American Political Science Review, March, 92*(1), 1–22. doi:10.2307/2585925

Ostrom, E. (1998b). Institutional analysis, design principles, and threats to sustainable community governance and management of commons. In E. Berge, & N. C. Stenseth (Eds.), *Law and the governance of renewable resources: Studies from Northern Europe and Africa* (pp. 27–53). Oakland, CA: ICS Press.

Ostrom, E. (Forthcoming). Reformulating the commons. In J. Burger, R. Norgaard, E. Ostrom, D. Policansky, & B. Goldstein, Eds., *The Commons Revisited: An Americas Perspective.* Washington, DC: Island Press.

Ostrom, E., Gardner, R., & Walker, J. (1994). *Rules, games, and common-pool resources.* Ann Arbor: University of Michigan Press.

Ostrom, E., & Walker, J. (1997). Neither markets nor states: Linking transformation processes in collective action Arenas. In D. C. Mueller, ed., *Perspectives on public choice: A handbook* (pp. 35–72). Cambridge: Cambridge University Press.

Pinker, S. (1994). *The language instinct.* New York, NY: W. Morrow.

Posner, R. A., & Rasmusen, E. B. (1999). Creating and enforcing norms, with special reference to sanctions. *International Review of Law and Economics, September, 19*(3), 369–382. doi:10.1016/S0144-8188(99)00013-7

Rabin, M. (1993). Incorporating fairness into game theory and economics. *American Economic Review, 83*, 1281–1302.

Ray, I., & Williams, J. (1999). Evaluation of price policy in the presence of water theft. *Arneriran Joumal of Agricultural Econmnirs, November, 81*, 928–941.

Schlager, E. (1994). Fishers' institutional responses to common-pool resource dilemmas. In E. Ostrom, R. Gardner, & J. Walker, Eds., *Rules, games, and common-pool resources* (pp. 247–265). Ann Arbor: University of Michigan Press.

Selten, R. (1991). Evolution, learning, and economic behavior. *Games and Economic Behavior, February, 3*(1), 3–24. doi:10.1016/0899-8256(91)90003-W

Sengupta, N. (1991). *Managing common property. Irrigation in India and the Philippines.* New Delhi: Sage.

Sethi, R., & Somanathan, E. (1996). The evolution of social norms in common property resource use. *American Economic Review, September, 86*(4), 766–788.

Tang, S. Y. (1992). *Institutions and collective action: Self governance in irrigation.* San Francisco, CA: ICS Press.

Trawick, P. (1999). *The moral economy of water: 'Comedy' and 'Tragedy' in the Andean Commons.* Lexington: University of Kentucky, Department of Anthropology, Working paper.

Varughese, G. (1999). *Villagers, bureaucrats, and forests in Nepal: Designing governance for a complex resource.* (Ph.D. dissertation). Indiana University.

Wade, R. (1994). *Village republics: Economic conditions for collective action in South India.* San Francisco, CA: ICS Press.

Yoder, R. D. (1992). Performance of the Chhattis Mauja Irrigation System, a Thirty-five Hundred Hectare System Built and Managed by Farmers in Nepal, Colombo, Sri Lanka. International Irrigation Management Institute.

The collective action theory path to contextual analysis

Paul Dragos Aligica[a] and Filippo Sabetti[b]

[a]F. A. Hayek Program for Advanced Study in Philosophy, Politics and Economics, George Mason University, Mercatus Center, Arlington, USA; [b]Department of Political Science, McGill University, Quebec, Canada

In 'Collective Action and the Evolution of Social Norms' Elinor Ostrom notes that '[c]ontextual variables are ... essential for understanding the initial growth and sustainability of collective action as well as the challenges that long-surviving, self-organized regimes must try to overcome' (2000, p. 153). Simply saying that context matters is not, however, sufficient. A more systematic approach, she notes, is needed. Our contribution takes a closer look at the idea of analysis that acknowledges the preeminent place of contextual and circumstantial configurations of variables in social science. Today the notion of contextual analysis and context sensitivity have spurred a whole domain that has grown up to the point that an entire *Oxford Handbook* has been dedicated to the theme (Goodin & Tilly, 2008). Ostrom was one of the pioneers of the idea as well as one of the first to think about methodical ways of dealing with the problems it poses. Our essay looks at this theme as well as a couple of pioneering insights articulated by Ostrom and her associates, regarding how we should deal with its methodological and epistemic challenges.

At the center of 'Collective Action and the Evolution of Social Norms' is the investigation of a two-step process, pivoting on two dilemmas that users of a common-pool resource face. The first-level dilemma is that each individual would prefer that others control their use of the resource, while he or she is able to use the resource freely. To solve it, a change of rules is necessary. Hence the problem of changing these rules generates a second-level dilemma, because 'the new rules that they share are a public good' (p.142). More precisely, Ostrom looks at the essence of the well-known collective action problem: cooperation is necessary but what she calls 'immediate best-response strategies' (p.143) for individuals may lead to suboptimal outcomes for all. In brief, the challenge is to understand the well-documented findings that, despite the problematic incentives an individual faces, groups of individuals manage to overcome in some cases both dilemmas.

Ostrom is thus part of a larger research program started in 1960 and focusing on collective action. Its objective: to understand the nature, processes, conditions of success of coordination and cooperation against the adverse and perverse incentives faced by social actors. This was indeed one of the most important research programs of the twentieth century, one of the best methodologically and analytically articulated social science investigation lines, extending over multiple disciplines and many decades. Ostrom was at the core of it, being one of the most influential scholars in the world in this respect. Following this research program unfolding, we can see that years of inquiry have led to the emergence of a very powerful epistemic, and theoretic idea: The circumstantial configurations of variables determining action arenas and action situations are crucial for the success or failure of collective actions. Context matters. Contextual analysis should be taken seriously as a distinct methodological, epistemological and theoretical possibility.

The importance of Ostrom's 2000 article in this respect is that in it she articulates with clarity these observations and the associated notions. When we are looking back at the current conclusions of the field, we see that they converge in reinforcing her initial observations made over the years with increasing sharpness. To understand collective action is to understand how institutional, cultural, and biophysical contexts affect collective action situations. 'Contextual variables are essential for understanding the initial growth and sustainability of collective action as well as the challenges that long-surviving, self-organized regimes must try to overcome', explains Ostrom. 'More work is needed to explain how a large array of contextual variables affects the processes of teaching and evoking social norms; of informing participants about the behavior of others and their adherence to social norms; and of rewarding those who use social norms, such as reciprocity, trust, and fairness' (Ostrom, 2000, p. 154).

This shift towards the diversity of configurations shaping human interactions and their collective action dimension has serious consequences for our approaches, models and theories. In affirming that context matters, we get a more nuanced understanding but at the same time we are forced to confront the limitations of our approaches. From experimental research we learn that contextual factors affect the rate of individual contribution to public goods; from field research we are alerted to the fact that 'an immense number of contextual variables' may hinder or facilitate endogenous collective action (Ostrom, 2000, p. 148). In brief, each further specification applied in order to capture context elements, leads to increasingly difficult generalizations. As Ostrom (1998, p. 15) put it, 'changes in one structural variable can lead to a cascade of changes in the others'. Just an apparently minor change in configuration or magnitude of a variable 'may suffice to reverse the predicted outcome'. We thus come to recognize 'how difficult it is to make simple bivariate hypotheses about the effect of one variable on the level of cooperation' (Ostrom, 1998, p. 15). This volatility and the unpredictability it entails, raise serious doubts about the possibility to identify the general social laws of collective action. Out of such investigative effort, one may gain a better understanding of the phenomenon, but no universal law, code or general model comes to be isolated and specified. The laws of collective action are elusive. One may identify and document a variety of mechanisms, processes and linkages relating possible configurations of variables, but one remains very far away from the ambitions of the broad initial generalizations of the 'Tragedy of the Commons' or the 'Logic of Collective Action' of the early literature of Olson and Hardin.

Consequently, in the years that have passed since that early literature, social scientists have been increasingly put in the position to reconsider their efforts to build 'the theory of collective action' based on 'the laws of collective action'. After all, this seems to be one of those domains in which 'it is not possible to relate all structural variables in one large causal model, given the number of important variables' (Ostrom, 1998, p. 14). Today, scholars are more than ever ready to acknowledge that 'there are many different issues and many different kinds of collective action and that one can shade into the other depending upon the structural characteristics of the situation' (Marwell & Oliver, 1993, p. 25). In fact, authors such as Oliver and Marwell (2001, pp. 292–293) go as far as to suggest that there is no single and unitary social phenomenon under that label. One needs 'a disciplined search for the distinctions among different types of collective action and the factors that distinguish them'. In such circumstances it is evident why the pursuit of comparable concepts and data about collective action remains a challenge (Poteete &

Ostrom, 2004). All of the above are very important conclusions, indeed. Their implications for the way we think about social research and institutional theory and design are considerable.

These insights and lessons from the decades-long research program on collective action are undoubtedly relevant for social sciences in general, converging with similar observations and conclusions reached in other domains and parallel research lines. Their most profound epistemological significance is well summarized by Goodin and Tilly (2008). The program of identifying simple general laws in social phenomena, they write, has yielded meager results. Both the epistemology and the method concentrated on finding general social laws conform badly with the empirical reality. The strength of the approach focused on seeking general laws lies more in identification of empirical regularities and not so much in the provision (or verification) of explanations. Generalities occur in social life but not at the scale and in the forms presumed by the 'covering laws' models of social science. As Clarke Kevin and Primo (2012) bluntly put it, today, nobody among those informed holds such an outdated and faulty understanding of how science operates. Therefore an increasingly larger number of scholars agree that we need to 'shift attention away from empirically grounded general laws to repeated processes and toward efficacious causal mechanisms that operate at multiple scales but produce their aggregate effects through their concatenation, sequences and interaction with initial conditions' (Goodin & Tilly, 2008, p. 20). At the same time, we need to be mindful of the fact, stressed by authors such as Vincent Ostrom (1997, pp. 89–111) or Karol Soltan (2014, p. 12), that the construction of causal explanations often leads to the neglect of the role of language, learning, knowledge, communication, artisanship and moral judgment in the exercise of human initiative and creativity required to fashion collective undertakings.

One may recognize in all these precisely the shift towards a context-focused approach. We need to reconsider our approaches and theoretical ambitions, recognizing the centrality of a variety of elements difficult to for in universal or grand-scale generalizable ways: historical, institutional, technological, psychological, cultural, demographic, ideological, and epistemological. When, where, in what settings, on what premises, under what conditions and circumstances, in what sequence, all these matter. Once when we realize that to answer the big questions of social science our reply is mostly invariably 'it depends', we realize that a major rethinking of our epistemic objectives and parameters is required.

As Goodin and Tilly (2008, pp. 8–9) explain, what is needed is a mixed strategy and a middle of the road between two extreme positions: The search of general laws is at one extreme. Its objective is to build empirical generalizations. The most general of them are called 'laws' because they are presumed to work the same in all conditions. In this approach, 'context' is just a noise, an interference or subversion in the transmission of the signal we are searching for. Research means to clear away the effect of context to discover the true regularities. At the other extreme is skepticism (these days under a 'postmodern' guise) that assumes that the search for regularities is an illusion. We struggle with elusive phenomena that we interpret the best we can, but there is no systematic component. Research means to offer contextual interpretations.

It is important to note that both extremes in fact deal with the reality of contextual factors. In the first case 'control of context' means to recognize that some aspects of context matter and make sure that they hold constant in the situation under study – recognizing its presence but trying to clear it up, to reach regularities. In the second, one may simply recognize it and then immerse in it without any general ambitions.

Context is everything and hence is nothing. In brief, to be sensitized to the effect of context is a necessary condition for analysis but it is not sufficient.

A truly effective contextual analysis needs to go beyond the two approaches and look at a third alternative, in which the researcher, taking context seriously but not succumbing to it, is trying to identify mechanisms, processes, patterns and their operating circumstances. This is what Goodin and Tilly (2008, pp. 23–24) call to 'correct for context': that is to say, taking systematically into account how different contexts might actually matter to the phenomena under study. This alternative method focuses on the logics of explanations to be used. It brings to the table a variety of epistemic and methodological approaches and strategies. Propensity explanation, for instance, 'consists of reconstructing a given actor's state at the threshold of action with that state variously stipulated as motivation, consciousness, need, organization or momentum'. Systemic explanations specify 'a place for some event, structure or process within a larger set of interdependent elements, showing how the event structure and process in question serves or results from interactions of the elements'. Mechanism-based explanations focus on 'a delimited class of events that change relations among specified set of elements in identical or closely similar ways over a variety of situations'. Processes-based explanations explore the 'frequently occurring combinations or sequences of mechanisms' (Goodin & Tilly, 2008, pp. 12–13).

From all of the above, it becomes evident that contextual analysis is not a mere illusory solution to a tough scientific problem but an approach that could be firmly grounded epistemologically and methodologically. It is rather clear that there are methods, approaches and instruments to implement it. Elinor Ostrom's observations were hence pointing out to a significant latent but emerging direction in social sciences and the philosophy of social sciences.

By the time she was writing 'Collective Action and the Evolution of Social Norms', Ostrom had already made important steps in articulating developing several concrete approaches to the problem. The article looks at the elements of the actions situations, at actors and their typologies in specific settings in a systematic and comparative perspective, as well as at the process aspect of moving from first-level dilemmas to second-level dilemmas. In so doing, it gives a hint regarding these important methodological approaches essential to contextual analysis. One cannot conclude our brief discussion without briefly introducing them.

Further developing the ideas illustrated in the 2000 article, Ostrom (2005) notes that even if general social laws are difficult to identify, one could nevertheless identify some 'basic units' that are pretty much the same in all cases. These are the 'elements' of social situations and the basic building blocks of social order and change. They get disposed and rearranged in various configurations generating different patterns of order and change. In fact, to identify configurations and patterns means to follow them and their relationships. The Ostrom strategy first aims at identifying these basic building blocks. Then, in function of case and context, to chart and reconfigure conceptually the different levels of combinations and arrangements of interest, for the case in point. The core of the procedure is a mapping of the institutional reality (structures and situations) that uses a set of basic units in order to chart any institutional domain of interest. The analogy with geographical maps and the way they generate growth of knowledge is telling: 'The advantage of a good set of geographic maps is that after centuries of hard work, multiple levels of detailed maps of most places are available and are nested in a consistent manner within one another. Most of us recognize that there is not one optimal map that can be used for all purposes. Each level of detail is useful for different purposes' (Ostrom, 2005, p. 8). The heuristic and context-driven nature of the approach is obvious: Ostrom is not looking for 'The Map' of institutional reality, she is looking for a map-making 'instrument' that would help us to generate specific maps of various contexts (Aligica, 2014).

The 'instrument' the Ostroms and their associates put forward is the Institutional Analysis and Development (IAD) framework. It has been defined as an analytical and heuristic device 'composed of nested sets of components within components' aimed at mapping diverse institutional arrangements, more precisely 'a series of nested conceptual maps of the explanatory space that social scientists can use in trying to understand and explain the diversity of human patterns of behavior' (Ostrom, 2005, p. 8).

Intrinsic to its application is 'a consistent method for overtly analyzing the deeper structures that constitute any particular action situation' (Ostrom, 2005, p. 7). It is a social agent-based tool, on the lines reflected in the 2000 article, integrating insights on how the environment and institutions impact and shape the incentives and individuals' behavior. At the same time, it has a clear heuristic and operational nature and function. We are, with this approach, at the core of current developments in social sciences. As Clarke and Primo (2012) explain, the approach to social sciences in which models and mapping are pivotal, challenges the outdated received vision of science (science revolves around general sentences or propositions to be verified) and advances the current vision (science revolves around models). Models are not true or false, they are instruments for achieving specific objectives. They should be seen as we see maps: useful or not, in function of the specific investigative purposes of the user. A map is not true or false, it is useful or not. Its epistemic status is strictly related to its pragmatic one and the circumstances of the user and the context of the case. Obviously a shift from general propositions to models and the mapping is also a shift in epistemology.

All of the above help us to understand better the other contextual analysis relevant idea that Elinor Ostrom introduced, while building on the insights coming from the application of the IAD framework: the notion of 'theoretical scenarios' (Ostrom, 1998, p. 14; Aligica, 2014). An alternative to grand generalizing and universal laws could be to build scenarios of how 'exogenous variables combine to affect endogenous structural variables'. It is possible, she explains, to 'produce coherent, cumulative, theoretical scenarios that start with relatively simple baseline models. One can then begin the systematic exploration of what happens as one variable is changed'. Again, the function is first and foremost heuristic: an instrument that facilities understanding. The logic of combinations and permutations, systematically reinforced by empirical verification drives the research, revealing the main facets of the phenomena in their context. Theoretical scenarios are hence a natural and flexible way of framing contextual analysis.

To conclude, Ostrom was one of the pioneers of the idea of contextual analysis – an idea unmistakably featured in 'Collective Action and the Evolution of Social Norms'. She also was one of the first scholars to methodically think about the ways of dealing with the analytical and methodological problems that an investigative focus on context may pose. Last but not least, it is important to note that one of the most important insights of her work in this respect is however one of huge normative implications. The approach she sketches ends up confronting us with, 'a world of possibility rather than of necessity'. In other words, 'we are neither trapped in inexorable tragedies nor free of moral responsibility for creating and sustaining incentives that facilitate our own achievement of mutually productive outcomes' (Ostrom, 1998, pp. 15–16). Social order and institutional arrangements are not predetermined; they are not a simple matter of mere impersonal variables, factors and forces, but a matter of human deliberation, decision and responsibility. In the end, humans as moral agents – conditional cooperators, rational egoists, willing punishers – being able to imagine and create alternative strategies and rules, and thus bear the responsibility for the alternative courses of action and institutional arrangements they create.

References

Aligica, P. (2014). *Institutional diversity and political economy. The Ostroms and beyond.* Oxford and New York: Oxford University Press.

Clarke Kevin, A., & Primo, D. M. (2012). *A model discipline: Political science and the logic of representations* (x + 220 Pages). New York, NY: Oxford University Press. USD 34.95 (paper).

Goodin, R. E. & Tilly, C. (Eds.). (2008). *The Oxford handbook of contextual political analysis.* Oxford and New York: Oxford Handbooks Online.

Marwell, G., & Oliver, P. (1993). The critical mass in collective action. Cambridge: Cambridge University Press.

Oliver, P. E., & Marwell, G. (2001). Whatever happened to critical mass theory? A retrospective and assessment. *Sociological Theory, 19*(3), 292–311. doi:10.1111/0735-2751.00142

Oliver, P., Gerald Marwell, E., & Teixeira, R. (1985). A theory of the critical mass. I. Interdependence, group heterogeneity, and the production of collective action. *The American Journal of Sociology, 91*(3), 522–556. doi:10.1086/228313

Ostrom, E. (1998). A behavioral approach to the rational choice theory of collective action: Presidential address, American Political Science Association, 1997. *The American Political Science Review, 92*, 1–22. doi:10.2307/2585925

Ostrom, E. (2000). Collective action and the evolution of social norms. *The Journal of Economic Perspectives, 14*(3), 137–158. doi:10.1257/jep.14.3.137

Ostrom, E. (2005). *Understanding institutional diversity.* Princeton: Princeton University Press.

Ostrom, V. (1997). Epistemic choice and public choice. In *The meaning of democracy and the vulnerability of democracies: Response to Tocqueville's challenge* (pp. 89–116). Ann Arbor: The University of Michigan Press.

Poteete, A., & Ostrom, E. (2004). In pursuit of comparable concepts and data about collective action. *Agricultural Systems, 82*, 215–232. doi:10.1016/j.agsy.2004.07.002

Soltan, K. (2014). The emerging field of a New Civics. In P. Levin & K. E. Soltan (Eds.), *Civic studies* (pp. 9–19). Washington, DC: Bringing Theory to Practice.

Contextualizing the influence of social norms, collective action on social-ecological systems

Tom P. Evans[a,c] and Daniel H. Cole[b,c]

[a]Department of Geography, Indiana University, Bloomington, IN USA; [b]Maurer School of Law, School of Public and Environmental Affairs, Indiana University, Bloomington, IN USA; [c]Ostrom Workshop in Political Theory and Policy Analysis, Indiana University, Bloomington, IN USA

1. Introduction

The influence of social norms in social-ecological systems is often dramatic but also deceptively complex. Ostrom's work elegantly leverages research from experimental economics and case studies of common-pool resource systems to demonstrate that many collective action dilemmas can be successfully resolved (Ostrom, 2000). This analysis was by no means suggested as a universal or generalizable foregone outcome as there are many cases of failures to overcome collective action problems. Furthermore, collective action problems only constitute a subset of social-ecological systems found globally. Thus, in order to understand the interplay between social norms and collective action in social-ecological systems it is necessary to contextualize these dynamics within a broader framework that encompasses a broad area of components in Social-Ecological Systems (SESs). Ostrom's later work did just this, with publications that were clearly inspired by her earlier foundational work. In particular, what has become known as the '*Social-Ecological Systems Framework*' (Ostrom, 2009) outlines numerous elements of social-ecological systems that received relatively little attention in the 2000 manuscript. And as was noted by Ostrom in 2000, 'empirical and theoretical work in the future needs to ask how a large array of contextual variables affects the processes of teaching and evoking social norms' (p. 154). Here we explore selected arenas that are of particular interest to the evolution of SESs while at the same time attempting to synthesize some of the work that followed after Ostrom's 2000 publication.

2. Missing pieces of the puzzle

First, it is necessary to draw a distinction between types of social-ecological systems. Ostrom herself was a diligent attendant to careful language and the particular context of the 2000 manuscript was more focused than the later work on SESs. Here we adopt the definition of a social-ecological system as 'a coherent system of biophysical and social factors that regularly interact in a resilient, sustained manner' (Redman, Grove, & Kuby, 2004, p. 163). For the moment we leave aside the question of what system boundaries mean with respect to an SES. But our point is to clarify that an SES may be considered a common-pool resource system but of course not all SESs are Common Pool Resources (CPRs). Ostrom's earlier work was inspired by the observation that actors are able to sustain governance arrangements with an emphasis on CPRs, but many and likely most

SESs are not dominated by CPR type arrangements. This is by no means meant as a criticism as Ostrom was simply using a set of case studies to demonstrate conditions under which actors may be able to sustain governance of a particular resource. But it does suggest that extending Ostrom's earlier work beyond CPRs to other types of SESs is an exceedingly complicated challenge given the diversity of social and biophysical dynamics found across global SESs. This can lead to some confusion as in some of Ostrom's later work she herself seemingly misses the opportunity to clarify what conditions tend to result in long-enduring common-pool resource systems as opposed to social-ecological systems more generally. Specifically, the section 'Design Principles and Robust Social-Ecological Systems' in *Understanding Institutional Diversity* (Ostrom, 2005) begins by reiterating the design principles for robust common-property institutions (Ostrom, 1990). So we can consider still unfinished the challenge of identifying the conditions that tend to lead to long-enduring social-ecological systems, much less the corresponding challenge of identifying the conditions that result in equitable distribution of resources across actors within SESs. But some guidance is given later in the chapter when Ostrom translates the design principles to a set of scoping questions including 'Are there functional and creative efforts by local appropriators to craft effective stewardship mechanisms for local resources that should be recognized?' (p. 271) and 'How do we create a multiple-layer, polycentric system that can be dynamic, adaptive, and effective over time?'. Here direct inspiration is taken from Vincent Ostrom's early work on polycentric governance (Ostrom, Tiebout, & Warren, 1961) and also recognition of the role of learning and adaptation for sustaining SESs.

3. Social-ecological systems, social learning and decision-making

Ostrom's connection to experimental work exemplifies her recognition that learning, adaptation and decision-making were important dimensions of social-ecological systems. She designed many experiments in collaboration with colleagues but also frequently referenced the emerging field of experimental economics as she developed theories of common-pool resource management (Ostrom, Gardner, & Walker, 1994). Much of this experimental work focused on the influence of communication (Ostrom & Walker, 1991), and this work was later extended by colleagues in subsequent experiments (Janssen, Anderies, & Joshi, 2011), including experiments that were translated from laboratory settings to the field (Janssen, Anderies, & Cardenas, 2011). This attention to decision-making in collective action settings was important but perhaps stopped short of a focus on individual-level decision-making in the way that cognitive science typically focuses. In these experiments it was the group outcome that was of particular interest and there was less attention afforded to an explanation of the diversity of individual-level decisions. Without a doubt the Prisoner's dilemma game and conditions under which a player would defect constitutes a recognition of individual-level decision-making, but overall learning and decision-making perhaps received less attention than the group outcome of successful collective action.

Other scholars of course have explored this terrain. There is a rich literature on social learning particularly with respect to water governance that provides a valuable complement to Ostrom's work on decision-making (Pahl-Wostl et al., 2007). In the same way that the Institutional Analysis and Development (IAD) framework provided a grounding force behind work at the Ostrom Workshop in Political Theory and Policy Analysis at Indiana University, complementary or alternative frameworks strengthen our understanding of the role of governance in SESs. Different types of actors hold different positions in an SES and may have different learning pathways. Critically, we can distinguish between different types of learning such as single-loop learning that leads to incremental changes in decision-making performance vs. so-called triple-loop learning that results in transformation in an SES that entails changing social norms and values towards environmental resources (Pahl-Wostl et al., 2007, 2008; Pahl-Wostl, Mostert, & Tàbara, 2008).

Extensive empirical work, critical theoretical development and rigorous data collection protocols laid the groundwork for what would become the SES Framework. Particularly important was the experience of designing coding protocols for the International Forestry Resources and Institutions program (IFRI) and similar protocols for coding CPR cases (Ostrom, Agrawal, Blomquist, Schlager, & Tang, 1989). This ultimately led to the vision for a framework that would enable case studies to be compiled into a single database using consistent definitions and procedures. The SES Framework only reached the stage of a framework but not an implemented system before Ostrom's passing. But this implementation work has proceeded in the form of extensions to and refinement of the SES Framework (McGinnis & Ostrom, 2014). A particularly important dimension for implementing the SES Framework is articulation of the environmental dynamics in SESs (Epstein, Vogt, Mincey, Cox, & Fischer, 2013). But as important are the learning mechanisms and signals that actors use to interpret those environmental dynamics (Pahl-Wostl et al. 2007). The question of what environmental data actors need to make effective decisions about environmental resources remains a scientific territory ripe for attention.

4. Social norms, rules-in-use and rules-in-form

In order to understand Ostrom's work, including her 2000 paper in the *Journal of Economic Perspectives*, the reader must appreciate certain conceptual definitions that informed almost everything she wrote (even though she did not always pay such close attention to her own definitions). First and foremost, when Ostrom (2000) wrote about rules and norms, she was writing about what she called (following North, 1990), 'institutions' or the 'rules of the game' that structure human actions and interactions (see also Ostrom, 2005, pp. 16–19). Also following North (1990), Ostrom (2005, p. 179) distinguished between formal rules, such as legislation, regulation, and court decisions, and informal rules, such as social norms, conventions, or habits.

This distinction relates to another between 'rules-in-use' (a.k.a., the 'working rules') and 'rules-in-form'. A 'rule-in-form' is, generally speaking, what is written on paper (e.g., by some legislative body). A 'rule-in-use' is what individuals and groups understand the rules to be in their interactions. The distinction seems clear enough, but actual relations between 'rules-in-form' and 'rules-in-use' are substantially richer and more complex than Ostrom sometimes acknowledged. A greater focus on 'rules-in-form', in addition to 'rules-in-use', would enhance our understanding of social interactions to resolve actual or experimental collective-action problems.

Ostrom (2000, p. 148) also distinguished 'rules' from 'norms' (based on Crawford and Ostrom, 1995), but that distinction may not add much to the formal/informal distinction discussed above. As Ostrom (2005, p. 166) has explained, '[b]oth formal and informal prescriptions can be classified as shared norms or rules', depending on the availability of punishments for noncompliance.

By focusing exclusively on 'rules-in-use' and 'social norms', Ostrom (2000) created (albeit unintentionally) an impression that formal rules (such as duly-enacted laws) do not much matter for interactions to resolve social or social-ecological dilemmas. In fact,

Ostrom understood quite well that formal rules matter, as exemplified by her close attention to the constitutional- and collective-choice action situations in her IAD framework (see, e.g., Ostrom, 2005). In her work on water allocation institutions in Southern California (e.g., Blomquist & Ostrom, 1985), she paid close attention to judicial adjudication of rights. Moreover, there is no reason to believe *ex ante* that a particular rule-in-use does not equal a particular rule-in-form. Not every formal legal (or constitutional) rule is subject to the kind of multiple, conflicting interpretations that can cause the rule-in-use to deviate from it. For example, there is no difference between the constitutional rule-in-form and the rule-in-use regarding the minimum age requirement for the office of President of the United States. Thirty-five years is both the rule-in-form and the rule-in use.

Many rules are of that clear and uncontroversial type, so that it would be a mistake to assume that rules-in-form amount to rules-in-use only in exceptional circumstances. However, divergence does occur, perhaps in the majority of cases, for a variety of reasons, including ignorance of formal rules, multiple reasonable but conflicting interpretations of them, or difficulties of enforcement. Sometimes, preexisting social norms, whether socially efficient or inefficient, are so strongly entrenched that formal rules have insufficient power to displace or amend them. Ellickson (2009) explained that not even the lawyers in Shasta County, California knew of the state's legal rules on fencing cattle in/ out. Like the neighbors they were advising, the lawyers were operating under the influence of informal norms of neighborliness that led in most cases to cost-sharing by neighboring ranchers and crop farmers of fence construction and maintenance. Ellickson showed that social norms – which North (1990) classified as informal 'rules of the game' – might be more efficient and prevail over the formal legal rules.

But informal social norms are not inevitably more efficient or otherwise better than formal rules. In some cases, formal rules are necessary to break down unfairly exclusionary and/or inefficient informal norms, such as anti-Semitism and racism, especially when those norms target 'discrete and insular minorities' (*United States v. Carolene Products,* 304 US 144, fn. 4, 1938). Uprooting bad social norms may be very difficult and take a long period of time. A legislative body, however well-meaning, cannot be expected to eradicate *de facto* (or even *de jure*) racism simply by passing a law (as the short history of constitutional amendments prohibiting sale and use of alcohol in the US exemplifies). It took a century for the 'equal protection' guarantee of the 14th Amendment to the US Constitution, aided by statutes such as the 1964 Civil Rights Act (Pub.L. 88–352, 78 Stat. 241) and the 1965 Voting Rights Act (42 U.S.C. §§ 1973–1973bb-1), along with Supreme Court decisions like *Brown v. Board of Education* (347 US 483, 1954) to even begin the process of leveling the playing field for African Americans. There is no doubting, however, that formal constitutional and legal rules played an important, perhaps necessary, role in eroding the mindsets and institutions (both formal and informal) that supported 'Jim Crow'.

Even on less socially weighty matters, formal rules and informal norms often interact in ways that make it necessary to focus not just on one or the other but both. Consider something as simple as the rules of the road (an example Ostrom, 2005, p. 18, also used). Under state laws, legal speed limits are posted on all public highways. Those posted limits represent the rules-in-form, and some motorists follow them strictly. But many motorists understand that enforcement is costly (and therefore imperfect) and that law enforcers are unlikely to pull them over unless they exceed the posted speed limit by a substantial amount. So, they follow an almost universal (at least in the US) social norm of driving approximately five miles per hour above the posted limit. Notice that the norm itself tells us nothing about the actual speed anyone is likely to drive on a given road (the rule-in-use), unless we also know the posted speed limit (the rule-in-form). Moreover, motorists know that reliance on the rule-in-form is not foolproof. Should a highway patrol officer choose to ticket a driver for exceeding the posted speed limit by only three miles per hour, a court of law will strictly enforce that decision, regardless of the prevailing social norm. The result would no doubt strike the unfortunate motorist as grossly unfair, but in case of conflict the rule-in-form would trump the rule-in-use.

The distinction between 'rules-in-form' and 'rules-in-use' can mislead social scientists into disregarding the former as insignificant. For example, Kingston and Cabelleros (2009, p. 158) refer to rules-in-form as 'dead letters' (and misattribute that view to Ostrom). Consequently, it might have been better for Ostrom to rely exclusively on her alternative conception of 'working rules', which intuitively seems more inclusive. Ostrom (2005, p. 19) defined 'working rules' as 'the set of rules to which participants would make reference if asked to explain and justify their actions to fellow participants'. Such reasons and justifications obviously might include references to either social norms or formal legal rules.

5. Concluding thoughts

The search for generalizable findings from research on the management of social-ecological systems is an elusive pursuit. Ostrom herself acknowledged that only through careful refinement and revision to research design can progress be made. This is demonstrated through the immense work done to refine the IFRI protocol over time as well as the starting point constituted by the SES Framework. What is remarkable about her work is the way that empirical research, theories and frameworks built on each other over time. It is hard to say to what degree Ostrom's vision to connect these elements more than 15 years ago included a path that would include the challenge of understanding the field of environmental governance beyond the seminal work on CPRs. But the rigor and meticulousness from her earlier work serves as both an example to follow as well as an inspiration to those who continue working on this challenge.

Funding

We acknowledge financial support for this work from the National Science Foundation [BCS-1115009, BCS-1026776].

References

Blomquist, W., & Ostrom, E. (1985). Institutional capacity and the resolution of a commons dilemma. *Review of Policy Research, 5*(2), 383–394. doi:10.1111/j.1541-1338.1985.tb00364.x

Crawford, S. and Ostrom E. (1995). A Grammar of Institutions. *American Political Science Review, 89*(3), 582–600.

Ellickson, R. C. (2009). *Order without law: How neighbors settle disputes.* Cambridge, MA: Harvard University Press.

Epstein, G., Vogt, J. M., Mincey, S. K., Cox, M., & Fischer, B. (2013). Missing ecology: Integrating ecological perspectives with the social-ecological system framework. *International Journal of the Commons, 7*(2), 432–453.

Janssen, M. A., Anderies, J. M., & Cardenas, J.-C. (2011). Head-enders as stationary bandits in asymmetric commons: Comparing irrigation experiments in the laboratory and the field. *Ecological Economics, 70*(9), 1590–1598. doi:10.1016/j.ecolecon.2011.01.006

Janssen, M. A., Anderies, J. M., & Joshi, S. R. (2011). Coordination and cooperation in asymmetric commons dilemmas. *Experimental Economics, 14*(4), 547–566. doi:10.1007/s10683-011-9281-9

McGinnis, M. D., & Ostrom, E. (2014). Social-ecological system framework: Initial changes and continuing challenges. *Ecology and Society, 19*(2), 30. doi:10.5751/ES-06387-190230

North, D. C. (1990). *Institutions, institutional change and economic performance.* Cambridge, England: Cambridge University Press.

Ostrom, E. (1990). *Governing the commons: The evolution of institutions for collective action.* Cambridge, England: Cambridge University Press.

Ostrom, E. (2000). Collective action and the evolution of social norms. *The Journal of Economic Perspectives, 14*(3), 137–158. doi:10.1257/jep.14.3.137

Ostrom, E. (2009). A general framework for analyzing sustainability of social-ecological systems. *Science, 325,* 419–422. doi:10.1126/science.1172133

Ostrom, E. (2005). *Understanding institutional diversity.* Princeton, New Jersey: Princeton University Press.

Ostrom, E., Agrawal, A., Blomquist, W., Schlager, E., & Tang, S. Y. (1989). *CPR Coding Manual.*

Ostrom, E., Gardner, R., & Walker, J. (1994). *Rules, games, and common-pool resources.* Ann Arbor, Michigan: University of Michigan Press.

Ostrom, V., Tiebout, C. M., & Warren, R. (1961). The organization of government in metropolitan areas: A theoretical inquiry. *The American Political Science Review, 55*(4), 831–842. doi:10.2307/1952530

Ostrom, E., & Walker, J. (1991). Communication in a commons: Cooperation without external enforcement. In Thomas R. Palfrey (Ed.), *Laboratory Research in Political Economy.* Ann Arbor, MI: University of Michigan Press. 287–322.

Pahl-Wostl, C., Craps, M., Dewulf, A., Mostert, E., Tabara, D., & Taillieu, T. (2007). Social learning and water resources management. *Ecology and society, 12*(2), 5.

Pahl-Wostl, C., Mostert, E., & Tàbara, D. (2008). The growing importance of social learning in water resources management and sustainability science. *Ecology and Society, 13*(1), 24.

Pahl-Wostl, C., Tàbara, D., Bouwen, R., Craps, M., Dewulf, A., Mostert, E., ... Taillieu, T. (2008). The importance of social learning and culture for sustainable water management. *Ecological Economics, 64*(3), 484–495. doi:10.1016/j.ecolecon.2007.08.007

Redman, C. L., Grove, J. M., & Kuby, L. H. (2004). Integrating social science into the long-term ecological research (LTER) network: Social dimensions of ecological change and ecological dimensions of social change. *Ecosystems, 7*(2), 161–171. doi:10.1007/s10021-003-0215-z

Collective Action and the Evolution of Social Norms: the principled optimism of Elinor Ostrom

Matthew R. Auer

Environmental Studies Program, Bates College, Lewiston, Maine, USA

Of her many contributions to the social, behavioral and applied natural sciences, which title by Elinor 'Lin' Ostrom towers over all others? Answering this question is no simple task. The amount of vital authorship by Ostrom rivals that of any political scientist over the past 50 years. Indeed, it is confining to situate Ostrom in the discipline of political science. Her highest honor, the Nobel Memorial Prize, was earned in economic sciences. And her theories, discoveries, and casework shape fields and specializations as wide ranging as complex economic systems (Ostrom, 2010) to community forestry (Wollenberg, Merino, Agrawal, & Ostrom, 2007) and from local policing (Ostrom & Parks, 1973) to rule-making in sports (Castronova & Wagner, 2009). As a seminal figure in the study of institutions, her insights are far-reaching, considering that institutions are found almost everywhere in human affairs. Pervasive as well as diverse, Ostrom's institutions are, Munger argues, akin to Darwin's 'endless forms' of ecological niches and biological variation (Munger, 2010).

Nevertheless, her 'Collective Action and the Evolution of Social Norms' which appeared in the *Journal of Economic Perspectives* (Ostrom, 2000) rightfully stands among her most important contributions to our understanding of human social behavior and the conditions by which people overcome self-interested and self-defeating outcomes involving things of value. The compact and comprehensive form of her argument makes it an especially accessible introduction to Ostrom's intellectual legacy. Yet, 'Collective Action and the Evolution of Social Norms' – henceforth, identified by its abbreviation, 'CAESN', and the broader implications of Ostrom's argument about the potential for trust and cooperation amidst uncertainty – are not universally embraced by all students of natural resource management regimes.

Ostrom's article is steeped in the literatures of political economy, new institutional economics, game theory, rational choice, and of course, collective action, with case material playing key supporting roles. She uses many of her references to carefully explore – and systematically dismantle – the basic assumptions of the so-called rational egoist. The first part of the present essay considers her critique of the rational egoist, 15 years after the publication of CAESN. Ostrom presents evidence that human personality is amenable to collective decision-making and considerations of equity. However, outcomes that are good for the collective occur because of participants' particular expectations and in-the-moment experiences. Over many years of observation, Ostrom found consistent evidence that a set of 'design principles' were at work for 'long-surviving' resource management regimes, including contexts involving easily accessed, easily depleted, costly-to-protect natural resources ('common pool resources' or CPRs). Ostrom notes in CAESN that to her knowledge, 'no empirical study has challenged (the) validity' of the 'design principles' (Ostrom, 2000, p. 149 *passim*). And yet, in the years since CAESN was published, challenges have been proffered. The second half of this essay explores the design principles in critical perspective. These considerations form a bridge to the essay's final concern, namely whether the design principles, and more broadly, Ostrom herself, was unjustifiably 'optimistic' about prospects for collective action.

Putting rational egoism to the test

CAESN begins with a recitation of Mancur Olson's famous assertion that 'no self-interested person would contribute to the production of a public good: "[u]nless the number of individuals in a group is quite small, or unless there is coercion or some other special device to make individuals act in their common interest..."' (Ostrom, 2000, p. 137). According to this 'zero contribution thesis', self-regarding behavior is expected even in instances when cooperation promises payoffs to individuals that exceed in value the non-cooperative alternatives. Exceptions include cases when private utility is so high, one actor or a 'small privileged group' has incentive to provide public goods (Keohane & Ostrom, 1995, p. 13). But more often than not, individual contributions to the provision of the public good is unlikely because 'rational, self-interested individuals will not act to achieve their common or group interests' (Ostrom, 2000, p. 137). The notion '...that individuals cannot overcome collective action problems and need to have externally enforced rules to achieve their own long-term self-interest' is the edifice that Ostrom carefully and methodically picks apart over the first half of the paper, drawing extensively on laboratory evidence of 'rational choice in collective action situations' (Ostrom, 2000, p. 139).

Importantly, Ostrom's critique of Olson is less a blanket refutation than an empirically-derived challenge to the rational egoist proposition. Over many years, Ostrom and her collaborators (e.g., Ostrom & Walker, 1997; Ostrom, Gardner, & Walker, 1994; Ostrom, Walker, & Gardner, 1992), among others (e.g., Offerman, 1997), devised experimental conditions that brought out self-serving behavior in subjects, and catalogued circumstances when mutual gains through cooperation prevailed. Rich evidence comes from highly-controlled laboratory tests, where participants (generally, college students) face trade-offs in allocating 'tokens' or other objects with symbolic or real value that yield private payoffs and/or group payoffs (Ostrom, Gardner, & Walker, 1994). In some experiments, full group cooperation (with all individuals contributing tokens to the public good) yields the highest payoffs to individuals. But the temptation to defect and free-ride increases as well, as individuals contemplate high private payoffs by not contributing to the public good, and hence, not incurring costs that 'cooperators' incur.

As neatly summarized in CAESN, among the key factors that proved important for cooperation and collective action was face-to-face communication. This proved true even in instances when conditions for free-riding were high. A prototypical circumstance for free-riding is the common pool resource dilemma. Ostrom, Gardner, and Walker (1994) found, for example, that in cases involving allocation of 'high-endowment' (comparatively rich) CPRs, when players had one and only one opportunity to communicate, these players enjoyed an average percentage of net yield above baseline of 55% compared to 21% for individuals who did not communicate. Yields increased when participants communicated in multiple rounds (73% versus 21%) and the yields were higher still when the CPR was low-endowment (Ostrom & Walker, 1997; Ostrom, Walker, & Gardner, 1992).

Ostrom and her collaborators speak of the efficiency-inducing benefits of face-to-face communication and how the power of communication produces higher joint outcomes, even when players start the game with dissimilar resource endowments (Hackett, Schlager, & Walker, 1994). Considering that Ostrom's findings frequently challenge and refute the rational egoist thesis, it is interesting, and perhaps ironic, that Ostrom invokes rationalist explanations for her observed outcomes, namely, that communication increases the flow of information, allowing for more efficient decision-making, and hence, more rational decisions. The paradox that rationalism is the framing for a series of experiments that discover the limits of rational egoism is accentuated by a footnote in CAESN (Ostrom, 2000, p. 140 *passim*). The author notes the 'startling' finding by Bohnet and Frey (1999) that 'simply allowing subjects to see the other persons with whom they are playing greatly increases cooperation as contrasted to completely anonymous situations'. Indeed, this finding is startling if one presumes that the players are one-dimensional utility-maximizers whose behavior is unobstructed by concerns of conscience or reputation. These experiments would suggest that even in highly controlled situations where decisions are stripped down to binary choices about contributing to the public good, it is difficult for players to suppress dimensions of personality and character that, fortunately, most psychologically healthy human beings exhibit.

The repeated rebuttal of the rational egoist expectation, even in Ostrom's and her colleagues' uncluttered laboratory tests, suggests first order problems with the premises of the rational egoism. Fundamental questions of salience crop up, namely, in the ordinary course of human affairs, where social interaction is pervasive, under what conditions might we actually expect to encounter unmitigated rational egoism? Is it conceivable that the rational egoist, in its unadulterated form, is the exception rather than rule? Whittaker argues that even Adam Smith appreciated the limits of the self-regarding actor precept. She writes,

> Both Ostrom and Smith recognize self-interest is part of human nature but also draw attention to the importance of other-regarding behavior, in Ostrom's case for addressing common pool resource problems, and in Smith's case for achieving a society of "human flourishing". (Whittaker, 2011, p. 33)

In CAESN, Ostrom mentions that collective action provided evolutionary advantages to ancestors of humans, dating to the Pleistocene era (Ostrom, 2000, p. 143). However, considering the evolutionary ascendancy of collectively-oriented social behavior, Ostrom does not clarify why it is necessary to perform experiments that, in a broad sense, affirm what is apparent in dozens of daily social interactions – namely that unmitigated self-interested behavior is anomalous. Indeed, this behavior is 'anti-social'; the prevailing norm is to be conscious of others' interests as well as that of one's own. But again, the significance of Ostrom's work has less to do with negating the rational egoist axiom than in demonstrating, at a granular level, the conditions and probabilities for cooperation, or alternatively, defection and self-interest, in a wide variety of situations or games. Explicating those specific conditions and the experts' various experimental protocols go beyond the scope of this essay. For interested readers, the best sources are Ostrom, Walker, and Gardner (1992) and Ostrom, Gardner, and Walker (1994).

Even if the student never dives deeply into the experiments, there is much to learn from CAESN about the basics of whom, exactly, is vital in the emergence and stability of collective action regimes. The most key players, Ostrom argues, are 'conditional cooperators' and 'willing punishers'. Conditional cooperators are 'individuals who are willing to initiate cooperative action when they estimate others will reciprocate' and who will 'repeat these actions as long as a sufficient proportion of others involved reciprocate' (Ostrom, 2000, p. 142). Willing punishers, meanwhile,

> ...punish presumed free riders through verbal rebukes or...use costly material payoffs when available. Willing punishers may also become willing rewarders if the circle of relationships allows them to reward those who have contributed more than the minimal level. (Ostrom, 2000, p. 142)

Ostrom and her colleagues found conditional cooperators well-represented in their lab experiments (Ostrom, 2000, p. 140). When participants were afforded an opportunity to communicate one time, they contributed between 40 and 60% of their endowments to the public good – an unpredicted outcome from a rational egoist perspective. And willing punishers were willing to expend personal resources to sanction players making 'below-average contributions to a collective benefit' (Ostrom, 2000, p. 141). These rebukes imply the existence of a group norm for cooperation and reciprocity as well as voluntary investment in and enforcement of that norm by the willing punishers.

Collective action by design

The second half of CAESN considers another of Ostrom's key contributions to the collective action literature, namely the 'design principles of long-surviving, self-organized resource regimes' (Ostrom, 2000, p. 149). The power of her insights are two-fold. First, the principles she enumerates are, arguably, more profound than the discoveries from the lab, because they are derived from the more complicated, multivariate world of field-based observation. Secondly, there is the tantalizing prospect of learning the secrets of 'long-surviving' resource regimes.

Ostrom (2000, pp. 149–152) succinctly defines eight design principles in CAESN; they are refined versions of concepts explored in Ostrom (1990), and they include: (1) clear boundary rules, (2) equitable rules-in-use that recognize biophysical limitations of the resource, (3) participation rules, (4) monitoring that is accountable to resource users, (5) graduated sanctions, (6) access to low-cost arenas for resolving conflicts, (7) recognition of local users' self-organization right by external authorities, and (8) nested rule-making in governance structures. Field-based corroboration of the validity of the design principles in the formation and long-term stability of resource regimes are too many to mention (see, for example, Poteete, Janssen, & Ostrom, 2010, p. 101), but it is worth noting the great variety of resource types and national and cultural contexts that have been examined (e.g., Sarker & Itoh, 2001 and Zabel & Holm-Müller, 2008).

Not all experts have applied the design principles and come away feeling persuaded about their applicability or robustness. Campbell et al. (2001), for example, found few examples of sustainably managed forests in Zimbabwe, but absence of institutions for resource management did not explain this trend. In fact, 'local customs and norms' – which are the formative elements of institutions – were firmly in place, and yet, served to hinder rather than promote sustainable forest management. The authors query whether Ostrom's design principles make more sense for 'other resource types – irrigation systems feature prominently' (in her work), or if her thesis is simply unrealistic in its optimism (Campbell et al., 2001, p. 595). No less skeptical, in Steins' (1999) studies of coastal resource management systems in Ireland, the United Kingdom, and the Netherlands, the author criticizes the design principles for failing to account for 'contextual factors' and for the tendency of the principles to be used as a 'blueprint' for determining successful CPR regimes.

Notably, Ostrom (2000, p. 153) does make reference to 'contextual variables' as 'essential for understanding the initial growth and sustainability of collective action as well as the challenges that long-surviving, self-organized regimes must try to overcome'. Those challenges include major migrations of resource users (in or out of the resource area), rapid changes in technology, corruption, and other forces. But Ostrom contends (2000, pp. 153–154):

> Simply saying that context matters is not, however, a satisfactory theoretical approach. Adopting an evolutionary approach is the first step toward a more general theoretical synthesis that addresses the question of how context matters. In particular, we need to address how context affects the presence or absence of conditional cooperators and willing punishers and the likelihood that the norms held by these participants are adopted and strengthened by others in a relevant population.

Responding to the 'context matters' crowd, Ostrom places particular emphasis on the salience of conditional cooperators and willing punishers. Arguably, these two actors occupy an even more essential role than the design principles because they are implicated in so many of those principles. The conditional cooperator and the willing punisher are arbiters of the proper functioning of the many rules embedded in the design principles – for example, the stinting rules described in design principle #2. The free-riders and other self-regarding participants in the resource regime cannot be expected to develop or enforce rules that generate joint benefits or long-term resource sustainability. Yes, context matters, Ostrom acknowledges. But she urges students of CPRs and of collective action to inquire how context affects incentives for participants in the community who are contemplating alternative payoff outcomes, over time.

Concluding thoughts: Ostrom as principled optimist

Ostrom and other exponents of the design principles (see, e.g., Acheson, 2006) appreciate that 'contextual factors' can stymie the formation of collective action or disrupt, alter, and overpower regimes that are already in place. To my knowledge, the notion of the design principles as a 'blueprint' for successful CPRs was never claimed by the concept's founder, and three of her collaborators went so far as to refute the blueprint claim (Cox, Arnold, & Villamayor-Tomas, 2010). Nevertheless, accusing Ostrom of optimism is not amiss, though more precisely, she was a 'principled optimist'. Her confidence in the rational, joint benefit-producing behavior of resource users was conditioned by the design principles. In recognizing that individuals can overcome selfish motives and temptations so as to manage contested resources, and having witnessed the formation of trust and reciprocity in repeated laboratory trials and in the field, Ostrom understandably felt sanguine about the noble possibilities of human nature. But she also understood that resource users' spontaneous discovery, adoption, and adherence to the design principles – and the presence of conditional cooperators and willful punishers – were key to the success and long-term stability of cooperative regimes. And she appreciated the many ways otherwise well-meaning individuals and groups of resource users could lose their way.

Ostrom's optimism was informed not only by an appreciation of peoples' ability to embrace collective action over short-term individualistic gain. She was also fascinated and heartened by self-organization as an alternative to dependence on outsiders. Solutions imposed from outside the community, including from state actors, were not always necessary for managing 'at-risk' resources, and indeed, interventions by outsiders could make matters worse. Ostrom was gratified to demonstrate, empirically, that people could be empowered, made more confident, and more competent, through their own, natural process of determining and enforcing community norms. If she was upbeat about the good things that could be accomplished by ordinary people, this part of her personality was informed by her own observations and experiments and those of many others. Lin Ostrom's optimism was grounded in a well-ordered process of trial and discovery that any skeptical scientist can appreciate.

References

Acheson, J. M. (2006). Institutional failure in resource management. *Annual Review of Anthropology*, *35*, 117–134. doi:10.1146/annurev.anthro.35.081705.123238

Bohnet, I., & Frey, B. S. (1999). The sound of silence in prisoner's dilemma and dictator games. *Journal of Economic Behavior and Organization*, *38*, 43–57. doi:10.1016/S0167-2681(98)00121-8

Campbell, B., Mandondo, A., Nemarundwe, N., Sithole, B., de Jong, W., Luckert, M., & Matose, F. (2001). Challenges to proponents of common property resource systems: Despairing voices from the social forests of Zimbabwe. *World Development*, *29*, 589–600. doi:10.1016/S0305-750X(00)00114-5

Castronova, E., & Wagner, G. G. (2009). Sports rules as common pool resources: A better way to respond to doping. *Economic Analysis and Policy*, *39*, 341–344.

Cox, M., Arnold, G., & Villamayor-Tomas, S. (2010). A review of the design principles for community-based natural resource management. *Ecology and Society*, *15*, 38.

Hackett, S., Schlager, E., & Walker, J. (1994). The role of communication in resolving commons dilemmas: Experimental evidence with heterogeneous appropriators. *Journal of Environmental Economics & Management*, *27*, 99–126. doi:10.1006/jeem.1994.1029

Keohane, R. O., & Ostrom, E. (1995). Introduction. In R. O. Keohane & E. Ostrom (Eds.), *Local commons and global interdependence* (pp. 1–26). London: Sage.

Munger, M. C. (2010). Endless forms most beautiful and most wonderful: Elinor Ostrom and the diversity of institutions. *Public Choice*, *143*, 263–268. doi:10.1007/s11127-010-9629-2

Offerman, T. (1997). *Beliefs and decision rules in public goods games: Theory and experiments.* Dordrecht: Kluwer.

Ostrom, E., & Parks, R. B. (1973). *Suburban police departments: Too many and too small?.* Thousand Oaks, CA: Sage.

Ostrom, E. (1990). *Governing the commons: The evolution of institutions for collective action.* New York, NY: Cambridge University Press.

Ostrom, E. (2000). Collective action and the evolution of social norms. *Journal of Economic Perspectives*, *14*, 137–158. doi:10.1257/jep.14.3.137

Ostrom, E. (2010). Beyond markets and states: Polycentric governance of complex economic systems. *American Economic Review*, *100*, 641–672. doi:10.1257/aer.100.3.641

Ostrom, E., Gardner, R., & Walker, J. (1994). *Rules, games, and common-pool resources.* Ann Arbor, MI: University of Michigan Press.

Ostrom, E., Walker, J., & Gardner, R. (1992). Covenants with and without a sword: Self-governance is possible. *The American Political Science Review*, *86*, 404–417. doi:10.2307/1964229

Ostrom, E., & Walker, J. (1997). Neither markets nor states: Linking transformation processes in collective action arenas. In D. C. Mueller (Ed.), *Perspectives on public choice: A handbook* (pp. 35–72). Cambridge: Cambridge University Press.

Poteete, A. R., Janssen, M. A., & Ostrom, E. (2010). *Working together: Collective action, the commons, and multiple methods in practice.* Princeton, NJ: Princeton University Press.

Sarker, A., & Itoh, T. (2001). Design principles in long-enduring institutions of Japanese irrigation common-pool resources. *Agricultural Water Management*, *48*, 89–102. doi:10.1016/S0378-3774(00)00125-6

Steins, N. A. (1999). *All hands on deck: An interactive perspective on complex common-pool resources management based on case studies in the coastal waters of the isle of Wight (UK), Connemara (Ireland) and the Dutch Wadden Sea*. Wageningen: Wageningen University.

Whittaker, J. (2011). The evolution of environmentally responsible investment: An adam smith perspective. *Ecological Economics*, *71*, 33–41. doi:10.1016/j.ecolecon.2011.08.006

Wollenberg, E., Merino, L., Agrawal, A., & Ostrom, E. (2007). Fourteen years of monitoring community-managed forests: Learning from IFRI's experience. *International Forestry Review*, *9*, 670–684. doi:10.1505/ifor.9.2.670

Zabel, A., & Holm-Müller, K. (2008). Conservation performance payments for carnivore conservation in sweden. *Conservation Biology*, *22*, 247–251. doi:10.1111/j.1523-1739.2008.00898.x

Crossing disciplinary boundaries

L. Schroeder

Emeritus Professor of Public Administration and International Affairs, Syracuse University, Syracuse NY, USA

Re-reading Elinor (Lin) Ostrom's 'Collective Action and the Evolution of Social Norms' (2000) provided the opportunity for me to review my own evolution of thinking about public goods and common pool resources (CPRs). It also reiterated to me the degree to which Lin's work was not bounded by traditional academic boundaries. As a graduate student of economics concentrating in public finance during the 1960s, it was easy for me to believe and subsequently teach that rational, self-interested actors will not contribute to the provision of public goods, including the subset of goods that exhibit rivalry but non-exclusion.

Fortunately I had the opportunity to work closely with Lin in the late 1980s on issues related to decentralized provision of public services in developing countries. My collaboration with her coincided with the completion of her *Governing the Commons: The Evolution of Institutions for Collective Action* (Ostrom 1990) so I soon learned that the theories I had been teaching in the classroom were often contradicted in the real CPR world. This additional knowledge prompted me to change substantially my classroom discussions of public goods and CPRs. However, it is probably the case that most economists, other than the new institutional economists led by Professors North and Williamson, were not aware of Lin's work in spite of the availability of *Governing the Commons*. Unfortunately, with high levels of academic specializations, there is often relatively little cross-fertilization of ideas.

Publication of the 'Collective Action...' article in the *Journal of Economic Perspectives* was an important outlet to inform a much wider range of economists of Elinor's contribution to the literature. This *Journal* was one of three that were published by the American Economic Association in 2000 and was distributed to a majority of economists in the US as well as many others around the world. As stated by the Association –

> The *Journal of Economic Perspectives (JEP)* attempts to fill a gap between the general interest press and most other academic economics journals. The journal aims to publish articles that will serve several goals: to synthesize and integrate lessons learned from active lines of economic research; to provide economic analysis of public policy issues; to encourage cross-fertilization of ideas among the fields of thinking; to offer readers an accessible source for state-of-the-art economic thinking; to suggest directions for future research; to provide insights and readings for classroom use; and to address issues relating to the economics profession.

Lin's article obviously is fully in line with those goals. Furthermore, the coverage of the paper with its inclusion of both results from laboratory experiments (then still a relatively new approach to empirical analysis in economics) and documentation of field-based studies, would make those not previously familiar with her work impressed with its breadth.

Publication of this article in a broadly circulated, main-line economics journal certainly helped make Lin and her work more recognized by a wider range of economists and, as such, probably helped her chances for subsequently being named a co-winner of the Nobel Prize in Economics – the only woman to have garnered that prize. In any event, of all the many articles that Elinor Ostrom authored or co-authored, her *Journal of Economic Perspectives* article is one of her top cited articles, with more than 1,800 citations, thus reflecting the importance scholars from within economics but also from other disciplines place on it.[1]

As is the case in many of her publications, the approach in the 'Collective Action ...' paper is both theoretical and empirical. Although published in an economics journal, this paper focuses on a concept that, until the emergence of the new institutional economics, had not commonly been used in economic theory – social norms (see Elster, 1989).[2] As such the paper relies on disciplines beyond economics and Lin's own formal discipline of political science. Indeed, this is one feature of much of her work throughout her career; it is very difficult to categorize her work within a single discipline or based on a single method. Or as Earl and Potts (2011) state, 'She is multi-methodological and multidisci-plinary' (p. 16); these attributes are illustrated well in this paper.[3] In fact, perhaps the most outstanding feature of the Workshop in Political Theory and Policy Analysis which Elinor and her husband, Vincent Ostrom, established at Indiana University was its interdisci-plinary nature. Membership in and, more importantly, participation in the weekly seminars would always include participants from a broader cross section of disciplines.

Other social sciences have, since the 2000 publication, become increasingly interested in the CPR issue and Professor Ostrom's approach to the study of institutional arrange-ments and how they evolve over time. For example Rudel (2011) argues that macro-sociological trends linked to economic and political development can be studied by sociologists to lead to a better understanding of common pool institutions. He focuses on how economic development can positively affect social capital in societies thereby enhancing the formation of common pool institutions but, at the same time, increases in economic activity are associated with greater globalization, trade and migration which may impede the formation of those institutions.

Acheson (2011) argues that, although a few anthropologists are currently researching the creation and evolution of rules or norms, Ostrom's work 'should resonate with anthropologists' (p. 320). Indeed, it seems to me that the in-depth ethnographic work carried out by anthropologists could yield important insights to the phenomena that underlie the evolution of social norms as posited in the 'Collective Action ...' paper. While laboratory experiments and other techniques associated with behavioral economics may provide some information, it is unlikely to be as complete as in-field observations of behaviors, the technique in which anthropologists excel.

The initial focus of Lin's empirical analysis of CPRs was oriented to rural activities – irrigation, fisheries, forests, and so on. Several of the factors mentioned in the 'Collective Action ...' paper help explain why collective action initiatives may be more likely to be successful in rural rather than in urban areas, particularly in developing countries. For example, migration into and from cities is much more likely in an urban environment; likewise in large urban spaces where many of those living nearby are basically strangers, it is less likely that interpersonal trust and reciprocity will be present. Furthermore, in urban areas, the costs of monitoring illicit behaviors could be considerably higher than in sparsely populated rural areas.

Nevertheless, during the past decade there has been expanding interest in the applica-tion of Elinor's CPR theories to urban areas and urbanization.[4] Just as in the case of rural overuse of an open pasture, urban parks can be overcrowded or improperly used. Parker and Johansson (2011) review some of the literature that has focused on CPRs in urban areas such as urban space, community gardens, or urban ecosystems including green areas and street trees. Even the green spaces reserved for dogs, that is, dog parks, have been examined as CPRs (see Matisoff & Noonan, 2012) . While these urban-oriented issues fall under the heading of CPRs, few of the contributions go the additional step of illustrating how self-governing institutions have been created to overcome the potential allocative inefficiencies associated with such resources. One exception to that is the paper by Wutich (2009) who analyzes the arrangements used to combat water scarcity in a squatter settlement in urban Cochabamba, Bolivia.[5]

Before closing this brief recollection of Elinor Ostrom, it is useful to return more directly to CPR issues associated with natural resources, specifically forestry. In an Occasional Paper prepared for the Center for International Forestry Research (CIEFOR) just prior to the *Journal of Economic Perspectives* paper, Ostrom (1999) documents that there are good positive examples of how forest users can cooperate to overcome the overconsumption tendencies of CPRs. She specifies a number of attributes of the resource (the forest) and a longer list of attributes of the users that, if present, will enhance the ability of the users to self-organize and govern the CPR.

But as Lin recognized and emphasized in numerous papers self-governing is not necessarily the same as formal 'Government'. And there are plenty of instances in which formal government policy can interfere with self-government and lead to failures of the CPR that the policies are intended to avoid. The Government of India adopted a National Forest Policy in 1988 and in 1990 issued a circular to operationalize that policy. A component of the circular was to support the creation of community forests through a policy termed 'joint forest management' or JFM.

For the past several years I have been working with members of the Indian Forest Service (IFS), a central service that provides forest officers throughout the country. It has been interesting that in conversations with many of the senior IFS officers (all with at least 20 years of experience in the service), only a small proportion are strong advocates of the JFM policy. There are some who argue quite strongly against this policy with the majority being at best skeptical about its efficacy. In fact, it is highly likely that the JFM, with its strong government role in the 'management' process can overwhelm any self-governing efforts on the parts of communities, something that Elinor Ostrom recognized and warned policy makers against in many of her papers.

An assessment of the JFM implementation in Indian states[6] by Damodaran and Engel (2003) found that there was considerable inter-state variability in the degree to which the policy had been implemented after more than a dozen years and that the Forest Department generally retained powers to disband local forest protection committees. Furthermore, often those committees were not given the rights to set their own rules and devise their own management plans. Obviously these provisions fly in the face of the general principles for successful self-governing institutions framed by Ostrom.

Perhaps most egregious is the example from the State of Uttrakhand (a state in the Himalayas region of India and created in 2000 from hill districts of the State of Uttar Pradesh). In this area of the country, local self-governing institutions known as *Van Panchayats* had been operating legally since the early 1930s, that is, even during the colonial period in India. According to Mukherjee (2004, p. 163) these local institutions 'have however their own set of working rules concerning forest use' in addition to rules regarding monitoring, sanctions and arbitration. He goes on to note that two initiatives, ironically intended to foster participatory governance create threats to the longer term sustainability of the *Van Panchayats* in Uttrakhand.

One threat came from the additional funds provided under the Government's (and often donor-supported) efforts to implement the JFM activities through the creation of 'new' *Van Panchayats*. These new organizations were not being created in response to the needs felt by local residents but, instead, were really supply driven. As such they often ignored the sorts of the design principles put forward by Professor Ostrom. Secondly, the Forest Department was simultaneously advocating creation of Village Forest Committees tied explicitly to the lowest level of local government, the Gram Sabhas.[7] Furthermore, the choice of eligible villages and creation of the Committees were apparently strongly influenced by the Forest Department. These efforts had the effect of undermining the existing and long-standing *Van Panchayats*.[8]

This is one example of Elinor Ostrom's concern, as expressed in the 'Collective Action ...' paper, that policies or initiatives of national governments and/or international donors can undermine the success of self-governing regimes overseeing CPRs. As mentioned above, my collaborations with Lin were centered on the general issue of decentralized institutional arrangements for the provision of public services. In many instances, this meant reliance upon formal local governments as opposed to groups governing specific natural resources. She and I had numerous discussions about the delicate policy dilemma of strengthening local governments and providing them with sufficient autonomy to operate effectively while minimizing the risk that stronger local governments dominate and undermine the sustainability of institutions that have heretofore effectively managed CPRs. Unfortunately, I am afraid that this is still a puzzle that has not been solved.

In summary, the article reprinted here marked an important entrance of Professor Ostrom's work into the mainstream of economic literature. It also illustrates the interdisciplinary and multi-methodological approaches that are the hallmarks of her research. Since its publication, it has spawned a large amount of additional research into the issues associated with governing and managing CPRs, including important contributions by Lin herself. But as the case from north India illustrates, top-down efforts to establish new institutional arrangements can, unfortunately, lead to the weakening and possible destruction of long-standing and self-governing natural resource organizations.

Notes

1. According to Google scholar, only the Presidential address to the American Political Science Association (Ostrom 1998) and her co-authored article in *Science* (Ostrom, Burger, Field, Norgaard, & Policansky, 1999) have, among her published articles, been cited more frequently. Not surprisingly her Cambridge University Press book is, by far, the most cited of her academic writings.
2. It is interesting to note that in 1996, after the publication of her *Governing the Commons* book, an article on the evolution of social norms was published in the *American Economic Review* by Sethi and Somanathan (1996). The paper, which acknowledged and cited Lin's book, contains a theoretical model that explains why cooperation today will generally be followed by cooperation and similarly defection at one point will generally lead to defection.
3. In a similar vein, Ostrom (2002) argues that analyses of public policies really must be interdisciplinary. Specifically she suggests that 'we need to think about how to overcome the disciplinary walls that have been erected in the contemporary university' (p. 46).
4. It is interesting that her early work was focused on urban questions, particularly police services in urban areas. See, for example, Ostrom, Parks and Whitaker (1978).
5. Although not directly focused on self-governing institutions to combat CPR issues, the paper by Mincey et al. (2013) uses the Institutional Analysis and Development (IAD) framework developed by Elinor and her colleagues to analyze urban forest management.

6. Since forestry in the Indian context is on the 'concurrent list' of subjects, the central government has the Constitutional power to make laws governing forestry, but implementation of those laws is carried out by the individual states

7. It is useful to keep in mind that the 73rd Amendment to the Indian Constitution came into force in 1993 which gave Constitutional status to self-governing institutions at the village level, the Gram Sabhas. Thus, almost simultaneous with the desire for greater local participation in the management of forest resources under the JFM policy, decentralization of governance was also occurring in the country.

8. My conversation with a senior IFS officer who has worked extensively in Uttrakhand was supportive of these generalizations. The officer also supports a policy giving *Van Panchayats* greater autonomy vis-à-vis the IFS.

References

Acheson, J. (2011). Ostrom for anthropologists. *International Journal of the Commons, 5*(2), 319–339.

Damodaran, A., & Engel, S. (2003). Joint Forest Management in India: Assessment of Performance and Evaluation of Impacts., ZEF Discussion Papers on Development Policy, No. 77. Zentrum für Entwicklungsforschung / Center for Development Research (ZEF), University of Bonn, Bonn. Retrived from http://hdl.handle.net/10419/84708

Earl, P. E., & Potts, J. (2011). A nobel prize for governance and institutions: Oliver williamson and elinor ostrom. *Review of Political Economy, 23*(1), 1–24.

Elster, J. (1989). Social norms and economic thoery. *Journal of Economic Perspectives, 3*(4), 99–117.

Matisoff, D., & Noonan, D. (2012). Managing contested greenspace: Neighborhood commons and the rise of dog parks. *International Journal of the Commons, 6*(1), 28–51.

Mincey, S. K., Hutten, M., Fischer, B. C., Evans, T. P., Stewart, S. I., & Vogt, J. M. (2013). Structuring institutional analysis for urban ecosystems: A key to sustainable urban forest management. *Urban Ecosystems, 16*(3), 553–571.

Mukherjee, P. (2004). Community rights and statutory laws: Politics of forest use at uttrakhand himalayas. *Journal of Legal Pluralism, 50*, 161–172.

Ostrom, E. (1990). *Governing the commons: The evolution of institutions for collective action.* New York, NY: Cambridge University Press.

Ostrom, E. (1998). A behavioral approach to the rational choice theory of collective action: Presidential address, american political science association, 1997. *The American Political Science Review, 92*(1), 1-22. doi:10.2307/2585925

Ostrom, E. (1999). Self-Governance and Forest Resources. Center for International Forestry Research, Occasional Paper No. 20. Jakarta: CIFOR.

Ostrom, E. (2000). Collective action and the evolution of social norms. *Journal of Economic Perspectives, 14*(3), 137–158. doi:10.1257/jep.14.3.137

Ostrom, E. (2002). Policy analysis in the future of good societies. *The Good Society, 11*(1), 42–48. doi:10.1353/gso.2002.0013

Ostrom, E., Burger, J., Field, C. B., Norgaard, R. B., & Policansky, D. (1999). Revisiting the commons: Local lessons, global challenges. *Science e, New Series, 284*(5412), 278–282.

Ostrom, E., Parks, R., & Whitaker, G. (1978). *Patterns of metropolitan policing.* Cambridge, MA: Ballinger Books.

Parker, P., & Johansson, M. (2011). *The Uses and Abuses of Elinor Ostrom's Concept of Commons in Urban Theorizing.* Paper presented at the International Conference of the European Urban Research Association 2011, Copenhagen. Retrieved from http://dspace.mah.se/dspace/bitstream/handle/2043/12212/EURA%20conf%20version3.pdf;jsessionid=B68D104308F29BF789DAA1ADFCCE2BE1?sequence=2

Rudel, T. K. (2011). The commons and development: Unanswered sociological questions. *International Journal of the Commons, 5*(2), 303–318.

Sethi, R., & Somanathan, E. (1996). The evolution of social norms in common property resource use. *The American Economic Review, 86*(4), 766–788.

Wutich, A. (2009). Water scarcity and the sustainability of a common pool resource institution in the urban andes. *Human Ecology: An Interdisciplinary Journal, 37*(2), 179–192.

Elinor Ostrom's challenge for laboratory experiments

Rick K. Wilson

Department of Political Science, Rice University, Houston, TX, USA

Elinor Ostrom's *Journal of Economic Perspectives* article (Ostrom, 2000) achieved exactly what one would hope for a review article. It established a clear set of findings, it challenged theorists and it suggested several new avenues for research. Since publication, the article has been important for the laboratory experimental community that has pressed ahead on many of the new topics Ostrom suggested. In this commentary I mention pockets of new research that were influenced by the article and I suggest several areas of research that are promising.

The article detailed seven general 'core facts' drawn from laboratory experiments on public goods. The standard public goods game involves individuals given an initial endowment and grouped together. Any portion of the endowment can be contributed to a group fund, the experimenter increases the size of the fund and everyone in the group receives an equal share of the augmented fund. Individuals always keep whatever they do not put into the group fund. The public goods dilemma stems from the fact that the marginal per capita rate of return from the group fund is somewhere on the interval [0,1]. The dilemma is that the group is always better off if everyone contributes their endowment to the group fund. However, every individual is better off free riding off the contributions of others. In a related game, the Common-Pool Resource (CPR), a similar problem occurs. Instead of contributing, individuals need to refrain from consuming the resource beyond its recharge rate. Of course, every individual has a strong incentive to consume as much of the resource as possible before it is fully consumed. Both settings have been well studied in the laboratory.

In her review Ostrom concluded that there are seven 'core facts': (1) subjects contribute, (2) contributions decay in a repeated setting, (3) beliefs about contributions by others affects one's contributions, (4) learning about the game leads to more cooperation, (5) face-to-face communication produces substantial increases in contributions, (6) if allowed, subjects will pay to punish those who make below-average contributions, and (7) various contextual factors including framing and competition affect the rate of contributions. That these core facts were well known now seems non-controversial. However, these points had never been clearly laid out and integrated into a critique of the standard model of rational behavior.

In a review of the continuing laboratory work on the provisioning of public goods, Chaudhuri (2011) points to three general areas that have been filled in since the Ostrom article. The first is that conditional cooperation is common. Much of conditional cooperation is built on beliefs about others and whether they will contribute to the public goods. Ostrom (2000) argued that conditional cooperation was central for understanding the resilience of norms. Pure cooperators would be quickly taken advantage of by pure free-riders. However, with a population mix of free-riders, pure cooperators and conditional cooperators, contributions to the public good can thrive. Much of the recent research reviewed by Chaudhuri (2011) points to mechanisms by which beliefs can be sustained and by which individuals can act strategically to ensure cooperation.

Second, Chaudhuri (2011) notes that costly punishment is common within groups. However, as Ostrom suspected, the findings point out that costly punishment creates a second-level public goods problem that requires a 'meta-norm' in which some are willing to punish (see for example the critique and discussion in Guala, 2012). In long-term interactions, the threat of punishment may be sufficient (a point well noted in Ostrom, Walker, & Gardner, 1992). A perverse finding has emerged in the literature on punishment showing that some individuals engage in anti-social punishment – punishing those who are contributing to the public good. It is not clear whether this is a leveling strategy that serves to enforce norms or whether it is about revenge. A concern detailed by this recent literature is that punishment may not be efficient. Anti-social punishment often will offset the gains from cooperation. The costs of punishment, when punishment is used, undermine many of the gains to cooperation. From a social efficiency standpoint, punishment is most valuable when it is not used.

Third, Chaudhuri (2011) details institutions that allow for ostracism and sorting among participants. Ostrom (2000) does not directly touch on this 'core fact' but points to it when discussing the role of boundary rules in natural settings. In the studies reviewed by Chaudhuri (2011), when subjects are able to build their own groups, selecting for cooperators, they do better. In effect subjects are allowed to define their own boundary rules and they select those who are also likely to cooperate. Ostrom's work directly influenced a number of researchers using laboratory experiments in political science (for example Ahn, Esarey, & Scholz, 2009; Ahn, Isaac, & Salmon, 2008; Eriksson & Strimling, 2012).

Ostrom also suggested other areas of study, including the effect of heterogeneity on the group. The central question is what happens to the provisioning of public goods when individuals in the group have different endowments. Do those who are wealthy behave differently from those who are poor? Manipulating differences in wealth is easy to do in the laboratory and a host of studies has taken up this question. The results are mixed. For example Chan, Mestelman, Moir, and Muller (1999) find that heterogeneous groups contribute less to the public good than homogeneous groups. The effect appears driven by the experimenter providing the endowment. In a similar study Cherry, Kroll, and Shogren (2005) obtain the same finding, but they manipulate the manner in which the endowment is provided and rule out endowment effects. By contrast, Buckley and Croson (2006) find a positive effect for heterogeneous groups with poorer individuals contributing as much as the wealthier. Context is important as is made amply clear by Reuben and Riedl (2013) where they look at heterogeneous groups and the possibility of punishment. They find that different punishment institutions help anchor the development of norms for contributions even when people differ in their endowments. Heterogeneity of groups appears to have a nuanced effect on the provision of public goods.

Ostrom also made it clear that it is important to understand what subjects bring with them into the laboratory. Laboratory experiments are often dismissed because they do not resemble the natural settings found in the field. While laboratory experiments allow researchers to carefully manipulate treatment variables, to what extent does the highly controlled, antiseptic, laboratory resemble the field? Cárdenas (2003) tackles this question by looking at the natural heterogeneity in the wealth of subjects and having them participate in a CPR (an extraction game) in the field. Like Cherry et al. (2005), he finds that inequality dampens cooperation. Cárdenas and Ostrom (2004) press this further by recruiting subjects from environments that are similar to the CPR setting used in the laboratory and letting individual characteristics provide differing levels of information and experience about the CPR. They find that subjects have no trouble making the link between the controlled experiment and the norms they use in their own settings. Habyarimana, Humphreys, Posner, and Weinstein (2007) rely on the ethnic differences of subjects to test different mechanisms by which public goods are under-provisioned. These only represent a handful of studies that are carrying out laboratory experiments-in-the-field and make use of the norms that subjects bring to the experiment (see also Baldassarri & Grossman, 2013; Cavalcanti, Schläpfer, & Schmid, 2010; Janssen, Anderies, & Cárdenas, 2011; Otto & Wechsung, 2014). It is clear from these findings that subjects have clear norms in mind that carry over into their behavior in the laboratory. It also means that the laboratory is a useful place to examine the resilience of norms.

Finally, Ostrom's article has been important for focusing scholars on the endogenous choice of institutions to solve public goods provisioning problems. Much of the laboratory research looks at settings in which subjects can choose levels of contributions and then vote on which to implement. Sometimes the choices are binding and sometimes not. Many of the designs use a variation of Ostrom et al. (1992) or Walker, Gardner, Herr, and Ostrom (2000). Kroll, Cherry, and Shogren (2007) add a punishment option and find that a non-binding allocation rule, coupled with punishment, increases contribution levels above a non-binding rule. This corroborates prior findings that graduated sanctions are important and helps enforce suggested norms (after all, this is precisely what a non-binding allocation rule is). Ertan, Page, and Putterman (2009) and Putterman, Tyran, and Kamei (2011) offer variations on the endogenous choice of punishment institutions and find much the same. Dal Bó, Foster, and Putterman (2010) argue that the endogenous choice of institutions affects the beliefs of individuals in the group. Since institutional change in these experiments occurs through voting, the degree to which the group votes for change provides information about the future behavior of others. Finally, Hamman, Weber, and Woon (2011) turn to a setting in which groups in a public goods game can elect a member to make binding contribution decisions for the group. This form of electoral delegation leads to higher rates of contributions. In a second experiment they examine what happens when groups can choose whether they want a delegation institution. When choice is coupled with communication, delegation is more likely and leads to higher contribution rates. An interesting variation on delegating coupled with punishment is found in Grossman and Baldassarri (2012). These studies all point to Ostrom's claim that when users of a resource can design their own rules, where they can enforce the rules, where they can revisit the rules and where they can effectively monitor contributions, such institutions will be successful in provisioning public goods.

While laboratory experiments have extended many of the points that Ostrom raised, a great deal remains unexplored. I take these to be opportunities for future research. Little work has been carried out in the laboratory about the effectiveness of graduated sanctions. While Ostrom stressed the importance of gradually ramping up sanctions, most experiments on sanctioning do not address the sanctioning strategies by individuals. Ostrom noted that exogenous shocks to the public goods environment can have a major impact. For example, the influx of a new group of people (in-migration) may upset well established beliefs about contributions, this has not received much attention in the laboratory. A key question about the persistence of norms has to do with the manner in which those norms are transmitted over generations. This is difficult to study in a natural setting, yet it would be relatively easy to implement in the laboratory. While the role of overlapping jurisdictions is considered important in natural settings, the precise mechanisms by which that overlap encourages the provisioning of public goods is not well elaborated or tested in the laboratory. Finally, while we suspect that corrupt institutions will decrease the provisioning of public goods, this is difficult to study in natural settings. Corruption is often hidden and is difficult to measure. Yet doing so in the laboratory is relatively straightforward. All of these present potentially valuable topics that those using experiments might further pursue.

The findings from laboratory experiments were a central part of Ostrom's thinking about norms. She appreciated what could be manipulated in the laboratory and how it was important to understand behavioral anomalies. Her seven 'core facts' led her to argue that incorporating 'norm-using' players would improve many of the workhorse theoretical models. In her discussion Ostrom concluded that 'one is forced by these well-substantiated facts to adopt a more eclectic (and classical) view of human behavior' (2000, p. 141). It has been heartening to see the new theoretical models that have been proposed in the past 15 years to handle concepts like inequality aversion (Fehr & Schmidt, 1999) or higher order beliefs about others (Dufwenberg & Kirchsteiger, 2004). As well we have seen growth in new areas such as Behavioral Game Theory and Neuroeconomics (for an overview, see Wilson, 2011). These developments and others were applauded by Ostrom as extending the accuracy of our models in order to allow us to provide better policy prescriptions.

References

Ahn, T. K., Esarey, J., & Scholz, J. T. (2009). Reputation and cooperation in voluntary exchanges: Comparing local and central institutions. *The Journal of Politics*, *71*, 398–413. doi:10.1017/S0022381609090355

Ahn, T. K., Isaac, R. M., & Salmon, T. C. (2008). Endogenous group formation. *Journal of Public Economic Theory*, *10*, 171–194. Retrieved from: http://www.blackwellpublishing.com/journal.asp?ref=1097-3923. doi:10.1111/j.1467-9779.2008.00357.x

Baldassarri, D., & Grossman, G. (2013). The effect of group attachment and social position on prosocial behavior. Evidence from lab-in-the-field experiments. *Plos One*, *8*, doi:10.1371/journal.pone.0058750

Buckley, E., & Croson, R. (2006). Income and wealth heterogeneity in the voluntary provision of linear public goods. *Journal of Public Economics*, *90*, 935–955. doi:10.1016/j.jpubeco.2005.06.002

Cárdenas, J. C. (2003). Real wealth and experimental cooperation: Experiments in the field lab. *Journal of Development Economics*, *70*, 263–289. doi:10.1016/s0304-3878(02)00098-6

Cárdenas, J. C., & Ostrom, E. (2004). What do people bring into the game? Experiments in the field about cooperation in the commons. *Agricultural Systems*, *82*, 307–326. doi:10.1016/j.agsy.2004.07.008

Cavalcanti, C., Schläpfer, F., & Schmid, B. (2010). Public participation and willingness to cooperate in common-pool resource management: A field experiment with fishing communities in Brazil. *Ecological Economics*, *69*, 613–622. doi:10.1016/j.ecolecon.2009.09.009

Chan, K. S., Mestelman, S., Moir, R., & Muller, R. A. (1999). Heterogeneity and the voluntary provision of public goods. *Experimental Economics*, *2*, 5–30. doi:10.1007/BF01669132

Chaudhuri, A. (2011). Sustaining cooperation in laboratory public goods experiments: A selective survey of the literature. *Experimental Economics*, *14*, 47–83. doi:10.1007/s10683-010-9257-1

Cherry, T. L., Kroll, S., & Shogren, J. F. (2005). The impact of endowment heterogeneity and origin on public good contributions: Evidence from the lab. *Journal of Economic Behavior & Organization*, *57*, 357–365. doi:10.1016/j.jebo.2003.11.010

Dal Bó, P., Foster, A., & Putterman, L. (2010). Institutions and behavior: Experimental evidence on the effects of democracy. *American Economic Review, 100*, 2205–2229. Retrieved from: http://www.aeaweb.org/aer/. doi:10.1257/aer.100.5.2205

Dufwenberg, M., & Kirchsteiger, G. (2004). A theory of sequential reciprocity. *Games and Economic Behavior, 47*, 268–298. doi:10.1016/j.geb.2003.06.003

Eriksson, L., & Strimling, P. (2012). The hard problem of cooperation. *PloS One, 7*, e40325. doi:10.1371/journal.pone.0040325

Ertan, A., Page, T., & Putterman, L. (2009). Who to punish? Individual decisions and majority rule in mitigating the free rider problem. *European Economic Review, 53*, 495–511. doi:10.1016/j.euroecorev.2008.09.007

Fehr, E., & Schmidt, K. M. A. (1999). A theory of fairness, competition, and cooperation. *The Quarterly Journal of Economics, 114*, 817–868. doi:10.1162/003355399556151

Grossman, G., & Baldassarri, D. (2012). The impact of elections on cooperation: Evidence from a lab-in-the-field experiment in Uganda. *American Journal of Political Science, 56*, 964–985. doi:10.1111/j.1540-5907.2012.00596.x

Guala, F. (2012). Reciprocity: Weak or strong? What punishment experiments do (and do not) demonstrate. *Behavioral and Brain Sciences, 35*, doi:10.1017/s0140525x11000069

Habyarimana, J., Humphreys, M., Posner, D. N., & Weinstein, J. M. (2007). Why does ethnic diversity undermine public goods provision? *American Political Science Review, 101*, 709–725. doi:10.1017/S0003055407070499

Hamman, J. R., Weber, R. A., & Woon, J. (2011). An experimental investigation of electoral delegation and the provision of public goods. *American Journal of Political Science, 55*, 738–752. doi:10.1111/j.1540-5907.2011.00531.x

Janssen, M. A., Anderies, J. M., & Cárdenas, J. C. (2011). Head-enders as stationary bandits in asymmetric commons: Comparing irrigation experiments in the laboratory and the field. *Ecological Economics, 70*, 1590–1598. doi:10.1016/j.ecolecon.2011.01.006

Kroll, S., Cherry, T. L., & Shogren, J. F. (2007). Voting, punishment, and public goods. *Economic Inquiry, 45*, 557–570. doi:10.1111/j.1465-7295.2007.00028.x

Ostrom, E. (2000). Collective action and the evolution of social norms. *Journal of Economic Perspectives, 14*, 137–158. doi:10.1257/jep.14.3.137

Ostrom, E., Walker, J., & Gardner, R. (1992). Covenants with and without a sword: Self-governance is possible. *The American Political Science Review, 86*, 404–417. doi:10.2307/1964229

Otto, I. M., & Wechsung, F. (2014). The effects of rules and communication in a behavioral irrigation experiment with power asymmetries carried out in North China. *Ecological Economics, 99*, 10–20. doi:10.1016/j.ecolecon.2013.12.007

Putterman, L., Tyran, J. -R. K., & Kamei, K. (2011). Public goods and voting on formal sanction schemes. *Journal of Public Economics, 95*, 1213–1222. doi:10.1016/j.jpubeco.2011.05.001

Reuben, E., & Riedl, A. (2013). Enforcement of contribution norms in public good games with heterogeneous populations. *Games and Economic Behavior, 77*, 122–137. doi:10.1016/j.geb.2012.10.001

Walker, J. M., Gardner, R., Herr, A., & Ostrom, E. (2000). Collective choice in the commons: Experimental results on proposed allocation rules and votes. *The Economic Journal, 110*, 212–234. doi:10.1111/1468-0297.00497

Wilson, R. K. (2011). The Contribution of Behavioral Economics to Political Science. *Annual Review of Political Science, 14*, 201–223. doi:10.1146/annurev-polisci-041309-114513

The evolution of social norms in conflict resolution

Lisa Blomgren Amsler

Keller-Runden Professor of Public Service, Indiana University School of Public and Environmental Affairs, Bloomington, IN, USA

In her classic essay 'Collective Action and the Evolution of Social Norms', Nobel laureate Elinor Ostrom (2000) made a major contribution to our understanding of human institutions. She developed the 'Indiana School's' Institutional Analysis and Development (IAD) Framework at Indiana University's Workshop on Political Theory and Policy Analysis. Her work has broad application to law and conflict resolution.

We are currently undergoing a wave of privatization of justice in the United States. Companies are imposing mandatory or adhesive arbitration clauses on employees (Baker, 2004) and consumers (Demaine & Hensler, 2004) that preclude them from joining class actions or resorting to the public justice system to enforce laws on discrimination or consumer protection (Bingham, 2004; Sternlight, 2005). The result is undermining the enforcement of public law.

This essay endeavors a brief application of Ostrom's work to these private justice systems.[1] It examines collective action and social norms in formal legal institutions and informal ones for managing conflict that have evolved outside the justice system. It introduces dispute system design (DSD) in the context of IAD. It applies IAD to examples of these systems. It concludes with issues, collective action and the development of social norms, for managing conflict in dispute resolution systems that have emerged in certain industries. Ostrom's work can help us address collective action problems in these private justice systems.

Institutional analysis and development

In the IAD framework, Ostrom identified an underlying set of universal building blocks for researching institutions and how they function (Ostrom, 2005, p. 6). Ostrom defines a framework as the level of analysis necessary to identify the elements and relationships among those elements necessary to engage in institutional analysis; it provides the most general set of variables for all settings and institutions (p. 28). This framework helps researchers focus on the action situation and the concept of the holons – 'nested sub-assemblies of part-whole units' (p. 7). Ostrom focuses on two holons in the action arena, defined as a unit of analysis in which participants (first holon) and the action situation (second holon) interact in ways affected by other outside variables and produce outcomes (p. 13). Structures are nested; families, firms, communities, industries, states, nations, transnational alliances, and others are all structures that can be viewed in isolation or as part of a larger whole (p. 11). To analyze an action situation, Ostrom uses seven categories of information:

(1) the set of participants [single individuals or corporate actors], (2) the positions to be filled by participants, (3) the potential outcomes, (4) the set of allowable actions and the function that maps actions into realized outcomes [action-outcome linkages], (5) the control that an individual has in regards to this function, (6) the information available to participants about actions and outcomes and their linkages, and (7) costs and benefits – which serve as incentives and deterrents – assigned to actions and outcomes.

(p. 32; *see generally*, pp. 32–68). Ostrom explains how game theory can structure laboratory experiments on these concepts (pp. 69–98).

To apply IAD to DSD, consider a court-connected mediation program as a holon nested in a court, nested in the judicial branch, nested in the state or federal government. A DSD that uses mediation affords participants more control over the outcome of the function of dispute resolution as an allowable action. The mediator assists them in negotiating; he or she has no power to decide the case. In contrast, a DSD using arbitration changes the allowable actions; it lets the arbitrator decide the outcome. Some DSDs limit discovery in arbitration; this restricts information availability to participants about actions and outcomes and their linkages. Courts usually afford broader discovery in litigation.

Ostrom (2005) suggests we understand the outside variables that affect the action arena in a two-stage process. First, the action arena now becomes a dependent variable subject to three categories of exogenous variables: '(1) the *rules* used by participants to order their relationships, (2) the attributes of the *biophysical world* that are acted upon in these arenas, and (3) the structure of the more general *community* within which any particular arena is placed' (Ostrom, 2005, p. 15). In DSD, parties in mediation negotiate in the shadow of the civil justice system; the trial is an action arena that follows in sequence upon a failed civil or commercial mediation. Parties in arbitration have limited access to the civil justice system; judicial review of awards is legally restricted.

Lawyers focus on gaming rules to advance their clients' interests in the action arena of the mediation, arbitration, administrative agency, court, or another forum. Ostrom (2005) describes how rules can emerge through democratic governance (p. 29), people who organize privately like corporations or membership associations, or within a family or work team (p. 19). Working rules evolve as a function of what individuals do in practice. They can encompass rules in DSD structures that governments create, that parties mutually negotiate, and that one corporate player imposes on a weaker party in an economic transaction.

IAD is aimed at all institutions – in an open, democratic society governed by the rule of law or other systems where rules and attempts to enforce them exist, but people generally seek noncompliance (p. 20). Rules-in-form may be consistent or inconsistent with rules-in-practice. Rules use language, an imperfect and sometimes ambiguous tool, and hence they depend upon a generally shared understanding of meaning in action situations; rules may or may not be predictable and produce stability in human action. Community mediation and restorative justice programs in theory allow neighbors to design and implement their own justice systems and rules, but they are nested in the legal system.

Compliance with rules is a function of monitoring and enforcement (p. 21). Most DSDs use a confidentiality rule that renders empirical research and monitoring for compliance difficult. How can we introduce rigor into the analysis of these emerging private justice systems using IAD?

Dispute system design (DSD)

Ostrom's framework can help identify the elements of DSD, which is best understood as institutional design as applied in practice. DSD includes choices that create rules for structures, including but are not limited to public, private, or nonprofit institutions, conflict subject matter, participants, timing, voluntariness, and interventions like facilitation, consensus-building, mediation, or arbitration (Bingham, 2008–2009, pp. 12–14, with a more detailed list of DSD elements). DSD must be embodied in some form of rule. Ostrom defines rules as 'shared understandings by participants about enforced prescriptions concerning what actions (or outcomes) are required, prohibited, or permitted' (2005, p. 18), and as instructions for successful strategies or principles that can be true or false, like the laws of physics. There are strategies, norms and rules: '[I]ndividuals adopt strategies in light of the norms they hold and within the rules of the situation within which they are interacting' (Ostrom, 2005, p. 175). To advance the field of institutional design, Ostrom proposes seven kinds of rules: rules regarding positions, boundaries, choice, aggregation, information, payoff, and scope (pp. 186–215).

Ostrom's IAD work provides the building blocks to help us understand DSD, a field that emerged in organizational workplace conflict (Ury, Brett, & Goldberg, 1988). DSD is the purposeful creation of an organization's program to manage conflict through steps or options for process (pp. 41–64). To manage conflict, organizations should focus primarily on human interests (pp. 3–19), rather than rights in contract or law. A healthy system should only use rights-based arbitration or litigation when disputants reached impasse; parties should avoid using economic or physical power. DSD takes many forms. It can be a multi-step procedure culminating in mediation, fact finding, and/or advisory or binding arbitration; ombudspersons give disputants many different process choices (Rowe, 1991). Recently, companies have imposed a single step binding arbitration DSD on employees and consumers: adhesive arbitration (Sternlight, 2005).

Applying Ostrom's IAD to arbitration DSDs, we ask questions like: who is eligible to use arbitration? This position rule defines participants. What kinds of cases does the arbitration clause cover? This is a boundary rule that defines the scope of the arbitrator's power. Is arbitration is voluntary, mandatory, or opt out? This is a choice rule because it defines what action set a participant has in relation to arbitration. Limits on class actions and collective class arbitration are aggregation rules that shape whether arbitration is affordable. If the claim is too small, it costs too much to arbitrate it unless a consumer can act collectively with others. Boundary rules can make arbitration unaffordable for consumers and nullify public laws for fair credit or consumer protection. DSDs that limit discovery have rules about what information participants can use as evidence. DSDs limit outcomes of arbitration by shifting attorneys' fees or arbitrator fees to the winner or loser; these are payoff rules. If we more systematically analyze the rule choices in arbitration DSDs, we can explain the differences in outcomes. Rules define substantive rights in the system.

Ostrom researched institutions for managing conflict over common pool environmental and natural resources (Ostrom, 2005, pp. 258–280). She wrote that robust institutions persist, are stable, and adapt to change (Ostrom, 1990). They include clearly defined boundaries of the resource and rights of individuals who can take it, proportional equivalence between benefits and costs, collective choice arrangements, monitoring, graduated sanctions, conflict resolution mechanisms, minimal recognition of rights to organize, and enterprises in which appropriation, enforcement, monitoring, conflict resolution, and governance are nested in layers.

Collective choice arrangements are those in which people who are subject to the rules are included in the group who can make or change the rules (Ostrom, 2005, p. 259). Arbitration DSDs in theory are subject to collective choice arrangements, minimal recognition of the rights to organize, monitoring, and governance, but in modern corporate practice, large companies impose adhesive or mandatory arbitration DSDs on employees and consumers without collective choice (Bingham, 2008–2009). Companies retain control over DSD (Bingham, 2002, 2004). DSD varies across two separate dimensions of disputant control: control over the full DSD, or control over a case using a specific process. Control over DSD is the power to choose the rules: for example, what cases, which process or sequence of processes, what due process rules, what discovery, and other structural aspects are in the DSD? Control over a case can address its process and/or outcome, but not other cases. In arbitration, parties can give control over outcome to the arbitrator.

Arbitration DSDs may reflect structural bias – the rules may favor one party. This depends on who designs the system, their goals, and how they exercise their power. DSDs fall into three categories: (1) third party design, in which a court or agency designs the system for the disputants; (2) disputant design, in which those subject to the system jointly design it, as in collective bargaining; and (3) one party design, in which the party with stronger economic power imposes a DSD on the other as in adhesive arbitration (Bingham, 2002, 2004). Companies in one party DSDs prevail significantly more frequently when they are repeat users of arbitration and use the same arbitrator repeatedly (Bingham, 1997, 1998; Colvin, 2011). Control over DSD allows them to use their advantages as repeat players. Ostrom's analysis of game theoretic research and its application to IAD is equally useful for institutions in the field of dispute resolution, and particularly, to arbitration.

Collective action and social norms in dispute resolution

In examining human evolution, collective action, and social norms, Ostrom (2000, p. 142) finds conditional cooperators are willing to cooperate estimating that others will reciprocate, and are willing to repeat based on experience. She finds that when 'users of a common-pool resource organize themselves to devise and enforce some of their own basic rules, they tend to manage local resources more sustainably than when rules are externally imposed on them....' (p. 148). She finds that these self-organized regimes frequently outperform government regimes that rely on externally enforced, formal rules. Factors include a group determining its own membership and rules, leading to developing greater trust and reciprocity, and group boundaries that define the community of members (p. 149). Ostrom observes that institutions with long-term survival and comparative effectiveness are shaped by eight key design principles (pp. 151–152, paraphrased):

(1) Clear boundary rules,
(2) Effective local rules-in-use assigning costs proportional to benefits,
(3) Members can participate in making and modifying the rules,
(4) Selecting their own monitors who are accountable,
(5) Graduated sanctions,
(6) Most significant for this essay, 'access to rapid, low-cost, local arenas to resolve conflict among users or between users and officials' (p. 152)

(7) Minimal recognition of the right to organize by a national or local government, and

(8) Governance activities in multiple layers of nested enterprises.

There are successful private justice systems that use arbitration characterized by Ostrom's eight key design principles. Two examples are the diamond (Bernstein, 1992) and cotton industries (Bernstein, 2001), both robust in Ostrom's sense of enduring, stable, adaptive, participatory, and characterized by collective choice rules.

Professor Bernstein (1992) studied the diamond industry's private justice system, the Diamond Dealers' Club (DDC). It operated a private arbitration system with mandatory pre-arbitration conciliation that settled approximately 85% of the 150 disputes submitted annually. Procedural rules for arbitration gave the parties control over the system, which entailed an initial fact-finding step with the Floor Committee (club members elected to two-year terms). If the Committee found a material issue of fact, the dispute went to arbitration before the Board of Arbitrators (again members elected to two-year terms). Proceedings and awards were confidential. The arbitration fee was small. The arbitrators allocated the expenses of arbitration, but they could also decide to refund the fee. Disputants could appeal to a five-arbitrator board (elected panel members who did not hear the original case). Parties had the right to counsel. If the DDC declined to arbitrate, the parties could resort to other remedies.

The cotton industry used two main arbitration DSDs: the Board of Appeals created by the American Cotton Shippers Association (ACSA) and American Textiles Manufacturers Institute (ATMI) primarily for disputes between merchants and mills, and the Memphis Cotton Exchange (MCE) arbitration tribunal primarily for disputes between merchants. Both tribunals are the result of a quasi-legislative process among the members of the respective professional associations.

The Board of Appeals consists of one arbitrator appointed based on industry experience, fairness, and integrity by the presidents of the ACSA and ATMI. It conducts a paper review of the case with parties' names redacted from documents. It publicly circulates the Board's written opinions with arbitrator names to discourage its members from systematically favoring one industry.

The MCE Board of Directors appoints seven arbitrators annually. The panel holds oral hearings, permits cross-examination of witnesses, but does not publish its written opinions. There is a norm of consensus decision-making. Both arbitration bodies permit limited discovery and representation by counsel. Professor Bernstein observes that this private legal system works 'extraordinarily well'; it resolves disputes expeditiously and inexpensively, and it keeps transaction costs, error costs, legal system costs, and collection costs low (Bernstein, 2001, p. 1725). It also yields a body of cases that reflect coherent jurisprudence, and which are both respected and promptly, voluntarily implemented.

These DSDs illustrate that members acting collectively where there are repeat dealings with each other can jointly create a fair justice system for commercial settings in the diamond and cotton industries. Membership is important to success in these businesses. They monitor and enforce shared rules. They establish precedent for the members to follow in their business dealings with each other. Because the members of the community have repeated dealings with each other, they are stable and have norms of fair business practices.

Conclusion

In her classic essay 'Collective Action and the Evolution of Social Norms', Elinor Ostrom (1990) provides us a guide to understanding not only collective action in institutions for managing common pool resources, but also to dispute system design in private systems of justice that increasingly characterize the economy of the United States. Her principles can help scholars work to improve access to justice.

Note

1. An early version of portions of this discussion first appeared in Bingham (2008–2009).

References

Baker, S. 2004. A risk-based approach to mandatory arbitration. *Oregon Law Review, 83*, 861–898.

Bernstein, L. 1992. Opting out of the legal system: Extralegal contractual relations in the diamond industry. *The Journal of Legal Studies, 21*, 115–157. doi:10.1086/467902

Bernstein, L. 2001. Private commercial law in the cotton industry: Creating cooperation through rules, norms, and institutions. *Michigan Law Review, 99*, 1724–1788. doi:10.2307/1290478

Bingham, L. B. 1997. Employment arbitration: The repeat player effect. *Employee Rights and Employment Policy Journal, 1*(1), 189–220.

Bingham, L. B. 1998. McGEORGE symposium on arbitration: On repeat players, adhesive contracts, and the use of statistics in judicial review of arbitration awards. *McGeorge Law Review, 29*(2), 223–260.

Bingham, L. B. 2002. Self-determination in dispute system design and employment arbitration. *University of Miami Law Review, 56*, 873–908.

Bingham, L. B. 2004. Control over dispute system design and mandatory commercial arbitration. *Law & Contemporary Problems, 67*(1&2), 221–251.

Bingham, L. B. 2008–2009. Designing justice: Legal institutions and other systems for managing conflict. *Ohio State Journal on Dispute Resolution, 24*, 1–50.

Colvin, A. J. S. 2011. An empirical study of employment arbitration: Case outcomes and processes. *Journal of Empirical Legal Studies, 8*(1), 1–23. doi:10.1111/j.1740-1461.2010.01200.x

Demaine, L. J., & Hensler, D. R. 2004. "Volunteering" to arbitrate through predispute arbitration clauses: The average consumer's experience. *Law & Contemporary Problems, 67*(1&2), 55–74.

Ostrom, E. 1990. *Governing the commons: The evolution of institutions for collective action.* Cambridge, UK: Cambridge University Press.

Ostrom, E. 2000. Collective action and the evolution of social norms. *The Journal of Economic Perspectives, 14*(3), 137–158. doi:10.1257/jep.14.3.137

Ostrom, E. 2005. *Understanding institutional diversity.* Princeton, NJ: Princeton University Press.

Rowe, M. P. 1991. The Ombudsman's role in a dispute resolution system. *Negotiation Journal, 7*, 353–362. doi:10.1111/j.1571-9979.1991.tb00630.x

Sternlight, J. R. 2005. Creeping mandatory arbitration: Is it just? *Stanford Law Review, 57*, 1631–1675.

Ury, W. L., Brett, J., & Goldberg, S. B. 1988. *Getting disputes resolved: Designing systems to cut the cost of conflict.* San Francisco, CA: Jossey Bass.

The evolution of elite and societal norms pertaining to the emergence of federal-tribal co-management of natural resources

Shane Day[a,b]

[a]School of Public Administration, University of New Mexico, Albuquerque, NM, USA; [b]Vincent and Elinor Ostrom Workshop in Political Theory and Policy Analysis, Indiana University, Bloomington, IN, USA

Elinor Ostrom's 'Collective Action and the Evolution of Social Norms' represents a concise yet sophisticated summary of the multi-method approach which informed so much of her work. I have always been struck by the diverse reactions that scholars have had to this work, as well as the multitude of subsequent research directions that have been influenced by the article. In regards to my own research agenda, Ostrom has been very influential in my approach to understanding the emergence of federal-tribal co-management of natural resources. In this article, I give a brief summary of the issue of co-management, and emphasize how the design principles, player types, and contextual factors identified in Ostrom's article inform my approach to understanding the diversity of federal-tribal co-management arrangements that have been initiated thus far. I also suggest how Ostrom's approach might be specifically adapted to the context of co-management, particularly through a differentiation between the norms held by elites as opposed to broader society, and how these evolve in such a way as to generate support or opposition to the inclusion of Native American stakeholders in the management of natural resources.

The concept of co-management

The burgeoning literature on 'new governance' and the enhanced role of non-state actors in the policy process identifies various buzzwords such as 'cooperation', 'participation', 'collaboration', 'co-management', and 'consultation', which are often used interchangeably with little common definition nor discrimination between what are distinct classes of policy activity. At a basic level, one can conceptualize a continuum ranging between 'no' and 'maximum' levels of participation by non-governmental actors in policy decision-making. From there, different approaches at characterizing the middle ground between 'no' and 'maximum' participation abound in the literature. The public management literature, for instance, identifies a continuum between 'cooperation' and 'service integration', with simple cooperation implying greater degrees of autonomous relationships among all actors which are overseen by a governmental actor with higher degrees of authority, while 'service integration' implies the greatest degree of interdependence between actors and less clear relational authority patterns (O'Leary, Gazely, McGuire, & Bingham, 2009).

Sidaway (2005) adopts a similar approach whereby different participatory techniques can be located on a continuum between non-participation and full empowerment. At one end is 'non-participation' in which public agencies make decisions unilaterally through closed decision processes. 'Information provision' is seen as slightly more participatory in that government provides the public with information to aid them in understanding public problems and the alternatives being considered in addressing them. 'Consultation' entails a range of activities that open the possibilities for citizen feedback. For instance, 'Information gathering', in the form of focus groups or surveys is seen as slightly more participatory given the active input citizens are making in the governance process, although this still implies little real decision-making as input is mostly restricted to the 'intelligence' and 'promotion' functions of the decision process (Lasswell, 1971). 'Collaboration' occurs when government actors actively delegate certain decision-making functions to non-state actors at various stages of the policy process, albeit in a context where the government maintains final say over any authoritative decisions. Finally, full 'empowerment' entails a situation where the public is involved at each successive stage of the decision process and have final decision-making authority that cannot be unilaterally overturned by government.

Co-management is generally defined as a process involving diverse stakeholders and government regulators working together to resolve shared dilemmas, divvying up the tasks of designing and implementing remedies to environmental problems (Carlsson & Berkes, 2005; Heikkila & Gerlak, 2005; Koontz & Johnson, 2004; Plummer & FitzGibbon, 2004). Given an 'official' definition of co-management as being 'a process of management in which government shares power with resource users, with each given specific rights and responsibilities relating to information and decision-making' (OECD, 2007, 114), I argue that co-management is a distinct policy-making milieu which exhibits the characteristics of 'service integration' and 'empowerment' discussed previously. Thus co-management goes above and beyond basic 'collaboration', 'participation', or 'consultation', which may be considered 'lesser' forms of cooperation due to the interdependence between stakeholders, joint ownership of decisions, and collective responsibility for the future of the partnership which is inherent in co-management as opposed to other forms of cooperation (O'Leary et al., 2009).

Thus co-management can also be situated along a continuum between pure governmental management and pure user group management without any real role for governmental actors (see for instance Sen & Nielsen, 1996), the latter situation which is of course so much of the emphasis of Ostrom's and others' field work on common pool resources. It is necessary to distinguish between co-management arrangements which entail very real decision-making authority on the one hand, while on the other simple programmatic functional tasks that are undertaken by tribes and negotiated through processes much more akin to contracting type of arrangements (see for instance, King, 2007).

Why federal-tribal co-management is distinct

Native American groups are distinct from other non-state actors which might be included in co-management arrangements, on account of their sovereign status. That being said, sovereignty does not mean that tribes have an automatic right to co-management authority. Contrary to the assertion that 'substantive' cases of federal-tribal co-management are tied to legal stipulations mandating their use (Nie, 2008), full-fledged co-management is not a specific legal requirement in any US legal statute that I am aware of. Instead, various legal mechanisms such as the National Environmental Protection Act and the Tribal Self Governance Act mandate consultation and negotiation with tribal groups in various circumstances, but this does not guarantee co-management arrangements to tribal groups in the United States. The question then that emerges is under what circumstances do tribes gain co-management authority? The answer to that question is complex, in that co-management authority has been attained by tribes through a variety of processes.

There are several distinct bases upon which tribes articulate a right to participate in co-management. First, co-management has been interpreted to emanate from reserved rights embodied in treaties, which frequently entail rights to conduct activities off-reservation (Ross, 1999; Singleton, 1998). The extension of co-management in these cases has largely been an outgrowth of protracted legal battles in which co-management rights have been judicially mandated, and are particularly associated with treaty rights pertaining to water resources and fish and wildlife (Blades, 2010; Pinel & Pecos, 2012; Singleton, 2002). Secondly, as an outgrowth of this authority to directly co-manage the resource itself, tribes have engaged in a variety of tribally-initiated processes to manage activities that have positive or negative impacts on fish and wildlife, as mentioned above (Ross, 1999; Singleton, 1998). Thirdly, co-management has been extended largely on an *ad hoc* basis through legislative mandate, in the form of the enabling statutes that create or extend certain tracts of protected lands (King, 2007; Sholar, 2004). Fourthly, the 1994 Tribal Self-Governance Act extends self-determination policy, in which tribes may petition the federal government for funding to directly implement Bureau of Indian Affairs (BIA) or Indian Health Services (HIS) programs they are eligible for on the basis of their status as Indians, to additional bureaus within the Department of Interior (DOI) that have control over 'programs of special geographic, historical, or cultural significance' to the tribes (King, 2007, pp. 498–499). Such a process is limited however to tribes that are certified as 'self-governance' tribes, and it only stipulates that the various DOI bureaus engage in negotiation of contracts and compacts which would turn over some degree of implementation authority to the tribes over various activities on public lands (King, 2007). While this does not necessarily result in true co-management, it has set up a pathway for negotiation between tribes and federal agencies in the area of co-management of protected lands. Within this context, it is useful to differentiate between processes that have been initiated by the tribes themselves, through petitioning bureaus such as the National Park Service (NPS), and processes that have been initiated by the various federal agencies (Pinel & Pecos, 2012). Finally, tribes have found themselves incorporated into *de facto* co-management arrangements in a limited number of situations in which they were instrumental in the creation of a particular tract of protected land (King, 2007).

It is important at this point to also clarify that the federal participants in co-management arrangements are highly varied. Regulatory authority of endangered species under the Endangered Species Act of 1973 (ESA) is held by either the US Fish and Wildlife Service (FWS) or the National Oceanic and Atmospheric Administration (NOAA). In the area of protected lands policy in particular, there are a range of regulatory agencies with responsibilities for particular tracts of protected lands. For instance, while the 59 National Parks are all managed by the NPS, the lead authority for management of National Monuments is split between the NPS, the Bureau of Land Management (BLM), the FWS, and the US Forest Service (USFS). These distinctions are important in that the particular organizational cultures of these various agencies may impact the willingness of specific agencies to initiate co-management negotiations and/or their receptiveness to tribally-initiated co-management negotiations.

Player types, contextual factors, and design principles informing the evolution of co-management

Ostrom's work provides a wide range of theoretical guidance for the study of co-management. I see the distinction of player types to be a useful starting point for the examination of the emergence of co-management arrangements. Certain *a priori* assumptions about the motivations of certain tribal and federal actors may serve as a useful starting point for examination. According to the closed model of organizational theory, bureaucracies tend to emphasize control over turf over all other considerations (Burns & Stalker, 1961; Wilson, 1989), which serves as a significant initial hurdle to co-management as bureaucracies resist devolution of control. Thus, the 'rational egoist' model of behavior, with utility conceptualized as control over authority, may best characterize the federal bureaucracy. Indeed, there is some degree of support in the literature on federal-tribal co-management for such an assumption (Pinel & Pecos, 2012). Conversely, it may be a fair assumption that tribal interests tend to veer towards the 'conditional cooperator' player type, for at least two reasons. First, Native American groups are commonly characterized in the anthropological literature as placing signifi-cant value on norms of fairness, reciprocity, trust, and listening. Second, tribal govern-ments are increasingly taking on more and more governance responsibilities in the current era of 'self-governance', and are frequently keen to seek out as many opportu-nities for consultation and governance responsibilities as possible, as each responsibility taken on represents an additional expression of sovereignty (see for instance Harvard Project, 2008).

Ostrom's insights into evolutionary processes of cooperation are very instructive at this juncture. If one accepts the starting condition of cautious/conditional cooperation on the part of tribal governments and the guarding of turf on the part of federal bureaucracies, it becomes difficult to see any way in which co-management could evolve. The principle that externally imposed rules tend to crowd out endogenous cooperative behavior (Ostrom, 2000, p. 147) is significant in that the implication is that co-management is more likely to evolve from a bottom-up process, presumably initiated by the party that is most open to cooperation and compromise. The question that emerges is under what conditions can tribally-initiated efforts at attaining co-management authority break through bureaucratic opposition? Additionally however, certain instances of co-manage-ment have been judicially mandated, which necessitated a change in bureaucratic leader-ship in order to accommodate the mandate for cooperation, thus necessitating a change in organizational culture and leadership (Day, 2012; Singleton, 1998). This points to the importance of face-to-face communication and trust-building (Ostrom, 2000, p. 140) between federal and tribal actors, as well as a potential barrier to cooperation on the part of tribal authorities whose preferences may be altered by bad experiences with federal representatives in other issues domains (Ostrom, 2000, p. 147).

I also believe that it is useful to differentiate between prevailing norms held by elites versus broader prevailing norms within society. For instance, the successful evolution of co-management in the Pacific salmon regime has been partially attributed to the aforemen-tioned turnover in bureaucratic leadership in order to meet judicial demands for cooperation despite an initial broad-based societal opposition to co-management, which has slowly become more favorable towards tribal inclusion over time (Singleton, 1998). Alternatively, the initiative of new leadership that has been relatively more open to the inclusion of tribal interests in protected lands management, if admittedly due to self-serving reasons, has been cited as an alternative conduit for the emergence of 'real' co-management authority (Pinel & Pecos, 2012). On the other hand, it is entirely possible that tribal elites can be relatively more supportive of co-management despite prevailing opposition from tribal membership. A theoretical construct based on these premises may be useful in differentiating between different evolutionary processes of co-management, with entirely different implications for the working relationships that exist on the ground. For instance, co-management mutually supported by elites but predominately opposed by both native and non-native societal interests is likely to look very different from processes where societal support may be relatively favorable despite elite opposition from one or both sides.

The rich array of contextual variables and design principles discussed in Ostrom's article provide further theoretical guidance to the exploration of these distinct processes of co-management development and evolution. Certain contextual variables, such as the issue salience or dependence of the federal and tribal actors on the good or resource in question, the role of institutional leadership, autonomy to make binding rules, levels of social capital, and the legacy of past experiences are all likely to frame the initial start-up conditions, and subsequent evolution, of co-management arrangements. In terms of the design principles identified by Ostrom, we can also extrapolate tentative hypotheses regarding the likelihood of successful negotiation of these arrangements. In particular, the principle that most individuals affected by the regime can participate in rule making may be suggestive of a barrier to successful long-lasting co-management to the extent that roles are restricted to just federal and tribal interests, and thus shutting out potentially significant third parties such as recreational users of protected lands, for instance. The fourth design principle, that regimes select their own monitors appears to be a significant component of existing co-management arrangements involving tribes insofar as monitoring functions appear to be key tasks commonly granted to tribal actors (King, 2007; Pinel & Pecos, 2012; Singleton, 1998) and could be the perceived utility of the tribal role from a federal perspective. The sixth design principle, the need for rapid, low cost conflict resolution mechanisms, could be a key characteristic of long-lasting co-management arrangements, and could be examined empirically in the context of comparative analysis should a comprehensive list of co-management arrangements be identified. The seventh design principle, that minimal recognition by government actors of the right to self-organize be afforded to local actors, is absolutely important in that in the current era of self-governance and self-determination policy, the federal government affords such a minimal level of recognition of tribal sovereignty. This represents a primary distinguishing characteristic of federal-tribal co-management in comparison to other types of co-management involving other non-state actors.

Conclusion

Ostrom's contributions in 'Collective Action and the Evolution of Social Norms' have been highly influential in a number of areas and will likely continue to instigate further refinements for decades to come. In the area of co-management, I believe that the differentiation between elite and social norms in particular, and how different initial contextual variables impact the start-up conditions and subsequent evolution of collaboration, holds promise for explaining the emergence of federal-tribal co-management regimes. It is also apparent that the design principles first identified in *Governing the Commons* (1990) will continue to be refined for certain situations (see for instance Cox, Arnold, & Tomas, 2010), and that refinements specific to federal-tribal co-management are possible through rigorous comparative analysis of existing cases. Finally, I propose that clearly distinguishing co-management from self-governance, collaboration, and other modalities of natural resource management, and adapting the design principles accordingly, represents a potentially fruitful endeavor which will guide my future work in the area of co-management of protected lands.

References

Blades, E. (2010). Using the legal system to gain control of natural resources on tribal lands: Lessons from the Confederated Salish and Kootenai Tribes and the Coeur D'Alene Tribe. *Idaho Law Review, 47,* 175–203. Retrieved from http://www.uidaho.edu/law/law-review

Burns, T., & Stalker, G. M. (1961). *The management of innovation.* London: Tavistock.

Carlsson, L., & Berkes, F. (2005). Co-management: Concepts and methodological implications. *Journal of Environmental Management, 75,* 65–76. doi:10.1016/j.jenvman.2004.11.008

Cox, M., Arnold, G., & Tomas, S. V. (2010). A review of design principles for community-based natural resource management. *Ecology & Society, 15*(4): 38–57. Retrieved from http://www.ecologyandsociety.org/

Day, S. D. (2012). *Indigenous group sovereignty and participatory authority in international natural resource management regimes* (Doctoral dissertation). Retrieved from ProQuest Dissertations and Theses. (1235652894). Bloomington, IN: Indiana University.

Harvard Project on American Indian Economic Development. 2008. *The state of the native nations: Conditions under U.S. policies of self-determination.* New York, NY: Oxford University Press.

Heikkila, T., & Gerlak, A. K. (2005). The formation of large-scale collaborative resource management institutions: Clarifying the roles of stakeholders, science, and institutions. *Policy Studies Journal, 33*(4): 583–612. doi:10.1111/j.1541-0072.2005.00134.x

King, M. A. (2007). Co-management or contracting? Agreements between native american tribes and the U.S. national park service pursuant to the 1994 tribal self-governance act. *Harvard Environmental Law Review, 31,* 475–530.

Koontz, T. M., & Johnson, E. M. (2004). One size does not fit all: Matching breadth of stakeholder participation to watershed group accomplishments. *Policy Sciences, 37,* 185–204. doi:10.1023/B:OLIC.0000048532.94150.07

Lasswell, H. D. (1971). *A pre-view of the policy sciences.* New York: American Elsevier.

Nie, M. (2008). The use of co-management and protected land-use designations to protect tribal cultural resources and reserved treaty rights on federal lands. *Natural Resources Journal, 48,* 585–647. Retrieved from http://lawschool.unm.edu/nrj

O'Leary, R., Gazely, B., McGuire, M., & Bingham, L. B. (2009). Public managers in collaboration. In R. O'Leary and L. B. Bingham, (Eds.), *The collaborative public manager: New ideas for the twenty-first century* (pp. 1–12). Washington, DC: Georgetown University Press.

Organization for Economic Cooperation and Development. 2007. *OECD glossary of statistical terms.* Paris: OECD.

Ostrom, E. (1990). *Governing the commons: The evolution of institutions for collective action.* New York, NY: Cambridge University Press.

Ostrom, E. (2000). Collective action and the evolution of social norms. *Journal of Economic Perspectives, 14*(3), 137–158. doi:10.1257/jep.14.3.137

Pinel, S. L., & Pecos, J. (2012). Generating co-management at Kasha Katuwe Tent Rocks National Monument, New Mexico. *Environmental Management, 49,* 593–604. doi:10.1007/s00267-012-9814-9

Plummer, R., & FitzGibbon, J. (2004). Co-management of natural resources: A proposed framework. *Environmental Management, 33,* 876–885. doi:10.1007/s00267-003-3038-y

Ross, H. (1999). New ethos – new solutions: Indigenous negotiation of co-operative environmental management agreements in Washington State. *Australian Indigenous Law Review, 4*(2), 1–28. Retrieved from http://www.ilc.unsw.edu.au/publications/australian-indigenous-law-review

Sen, S., & Nielsen, J. R. (1996). Fisheries co-management: A comparative analysis. *Marine Policy, 20,* 405–418. doi:10.1016/0308-597X(96)00028-0

Sholar, C. (2004). Glacier National Park and the Blackfoot Nation's reserved rights: Does a valid tribal co-management authority exist? *American Indian Law Review, 29,* 151–172. doi:10.2307/20070724

Sidaway, R. (2005). *Resolving environmental disputes: From conflict to consensus.* London: EarthScan.

Singleton, S. (1998). *Constructing cooperation: The evolution of institutions of comanagement.* Ann Arbor, MI: University of Michigan Press.

Singleton, S. (2002). Collaborative environmental planning in the American west: The good, the bad, and the ugly. *Environmental Politics, 11*(3), 54–75. doi:10.1080/714000626

Wilson, J. Q. (1989). *Bureaucracy: What government agencies do and why they do it.* New York, NY: Basic Books.

The Allocation of Energy Resources

William Nordhaus

For the full text, see: *Brookings Papers*, 3 (1973), pp. 529–576.

Modeling long term energy futures after Nordhaus (1973)

Gregory F. Nemet[a,b]

[a]La Follette School of Public Affairs, University of Wisconsin-Madison, Madison, WI, USA;
[b]Nelson Institute Center for Sustainability and the Global Environment (SAGE), University of Wisconsin-Madison, Madison, WI, USA

1. Introduction

Nordhaus' (1973) prescient analysis is seminal – and has been cited hundreds of times – in part because of the insights it provides about the energy system and also because it serves as a model model. The approach, modeling a complex system over several decades, identified issues that remain contentious even today, including time preferences, assumptions about future technology, and interpreting the reliability of the results. The historical context is itself important to understanding the approach. Nordhaus wrote it in the wake of a set of studies warning of impending collapse due to population growth (Ehrlich & Holdren, 1971) and resource depletion (Meadows, Meadows, Randers, & Behrens, 1972). Concerns about the environment had been building for several years and the US Congress passed the National Environmental Policy Act in 1969 and the Clean Air Extension Act in 1970. US oil production peaked that same year and just before publication of Nordhaus' article, a group of Arab and North African countries shocked the world by halting oil sales to the US – although clearly Nordhaus performed much of his analysis prior to that event. President Nixon was about to make energy a focus of his 1974 State of the Union speech. A sense of crisis was pervasive. However, 'Allocation' is a precursor of Nordhaus' approach in later work in that the analysis includes both a long-term and a near-term perspective. It encourages looking beyond the crisis toward the longer term, while acknowledging that optimal decisions will value near impacts substantially more than long-term ones.

Nordhaus is sympathetic with the earlier studies in his emphasis that resource scarcity is something society should take seriously. That, itself, was something new in that the country had just experienced a quarter century of unprecedented abundance, on many dimensions. His approach is that this scarcity could be more effectively managed by modeling. There is an optimal strategy for allocating these scarce resources that minimizes the social costs of meeting energy demand over time. Given the size of the humanity's endowment of fossil energy, scarcity depends on taking a long view of future consumption. Despite the shared concern about scarcity and the use of modeling, the article adopts a less strident, and notably less pessimistic tone than the earlier long-term studies. This difference occurs, perhaps in part because of more realistic discounting, and in part due to its consideration of technological change as a factor offsetting population growth and resource depletion. Nordhaus' concern is not so much about running out, but about under-consumption. If new, more resource-efficient technologies beckon, and if discounting focuses attention on the nearer term, then it would be folly to miss out on the improvements to well-being that will accrue from making optimal use of our energy resources. Instead of focusing on the crisis, now (1973) is the time to invest in the longer term to enhance the possibility that new technologies will be available to help society deal with resource scarcity later. Note also his counterintuitive response to the oil crisis; rather than pursuing self-sufficiency, which Nixon championed with his 'Project Independence', Nordhaus emphasized that the US should continue to pursue freer trade. The gains from trade were more important than increasing security of supply since the latter could be improved by other means. For Nordhaus, emergency reserves were the response to the then imminent possibility of further short-term disruptions.

2. What is still true and what has changed

Many aspects of the problems Nordhaus was analyzing are still with us today. The availability of abundant energy supplies at low prices remains fundamental to a highly industrialized economy like the United States. Even though, on many measures, the US is now much more efficient in converting energy into well-being, one cannot make the case that our lifestyle is not dependent on energy. Indeed, the pervasive influence of information and communications technologies makes modern life more vulnerable to disruptions, than the economy of four decades ago. The major difference now is that the problems of resource scarcity are inherently global ones; as the 80% of the people in the world that live in developing countries are in the midst of, or are aspiring to, an energy-intensive process of industrialization. Global markets are linked financially and physically in ways they were not before, such that the relevant demand for US resource security is truly a global one.

Oil prices continue to be an area of intense interest, for policy makers and for investors. Arguments about energy self-sufficiency appeal on many levels – even as they inherently conflict with efforts to reduce barriers to trade and increase the gains from trade. Every President since Nixon has talked about the need for energy self-sufficiency. In 1975, the US created a Strategic Petroleum Reserve to provide the buffer, about 2 months' worth of imports, which Nordhaus suggested would be more prudent than pursuing independence. Today, 28 other countries in the world have agreed to maintain similarly sized reserves.

A few things that Nordhaus discusses are quite different now. For one, the 10% discount rate he uses is high relative to those used in long-term models today, both due to changes in capital markets and also in terms of incorporating philosophical issues such as intergenerational rights into time preferences. The argument that Nordhaus seems to take issue with most, that we should conserve our scarce energy for later, has many fewer proponents now. Instead, current arguments are dominated by (1) those that advocate expanding ways to get more energy out of the ground faster and more cheaply, and (2) those that say we should keep a substantial portion of our energy reserves in the ground, not so we can use them in the future, but so we can keep their combustion products out of the atmosphere. The notion of the Green Paradox reconciles both by suggesting that expected future limitations on carbon emissions will lead to near-term acceleration in fossil resource consumption so that entities can produce emissions before more stringent restrictions are put in place (van der Ploeg & Withagen, 2012). Clearly the paper precedes widespread consideration of climate change, although note in the 'Comments and Discussion' Nordhaus' suggestion of the possibility of a 'limit to the earth's tolerance for energy derived from nonhydro or nonsolar sources' (p. 576).

Finally, we still depend on Nordhaus' 'unproven technologies' (p. 568) to address our long-term energy issues. Nordhaus laid out a case for synthetic liquid fuels in the near term and breeder reactors in the longer term. The US federal government was active in both areas in the years after this article. Breeders were abandoned under the Ford Administration due to proliferation concerns (Ford, 1976). Synfuels were abandoned after a decade and $4.5billion invested in pilot plants; very little useful fuel was produced although the program did generate commercial technology, some of which is now being applied in China (Anadon & Nemet, 2013). Aside from the technology specifics, Nordhaus' modeling raises the question: to what extent should we bet on new unproven technology to help us achieve societal goals in the future?

3. Crucial assumptions: technological change

Nordhaus appears to be a technology optimist; his prices and optimal depletion path depend on an optimistic view of breeders and synfuels. But by being specific about the technologies that might be possible, and importantly, the distinct energy services that each might provide, Nordhaus was explicit about his technology assumptions. This was not a general sentiment about human creativity in the face of constraints (Simon, 1981); it provided readers with a clear set of technological assumptions, whose likelihood could be debated. For example, in discussing the paper, Robert Solow says the model has a 'conservative bias' (p. 574) because it excludes 'exotic' (p. 574) energy technologies like solar (no longer exotic today) and fusion (still exotic). This reflects general findings from the history of technological change that people tend to over-estimate the impact of technologies in the medium term but under-estimate the most important of them over the long term.

Characterization of future technology also presaged a large body of work that began to emerge in the 1990s that made the case that long-term energy futures – whether about supply, prices, and pollution – depend crucially on assumptions about the state, over time, of technologies, also referred to as technological change (Azar & Dowlatabadi, 1999; Goulder & Schneider, 1999; Grübler, Nakićenović, & Victor, 1999). Nordhaus' scenario of a world shifting to synfuels and breeder reactors, and the debates about them in the discussion papers that accompany his article, make this point as clearly as any of the papers that came two and three decades later. As important as technology assumptions are for optimal consumption amidst resource scarcity, they are even more so for optimal consumption with a scarcity of storage space for greenhouse gases in the atmosphere. Nordhaus' own later work with the Dynamic Integrated Climate Economy (DICE) model and its descendants, has always kept assumptions on technological change prominent and explicit, even if less technologically specific than those in his 1973 article (Nordhaus, 1992, 2008, 2013).

A now substantial literature on the empirics of technological change provides modelers with a basis on which to make assumptions (Grübler, 1998). While truly general findings have proven scarce, one can confidently claim that the technologies that exist today are a poor proxy for those that will exist in 10, 20, 50 or 100 years. Assuming frozen technology is certain to be wrong, so one must come up with other assumptions. Modeling long-term energy futures forced the issue by making modelers explicit about what to expect about future technologies. Subsequently, modelers began to build in characterizations of technological change, using for example, exogenous rates of technological improvement, learning curves, and estimates of expected returns to R&D investments, some of which have come from expert elicitation techniques (Azar & Dowlatabadi, 1999). Key research questions today involve these assumptions:

to what extent will scarcity, whether geologic or atmospheric, induce the private sector to invest and affect the rate and direction of technological change? To what extent should government policy create such incentives? To what extent can governments affect technological change on their own? Can government R&D portfolios create outcomes that are robust to inherently unknowable technological outcomes? Is there a conservative or optimistic bias regarding assumptions about new technology in the long-term future? A crucial point in the 1973 paper, as well as subsequent modeling, is that, despite the long-term perspective, these questions are relevant for near-term policy decisions.

4. Why model the long-term future if we are always wrong?

Despite the importance of the questions raised by modeling the long-term future, one still must ask whether modeling long-term outcomes is worthwhile if answers to those questions are elusive – especially if they remain elusive over decades. George Box said, 'all models are wrong, but some are useful' (p. 424) (Box & Draper, 1987). Despite its multiple contributions, Nordhaus' model's predictions about our current electricity system over predict use of nuclear power; what makes it useful? Some contemporary discussants of Nordhaus' paper had a clear perspective, with William Poole questioning the reliability of the model, specifically because of the uncertainty surrounding technological change. James Duesenberry gave the example that oil firms limit their planning to short time horizons because technological change makes planning beyond that 'ineffective'. Moreover, the record of retrospective analyses of past predictions in energy is quite damning, including those of energy demand (Craig, Gadgil, & Koomey, 2002; Winebrake & Sakva, 2006), supply technologies (Hultman & Koomey, 2007), and end-use devices (Dale, Antinori, McNeil, McMahon, & Sydny Fujita, 2009). We know from elicitation studies that experts are typically over-confident in their predictions, that is, they underestimate the appropriate confidence interval around their predictions (Lin & Bier, 2008; Speirs-Bridge et al., 2010). In the realm of climate change, where Nordhaus has been a prolific contributor, concerns about the utility of models have also been raised (Cullenward, Schipper, Sudarshan, & Howarth, 2011; Rosen & Guenther, 2014).

Some agree with Duesenberry and the oil producers, characterizing long-term predictions as futile, or more descriptively, 'basing policies on computerized fairy tales is inadvisable' (p. 154) (Smil, 2008). Other observers who acknowledge the poor track record point to ways that wrong forecasts can still be useful, for example by expanding consideration of alternatives (Morgan & Keith, 2008), by illuminating interactions and systemic properties (Hanson, 1985), and by acknowledging that existing technologies, not just new ones, improve (Bezdek & Wendling, 2002). And even Vaclav Smil, who dismisses most forecasts as 'fairy tales', does acknowledge they can be useful in identifying no regrets actions, those that are robust to the full range of possible outcomes (Smil, 2003). For some problems, we do not really have a choice. Scarcity of greenhouse gas storage in the atmosphere is not an issue if we constrain our view to the time frame over which we are most confident, the near term; nor is fossil fuel resource depletion an issue. In short, wrong and useful modeling can help us to focus on what is important and not chase red herrings. Nordhaus' modeling, in 1973 and since, has embraced these best practices; it is explicit about uncertainty, it increasingly addresses robustness, and it has evolved to take into account new information and occasionally new parameters. But this value of long term modeling – pointing to what is important – is only available if the tool is accessible, transparent, and replicable.

5. Tradeoffs between model complexity and transparency

Since 'Allocation', Nordhaus has led the way on these three attributes. This approach is in sharp contrast to important critiques of integrated assessment models, that they are black boxes, difficult to unpack and to compare (NCC, 2015; Rosen & Guenther, 2014). Nordhaus' main assumptions are included in the paper and an appendix provides the detail. The original DICE model had 13 equations. Subsequent versions have expanded detail, but only to the extent that there are a couple of dozen now. If one disagrees with the results of the latest version, one can go to Nordhaus' website, download the most recent code, and run it in GAMS with one's alternative values. There is no training needed, nor any withholding of the model's innards due to concerns about the model being abused if put in the wrong hands. On this basis, Nordhaus' is probably the most scientific approach to integrated assessment. To be fair to the other models, credibility is likely derived from a tradeoff between transparency and sophistication, rather than simply maximizing transparency. Other models have much more detail, whether about energy technology, agriculture, the carbon cycle, and its possible feedback processes. There are so many assumptions involved that transparency becomes somewhat intractable, replication less feasible. This comes at the price of credibility. The difficulties in replicating and the immense efforts required to run insightful model comparisons raise questions about whether the detail obscures more than it enlightens or whether the detail provides different or more robust conclusions. Nordhaus appears to have a clear perspective on this question – especially when one considers that the most recent DICE model is in a much more reduced form than the Allocation model of 40 years ago.

Disclosure statement

No potential conflict of interest was reported by the author.

References

Anadon, L. D. & Nemet, G. F. (2013). The US synthetic fuels corporation: Policy consistency, flexibility, and the long-term consequences of perceived failures. In A. Grübler & C. Wilson (Eds.), *Energy technology innovation: Learning from historical successes and failures* (pp. 257–273). Cambridge: Cambridge University Press.

Azar, C. & Dowlatabadi, H. (1999). A review of technical change in assessment of climate policy. *Annual Review of Energy and the Environment, 24*(1), 513–544. doi:10.1146/energy.1999.24. issue-1

Bezdek, R. H. & Wendling, R. M. (2002). A half century of long-range energy forecasts: Errors made, lessons learned, and implications for forecasting. *Journal of Fusion Energy, 21*(3/4), 155–172. doi:10.1023/A:1026208113925

Box, G. & Draper, N. R. (1987). *Empirical model-building and response surfaces.* Oxford: John Wiley & Sons.

Craig, P. P., Gadgil, A., & Koomey, J. (2002). What can history teach us? A retrospective examination of long-term energy forecasts for the United States. *Annual Review of Energy and the Environment, 27*, 83–118. doi:10.1146/energy.2002.27.issue-1

Cullenward, D., Schipper, L., Sudarshan, A., & Howarth, R. (2011). Psychohistory revisited: Fundamental issues in forecasting climate futures. *Climatic Change, 104*(3–4), 457–472. doi:10.1007/s10584-010-9995-2

Dale, L., Antinori, C., McNeil, M., McMahon, J. E., & Sydny Fujita, K. (2009). Retrospective evaluation of appliance price trends. *Energy Policy*, *37*(2), 597–605. doi:10.1016/j.enpol.2008.09.087

Ehrlich, P. R. & Holdren, J. P. (1971). Impact of population growth. *Science*, *171*(3977), 1212–1217. doi:10.1126/science.171.3977.1212

Ford, G. (1976). Statement on Nuclear Policy. Online by Gerhard Peters and John T. Woolley, The American Presidency Project. Retrieved from http://www.presidency.ucsb.edu/ws/?pid=6561

Goulder, L. H. & Schneider, S. H. (1999). Induced technological change and the attractiveness of CO2 abatement policies. *Resource and Energy Economics*, *21*, 211–253. doi:10.1016/S0928-7655(99)00004-4

Grübler, A. (1998). *Technology and global change*. Cambridge: Cambridge University Press.

Grübler, A., Nakićenović, N., & Victor, D. G. (1999). Dynamics of energy technologies and global change. *Energy Policy*, *27*, 247–280. doi:10.1016/S0301-4215(98)00067-6

Hanson, M. (1985). Modeling for forecasting versus modeling for understanding: Observations from energy planning. Journal of Planning Education and Research, 6(1), 50–59.

Hultman, N. E. & Koomey, J. G. (2007). The risk of surprise in energy technology costs. *Environmental Research Letters*, *2*(3), 034002.

Lin, S.-W. & Bier, V. M. (2008). A study of expert overconfidence. *Reliability Engineering & System Safety*, *93*(5), 711–721. doi:10.1016/j.ress.2007.03.014

Meadows, D. H., Meadows, D. L., Randers, J., & Behrens III, W. W. (1972). *The limits to growth*. New York: Universe.

Morgan, M. & Keith, D. (2008). Improving the way we think about projecting future energy use and emissions of carbon dioxide. *Climatic Change*, *90*(3), 189–215. doi:10.1007/s10584-008-9458-1

NCC. (2015). IAM helpful or not? [Editorial]. *Nature Climate Change*, *5*(2), 81–81. doi:10.1038/nclimate2526

Nordhaus, W. D. (1973). The allocation of energy resources. *Brookings Papers on Economic Activity*, *3*, 529–576.

Nordhaus, W. D. (1992). An optimal transition path for controlling greenhouse gases. *Science*, *258* (5086), 1315–1319. doi:10.1126/science.258.5086.1315

Nordhaus, W. D. (2008). *A question of balance: Weighing the options on global warming policies*. New Haven: Yale University Press.

Nordhaus, W. D. (2013). *The climate casino: Risk, uncertainty, and economics for a warming world*. New Haven: Yale University Press.

Rosen, R. A. & Guenther, E. (2014). The economics of mitigating climate change: What can we know? *Technological Forecasting and Social Change*, 91, 93–106.

Simon, J. L. (1981). *The ultimate resource*. Princeton: Princeton University Press.

Smil, V. (2003). *Energy at the crossroads: Global perspectives and uncertainties*. Cambridge, MA: MIT Press.

Smil, V. (2008). Long-range energy forecasts are no more than fairy tales. *Nature*, *453*(7192), 154–154. doi:10.1038/453154a

Speirs-Bridge, A., Fidler, F., McBride, M., Flander, L., Cumming, G., & Burgman, M. (2010). Reducing overconfidence in the interval judgments of experts. *Risk Analysis*, *30*(3), 512–523. doi:10.1111/risk.2010.30.issue-3

van der Ploeg, F. & Withagen, C. (2012). Is there really a green paradox? *Journal of Environmental Economics and Management*, *64*(3), 342–363. doi:10.1016/j.jeem.2012.08.002

Winebrake, J. J. & Sakva, D. (2006). An evaluation of errors in US energy forecasts: 1982–2003. *Energy Policy*, *34*(18), 3475–3483. doi:10.1016/j.enpol.2005.07.018

The allocation of energy resources in the very long run

Roger Fouquet

Grantham Research Institute on Climate Change and the Environment, London School of Economics and Political Science (LSE), London, UK

1. Introduction

A central concern to energy economists in the 1970s was the threat of energy resource limits to economic growth. William Nordhaus' (1973) article on The Allocation of Energy Resources was one of the finest and grandest examples of this effort to understand how an economy can continue to grow despite limited fossil fuel resources.

Strongly influenced by his supervisor Robert Solow (1974), William Nordhaus became highly proficient at developing 'small models applied to real problems, blending real-world observation and a little mathematics to cut through to the core of an issue' (Krugman, 2015, p. 1). Shortly after he completed his PhD in 1967, energy economics began to benefit from the skills and imagination of this innovative researcher coming out of the golden age of MIT's PhD program.

This is particularly interesting, since he had identified the crucial role energy played in the economy before the oil price hike of 1973. Naturally, other scholars had already alerted economists and the world of this role – particularly Mori Adelman (1972) at MIT, Sam Schurr and his colleagues (Schurr & Netschert, 1960) at Resources for the Future, and, of course, the 'Limits to Growth' team (Meadows, Meadows, Randers, & Behrens, 1972). Yet, just as he pre-empted the importance of the economics of climate change and of technological development (Nordhaus, 1977, 1991, 1997), he was at the right place, at the right time.

As his research assistant on the project, Paul Krugman offered some insight into the evolution of the paper.

> The first summer I worked for him, Nordhaus began with only a vague sense of how to think about the problem of appropriate pricing of energy. I was able to watch the process by which he crystallized that vague sense into a model, and then was able to see the way in which that model transformed everyone's perception of the issue. (Krugman, 2015, p. 1)

Nordhaus (1973) was interested in identifying how energy resources would be allocated, both positively and normatively. In other words, first, how do markets allocate energy resources? As he said '[i]t takes an act of faith to believe that "the market" can somehow see the proper allocation through this tangle of complexity, uncertainty, and politics' (Nordhaus, 1973, p. 538). And, second, how energy resources should be allocated? Always the pragmatist, he tried to provide 'a middle ground between .. summon [ing] ... all current and future citizens ... into Yankee Stadium' (Nordhaus, 1973, p. 538) to decide on how to allocate resources, and developing a model that forecasts all present and future prices. Indeed, his model offered a very long run perspective, looking 200 years into the future.

Given his very long run perspective, this special issue offers an opportunity to examine the Nordhaus (1973) framework, and comment on how energy markets have allocated resources in the very long run. Therefore, the focus in this paper is to look at backstop energy resources, extraction costs and royalties, as well as transport costs, taxes and interest rates, over more than 500 years in Britain. The focus is on coal markets from the thirteenth century until the mid-twentieth century, because they provide a case study in which governments had limited influence over prices, and markets dominated the allocation of energy resources. This data analysis provides a crude test of his model.

This brief historical analysis builds on and greatly extends a discussion in Fouquet (2011a) on long run energy prices. For those interested in the sources of the data presented in this paper, the extensive data collection exercise by Thorold Rogers (1865, 1882, 1886) on agricultural prices in market towns across England provided indicators of the cost of fuels as far back as the eleventh century. William Beveridge (1894) then gathered reliable data from the sixteenth century onwards, creating long run series reflecting the price of energy faced by individual institutions. The institutions included some of the Oxford and Cambridge colleges, the Eton and Westminster Colleges and the Navy, as well as long-standing hospitals. They have been combined to get an average price of individual fuels in Southern England, where most of the institutions were based. Gregory Clark (2010) has recently added to the data sets. All the costs and prices are converted into values in the year 2000 using the price index data from Allen (2007).

2. Backstop and non-renewable energy sources

Nordhaus (1973) presented a model of a relatively cheap non-renewable resource and an abundant but expensive backstop technology – he proposed either a fast breeder or fusion nuclear power source.[1] For much of its history, the backstop energy source in Britain was woodfuel. Although limited in England and, to a lesser extent, in Wales and Scotland, it could also be imported from overseas. It effectively was between 1650 and 1800, since England and Wales imported two-thirds of its bar iron from Sweden and Russia (King, 2005). At the height of imports, in the 1780s, the 50,000 tonnes of bar iron imported into England and Wales would have required 170,000 tonnes of charcoal and coppiced woods equivalent to 3% of England's surface area (Fouquet, 2008, p. 60).

Naturally, there was a limit to the abundance of this backstop energy source, especially when considering the demands of a global economy. However, until the twentieth century, Britain could have considered woodfuel a genuine backstop energy source. Between 1700 and 1900, total energy consumption increased 16-fold (from 1.4 to 22.2 million tonnes of oil equivalent), which could have been supplied to a large extent by imports of fuelwood, charcoal or the goods produced from these fuels. After all, Sweden was nine times larger than England, and Russia was 340 times larger. Clearly, the rising prices from using woodfuels would have greatly reduced energy consumption and impeded economic growth and development, but it was a more realistic backstop energy source then than nuclear fusion or even probably fast breeder reactors are today (Hatcher, 1993).

Nordhaus (1973, p. 533) explains that, for a non-renewable resource, '[t]here are three important elements in determining current royalty . . .: the cost of the backstop technology, the interest rate, and the switch date'. Figure 1 presents the prices of both the backstop, charcoal, and the non-renewable energy source, coal. In the fourteenth century, the dominant source was the backstop energy source, because coal markets and technologies

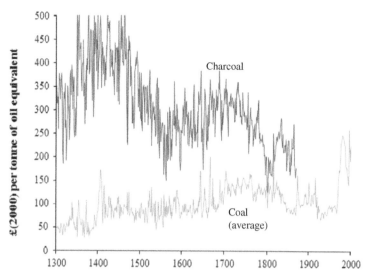

Figure 1.   (Colour online) Average charcoal and coal prices in England, 1300–2000.
Source: Fouquet (2011a).

had not yet been fully developed. The rising population placed significant pressures on woodfuel and charcoal prices. After the Black Death, and the near halving of the population, woodfuel prices dropped. Prices began to rise again as population grew once more in the sixteenth century.

In sixteenth-century England, the introduction of grates for burning coal and chimneys to externalize emissions enabled households in urban areas to switch from woodfuels to coal. The experience of the 1300s suggests that woodfuel prices would have increased a great deal further in the sixteenth century (above £300 in 2000 values) without the slow transition towards coal for residential heating demands (Fouquet, 2010). Similarly, in a number of industries, methods were developed to use coal rather than charcoal – although it took until the eighteenth century for adequate and affordable techniques to be developed in the large iron industry.

The transition from woodfuels and other biomass sources to coal took roughly 300 years. In 1700, coal already provided 73% of all primary (non-agricultural) energy consumption. By 1800, its share had reached 95%. King Coal was at the heart of British economic growth (Flinn, 1984).

Reflecting this transition, the prices of charcoal and of coal varied considerably. In the seventeenth century, the differential between the two prices was certainly increasing, with the former triple the latter. But, in the eighteenth century, the gap was closing; by 1800, there was less than 50% difference in prices. According to Nordhaus' (1973) model, this should have been captured in higher royalties for the producers (see below).

3.   Long run trend in taxes and transport costs

In the Introduction, it was proposed that governments had little influence over coal markets. While this is broadly true, the government did alter the course of price trends by introducing and varying the tax facing many consumers in Britain. Certainly, average

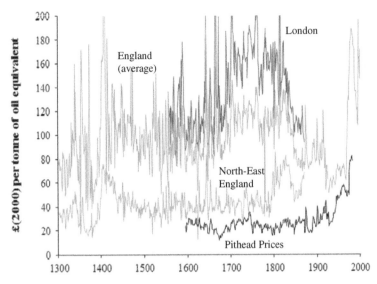

Figure 2.   (Colour online) Pithead and regional coal prices in England, 1300–2000.
Source: Fouquet (2011a).

coal prices appear to have risen between 1600 and 1800, and the main explanation for this rise in coal prices to the consumer from the late 1600s (see Figures 1 and 2) was the introduction of taxes on coal to pay for wars. The tax stood at an average of 12% between 1691 and 1697, and then increased to 33% in 1698, peaking at 38% from 1714 to 1758, varying between 29% and 34% throughout the second half of the eighteenth century, and then dropping to 15% in 1816, after the Battle of Waterloo. In 1831, national duties on coal were removed, although modest local taxes of about 5% remained until 1903 (Hausman, 1987, p. 592). Therefore, average consumer coal prices increased as consumption grew, reflecting the government's ability to capture some of the consumer surplus associated with a relatively inelastic demand.

Figure 2 presents more detailed trends in coal prices over 700 years in England. It shows prices in London, in England (on average) and in the North-East (without the tax). From 1500, coal prices in the North of England stayed close to £40 (in 2000 values) per tonne for 300 years. Removing the taxes from the average England and London series creates three parallel trends, indicating the cost of distributing coal around the country. The average English transport costs of coal were 60% of the untaxed value from 1300 until about 1700. In other words, transport costs (and middlemen) were a large component of the price faced by the consumer.

From the beginning of the eighteenth century, transport costs fell to about 45%. They dropped substantially as a result of the expansion of canals, especially in certain regions (such as South Wales, East Midlands and Lancashire, Turnbull, 1987, p. 549). Others benefitted from improving coastal trade (Ville, 1986). London prices were consistently about 10% higher than the average and, there, reductions in distribution costs only occurred from the 1790s. Then, from the 1840s, and the advent of the railways, coal prices across England fell towards the price paid in the North East – though, more slowly for London prices.

4. Long run trends in extraction costs

In analyzing non-renewable resource prices, Nordhaus (1973, p. 531) 'distinguish[ed] between extraction costs, the vector z(t), or the marginal cost per unit of output excluding rents and royalties; and royalties, the vector y(t), which are a reflection of the presumed scarcity of a particular resource'. From 1600, there were data on pithead prices, which act as an indicator of the extraction costs (see Figure 2). The trend was generally flat (in the $20–$30 per tonne of oil equivalent range) from the seventeenth to the end of the nineteenth century, which is impressive given that coal mines had to be dug deeper to meet rapidly growing demands. In fact, there were declines in extraction costs in the second half of the seventeenth and of the eighteenth centuries – although prices gravitated back to the $20–$30 range. The latter period probably reflected the ability to use early steam engines to pump water out of the deeper mines. Thus, for 300 years, the greater difficulties of extraction were balanced-out by improvements in technical ingenuity.

It also indicated that until the end of the nineteenth century, there was an elastic supply of labor. In 1913, the peak year of coal production in Britain, there were 1 million coal miners – 7% of the male work force was extracting coal. However, from the 1870s until the 1920s, miners' strikes signaled the demands for higher wages and better working conditions – there were more than 2200 coal-mining related deaths in 1913 (Fouquet, 2011b). British mines became more mechanized, but overall production costs rose substantially, because coal mines still needed many workers and could never be completely mechanized (see Figure 1). More generally, one can expect that where substitutability between capital and labor is limited for technical reasons, as in coal mines, the trend in extraction costs will tend to increase, as the economy develops (Ayres & Warr, 2009). In other words, if energy is fueling economic growth and development, then, wages will rise, thus, so will labor costs and, ultimately, energy prices.

5. Long run trends in royalties

Having a proxy for extraction costs (i.e., pithead prices) and prices near the mines (e.g., the North East of England) in Figure 2, it is possible to estimate a crude indicator of royalties. As mentioned, between 1500 and 1800, coal prices in North East England stabilized around $40 per tonne of oil equivalent. Thus, given that extraction costs were in the $20–$30 range, the royalties were roughly one quarter to one half of the costs – though this does ignore (presumably modest) local supply costs. Then, from just before 1800, they increased dramatically.

Nordhaus (1973, p. 534) explains '… if the interest rate is high, then the royalty on energy resources is relatively low. Conversely, if these conditions are reversed, the royalty on energy resources is high'. Looking at the last 250 years, for which real interest rates exist, Figure 3 suggests that this relationship seems to hold in a few historical periods, but is far from the norm. For instance, in the late eighteenth century, 10-year average real interest rates fell from 4% to 0% and royalties jumped from 40% to almost 70%. Then, around 1800, real interest rates rose again and royalties declined. However, for much of the nineteenth century, there is little correlation. And, then, from 1880, the opposite occurs, and the two variables appear to be positively correlated – real interest rates drop from 4% to 2% and then fall into negative values during the First World War, and royalties on coal seem to follow. Then, from 1950, the negative relationship seems to return. Real interest rates jumped from −2% to 2%, and royalties fell to 20%. In 1965, real interest rates drop back down to −2% and royalties bounce back to 60%. However, this was also a period of heavy

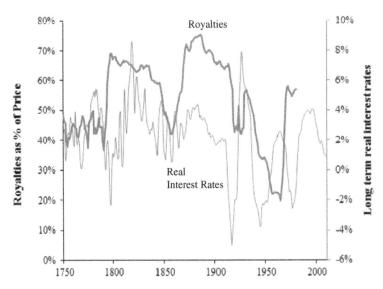

Figure 3. (Colour online) Royalties on coal prices and real interest rates in England, 1750–2010. Source: Royalties: see Figure 2; Interest Rates: Officer (2012) and Allen (2007) – 10-year average.

government intervention, and institutional factors might have played a stronger role than interest rates in determining royalties. Overall, the historical evidence is inconclusive, and a more thorough econometric analysis would be required to discern the influence of interest rates on royalties and, thus, on trends in coal prices.

More importantly, as Nordhaus (1973) emphasized, royalties reflected resource scarcity. He proposed that the 'switch date' – that is, the year in which the economy has to make the transition to the abundant, but expensive backstop energy source – imposes upward pressure on royalties and, therefore, prices. The sooner the date at which the economy needs to begin the transition to the backstop energy source, the higher will be the price.

So, when was the perceived switch date? As a young economist, William Stanley Jevons (1865) made his name by effectively asking this question. He famously proposed the paradox that efficiency improvements would lead to an increase in coal consumption, rather than a decrease, because of what is now known as the 'rebound effect' (Madureira, 2012, p. 409). He combined this idea with long run projections of British population and economic growth to forecast coal consumption over the next 100 years – which he proposed would grow by 3.5% per year, reaching 2.6 billion tons in 1961 (Jevons, 1865, p. XII.23) – equivalent to 1.6 billion tonnes of oil.[2] Jevons estimated that, at this growth rate, the country would consume roughly 100 billion tons of coal between 1860 and 1960. However, he also used geological estimates of coal reserves to indicate that, at that rate, Britain's main fuel would disappear in 80 years (Madureira, 2012, p. 410).

Two years before, an industrialist, William George Armstrong, had already made a forecast, using more simple linear assumptions about consumption patterns, that Britain's coal reserves would last 212 years (Madureira, 2012, p. 410). Two years before that, in 1861, the geologist Edward Hull 'had estimated the recoverable resources as assessed by the Geological Survey for England, Wales and Scotland amounted to about 80,000 million tons of coal, which, at the rate of production in the late 1850s, would last for 1100 years' (Madureira, 2012, p. 403). Thus, the markets might have believed that the switch date to a backstop energy source had fallen from 1100 years (in the future) in 1861 to 80 years in

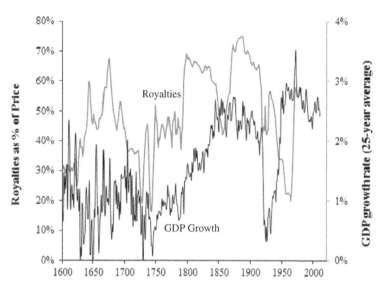

Figure 4. (Colour online) Royalties on coal prices and GDP growth rates (25-year average) in England/Britain/United Kingdom, 1600–2010.

Source: Royalties: see Figure 2; GDP: Broadberry, Campbell, Klein, Overton, and van Leeuwen (2015).

1865. It may be a coincidence, but royalties increased from around 40% of the pre-tax price in 1857 to 70% in 1872.

Certainly, just as the US has been concerned about oil supplies since the 1970s, British industrialists and politicians were fearful about dwindling coal reserves in the mid-nineteenth century. As Figure 4 shows, the (25-year average) growth rate of British GDP, which had been fueled by deeper and longer coal mines, had been accelerating since the 1750s.

> British leaders viewed the linkage between coal and the empire as the mainstay of their strategic clout, which was then consolidated through trade networks, industrial advantage, shipbuilding industries and naval power. More than a commodity, what was at stake was a string of economic interdependencies with repercussions for the British way of life. There was such anxiety about coal's interlocking effects that the slightest sign of disturbance could escalate into sweeping policy issues. Irrespective of the different political positions of economists and geologists, they both shared the view that industrial ascendancy and world supremacy was closely bound up with coal. Madureira (2012, p. 419)

Royalties peaked in the mid-1880s at 75% of the pre-tax price, which coincided with the peak of British long-run average GDP growth rate (see Figure 4). Both the growth rate and royalties fell a little over the next 30 years. Then, as economic growth rates collapsed, royalties fell from 65% in 1913 to 42% in 1919. Afterwards, the British economy was no longer as fundamentally tied to coal, and royalties fell to 20%. Coal was no longer king in Britain, and was no longer scarce (Church, 1987).

6. Conclusion

Given the growing concern about the ability for economies to continue to grow despite limited fossil fuel reserves, William Nordhaus (1973) sought to ask 'how do markets allocate energy resources?' and 'how can energy resources be allocated efficiently?' The purpose of this paper was to offer a crude test of the model he developed to answer the first question. The model is tested by using energy prices over more than 500 years.

The model is based on the relationship between royalties associated with the production of a non-renewable energy resource and (1) the cost of the backstop energy source, (2) the interest rate and (3) the switching date to the backstop energy source. Although elegant and simple, a general weakness of the model is that, both to the market and to the analyst, a backstop technology may not be clearly identified. As a result, the cost and the switching date may be highly uncertain.

Despite this general limitation, for the history of Britain, it was possible to identify a backstop energy source, woodfuel (i.e., firewood and charcoal), which could have been an expensive alternative to coal. For most of the period, there is little evidence of concern for the switching date to the backstop. However, a fear of running-out of coal did take hold of Britain in the mid-nineteenth century. This was a remarkable period of 100 years of accelerating economic growth rates and popular fears of resource scarcity developed. In turn, the markets translated this fear into a dramatic increase in royalties, though with more ambiguous effects on national average coal prices. Nevertheless, this led to the discovery of new coal reserves, new methods of extraction, more efficient ways of consuming energy and, ultimately, substitutes for coal, in the form of new energy sources (such oil, gas and electricity) rather than the backstop technology. It ultimately led to the gradual decline of coal use in Britain, perhaps like the energy crisis in the 1970s was a signal of the beginning of a gradual decline of oil use in industrialized economies.

This paper only offered a crude attempt to test the Nordhaus (1973) model of resource allocation – and the model needs and deserves a more rigorous analysis. The general impression the very long run data and this crude test provided was that energy markets tend to be myopic, unaware of the limits of the non-renewable resource being traded and of a backstop technology. Only in moments of crisis does it consider the finiteness of the resource and, then, perhaps too dramatically, triggering major new technological, infrastructure and R&D investments. Yet, these create the new landscape of future energy markets.

Acknowledgement

I would like to acknowledge that this research was funded by the Grantham Foundation and the Economic and Social Research Council.

Disclosure statement

No potential conflict of interest was reported by the author.

Notes

1. The former is still seen as very expensive 40 years later, while the latter cannot realistically be considered one, due to current scientific and engineering limitations.
2. Out of interest, United Kingdom's peak year of coal consumption was 1913, reaching 160 million tonnes of oil equivalent, which was 50% of the Jevons' forecast for 1913 and 10% of the Jevons' peak (i.e., 1961) forecast. Nevertheless, he was partially correct about the impact of rebound effects on energy consumption, although only for a few decades in the second half of the nineteenth century (Fouquet, 2014).

References

Adelman, M. A. (1972). Is the oil shortage real? Oil companies as OPEC tax-collectors. *Foreign Policy, 9*(4), 69–107.

Allen, R. C. (2007). *Pessimism preserved: Real wages in the British industrial revolution* (Economics Series Working Papers 314). Department of Economics, University of Oxford. Retrieved from http://www.economics.ox.ac.uk/materials/working_papers/paper314.pdf

Ayres, R., & Warr, B. (2009). *The economic growth engine: How energy and work drive material prosperity*. Cheltenham, UK: Edward Elgar.

Beveridge, W. (1894). *Prices and wages in England: From the twelfth to the nineteenth century*. London: Longmans, Green.

Broadberry, S. N., Campbell, B., Klein, A., Overton, M., & van Leeuwen, B. (2015). *British economic growth, 1270–1870*. Cambridge: Cambridge University Press.

Church, R. (1987). *The history of the British coal industry. Vol 3. 1830–1913*. Oxford: Clarendon Press.

Clark, G. (2010). The macroeconomic aggregates for England, 1209–1869. *Research in Economic History, 27*, 51–140.

Flinn, M. W. (1984). *The history of the British coal industry. Vol 2. 1700–1830*. Oxford: Clarendon Press.

Fouquet, R. (2008). *Heat, power and light: Revolutions in energy services*. Cheltenham, UK: Edward Elgar.

Fouquet, R. (2010). The slow search for solutions: Lessons from historical energy transitions by sector and service. *Energy Policy, 38*(11), 6586–6596. doi:10.1016/j.enpol.2010.06.029

Fouquet, R. (2011a). Divergences in long run trends in the prices of energy and energy services. *Review of Environmental Economics and Policy, 5*(2), 196–218. doi:10.1093/reep/rer008

Fouquet, R. (2011b). Long run trends in energy-related external costs. *Ecological Economics, 70* (12), 2380–2389. doi:10.1016/j.ecolecon.2011.07.020

Fouquet, R. (2014). Long-run demand for energy services: Income and price elasticities over two hundred years. *Review of Environmental Economics and Policy, 8*(2), 186–207. doi:10.1093/reep/reu002

Hatcher, J. (1993). *The history of the British coal industry* (Vol. I). Oxford: Clarendon Press.

Hausman, W. J. (1987). The English coastal coal trade, 1691–1910: How rapid was productivity growth? *Economic History Review, 40*(4), 588–596.

Jevons, W. S. (1865). *The coal question*. London: Macmillan.

King, P. (2005). The production and consumption of bar iron in early modern England and Wales. *The Economic History Review, 58*(1), 1–33. doi:10.1111/ehr.2005.58.issue-1

Krugman, P. (2015). Incidents from my Career. Retrieved from http://web.mit.edu/krugman/www/incidents.html

Madureira, N. L. (2012). The anxiety of abundance: William Stanley Jevons and coal scarcity in the nineteenth century. *Environment and History, 18*(3), 395–421. doi:10.3197/096734012X13400389809373

Meadows, D. H., Meadows, D. L., Randers, J., & Behrens, W. (1972). *The limits to growth*. New York, NY: Universe Books.

Nordhaus, W. D. (1973). The allocation of energy resources. *Brookings Papers on Economic Activity, 3*, 529–576.

Nordhaus, W. D. (1977). Economic growth and climate: The carbon dioxide problem. *American Economic Review, 67*(1), 341–346.

Nordhaus, W. D. (1991). To slow or not to slow: The economics of the greenhouse effect. *The Economic Journal, 101*(4), 920–937.

Nordhaus, W. D. (1997). Do real output and real wage measures capture reality? The history of lighting suggests not. In T. F. Breshnahan & R. Gordon (Eds.), *The economics of new goods*. Chicago, IL: Chicago University Press.

Officer, L. H. (2012) What was the interest rate then? MeasuringWorth. Retrieved from http://www.measuringworth.com/interestrates/

Rogers, J. E. T. (1865). *A history of agriculture and prices in England* (Vols. I–VI). Oxford: Clarendon Press.

Rogers, J. E. T. (1882). *A history of agriculture and prices in England* (Vols. I–VI). Oxford: Clarendon Press.

Rogers, J. E. T. (1886). *A history of agriculture and prices in England* (Vols. I–VI). Oxford: Clarendon Press.

Schurr, S., & Netschert, B. (1960). *Energy in the American economy, 1850–1975*. Baltimore, MD: John Hopkins Press.

Solow, R. M. (1974). Intergenerational equity and exhaustible resources. *Review of Economic Studies, 41*(5), 29–46.

Turnbull, G. (1987). Canals, coal and regional growth during the industrial revolution. *Economic History Review, 40*(4), 537–560.

Ville, S. (1986). Total factor productivity in the English shipping industry. *Economic History Review, 39*(3), 355–370.

The world before climate change

Frank Ackerman

Synapse Energy Economics, Inc., & Massachusetts Institute of Technology, Cambridge, MA, USA

William Nordhaus is best known today for his long career of path-breaking research on the economics of climate change, beginning in the late 1970s. It is intriguing to look back even farther in time, to his 1973 projection of long-term world energy futures (Nordhaus, 1973) – both for the successes and failures of that projection, and for the ways in which it foreshadowed the author's later work on climate change.

Now that the first 40 years of his 1973 forecast have slipped from the future into the past, it is impressive to see some striking successes. Who else predicted, back then, that shale oil supplies would eventually be developed, reducing US oil imports, by about 2020? Perhaps less remarkable, but clearly on the mark, was the anticipation of environmental restrictions on power plants, particularly those burning coal; it was, after all, several years after the passage of the Clean Air Act and the creation of the Environmental Protection Agency. The identification of natural gas as the least-cost fuel for US electricity production in the near term was also accurate in retrospect.

But prediction is especially difficult for the future, as the saying goes, because it has not happened yet. The young Nordhaus, as energy forecaster, failed to foresee the rapid rise of renewable energy, or the importance of the Organization of the Petroleum Exporting Countries (OPEC) and the heights which oil prices would soon reach. His assumption that coal, often liquefied, would be widely used in twenty-first century America does not currently look accurate. Writing years before Three Mile Island, let alone Chernobyl and Fukushima, he was remarkably sanguine about the prospects for nuclear power, discussing 'the inevitable transition from exhaustible fossil fuels to nuclear fuels... this basic pattern is all but invariant to such things as modifications in cost' (Nordhaus, 1973, p. 553).

It was, however, several years after Detroit Edison's disastrous attempt at building a fast breeder reactor, now largely forgotten but memorialized at the time in a book and a popular song titled 'We Almost Lost Detroit'. This experience may be reflected in Nordhaus' discussion of the risk that breeder reactor technology, often seen as the key to extending limited supplies of nuclear fuel, might not prove successful – even though his basic projections assumed that breeder reactors would become increasingly important in the twenty-first century and beyond (Nordhaus, 1973, p. 552, Table 5).

Nordhaus, as of 1973, also failed to anticipate the importance of the issue that he later became so well-known for studying – the economics of climate change. Indeed, almost no one was talking about global warming at the time. While the basic science underlying climate change is much older, widespread awareness of the urgency of the problem only surfaced in the 1980s. Yet on a deeper level, many of the themes of Nordhaus' later work are anticipated in his early work on energy futures.

In both arenas, Nordhaus starts with a framework from conventional economic theory and applies it to an empirical problem of global scope and multi-century duration. An intentionally simple logical structure, combined with heroic extrapolation from limited available data, yields interesting estimates that are arguably better than complete ignorance, representing ambitious attempts at creating the best available or least bad forecasts. (When I was an undergraduate, the campus newspaper had a slogan on the wall in its editorial office: 'Something inaccurate is better than nothing at all'. This may be better guidance for some kinds of forecasting than for newspaper writing.)

In both cases Nordhaus offers a vision of the uncertain future that is imbued with technological optimism. For climate change this has often meant a comfortably modest estimate of the pace of climate change and the extent of the resulting damages; the assumption of a carbon-free backstop fuel, or complete decarbonization option, available at a moderately large but imaginable price; and, in some early analyses, over-reliance on cheap nuclear power,[1] and a geoengineering strategy that would solve the entire climate crisis at a very low cost.

The simplicity of Nordhaus' analyses, in climate change as in the 1973 energy forecast, may seem frustrating at times. It is, however, a conscious choice, designed for comprehensibility rather than completeness. His DICE (Dynamic Integrated Climate-Economy) model is one of the first and simplest of the integrated assessment models of climate economics. Even after decades of development, it still represents the entire long-run dynamics of the global economy, the climate, and their interactions, with only 18 equations and 44 parameters (Nordhaus, 2011). This offers a skeletal clarity about the assumed mechanisms, at the price of ruthless oversimplification. In defense of this approach, Nordhaus has argued that the complexity of more elaborate models implies that they will inevitably have a significant rate of errors, with unintended consequences for model results. My own work (Ackerman & Munitz, 2012), which identified a glaring algebraic error in a more complex integrated assessment model, provides one of his examples (Nordhaus with Sztorc, 2013, pp. 51–54).

The good news about this approach is that it has led to widespread understanding of DICE, and has created a community of users who have experimented with incremental changes to the model. Nordhaus' longstanding policy of making the code freely available, and making no attempts to police anyone else's use of it, has made DICE a *de facto* open-source standard for climate economics. Rigorous simplicity and intense public scrutiny ensure that there are no hidden errors or unintended glitches in the DICE software.

The bad news is that those 18 equations and 44 parameters leave out a lot of things about climate change that we know are very important. Particularly in its early, extremely optimistic versions, DICE could be, and often was, cited as proof that sound economic analysis shows climate change to be a minor problem, fully solvable without major expenditures or policy initiatives. The transparency of DICE has allowed critics, myself included, to rake over the model in search of the sources of this unwarranted optimism. Once the geoengineering and cheap nuclear power panaceas were abandoned, a while back, the principal remaining questions, from my perspective, concerned the discount rate, the near-absence of tipping-point risks of discontinuous or catastrophic outcomes, and the shape of the damage function. The discount rate may be the most important factor: in his widely cited critique of the Stern Review, Nordhaus emphasized Stern's use of a much lower discount rate as the root cause of their disagreement (Nordhaus, 2007). Regarding the damage function, a single equation in DICE projects a rather leisurely growth of total climate damages as global temperatures rise. Reasonable alternatives have very different implications for the costs and severity of climate impacts (Ackerman & Stanton, 2012).

Fortunately, the story does not end there. Fascination with the data and curiosity about what it implies, visible in Nordhaus' early work on energy futures, has continued to inform his latter-day work on climate change. For example, after Hurricane Katrina he demonstrated that hurricane damages rise extraordinarily rapidly as wind speed increases. Basic physics suggests that damages should be proportional to the cube of wind speed, a relationship that is assumed in many models.[2] Empirically, Nordhaus found, the relationship is much steeper, with damages proportional to the ninth power of wind speed (Nordhaus, 2010). This is plausible, he suggested, because many structures are little affected by strong winds up to a breaking point, at which point they experience large, discontinuous increases in damages. When wind speeds first exceed the breaking points of many structures, aggregate damages can rise quite steeply. Other researchers have found similar, if not quite as extreme, patterns in hurricane damages as a function of wind speed (Bouwer & Wouter Botzen, 2011).

In the bigger picture, Nordhaus has gradually shifted his estimates of the severity of climate risks, nudging the damage function upward with each revision. There is also a larger, noteworthy change in his latest book, *The Climate Casino* (Nordhaus, 2013). As well as presenting a new revision of DICE, he emphasizes that there are critical impacts of climate change that cannot easily be quantified or monetized, and hence cannot be incorporated into a model of this type. The title of the book reflects his focus on unpredictable, extreme risks as the most serious problem of climate change, justifying policy responses beyond those literally recommended by the DICE model. It is still not the book I would have written on these issues; Martin Weitzman's appreciative critique seems to me to strike many of the right notes (Weitzman, 2015). But *The Climate Casino* is more than just an update of earlier books by Nordhaus. In public debate, Nordhaus appears to have concluded that the Stern Review and others calling for more drastic action are less of a threat than the rising tide of climate science denial in American politics. He has spoken out forcefully to emphasize that the problem is real, and inaction is not a survivable option (Nordhaus, 2012).

Finally, more than 40 years on from the publication of his global energy forecast, Nordhaus provides an exemplary model of scholarly activity. We all have met people who, by this stage in their careers, are so absorbed in pride or defensiveness about their past accomplishments that they are no longer really open to discussion of new and different perspectives. Nordhaus, despite his fame, remains impressively humble and curious about the views of others, seeking out some of his harshest critics (I am speaking from personal experience here) to be sure he understands where they disagree with him. This sort of behavior threatens to give academic careers a good name. In the words of a television show that was popular when Nordhaus published his early energy projections, 'Live long and prosper'.

Disclosure statement

No potential conflict of interest was reported by the author.

Notes

1. He commented in one of his first analyses of climate change that prohibition on nuclear power would make the cost of meeting carbon constraints about five times as large (Nordhaus, 1977, p. 346).
2. The kinetic energy of an air molecule is proportional to the square of wind speed. The number of molecules striking a fixed structure per unit of time is proportional to wind speed. The impact on a fixed structure per unit of time is the product of these two factors.

References

Ackerman, F., & Munitz, C. (2012). Climate damages in the FUND model: A disaggregated analysis. *Ecological Economics, 77*, 219–224. doi:10.1016/j.ecolecon.2012.03.005

Ackerman, F., & Stanton, E. A. (2012). Climate risks and carbon prices: Revising the social cost of carbon. *Economics E-journal, 6*, 2012–10.

Bouwer, L. M., & Wouter Botzen, W. J. (2011). How sensitive are us hurricane damages to climate? Comment on a paper by W.D. Nordhaus. *Climate Change Economics, 2*, 1–7. doi:10.1142/S2010007811000188

Nordhaus, W. D. (1973). The allocation of energy resources. *Brookings Papers on Economic Activity, 3*, 529–570.

Nordhaus, W. D. (1977). Economic growth and climate: The carbon dioxide problem. *American Economics Review, 67*, 341–346.

Nordhaus, W. D. (2007). A review of the *Stern Review on the Economics of Climate Change*. *Journal of Economic Literature, 45*, 686–702. doi:10.1257/jel.45.3.686

Nordhaus, W. D. (2010). The economics of hurricanes and implications of global warming. *Climate Change Economics, 1*, 1–20. doi:10.1142/S2010007810000054

Nordhaus, W. D. (2011). Integrated economic and climate modeling. Cowles Foundation, Retrieved from http://dido.econ.yale.edu/P/cd/d18a/d1839.pdf

Nordhaus, W. D. (2012, March 22). Why the global warming skeptics are wrong. *New York Review of Books, 59*(5), 32–34.

Nordhaus, W. D. (2013). *The climate casino: Risk, uncertainty, and economics for a warming world*. New Haven, CT: Yale University Press.

Nordhaus with Paul Sztorc. (2013). "DICE 2013R: Introduction and User's Manual," Retrieved from http://www.econ.yale.edu/~nordhaus/homepage/documents/DICE_Manual_103113r2.pdf

Weitzman, M. L. (2015). Book review–a review of William Nordhaus' *The Climate Casino: Risk, Uncertainty, and Economics for a Warming World*. *Review of Environmental Economics and Policy, 9*, 145–156. doi:10.1093/reep/reu019

Energy modeling post 1973

John Feddersen[a,b,c], Florian Habermacher[a,d], Jan Imhof [a,e] and Rick van der Ploeg[a,f]

[a]Aurora Energy Research, Oxford, United Kingdom; [b]New York University Abu Dhabi, Abu Dhabi, United Arab Emirates; [c]Smith School of Enterprise and the Environment, University of Oxford, Oxford, United Kingdom; [d]Department of Economics, University of St. Gallen, St. Gallen, Switzerland; [e]Departement of Management, Technology and Economics, ETH Zurich, Zurich, Switzerland; [f]Department of Economics, University of Oxford, Oxford, United Kingdom

Nordhaus (1973) has in his seminal contribution addressed two emerging questions in the field of energy economics. First, how do current market prices of natural resources reflect true scarcity from a theoretical perspective? He shows that the absence of complete markets implies that discount rates are critical as myopic agents are not kept in check and the instability in spot market prices will cause suboptimal resource extraction rates. More succinctly, 'markets in their current form may be unreliable ways to allocate exhaustible resources' (p. 537). Second, how well do current prices of resources empirically reflect true scarcity? Nordhaus (1973, p. 537) rightly states that 'unfortunately, an estimate of whether current usage is too fast or too slow can emerge *only* from a carefully constructed econometric and engineering model of the economy'. He then proceeds to lay out such a carefully constructed model, solve it, and draw out a large number of conclusions.

With the benefit of hindsight, it is difficult to see the rudimentary model deployed as sufficient for the task. The assumptions are heroic given the seriousness with which the results are treated. The predictions and assumptions about technology have proven to be inaccurate: for example, nuclear costs have ballooned, coal is unlikely to remain the dominant fuel source throughout the 2020s, the shale boom in the US ensures that it will not be a liquefied natural gas (LNG) importer over even the long run, and oil shale, as opposed to shale oil, is still a very long way from living up to the promise that it indicated in the 1960s and 1970s. Of course, anyone would have found it difficult to correctly predict these developments, but Nordhaus (1973) has taught us the importance of modeling energy developments in a consistent manner.

We first reflect on the critical assumptions made by Nordhaus (1973) and evaluate whether one would still make these today. We then discuss the advances made in energy modeling during the last four decades, both theoretically and in practical modeling. Finally, we indicate promising areas for future research to take forward the agenda inspired by Nordhaus' seminal work.

Reflections on validity of Nordhaus' critical assumptions

Nordhaus (1973) infers the discount rate from market capital returns. Market returns arguably form a sound basis for this key parameter, since gains from fuel use can be invested and returns distributed to future generations. The adopted rate of 10% per annum seems high given that it is corrected for inflation and depreciation, but it also includes a premium to capture economic and political risk. While the model holds the rate constant throughout time, past decades have shown that annual returns of 4–5% and above in mature economies cannot be taken as much for granted as earlier in the twentieth century. Uncertainty about future growth and rates of return suggests that using a lower discount rate is appropriate (Weitzman, 2009). In later work, Nordhaus (2007) derives a discount rate of 4% from a variety of relevant returns that lie mainly in the range 5–6% (not adjusted for risk). The importance of Nordhaus' assumption cannot be stressed enough, because 10% per annum means weighting real revenue after 50 years by only 0.5% and after 100 years by a mere 0.03%. It explains his key finding that scarcity rents on natural resources are very low (Nordhaus, 1973, p. 554, Table 6).

In the deterministic analysis of Nordhaus (1973) an abundant backstop meets energy demands at limited costs for an indefinite future. This happy ending based on nuclear fusion is, however, uncertain, and generations far in the future may instead have to rely on limited amounts of costly renewables. Factoring in this possibility will, especially with limited discount rates, delay the efficient consumption of fossil fuel energy. Nordhaus (1973) further disregarded climate change, but neglecting the social cost of carbon biases fossil fuel use towards the present.

Of course, in 1973 a good basis for quantitative assessment of global warming and expected damages was lacking and Nordhaus has during the last few decades become the most prominent modeler of growth and climate change, and his 1973 model was one of the earliest precursors to the Dynamic Integrated Climate-Economy (DICE) model (Nordhaus, 2007). Energy resources affect the evolution of energy demand and technological progress, and are a major driver of economic growth. In contrast to modern general equilibrium studies, Nordhaus (1973) abstracted from the endogenous nature of energy demand and supply.

Nordhaus (1973) accounted for the increasing importance of electricity, but disregarded central features of its efficient production. Diurnal and seasonal variations of demand imply a relative advantage for technologies with the lowest fuel costs (coal, nuclear) for base-load production and use of technologies with lower capital costs (gas) for covering demand peaks. This limits the substitutability of electricity technologies. Nordhaus (1973) assumes perfect substitutability, which implies that at each point in time only one type of energy is allocated as input to electricity production (p. 552, Table 5). In reality, the imperfect substitutability warrants periods with simultaneous use of multiple technologies.

Limiting the focus to direct energy goods allowed Nordhaus (1973) to cut down the computational burden of the equilibrium calculations. But it meant ignoring how other inputs can substitute energy in the production of the demanded services, such as when the effect of higher energy prices on heating costs can be mitigated by better insulation.

Nordhaus (1973) adopted extreme positions in response to the lack of generalizable data on price and substitution elasticities of energy demands. For individual energy demand categories, he assumed no price dependence of the energy quantities demanded, hence blocking key equilibrium responses on the fuel market. His assumption of resources being perfect substitutes is a strong simplification of a more complex world, notably regarding the electricity market. Imperfect substitutability suggests that the depletion of fuels may in reality be less easily compensated for by other fuels than in the model, likely increasing the social cost of depletion of individual fuels.

Progress in energy modeling during the last 40 years

The tools and approaches have not changed greatly. To a modern energy economist it would be no surprise that the forefront of research in energy economics has benefited from Tjalling Koopmans (mathematician), Alan S. Manne (a computer scientist), and Paul

Krugman (theorist in international economics). Since publication of Nordhaus' pioneering study, energy modeling has made much progress. Climate discussions – absent in Nordhaus – increasingly dominate the debate, with concerns about carbon costs partly replacing those about resource scarcity: climate risks are thought to limit the fuel amounts society may rationally want to extract, replacing physical constraints on how much can be extracted (e.g., Nordhaus, 2007).

Pure-time preferences and growth-related factors are often explicitly considered in discounting of future fuel utility and climate damages, and Schelling (1995) pointed out that market interest rates are no sufficient statistic for current generations' preferences. Nordhaus (1973) aimed to find an efficient allocation and was less concerned with representing the preferences of current generations. Nevertheless, newer studies implicitly acknowledge that risky returns from high-yield investments are not directly applicable. Nordhaus (2007) reduced discount rates to 4%, quoting bond returns besides equity rates as a basis: opportunity cost calculations cannot ignore reasons for investments also in low-yield assets.

Past price decreases suggest that renewables, increasingly the focus of studies, might plausibly cover a sizeable share of future energy use. While Nordhaus considered breeder reactors as a backstop available at constant cost and infinite quantities, renewables costs may decrease over time, but increase in quantities demanded.

Computational general equilibrium (CGE) models churn out prices that clear markets for the various types of energy and allow for substitution between energy goods and other goods and services. CGE models also have durable goods and gradual capital stock adjustments, which lead to more realistic dynamics. Dozens of sectors of regional economies can be simulated with the current breed of CGE models, where interactions are calibrated with statistical data in the form of input–output tables and accounting matrices, trade-flows, prices, and substitution elasticities. Many CGE models have imperfect substitutability between different fuels for electricity production using constant elasticity of substitution (CES) production functions (e.g., Paltsev et al., 2005) and allow for gradually increasing fuel extraction costs as resources deplete (e.g., Manne & Richels, 2000).

Since the 1930s two different computational approaches have been developed to tackle energy economic issues. First, the class of economy-wide or top-down models started with Leontief's input–output system (Leontief, 1936, 1941) and were developed into different directions by Sandee (1960), Manne (1963), Evans (1972) and, of course, Nordhaus (1973). Lack of computational power, as well as restrictions in the available solution algorithms and theoretical concepts, made it tough to move beyond very simplified frameworks. In those economy-wide models the behavior of the agents was not well defined. The model of Nordhaus (1973) finds the cost-minimizing technology mix to satisfy an exogenously defined demand for energy services. He already notes that 'It would be desirable to test the sensitivity of the results to some price elasticity of final demand' (Nordhaus, 1973, p. 541). While Johansen (1960) already modeled consumer behavior by founding what is now called CGE modeling, his representation of the productive sectors of the economy was somewhat simplified and did not allow for many details of the energy side of the economy.

The following decades saw quick development of computational power and theoretical and applied advancements. Further developments of Johansen's framework led to the development of CGE modeling, mainly at Monash University (Dixon & Rimmer, 2010), while the theoretical work on general equilibrium theory of Arrow and Debreu made it possible for Manne to further develop CGE modeling techniques. Both kinds of CGE models have been widely applied to various energy policy issues over the past four decades. Although those economy-wide models are advanced, they lack an adequate representation of engineering details in the energy sectors.

A second branch of energy modeling is thus the application of simulation and optimization models in the engineering sciences. So-called bottom-up models with technology-rich representations of a partial equilibrium have been applied widely to study the evolution and specific policy questions surrounding energy markets. Such techniques can be applied to study dispatch decisions for minute long-load segments in models that look only hours ahead, as well as in models that investigate investment and capacity decisions over the course of decades. These engineering models lack economic feedback mechanisms that might arise through developments in markets that are not modeled.

The shortcomings of those two approaches inspired the rise of a new class of models. Such hybrid models aim at combining the advantages of both modeling philosophies, which was only feasible thanks to advancements in theory and huge improvements in computational capacities. The literature on integrating 'top-down' and 'bottom-up' models overcomes the shortcomings of both CGE and partial-equilibrium engineering approaches. Böhringer and Rutherford (2008) provide an overview of hybrid modeling efforts in energy policy evaluation. Some important contributions to hybrid modeling include the Model for Evaluating the Regional and Global Effects of Greenhouse Gas Reduction Policies (MERGE, Manne, et al., 1995), Messner & Schrattenholzer (2000), the World Induced Technical Change Hybrid (WITCH) model (Bosetti, Carraro, Galeotti, Massetti, & Tavoni, 2006) or Strachan and Kannan (2008). In many applications the bottom-up components have focused on power dispatch, as the specific characteristics of power supply and demand make it necessary to look at the issue in greater detail and mainly with higher time resolution (e.g., Lanz & Rausch, 2011; Sue Wing, 2008).

Future steps for energy modeling

However, in CGE, engineering and hybrid models, little emphasis has been paid to the resource extracting sectors which were at the core of Nordhaus' (1973) considerations. One recent model that aims at including the role of resource extraction for the global economy and that can demonstrate the idea behind iteratively solved hybrid models is Aurora's Global General Equilibrium (AER-GLO) model. This model is a representation of the global economy split into 21 countries and regions, 13 final demand goods, five primary factors and 11 resource extraction categories.

At the core of AER-GLO is a recursive dynamic CGE model with annual time steps. The demand side of the economy is characterized by a representative consumer in each region, who maximizes her utility subject to her budget constraint. The consumer pays for her consumption by selling her primary factor endowments. The savings rate in each region depends on the current and expected future rates of return and current and expected future prices. Production of goods and services – with the exception of electricity and resource extraction – are modeled by assuming that firms maximize their profits under perfect competition, taking nested CES production technologies as given. Prices of goods and factors are determined by assuming that all markets clear in all periods.

To account for the special characteristics of power–dispatch decisions, we model electricity production outside of the CGE model. The power–dispatch model minimizes the system cost of the electricity sector in each modeled country and takes as given generation capacities, the annual demand for electricity, the load curve and technological parameters.

Natural resource extraction is modeled in a large set of sub-modules. Those forward-looking sub-modules determine extraction of five different crude oil resources, four natural gas extraction technologies and two coal types in each region by maximizing the profit from resource extraction over a 100 years horizon. The sub-modules take into account current resource and input prices, extraction costs, decline rates of wells, taxes and royalties, building time of new projects and remaining resource stocks.

To solve the different modules of AER-GLO consistently, we apply a decomposition algorithm proposed by Böhringer and Rutherford (2009). Once the models are decomposed, we can solve the CGE model component with fixed supplies of electricity and primary resources. The top-down model determines prices for all goods by assuring market clearance. We then feed the resulting prices into the bottom-up electricity dispatch and the resource extraction models which determine supply of electricity, crude oil, natural gas and coal in turn. Once this is done, we fix supply levels of those energy goods in the CGE model to their new levels and solve the CGE model for the new market clearing prices. Those prices are fed into the partial equilibrium models to update supply. We proceed with the iterative approach until prices and quantities do not change anymore.

Summing up, after four decades, and in spite of a proliferation of tools and methods for modeling the energy sector, we do not appear to be much closer to quantifying the optimal extraction path for exhaustible energy resources. Nordhaus' (1973) bold exercise provided an intellectual foundation for subsequent generations of energy modelers to take this work forward. Specifically, energy modeling during the last four decades has been inspired by imposing that everything depends on everything, as is common in CGE models, and by allowing for micro bottom-up engineering details. More recently, the detailed modeling of resource scarcity, inspired by the seminal work of Nordhaus (1973), has been taken to the fore in the context of advanced hybrid energy models.

Disclosure statement

No potential conflict of interest was reported by the authors.

References

Böhringer, C., & Rutherford, T. F. (2008). Combining bottom-up and top-down. *Energy Economics*, 30(2), 574–596.

Böhringer, C., & Rutherford, T. F. (2009). Integrated assessment of energy policies: Decomposing top-down and bottom-up. *Journal of Economic Dynamics and Control*, 33, 1648–1661. doi:10.1016/j.jedc.2008.12.007

Bosetti, V., Carraro, C., Galeotti, M., Massetti, E., & Tavoni, M. (2006). WITCH: A world induced technical change hybrid model. *Energy Journal*, Special Issue 2, 13–38.

Dixon, P. B., & Rimmer, M. T. (2010). *Johansen's contribution to CGE modelling: Originator and guiding light for 50 years* (Working Paper 9-203). Canada: Centre of Policy Studies/IMPACT Centre, Victoria University.

Evans, H. D. (1972). *A general equilibrium analysis of protection: The effects of protection in Australia*. Contributions to Economic Analysis 76. North-Holland, Amsterdam.

Johansen, L. (1960). *A Multisectoral Study of Economic Growth*. Contributions to Economic Analysis 21, North-Holland, Amsterdam.

Lanz, B., & Rausch, S. (2011). General equilibrium, electricity generation technologies and the cost of carbon abatement: A structural sensitivity analysis. *Energy Economics*, *33*, 1035–1047. doi:10.1016/j.eneco.2011.06.003

Leontief, W. W. (1936). Quantitative input-output relations in the economic system of the United States. *The Review of Economics and Statistics*, *18*(3), 105–125.

Leontief, W. W. (1941). *The structure of the American economy 1919–1929*. Cambridge, MA: Harvard University Press.

Manne, A. S. (1963). Key sectors of the Mexican economy 1960–1970. In A. S. Manne & H. M. Markowitz (Eds.), *Studies in process analysis* (pp. 379–400). New York, NY: Wiley.

Manne, A. S., Mendelsohn, R., & Richels, R. G. (1995). MERGE: A model for evaluating regional and global effects of GHG reduction policies. *Energy Policy*, *23*, 17–34. doi:10.1016/0301-4215 (95)90763-W

Manne, A. S., & Richels, R. G. (2000). The Kyoto protocol: A cost-effective strategy for meeting environmental objectives? In C. Carraro (Ed.), *Efficiency and equity of climate change policy* (pp. 43–61). Dordrecht, Netherlands: Springer.

Messner, S., & Schrattenholzer, L. (2000). MESSAGE-MACRO: Linking an energy supply model with a macroeconomic module and solving iteratively. *The International Energy Journal*, *25*(3), 267–282. doi:10.1016/S0360-5442(99)00063-8

Nordhaus, W. D. (1973). *The allocation of energy resources*. Brookings Papers on Economic Activity, 529–576.

Nordhaus, W. D. (2007). *The challenge of global warming: Economic models and environmental policy* (Vol. 4). New Haven, CT: Yale University.

Paltsev, S., Reilly, J. M., Jacoby, H. D., Eckhaus, R. S., McFarland, J. R., Sarofilm, M. C., ... Babiker, M. H. (2005). *The MIT Emissions Prediction and Policy Analysis (EPPA) model: Version 4*. Cambridge, MA: MIT Joint Program on the Science and Policy of Global Change.

Sandee, J. (1960). *A long-term planning model for India*. New York, NY: Asia Publishing House, Statistical Publishing Company, Calcutta, India.

Schelling, T. C. (1995). Intergenerational discounting. *Energy Policy*, *23*(4–5), 395–401. doi:10.1016/0301-4215(95)90164-3

Strachan, N., & Kannan, R. (2008). Hybrid modelling of long-term carbon reduction scenarios for the UK. *Energy Economics*, *30*, 2947–2963. doi:10.1016/j.eneco.2008.04.009

Sue Wing, I. (2008). The synthesis of bottom-up and top-down approaches to climate policy modeling: Electric power technology detail in a social accounting framework. *Energy Economics*, *30*, 547–573. doi:10.1016/j.eneco.2006.06.004

Weitzman, M. L. (2009). On modeling and interpreting the economics of catastrophic climate change. *The Review of Economics and Statistics*, *91*(1), 1–19. doi:10.1162/rest.91.1.1

The allocation of energy conservation

Franz Wirl

Faculty of Business, Economics, and Statistics, University of Vienna, Oskar Morgenstern Platz 1, Austria

Introduction

Conservation is considered to be an important source of future energy, for example, in the International Energy Agency (2013), due to a claimed efficiency gap resulting from distorted consumer decisions. This claim led to many proposals and the EU's politicians being 'committed' to a 20% reduction in energy consumption. This paper departs from Nordhaus (1973), but focuses on this specific source of energy conservation and draws attention to other characteristics of Nordhaus' work. First, whether an 'energy efficiency gap' exists and whether it can be attributed to consumers discounting too high (compare Nordhaus' (2007) review of Stern (2007)). Second, if existing, how can one correct and what are the obstacles. Third, limits of politics (compare Nordhaus (1991)).

Conservation is programs involve three parties: governments, utilities and consumers. The literature concentrates on regulatory aspects, but neglects how incentives affect consumer decisions. The unintended consequences of intentional human actions, the analysis of which should be the major task of social sciences, according to Popper (1972, p. 342), render proposed conservation programs ineffective.

Demand

Consumers are concerned about services like thermal comfort, lighting, mobility, among others, and not about kWhs. Simplifying as Wirl (1997), service s is the product of the energy efficiency η and energy e:

$$s = \eta e. \tag{1}$$

Consumers maximize the net present value of their surplus (U):

$$\max_{e,\,\eta} U(e,\,\eta) := D[u(e\eta) - pe] - K(\eta) = \max_{\eta}\{D \max_{e} [u(e\eta) - pe] - K(\eta)\}. \tag{2}$$

$$:= w(\eta, p),\ w_\eta = u'e,\ w_p = -e$$

This surplus consists of the consumer's benefit, $u(s)$ satisfies standard requirements, and the expenses for energy e (at the price p for a unit) and the appliance depending on efficiency η, $K' > 0$, $K'' > 0$. This optimization can be separated into the *ex-ante* choice of efficiency and the *ex-post* choice of energy. The latter maximization renders the surplus

$w(\eta,p)$. The parameter D denotes the subjective 'payback time' depending on the lifetime of the equipment, L, and on individual discounting, $\delta > r = $ social discount factor,

$$D(\delta,L) := \int_0^L \exp(-\delta t)dt \leq R := \int_0^L \exp(-rt)dt, \tag{3}$$

Given the efficiency, the choice of energy must satisfy,

$$e = E(\eta,p) := \arg\max_e \; (u(e\eta) - pe)$$
$$=> u'\eta = p, \alpha := - \partial lnE/\partial lnp, -\partial lnE/\partial ln\,\eta = 1 - \alpha \tag{4}$$

The condition, marginal service benefit (u') = marginal costs of the service (p/η), defines the short run demand $E(\eta,p)$ with price elasticity α and the efficiency elasticity $(1 - \alpha)$. Therefore, more efficient appliances raise the service demand due to reduced marginal service costs, which is the so called 'rebound effect', see Khazzoom (1987). The long term view in Saunders (2015) documents a large effect. Therefore, efficiency improvements alone cannot provide the silver bullet to climate change mitigation, although most politicians try to convince the population that this plus some renewable energy is all that is needed.

The optimal choice of efficiency must satisfy the usual equality between marginal benefit and marginal costs:

$$w_\eta = u'e = K'/D => - (K'/D)/E_\eta = -w_\eta/E_\eta = p/(1 - \alpha). \tag{5}$$

Thus, consumers' annual expenditures (based on the subjective payback time) for conserving an incremental kWh, $[-(K'/D)/E_\eta]$ must equal the gross benefit, $- w_\eta/E_\eta = p/(1 - \alpha)$. Therefore, an increase of efficiency that reduces energy consumption by 1 kWh is worth $p/(1 - \alpha)$ and thus exceeds the costs per kWh; see Wirl (1997).

The conditions Equations (4) and (5) determine the outcome for given market and policy failures, denoted by $e_0 = e_0(D,p)$ and $\eta_0 = \eta_0 (D,p)$.

The social optimum must consider the supply side, too. The supply of efficiency is competitive, independent of conservation incentives, and involves no externalities. In contrast, the supply and use of energy includes external costs $C(e) > c(e)$ that exceed the out of pocket expenditures c. Considering the payback time R, the social welfare objective is to

$$\max_{e,\; \eta} W(e,\eta) := R[u(e\,\eta) - C(e)] - K(\eta), \tag{6}$$

which implies the first order conditions:

$$u'\eta = C', \tag{7}$$

$$u'e = pK'. \tag{8}$$

Solving Equations (7) and (8) yields the first best social optimum, (e_1, η_1). These conditions differ from the consumer's only on the right hand side by using in Equation (7) the full social marginal costs of energy instead of the price in Equation (4) and the social payback time in Equation (8) but the individual one in Equation (5).

Market failures

A chosen piece of equipment should maximize the net present value of benefits over expenditures over its lifetime, based on the correct discount rate. Otherwise, an energy efficiency gap results that is reflected by $D \leq R$. This seems empirically supported since Hausman (1979). Therefore, regulations could save money. This is, however, wrong because often the lifetime of a piece of equipment is different from its economic use due to individual circumstances unknown to outsiders, that is, small values of D are perfectly compatible with fully rational agents. First, short planning horizons due to individual circumstances are not a market failure, neither for young, nor for old people, nor for firms with short run opportunities (e.g., during the World Soccer Championship 2014 in Brazil). Second, observing a low value of D is compatible with rational behavior accounting for option values, as in Dixit and Pindyck (1994), due to further technological improvements. Third, consumers do not expose high discounting and thus do acquire highly energy efficient equipment in many cases, for example, most Austrian car owners opt for highly efficient and thus expensive diesel engines, which can only be rationalized assuming very low discount rates.

Policy failures

Although too low energy prices, $p < C'$, are often labeled as a market failure, they are actually a policy failure since governments can internalize external costs in a way Pigou (1920) advocated almost a hundred years ago. In fact, energy, in particular gasoline, is one of the few goods where this internalization has been practiced for many decades. This internalization may be insufficient, but then it must be even more so, due to a policy failure. This policy failure is observable in many developing countries that even subsidize energy, and also in industrialized countries since no country, except Denmark, introduced a carbon tax and others withdrew their proposal during 2008.

Another important source of policy failures is the inability of governments to commit. This is not only a consequence of democracy with the possibility to change governments every four years. Examples are manifold and not restricted to developing countries with poor governance. A topical example is the financial crisis in the European Union when it turned out that governments were unable to stick to their no-bail out commitment when facing Greece's debt overhang. This impossibility to commit has far reaching consequences on energy policy with many examples in the past: oil price regulation in the US in 1973, Labour's windfall profit tax for utilities in the UK, photovoltaic (PV) feed-in tariffs in Spain, among others. Consider the example of electric cars which are just appearing from different suppliers such as GM, Nissan and Renault. What is the basic incentive to buy such expensive cars? The major objective, green posturing and signaling aside, is to escape petrol taxes. But for how long? If many take this action, the treasuries will impose, *ex post*, a levy for sure. Therefore, it is naïve to base individual profitability considerations on current electricity prices relative to petrol prices. If only few do, they will enjoy the cheap ride, but a strong tendency to use electric cars will deter their individual purchase, due to an unintended consequence.

Conservation incentives

Government

If the only market imperfection is that consumers do not discount properly, then means exist to correct. For example, prescribing the first best efficiency standard (η_1) eliminates any kind of inefficiency if energy is priced at the social marginal costs. Therefore, the emphasis on consumers failing to discount properly and the need to run conservation initiatives seems out of proportion. Of course, fixing η_1 for each type of appliance and accounting in addition for variations in service demand is impossible in practice.

How does a benevolent and paternalistic regulator design incentive compatible conservation? Paternalism, compare Wirl (1999), means that the regulator uses the consumer's objective but substitutes the social discount rate, that is, the corresponding net present value aggregate R. Since a consumer's attribute $D \leq R$ is unknown to all outsiders, the benevolent government maximizes the expected social welfare, denoted V,

$$\max V := \int_{-D}^{R} \{Rw(\eta, C') - K(\eta) - mt)\}\mathrm{d}F, \qquad (9)$$

considering D as a random variable with distribution $F(D)$. Producer surplus and external costs cancel due to the assumption of $p = C'$. The maximization of the social surplus may require subsidies (t) that have social costs m (per \$). In other words, the government 'bribes' consumers so that they choose higher efficiencies, $\eta(D) > \eta_0(D)$.

Carrying the paternalistic attribute to its extreme, subsidies do not count similar to transfers in traditional welfare considerations, implies: Asymmetric information and the possibility of strategic behavior does not affect the social optimum. The optimal subsidy has to cover the difference between the costs of meeting the first best efficiency target η_1 and the costs for the least efficient equipment, irrespective of a consumer's type. This is expensive, but incentive compatible, as no agent can gain from cheating.

Now assume the opposite: Subsidies have the full opportunity costs, $m = 1$, then, no incentives are justified if the hazard rate is less than for the uniform distribution. Only distributions with higher hazard rates justify incentives if the full opportunity costs for transfers have to be paid, see Wirl (1999). As a consequence, an optimistic prior distribution (high types are more likely) cannot justify public conservation initiatives with significant costs of public funds; only a pessimistic one can.

Even if subsidies are too costly due to the high costs of public funds, and standards are ruled out, one instrument is still left: the price of electricity. Given the distortion in the efficiency market, deviations from marginal cost tariffs improve the social surplus, of course evaluated at the paternalistic payback time R. More precisely, electricity prices above the marginal social costs, $p > C'$, can be used in a typical second best manner to counteract the failure in the efficiency market.

Utility conservation programs

The upshot of the above subsection is that government programs cannot be justified if the government faces the full opportunity costs and has an optimistic prior distribution about D. Thus, following the conservation literature and practice, it may be advisable to leave conservation to the utility, which has in addition a better knowledge of the market. Eric Hirst (1992, p. 77) argues that: 'Utilities can help overcome these barriers and do so at low cost' and Amory Lovins (1985) claims that utilities can make 'gigabucks with negawatts'.

Recently, Bertoldi, Labanca, Rezessy, Steuwer, and Oikonomou (2013) have argued that utilities shall be placed under an obligation to save energy. How can a utility be motivated, given that even benevolent governments are reluctant to run conservation programs in theory and practice? Indeed, the idea of utility conservation and in particular the recent resurrection in the European Union (white certificates force utilities and firms to invest in conservation in a way similar to the already existing renewable energy quota) and in some US states is ill-conceived, the huge and supporting literature notwithstanding. First, utility conservation faces the problem of 'a butcher selling fish', see Larry Ruff (1988). Second, the billions actually spent are no proof of efficiency. Conservation was the only legal means to avoid serving unprofitable segments of demand due to prices regulated below marginal costs faced by the utility, that is, $C' > c' > p$, see Cicchetti and Hogan (1989). Rate of return regulation (thus $p > c'$) combined with shared savings (based on engineering data) encourages utilities to undertake conservation programs that are expensive but save little energy, see Wirl (1997). Therefore it is not surprising that the effects of these US programs in the 1980s and early 1990s are invisible in spite of micro-'evidence' of conservation, see Wirl and Orasch (1998).

Final remarks

This paper tries to address the allocation of energy conservation 40 years after Nordhaus' seminal paper on all energy resources. However, its narrow focus is complemented by including often omitted features like (private) information and political constraints. Unfortunately, the implications from this analysis are not promising. First, energy efficiency investments cannot provide the proclaimed silver bullets to mitigate climate change because expected conservation will not materialize due to the rebound effect. Second, commanding standards will burden many consumers and firms with unnecessary costs. Third, governments face the issue of time inconsistency when designing inter-temporal conservation initiatives. Fourth, any conservation incentive faces private information of consumers or firms which either leads to cheating or requires incentives with substantial deadweight loss. In fact, even accepting market failures, the optimal government intervention may be no incentive. Fifth, the inclusion of a utility as a conservation angel is hard to explain, given the poor past performance and the absence of an economic justification. Given all these obstacles, it is a big puzzle how such claims could enter public policies. Of course, there exist precedents, like joint implementation and clean development mechanism, which led to cheating and even fraud, which anyone familiar with private information could tell in advance (Wirl, Huber, & Walker, 1998). A major reason seems to be that the public and, in particular, the media and consequently politicians tend to evaluate a policy by its intentions (who can be against energy conservation?) rather than its consequences.

Disclosure statement

No potential conflict of interest was reported by the author.

References

Bertoldi, P., Labanca, N., Rezessy, S., Steuwer, S., & Oikonomou, V. (2013). Where to place the saving obligation: Energy end-users or suppliers? *Energy Policy, 63*, 328–337. doi:10.1016/j.enpol.2013.07.134

Cicchetti, C. J., & Hogan, W. W. (1989, June, 8). Including unbundled demand side options in electric utility bidding programs. *Public Utilities Fortnightly*, 9–20.

Dixit, A. K., & Pindyck, R. S. (1994). *Investment under uncertainty*. Princeton, NJ: Princeton University Press.

Hausman, J. A. (1979). Individual discount rates and the purchase and utilization of energy-using durables. *Bell Journal of Economics*, *10*, 33–54.

Hirst, E. (1992). Price and cost impacts of utility DSM programs. *The Energy Journal*, *13/4*, 75–90.

International Energy Agency. (2013). *World energy outlook 2013*. Paris: OECD.

Khazzoom, D. J. (1987). Energy saving resulting from the adoption of more efficient appliances. *The Energy Journal*, *8*(4), 85–89.

Lovins, A. (1985). Saving gigabucks with negawatts. *Public Utilities Fortnightly*, *115/6*, 19–26.

Nordhaus, W. D. (2007). A review of the stern review on the economics of climate change. *Journal of Economic Literature*, *45*, 686–702. doi:10.1257/jel.45.3.686

Nordhaus, W. D. (1973). The allocation of energy resources. *Brookings Papers*, *3*, 529–576.

Nordhaus, W. D. (1991). The political business cycle. *Review of Economic Studies*, *42*, 169–190.

Pigou, A. C. (1920). *The economics of welfare*. London: MacMillan.

Popper, K. R. (1972). *Conjectures and refutations* (4th revised edition (paperback)). London: Routledge and Kegan Paul.

Ruff, L. E. (1988, April 28). Least-cost-planning and demand-side-management: Six common fallacies and one simple truth. *Public Utilities Fortnightly*, 19–26.

Saunders, H. D. (2015). Recent evidence for large rebound: Elucidating the drivers and their implications for climate change models. *The Energy Journal*, *36*(1), 23–48.

Stern, N. (2007). *The economics of climate change: The stern review*. Cambridge: Cambridge University Press.

Wirl, F. (1997). *The economics of conservation programs*. Boston, Dordrecht, London: Kluwer Academic Publishers.

Wirl, F. (1999). Paternalistic principals. *Journal of Economic Behavior & Organization*, *38*, 403–419. doi:10.1016/S0167-2681(99)00018-9

Wirl, F., Huber, C., & Walker, I. O. (1998). Joint implementation: Strategic reactions and possible remedies. *Environmental and Resource Economics*, *12*, 203–224. doi:10.1023/A:1008272620797

Wirl, F., & Orasch, W. (1998). Analysis of United States' utility conservation programs. *Review of Industrial Organization*, *13*, 467–486. doi:10.1023/A:1007707523605

A retrospective on *The Allocation of Energy Resources* by William D. Nordhaus

P. Koundouri[a,b,c], D. Reppas[c] and I. Souliotis[a,c]

[a]Department of International and European Studies, Athens University of Economics and Business, School of Economics, Athens, Greece; [b]Grantham Research Institute on Climate Change and the Environment, London School of Economics, UK; [c]International Centre for Research on the Environment and the Economy (ICRE8), Athens, Greece

Nordhaus (1973) does have important implications in energy policy. Nordhaus develops a general equilibrium model to determine the path of prices of energy resources and efficiently allocate four main energy resources (petroleum, coal, natural gas, and uranium-235) over time, space and different energy demand categories. Additionally, he explores whether the resulting optimal price paths are close to market-determined ones. His formulation of the model follows a standard dynamic optimization problem; and thus the price paths associated with his optimal solution (shadow prices for resources over time) are interpreted as rents that a competitive market would impute to scarce resources (Hotelling's Rule). The main empirical conclusion of the paper is that the calculated prices are not very far from the actual market ones, with the exception of petroleum products and coal.

According to natural resources economic theory, in an efficient allocation, resources are extracted such that the stream of discounted profits (from selling a unit of the resource at each time period) is maximized. The time horizon, nevertheless, Nordhaus considers, is a very long one (200 years). Furthermore, in discounting future values, Nordhaus applies a constant interest rate.[1] The following paragraphs discuss how both these aspects in natural resources modeling have been questioned by economists.

Economists have argued extensively, in the context of Net Present Value criterion (in Cost Benefit Analysis, CBA), over the choice of the appropriate discount rate. The conclusion of the debate is that the choice of the discount rate depends on the extent to which a project is funded by consumption or private investment. For example, if the project is entirely funded by consumption, then it has been argued that it should be discounted by the Social Rate of Time Preference; while if it is funded by displaced investment, then it should be discounted by the Private Return to investment (other economists have argued we may want to use a mix of these two). In any case, the standard practice has been to use the same value for discount rate across all time periods, the latter thus leading to exponential discounting.

Nevertheless, the classic constant discount rates have been proven to perform well in short–medium time horizons. However, over the recent years, economists have shown that discounting at a constant positive rate is problematic, particularly in long-run environmental problems (such as climate change, nuclear waste, or biodiversity loss). The reason is that a constant discount rate over time discounts so heavily the welfare (costs or benefits) of future generations, such that it appears small (in present value terms). The proposed solution in the literature has been the use of a declining discount rate (DDR) over time: a DDR increases the weight attached to welfare of future generations; and thus corrects the insufficient representation of future generations.

In a series of papers, Gollier, Koundouri, and Pantelidis (2008), Pearce, Groom, Hepburn, and Koundouri (2003), Hepburn, Koundouri, Panopoulou, and Pantelidis (2009), and Groom, Hepburn, Koundouri, and Pearce (2005) show that a declining pattern of discount rates is justified both theoretically and empirically (i.e., from historical data). All papers suggest that standard discounting is more suitable for formulating policies in the short or medium term, but DDRs should be used in CBA with long time horizons.

Regarding the theoretical justifications for using a DDR, Groom et al. (2005, 2007) explain how DDRs can emerge in a deterministic world, but focus mainly on the case of uncertainty, and show how the case for DDRs is then even more compelling. In short, in an uncertain economic environment, the persistence of shocks on the growth rate of consumption (consumption-based approach), and the persistence on short-term rates of return to capital (production-based approach), both imply a declining pattern in discount rates. The results are intuitive: when there is uncertainty about how consumption will grow in the future, we want to apply a smaller discount rate, that is, sacrifice a larger amount of our current consumption in favor of future generations (formally, the Ramsey rule is extended by the 'precautionary saving motive'). In the production-based approach, the authors show how uncertainty in the equilibrium interest rate in the economy, together with persistence of interest rates (persistence meaning that high discount rates tend to clump together over time; they are 'sticky') can lead to DDRs.

But, whether this persistence in the shocks exists or not, is clearly an empirical question. Therefore, Gollier et al. (2008) estimate country-specific trajectories for the social discount rates (based on the production-based approach) from historic data: a series of discount factors and DDRs is estimated (from data on risk-free market interest rates) for France, India, Japan, and South Africa based on the simulation procedure of Newell and Pizer (2003); the simulation for Australia, Canada, Germany, and the UK, was based on the model of Hepburn et al. (2009); while for the US, it was based on Pearce et al. (2003). In short, the empirical estimation is described by a univariate time series model, in which future interest rates are determined by past values, that is, past behavior reveals useful information about the future dynamics of the series. In the univariate time series model, uncertainty about the future path of interest rates is captured by the uncertainty of the estimated parameters of a two-regime switching model. All papers conclude that the decision to replace constant discount rates with DDRs has significant policy implications (for instance, in estimating the social cost of carbon in climate change policies). Furthermore, there is significant country heterogeneity in terms of the empirically esti-mated discount rates; therefore, transferring a discount rate scheduled from one area to another would be unwise (Hepburn et al., 2009). The aforesaid statement could imply that (1) the discount rate that Nordhaus uses in the description of the problem should not be constant over time, and (2) adding to the previous proposition, a subscript denoting the country where the resources of the model are located, should be added to the variable that describes the discount rate informing that each one of the countries is assigned a different rate of discounting.

In the light of the above theoretical justifications and empirical findings towards the use of declining rather than constant discount rates (particularly in the context of long-term horizon problems), it seems that Nordhaus' optimal price paths for energy resources, over a 200-year horizon, will follow different trajectories from the ones simulated.

Apart from the issue of choosing the appropriate pattern of discount rates in an optimization problem, another issue that has been questioned by the literature is the monotonic quadratic trend of natural resource prices over time. A strand of the literature has considered stochastic trends in the evolution of prices; however, there is not strong evidence to support such specifications. Antypas, Koundouri, and Kourogenis (2013) have also challenged the standard theoretical finding for prices of natural resources. The authors provide evidence that oscillatory behavior in real natural resource prices is more common than the existence of a long-run quadratic trend. More specifically, the authors estimate four specifications for the trends of prices for 11 major natural resources (their specifications allow for a more general than the standard quadratic trend model; that is, they nest both oscillatory and quadratic trends). The competing specifications are then evaluated, for each natural resource, based on three informa- tion criteria (where the criteria disagreed, they performed a simulation study to decide on the best specification). Overall, the results showed that in nine out of the 11 examined natural resources, a trigonometric trend function captured better the dynamics of prices than a quadratic function alone (the latter was selected only for aluminum and perhaps for nickel). The reason behind the failure of simple quadratic functions to empirically capture the long-term evolution of prices of natural resources is that quadratic functions are explosive. These empirical findings allow authors to restate Hotelling's rule as follows: the price of an exhaustible resource which corresponds to a competitive (or efficient) utilization path will oscillate around the interest rate. This provides evidence that projects with high extraction costs should consider upper bounds of the prices of the real prices.

The motivation for Nordhaus's work was the 'insatiable appetite for energy' that caused anxiety given the limited amount of energy resources. He notes that apart from hydrogen, other renewable resources were not of much use in the 1970s. Therefore, the wide spectrum of renewable resources was not taken into account in the analysis. However, from that time there has been a significant increase in the production of energy with the use of renewable resources. This trend has been facilitated by technological developments. Additionally, due to the increase in the price of conventional sources of energy, their low limited quantity and the environmental effects their use yields, renew- able sources of energy have been considered the most appropriate solution to the energy problem, simultaneously satisfying the environmental constraints related to production of emissions and exacerbation of greenhouse gas emissions and their impacts on ecosystems.

The consideration of renewable resources in the problem would have definitely had an impact in the solution of the problem, that is, the allocation of energy over time, space. This is due to the fact that the resources are not – at least a part of them – exhaustible; therefore, the increasing production of energy through renewable resources could lead to depleting scarcity cost of resources. Intuitively, this will be observed at times when the decreasing rate of stock natural energy resources is lower than the increasing rate of growth of quantity of renewable energy resources. Undoubtedly, such an occurrence has an effect on the long-run price path of energy. More specifically, since some of the resources will be replenished in the end of each extraction period, Hotelling 's rule should be transformed to one that takes into account the growth rate of the renewable resources. This might lead to further restate Hotelling's rule as: the price of an exhaustible resource, which corresponds to a competitive (or efficient) utilization path will oscillate around the interest rate minus the growth rate. Overall, the price of energy over time might be lower due to the inclusion of the growth rate. This, however, needs to be empirically justified.

Disclosure statement

No potential conflict of interest was reported by the authors.

Note

1. Nordhaus considers a 10% interest rate in the baseline scenario and several alternate values (but still constant over time) in the sensitivity analysis.

References

Antypas, A., Koundouri, P., & Kourogenis, N. (2013). *Hotelling rules: Oscillatory versus quadratic trends in natural resource prices (No. 126)*. Grantham Research Institute on Climate Change and the Environment.

Gollier, C., Koundouri, P., & Pantelidis, T. (2008). Declining discount rates: Economic justifications and implications for long-run policy. *Economic Policy, 23*(56), 757–795. doi:10.1111/ecop.2008.23.issue-56

Groom, B., Hepburn, C., Koundouri, P., & Pearce, D. (2005). Declining discount rates: The long and the short of it. *Environmental & Resource Economics, 32*(4), 445–493. doi:10.1007/s10640-005-4681-y

Groom, B., Koundouri, P., Panopoulou, E., & Pantelidis, T. (2007). Discounting the distant future: How much does model selection affect the certainty equivalent rate? *Journal of Applied Econometrics, 22*(3), 641–656. doi:10.1002/(ISSN)1099-1255

Hepburn, C., Koundouri, P., Panopoulou, E., & Pantelidis, T. (2009). Social discounting under uncertainty: A cross-country comparison. *Journal of Environmental Economics and Management, 57*(2), 140–150. doi:10.1016/j.jeem.2008.04.004

Newell, R. G., & Pizer, W. A. (2003). Discounting the distant future: How much do uncertain rates increase valuations?. *Journal of Environmental Economics and Management, 46*(1), 52–71. doi:10.1016/S0095-0696(02)00031-1

Nordhaus, W. D. (1973). The allocation of energy resources. *Brookings Papers on Economic Activity, 4*(3), 529–576.

Pearce, D., Groom, B., Hepburn, C. & Koundouri, P. (2003). Valuing the future. *World economics, 4*(2), 121–141.

Backstop technology: model keystone or energy systems transition guide

Aviel Verbruggen

Engineering Management Department, University of Antwerp, Antwerp, Belgium

Few papers by young academics have been as influential on energy economics as 'The Allocation of Energy Resources' by William Nordhaus (1973). To me, the influence of Nordhaus' work causes mixed feelings. His 'backstop technology' concept is a source of inspiration. Although mainly used as keystone to seal his model, his square choice for nuclear power as backstop supply was unfounded. The enduring influence of 'econometric-engineering' models on public energy policy-makers often precludes a necessary broader decision-making approach.

Eye catcher and eye opener

'The Allocation of Energy Resources' was published in 1973 at the right time, was launched at an outstanding forum (Brookings Institute), and was refereed and discussed by a panel of highly respected experts. The fertile sowing ground was receptive for Nordhaus' fresh and ambitious addressing of the USA's major and painful energy questions at that time: Will oil scarcity cause economic doom? Is saving oil (and other fossil fuels) desirable, viz. necessary? Is USA oil autarky a recommendable target? In a period of much confusion and debate, the young economist provided clear 'NO' answers, backed by his 'econometric-engineering' model. By today's data availability, processing capabilities, and methodological refinements, the 1973 model is a simple one. Also, the analysis supported by the model was limited. Although the overall scope was global, very long-term and multi-sector supply and demand, the detailing of several crucial components remained poor. For example: 'A serious practical problem is Nordhaus' assumption that all demand elasticities are zero' (p. 572, Houthakker); 'Environmental constraints could embody a significant cost and their exclusion from the model is unfortunate' (p. 574, Solow). Also, markets and policy sector interactions, assessment of energy supply technologies, contentious aspects of nuclear power, non-hydro renewable energy, demand side and energy end-use efficiency, ... were all issues under debate at that time in the USA (Daly, 1973; Freeman et al., 1974), but not taken up by Nordhaus. Several criticisms are repeated here, not for blaming the contribution by the young academic, but as warning for reckless use of unbalanced economic logic and recommendations.

Precarious 'econometric-engineering' models

Nordhaus stepped over the limitations of his analysis and model in his search for answers on the major energy questions confronting the USA constituency and policy-makers. Although the models of the twenty-first century are far more extended and sophisticated, 'stepping over' remains accepted practice. Two issues are highlighted here.

Long-term scenarios versus consecutive recommencing

Nordhaus' temporal forward perspective runs through four 50-year periods, with the year 2170 as the end of the study period. I skip the discount rate problem (Lind et al., 1982; Portney & Weyant, 1999), and discuss backstop technology later, and focus on how the model incorporates future timelines.

Nordhaus (1973, p. 536) mentions 'myopic decisions' as 'possible complication', with: 'In the present context "myopia" means that the planning horizons of economic agents are relatively short'. Shortness in forward looking by most economic agents (and politicians!) is real because it corresponds to individual efficient behavior. Modelers extrapolate evolutions very far in the future, beyond the capacity of human control and imagination. They project scenarios, as would the future follow today's script within predictable and orderly environments. Real life at personal, community, national and global levels is regularly disrupted by unforeseen events and developments. Understanding what is going on today is already a hell of a job; it is impossible to foresee what will occur in the next century, neither is it necessary in a numerical sense. Processing future time as a sequence of relatively short (for example 5 or 10 years) time slots is the appropriate substitute for prolonged scenarios. Then, one deals with 'myopia' not as a 'possible complication' but as a natural phenomenon: life is a consecution of rather short-running periods. The present is not only today's present, but over and over again the beginning of every new future period, considering the accumulated history and adapted expectations and plans for the future.

Time sequential analysis was at the core of decision analysis theory deployed in the 1960s. Its concepts and rules penetrated public decision-making slowly, for example, as quasi option theory (Arrow & Fisher, 1974). Dixit and Pindyck (1994) discussed time sequential analysis in investment theory. In the 1990s USA scholars employed decision theory for finding the proper pace of mitigating carbon dioxide emissions from combusting fossil fuels (Kolstad, 1996; Manne & Richels, 1991). Nordhaus (2013) shared in the debate with his Dynamic Integrated model of Climate and the Economy (DICE) model.

Models are helpful tools when applied within their proper context, respecting limits on human foreseeing imposed by distant time, uncertainty, ignorance, and irreversible processes. When the latter conditions prevail, models often turn into concealing the impossibility to know the unknown. However, this impossibility is no one's responsibility and is better recognized than obscured. Decision-making processes other than cost–benefit based model logic are more apt to deal with contentious choices stretching awesomely far in the future (Ethics Commission on a Safe Energy Supply, 2011).

Uniformity versus specificity

In 1973, Nordhaus had the ambition to cover the supply side and demand side of the energy markets. He stated: 'Unfortunately, the calculation required to get the answers is extremely complex. Since there are many sources and grades of energy resources, many uses, and many demand categories, each with peculiar specifications, calculation of the optimal and the switch points for different resources is cumbersome' (Nordhaus, 1973, p. 537). Nordhaus experiences that the real world is fully diverse, and that diversity is cumbersome to fit in economic models. Economic model results remain contingent on many simplifications and assumptions embedded in the models. Economic theory adopts uniformity as a key attribute for increasing efficiency, whereas diversity is considered as costly (Weitzman, 1992). The lack of specificity in economic analysis and modeling creates problematic failures. For example, most model algorithms juxtapose low-carbon electricity supply capacities or deliveries (in case: nuclear and renewable flow supplies like wind, photovoltaic power, non-dam hydro), notwithstanding ample logical and practical evidence that they are mutually exclusive (IEA [International Energy Agency], 2013; Verbruggen, 2008).

Yet, since the 1970s the economists' modeling discourse has grown overly influential. For example, in the latest Intergovernmental Panel on Climate Change (IPCC) Working Group III report (IPCC, 2014) integrated assessment models play a predominant role.

Backstop technology

The 1973 events in global oil markets were mainly an overnight quadrupling of crude oil prices, with repositioning of power among countries on a scene of warfare between Arabic countries and Israel, and of Western concerns about limits to growth. Oil prices and depletion of fossil fuel, in particular oil, resources were focal points of societal debate and of academic research.

Nordhaus presented an inventive coupling of both issues. He writes the price of oil as the sum of the marginal cost of oil extraction plus royalties 'which are a reflection of the presumed scarcity of a particular resource' (Nordhaus, 1973, p. 531). The scarcity price would rise exponentially at the interest rate (for a given resource base in a world of certainty), and its use would run unto 'a time horizon of T years', with as footnote: 'The terminal point can be a sticky issue. If there exists what I later call a "backstop technology" (roughly, a substitute process with infinite resource base), then T is the time at which transition to it is completed; if resources are finite and essential, and no backstop technology exists, T is the time of extinction'. He continues (p. 532): 'Over the next century or so, many low-cost energy resources will be largely depleted, leaving more abundant but also more expensive resources. Ultimately, if and when the transition is completed to an economy based on plentiful nuclear resources (either through breeder or fusion reactors), the economic importance of *scarcity* of resources will disappear, and capital and labor costs alone will determine prices. This ultimate technology—resting on a very abundant resource base—is the "backstop technology" and is crucial to the allocation of scarce energy resources'.

By the ingenious concept of 'backstop technology' Nordhaus is, presumably unintended, an early prophet of the transitions movement (www.transitionsnetwork.org). Modern energy system transitions are pushed not by fossil fuel scarcity but by limited atmospheric capacity in greenhouse gas emissions assimilation without irreversible climate change impacts. Striking innovations in renewable energy technologies and in end-use energy efficiency further pull transitions forward. Overall, where in practice the transition from fossil fuels to low-carbon backstop technology is ongoing (Germany is an example in case, see Agora Energiewende, 2013), the experiences reveal an opposite reality as the one projected by Nordhaus' long-term model scenarios. Major differences are highlighted here.

First, there exists no constraining scarcity in fossil fuel resources. Contrary, there are massive reserves and resources that have to be kept underground when carbon dioxide emissions mitigation is organized to keep global temperature increase below 2°C with safe likelihood (IEA, 2013; IPCC, 2014).

Second, environmental issues, receiving minor attention by Nordhaus in 1973 (this fully changed afterwards, e.g., Nordhaus, 2013), are actually determining which energy technologies are acceptable by developed societies. The energy systems' future must match the imperatives of sustainable development (World Commission on Environment Development [WCED], 1987). Energy is an important, yet subordinate part of the sustainability paradigm, in 1992 at the Rio Summit, globally accepted by the world leaders.

Third, technological innovations were the most dynamic and to a large degree unpredictable (r)evolutions, shaping the post-World War II economies and societies, also supporting their globalization. Technological innovation is the determining factor of making energy transition paths, yes or no, economically feasible. Nuclear power, the technology favored by Nordhaus as the backstop solution, has not delivered. Renewable energy technology, ignored by Nordhaus, did surf on the most successful innovation waves: electronics, IT, special materials, and so on.

Fourth, energy end-use efficiency has brought more productivity and comfort, with less energy input than the consumptive USA lifestyle in the postwar decades. Nordhaus opened his 1973 paper with 'abundant energy at low cost is fundamental to a high-industrialized economy like the United States' (p. 529), and in his model demand price elasticity was set at zero. Disregarding half of the market, the demand side, distorts the analysis and results.

After 1973 another world has taken shape, more in the direction of cross-views developed by mainly non-economists (e.g., Freeman et al., 1974; Lovins, 1977), than along the engineering-econometric model projections. This is illustrated by the substitution of renewable energy for nuclear power as backstop technology, and by the prominent role of end-use energy intensity at the demand side.

Figure 1 shows the major components of the energy demand and supply context. Gross Domestic Product (GDP) is the sum of spending on numerous (priced) activities, being generic or specific. The activities are assigned to various sectors, and their performances require a set of energy services. Energy intensity expresses the quantities of energy used in creating value hold by the activities.

There are three energy supply sources: renewable, nuclear, and fuels (fossil and bio). Electricity is the major conveyor of commercial end-use energy, converted from the three supply sources. When nuclear energy is assigned the backstop role, electricity obtains a pole position in the analysis, because commercial nuclear energy is limited to power generation. Renewable energy is a versatile energy source, with direct energy services (e.g., daylight, natural ventilation), delivery of biofuels, input for electricity generation, low-carbon and truly inexhaustible.

Nordhaus (1973) presented nuclear power as apparent backstop energy supply technology with little consideration of its technological attributes and its real performance. However, his referees Houthakker and Solow ventilated criticisms, in particular on breeders, for Nordhaus being the ticket to inexhaustible supplies. Already, before 1973, evidence accumulated that nuclear power was not delivering, and was subject to major, costly risks. Breeders failed in the USA (in 1966, meltdown at Fermi-1, Michigan) and in Europe (Superphénix, Kalkar).

In 1973, Solow (p. 574) labeled fusion and solar power as 'really exotic energy technologies'. Indeed, nuclear fusion is energy Eden on Earth whose advent is receding

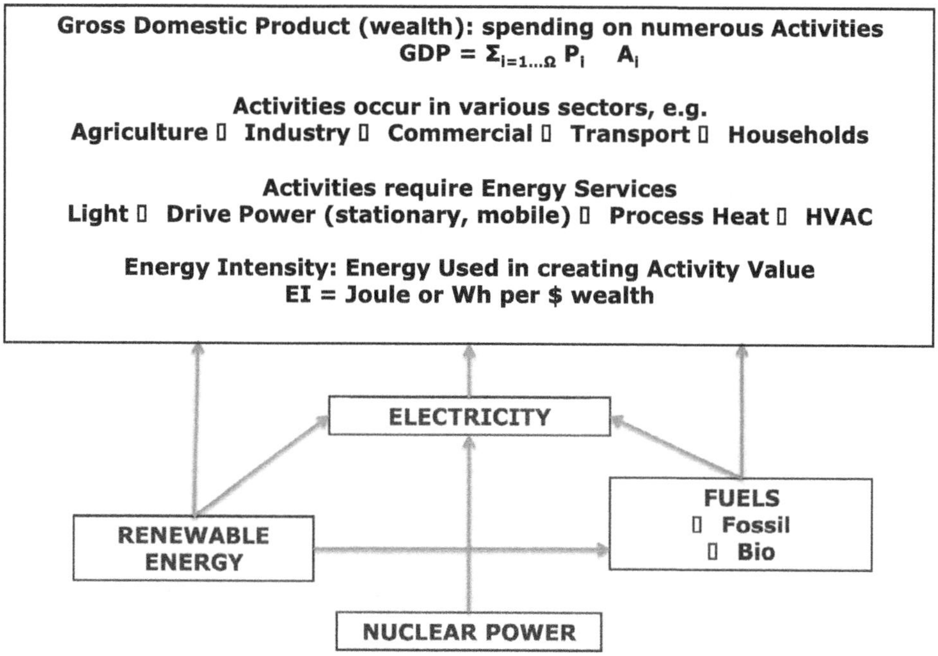

Figure 1. (Colour online) Economic activities linked to energy services and energy supplies.

with time elapsing. Contrary, after too long smoldering, solar power witnessed technological breakthroughs and falling production costs (IPCC, 2012).

Nordhaus' nuclear backstop technology was unilaterally positioned at the energy supply side as a horizontal line (inexhaustible supplies) and at a high unit price. Only when fossil resources became scarcer, their sloping-up marginal cost line would hit the horizontal ceiling line, triggering the transition. Exclusive attention for nuclear shrinks the analysis to electricity supplies. Figure 2 shows the horizontal supply curve with Electricity Intensity as demand variable dependent on the kWh price. Based on panel data of the most wealthy Organization for Economic Cooperation and Development (OECD) countries, Verbruggen (2006) found that $EI = \alpha.P^{\beta}$ with $\beta \approx -1$, or $EI \times P \approx$ the constant α, indicating the share of GDP spent by a country on electricity supplies. Given the panel statistics cover limited ranges of price and intensity data, the observed section of the orthogonal hyperbole curve $\alpha.P^{\beta}$ is a limited segment of the cross-sectional long-run relationship. Assuming the curve can be extrapolated, the abscissa of the crossing point S is called the 'backstop electricity intensity', where the rectangle with diagonal OS reflects α. Economies performing low electricity intensity maintain their shares of GDP spent on electricity supplies constant; what makes the transition to backstop supplies affordable.

Further, Verbruggen (2006) extended the conditions for a backstop supply technology from only inexhaustible to fully sustainable in the basic meaning assigned by the UN World Commission on Environment and Development (WCED, 1987). In addition, evidence is established that the backstop supply curve is not a fixed horizontal line, but shifts by learning and experience. Here again, nuclear power is losing ground compared to renewable energy. Grübler (2010) shows how the cost–price curve of nuclear power is increasing over time, plagued by 'negative learning'. The cost–price curves of

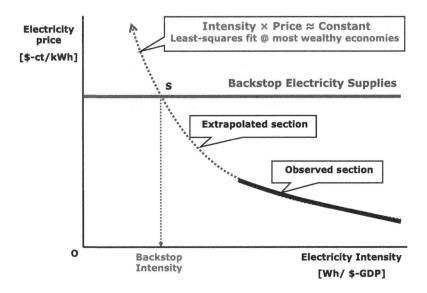

Figure 2. (Colour online) Backstop electricity intensity makes backstop electricity supplies affordable.

flow renewable energy supplies (mainly wind and PV-solar) are quickly decreasing (IPCC, 2012). Decreasing backstop supply costs and prices can accept higher electricity intensities with easier affordability of the energy transitions.

Epilogue

Transition of the energy systems of the world is climbing on the global agenda, mainly pushed by the risks of irreversible climate change. Nordhaus (1973) pioneered the transition concept by introducing 'backstop supply technology'. Nuclear fission (stranded, exhaustible (American Nuclear Society, 2001)), and ramping up costs (Grübler, 2010), breeders (tested, and failed) or fusion (stays in the announcement phase with receding horizons of availability) are no valid options in realizing the urgent transitions. With sustainable development adopted as global paradigm in 1992, the backstop technology also should meet the criteria of such development (WCED, 1987). Nuclear is failing on most criteria (Verbruggen, Laes, & Lemmens, 2014). Renewable energy is ready to fill the gap (IPCC, 2012).

The concept of backstop energy supply can be combined with the demand-side concept of backstop energy-use intensity, with the role of electricity intensity growing in importance.

Disclosure statement

No potential conflict of interest was reported by the author.

References

Agora Energiewende. (2013). 12 Insights on Germany's Energiewende. Retrieved from http://www.agora-energiewende.de

American Nuclear Society. (2001). Generation IV Roadmap: Fuel Cycle Crosscut Group. Winter Meeting Reno. Retrieved from http://gif.inel.gov/roadmap/pdfs/fuel_cycles.pdf

Arrow, K. J., & Fisher, A. C. (1974). Environmental preservation, uncertainty, and irreversibility. *Quarterly Journal of Economics*, *88*, 312–319.

Daly, H. E. (1973, 1980). *Economics, ecology, ethics: Essays toward a steady-state economy*. San Francisco, CA: W.H. Freeman and Company.

Dixit, A. K., & Pindyck, R. S. (1994). *Investment under uncertainty*. Princeton, NJ: Princeton University Press.

Ethics Commission on a Safe Energy Supply. (2011). *Germany's energy turnaround: A collective effort for the future*. Berlin: Ethics Commission on a Safe Energy Supply.

Freeman, D., Baldwin, P., Canfield, M., Carhart, S., Davidson, J., Dunkerley, J., Eddy, C., Gillman, K., Makhijani, A., Saulter, K., Sheridan, D., & Williams, R. (1974). *A time to choose: America's energy future*. Cambridge, MA: Energy Policy Project of the Ford Foundation, Ballinger Publishing Company.

Grübler, A. (2010). The costs of the French nuclear scale-up: A case of negative learning by doing. *Energy Policy*, *38*, 5174–5188. doi:10.1016/j.enpol.2010.05.003

IEA. (2013). *World energy outlook*. Paris: International Energy Agency.

IPCC. (2012). Renewable energy sources and climate change mitigation. Working Group III Special Report. Retrieved from http://www.ipcc.ch

IPCC. (2014). Intergovernmental Panel on Climate Change. Fifth Assessment Report, Working Group III 'Mitigation of Climate Change'. Retrieved from http://www.ipcc.ch

Kolstad, C. D. (1996). Fundamental irreversibilities in stock externalities. *Journal of Public Economics*, *60*, 221–233. doi:10.1016/0047-2727(95)01521-3

Lind, R.C., Arrow, K.J., Corey, G.R., Dasgupta, P., Sen, A.K., Stauffer, T., Stiglitz, J.E., Stockfisch, J.A., & Wilson, R. (1982). *Discounting for time and risk in energy policy*. Washington, DC: Resources for the Future.

Lovins, A. B. (1977). *Soft energy paths: Towards a durable peace*. New York, NY: Harper & Row.

Manne, A. S., & Richels, R. G. (1991). Buying greenhouse insurance. *Energy Policy*, *19*(6), 543–552. doi:10.1016/0301-4215(91)90034-L

Nordhaus, W. (1973). The allocation of energy resources. *Brookings Papers on Economic Activity*, *3*, 529–576.

Nordhaus, W. (2013). *The climate casino: Risk, uncertainty, and economics for a warming world*. New Haven & London: Yale University Press.

Portney, P. R., & Weyant, J. P. (eds). (1999). *Discounting and intergenerational equity*. Washington, DC: Resources for the Future.

Verbruggen, A. (2006). Electricity intensity backstop level to meet sustainable backstop supply technologies. *Energy Policy*, *34*, 1310–1317. doi:10.1016/j.enpol.2005.12.007

Verbruggen, A. (2008). Renewable and nuclear power: A common future? *Energy Policy*, *36*, 4036–4047. doi:10.1016/j.enpol.2008.06.024

Verbruggen, A., Laes, E., & Lemmens, S. (2014). Assessment of the actual sustainability of nuclear fission power. *Renewable and Sustainable Energy Reviews*, *32*, 16–28. doi:10.1016/j.rser.2014.01.008

WCED. (1987). *Our common future. World commission on environment and development*. Oxford: Oxford University Press.

Weitzman, M. (1992, May). On diversity. *The Quarterly Journal of Economics*, *107*, 363–405. doi:10.2307/2118476.

Caveats for climate policy from Nordhaus's *The Allocation of Energy Resources*

Isabel Galiana

Department of Economics, McGill University, Montreal, Canada

Over 40 years ago, in the midst of an oil embargo and rapidly rising energy prices, Nordhaus wrote the seminal piece *The Allocation of Energy Resources* (Nordhaus, 1973). While there are many disparities between the times in which Nordhaus posed the questions 'how do markets allocate scarce resources?' and 'how should resources be efficiently allocated?' and the current global context, he presented a number of issues and solutions that are still integral to energy and climate policy modeling. Written in 1973, following years of rapid economic expansion, slow growth in proven energy reserves and in the midst of the oil embargo, it was a time of increasing energy security concerns and the beginning of the notion of peak oil. The decade leading up to 2015, however, has been characterized by a global recession, rapid expansion of proven reserves, the weakening monopoly power of the Organization of Petroleum Exporting Countries (OPEC) and a growing recognition of the impact of fossil fuels on climate change. Moreover, energy has experienced unforeseen changes in both the geographic distribution of supply and demand as well as in the types of energy sources used. Despite these massive shifts in both supply and demand of energy, Nordhaus's analyses and discussions remain current in a time of apparent energy abundance. Here, I focus on the lessons that can be extracted for climate policy from *The Allocation of Energy Resources*. While Nordhaus acknowledges the potential impacts of environmental constraints on the optimal allocation of energy resources, his analysis could not foresee the extent to which we are moving towards a carbon-constrained world. Long-run issues, such as the inclusion of backstop technologies, technology forecasting in general and the need for reliable, base-load energy production, although written in the context of energy security, are critical to developing coherent climate policies. I will examine each within the current global context and discuss the amazing foresight exhibited in *The Allocation of Energy Resources*.

Climate change

Climate change is fundamentally an energy technology problem (Galiana & Green, 2012; Kriegler et al., 2014). The overwhelming majority of greenhouse gas emissions come from the burning of fossil fuels either for electricity, transportation or direct heating. Fossil fuels, currently the largest source of primary energy, contribute about 10 billion tons of CO_2 a year to the atmosphere, as well as significant amounts of ozone, sulfur dioxide, nitrogen dioxide and particulate matter. The complementarity of energy and climate policy is now widely accepted and in fact essential to successfully address energy needs while ensuring a liveable planet. At the UN General Assembly in 2010 a resolution was passed designating 2012 as the International Year of Sustainable Energy for All. Energy access and security remains a top priority globally but with the qualification that it be 'sustainable'. The Sustainable Energy for All (SE4ALL) focuses on drawing attention and financing to three objectives. First, ensuring universal access to modern energy services by 2030 that implies accelerating the growth in energy demand. Second, to double the rate of improvements in energy efficiency by 2030. This is helpful in mitigating energy demand growth but not sufficient to offset the economic development imperative. Third, to double the share of renewable energy up to 30% of the global energy mix by 2030. This last objective was not of interest in 1973, unless one includes nuclear as a renewable technology. Nordhaus acknowledges the lack of environmental constraints in his work, briefly commenting on climate change, which, 42 years ago, was extremely forward thinking.

In his analyses, Nordhaus finds the price of fossil fuels to be inexplicably high, arguing that this may be explained by monopoly power or technological pessimism about the ability to meet certain constraints. With regard to the ability to meet environmental constraints and referring to sulfur emission standards he states, 'this assumption (that technologies will be a hundred times more expensive than current estimates) implies that coal cannot be economically used for electricity generation because the sulphur emission standards cannot be easily met' (p. 559). An interesting parallel can be drawn with climate change. If we were to attempt to meet the emission-targets necessary to stabilize temperatures at a two-degree increase from preindustrial levels, fossil fuels would be rendered uneconomical. Unfortunately, we are currently incapable of meeting global energy demand with existing low-carbon energy sources, save for perhaps nuclear, which faces many nontechnical challenges discussed below.

Changing landscape of energy supply

Nordhaus identifies four important energy resources; petroleum, coal, natural gas and uranium-235 that he deems likely to provide the bulk of energy for the US over the next 200 years. He forecasts that petroleum and natural gas will dominate until the beginning of the twenty-first century, at which point coal and nuclear become large players. He also forecasts that fossil fuels will be exhausted by 2120 and the economy will run entirely on an electric–hydrogen technology.

The reality is that despite the fears of declining stocks and peak oil, the last 45 years have seen a dramatic increase in reserve to production ratios[1] (R/P) of all fossil fuels. Even in the face of a 222%[2] increase in global consumption of energy, new discoveries and extraction technologies have progressed at an even greater rate, thus offsetting depletion. In fact, the availability and access to primary energy sources has never been greater. The past two decades have revealed an abundance of previously inaccessible energy, particularly in developed countries where both technology and capital are plentiful. Oil prices have dropped over 50% in the last year, renewables are driving the spot price of electricity down, and technologies allowing for the extraction of shale gas have pushed coal to the wayside in the US. We are, by all measures, in the midst of a radical shift in production of energy. In the context of climate change, greater reserves and consumption plainly imply earlier and greater temperature increases. Greater reserves are also associated with lower fossil fuel prices that in turn may make policies to mitigate emissions less effective.

The geographic distribution of energy supply has also experienced a massive shift. Much of the increased supply is due to the 'shale gas revolution'. Shale gas, until recently economically infeasible, is now part of the energy lexicon as techno-logical innovation has increased proven gas reserves to unprecedented levels. Both government policy and export constraints interfere with the ability of resource-rich regions to move their product to external markets, thus keeping local shale prices artificially low. High oil prices up to 2014 allowed for massive investment in otherwise uneconomical reserves in much of the US and Western Canada. In addi-tion, where OPEC once exerted strong monopoly power due to their low production costs, recent technological innovations have allowed unconventional deposits to become more cost-effective thus reducing OPEC's share of global supply.

The recent evolution of energy supply in Japan and its global consequences for climate policy provide an interesting case with which to understand the complexity of technology forecasting. Nordhaus soundly models Japan as one of the five energy intensive regions in his optimization. Following World War II, Japan emerged as an economic giant with energy-intensive industries such as steel. It invested heavily in nuclear energy facilities for electricity generation ahead of the expectation for the US in Nordhaus's model. Nuclear power plants, although expensive to build, are relatively inexpensive to operate and can produce vast amounts of carbon-free energy at low cost. Prior to the earthquake in 2011, 30% of Japan's electricity came from its 40,000 MW nuclear generating facilities. However, following the incidents at Fukushima, Japan systematically shut down the country's nuclear fleet, and at present Japan's energy needs are being met by coal, oil and liquefied natural gas. As Japan's carbon-free nuclear energy was replaced with higher carbon sources, the country's carbon emissions have increased. While there appears to be unusual trepidation from policy makers globally with respect to expanding the role of nuclear energy, the climate implications of switching from carbon-free to carbon-intensive sources is clear. Germany's Energiewende (exemplary of a European wide phenom-enon) which supported the closure of nuclear facilities and the subsidization of renewable, but non-dispatchable, energy sources, has seen its emissions increase as base load coal facilities are required to offset the nuclear closures. This example highlights the difficulties in predicting technological evolution and limits to energy adoption beyond availability and price. Nordhaus assumes widespread up-take of nuclear but cannot foresee the political and institutional barriers exemplified by opposition to nuclear.

Nordhaus all but dismisses non-hydro renewables with only a casual mention of solar and biofuels as not being up to the task. How could he have imagined the massive growth in intermittent renewables? While issues have arisen due to over-subsidization, intermittency and lack of storage, these technologies, such as wind and solar photovoltaic (PV), have the potential to be deployed at a small scale in remote areas. Renewables currently provide 18% of global energy production, up from less than 1% in 1973.

These examples are not to dismiss the Herculean effort made by Nordhaus in fore-casting energy use in the midst of what was a state of flux and uncertainty. They do provide a cautionary tale for the use of long-run technology forecasting in policy design. At the very least it suggests the need for policy to be designed with an awareness of potential game-changing energy transformations.

Innovation and backstop technologies

Historical evidence suggests that innovation in energy technologies occurs through learning-by-doing and marginal efficiency improvements. However, every so often, a radical Schumpeterian shift occurs that alters the energy landscape. As Schumpeter elucidated in 1942, revolutions occur in discrete rushes separated by spans of comparative quiet. What is clear from historical radical shocks in energy supply technologies is that they are extremely difficult to predict and once initiated fairly rapid to diffuse (Fouquet & Pearson, 2006; Gales, Kander, Malanima, & Rubio, 2007). Much of the literature on climate policy focuses on the diffusion of existing technologies. Unfortunately, in order to meet growing energy demand and given large fossil fuel reserves effectively addressing climate change will require one of the Schumpeterian shifts. Nordhaus has a great deal to contribute in this respect! One of the most innovative aspects of his paper is the coining of the term 'backstop technology' (p. 531). This notion that a technology would appear at a given (high) price that was capable of meeting infinite demand requirements was designed to ensure a feasible solution to the optimal energy allocation problem. The 'backstop technology' is now a key aspect of any integrated assessment model[3] used to evaluate and/or define climate policy with the additional requirement that the technology be emission free. This is a valuable contribution to the modeling of optimal resource use. Here, we consider both fossil fuels and the use of the atmosphere as a sink for GhGs as finite resources. Unfortunately, this backstop technology is often modeled as an exogenous factor, and successful climate stabilization depends on the existence of said backstop (Bosetti & Tavoni, 2009). Just as in the standard Hotelling model where the next most expensive reserve acts as a price cap for the current extraction site, Nordhaus's backstop acts as a price cap for all non-renewable resources. Moreover, it limits the costs of climate policy at a social cost of carbon defined by the cost of the backstop. The issue here is the widespread use of the backstop with little regard to its actual technological feasibility or its development (Galiana & Green, 2009). In fact, backstop technologies, the technology of choice *du jour* being BECCS,[4] have become our Holy Grail for climate change mitigation (Edmonds, Calvin, Clarke, Kyle, & Wise, 2012, IPCC, 2014; Kriegler et al., 2014). There is a recent surge in research evaluating the effects of the timing of availability and the price of the backstop, with radically different policy recommendations resulting (for example, Fuss et al., 2014). Our dependence on a backstop technology, and the lack of explicit means to ensure its existence, leads us to a discussion of innovation policy.

Nordhaus recognizes that the prices of appropriable resources (e.g., petroleum, coal, natural gas) have had limited, if any, public intervention and thus are left to be determined by market forces. Regrettably the non-appropriable resource of basic low-carbon innovation, including backstop technologies, has also suffered from weak public intervention (Nemet & Kammen, 2007). The dangers of including an exogenous backstop technology in climate policy modeling and the extreme technological optimism it embodies should be moderated with active innovation policy. Indeed, much of the current work in climate policy deals with understanding the drivers of low-carbon technological innovation (Le Quéré et al., 2015).

The changing landscape of energy demand

Similarly, our demand for energy is undergoing, if not unprecedented, rare shift, both in geographic distribution and type. Nordhaus very rationally chose six regions to model: the United States, Western Europe, Japan, the Persian Gulf, North Africa and the rest of the world (ROW). Of course the current situation is very different. Between 1990 and 2010, the Chinese and Indian economies grew by an average of 10.4 and 6.4% per year, respectively. And although since 2010, the growth rates in both those countries have fallen slightly, the solid GDP growth experienced continues to necessitate further coal use. The US Energy Information Administration (EIA) estimates Chinese coal consumption tripled in the period between 2000 and 2010, and in 2011 China became the largest coal importer in the world, although these imports represent only 5% of the country's total coal consumption; China alone consumed 47% of global coal in 2012 and accounted for 82% of the global incremental coal demand in that year. In 2012, 41% of the world's electricity generation was coal-fired, although the distribution of coal, as a primary energy source in electricity production, is not uniform. In 2012, the top three importers of coal for steam-fired electricity production were China, Japan and India. Japan's coal necessity is due to the closure of its nuclear facilities although it appears that the new government in place is willing to reconsider the nuclear option. For China and India, strong economic growth, which is closely tied to energy consumption, was responsible for the increase. Rapid urbanization has been a significant contributor to the increase in greenhouse gas emissions. The lesson here is that it is extremely difficult to forecast how countries will evolve. Weak forecasts for energy demand imply that climate policy measures will be easier to implement than under higher growth.

Concluding remarks

Nordhaus's paper had many important insights and I have used but a few to raise parallel questions for the relationship between energy use and climate change policy. In my view there are two important takeaways, first, it is extremely difficult to predict long-run changes in energy supply and demand, and second, we are not guaranteed the existence of a backstop technology policy dependent on forecasts of these factors will inevitably be mired with high levels of uncertainty and the associated risk. In an era of energy abundance, how do we resolve the climate/energy nexus?

> 'We should not be haunted by the specter of the affluent society grinding to a halt for lack of energy sources (p. 570) ... the radical shift in relative prices, making environmental resources very costly goods, will promote technological change aimed at saving these resources, although this may take time' (p. 550).

We should, however, be haunted by the specter of depleted absorptive capacity of the earth. Although Nordhaus's optimism is infectious, it is my view that only with the appropriate willingness to support the development of a low-carbon energy backstop can we simultaneously overcome energy scarcity and climate change.

Disclosure statement
No potential conflict of interest was reported by the author.

Notes
1. The R/P ratio (reserves/production) gives the years left to depletion at the given extraction rate and with no increase in reserve size

2. BP statistical review of world energy 2014
3. See for example DICE; WITCH, among others
4. BECCS – Bioenergy carbon capture and storage

References

Bosetti, V., & Tavoni, M. (2009). Uncertain R&D, backstop technology and GHGs stabilization. *Energy Economics*, *31*(Supplement 1), S18–S26. doi:10.1016/j.eneco.2008.03.002

Edmonds, J., Calvin, K., Clarke, L., Kyle, P., & Wise, M. (2012). Energy and technology lessons since Rio. *Energy Economics*, *34*, S7–S14. doi:10.1016/j.eneco.2012.08.037

Fouquet, R., & Pearson, P. J. (2006). Seven centuries of energy services: The price and use of light in the United Kingdom (1300–2000). *The Energy Journal*, 139–177.

Fuss, S., Canadell, J. G., Peters, G. P., Tavoni, M., Andrew, R. M., Ciais, P. . . . Yamagata, Y. (2014). Betting on negative emissions. *Nature Climate Change*, *4*(10), 850–853. doi:10.1038/nclimate2392

Gales, B., Kander, A., Malanima, P., & Rubio, M. (2007). North versus South: Energy transition and energy intensity in Europe over 200 years. *European Review of Economic History*, *11*(2), 219–253. doi:10.1017/S1361491607001967

Galiana, I., & Green, C. (2009). Let the global technology race begin. *Nature*, *462*(7273), 570–571. doi:10.1038/462570a

Galiana, I., & Green, C. (2012). *A technology-led climate policy in a changing landscape*. Global Problems, Smart Solutions, Cambridge University Press, UK.

IPCC. (2014). Working Group III, Cliamte Change 2014, Mitigation of Climate Change. Fifth Assessment Report IPCC, Geneva.

Kriegler, E., Weyant, J. P., Blanford, G. J., Krey, V., Clarke, L., Edmonds, J. . . . Van Vuuren, D. P. (2014). The role of technology for achieving climate policy objectives: Overview of the EMF 27 study on global technology and climate policy strategies. *Climatic Change*, *123*(3–4), 353–367. doi:10.1007/s10584-013-0953-7

Le Quéré, C., Capstick, S., Corner, A., Cutting, D., Johnson, M., Minns, A., Schroeder, H., Walker-Springett, K., Whitmarsh, L., & Wood, R. (2015). Towards a culture of low-carbon research for the 21 st Century. Tyndall Centre for Climate Change Research, Working paper #161.

Nemet, G. F., & Kammen, D. M. (2007). U.S. energy research and development: Declining investment, increasing need, and the feasibility of expansion. *Energy Policy*, *35*(1), 746–755. doi:10.1016/j.enpol.2005.12.012

Nordhaus, W. D. (1973). The allocation of energy resources. *Brookings Papers on Economic Activity*, 529–576.

Professor Robert M. Solow

RICHARD T. ELY LECTURE

The Economics of Resources
or the Resources of Economics*

ROBERT M. SOLOW
Professor of Economics, Massachusetts Institute of Technology

It is easy to choose a subject for a distinguished lecture like this, before a large and critical audience with a wide range of interests. You need a topic that is absolutely contemporary, but somehow perennial. It should survey a broad field, without being superficial or vague. It should probably bear some relation to economic policy, but of course it must have some serious analytical foundations. It is nice if the topic has an important literature in the past of our subject—a literature which you can summarize brilliantly in about eleven minutes—but it better be something in which economists are interested today, and it should appropriately be a subject you have worked on yourself. The lecture should have some technical interest, because you can't waffle for a whole hour to a room full of professionals, but it is hardly the occasion to use a blackboard.

I said that it is easy to choose a subject for the Ely Lecture. It has to be, because twelve people, counting me, have done it.

I am going to begin with a quotation that could have come from yesterday's newspaper, or the most recent issue of the *American Economic Review*.

> Contemplation of the world's disappearing supplies of minerals, forests, and other exhaustible assets has led to demands for regulation of their exploitation. The feeling that these products are now too cheap for the good of future generations, that they are being selfishly exploited at too rapid a rate, and that in consequence of their excessive cheapness they are being produced and consumed wastefully has given rise to the conservation movement.

The author of those sentences is not Dennis Meadows and associates, not Ralph Nader and associates, not the President of the Sierra Club; it is a very eminent economic theorist, a Distinguished Fellow of this Association, Harold Hotelling, who died at the age of seventy-eight, just a few days ago. Like all economic theorists, I am much in his debt, and I would be happy to have this lecture stand as a tribute to him. These sentences appeared at the beginning of his article "The Economics of Exhaustible Resources," not in the most

---

*Originally published in: *The American Economic Review*, Vol. 64, No. 2, Papers and Proceedings of the Eighty-sixth Annual Meeting of the American Economic Association (May, 1974), pp. 1–14. Reproduced with kind permission of the American Economic Association.

recent *Review*, but in the *Journal of Political Economy* for April 1931. So I think I have found something that is both contemporary and perennial. The world has been exhausting its exhaustible resources since the first cave-man chipped a flint, and I imagine the process will go on for a long, long time.

Mr. Dooley noticed that "th' Supreme Coort follows the iliction returns." He would be glad to know that economic theorists read the newspapers. About a year ago, having seen several of those respectable committee reports on the advancing scarcity of materials in the United States and the world, and having, like everyone else, been suckered into reading the *Limits to Growth*, I decided I ought to find out what economic theory has to say about the problems connected with exhaustible resources. I read some of the literature, including Hotelling's classic article—the theoretical literature on exhaustible resources is, fortunately, not very large—and began doing some work of my own on the problem of optimal social management of a stock of a nonrenewable but essential resource. I will be mentioning some of the results later. About the time I finished a first draft of my own paper and was patting myself on the back for having been clever enough to realize that there was in fact something still to be said on this important, contemporary but somehow perennial topic just about then it seemed that every time the mail came it contained another paper by another economic theorist on the economics of exhaustible resources.[1] It was a little like trotting down to the sea, minding your own business like any nice independent rat, and then looking around and suddenly discovering that you're a lemming. Anyhow, I now have a nice collection of papers on the theory of exhaustible resources; and most of them are still unpublished, which is just the advantage I need over the rest of you.

A pool of oil or vein of iron or deposit of copper in the ground is a capital asset to society and to its owner (in the kind of society in which such things have private owners) much like a printing press or a building or any other reproducible capital asset. The only difference is that the natural resource is not reproducible, so the size of the existing stock can never increase through time. It can only decrease (or, if none is mined for a while, stay the same). This is true even of recyclable materials; the laws of thermodynamics and life guarantee that we will never re- cover a whole pound of secondary copper from a pound of primary copper in use, or a whole pound of tertiary copper from a pound of secondary copper in use. There is leakage at every round; and a formula just like the ordinary multiplier formula tells us how much copper use can be built on the world's initial endowment of copper, in terms of the recycling or recovery ratio. There is always less ultimate copper use left than there was last year, less by the amount dissipated beyond recovery during the year. So copper remains an exhaustible resource, despite the possibility of partial recycling.

A resource deposit draws its market value, ultimately, from the prospect of extraction and sale. In the meanwhile, its owner, like the owner of every capital asset, is asking: What have you done for me lately? The only way that a resource deposit in the ground and left in the ground can produce a current return for its owner is by appreciating in value. Asset markets can be in equilibrium only when all assets in a given risk class earn the

---

[1]*The Review of Economic Studies* will publish a group of them in the summer of 1974, including my own paper and others by Partha Dasgupta and Geoffrey Heal, Michael Weinstein and Richard Zeckhauser, and Joseph Stiglitz, from all of which I have learned a lot about this subject. (This paper was actually published in the *Review of Economic Studies* in 1974—Editor.) I would especially like to thank Zeckhauser for conversation and correspondence, and for the kind of reading of the first draft of this Lecture that one only dares to hope to get because it is so close to Christmas. The final version reflects his comments.

same rate of return, partly as current dividend and partly as capital gain. The common rate of return is the interest rate for that risk class. Since resource deposits have the peculiar property that they yield no dividend so long as they stay in the ground, in equilibrium the value of a resource deposit must be growing at a rate equal to the rate of interest. Since the value of a deposit is also the present value of future sales from it, after deduction of extraction costs, resource owners must expect the net price of the ore to be increasing exponentially at a rate equal to the rate of interest. If the mining industry is competitive, net price stands for market price minus marginal extraction cost for a ton of ore. If the industry operates under constant costs, that is just market price net of unit extraction costs, or the profit margin. If the industry is more or less monopolistic, as is frequently the case in extractive industry, it is the marginal profit-marginal revenue less marginal cost—that has to be growing, and expected to grow, proportionally like the rate of interest.

This is the fundamental principle of the economics of exhaustible resources. It was the basis of Hotelling's classic article. I have deduced it as a condition of stock equilibrium in the asset market. Hotelling thought of it mainly as a condition of flow equilibrium in the market for ore: if net price is increasing like compound interest, owners of operating mines will be indifferent at the margin between extracting and holding at every instant of time. So one can imagine production just equal to demand at the current price, and the ore market clears. No other time profile for prices can elicit positive production in every period of time.

It is hard to overemphasize the importance of this tilt in the time profile for net price. If the net price were to rise too slowly, production would be pushed nearer in time and the resource would be exhausted quickly, precisely because no one would wish to hold resources in the ground and earn less than the going rate of return. If the net price were to rise too fast, resource deposits would be an excellent way to hold wealth, and owners would delay production while they enjoyed supernormal capital gains.

According to the fundamental principle, if we observe the market for an exhaustible resource near equilibrium, we should see the net price—or marginal profit—rising exponentially. That is not quite the same thing as seeing the market price to users of the resource rising exponentially. The price to consumers is the net price plus extraction costs, or the obvious analogy for monopoly. The market price can fall or stay constant while the net price is rising if extraction costs are falling through time, and if the net price or scarcity rent is not too large a proportion of the market price. That is presumably what has been happening in the market for most exhaustible resources in the past. (It is odd that there are not some econometric studies designed to find out just this. Maybe econometricians don't follow the iliction returns.) Eventually, as the extraction cost falls and the net price rises, the scarcity rent must come to dominate the movement of market price, so the market price will eventually rise, although that may take a very long time to happen. Whatever the pattern, the market price and the rate of extraction are connected by the demand curve for the resource. So, ultimately, when the market price rises, the current rate of production must fall along the demand curve. Sooner or later, the market price will get high enough to choke off the demand entirely. At that moment production falls to zero. If flows and stocks have been beautifully coordinated through the operations of futures markets or a planning board, the last ton produced will also be the last ton in the ground. The resource will be exhausted at the instant that it has priced itself out of the market. The Age of Oil or Zinc or Whatever It Is will have come to an end. (There is a limiting case, of course, in which demand goes asymptotically to zero as the price rises to infinity, and the resource is exhausted only asymptotically. But it is neither believable nor important.)

Now let us do an exercise with this apparatus. Suppose there are two sources of the same ore, one high-cost and the other low-cost. The cost difference may reflect geographical accessibility and transportation costs, or some geological or chemical difference that makes extraction cheap at one site and dear at the other. The important thing is that there are cost differences, though the final mineral product is identical from both sources.

It is easy to see that production from both sources cannot coexist in the market for any interval of time. For both sources to produce, net price for each of them must be growing like compound interest at the market rate. But they must market their ore at the same price, because the product is identical. That is arithmetically impossible, if their extraction costs differ.

So the story has to go like this. First one source operates and supplies the whole market. Its net price rises exponentially, and the market price moves correspondingly. At a certain moment, the first source is exhausted. At just that moment and not before, it must become economical for the second source to come into production. From then on, the world is in the single-source situation: the net price calculated with current extraction costs must rise exponentially until all production is choked off and the second source is exhausted. (If there are many sources, you can see how it will work.)

Which source will be used first? Your instinct tells you that the low-cost deposit will be the first one worked, and your instinct is right. You can see why, in terms of the fundamental principle. At the beginning, if the high-cost producer is serving the market, the market price must cover high extraction costs plus a scarcity rent that is growing exponentially. The low-cost producer would refrain from undercutting the price and entering the market only if his capital gains justify holding off and entering the market later. But just the reverse will be true. Any price high enough to keep the high-cost producer in business will tempt the low-cost producer to sell ore while the selling is good and invest the proceeds in any asset paying the market rate of interest. So it must be that the low-cost producer is the first to enter. Price rises and output falls. Eventually, at precisely the moment when the low-cost supply is exhausted, the price has reached a level at which it pays the high-cost producer to enter. From then on, *his* net price rises exponentially and production continues to fall. When cumulative production has exhausted the high- cost deposit, the market price must be such as to choke the demand off to zero—or else just high enough to tempt a still higher-cost source into production. And so it goes. Apart from market processes, it is actually socially rational to use the lower-cost deposits before the higher-cost ones.

You can take this story even further, as William Nordhaus has done in connection with the energy industry. Suppose that, somewhere in the background, there is a technology capable of producing or substituting for a mineral resource at relatively high cost, but on an effectively inexhaustible resource base. Nordhaus calls this a "backstop technology." (The nearest we now have to such a thing is the breeder reactor using U^{238} as fuel. World reserves of U^{238} are thought to be enough to provide energy for over a million years at current rates of consumption. If that is not a back- stop technology, it is at least a catcher who will not allow a lot of passed balls. For a better approximation, we must wait for controlled nuclear fusion or direct use of solar energy. The sun will not last forever, but it will last at least as long as we do, more or less by definition.) Since there is no scarcity rent to grow exponentially, the backstop technology can operate as soon as the market price rises enough to cover its extraction costs (including, of course, profit on the capital equipment involved in production). And as soon as that happens, the market price of the ore or its substitute stops rising. The "backstop technology" provides a ceiling for the market price of the natural resource.

The story in the early stages is as I have told it. In the beginning, the successive grades of the resource are mined. The last and highest-cost source gives out just when the market price has risen to the point where the backstop technology becomes competitive. During the earlier phases, one imagines that resource companies keep a careful eye on the prospective costs associated with the backstop technology. Any laboratory success or failure that changes those prospective costs has instantaneous effects on the capital value of existing resource deposits, and on the most profitable rate of current production. In actual fact, those future costs have to be regarded as uncertain. A correct theory of market behavior and a correct theory of optimal social policy will have to take account of technological uncertainty (and perhaps also uncertainty about the true size of mineral reserves). Here is a mildly concrete illustration of these principles. There is now a workable technology for liquefying coal-that is, for producing synthetic crude oil from coal.[2] Nordhaus puts the extraction-and-preparation cost at the equivalent of seven or eight 1970 dollars per barrel of crude oil, including amortization and interest at 10 percent on the plant; I have heard higher and lower figures quoted. If coal were available in unlimited amounts, that would be all. But, of course, coal is a scarce resource, though more abundant than drillable petroleum, so a scarcity rent has to be added to that figure, and the rent has to be increasing like the rate of interest during the period when coal is being used for this purpose.

In the meanwhile, the extraction and production cost for this technology is large compared with the scarcity rent on the coal input, so the market price at which the liquefied-coal-synthetic-crude activity would now be economic is rising more slowly than the rate of interest. It may even fall if there are cost-reducing technological improvements; and that is not unlikely, given that research on coal has not been splashed as liberally with funds as research on nuclear energy. In any case, political shenanigans and monopoly profits aside, scarcity rents on oil form a larger fraction of the market price of oil, precisely because it is a lower cost fuel. The price of a barrel of oil should therefore be rising faster than the implicit price at which synthetic crude from coal could compete. One day those curves will intersect, and that day the synthetic-crude technology will replace the drilled- petroleum technology.

Even before that day, the possibility of coal liquefaction provides a kind of ceiling for the price of oil. I say "kind of" to remind you that coal-mining and moving capacity and synthetic-crude plant cannot be created overnight. One might hope that the ceiling might also limit the consuming world's vulnerability to political shenanigans and monopoly profits. I suppose it does in some ultimate sense, but one must not slide over the difficulties: for example, who would want to make a large investment in coal liquefaction or coal gasification in the knowledge that the current price of oil contains a large monopoly element that could be cut, at least temporarily, if something like a price war should develop?

The fundamental principle of the economics of exhaustible resources is, as I have said, simultaneously a condition of flow equilibrium in the market for the ore and of asset equilibrium in the market for deposits. When it holds, it says quite a lot about the probable

---

[2]As best one can tell at the moment, shale oil is a more likely successor to oil and natural gas than either gasified or liquefied coal. The relevant costs are bound to be uncertain until more research and development has been done. I tell the story in terms of liquefied coal only because it is more picturesque that way.

pattern of exploitation of a resource. But there are more than the usual reasons for wondering whether the equilibrium conditions have any explanatory value. For instance, the flow market that has to be cleared is not just one market; it is the sequence of markets for resource products from now until the date of exhaustion. It is, in other words, a sequence of futures markets, perhaps a long sequence. If the futures markets actually existed, we could perhaps accept the notion that their equilibrium configuration is stable; that might not be true, but it is at least the sort of working hypothesis we frequently accept as a way of getting on with business. But there clearly is not a full set of futures markets; natural-resource markets work with a combination of myopic flow transactions and rather more farsighted asset transactions. It is legitimate to ask whether observed re- source prices are to be interpreted as approximations to equilibrium prices, or whether the equilibrium is so unstable that momentary prices are not only a bad indicator of equilibrium relationships, but also a bad guide to resource allocation.

That turns out not to be an easy question to answer. Flow considerations and stock considerations work in opposite directions. The flow markets by themselves could easily be unstable; but the asset markets provide a corrective force. Let me try to explain why.

The flow equilibrium condition is that the net price grow like compound interest at the prevailing rate. Suppose net prices are expected by producers to be rising too slowly. Then resource deposits are a bad way to hold wealth. Mine owners will try to pull out; and if they think only in flow terms, the way to get out of the resource business is to increase current production and convert ore into money. If current production increases, for this or any other reason, the current price must move down along the demand curve. So initially pessimistic price expectations on the part of producers have led to more pressure on the current price. If expectations about future price changes are responsive to current events, the consequence can only be that pessimism is reinforced and deepened. The initial dise-quilibrium is worsened, not eliminated, by this chain of events. In other words, the market mechanism I have just described is unstable. Symmetrical reasoning leads to the conclusion that if prices are initially expected to be rising too fast, the withholding of supplies will lead to a speculative run-up of prices which is self-reinforcing. Depending on which way we start, initial disequilibrium is magnified, and production is tilted either toward excessive current dumping or toward speculative withholding of supply. (Still other assumptions are possible and may lead to qualitatively different results. For instance, one could imagine that expectations focus on the price level rather than its rate of change. There is much more work to be done on this question.)

Such things have happened in resource markets; but they do not seem always to be happening. I think that this story of instability in spot markets needs amendment; it is implausible because it leaves the asset market entirely out of account. The longer run pros-pect is not allowed to have any influence on current happenings. Suppose that producers do have some notion that the resource they own has a value anchored somewhere in the future, a value determined by technological and demand considerations, not by pure and simple speculation. Then if prices are now rising toward that rendezvous at too slow a rate, that is indeed evidence that owning resource deposits is bad business. But that will lead not to wholesale dumping of current production, but to capital losses on existing stocks. When existing stocks have been written down in value, the net price can rise toward its future rendezvous at more or less the right rate. As well as being destabilized by flow reactions, the market can be stabilized by capitalization reactions. In fact the two stories can be made to merge: the reduction in flow price coming from increased current production can be read as a signal and capitalized into losses on asset values, after which near-equilibrium is reestablished.

I think the correct conclusion to be drawn from this discussion is not that either of the stories is more likely to be true. It is more complex: that in tranquil conditions, resource markets are likely to track their equilibrium paths moderately well, or at least not likely to rush away from them. But resource markets may be rather vulnerable to surprises. They may respond to shocks about the volume of reserves, or about competition from new materials, or about the costs of competing technologies, or even about near-term political events, by drastic movements of current price and production. It may be quite a while before the transvaluation of values—I never thought I could quote Nietzsche in an economics paper—settles down under the control of sober future prospects. In between, it may be a cold winter.

So far, I have discussed the economic theory of exhaustible resources as a partial-equilibrium market theory. The interest rate that more or less controls the whole process was taken as given to the mining industry by the rest of the economy. So was the demand curve for the resource itself. And when the market price of the resource has ridden up the demand curve to the point where the quantity demanded falls to zero, the theory says that the resource in question will have been exhausted.

There is clearly a more cosmic aspect to the question than this; and I do not mean to suggest that it is unimportant, just because it is cosmic. In particular, there remains an important question about the social interest in the pace of exploitation of the world's endowment of exhaustible natural resources. This aspect has been brought to a head recently, as everyone knows, by the various Doomsday forecasts that combine a positive finding that the world is already close to irreversible collapse from shortage of natural resources and other causes with the normative judgment that civilization is much too young to die. I do not intend to discuss those forecasts and judgments now—this convention already has one session devoted to just that—but I do want to talk about the economic issues of principle involved.

First, there is a proposition that will be second nature to everyone in this room. What I have called the fundamental principle of the economics of exhaustible re- sources is, among other things, a condition of competitive equilibrium in the sequence of futures markets for deliveries of the natural resource. This sequence extends out to infinity, even if the competitive equilibrium calls for the resource to be exhausted in finite time. Beyond the time of exhaustion there is also equilibrium: supply equals demand equals zero at a price simultaneously so high that demand is choked off and so low that it is worth no one's while to lose interest by holding some of the resource that long. Like any other competitive equilibrium with the right background assumptions, this one has some optimality properties. In particular, as Hotelling pointed out, the competitive equilibrium maximizes the sum of the discounted consumer-plus-producer surpluses from the natural resource, *provided* that society wishes to discount future consumer surpluses at the same rate that mine owners choose to discount their own future profits.

Hotelling was not so naive as to leap from this conclusion to the belief that *laissez-faire* would be an adequate policy for the resource industries. He pointed to several ways in which the background assumptions might be expected to fail: the presence of externalities when several owners can exploit the same underground pool of gas or oil; the considerable uncertainty surrounding the process of exploration with the consequent likelihood of wasteful rushes to stake claims and exploit, and the creation of socially useless windfall profits; and, finally, the existence of large monopolistic or oligopolistic firms in the extractive industries.

There is an amusing sidelight here. It is not hard to show that, generally speaking, a monopolist will exhaust a mine more slowly than a competitive industry facing the same demand curve would do. (Hotelling did not explore this point in detail, though he clearly knew it. He did mention the possibility of an extreme case in which competition will exhaust a resource in finite time and a monopolist only asymptotically.) The amusing thing is that if a conservationist is someone who would like to see resources conserved *beyond* the pace that competition would adopt, then the monopolist is the conservationist's friend. No doubt they would both be surprised to know it.

Hotelling mentions, but rather pooh-poohs, the notion that market rates of interest might exceed the rate at which society would wish to discount future utilities or consumer surpluses. I think a modern economist would take that possibility more seriously. It is certainly a potentially important question, because the discount rate determines the whole tilt of the equilibrium production schedule. If it is true that the market rate of interest exceeds the social rate of time preference, then scarcity rents and market prices will rise faster than they "ought to" and production will have to fall correspondingly faster along the demand curve. Thus the resource will be exploited too fast and exhausted too soon.

The literature has several reasons for expecting that private discount rates might be systematically higher than the correct social rate of discount. They fall into two classes. The first class takes it more or less for granted that society ought to discount utility and consumption at the same rates as reflective individuals would discount their own future utility and consumption. This line of thought then goes on to suggest that there are reasons why this might not happen. One standard example is the fact that individuals can be expected to discount for the riskiness of the future, and some of the risks for which they will discount are not risks to society but merely the danger of transfers within the society. Since there is not a complete enough set of insurance markets to permit all these risks to be spread properly, market interest rates will be too high. Insecurity of tenure, as William Vickrey has pointed out, is a special form of uncertainty with particular relevance to natural resources.

A second standard example is the existence of various taxes on income from capital; since individuals care about the after-tax return on investment and society about the before-tax return, if investment is carried to the point where the after-tax yield is properly related to the rate of time preference, the before-tax profitability of investment will be too high. I have nothing to add to this discussion.

The other class of reasons for expecting that private discount rates are too high and will thus distort intertemporal decisions away from social optimality denies that private time preference is the right basis for intertemporal decisions. Frank Ramsey, for instance, argued that it was ethically indefensible for society to discount future utilities. Individuals might do so, either because they lack imagination (Bohm-Bawerk's "defective telescopic faculty") or because they are all too conscious that life is short. In social decision- making, however, there is no excuse for treating generations unequally, and the time-horizon is, or should be, very long. In solemn conclave assembled, so to speak, we ought to act as if the social rate of time preference were zero (though we would simultaneously discount future *consumption* if we expect the future to be richer than the present). I confess I find that reasoning persuasive, and it provides another reason for expecting that the market will exhaust resources too fast.

This point need not be divorced so completely from individual time preference. If the whole infinite sequence of futures markets for resource products could actually take place and find equilibrium, I might be inclined to accept the result (though I would like to know who decides the initial endowments within and between generations). But of course they cannot take place. There is no way to collect bids and offers from everyone who will ever live. In the markets that actually do take place, future generations are represented only by us, their eventual ancestors. Now generations overlap, so that I worry about my children, and they about theirs, and so on. But it does seem fundamentally implausible that there should be anything *ex post* right about the weight that is actually given to the welfare of those who will not live for another thousand years. We have actually done quite well at the hands of our ancestors. Given how poor they were and how rich we are, they might properly have saved less and consumed more. No doubt they never expected the rise in income per head that has made us so much richer than they ever dreamed was possible. But that only reinforces the point that the future may be too important to be left to the accident of mistaken expectations and the ups and downs of the Protestant ethic.

Several writers have studied directly the problem of defining and characterizing a socially-optimal path for the exploitation of a given pool of exhaustible resources. The idea is familiar enough: instead of worrying about market responses, one imagines an idealized planned economy, constrained only by its initial endowment, the size of the labor force, the available technology, and the laws of arithmetic. The planning board then has to find the best feasible development for the economy. To do so, it needs a precise criterion for comparing different paths, and that is where the social rate of time preference plays a role.

It turns out that the choice of a rate of time preference is even more critical in this situation than it is in the older literature on optimal capital accumulation without any exhaustible resources. In that theory, the criterion usually adopted is the maximization of a discounted sum of one-period social welfare indicators, depending on consumption per head, and summed over all time from now to the infinite future. The typical result, depending somewhat on the particular assumptions made, is that consumption per head rises through time to a constant plateau defined by the "modified Golden Rule." In that ultimate steady state, consumption per head is lower the higher is the social rate of disount; and, correspondingly, the path to the steady state is characterized by less saving and more interim consumption, the higher the social rate of discount. That is as it should be: the main beneficiaries of a high level of ultimate steady-state consumption are the inhabitants of the distant future, and so, if the planning board discounts the future very strongly, it will choose a path that favors the near future over the distant future.

When one adds exhaustible resources to the picture, the social rate of time preference can play a similar, but even more critical, role. As a paper by Geoffrey Heal and Partha Dasgupta and one of my own show, it is possible that the optimal path with a positive discount rate should lead to consumption per head going asymptotically to zero, whereas a zero discount rate leads to perpetually rising consumption per head. In other words, even when the technology and the resource base could permit a plateau level of consumption per head, or even a rising standard of living, positive social time preference might in effect lead society to prefer eventual extinction, given the drag exercised by exhaustible resources. Of course, it is part of the point that it is the planning board in the present that plans for future extinction: nobody has asked the about-to-become-defunct last generation whether *it* approved of weighting its satisfactions less than those of its ancestors.

Good theory is usually trying to tell you something, even if it is not the literal truth. In this context, it is not hard to interpret the general tenor of the theoretical indications. We know in general that even well-functioning competitive markets may fail to allocate resources properly over time. The reason, I have suggested, is because, in the nature of the case, the future brings no endowment of its own to whatever markets actually exist. The intergenerational distribution of income or welfare depends on the provision that each generation makes for its successors. The choice of a social discount rate is, in effect, a policy decision about that intergenerational distribution. What happens in the planning parable depends very much—perhaps dramatically—on that choice; and one's evaluation of what happens in the market parable depends very much on whether private choices are made with a discount rate much larger than the one a deliberate policy decision would select. The pure theory of exhaustible resources is trying to tell us that, if exhaustible resources really matter, then the balance between present and future is more delicate than we are accustomed to think; and then the choice of a discount rate can be pretty important and one ought not to be too casual about it.

In my own work on this question, I have sometimes used a rather special criterion that embodies sharp assumptions about intergenerational equity: I have imposed the require-ment that consumption per head be constant through time, so that no generation is favored over any other, and asked for the largest steady consumption per head that can be main-tained forever, given all the constraints including the finiteness of resources. This criterion, like any other, has its pluses and its minuses and I am not committed to it by any means. Like the standard criterion—the discounted sum of one-period utilities—this one will always pick out an *efficient* path, so one at least gets the efficiency conditions out of the analysis. The highest-constant-consumption criterion also has the advantage of highlighting the crucial importance of certain technological assumptions.

It is clear without any technical apparatus that the seriousness of the resource- exhaustion problem must depend in an important way on two aspects of the technology: first, the like-lihood of technical progress, especially natural-resource-saving technical progress, and, second, the ease with which other factors of production, especially labor and reproducible capital, can be substituted for exhaustible resources in production.

My own practice, in working on this problem, has been to treat as the central case (though not the only case) the assumption of zero technological progress. This is not because I think resource-saving inventions are unlikely or that their capacity to save resources is fundamentally limited. Quite the contrary—if the future is anything like the past, there will be prolonged and substantial reductions in natural-resource requirements per unit of real output. It is true, as pessimists say, that it is just an assumption and one cannot be sure; but to assume the contrary is also an assumption, and a much less plausible one. I think there is virtue in analyzing the zero-technical-progress case because it is easy to see how technical progress can relieve and perhaps eliminate the drag on economic welfare exercised by natural-resource scarcity. The more important task for theory is to try to understand what happens or can happen in the opposite case.

As you would expect, the degree of substitutability is also a key factor. If it is very easy to substitute other factors for natural resources, then there is in principle no "problem." The world can, in effect, get along without natural resources, so exhaustion is just an event, not a catastrophe. Nordhaus's notion of a "back- stop technology" is just a dramatic way of putting this case; at some finite cost, production can be freed of dependence on exhaustible resources altogether.

If, on the other hand, real output per unit of resources is effectively bounded—cannot exceed some upper limit of productivity which is in turn not too far from where we are now—then catastrophe is unavoidable. In-between there is a wide range of cases in which the problem is real, interesting, and not foreclosed. Fortunately, what little evidence there is suggests that there is quite a lot of substitutability between exhaustible resources and renewable or reproducible resources, though this is an empirical question that could absorb a lot more work than it has had so far.

Perhaps the most dramatic way to illustrate the importance of substitutability, and its connection with Doomsday, is in terms of the permanent sustainability of a constant level of consumption. In the simplest, most aggregative, model of a resource-using economy one can prove something like the following: if the elasticity of substitution between exhaustible resources and other inputs is unity or bigger, and if the elasticity of output with respect to reproducible capital exceeds the elasticity of output with respect to natural resources, then a constant population can maintain a positive constant level of consumption per head forever. This permanently maintainable standard of living is an increasing, concave, and unbounded function of the initial stock of capital. So the drag of a given resource pool can be overcome *to any extent* if only the initial stock of capital is large enough. On the other hand, if the elasticity of substitution between natural resources and other inputs is less than one, or if the elasticity of output with respect to resources exceeds the elasticity of output with respect to reproducible capital, then the largest constant level of consumption sustainable forever with constant population is—zero. We know much too little about which side of that boundary the world is on—technological progress aside—but at least the few entrails that have been read seem favorable.[3]

Perhaps I should mention that when I say "forever" in this connection, I mean "for a very long time." The mathematical reasoning does deal with infinite histories, but actually life in the solar system will only last for a finite time, though a very long finite time, much longer than this lecture, for instance. That is why I think it takes economics as well as the entropy law to answer our question.

I began this lecture by talking of the conditions for competitive equilibrium in the market for natural resources. Now I have been talking of centralized planning optima. As you would expect, it turns out that under the standard assumptions, the Hotelling rule, the fundamental principle of natural-resource economics, is a necessary condition for efficiency and therefore for social optimality. So there is at least a prayer that a market-guided system might manage fairly well. But more than the Hotelling condition is needed.

I have already mentioned one of the extra requirements for the intertemporal optimality of market allocations: it is that the market discount future profits at the same rate as the society would wish to discount the welfare of future inhabitants of the planet. This condition is often given as an argument for public intervention in resource allocation because as I have also mentioned there are reasons to expect market interest rates to exceed the social rate of time preference, or at least what philosophers like us think it ought to be. If the analysis is right, then the market will tend to consume exhaustible resources too fast, and corrective public intervention should be aimed at slowing down and stretching out the exploitation of the resource pool. There are several ways that could be done, in principle, through conservation subsidies or a system of graduated severance taxes, falling through time.

---

[3]See pp. 60–70 in William D. Nordhaus and James Tobin.

Realistically speaking, however, when we say "public intervention" we mean rough and ready political action. An only moderately cynical observer will see a problem here: it is far from clear that the political process can be relied on to be more future-oriented than your average corporation. The conventional pay-out period for business is of the same order of magnitude as the time to the next election, and transferring a given individual from the industrial to the government bureaucracy does not transform him into a guardian of the far future's interests. I have no ready solution to this problem. At a minimum, it suggests that one ought to be as suspicious of uncritical centralization as of uncritical free-marketeering. Maybe the safest course is to favor specific policies—like graduated severance taxes—rather than blanket institutional solutions.

There is another, more subtle, extra requirement for the optimality of the competitive market solution to the natural-resource problem. Many patterns of exploitation of the exhaustible-resource pool obey Hotelling's fundamental principle myopically, from moment to moment, but are wrong from a very long-run point of view. Such mistaken paths may even stay very near the right path for a long time, but eventually they veer off and become bizarre in one way or another. If a market-guided system is to perform well over the long haul, it must be more than myopic. Someone—it could be the Department of the Interior, or the mining companies, or their major customers, or speculators—must always be taking the long view. They must somehow notice in advance that the resource economy is moving along a path that is bound to end in disequilibrium of some extreme kind. If they do notice it, and take defensive actions, they will help steer the economy from the wrong path toward the right one.[4] Usually the "wrong" path is one that leads to exhaustion at a date either too late or too soon; anyone who perceives this will be motivated to arbitrage between present and future in ways that will push the current price toward the "right" path.[5]

It is interesting that this need for someone to take the long view emerged also when the question at hand was the potential instability of the market for natural resources if it concentrates too heavily on spot or flow decisions, and not enough on future or stock decisions. In that context too, a reasonably accurate view of the long-term prospects turns out to be a useful, maybe indispensable, thing for the resource market to have.

This lecture has been—as Kenneth Burke once said about the novel—words, all words. Nevertheless, it has been a discourse on economic theory, not on current policy. If some of you have been day-dreaming about oil and the coming winter, I assure you that I have been thinking about shadow prices and transversality conditions at infinity. If I turn briefly to policy at the end, it is not with concrete current problems in mind. After all, nothing I have been able to say takes account of the international oil cartel, the political and economic ambitions of the Middle Eastern potentates, the speeds of adjustment to surprises in the supply of oil, or the doings of our own friendly local oligopolists. The only

---

[4]This sort of process has been studied in a different context by Frank Hahn and by Karl Shell and Joseph Stiglitz.
[5]For example, suppose the current price is too low, in the sense that, if it rises according to the current principle, the demand path will be enough to exhaust the resource before the price has risen high enough to choke demand to zero. A clever speculator would see that there will be money to be made just after the date of exhaustion, because anyone with a bit of the resource to sell could make a discrete jump in the price and still find buyers. Such a speculator would wish to buy now and hold for sale then. But that action would tend to raise the current price (and, by the fundamental principle, the whole price path) and reduce demand, so that the life of the resource would be prolonged. The speculation is thus corrective.

remarks I feel entitled to make are about the long-run pursuit of a general policy toward exhaustible resources.

Many discussions of economic policy—macroeconomics aside—boil down to a tension between market allocation and public intervention. Marketeers keep thinking about the doughnut of allocative efficiency and informational economy and *dirigistes* are impressed with the size of the hole containing externalities, imperfections, and distributional issues. So it is with exhaustible resources. One is impressed with what a system of ideal markets, including futures markets, can accomplish in this complicated situation; and one can hardly miss seeing that our actual oligopolistic, politically involved, pollution-producing industry is not exactly what the textbook ordered. I have nothing new to add to all that. The unusual factor that the theory of exhaustible resources brings to the fore is the importance of the long view, and the value of reasonable information about reserves, technology, and demand in the fairly far future.

This being so, one is led to wonder whether public policy can contribute to stability and effi-ciency along those lines. One possibility is the encouragement of organized futures trading in natural resource products. To be useful, futures contracts would have to be much longer-term than is usual in the futures markets that now exist, mostly for agricultural products. I simply do not know enough to have an opinion about the feasibility of large scale futures trading, or about the ultimate contribution that such a reform would make to the stability and efficiency of the market for resource products. But in principle it would seem to be a good idea.

The same considerations suggest that the market for exhaustible resources might be one of the places in the economy where some sort of organized indicative planning could play a constructive role. This is not an endorsement of centralized decision-making, which is likely to have imperfections and externalities of its own. Indeed it might be enough to have the government engaged in a continuous program of information-gathering and dissemination covering trends in technology, reserves and demand. One could at least hope to have professional standards govern such an exercise. I take it that the underlying logic of indicative planning is that some comparison and coordination of the main partici-pants in the market, including the government, could eliminate major errors and resolve much uncertainty. In the case of exhaustible resources, it could have the additional purpose of generating a set of consistent expectations about the distant future. In this effort, the pooling of information and intentions from both sides of the market could be useful, with the effect of inducing behavior that will steer the economy away from ulti-mately inferior paths. It is also likely, as Adam Smith would have warned, that a certain amount of conspiracy against the public interest might occur in such sessions, so perhaps they ought to be recorded and the tapes turned over to Judge Sirica, who will know what to do with them.

REFERENCES

P. Dasgupta and G. Heal, "The Optimal Depletion of Exhaustible Resources," *Rev. Econ. Stud.*, forthcoming, 1974. (This paper was actually published in 1974 in the *Rev. Econ. Stud.*, pp. 3–28—Editor.)

F. H. Hahn, "Equilibrium Dynamics with Heterogeneous Capital Goods," *Quart. J. Econ.*, Nov. 1966, *80*, 633–646.

H. Hotelling, "The Economics of Exhaustible Resources," *J. Polit. Econ.*, April 1931, *39*, 137–175.

W. D. Nordhaus, "The Allocation of Energy Resources," *Brookings Papers on Econ. Activ.*, forthcoming.

——— and J. Tobin, "Is Economic Growth Obsolete?" in National Bureau of Economic Research, *Economic Growth*, 50th Anniversary Colloq. V, New York 1972.

K. Shell and J. E. Stiglitz, "The Allocation of Investment in a Dynamic Economy," *Quart. J. Econ.*, Nov. 1967, *81*.

R. M. Solow, "Intergenerational Equity and Exhaustible Resources," *Rev. Econ. Stud.*, forthcoming, 1974.

J. E. Stiglitz, "Growth with Exhaustible Natural Resources," *Rev. Econ. Stud.*, forthcoming, 1974.

M. Weinstein and R. Zeckhauser, "Use Patterns for Depletable and Recyclable Resources," *Rev. Econ. Stud.*, forthcoming, 1974.

Reflections on Solow's *The Economics of Resources or the Resources of Economics*

PETER BERCK

University of California at Berkeley, Berkley, CA, USA

Robert M. Solow's Richard T. Ely Lecture seems almost as fresh today as when Bob explained these views to us as young graduate students in 1974. Now, as then, everyone has oil on the brain (though Bob has famously said that everything reminds him of sex). There are many similarities between these years and those, and, perhaps, that accounts for the timeliness of his Lecture.

The year of 1974 followed the first OPEC oil-price run-up. In retrospect, the price spike following the Yom Kippur War was just small potatoes. It was not until 1979 that oil prices truly rose and, shortly thereafter, collapsed. Now, they have, again, risen and finally eclipsed, in real terms, the 1979 highs. High prices do wonderfully concentrate the mind on natural resources (see Figure 1).

In 1974, Bob was 'suckered' into reading the Meadows and Meadows (Meadows *et al.*, 1972) grim predictions of running out of resources. The end was near, but, apparently, nowhere near that near. Another of the Meadows and Meadows' predictions was that, if the world did not run out of resources, such as oil and coal, the atmosphere would be a great wreck from burning fossil fuels. That is not a possibility that was considered in the Ely Lecture. In those years the idea of global-scale pollution was not widely discussed. But the grim prognosis, now of global warming and then of running out of everything, was in the air.

The guts of the Ely Lecture concerned the resurrection of Hotelling's (1931) article on natural resources. In the Ely Lecture, Bob reinterpreted Hotelling's 'price goes up at the rate of interest conclusion' as a condition of capital-market equilibrium rather than as firm efficiency. That has turned out to be a better way for empiricists to think about natural resources as it opens the door to using all of the financial-analysis tools. Indeed, many of us have tested the Hotelling hypothesis, which Bob suggested that we do.

Does the Hotelling hypothesis hold up? My work on trees (Berck & Bentley, 1997) gives the example where the hypothesis is most robust. It really is true that trees function like capital assets. For all other resources, up until the present, the empirical evidence was very mixed. Slade (1982) and Smith (1978) are two early examinations of the theory. There are many reasons why it might be difficult to detect an increase in resource rents. For instance, they are small relative to extraction or transport costs. In that case one should be able to

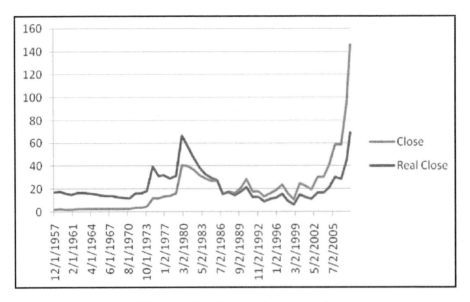

Figure 1. Brent Crude real and nominal.

detect the rents eventually. Perhaps, now with the current high oil prices, 'eventually' has come. Another alternative opened by Bob's view of resources as assets and Hamilton's (1983) observation that oil prices are countercyclical is that the risk premium on oil is negative. Therefore, price should go up at an interest rate that is near zero. This line of thinking makes the most sense of the existing data and was covered by Roberts (2000).

Bob wondered about time paths that had the price rising at the rate of interest but had the transversality condition wrong. All would look good in the short run but, then, either there would be lots of oil left long after mankind had found a better source of energy or, one bright day, there would be none left. It is easy to tell stories in which everything goes right. After all, economists are great at producing models of rational expectations. The 1979 price spike and collapse was exactly what Bob was talking about. Currently, oil price seems to have peaked at $146 per barrel and, as of this writing, has fallen to $124. People can, and do, get prices very wrong.

The Stern Report (Stern, 2006), perhaps today's version of Meadows *et al.* (1972), differs from the rest of the mainstream economic effects of climate-change models in its idea about what the interest rate ought to be. Stern argued for a very low rate of interest. With a low rate of interest, the damages from global warming are quite large in present-value terms. Others have assailed him for this assumption. In the Ely Lecture, Solow considered the same question. What should be the rate of interest used in computing the optimal rate of depletion of a natural resource? Bob went over many of the arguments: Individuals have more risk than collections of individuals and so demand a higher risk premium (they might die and never collect). People today may not care very much about people in the future. The latter argument Bob found to have a technical, but not a practical, solution.

The technical solution is to consider extraction plans that leave all generations with the same consumption. Indeed, there has been much research on such plans and their feasibility depends on, for example, the substitutability of resources for other capital and on the rate of technical progress. Bob was less happy about the possibility of a more conservative plan. Why, he asked, would a politician who needed to be elected every four years pay much more attention to the future than a businessperson who needed to recover his investment in about four years? The orgy of deficit spending that has gone along with the Iraq War surely bears out Bob's intuition that politicians are not focused on the long run.

The idea of a backstop technology, something society uses for energy when it runs out of oil, was named by Nordhaus (1973). Bob considered breeder reactors and uranium to be, if not a backstop, at least a catcher that does not allow many passed balls. In the next 30 years, nuclear power became a pariah in America, first because of cost (Zimmerman, 1982) and then because of accidents. With global warming and high oil prices, nuclear power seems to be coming back into favour along with good old-fashioned windmills and various direct solar-power schemes. What has remained constant over the last three decades is that there is nothing that provides energy at a private cost as cheap as coal, which basically brings us full circle.

In 1974 there was a real belief that conventional resources, such as oil and coal, were finite and were being used too fast. The underlying reasoning was that the economy acted too impatiently. Now, 34 years later, it does appear that fossil fuels were burned at too quick a rate. However, the reason for our regret is that the atmosphere is also a resource of the near-term exhaustible type. Think of it as a large hole into which one pours carbon dioxide. The more one fills it, the worse the damage. Unlike most energy minerals, the atmosphere suffers from an open-access problem. It belongs to everyone and no one. It spans all countries. Agreements on a very large scale are needed to insure its integrity. If it is difficult for one country's politicians to look to the future, imagine the challenge of politicians of all countries having to look to the future and agree with each other! It is no surprise that this resource is overexploited and used up too fast.

When we think of the atmosphere, all of the same things that make resource exhaustion less frightening could also work. There could be technical progress in energy production—carbon sequestration, cheap and safe nuclear energy, cheap solar cells, more efficient cars and appliances, less energy-demanding buildings. There could be substitution on the consumption side—modern dance at home instead of skiing away, walking instead of driving to the gym. And there could be substitution in production—more gears in cars to save gas, a trade of capital for energy and so on. In another of his well-known essays (Solow, 1992), Bob explains all margins by which consumption can be sustained in the face of resource depletion.

Bob said that theorists read the newspapers the same way that the 'supreme court reads the illection results'. He hoped that his audience would endure an hour-long talk out of more than kindness to the speaker. Yet, when we read today's paper, his 1974 talk still seems to be timely and we would still do well to ponder how we can bequeath a bit more of an atmosphere to our children.

References

Berck, P. & Bentley, W. R. (1997) Hotelling's theory, enhancement, and the taking of the Redwood National Park, *American Journal of Agricultural Economics*, 79(2), pp. 287–298.

Hamilton J. (1983) Oil and the macroeconomy since World War II, *Journal of Political Economy*, 91(2), pp. 228–248.

Hotelling, H. (1931) The economics of exhaustible resources, *The Journal of Political Economy*, 39(2), pp. 137–175.

Meadows, D. H., Meadows, D. L, Randers, J. & Behrens, W. W. (1972) *The Limits to Growth* (New York: Universe Books).

Nordhaus, W. D. (1973) The allocation of energy resources, *Brookings Papers on Economic Activity*, 4(3), pp. 529–576.

Roberts, M. J. (2000) *Hotelling Reconsidered: The Implications of Asset Pricing Theory on Natural Resource Price Trends*. PhD thesis, University of California at Berkeley.

Slade, M. E. (1982) Trends in natural resource commodity prices: An analysis of the time domain, *Journal of Environmental Economics and Management*, 9(2), pp. 122–137.

Smith, V. K. (1978) Measuring natural resource scarcity: Theory and practice, *Journal of Environmental Economics and Management*, 5(2), pp. 150–171.

Solow, R. M. (1992) *An Almost Practical Step Toward Sustainability* (Washington, DC: Resources for the Future).

Stern, N. (2006) *The Economics of Climate Change: The Stern Review* (Cambridge: Cambridge University Press).

Zimmerman, M. B. (1982) Learning effects and the commercialization of new energy technologies: The case of nuclear power, *The Bell Journal of Economics*, 13(2), pp. 297–310.

What Does the Empirical Work Inspired by Solow's *The Economics of Resources or the Resources of Economics* Tell Us?

ROBERT HALVORSEN

Department of Economics, University of Washington, Seattle, WA, USA

At the time of Robert Solow's Richard T. Ely Lecture in December 1973, the scarcity of exhaustible natural resources was a highly topical issue in the United States.[1] *Limits to Growth*, with its famous predictions of imminent doom, had been published in the previous year (Meadows *et al.*, 1972), and the issue had been covered at length in the major news media. However, it was Solow's lecture, and its subsequent publication in the May 1974 *American Economic Review*, that was principally responsible for introducing a rigorous analysis of the issue to mainstream economists.

The first half of Solow's lecture is devoted to a positive analysis of the operation of exhaustible natural resource markets. The analysis in this part exposits and extends the analysis in Harold Hotelling's 'The economics of exhaustible resources' (Hotelling, 1931) and concludes that the Hotelling rule, that a resource's net price should increase at the rate of interest, is the fundamental principle of the economics of exhaustible natural resources. The second half of the lecture contains a normative analysis of the rate of exploitation of the world's endowment of exhaustible natural resources and draws in part on his paper in the *Review of Economic Studies* (Solow, 1974a).

The analysis throughout is theoretical, with the only reference to empirical data being an implicit recognition that market prices for most exhaustible resources had not risen over time (Solow, 1974b, p. 3). Solow does, however, make two suggestions for additional econometric research. The first is to investigate whether the non-increasing behaviour of market prices was caused by the rise in the net price being offset by a fall in extraction costs. This can be interpreted more generally as empirically testing the consistency of market data with Hotelling's rule. Second, having noted the importance of the degree of substitutability between exhaustible resources and other inputs for sustainability, Solow suggests that much more empirical work on this topic would be useful.

The 1970's saw a rapid expansion of theoretical work on the issues discussed by Solow, with the number of studies published between 1973 and 1980 far exceeding the number published between 1931 and 1973 (see, for example, Devarajan & Fisher, 1981).

However, there was little empirical work on the topics suggested by Solow. With the exception of a few inconclusive studies of the elasticity of substitution between capital and resources,[2] the focus of most empirical work was on testing the hypothesis of increasing scarcity of natural resources, as pioneered earlier by Barnett and Morse (1963), rather then on testing the consistency of market data with the theory of exhaustible resources. Smith (1980) reviews the results of both the elasticity of substitution and scarcity index studies.

Subsequent attempts to explicitly test the empirical relevance of the theory of exhaustible resources have obtained results that can be best described as mixed to negative. The first published study appears to be Heal and Barrow (1980), whose results indicate that interest rate changes, but not levels, are significantly related to metals prices. Stollery (1983) obtains more positive results with data for Inco, the then largest firm in the international nickel industry. However, Cairns (1986) argues that the results are also consistent with a mark-up pricing model, and Ellis and Halvorsen (2002) find that the market power mark-up for Inco was a much more important determinant of output price than the resource's user costs. Krautkraemer (1998) surveys a number of other econometric studies, most of which do not provide empirical support for the theory.

It should be noted that the econometric models that were estimated were not limited to the restrictive version of Hotelling's model and rule that Solow used for expository purposes. For example, the models generally allowed for cumulative extraction to affect extraction costs, which implies that the growth rate of the net price might be negative. And the theoretical models have in fact become much more general over time, with one stimulus being the attempt to reconcile the theory with the empirical results (see, for example, Gaudet, 2007).

Taken at face value, rejection of the empirical validity of the theory of exhaustible resources would imply that normative conclusions drawn from the theory's predictions of market outcomes have little or no practical relevance. There are three plausible explanations for the negative results. First, the econometric studies are subject to criticism in terms of the quality of the available data and the necessarily large number of maintained hypotheses (see, for example, Berck, 1995).

Second, even if these problems did not exist, econometric studies are necessarily conducted on ex-post data that reflect uncertain events that could not be anticipated by market participants, including shocks to demand, input prices, reserve estimates and technology. Even if the Hotelling rule provides market participants the best available prediction of future resource prices, unanticipated changes in expectations due to the arrival of information will cause the actual time paths of resource prices to deviate from the Hotelling predictions (Swierzbinski & Mendelsohn, 1989).

Third, the net price, or user cost, for the exhaustible resources considered in the econometric studies may be too small to dominate the decisions of the resource-owning firms. For example, the average user cost for nickel has been estimated in three studies applying different methodologies to similar data. Cairns (1981) uses aggregate data for the Canadian nickel industry to estimate the user cost as the present value of future additional costs of production caused by current extraction and concludes that it is unlikely that the user cost exceeds 5% of the price of nickel.[3] Stollery (1983) calculates the user cost for Inco as the difference between econometric estimates of marginal revenue and marginal cost and finds it averages 20% of price. Ellis and Halvorsen (2002) estimate Inco's user cost as the derivative of estimated restricted cost with respect to the quantity of ore extracted and obtain an average estimate of 8% of price.

Using more aggregate data, Weitzman (1999) calculates the user cost for the 14 most significant exhaustible minerals using World Bank estimates of world prices and unit costs. For nine of the 14 minerals, his results imply that user costs are equal to less than 25% of output price.[4] If user costs are small, resource firms' extraction paths may be dominated by other concerns than the growth rate of user cost. This would be consistent with the Hotelling rule's lack of explanatory power, given that even the most generalized Hotelling models abstract from many complexities of production processes.

For normative purposes, the critical question is whether user costs are low because most exhaustible resources are in fact not scarce, or because resources are scarce but markets fail to recognize their scarcity, perhaps because of incomplete futures markets as suggested by Solow (1974b, p. 9). Weitzman (1999) assumes that markets do correctly assess resource values and estimates how much the exhaustibility of resources reduces welfare compared to the counterfactual case in which the resources considered could be supplied forever at their current quantities and extraction costs. He shows that this can be estimated as the ratio of world user costs to NDP and obtains an estimate of only about 1.5%, and even less when technological progress is allowed for.

While these results are striking, they are not necessarily inconsistent with Solow's theoretical analysis. Solow notes that the seriousness of the resource-exhaustion problem depends on the 'likelihood of technical progress' and 'the ease with which other factors of production . . . can be substituted for exhaustible resources in production' (Solow, 1974b, p. 10). He expresses some optimism with respect to both, and suggests more empirical work on substitutability would be useful.[5]

In conclusion, the results of the empirical work inspired by Solow's classic article have to be considered quite disappointing. Econometric tests of the implications of the theory of exhaustible resources have not in general been supportive, but at the same time do not provide convincing evidence against the theory. And reliable estimates of the critical parameters of the theoretical models, including future rates of technological progress and elasticities of substitution between resources and other inputs, do not appear to be obtainable.

One line of empirical research that remains promising is the investigation of whether the user costs that enter actual economic decisions by exhaustible resource firms are as small as suggested by some of the studies reviewed here. Of course, the interpretation of such a finding may ultimately depend on whether one is an optimist or a pessimist.

Notes

1. In recognition that renewable as well as nonrenewable natural resources are subject to exhaustion, the phrase 'exhaustible natural resources' is now generally replaced by 'nonrenewable natural resources'. I have retained the earlier terminology for consistency with Solow.

2. One difficulty in econometrically estimating elasticities of substitution of resources with other inputs is the lack of data on the net prices of the resources. Halvorsen and Smith (1986) show how a restricted cost function approach can resolve this issue and obtain some promising results for the Canadian mining industry. However, estimates based on historic data may not be reliable guides to what the elasticities will be in the future, when there will presumably be a substantially larger capital-resource ratio.

3. As Levhari and Liviatan (1977) discuss, when the cost of extraction is a function of cumulative extraction, the user cost of an exhaustible resource is equal to the Hotelling rent (the present value of the marginal contribution to profit of the last unit extracted at the terminal point) plus the present value of all future additional costs of production caused by the marginal unit extracted currently. For a resource with stationary demand and production costs that are an increasing function of cumulative extraction, it is possible that the stock of the resource will not be exhausted at the terminal point. In this case, the Hotelling rent would be equal to zero, but

the resource would still have a positive user cost because of the second component, which can be thought of as a Ricardian stock rent.

4. Weitzman's estimate for nickel, 16.5%, is consistent with the studies using less aggregate data.

5. In a later paper Solow (1978) draws on the limited empirical data then available to conclude, '. . . past economic growth would not have gained very much from cheaper or more abundant access to nonrenewable resources, nor lost very much from the opposite. Political events aside, the evidence is that the future will be rather like the past. I do not regard this as a very strong conclusion; but it is safe to say that the opposite conclusion has considerably less evidence or none at all going for it' (p. 11).

References

Barnett, H. J. & Morse, C. (1963) *Scarcity and Growth: The Economics of Mineral Extraction* (Baltimore: Johns Hopkins).

Berck, P. (1995) Economic consequences of the Hotelling principle, in: David Bromley (Ed) *Handbook of Environmental Economics*, pp. 202–221. Oxford: Blackwell.

Cairns, R. D. (1981) An application of depletion theory to a base metal: Canadian nickel, *Canadian Journal of Economics*, 14(4), pp. 635–648.

Cairns, R. D. (1986) More on depletion in the nickel industry, *Journal of Environmental Economics and Management*, 13, pp. 93–98.

Devarajan, S. & Fisher, A. C. (1981) Hotelling's 'Economics of Exhaustible Resources': fifty years later, *Journal of Economic Literature*, 19(1), pp. 65–73.

Ellis, G. M. & Halvorsen, R. (2002) Estimation of market power in a nonrenewable resource industry, *Journal of Political Economy*, 110(4), pp. 883–899.

Gaudet, G. (2007) Natural resource economics under the rule of Hotelling, *Canadian Journal of Economics*, 40(4), pp. 1033–1059.

Halvorsen, R. & Smith, T. R. (1986) Substitution possibilities for unpriced natural resources: restricted cost functions for the Canadian metal mining industry, *Review of Economics and Statistics*, 68(3), pp. 398–405.

Heal, G. & Barrow, M. (1980) The relationship between interest rates and metal price movements, *Review of Economic Studies*, 47, pp. 161–181.

Hotelling, H. (1931) The economics of exhaustible resources, *Journal of Political Economy*, 39(2), pp. 137–175.

Krautkraemer, J. A. (1998) Nonrenewable resource scarcity, *Journal of Economic Literature*, 36, pp. 2065–2107.

Levhari, D. & Livatan, N. (1977) Notes on Hotelling's economics of exhaustible resources, *Canadian Journal of Economics*, 10(2), pp. 177–192.

Meadows, D. H., Meadows, D. L., Randers, J. & Behrens, W. W. (1972) *The Limits to Growth: A Report for the Club of Rome's Project on the Predicament of Mankind* (New York: Universe Books).

Smith, V. K. (1980) The evaluation of natural resource adequacy: elusive quest or frontier of economic analysis?, *Land Economics*, 56(3), pp. 257–298.

Solow, R. M. (1974a) Intergenerational equity and exhaustible resources, *Review of Economic Studies, Symposium on the Economics of Exhaustible Resources*, pp. 29–45.

Solow, R. M. (1974b) The economics of resources or the resources of economics, *American Economic Review*, 64(2), pp. 1–14.

Solow, R. M. (1978) Resources and economic growth, *American Economist*, 22(2), pp. 5–11.

Stollery, K. R. (1983) Mineral depletion with cost as the extraction limit: a model applied to the behavior of prices in the nickel industry, *Journal of Environmental Economics and Management*, 10, pp. 151–165.

Swierzbinski, J. & Mendelsohn, R. (1989) Information and exhaustible resources: a Bayesian analysis, *Journal of Environmental Economics and Management*, 16, pp. 193–208.

Weitzman, M. L. (1999) Pricing the limits to growth from minerals depletion, *The Quarterly Journal of Economics*, 114(2), pp. 691–706.

What Would Solow Say?

JOHN M. HARTWICK

Queen's University, Kingston, Ontario, Canada

Introduction

Robert M. Solow (RMS) indicated that his Ely Lecture to the American Economics Association in December, 'The Economics of Resources or the Resources of Economics' (EROTRE), was a summary of what 'economic theory has to say about the problems connected with exhaustible resources'. Motivating his address was his dissatisfaction with the then-popular doomsday study *Limits to Growth*.

Solow's response, his EROTRE, though devoid of equations, is first of all about the centrality of dynamic efficiency (Hotelling's Rule) and capital theory more generally to the study of exhaustible resources;[1] secondly, about the substitutability of produced capital for natural capital; and finally, about discounting. On the topic of substitutability, there is the much cited remark, 'If it is very easy to substitute other factors for natural resources, then there is, in principle, no 'problem'. The world can, in effect, get along without natural resources' (p. 11 of EROTRE).

In his 'Is the end of the world at hand?' (Challenge, March 1973), he gave evidence for substitutability by providing data showing low rates of growth in the consumption of extracted resources over a few decades. His classic paper, 'Intergenerational Equity and Exhaustible Resources' (1974) showed mathematically that the substitution of produced capital for a dwindling stock of natural capital—such as oil—constitutes a central mechanism for obtaining 'the permanent sustainability of a constant level of consumption' (EROTRE). Note his unforced use of the term 'sustainability', well before Mrs. Brundtland made it famous in her report to the United Nations, *Our Common Future* (1987).

It is pretty clear that the second half of Solow's EROTRE is a non-technical walk-through of Solow (1974). I wrestled with this latter paper for some time after RMS kindly turned over his galleys to me when I was visiting MIT in 1973–74 as a young post-doc. Having just audited his new graduate course in resource economics, I was well-prepared and motivated. An exchange of letters between him and me when I was back at Queen's brought forth the 'invest exhaustible resource rents' rule that was implicit in Solow (1974). With characteristic generosity, he swatted up a brief, quite general paper on investing exhaustible resource rents and titled it 'Hartwick's Rule'.

It seems reasonable to ask here what RMS might change in EROTRE today if he were returning to the question of exhaustible resource scarcity. I doubt he would change much. He might abbreviate his discussion of Hotelling, since the importance of capital theory to the study of natural resource use is now commonly understood. He might expand a bit on his thinking about discounting since there has been much work on this topic since 1973. He would likely reflect on the global warming externality associated with hydrocarbon extraction and use, and he might consider the implications to Solow (1974) of relaxing his assumption of a constant population. There have, in fact, been many papers in many different journals that descend from Solow (1974), some of which address population growth and global warming.

Population Increase

Let us take up population increase first. Population was constant (i.e. population growth was zero) in the basic Solow model,[2] and the accumulation of produced capital that made sustainability possible was being funded by rents earned from exhaustible resource extraction (Hartwick's Rule). Dasgupta and Heal (1979, ch. 10) spelled out that one could contemplate a Solow future with aggregate consumption actually rising, if society were to invest more than current exhaustible resource rents.[3] Mitra apparently realized that this extra consumption achievable at each date could go to support a population increment, and in Mitra (1983) he showed that the Solow model could accommodate an ever-increasing population with constant per capita consumption, under certain conditions.

The Mitra model employed the usual Cobb–Douglas specification of the aggregate production function. The population both worked and consumed. The type of population growth found to be consistent with sustainability of consumption is limited, as you might expect. The admissible form of population growth is quasi-arithmetic,[4] something considerably less than exponential but nevertheless better than asymptotic to a bound. Mitra's remarkable line of analysis was ignored by everyone, it seems, but was re-opened some two decades later by Asheim et al. (2007) who took up the question of how much a society needed to save in excess of resource rents in order to achieve constant consumption for any particular 'level' of quasi-arithmetic population increase. The required 'extra' savings turns out to take a simple form: 'extra' savings should be a specific constant fraction of current aggregate output, the fraction being a function of the 'level' of quasi-arithmetic population increase.

The bottom line, then, is that the basic Solow model can accommodate sustainable per capita consumption under the condition of finite oil supplies, even with population ever increasing. The trick is to have population increase not too rapidly and to have aggregate savings be in excess of exhaustible resource rents. Sustainable per capital consumption still turns on the assumption of a Cobb–Douglas production function. One requires 'lots of' substitutability among inputs.[5]

What are we to make of sustainable per capita consumption with exhaustible resources and an ever-increasing population? It would be hard to draw out immediate policy implications of this work. RMS always kept one eye cocked on relevance, broadly defined. His original model showed that the dependence of current GDP on exhaustible resources need not spell future collapse or long-term economic impairment. Sufficient substitutability of produced capital, combined with the discipline to save resource rents, can avert these woes. This 'result' was surprising to many economists and there has been a steady stream of debunkers of 'Solow sustainability'.[6] Solow sustainability with population growth strikes one as even more surprising but it would be cavalier to draw out policy guidelines from this abstract reconnaissance work.

Cheviakov and Hartwick (2007) probed the Asheim et al., (2007) version of the Solow model to see what effect depreciation of capital would have. Given so-called radioactive decay of capital, economic collapse turns out to be inevitable. Cheviakov and Hartwick then included exogenous technical change to offset the decay in produced capital and found that sufficient technical change can indeed restore sustainability. (This analysis is related to but different from that in Stiglitz (1974).)

A technical digression: The basic Solow model, which solves maximization of the stream of future consumption for a society, results in produced capital (K) increasing linearly with time while investment each period remains constant. In Asheim et al. (2007), aggregate saving and investment are linear in current output, but produced capital increases quasi-arithmetically. The Cobb–Douglas assumption on technology keeps the solution from getting too technically daunting.[7] The Cheviakov–Hartwick extension solves by less direct arguments and involves a messier produced capital growth function.[8] Stollery (1998) was able to exploit the linear-in-time form of growth in produced capital in his extension of the basic Solow model to incorporate global warming arising from oil extraction. Let us now turn to some analysis of global warming, with the basic Solow model at its core.

Global Warming

Stollery[9] kept population constant in his version of the Solow model, but made temperature rise with cumulative oil extraction. He attached the temperature variable to the aggregate production function and to consumption in the utility function, such that current temperature impacted both production and utility negatively.

Stollery derived a Pigouvian tax on oil extraction such that Hotelling's Rule, in which the new tax shows up, plus the usual Hartwick's Rule are sufficient for constant utility (so-called maximin utility). Stollery then specialized his model to a Cobb–Douglas production function, an exponential temperature-increase function, and a non-temperature-sensitive utility function. For this specification he obtained a closed form solution, one where produced capital grows linearly over time. Since the initial oil stock is finite, the limiting temperature in the model is also finite. The model is remarkably well-behaved and seems a natural extension of Solow (1974).

Intrigued with Stollery's progress, d'Autume et al. (2008) took on extending his work to the case of a non-zero effect of temperature on utility.[10] Solutions for maximin utility were obtained for the case of a Cobb–Douglas utility function. Produced capital tends to increase linearly in time, now in the limit. Since temperature can only rise, aggregate consumption must also rise to prevent utility from deteriorating. And with temperature approaching a bound, consumption also tends to a bound in the limit.

Of interest in the d'Autume et al. analysis is the impact of a change in the strength of the temperature effect on utility. One observes that the consumption profile twists, with an increase in the negative effect of temperature on utility: early consumption declines and later consumption tends to a higher bound. An observer faced with this consumption profile would infer something about the strength of discounting, and a larger impact of temperature on utility would presumably be translated into the inference of 'stronger discounting'. But of course there is not explicit discounting of utility in the model. Instead, utility is unchanging *a priori* (a maximin model).

This extended Stollery model raises the issue of when to get serious about global warming. A hands-off person might say that since all the oil will be extracted in the end anyway, and the full impact of carbon dioxide accumulation will ultimately be felt, why bother taxing oil extraction on our way to the inevitable. A hand-on person might say we should regulate oil extraction and burning so as to have this inevitable extraction cause the least harm possible. Such a person is selecting the best consumption profile among many and, given the associated Pigouvian tax, the maximum level of utility. These two prescriptions deserve serious reflection. There is no reason to doubt that RMS would endorse so-called carbon taxes if they could capture the relevant externality properly. In EROTRE he contemplated 'conservation subsidies or a system of graduated severance taxes' to deal with a possible wedge between the private rate of discount and the social rate. Such interventions have been advocated by Nicholas Stern to address the risk of a possible huge future cost from continued global warming.

Other Spin-Offs

As we have already seen, the basic Solow model has served as the foundation for many variations on the general equilibrium resource exhaustion problem. Geir Asheim (1986) explored how Solow (1974) could be adapted to deal with international trade, say between a country having an oil stock and the other country an importer without oil. Hartwick (1995) returned to this work and came up with a model of a small, open oil-exporting nation (a 'Kuwait model') which has been extended by Vincent *et al.* (1997), Okumura and Cai (2007), Hamilton and Hartwick (2008), and others.

In an effort to better understand the so-called resource curse, Van der Ploeg (2008) has developed a common property model with many oil extractors in a constant consumption setting and observes that each extractor must invest more than her current exhaustible resource rents in order to remain on a constant consumption trajectory. Leonard and Long (1992), Cairns and Long (2007), and d'Autume and Schubert (2008) have researched new ways to solve for maximin programs as optimality problems instead of directly as a system of differential equations. Sato and Kim (2002), and Martinet and Rotillon (2007) have brought 'conservation law' theory to the study of maximin problems of the Solow type. And Pearce and Atkinson (1993) explored the measurement of an economy's sustainability with an expanded notion of investing resource rents—that of 'genuine savings'. This preliminary work has been taken up in more detail and with more sophistication over a number of years by Kirk Hamilton at the World Bank.

I am aware of very high quality journal articles deriving from Solow (1974) that I have neglected to mention due to the word limit governing this paper: I apologize.

Physicists are fond of remarking that Faraday, who was working before Nobel Prizes existed, made contributions that easily would have qualified him for six prizes in physics and chemistry combined. Robert M. Solow would seem a worthy candidate for a second Nobel for his seminal contributions to the development of the economics of natural resources.

Notes

1. The Solow–Wan (1975) article on extraction costs also is discussed in the first half of EROTRE.
2. Also, extraction of oil was governed by dynamic efficiency (Hotelling's Rule), and investment in produced capital was governed by the requirement to invest resource rents (Hartwick's Rule).
3. Another early contribution Dixit *et al.* (1980) took up the question of whether a constant consumption program implied Hartwick's Rule, the converse of Solow's approach. The answer is 'yes', given a regularity condition. The issue was re-investigated by Withagen and Asheim (1998). Hamilton and Hartwick (2005) observed that the Dixit, Hammond, Hoel regularity condition also characterizes peak consumption (a locally constant consumption) in the Dasgupta–Heal (1974) model. See also Hamilton and Withagen (2007).
4. Quasi-arithmetic is defined here as $N = \Gamma^* [A + Bt]^{\xi}$, for t time and the parameters positive.
5. Tapan Mitra in fact investigated the role of substitutability in the production function in the Solow model in a number of papers over a number of years, the most recent being one with David Cass (1991). Whatever production function 'works' must have properties very similar to the Cobb–Douglas function.
6. Recall Problem 6, Chapter 7 of George Stigler's *Theory of Price* which pointed out that sufficient substitutability between land and labour in the production function for wheat would allow the world's wheat to be 'grown in a flower pot, if the pot were small enough'.
7. The marginal product of produced capital declines in $1/[A + Bt]$, the parameters positive. And this property makes solving fairly direct.
8. Alexei Cheviakov is a practicing math professor–researcher, currently appointed at the University of Saskatchewan.
9. Hamilton and Ulph (1995) independently came up with a somewhat similar Solow model with global warming.
10. The 'technology' for this analysis had been developed by d'Autume and Schubert (forthcoming) in their analysis of the Solow problem with the exhaustible resource stock in the utility function, operating as some sort of amenity value (Krautkramer (1985)) Figuieres and Tidball (2006) have an instructive paper on the Krautkramer problem.

References

Asheim, G. B. (1986) Hartwick's rule in open economies, *Canadian Journal of Economics*, 19, pp. 395–402.

Asheim, G. B., Buchholtz, W., Hartwick, J. M., Mitra, T. & Cees W. (2007), Constant saving rates and quasi-arithmetic population growth under exhaustible resource constraints, *Journal of Environmental Economics and Management*, 53(2), pp. 213–239.

Cairns, R. & Long, N. Van (2006) Maximin: A direct approach to sustainability, *Environment and Development Economics*, 11(3), pp. 275–300.

Cass, D. & Mitra, T. (1991) Indefinitely sustained consumption despite exhaustible natural resources, *Economic Theory*, 1991, 1(2), pp. 119–146.

Cheviakov, A. F. & Hartwick, J. M. (2007) Constant consumption with exhaustible resources: New scenarios, typescript, presented at the Canadian Economics Association meetings, Halifax, Nova Scotia, May 2007.

Dasgupta, P. & Heal, G. M. (1974) The optimal depletion of exhaustible resources, *Review of Economic Studies*, Symposium, pp. 3–28.

Dasgupta, P. & Heal, G. M. (1979) *Economic Theory and Exhaustible Resources* (New York: Cambridge University Press).

D'Autume, A., Hartwick, J. M. & Schubert, K. (2008) On Stollery's global warming model, typescript.

D'Autume, A. & Schubert K. (forthcoming) Hartwick's rule and maximin paths when the exhaustible resource has an amenity value, *Journal of Environmental Economics and Management*.

Dixit, A. K., Hammond, P. & Hoel, M. (1980) On Hartwick's rule for regular maximin paths of capital accumulation and resource depletion, *Review of Economic Studies*, 47, 3, pp. 551–556.

Figuieres, C. & Tidball, M. (2006) *Sustainable Exploitation of a Natural Resource: a Satisfying Use of Chichinilsky's Criterion* UMR LAMETA, Research Paper, Montpellier, France.

Krautkramer, J. A. (1985) Optimal growth, resource amenities and the preservation of natural environments, *Review of Economic Studies*, 52, pp. 153–170.

Hamilton, K. & Hartwick, J. (2005) Investing exhaustible resource rents and the path of consumption, *Canadian Journal of Economics*, 38, 2, pp. 615–621.

Hamilton, K. & Hartwick, J. (2008) Oil stock discovery and Dutch disease, typescript.

Hamilton, K. & Ulph, D. (1995) The Hartwick rule in a greenhouse world, unpublished manuscript, University College, London.

Hamilton, K. & Withagen, C. (2007) Savings growth and the path of utility, *Canadian Journal of Economics*, 40(2), pp. 703–713.

Hartwick, J. M. (1977) Intergenerational equity and the investing of rents from exhaustible resources, *American Economic Review*, 66, pp. 253–256.

Hartwick, J. M. (1995) Constant consumption paths in open economies with exhaustible resources, *Review of International Economics*, 3(3), pp. 275–283.

Leonard, D. & Long, N. V. (1992) *Optimal Control Theory and Static Optimization in Economics* (Cambridge: Cambridge University Press).

Martinet, V. & Rotillon, G. (2007) Invariance in growth theory and sustainable development, *Journal of Economic Dynamics and Control*, 31(8), pp. 2827–2846.

Mitra, T. (1983) Limits on population growth under exhaustible resource constraints, *International Economic Review*, 24, pp. 155–168.

Okumura, R. & Cai, D. (2007) Sustainable constant consumption in a semi-open economy with exhaustible resources, *Japanese Economic Review*, 58(2), pp. 226–237.

Pearce, D. W. & Atkinson, G. D. (1993) Capital theory and the measurement of sustainable development: an indicator of 'weak' sustainability, *Ecological Economics*, 8(2), pp. 103–108.

Sato, R. & Kim, Y. (2002) Hartwick's rule and economic conservation laws, *Journal of Economic Dynamics and Control*, 26(3), pp. 437–449.

Solow, R. M. (1974) Intergenerational equity and exhaustible resources, *Review of Economic Studies*, Symposium, pp. 29–46.

Solow, R. M. & Wan, F. Y. (1975) Extraction costs in the theory of exhaustible resources, *Bell Journal of Economics*, 7(2), pp. 359–370.

Stiglitz, J. E. (1974) Growth with exhaustible natural resources: Efficient and optimal growth paths, *Review of Economic Studies*, Symposium, pp. 123–137.

Stollery, K. R. (1998) Constant utility paths and irreversible global warming, *Canadian Journal of Economics*, 31(3), pp. 730–742.

Van der Ploeg, F. (2008) Genuine saving and the Voracity Effect, typescript.

Vincent, J. R., Panayotou, T. & Hartwick, J. M. (1997) Resource depletion and sustainability in small open economies, *Journal of Environmental Economics and Management*, 33, pp. 274–286.

Withagen, C. & Asheim, G. B. (1998) Characterizing sustainability: The converse of Hartwick's rule, *Journal of Economic Dynamics and Control*, 23(1), pp. 159–165.

Reflections on Solow's 1974 Richard T. Ely Address

ALAN RANDALL

Ohio State University, Columbus, Ohio USA

Robert M. Solow began his Richard T. Ely lecture by noting that the ideal topic for a featured address must be contemporary but perennial. His topic, the economics of exhaustible resources, was front-page news when it engaged the great Harold Hotelling in the 1930s, highly topical again in the 1970s, and yet again in 2008. But Solow's staying power is not limited to choice of topic—after 35 years, the reader cannot help but admire the extent to which Solow achieved a contemporary but perennial analysis.

Solow addressed five major aspects of the exhaustible resources problem, and I will start by conveying a little of the flavour of what he had to say about each, viewed from today's perspective.

The Hotelling Rule

Hotelling (1931) derived his rule as a flow condition: to induce some extraction in each period, rents must grow at the rate of interest. Viewed that way, the Hotelling rule threatens instability in markets for exhaustible resources—why wouldn't an owner of reserves be inclined to withhold minerals from the market when prices were rising, thereby exacerbating the scarcity that drives up prices? Solow viewed the rule as also and perhaps primarily a stock condition, which opens the door to the stabilizing influence of asset market adjustments to changing scarcity conditions. Solow got it right—rather than declaring that due to the beneficence of asset markets all is well in the markets for minerals, he recognized both stabilizing and destabilizing influences[1]—and I was surprised to rediscover just how much my treatment of this topic in dozens of college classes and in my textbook (1987, p. 294) owes to Solow's 1974 exposition.

The Social Rate of Discount

Solow's discussion of discounting touched on the major issues of the day—the distinction between private and social discount rates, the centrality of time preference, the self-evident myopia reflected in private discount rates and the difficulty of inferring time preference from observations of financial markets that are influenced also by risk, insecurity of tenure, taxes and inflationary expectations. The contemporary discussion is perhaps less concerned with myopic time preferences, and rather more concerned with inter-temporal incentives to restrain borrowing and consumption, and encourage saving and investment. Given Solow's extensive immersion in growth theory, his relative inattention in the Ely address to the productivity of capital as a driver of the interest rate seems surprising.

It is clear that Solow viewed the choice of social discount rate as a policy decision. Perhaps so, in a tautological kind of way, but (as I argue below) a government that respects the welfare claims of both present and future generations in fact enjoys few degrees of freedom in the search for the optimal discount rate policy.

Substitutability of Capital for Natural Resources

Solow identifies substitutability of capital, K, for natural resources, D, as the primary source of optimism that welfare might be sustainable in an economy dependent on exhaustible resources. He foreshadowed (1974, p. 11) a result demonstrated later by Dasgupta and Heal (1979): if the elasticity of substitution between capital and natural resources is less than 1, production and consumption must fall eventually, implying that the economy is not sustainable. As it happens, we still know very little, empirically, about the elasticity of D-K substitution and whether it has been changing over time (Markandya & Pedroso, 2005; Andre & Cerda, 2005).

Technological Progress as a Factor Mitigating Scarcity of Exhaustible Resources

The prominent role Solow accorded to technological progress reflects his extensive and pioneering work in growth theory, and it serves as a lightning rod for critics who worry that economists are just too optimistic about sustainability.

The Role of Markets Versus Planning

Solow identified the potential for market failure, broadly defined, in several contexts. He was quite explicit regarding the scope for instability in markets for exhaustible resources and the divergence between market interest rates and the social rate of discount, but market failure also underpins at least implicitly his worries about whether market forces will optimize technological progress and direct it toward enhancing D-K substitutability. The Solow of 1974 was on balance more willing to take planning seriously than many of today's commentators. Nevertheless, he was clearly under no illusion that government is in practice dedicated single-mindedly to the public good and efficient in attaining it.

Discounting and Sustainability—Some Comments on Developments Since 1974

I conclude with a rather selective review of some developments since 1974 regarding discounting and sustainability. Solow took myopia for granted—he took it as obvious that markets would short-change the future, and that the culprit was human frailty in the form of impatience for gratification. In the intervening 35 years, economists have revisited the myopia issue from at least two perspectives. First, there is a stream of commentary on discounting and welfare for the very long run that evinces more concern with the productivity of capital and less concern with myopic time preferences than Solow did in 1974. Second, those who worry about human impatience have developed much more elaborate accounts of myopia including, but not limited to hyperbolic discounting. I will review these two streams of thought, and finish with some comments on implications for sustainability.

It is not surprising that academic economists, being former students in a student-dominated environment, find it easy to assume that humans are programmed strongly for myopia. Yet, many economists today, myself among them, argue that utility discounting should play no part in determining the proper discount rate for the long run.

The evidence for myopia is questionable. Consider lifecycle earning, borrowing, consumption, saving and investment behaviour in well-off societies. The young do indeed borrow, and they may be net borrowers for many years, for good reasons—it may take a long while to acquire an education, establish a household and subsidize the college education of one's children. But we find net saving not only in middle age but also among the better-off seniors. In short, the lifecycle behaviour of people supports the hypothesis of intertemporal consumption-smoothing, but not of systematic myopia. Furthermore, positive time preference at the margin is entirely consistent with *the absence of* myopia: given a preference for consumption smoothing, r must be positive to induce an individual to deviate from a flat consumption path by saving. Nothing about a preference for consumption-smoothing implies indifference to the timing of consumption.

Myopia is not necessary for explaining persistent positive interest rates in a productive economy. Where capital is productive and the young need to borrow it in order to command resources to complement their labour (such a world sounds familiar, I think), positive discount rates emerge and are sustained even in the absence of myopia (Farmer & Randall, 1997). If the productivity of capital drives r, it follows that $r = MEC$, the marginal efficiency of capital, for marginal investments. This suggests a social discount rate upper-bounded by the marginal efficiency of capital and converging on the growth rate of aggregate output or welfare, g, as projects become very large and/or time horizons become very long (Dasgupta & Heal, 1979).

At this point, I pause to consider skeptically some of the standard arguments for the systematic application of 'low' discount rates when evaluating public policies with long-run consequences. First, a literature has grown around the idea of hyperbolic discounting (Cropper & Laibson, 1999). Psychologists and economists using surveys and experiments have found that individuals tend to discount hyperbolically, applying very high discount rates to (say) the next meal, but much lower discount rates to housing, consumer durables and retirement planning.[2] I confess to finding the hyperbolic discounting hypothesis not very interesting—the human body has time-sensitive needs for food, shelter, warmth and the like, and servicing those needs acquires a genuine urgency in which human motivations are quite different from those that mediate the choice in well-off societies between discretionary consumption and saving for the future. The implications of the hyperbolic discounting hypothesis for sustainability policy are unclear—if other considerations (above) suggest discounting long-run prospects at the rate of g, would hyperbolic discounting suggest an even lower rate?

Weitzman (2001) offers another argument for hyperbolic discounting. It makes sense (he writes) to reject exponential compounding in favour of limiting the number of compounding operations, which would tend to generate a hyperbolic path. While one can question the general idea of earning interest on interest *ad infinitum*, Weitzman's 'gamma discounting' seems based on *ad hoc* theorizing and capable only of *ad hoc* implementation.

On a different tack, Weitzman (1998) argued that uncertainty about future discount rates implies that the lowest possible rate should be used in prescriptive policy analysis, because present values calculated at lower rates trump other present values. Pindyck (2007) illustrates this reasoning with an accessible numerical example: the expected present value of $100 promised 100 years from now, with a discount rate of 10% or 0 equally likely, is about $50, yet a discount rate of about 0.7% (not 5%) must be applied to yield a present value of $50.

Perhaps so, but something about the reasoning of Weitzman and Pindyck seems odd. After all, the task is not to choose the future discount rate; it is to choose the optimal portfolio to carry forward, given that the discount rate is *ex ante* uncertain. If we are uncertain about r, then we will be right or wrong *ex post* in the r we choose *ex ante*. If we are wrong, high or low, we will carry forward a sub-optimal portfolio and experience a concomitant loss of future welfare, and the welfare cost will be increasing in the size of our error. It cannot be true, by this logic, that when in doubt the lowest possible discount rate is the best.

Instead of Pindyck's calculation, one could calculate the optimal investment today to yield an expected value of $100 in 100 years' time. If we invested $50 today with r of 10% or 0 equally likely, the expected value 100 years from now would be $344,765 rather than $100. The optimal solution to the problem I have posed requires an interest rate of about 9.2% and a correspondingly lower initial investment. Viewing the problem as one of delivering future welfare under an uncertain r regime, the right r approaches the higher of the possible rates. This is enough to question the Weitzman–Pindyck argument—if arguments can be found for approaching both the lowest and the highest possible rates, perhaps a more complete analysis will converge on the *ex ante* expected value of r.

Whatever the prospects of future generations, a policy of suppressing the discount rate would only reduce those prospects (Farmer & Randall, 1997). K matters: we could fail the future in not one but two ways—failing to save enough D and failing to save enough K. However, it seems the D problem we face is not about exhausting a homogeneous cake (the real-world analogy would be running out of everything simultaneously), but about exhausting some particular and crucial natural resource(s), D_i. These considerations suggest that we should set $r = MEC$, which approaches g in the long run, to take care of K and implement some particular D_i policy(ies) to take care of D. Rather than interest rate suppression, safe minimum standards of conservation, for example, may be more appropriate instruments for addressing sustainability problems.

The appropriate rate of discount is that which reflects the productivity of the society—and this makes perfect sense: the whole purpose of discounting is to guard against allocating capital to less productive uses. People who are worried about sustainability issues may well have a point. But repressing the discount rate is not just a crude instrument, it is a counterproductive instrument, to promote sustainability.

Notes

1. Solow looked to futures markets for additional stabilizing influence, and lamented the relatively underdeveloped state of futures markets in extractive resources. However, he may have understated the extent of futures markets in extractive resources operating in 1974. Futures contracts for copper and tin have been traded on the London Metal Exchange since 1881 and, by the outbreak of World War I, zinc and lead were also listed (Wolff, 1991).
2. The behavioural evidence for decreasing impatience as the time-delay lengthens seems strong, but Read (2001) has questioned the hyperbolic discounting explanation. He presents experimental evidence that is consistent not with hyperbolic discounting but with subadditive discounting.

References

Andre, F. J. & Cerda, E. (2005) On natural resource substitution, *Resources Policy*, 30(4), pp. 233–246.

Cropper, M. & Laibson, D. (1999) The implications of hyperbolic discounting for project evaluation, in: P. R. Portney & J. P. Weyant (Eds) *Discounting and Intergenerational Equity*, pp. 163–172 (Washington, DC: Resources for the Future, Inc).

Dasgupta, P. S. & Heal, G. M. (1979) *Economic Theory and Exhaustible Resources* (Cambridge: Cambridge University Press).

Farmer, M. & Randall, A. (1997) Policies for sustainability: lessons from an overlapping generations model, *Land Economics*, 73, pp. 608–622.

Hotelling, H. (1931) The economics of exhaustible resources, *Journal of Political Economy*, 39, pp. 137–175.

Markandya, A. & Pedroso, S. (2005) How substitutable is natural capital? World Bank Policy Research Working Paper 3803.

Pindyck, R. S. (2007) Uncertainty in environmental economics, *Review of Environmental Economics and Policy*, 1(1), pp. 45–65.

Randall, A. (1987) *Resource Economics: An Economic Approach to Natural Resource and Environmental Policy*, 2nd ed. (New York: John Wiley and Sons).

Read, D. (2001) Is time-discounting hyperbolic or subadditive?, *Journal of Risk and Uncertainty*, 23, pp. 5–32.

Solow, R. M. (1974) The economics of resources or the resources of economics, *American Economic Review Papers and Proceedings*, 64, pp. 1–14.

Weitzman, M. L. (1998) Why the far-distant future should be discounted at the lowest possible rate, *Journal of Environmental Economics and Management*, 36, pp. 201–208.

Weitzman, M. L. (2001) Gamma discounting, *American Economic Review*, 91, pp. 260–271.

Wolff, R. & Co., Ltd. (1991) *Wolff's Guide to the London Metal Exchange* (New York: Metal Bulletin Books).

The Economics of Resources and the Economics of Climate*

R. DAVID SIMPSON

National Center for Environmental Economics, United States Environmental Protection Agency, Washington DC, USA

It is a very humbling experience to write a paper on one of Robert Solow's many contributions. I doubt that I would have the acumen even to *identify* among today's academic fads a 'topic that is absolutely contemporary, but somehow perennial', as Professor Solow did for the subject of his Richard T. Ely lecture in 1974 (p. 1). I would certainly have no expectation of being as spectacularly right in that topic choice as he is now, 35 years later. I would not have the command of the current literature he did, nor could I make any claim to having myself made such important contributions to its advancement. Most importantly, I could never hope to match the easy, engaging, always light, but nevertheless deeply illuminating, prose style of which Professor Solow is, almost uniquely among our profession, such a master. As someone whose own modest efforts in the field of resource economics have been aided greatly by Professor Solow's work, however, I feel I cannot decline this opportunity to express some gratitude for those achievements.[1]

In this brief paper I will attempt to do three things. The first is simply to review those aspects of Professor Solow's paper that I intend to emphasize. Second, I will note an interesting, and almost exact, parallel. The formal constructs Solow reviewed in the economics of rival, excludable *exhaustible* resources, as exemplified by fossil fuels, are almost directly analogous to those that would be prescribed for the efficient management of the *accumulation* of a nonexcludable public good, as exemplified by greenhouse gas emissions resulting from the combustion of fossil fuels. Finally, apropos of the second point, I'll ask what we might infer from the analysis of private exhaustible resources for the prospect of effective management of a global commons.

'The Economics of Resources or the Resources of Economics' appeared at an interesting time. Then, as now, two interrelated but distinct concerns drove interest in the future of oil use. The first was the Arab oil embargo that began in mid-October 1973 and pushed prices to then-record levels. The second was a concern for the 'limits to growth', to borrow the title of the famous 1972 Club of Rome report (Meadows *et al.* 1972). The former concern

---

*The views expressed in this paper are those of the author and do not necessarily represent those of the US Environmental Protection Agency. No official Agency endorsement should be inferred.

was largely a question of the adequacy of resources and the impacts of scarcity for the economy. To a large extent, so was the latter. However, coming out at roughly the same time as the first Earth Day, the founding of the United States Environmental Protection Agency, the Stockholm Conference on the Human Environment and similar events, *Limits to Growth* also reflected new concerns with the depletion and degradation of public, as well as private, resources.

In his paper Solow deals almost exclusively with the private-good aspects of resource depletion.[2] 'The economics of resources' surveyed for a broader audience of economists both Harold Hotelling's (1931) seminal contribution to the theory of exhaustible resources and the important work then being done on the topic by Solow himself and a number of other distinguished contributors. These contributions—particularly those collected in the now almost legendary *Review of Economic Studies Symposium* issue of 1974—are most noted now for extending Hotelling's theory of exhaustible resources from a partial to a general equilibrium framework. This led to crucial insights concerning the importance of substitution possibilities (Solow, 1974b; Dasgupta & Heal, 1974) and technological progress (Stiglitz, 1974) in determining the long-run consequences of resource depletion for prosperity. These contributions, in combination with William Nordhaus's (1973) complementary work on 'backstop technologies' established both the parameters and the lexicon for future policy discussions of resource exhaustion.

By and large, the work of the early- and mid-1970's confirmed an impression that had prevailed among most economists since at least the time of the seminal Resources for the Future study on *Scarcity and Growth* (Barnett & Morse, 1963): long-term price trends showed that vital resources were becoming more, rather than less, readily available, and technology stood ready to compensate for the effects of depletion on the availability of resources. While the brief blips of the first, and later the second oil embargo of 1979–80 provoked public concern for resource depletion and its consequences, optimists generally prevailed among economists (see, e.g. Smith, 1979 and the papers collected therein). This optimism was reinforced by the sharp drop of oil prices in the 1980s and their general stability until the early years of this century.

However, the return of relative abundance in fossil fuel and other private resource markets heightened concerns with the depletion of a *public* resource: the climate regulation capacity of the atmosphere. The Hotelling model that has been the work-horse of exhaustible resource management may be inverted to model the optimal *accumulation* of a pollution stock. It is an indication of how well established the principles Professor Solow reviewed in 1974 have become that it is now a relatively easy exercise to construct the optimization conditions characterizing this accumulation path. Probably the easiest way to think of this is to consider a sort of mirror image to an approach employed by the late Jeffrey Krautkraemer (1985) to model the depletion of a resource when both its stock and the services derived from its consumption enter into utility. In the case of climate, we might suppose that utility depends positively on the consumption of fossil fuels but negatively on the accumulation of greenhouse gases in the atmosphere. Then, analogously to the Krautkraemer paper, an optimal consumption path is one in which the marginal utility of consumption grows at the rate of interest less a term to reflect the shadow price of increased atmospheric concentrations of greenhouse gases. The model may be embellished to show how some of the other conditions Professor Solow described for optimal management of an exhaustible resource would be extended to the case of accumulation rather than depletion; really, they involve little more than a change in sign. One can work out the boundary conditions that would obtain when limits on accumulation are approached, partial vs. general equilibrium analysis, the timing by which the maximum accumulation would be reached simultaneously with the availability of a non-polluting backstop technology, etc.

Hotelling's model, as elaborated by Professor Solow and the other distinguished economists I have cited (for a more general review of similar literatures, see Geoffrey Heal's 2007 survey) has proved to be of great use to theorists. However, it cannot—and could not reasonably be expected to—explain all the movements of complicated real-world markets. Certainly the oil embargoes of the 1970s are aberrations, and we must agree with Solow that the theorist should not necessarily be judged by his ability to predict the vagaries of geopolitics, natural disasters, or the combinations of them and 'animal spirits' that fed the dizzying gyrations of the international oil market in 2008.

It is not the volatility of resource markets per se so much as the implications of analogous volatility in related markets that I want to emphasize in closing, however. One of Professor Solow's greatest strengths as a writer is his mastery of the evocative turn of phrase, a skill that he could apparently loose at will, explaining in part his great popularity with his students. In 'The Economics of Resources' he writes

[Free] marketeers keep thinking about the doughnut of allocative efficiency and informational economy and *dirigistes* are impressed with the size of the hole containing externalities, imperfections, and distributional issues. So it is with exhaustible resources. (p. 13)

However, in 'The Economics of Resources' he does not offer more than a few observations concerning the correction of failures in the markets for exhaustible resources.[3] His choice is easy to defend as, notwithstanding the contrary perceptions of the public and many of its elected representatives, there are no generic market failures in markets for rival, excludable exhaustible resources.

While the formal parallels between the problems of exhaustible resource management Professor Solow addressed and that of cumulative pollution management that now characterizes climate change policy are almost exact, there is a tremendous institutional difference between the applications. Nicholas Stern (2007) has characterized greenhouse gas emissions as the greatest market failure in history. While the optimal solutions to the exhaustible resource and cumulative greenhouse gas problems may be characterized in very similar formal terms, the latter require far more in the way of political coordination and oversight. Most in our profession would be content to let the market decide how quickly oil is to be consumed and what price path will mediate that consumption, at least if we think the market reflects all social costs and benefits of oil consumption. With the accumulation of pollution, however, the profession generally agrees that techno- and bureaucrats will have to make the analogous decisions.

Thus, in addressing the 'new scarcity' of declining public goods,[4] we face a problem even more daunting than the 'old scarcity' of declining private goods that Professor Solow considered and illuminated. Not only must we derive the technical tools to describe the optimal intertemporal path, but also the institutional adaptations to set ourselves upon them. This work is now being undertaken by a number of distinguished scholars, and we can only hope that someday soon someone among them will be able to summarize the essence of their findings with the same concision and wit as did Professor Solow in his work.

Notes

1. I must also confess that I'm moved by personal sentiment in accepting this opportunity to write on Professor Solow's contributions. When I came to graduate school after spending my formative years in Gig Harbor and Walla Walla, Washington, I found the East Coast a very strange and intimidating place indeed. I met fewer great people than I did great economists, but I've always felt that Professor Solow was both someone with the genius to revolutionize our profession, but who also had the time, willingness and good cheer to engage with even the lowliest of newly arrived, confused students. This is an aspect of a man's career I think we should celebrate at least as much as his publications and prizes.
2. It is an interesting comment on the circumstances of Professor Solow's article that the words 'climate', 'carbon', 'greenhouse' or even 'green' do not appear—just as it is an interesting comment on how much easier the task of research has become that one can now so easily search documents to discern such facts!
3. It is interesting to note that Professor Solow suggests that efficiency might be improved by promoting better organized and informed futures markets. At the time I am writing this paper our elected leaders are debating whether and how much to *restrain* such markets.
4. I borrow the term from the late Professor David Pearce, who was also a man of Solowian virtues: a great economist, but even a finer person.

References

Barnett, H. & Morse, C. (1963) *Scarcity and Growth* (Washington, DC: Resources for the Future).

Dasgputa, P. & Heal, G. (1974) The optimal depletion of exhaustible resources, *Review of Economic Studies* 42 (Symposium), pp. 3–28.

Heal, G. M. (2007) A celebration of environmental and resource economics, *Review of Environmental Economics and Policy*, 1(1), pp. 7–25.

Hotelling, H. (1931) The economics of exhaustible resources, *Journal of Political Economy*, 39, pp. 137–175.

Krautkraemer, J. (1985) Optimal growth, resource amenities, and the preservation of natural environments, *Review of Economic Studies*, 52(1), pp. 153–170.

Meadows, D. H., Meadows, D. L., Randers, J., & Behrens III, W. W. (1972) *The Limits to Growth* (New York: Universe Books).

Nordhaus, W. (1973) The allocation of energy resources, *Brookings Papers on Economic Activities*, 4(3), pp. 529–576.

Pearce, D. W. (2005) Environmental policy as a tool for sustainability, in: R. D. Simpson, M. A. Toman & R. U. Ayres (Eds) *Scarcity and Growth Revisited: Natural Resources and the Environment in the New Millennium*, pp. 198–224. (Washington, DC: Resources for the Future).

Smith, V. K. (1979) *Scarcity and Growth Reconsidered* (Washington, DC: Resources for the Future).

Solow, R. M. (1974) The economics of resources or the resources of economics, *American Economic Review*, 64(2) (Papers and Proceedings), pp. 1–14.

Solow, Robert M. (1974b) Intergenerational equity and exhaustible resources, *Review of Economic Studies*, 42 (Symposium), pp. 29–45.

Stern, N. (2007) *The Stern Review on the Economics of Climate Change* Final Report, London: Her Majesty's Treasury.

Stiglitz, J. (1974) Growth with exhaustible natural resources, *Review of Economic Studies* 42(Symposium), pp. 122–152.

Celebrating Solow: Lessons from Natural Resource Economics for Environmental Policy

V. KERRY SMITH

Introduction

Some Richard T. Ely Lectures have a larger impact than others. Surely Robert Solow's essay 'The Economics of Resources or the Resources of Economics' published 35 years ago is, by any standard, one of the series' 'home runs'. When I started this commentary sustainability and climate change, the importance of renewable sources for a national energy policy and the 'drill-baby-drill' mantra were all part of the national dialogue as the US faced a historic election. Just a few days later, in editing the final draft of this paper, the US financial markets experienced the largest one-day drop in the Dow Jones Industrials in history, nearly 800 points. Financial market instabilities here in the US and abroad are part of the daily news. As a result, it seemed impossible to ignore these issues and proceed, as if the economics of natural resources were all that mattered. Fortunately, there is a connection between the themes I wanted to highlight from Solow's paper, the challenges facing resource and environmental economics, and these very recent events. As a result, I can begin my comments with my bottom line conclusion, use it to establish the connection, and then proceed to outline this short paper.

Solow's essay does a masterful job of explaining in straightforward terms the Hotelling (1931) principle for efficient extraction of a non-renewable resource. Under competitive markets, owners of such resources can expect the net price (the market price less marginal extraction costs) to be increasing exponentially at a rate equal to the rate of interest for an asset of comparable risk and maturity. This conclusion was not surprising to readers at the time he summarized it so clearly. After all, as Solow acknowledged, Hotelling had developed the theory over forty years earlier. An insight I had not fully appreciated until Solow highlighted its importance is the point of this note. In discussing the possibility of instability in the markets for ore from non-renewable resources, he observed asset markets for deposits can be stabilizing influences. That is, the fundamental principle describing efficient extraction is

. . . simultaneously a condition of the flow equilibrium in the market for ore and of asset equilibrium in the market for deposits. (p. 8)

The events in the stock market are reminders that these interconnections between flow and asset markets are not confined to natural resources. When new assets were defined based on the interest income from home mortgages, the prices (and risks) attributed to these securities relied on the returns that follow from ability of borrowers to continue servicing their mortgages as well as the value of the assets (e.g. the homes) providing collateral for the debt. A complex web of other derivatives was defined from this simple structure. The bottom line for our purposes is a *multiplicity of interconnections* between asset and flow markets. These linkages can be either stabilizing, or in today's world, destabilizing influences. Shocks to the housing market, a lynchpin to the tiered structure of 'engineered' assets, caused updating in the perceived risks embedded in the system. Markets spread the effects quickly as we have seen.

To be sure the complexity of the assets makes it difficult to anticipate what is next. Nonetheless the economic principles underlying the linkages are what Solow explained. My focus here is on other assets that provide flows of services. These are outside the market. Moreover, both the flows *and* the stocks are linked in important ways to economic activities. However, there are no markets to signal the relative importance of these flows and stocks. They involve environmental assets and can be regional ecosystems or components of the global atmosphere. Nonetheless, the issues are the same. Each provides services. The state of each asset is important to the processes that assure they will continue to provide these services, but we get no signals of their relative scarcity. In this case, markets don't reflect these important connections.

Much of environmental economics is about how private actions affect the amount and quality of the flows of amenity and life supporting services from environmental assets. Externalities and the properties of policies to efficiently address them relate to the flows of these services. They are a necessary part of the public intervention that substitutes for the efficient regulation and signaling properties we attribute to ideal markets and private exchange. However, even under the best of circumstances we are beginning to recognize these approaches are incomplete because they overlook the flow-stock linkages.

It should not be surprising that when Solow was asked to discuss the concept of sustainability nearly 20 years after his Ely lecture that he was drawn to this linkage. His essay on sustainability can be interpreted as saying that sustainability concerns arise in part because the flow/stock link was missing in economic analyses and the associated policies related to most environmental problems.

This commentary has three parts after these introductory remarks. Section two discusses Solow's comments on the long term importance of non-renewable resources and highlights the Barnett–Morse (1963) qualification. Section three describes how non-market assets and their services matter. The last suggests next steps in the research needed to address these issues.

The Long Run Importance of Natural Resources

Solow tells us the long term view of non-renewable natural resources requires a 'delicate' balance between the present and future when those resources 'really matter'.[1] How can we decide which resources are important? Not surprisingly, and without significant modelling, most observers would agree that a judgment about importance depends on whether we can assume technological progress will consistently reduce our needs for resources that are limited or, equivalently, there is nothing really special about the resources because other relatively abundant inputs offer ready substitutes.

Thirty five years after Solow's essay we are not, in my opinion, any closer to answering these empirical questions. Recently, I reviewed the literature on technical change to consider what we could expect in response to an aggressive policy to reduce greenhouse gases (see Smith, 2008). The literature offered little basis for estimating what to expect or provide a basis for favouring one policy instrument over another for controlling these emissions due to its preferred incentive effects for new innovations. Our record in estimating whether labour and capital substitute for natural resources is no better. Indeed Nordhaus' (2008) most recent update of his Dynamic Integrated model of Climate and the Economy (DICE) avoids the issue by assuming industrial carbon emissions are a multiple of aggregate output that depends on effort devoted to abatement. No attempt is made to consider how energy and non-renewable resources contribute.[2]

Thus, we cannot answer Solow's two key questions determining whether natural resource really matter. So it would seem we need Solow's 'long run someone' who is always taking the long view, so they can notice whether the market based resource use path is heading toward disequilibrium with extreme consequences.

For market resources I think we have a better chance to meet this need. In a recent paper Nordhaus (2007) illustrates how we might do this. He uses macro-data along with oil price information to construct shock indexes for 'large' exogenous oil price movements and a 'surprise' index to evaluate their relative magnitude.[3] His analysis integrates both measures to conclude the US economy is less sensitive to oil price shocks. I believe this is the type of long term perspective Solow called for. Nonetheless, this flow market analysis might benefit, as Solow suggested, from integrating evidence on asset markets. Unfortunately, the record for non-market environmental services and their associated assets has been virtually ignored.

Non-Market Resources—Flows and Stocks

The classic reference providing a comprehensive assessment of the scarcity of natural resources was Barnett and Morse's *Scarcity and Growth*. They found no evidence of growing resource scarcity.[4] They attributed this outcome to technical change as the 'renewing resource'. For them

> . . . the resource problem is one of continual accommodation and adjustment to an ever changing economic resource quality spectrum. The physical properties of the natural resource base impose a series of initial constraints on the growth and press of mankind, but the resource spectrum undergoes kaleidoscopic change thru time. . . . man's technological ingenuity and organizational wisdom offers those who are nimble a multitude of opportunities for escape. (p. 244)

They did offer some qualifications to this largely optimistic assessment. Serious threats to maintaining and enhancing well-being arose, in their view, from changes in environmental conditions that affect the quality of life.[5] These were not reflected in the market signals that helped to ensure technology relieved resource stringencies.

Non-market environmental assets are another matter. These issues have not been completely ignored. Economic analyses of renewable resources, especially fisheries, have emphasized the interactions between market incentives and fisheries. However, the focus has been on the flow market. The implications of open access conditions and the resulting dynamic properties of the fishery as an asset providing output have been discussed, but recognizing that policies affect the flow/stock linkage are only now being discussed in these terms.

As for the rest of environmental economics, this recognition is lagging behind. One of the reasons is strategic separability assumptions imposed on the specifications used to describe preferences and production relationships. Most models of the effects of externalities, especially the recent work evaluating the second best implications of environmental policy (i.e. the literature on the potential for a double dividend from carbon taxes with revenue recycling), treats the enhanced quality as separable from other goods and services. So market goods and services are assumed to be average substitutes for environmental services. This relationship assures there are no feedback effects of policies affecting carbon or other pollution sources on the composition of the demands for market goods and services.

What happens if we change this assumption? Changes in the separability assumption for consumer preferences can lead to large changes in the policy conclusions of these models. The specific findings depend on the nature of the linkages between private commodities and these non-market services (see Carbone & Smith, 2008a). How about the effects of incorporating the connections assumed about environmental assets and their capacities to continue to provide services? This area is the one that genuinely needs attention. Some insights are offered by recent work Jared Carbone and I have undertaken extending the earlier research using static computable general equilibrium (CGE) models (see Carbone & Smith, 2008b). We consider three non-market resources potentially affected by acidic deposition—fish populations, landscapes and scenic views (a use-related service) and a composite asset described as providing non-use services and linked to the other two, use-related flows. The model is static so the dynamic properties of linkages can not be considered. Our focus is on the effects of altering the preference structure to include non-separabilities and the importance of changes in non-use services for people's behaviour.

Figure 1 provides a schematic diagram for the structure of the preferences specified for a representative individual. One tree in the nested constant elasticity of substitution structure describing preferences contains most of the private consumption goods; the second tree has two components—use-related services of environmental resources (on the right side) together with leisure time and non-use services. The use-related part of this nest combines a sub-nest that includes fishing services, scenic views and one private good–consumer service as a group with leisure time. Thus use-related consumption is not completely separable from non-use services. Rather those with intense use-related demands for environmental services might, all else equal, be likely to make larger trade-offs to protect the non-use services which could be considered to resemble natural assets. Each component of the tree has a separate elasticity of substitution describing the ease with which its component part exchange for each other, holding the composite index for each nest constant. These are the sigmas (σ) beside each nest.

They control the magnitude of the inter-linkages. So to my question, paralleling Solow's link between flow and asset markets for equilibrium with natural resources. Do non-use like services affect the evaluation of market behaviours and do policies

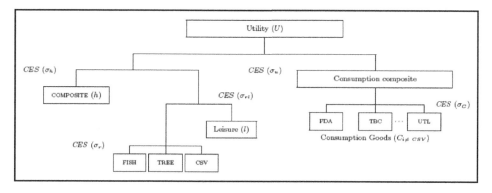

Figure 1. Nesting in household consumption.
Source: Carbone and Smith (2008b)

directed at use-related services influence the relative values of the non-use? Table 1 provides suggestive evidence, using our CGE model adapted from Goulder and Williams (2003). In our structure the environmental services—fishing, scenic views, and overall habitat are treated as quasi-fixed from the representative individual's perspective. They are outside his/her control, changing as the mix of market goods change with policy but not subject to direct choice. Thus policies can influence them, but only indirectly, yet their effects feedback and influence the demands for market goods and services due to the non-separability of preferences.

The policy considered in Table 1 is one that would reduce SO_2 and NO_x emissions by 20%. These pollutants are generated primarily by the transportation, utilities, primary energy

Table 1. Virtual prices and WTP for tax policy to reduce SO_2 and NO_x by 20%[a]

Preferences for Composite Asset	% Δ Virtual Price[b]			WTP[c]	
	Fish	Views	Composite	GE Price and Amenities	Price Change Only
Complements	−32.99	−26.84	−26.98	−947.78	−1047.94
Neutral	−32.58	−26.50	−14.42	−955.24	−1047.78
Substitutes	−32.42	−26.36	−7.54	−957.89	−1047.72

Notes: [a] This analysis is based on CGE model extending Goulder and William (2003) for the US as adapted by Carbone and Smith (2008b). It includes five final consumption goods, four intermediate sectors and one primary factor. The model includes a pre-existing labour tax as a distortion. The policy considered here corresponds to the least cost taxes that would reduce emission of SO_2 and NO_x (precursors to acidic deposition) by 20% assuming the neutral specification for preferences. The complementary, neutral and substitution preference specifications correspond to the non-use/use link relative to the top nest of: good versus non-market goods. We used the formulation σ_μ for this top next and σ_h for the use/nonuse with $\sigma_h = k \, \sigma_\mu$, and the remaining elasticities to designate complementary, neutral, and substitution relationships between market and non-market contributions. These relative sizes are designated by (σ_h, σ_r, σ_{rl}) as (1, 1, 2) (2, 1, 2) and (4, 1, 2) respectively. σ_r refers to the use aggregate, and σ_{re} to the composite of leisure and use related services. See Carbone and Smith (2008a,b) for details. [b] These percentage changes are for the Marshallian virtual prices defined as V_{qj}/V_m where q_j refers to the quasi-fixed environmental service and m is income V is the indirect utility function and V_k is the partial derivative. [c] WTP refers to the Hicksian willingness to pay for the policy. GE refers to the effects of the policy in a general equilibrium system that acknowledges pre-existing distortions (i.e. an income tax) and considers the tax increase to reduce emissions by 20% and the changes in environmental quality that result.

and manufacturing sectors in the model. The least cost set of taxes is selected (assuming preferences that display average substitution between market and non-market goods). What is important from our perspective is the ability to detect the impact of market to non-market feedbacks—as reflected in the substitution relationship between market and non-market sectors. This connection arises in the table with the labelling of each row in the table. Each is a separate solution to the model. The complements, neutral and substitutes cases refer to the use and non-use connection relative to non-market and market connection. The complements case is when non-use and the leisure use-related services are more complementary compare to the market to non-market linkage. Substitutes is where they are stronger substitutes and neutral is where they have the same elasticities. The effects of these differences in the linkages between the market and non-market sectors are picked up through the virtual price of the resource we defined to resemble one of Solow's stock effects.

Conventional welfare measures don't change with the differences in these linkages. General equilibrium measures of Willingness to Pay (WTP) (considering both the environmental quality changes and the relative price effects) and partial equilibrium measures considering only the effects of the policy on the relative prices of market goods do not signal its potential importance. Similarly the marginal values (virtual prices) of the use related environmental services also fail to signal the importance of feedbacks for the non-use contribution (designated here as the composite resource). Thus the structure of these connections matters.

In the case of environmental policy this connection between flows and assets has been missing. When we revisit Solow's discussion in his Ely and Sustainability lectures we see that he was signalling this connection is just as important for these assets as it is for marketed natural resources. Our simple exercise supports his insight in a static context.

Implications

Solow's Ely lecture had many important insights. I have used one of them as a rhetorical platform to raise parallel questions for the relationship between environmental services and the assets that provide them *outside markets*. Environmental economists have failed to appreciate the significance of Solow's advice. These linkages seem likely to transform the design and evaluation of environmental policy. Indeed, the research needed for sustainable environmental and economic policies seems directly related to understanding non-market linkages.

What is next? We need to move beyond the taxonomic approach of the Millennium Ecosystem Assessment (2005) in describing how to integrate economic models with ecosystem services. Economic policies affect *both* the flow (and quality) of services and the character of the natural assets that provide them. This issue may well provide a more compelling reason for the indicative planning Solow called for at the end of his Ely lecture. The balance sheet for environmental assets surely demands that:

'Someone . . . must always be taking the long view' (p. 12)

Notes

1. This discussion is in the context of selecting social rates of discount and is certainly a key part of the recent debate about the Stern report on climate policy. See the special section of the *Review of Environmental Economics and Policy*, 2, 2008 for commentaries on this topic.

2. Nordhaus' model assumes they are multiples of aggregate output depending on a fixed coefficient and a time profile of abatement activities. None of the issues associated with energy and materials balances and their roles for production are considered.
3. Nordhaus' surprise index is defined as the absolute value of the quarterly price change to the 25 year moving average of the standard deviation of price changes.
4. Their analysis did not use Hotelling rents but rather a measure of real unit costs. For a discussion of their index as a measure of resource scarcity see Smith (1980).
5. See chapter 12 of Barnett and Morse (1963) for a far-reaching discussion that anticipates many of the questions raised as part of discussing sustainability today.

References

Barnett, H. J. & Morse, C. (1963) *Scarcity and Growth* (Baltimore: Johns Hopkins University).

Carbone, J. C. & Smith, V. K. (2008a) Evaluating policy interventions with general equilibrium externalities, *Journal of Public Economics*, 92(June), pp. 1254–1274.

Carbone, J. C. & Smith, V. K. (2008b) *Environmental Feedbacks in a Joint-System General Equilibrium* revised CSEEP working paper, October.

Goulder, Laurence H. & Williams III, Roberton C. (2003) The substantial bias from ignoring general equilibrium effects in estimating excess burden and a practical solution, *Journal of Political Economy*, 3(4), pp. 898–927.

Hotelling, H. (1931) The economics of exhaustible resources, *Journal of Political Economy*, 39(2), pp. 137–175.

Millennium Ecosystem Assessment (2005) *Ecosystems and Human Well-Being: Synthesis* (Washington, D.C.: Island Press).

Nordhaus, W. D. (2007) Who's afraid of a big bad oil shock?, *Brookings Papers on Economic Activity*, 2, pp. 1–19.

Nordhaus, W. D. (2008) *The Challenge of Global Warming: Economic Models and Environmental Policy* (New Haven, CT: Yale University Press).

Smith, V. K. (1980) The evaluation of natural resource adequacy: Elusive quest or frontier of economic analysis, *Land Economics*, 56(August), pp. 257–298.

Smith, V. K. (2008) Reflections on the literature, *Review of Environmental Economics and Policy*, 2(Fall), pp. 130–145.

Solow, R. M. (1974) The economics of resources or the resources of economics, *American Economic Review, Proceedings*, 64(May), pp. 1–14.

Solow, R. M. (1992) *An Almost Practical Step Toward Sustainability* lecture for Resources for the Future's Fortieth Anniversary, 8 October.

Paul A. Samuelson

Economics of Forestry in an Evolving Society*

PAUL A. SAMUELSON
Massachusetts Institute of Technology

ABSTRACT   *A debate that has raged for centuries is unlikely to be resolved by me in one lecture. However, I shall do my best to set forth the issues and indicate what ought to be the crucial factors that a jury should consider in rendering its verdict on the matter. The issue is one between forestry experts and the general public on the one side and professional economists and profit-conscious businessmen on the other. At first blush this would seem to suggest that economists are on the side of the interests and are not themselves members of the human race. But, as I hope to show, sound economic analysis is needed to do justice to the cases put forward by either of the adversary parties.*

Sustain or not Sustain?

To vulgarize and oversimplify, *there has been a tradition in forestry management which claims that the goal of good policy is to have sustained forest yield, or even "maximum sustained yield" somehow defined*. And, typically, economists have questioned this dogma.

If laissez-faire enterprisers tended to be led by that invisible hand Adam Smith talked about to achieve in fact sustained forest yields, and even maximum sustained forest yields, no doubt there would be a school of economists called into existence to give their blessings to the doctrine of maximum sustained yield. In that case there would be no great debate. The economists in the liberal arts division of the university, on those rare occasions when they deign to think about the practical problems of forest management, would come out with the same conclusions and dicta as would the professional foresters in the school of forestry. Moreover, the professors in the biological departments, and the lay public generally, would heartily approve of the actual solution in this best of all possible worlds.

Life is not like that and it hasn't been for a long time. The medieval forests of Britain, and of Europe, tended to be chopped down as society moved into the Industrial Revolution. The virgin forests that graced the New World when Columbus arrived here have increasingly been cut down once the calculus of dollar advantage began to apply. When I informed

---

*This paper was presented initially as a lecture at a symposium on "The Economics of Sustained Yield Forestry," at the University of Washington, Seattle, Washington, November 23, 1974. I owe thanks to the National Science Foundation for financial aid, and to Kate Crowley for editorial assistance. Also to Vicki Elms for help with the bibliography, and to Barbara Feldstein for composition. It was Professor Barney Dowdle of the University of Washington who, knowing of my innocence of forestry economics, inveigled me into making these preliminary researches.

a graduate student that I was preparing this lecture, he mentioned to me the rumor that a nearby consulting firm had applied dynamical programming analysis to the problem of how old—or rather how young—a tree should be when it is to be optimally cut in the steady state. Allegedly, its computer spun out of control and generated a negative, or for all I know, imaginary, root for the equation: apparently at realistic profit rates, it doesn't pay to keep a forest in existence at all. This is probably only a tall story, but it does well illustrate the fact that standard managerial economics, and actual commercial practice, both tend to lead to an optimal cutting age of a forest that is much shorter than the 80 or even 100 years one often encounters in the forestry literature.

Externalities and Intervention

This apparent clash between economists and foresters is not an isolated one. Biological experts in the field of fisheries are sometimes stunned when they meet economists who question their tacit axiom that the stock of fish in each bank of the ocean ought to be kept as a goal at some maximum sustained level. Similarly, hard-boiled economists are greeted with incredulity if and when they opine that it may be optimal to grow crops in the arid plain states only until the time when the top soil there has blown away to its final resting place in the ears and teeth of Chicago pedestrians.

Everybody loves a tree and hates a businessman. Perhaps this is as it should be, and perhaps after the profession of economics is 1,000 rather than 200 years old, the human race will be as conditioned to abhor economists as it has become to abhor snakes. But really, these matters need arguing in court so the informed jury, and I do mean the informed jury of human beings, can make up its mind.

Let me say in advance of the argument, there is no ironclad presumption that profit seeking laissez-faire will lead to the social optimum. Thus, suppose that a living redwood tree helps purify the air of smoggy Los Angeles. Suppose sowing the land to short-lived pine trees prevents floods 500 miles downstream. Then we may well have here a case of what modern economists recognize as "externalities." We economists these days spend much of our time analyzing the *defects* of competitive free entry and push-shove equilibrium when important externalities are involved. If therefore in the great historic debate on sustained yields, foresters and conservationists had brought into court an elaboration of the respects in which forestry is an activity beset with important externalities, carefully and objectively described, Ph.D.'s in economics would be found on both sides of the case under trial. Indeed, if the externalities involved could be shown to be sufficiently important, I am naive enough to believe that all economists would be found on the side of the angels, sitting thigh next to thigh with the foresters. (All economists agree? Well, almost all.)

"Private" versus "Common" Property

Earlier I mentioned fisheries. Even those economists who ostrich-like tend always to play down externalities if they can, have long recognized that there is a "common property" element in hunting and fishing: even though I were to have to pay rent to someone who owns a particular acre of the ocean in order to put down my net there, my act of fishing there can hope to draw on fish with might migrate from nearby acres. So we have in the case of fisheries a special kind of externality that makes it nonoptimal to have *decentralized rent-charging owners* of subdivisions of a common fishing bank. Government regulation and centralized decision making for the whole fishing pool, if it can be arranged in this age of nationalism, is obviously preferable to free competition as Gordon (1954), Scott (1955), and Crutchfield (1962) have analyzed.

From a cursory glance at the literature of forestry, both technical and economic, I do not perceive foresters to be making as a case for timber what is true for fisheries, or for oil drilling. It is true that forest fires are a hazard that adjacent timber lands may face in common. And if the units of land owned by each forester-owner were very, very small, the externalities between adjacent plots would render decentralized competitive decision-making nonoptimal. However, for the most part, timber ownership will not under laissez-faire tend to stay so pulverized, since it is quite feasible to have the span of ownership widened to the optimal degree without creating monopoly or vitiating the assumptions of workable competition.

At the beginning, therefore, even before entering into the serious argument, let us make a deposition that the following would be a false issue in the debate:

Abolishing private ownership in land or abandoning public regulation of forest land owned by the government is not an alternative to maximum sustained yield that is advocated by anybody. This would certainly result in unnecessary decimation of the forest. Indeed, as Vernon Smith (1968) has shown in one of his models, it could in extinction of *all* forests; but even if a realistic model of complete push-shove free-free entry led to a maintainable sustained-yield steady state, the average age of the forest stands in such a Hobbesian jungle might well involve rotation periods so short as to be absurd, which is why in medieval Germany severe limits were properly placed on the use by the public of crown and public forest lands.

Competitive Land Rents

The economists who oppose maximum sustained-yield do not advocate any such absurd push-shove procedure. They assume that the cultivator who plants a tree on one acre of land owns or rents the right to exclusive garnering of the fruits of that which he has planted. Similarly, if I own yonder acre or have leased it from a public or private owner, and if I desist in chopping down a tree that is not yet ripe, I expect to find it still there when I do come to chop it down. In return for this exclusive use of my own area of cultivation, I expect to pay a land rent. If I own the land outright, I pay it *to myself* at an opportunity cost rate that is perfectly well determined in a freely competitive market. Or I pay the rent to a private owner, who knows he can rent that land to somebody else like me if not to me. Or I pay a rent to a government that owns the land.

This rate of land rental can be high or low. If the total amount of land available for growing the timber that society needs, and which is close enough to the market to be able to avoid heavy transportation charges, is severely limited in amount, then the appropriate competitive land rent will be high. If on the other hand land is extremely plentiful, its scarcity rent will be very low. It will not even matter for the purpose of our analysis if well-located land is so plentiful as to be redundant. In that case, its competitive land rent will be zero, but even though land rent is zero I shall still need to have *exclusive* rights to the fruits of my earlier labor and other investment inputs, independently of whether in other acres of the redundant territory push-shove free-free entry is permitted.

Assumptions for the Analysis

Let me first review the correct economic principles that would be applicable if forestry can be regarded simply as sources of wood saleable in competitive markets. This initially assumes away externalities such as flood control, pollution abatement, species preservation, vacationers' enjoyments, etc.

Although I am not a specialist in the field of forest economics, I have been reading a couple of dozen different analyses ranging over the last two centuries that grapple with optimal steady-state rotation periods. The economic analysis in most of them is wrong. In some it is very wrong. In others it is not quite right. In at least one case, the remarkable 1849 German article by Martin Faustmann, the analysis does come close to an essentially correct solution.

These remarks are not intended to give a harsh indictment of foresters or of economists who have worked in the field of forestry. The mistakes made in the forestry literature can be duplicated aplenty in the intermediate textbooks of pure economics.

Thus, Irving Fisher was the greatest single economic writer on interest and capital, and his 1930 *Theory of Interest* summarized his life work in that field. Yet at MIT we ask graduate students on quizzes to identify and correct Fisher's false solution as to when a tree should be cut (a false solution that he seems to share with the great von Thunen (1826) and the brilliant Hotelling (1925) as well as with some excellent economists who have written on forestry in recent decades). Again, Kenneth Boulding is one of our leading economists; but his rule of maximizing the so-called "internal rate of return" has led many a forestry economist down the garden path (Boulding 1935). A 1960 review of the literature by G.K. Goundrey comes out with the wrong Boulding solution, and yet his analysis purports to lean on such excellent authorities as Wicksell, Scitovsky, Kaldor, Metzler, and Scott; alas, it did not lean more heavily on Faustmann (1849), Preinrich (1938), Alchian (1952), Bellman (1957), Gaffney (1957), Hirshleifer (1958), and perhaps Samuelson (1937).

If an unambiguous solution to the problem is to be definable, of course certain definite assumptions must be made. If the solution is to be simple, the assumptions must be heroic. These include: (1) knowledge of future lumber prices at which all outputs can be freely sold, and future wages of all inputs; (2) knowledge of future interest rates at which the enterprise can both borrow and lend in indefinite amounts; and (3) knowledge of technical lumber yields that emerge at future dates once certain expenditure inputs are made (plantings, sprayings, thinnings, fellings, etc.). Finally, it is assumed (4) that each kind of land suitable for forests can be bought and sold and rented in arm's length transactions between numerous competitions; or, if the government owns public lands, it rents them out at auction to the highest of numerous alternative bidders and conducts any of its own forestry operations so as to *earn the same maximum rent* obtainable at the postulated market rate of interest. For the special steady-state model, the future prices and interest rates must be assumed to be known constants. Moreover, our problem is not one merely of managerial economics; rather we must deduce the competitive prices that clear the industry's market.

Assumptions would not be heroic if they could be easily taken for granted as being exactly applicable, Stochastic factors of climate, lightning, forest fires, and disease must in real life qualify the technical assumptions made in (3) above. At the least, therefore, as a second approximation, one must introduce probabilities and expected values into the decision calculus.

Similarly, tomorrow's lumber price is not knowable exactly, much less the price of lumber a score of years from now when today's seedling will mature. So, in other than a first approximation, the assumptions under (1) need to be complicated.

Finally, future interest rates are not knowable today, Moreover, the inherent uncertainties involved in interest and profit yields also serve to falsify the assumption in (2) that the enterprise is able at each date both to borrow and to lend in indefinite amounts at one interest rate (even one knowable at *that* date if not now). Once we recognize that the enterprise is in an imperfect capital market, we will not be able to deduce its optimal forestry decisions independently of knowledge about its owners' personal preferences concerning consumption outlays of different dates (and concerning their "liquidities" at different dates).

Correct Capital Analysis

Our problem is now well posed. What principles provide its solution? What is the exact nature of the solution?

(i) Does it yield a steady-state rotation period as long as that which achieves the foresters' traditional "maximum sustained yield"?

(ii) Is the optimal rotation that *shorter* period which maximizes the present discounted value over the first planting cycle of the cash receipts that come from the sale of cut lumber minus the cash expenses of planting and cutting inputs (excluding from the net cash receipts stream any adjustments for implicit and explicit land rent)?

(iii) Is the optimal rotation period that still shorter period which maximizes Boulding's "Internal Rate of Return," computed as that largest rate of interest which when applied to the net doller cash receipts over one complete cycle reduces the resulting present discounted value to zero (and, be it noted, ignores land rent in setting up the net algebraic cash receipts!)?

(iv) Alternatively, is the optimum the rotation period that results from maximizing (a) the present discounted value of all net cash receipts excluding explicit or implicit land rents, but calculated over the *infinite chain* of cycles of planting on the given acre of land from now until Kingdom Come; or (b) what may sound like a different criterion, the rotation period that results from maximizing the present discounted value of net algebraic receipts over the first cycle, but with the market land rental included in those receipts, it being understood that the land rental that each small enterprise will be confronted with will be the *maximum* rental that ruthless Darwinian competition can contrive?

If you have been testing yourself by trying to answer the objective-type quiz that I have just propounded, you will receive a perfect A + if you gave the following answers:

(i) No, the rotation period that maximizes sustained yield is so long that, at the postulated positive interest rate and inevitable market rent for land, it will bankrupt any enterprise that endeavors to realize it.

(ii) No, maximizing the present discounted value, over *one* plating cycle, of cash receipts from cut timber sold minus cash receipts for inputs that do planting, thinning, and cutting will give you a somewhat too long rotation period and will not enable you to cover the land rent that will be set by your more perspicacious competitors. However, your error will not be so very great in the case the length of each cycle is very great and/or the rate of interest per annum is very large, so that the discounted value today of a dollar payable at the end of the cycle is negligible. Still, employing this method that is so frequently advocated by sophisticated economists will lead you to the following absurdity: an increase in initial planting cost will have *no effect at all* on your optimal rotation period, up to the point that it makes it unprofitable to put the land you own into lumber, even when you are philanthropic enough to forego obtainable positive land rent. It is a solution that pretends that the Archimedean forest lever never needs the land fulcrum to work with.

(iii) No, ignoring land rent and maximizing the internal rate of return will give you so short a rotation period that, at the postulated interest rate, you will not be able to pay yourself the positive land rental set by competition. Moreover, maximizing the interal rate of return will give you the nonsensical result that you should select the same rotation period when the interest rate, the price of time, is high or low; and, when initial planting costs are zero, it will give a meaningless infinite return.

(iv) Finally, yes, (a) and (b), which really are exactly the same method, constitute the only correct method. The first formulation, in terms of an infinite chain of repeated cycles, was already proposed in the brilliant 1849 German article by Martin Faustmann. A glance at its recent English translation convinces me of his remarkable merit, even though at first glance one does not find in it the exact explicit conditions for optimal cutting age of the forest stand. I do not know that the economics literature caught up with this degree of sophistication prior to the 1938 *Econometrica* survey article on depreciation by Gabriel Preinrich, which was itself a notable anticipation of the dynamic programming that Richard Bellman made routine in the postwar period. The second approach, which I cannot recall seeing explicitly in print, will perhaps be more intuitively understandable at a first approach to the subject; and, in any case, land rent has tended not to be given the proper analysis it needs.

In a moment I shall illustrate all this by means of a specific model, which though not very realistic will be familiar to economists since the time of Stanley Jevons. From it, you will infer the presumption that commercial exploitation of forestry will lead to a departure from the goal of maximum sustained yield even greater than may have been realized by adherents and critics of forestry dogmas. The higher the effective rate of interest, the greater will be the shortfall of the optimal rotation age compared to the age that maximizes steady-state yield. As the interest rate goes to zero, the economists' correct optimum will reach the limit of the foresters' target of maximum sustained yield. Only if an explicit land rent charge is introduced into the cash stream will Boulding's maximized internal rate of return avoid incorrect results; but in that case, Ockham's razor can cut it down as redundant (worse than that, as involving incomplete, implicit theorizing.) Actually, as we have seen in (b) above, including in competitive land-rent can save from error the popular method of maximizing present discounted value calculated over only the first cycle; however, to know *how much* rent so to include, one must impose the condition that it be just large enough to reduce to zero that maximized discounted value over one cycle, and this rent so calculated will turn out to be after capitalization exactly what the Faustmann-Preinrich-Bellman-Hirshleifer solution deduced. It should be noted that, in the special case where the land for timber growth is redundant and therefore free, maximizing over a single cycle will singularly give the correct answer, and maximizing the internal rate of return will with equal singularity also give the same answer. Since at least one writer, Goundrey (1960), has alleged that timber land in Canada is so plentiful as to be free, it is worth emphasizing that even in this case the three methods nominated by economists will deduce a rotation period significantly shorter than the foresters' maximum because of the positive interest rate. The foresters, without realizing it, are correct only when the true interest rate is literally zero.

The Bogey of Compound Interest

I cannot conclude this general survey of wrong and right ways of analyzing the actual equilibrium that will emerge in the competitive steady-state without expressing my amazement at the low interest rates which abound in the forestry literature. Faustmann, writing in the middle of the nineteenth century, uses a four percent rate. Thunen, writing at the same time, uses a five percent interest rate. The 1960 Goundrey survey also uses a five percent rate. These will seem to an ordinary economist and businessman as remarkably low. The notion that for such gilt-edge rates I would tie up my own capital in a 50-year (much less a 100-year) timber investment, with all the uncertainties and risks that the lumber industry is subject to, at first strikes one as slightly daft. I can only guess that such low numbers have been used either as a form of wishful thinking so foresters or forest economists can avoid rotation ages so short they show up the forester's "maximum sustained yield"; or because the writers have not had the heart to face up to the discounting almost out of existence of receipts payable half a century from now.

Let us make no mistake about it. The positive interest rate is the enemy of long-lived investment projects. At six percent interest, money doubles in 12 years, quadruples in 24, grows 16-fold in 48 years, and 256-fold in 96 years. Hence, the present discounted value today of $1 of timber harvest 96 years from now is, at six percent, only 0.4 of one cent!

Foresters know this and fight against compound interest. Thus, an economist cannot help but be amused at the 1925 gem by the Assistant Chief, Board of Research, U.S. Forest Service, Ward Shepard. Entitled "The Bogey of Compound Interest," this argues that if you have a forest stand in the steady state, no interest need be involved: your cutting receipts exceed your planting expenses! This is so absurd as to be almost believable to the layman — up to the moment when the economist breaks the news to the farmer, lumber-company president, or government official that he can mine the forest by cutting it down without replanting and sell the land, thereafter putting the proceeds into the bank or into retiring the public dept and subsequently earn interest forever.

"Bogey" has two meanings. The first, which is Shepard's naive meaning, is that compound interest is a fictitious entity which, like the Bogey Man, is wrongfully used to frighten little children. The second and here more legitimate meaning of bogey is that defined in Webster's Dictionary as "a numerical standard of performance set up as a mark to be aimed at in competition." Compound interest is indeed the legitimate bogey that competitors must earn in forestry if they are not to employ their land, labor, and disposable funds in other more lucrative uses.

Competitive theory can be reassuring as well as frustrating to the forester. There is a popular notion that interest calculations may be applied to decisions for next year as against the immediately following years. "But," it is not infrequently argued, "when what is at issue is a tree or dam whose full fruits may not accrue until a century from now, the brute fact that our years are numbered as three score and ten prevents people from planting the trees that will not bear shade until after they are dead—altruism, of course, aside."

To argue in this way is to fail to understand the logic of competitive pricing. Even if my doctor assures me that I will die the year after next, I can confidently plant a long-lived olive tree, knowing that I can sell at a competitive profit the one-year-old sapling. Each person's longevity and degree of impatience to spend becomes immaterial in a competitive market place with a borrowing, lending, and capitalizing interest rate that encapsulates all which is relevant about society's effective time preferences.

Inflation and Income Taxes

What interest rate is appropriate for forestry? I hesitate to pronounce on such a complex matter. A dozen years ago I might incautiously have said 12 percent or more. And, just recently you could have got 12 percent per annum on $100,000 left with safety in the bank for three months. But this of course represented in part the 1974 10+ percent annual inflation rate, a rate which the price rise in lumber could also presumably share. Indeed timber lands are often recommended as an inflation hedge: if the interest rate is 12 percent and the price of lumber rises at 12 percent per annum, it is a standoff and in effect there is a zero real interest rate.

Fortunately, I was able to show back in 1937, correcting a misleading interpretation in Keynes' 1936 *General Theory*, that so long as price changes are anticipatable, it does not matter in what "own-rates-of-interest" you calculate to make decisions (such as at what optimal age to cut a tree), the optimal physical decision will always be invariant. This means that essentially all we need in order to discuss forest economics correctly is to concentrate on (1) the *real* rate of interest (i.e., the actual interest rate on money minus the presumed known rate of overall price inflation), and (2) the real price of lumber outputs and inputs (i.e., the percentage real rate of rise for $P_{lumber}/P_{general}$).

There is another complication. If marginal tax rates are (say) 50 percent, a 12 percent yield before tax is a 6 percent yield after tax. It would seem to make quite a difference for optimal rotation decisions whether we must use a 12 or a 6 percent discount rate. Actually, and this may seem discouraging to the foresters' dream of maximum sustained yield, one can correctly use the higher pre-tax rate in making optimal decisions provided the income tax authorities really do properly tax true money income at uniform prices. More specifically, I showed in Samuelson (1964) that, if foreseeable depreciation and appreciation are taxed when they occur, a person always in the 50 percent (or 99 percent) bracket will make the same optimal decisions as a person always in the zero percent bracket.

But are actual U.S. or Canadian tax systems "fair" in their income taxation? Of course not. As a forest grows in size and value, instead of taxing this certain accretion of true income in the Henry Simons fashion, the tax is deferrable until the wood is cut. So forestry may provide a "tax loophole," which can distort decisions toward the longer rotation period of the foresters' maximum sustained yield, particularly if capital-gains tax-treatment is available at lower rates.

To sum up, I might mention that William Nordhaus (1974) recently showed at Brookings that *real* profit yields have been falling in recent years. Thus, his Table 5 suggests that real before-tax yields on corporate capital have tended to average only about 10 percent in the early 1970's as against over 15 percent 20 years earlier. This seems better for forest economics than in earlier decades, but still bad enough. Tax loopholes may further improve the viability of longer rotation periods. Also, I remember Frank Knight's being quoted as saying that, in effect, *real* lumber prices have risen historically about enough to motivate holding on to forest inventories—a dubious generalization, but one that reminds us that lumber price cannot be taken as a hard constant in realistic analysis. Before a nation, or regions it trades with, completely depletes a needed item, the price of that item can be expected to rise.

Defining Maximum Sustained yield in a Classic Case

You might think that the practical man's notion of sustained yield, or of maximum sustained yield, would be clear-cut. But if you do, you haven't had much experience with analyzing so-called common sense notions. Certainly maximum sustained yield in forestry does not suggest all land wasted on soybeans and other goodies should be plowed and planted with trees. Nor does it mean that land devoted to forests should be manicured and fertilized by all the labor in society, labor not needed for subsistence calories and vitamins, in order to produce the most lumber that land is capable of in the steady state.

The amount of lumber a virgin forest is capable of producing in a wild state approaches closer to the notion's content. But biologists have long realized that Darwinian evolution leads to an ecological equilibrium in which many trees grow to be too old in terms of their wood-product efficiency; and, in any case, a virgin forest left unmolested by man is like a librarian's perverted dream of a library where no books are ever permitted to be taken out so that the inventory on the shelves can be as complete as possible.

One presumes that "maximum sustained yield" is shorthand for a reasonable notion like the following:

Cut trees down to make way for new trees when they are past their best growth rates. Follow a planting, thinking, and cutting cycle so the resulting (net?) lumber output, averaged over repeated cycles or, what is the same thing, averaged over a forest in a synchronized age class distribution, will be as large as possible.

Jevons, Wicksell, and other economists have for a century analyzed a simple "point-input point-output, time-phased" model that can serve as the paradigm of an idealized forest. Labor input of L, does planting on an acre of forest land at time t. Then at time $t + T$, I can cut lumber of Q_{t+T}, freeing the land for another input of L_{t+T} and output $Q_{t+2T}, \ldots$, and so forth in an infinite number of cycles. Biology and technology give me the production function relating inputs and output, namely

$$Q_{t+T} = f(T)$$
$$f'(T) > 0, a < T < b; f'(b) = 0$$

(1)

Actually, as we'll see, $f(T)$ is short for $f(s, L; T)$, where L is labor input at the beginning of one planting cycle and s is the land used throughout that complete cycle (which can be set at $s = 1$).

In the steady state, a new part of each forest is being planted at every instant of time, an old part is being cut down at age T, and forest stands of all ages below T are represented in equal degree. If we wish to calculate the average product per unit of land of the synchronized forest, we can follow one cycle on one part of the forest, and divide the Q it produces in T periods by T to get average product per year. So one measure of gross sustained yield would be $f(T)/T$. However, this neglects the fact that workers must be paid wages. These are payable in dollars at rate W; and the lumber is sold in dollars at the competitive price P. But we could think of the workers who do the initial planting as being paid off in kind, in lumber they can sell at price P. So their wage in lumber, $(W/P) L$, must be subtracted from gross output $f(T)$ in order to form "average sustainable net lumber yield" of $[f(T) - (W/P)L]/T$.

Figure 1 shows the story. The point of maximum $f(T)$ is shown at B, where $f'(b) = 0 > f''(b)$. The point of maximum sustained gross yield T_q, is shown where a ray through the origin, OG, is tangent to the $f(T)$ curve. The point of maximum sustained net yield, is given by tangency at T_r of a similar ray, EN, from the expense point, E, to the net curve $f(T) - (W/P)L$.

Maximum sustained gross yield, as here defined, is at a maximum, not when $T = b$. To wait until each tree slowly achieves its top lumber content is to fail to realize that cutting the tree to make the land available for a faster-growing young tree is truly optimal. Ignoring all wage subtractions, sustained yield of gross lumber is maximized at the lower rotation age, T_g, defined by

$$\underset{T}{Max}\ [f(T)/T] = f(T_g)/T_g, \tag{2}$$

where

$$f'(T_g) = f(T_g)/T_g,\ T_g < b.$$

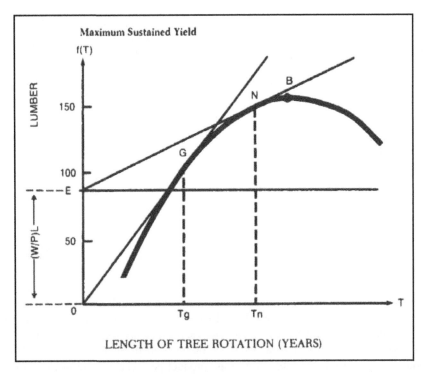

Figure 1. T_g is rotation period for maximum *gross* sustained yield irrespective of initial planting costs. T_n is rotation period for maximum *net* sustained yield.

Since a short rotation period makes us pay the same wages more often, once we introduce wage subtractions, we arrive at a forester's true "maximum sustained (net) yield" at a rotation age somewhat greater than T_g, namely at T_n defined as

$$\underset{T}{Max}\ [f(T) - (W/P)L]\ T = [f(T_n) - (W/P)L]/T_n, \tag{3}$$

where[1]

$$f'(T_n) - f(T_n)/T_n = -(W/P)L/T_n,\ T_g < T_n < b.$$

This provides us with an unambiguous and useful definition of "maximum sustained net yield." And it is this definition of sustained yield that I shall compare with what will actually emerge as steady-state competitive equilibrium, and with the various optima that one or another economist has proposed when poaching on the territory of forest economics.

The True Competitive Solution

The above Jevons model will illustrate the false economic solutions and the correct solution.

First, consider the most popular method which maximizes present discounted value or PDV, calculated over one planting cycle only and involving cash receipts other than land rent. This gives T_1, defined by the equations below as

$$f(T_1)e^{-rT_1} - (W/P)L \geq 0 = \underset{T}{Max}[f(T)e^{-rT} - (W/P)L], \tag{4}$$

where

$$f'(T_1)/f(T_1) = r$$

and

$$T_1 < b \text{ when } r > 0,$$

where r is the market-given competitive interest rate at which everyone can borrow and lend in unlimited amounts. This is the famous Jevons relation, which had already been glimpsed by Thunen and which Fisher was later mistakenly to apply to a forest growing on limited land. (Only if land is so abundant as to be redundant and rent-free, so that P/W falls to equal $f(T_1)L^{-1}$, will T_1 give the correct competitive rotation period of the forest. As we'll see, the correct rotation period, call it T_∞, will be shorter than T_1; but unlike T_1 it must always fall short of T_n.)

A defect in many good economic discussions is to present alternative maximum criteria, as if it were a matter of choice which to adopt. One such is to maximize the so-called internal rate of return, defined by

---

[1] Note that, as $(W/P) \rightarrow f(T)/L$, so that land rent is zero even at $r = 0$, $T_n \rightarrow b$.

$$\underset{T}{Max}\, Q = \underset{T}{Max}\{T^{-1} log\, [f(T)(P/WL)]\} = r_i = f'(T_i)/f(T_i),$$

$$= T_i^{-1} log[f(T_i)(P/WL)] = r_i$$

(5)

where

$$f'(T_i)/f(T_i) = T_i^{-1} log[f(T_i)(P/WL)]$$

$$T_i < T_1 \text{ when } r_i > r.$$

Anyone who misguidedly adopts this foolish T_i rotation period will find that he either goes broke or is permanently sacrificing return on original capital that could be his. (To prove that $T_i < T_1$, note that increasing r can be shown to lower T_1; also note that for $r = r_i$, T_1 and T_i would coincide. Hence, the T_1 for smaller r would be greater than T_i. Q.E.D.)

Finally, as Faustmann showed in 1849, the correct description of what will emerge in competitive forest-land-labor-investment equilibrium is an optimal rotation period shorter than the forester's T_n and Thunen-Fisher's T_1, but longer than Boulding's T_i, namely T_∞ as defined by either of the following equivalent formulations.

$$R_\infty \underset{T}{Max}\, Rs = \underset{T}{Max}\, R \text{ for } s = 1, \text{subject to}$$

$$0 = \underset{T}{Max}\, \{Pf(T)e^{-rT} - WL - R \int_O^T e^{-rT} dt\}$$

(6a)

$$= Pf(T_\infty)e^{-rT_\infty} - WL - R_\infty[1 - e^{-rT_\infty}]r^{-1}$$

or,

$$\underset{T}{Max}\, [Pf(T)e^{-rT} - WL][1 + e^{-rT} + (e^{-rT})^2 + \ldots]$$

$$= \underset{T}{Max}\, [Pf(T)e^{-rT} - WL]/[1 - e^{-rT}]$$

(6b)

$$= \underset{T}{Max}\, (R/r) = [Pf(T_\infty)e^{-rT_\infty} - WL]/[1 - e^{-rT_\infty}] = R_\infty/r,$$

land's value, where

$$f'(T_\infty) - rf(T_\infty) = +r[Pf(T_\infty)e^{-rT_\infty} - WL]/[1 - e^{-rT_\infty}]$$

$$= r(R_\infty/r) = r \text{ land value} = R_\infty$$

(6c)

$$T_i < T_\infty < T_i \text{ and } T_\infty < T_n \text{ for } R_\infty > 0$$

The first line of (6b) is the correct Faustmann-Gaffney-Hirshleifer formulation. Its equivalence with the maximum-land-rent formulation of (6a) is seen from solving the last

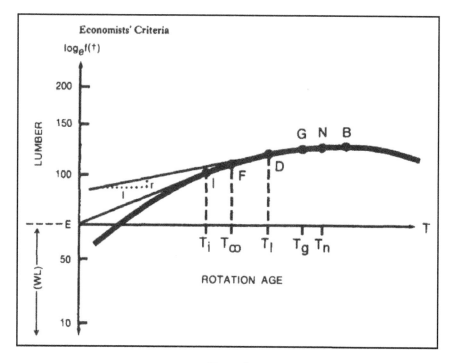

Figure 2.

relation of (6a) for R and noting its equivalence with the second relation of (6b) except for the extraneous constant r.

Figure 2 shows the familiar relation among the different rotation periods. Note that a reduction in P/W would lower the curve in the figure until at the zero-land-rent state the line through E with slope r would just touch the new curve at the new *coinciding* points T_i and T_1 and T_∞. It can be shown that, as $r \to 0.[2]$

---

[2] This is better brought out by my maximum rent formulation of (6a) than by Faustmann's infinite number of cycles as in (6b) here. Thus for $r = 0$ (6a) becomes equivalent to

$$\text{subject to } 0 = \underset{T}{Max} \ \{f(T) - (W/P)L - R \int_0^T dt\}$$

Maximize R, namely

$$\underset{T}{Max} \ \{[f(T) - (W/P)L]/T\} = [f(T_n) - (W/P)L]/T_n$$

where T_n is defined by my earlier equation (3). B. Ohlin, I now learn, worked out much of this as a graduate student: cf. Ohlin (1921).

Digression: Labor and Land Variable

The general problem recognizes that Q_{t+T} output can, for each T, be affected by how much labor, L_t, one uses initially and how much land, $s_{t:t+T}$, one uses throughout the time interval t to $t+T$. Hence, we replace $f(T)$ in the steady state by

$$Q = f(s, L; T) \equiv \lambda^{-1} f(\lambda s, \lambda L; T) \tag{1}$$

and $f()$ concave in (s, L) jointly; $f()$ can be smoothly differentiable in the neoclassical fashion, or it can take the fixed-coefficients form $f(Min[s/\alpha, L/\beta]; T)$ where (α, β) are positive constants that can be set equal to unity by proper choice of input units. For brevity, I analyze the neoclassical case.

Using the rate of interest (r) as a discount factor, economists like von Thünen and Irving Fisher favored cutting trees when percentage growth of gross lumber just equals the interest rate, giving T_1 as optimal age where D's slope just equals r on ratio chart. Boulding and those who say, maximize internal rate of return, select lower T_i where slope of ray through E is at its steepest because of tangency at I. Correct competitive solution is that of Martin Faustmann (1849), which maximizes *present discounted* value over infinity of cycles (not just one cycle as with Fisher): correct T_∞ is between T_i and T_1 and maximizes land rent of steady-state forest. If $r \to 0, T_\infty \to T_n$, the point at which the net sustained yield is maximized.

Competitive equilibrium requires, for given $(r, W/P)$,

$$0 = \underset{T,s,L}{Max} \{f(s, L; T)e^{-rT} - (W/P)L - (R/P)s \int_0^T e^{-rt} dt\} \tag{7}$$

$$= f(s_\infty, L_\infty; T_\infty)e^{-rT_\infty} - (W/P)L_\infty - (R/P)_\infty s[1 - e^{-rT_\infty}]r^{-1}$$

where $[L_\infty/s_\infty, T_\infty, (R/P)_\infty]$ are roots of

$$e^{-rT} \partial f(1, L/s; T)/\partial L = W/P \tag{8a}$$

$$e^{-rT} \partial f(1, L/s; T)/\partial s = (R/P)[1 - e^{-rT}]r^{-1} \tag{8b}$$

$$\partial f(1, L/s; T)/\partial T - rf(1, L/s; T) = (R/P) \tag{8c}$$

These equations are not all independent; and, of course, even if total land available for forestry, $\bar{s}$, is knowable in advance because such land has no other viable use, we need to know the consumer's demand for labor, and the workers' supply of labor to forestry as against alternative uses, before the extensive scale of (Q_∞, L_∞) are determined. It is worth noting that, in the steady state, there is a fundamental three-variable factor-price frontier of the form

$$r = \psi(W/P, R/P) \tag{9}$$

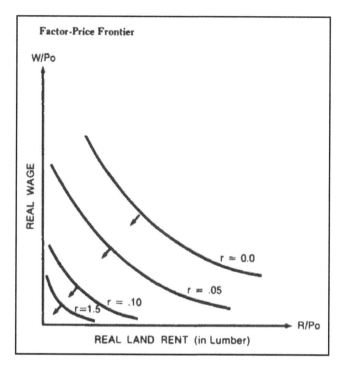

Figure 3. The higher the rate of interest, the lower will be the land rent that can be earned in forestry for each real wage given in terms of lumber price. The tradeoff between such real wage rates and land rents will be the convex contours of frontiers shown here; however, equal increments of profit rate may have quite unequal shift effects upon contours.

where ψ is a monotone-decreasing function that has contours that are convex. Figure 3 shows such contours for equi-spaced values of r: the fact they are alternately bunched and spread out indicates that, in the Sraffa fashion, the relation between r and any one variable can be wavy, with variable curvature.

Simple General Equilibrium: Static and Dynamic

An oversimplified case can illustrate the general equilibrium of lumber and other prices, and can show that some efficiency properties are produced by that equilibrium. Suppose the total supply of land is fixed at $s = \bar{s}$, and that it is suitable only for forestry. Suppose the total steady-state supply of labor is fixed at $\bar{L}$, to be divided between L for forestry and $\bar{L} - L$ for the other (composite) good. Let Q be the steady-state output of wood, as produced by the production function in (1′); and let C be the output of the other good, which is producible instantaneously from $\bar{L} - L$ alone, by $C = (\bar{L} - L)/c$. Finally, suppose everyone spends his income on lumber and the other good in the same way whether rich or poor, and in the same way as does any other person. Therefore, demand curves can be regarded as generated by the "homothetic" collective utility function, $U[C, Q] \equiv \lambda^{-1}U[\lambda C, \lambda Q]$, where U is a concave first-degree-homogeneous function with standard regularity properties. With the interest rate at which society neither saves nor dissaves given by time preference rate ϱ, so that $r = \varrho > 0$, the full equilibrium is defined by

$$C = (\bar{L} - L)/c$$

$$Q = f(\bar{s}, L; T) \tag{10a}$$

$$W/P_c = c^{-1}$$

$$W/P_Q = e^{-\rho T} \partial f(\bar{s}, L; T) \partial L \tag{10b}$$

$$P_Q/P_c = c^{-1} e^{\rho T} [\partial f(\bar{s}, L; T)/L]^{-1}$$

$$\partial f(1, L/\bar{s}; T)/\partial T - \varrho f(1, L/\bar{s}; T) = (R/P_Q) \tag{10c}$$

$$P_Q/P_c = \frac{\partial U(C, Q)/\partial Q}{\partial U(C, Q)/\partial C} \tag{10d}$$

Here (10a) gives the steady-state production functions. (10b) gives the labor and land marginal productivity relations, discounted when necessary, and with the implied steady-state price rations. (10c) gives the Faustmann optimal-rotation relation to determine T_∞. (10d) gives the needed demand relations. Note that, with T determined, we can use (10a) to express the right-hand side of (10d) in terms of L as the only unknown; substituting the right-hand side of (10b)'s last relation into the left-hand side of (10d), (10d) become one implicit equation for the one unknown, namely L. So an equilibrium does exist (and, under strong sufficiency conditions, it may well be unique). However, is there anything at all socially optimal about this positivistic competitive solution? Is there ever any "intertemporal efficiency" to this market equilibrium? The answer can be shown to be yes in a certain definable sense.

Specifically, imagine a Ramsey planner who maximizes an integral of discounted social utility, with discounting at an exponential rate of time preference, $r = \varrho$, in $\exp(-\varrho t)$. His steady-state optimality relations will be of the exact same form as the steady-state competitive relations.

The following simple example can help to illustrate the general principles involved.

Optimal Programming and Forestry Rotation

Thus, restrict T to only integral values—say to either $T = 1$ or $T = 2$; and replace the equality in (10c) that determines T_∞ by a corresponding inequality condition. And suppose a planner for this society acts to solve a Ramsey (1928) optimal-control problem, namely for t restricted to integral values,

$$Max \sum_{t=0}^{\tilde{\tilde{}}} U[C(t), Q(t)]e^{-\rho t} \text{subject to}$$

$$C(t) \le c^{-1}[L - L_1(t) - L_2(t)]$$

$$\bar{S} \ge S_1(t) + S_2(t) + S_3(t) \tag{11}$$

$$L_i(t) \ge 0, S_i(t) \ge 0$$

$$Q(t) = f[S_1(t-1), L_1(t-1); 1]$$

$$+ f[Min[S_2(t-2), S_3(t-1)], L_2(t-2)],$$

with specified initial conditions

$$L_1(-1), S_1(-1), S_2(-2), S_2(-1), S_3(-1).$$

Such a problem is known to have a determinate solution, with implied optimal T_∞ rotation periods that can prevail at each time. And normally it will have the property that as $t \to \infty$, the optimal solution approaches the "turnpike" defined by the steady-state equations (10) above, once they are modified for discrete time periods. Of course, for still lower Q, a different solution will be optimal, and presumably the optimal T_∞, call it $T_\rho = 1$, becomes optimal in the steady state. See Samuelson (1973) for indicative analysis concerning the dynamic aspects of profit-including prices.

Non-Steady-State Considerations

The forester's notion of sustained yield is a steady-state notion. The economist's shorter rotation period for the forest, due essentially to a positive interest rate, is also a steady-state notion. But life is not now in a steady-state. It never was. It never will be. Incessant change is the law of life. You might correctly infer from this that economists' simple notion of stationary equilibrium needs to be generalized and replaced by the notion of a perpetual Brownian motion, as dramatized by the perpetual dance of the colloidal particles one sees in the microscope as they are buffeted to and fro around an average position of equilibrium by ever present molecules, numerous and random, but unseen. A beginning has been made at the frontier of modern economics toward replacing equilibrium by an *ergodic probability distribution*. Since my time here is limited, I shall only refer to the works of Mirrlees (1965), Brock and Mirman (1972), R.C. Merton (1973), Samuelson (1971). But it is not the purely probabilistic perturbation of equilibrium that is important for the great debate on sustained yield. What is important is the realistic presence of *systematic trends* or *transients*, which move away from one steady-state equilibrium and which need not settle down to a newer one. It is no paradox that steady-state analysis is useful in the understanding of realistic trend analysis.

Foresters are concerned with sustained yield precisely because they have livèd in a world where virgin stands have been decimated. It is only too easy to understand why, with new technologies and consumer tastes and with the cheapening of transport of exports to affluent

North America and Western Europe, much land that was once devoted here to trees is transferred to other uses.

We have seen that the rotation age in the virgin forest is greater than what competitive enterprise will countenance. Indeed, were it not that, so to speak by accident, historical governments own much timber land, there would be even fewer trees in North America today. Our analysis warns that applying what is sound commercial practice to government's own utilization of public forests, or what is the same things, renting out public land to private lumbering interests at the maximum auction rent competition will establish—this is a sure prescription for future chopping down of trees.

No Trees Left?

Is this prospect a good or bad things? That cannot be decided in advance of lengthy discussion. Surely, from the vantage point of the final third of the twentieth century, few will agree with the beginning-of-the-century claim of Dean Fernow (1913) that wood is our most important necessity, second only to food in societal importance. Wood is only wood, just as coal is only coal, plastics are only plastics, and, some would say, as bubblegum is only bubblegum. Proper transient analysis does not justify the implied fear that, once forests cease to be cultivated at maximum sustained yield, the descent is inevitable to the hell of zero timber anywhere in the world where we engage in trade. As wood becomes scarce, it will become more expensive. As it becomes expensive, people will economize on its use. But so long as there remain important needs for wood that people will want to satisfy, the price of wood will rise to the level necessary to keep a viable supply of it forthcoming. This in a sense is a "doctrine of sustained yield," but of course not the traditional forester's doctrine of maximum sustained yield. Indeed, by contrast with deposits of oil, coal peat, and high-concentration ores, all of which are constantly being irreversibly mined, trees bottle up sunshine into cellulose in a reversible cycle.

Nothing said so far should rule out that, in a world where preparation for war is only prudent, governments may have some interest in subsidizing activities that will lower the probability that in emergency times the nation will find itself bereft of steel, uranium, food, energy, and certain kinds of wood. This is not ruled out by sound economics; but it is only fair to mention that economists have a good deal to say by way of criticism of the efficiency with which governments program their subsidies for national defense purposes.

Conservation and Flood Control

When people in a poor society are given a choice between staying alive in lessened misery or increasing the probability that certain species of flora and fauna will not go extinct, it is understandable that they may reveal a preference for the former choice. Once a society achieves certain average levels of well-being and affluence, it is reasonable to suppose that citizens will democratically decide to forego some calories and marginal private consumption enjoyments in favor of helping to preserve certain forms of life threatened by extinction. It is well-known that clearcutting forests is one way of altering the Darwinian environment. Therefore, pursuit of simple commercial advantage in forest management may have as a joint product reversible or irreversible effects upon the environment. When information of these tradeoffs is made available to the electorate, by that same pluralistic process which determines how much shall be spent on defense and other social goods, and how much shall be taxed for interpersonal redistributions of income, the electorate will decide to interfere with laissez-faire in forest management. This might show itself, for example, in forest sanctuaries of some size located in some density around the nation: the optimal cutting age there and indeed the whole mode of timber culture will have little to do with Faustmann copybook algorithm. Or, putting the matter more accurately, I would have to say the future vector of real costs and real benefits of each alternative will have to be scrutinized in terms of a generalization of the spirit and letter of the Faustmann-Fisher calculus.

Everything said about species conservation can, with appropriate and obvious modifications, be said about the programming of a nation's geographical resources to provide benefits for vacationers, campers, sportsmen, and tourists. Even the unspeakable fox hunter is an endangered species, and it is part of the political decision-making process to decide at what sustained level he is to be permitted to flourish.

Beyond pointing out these simple truisms, I need only mention in the present connection that, when a sophisticated cost-benefit calculus is applied to each of these areas, it is unlikely the optimal solution will include many virgin forests located in inaccessible places. Land use is shot through with externalities. Zoning, public regulations, and various use taxes will presumably be the rational way recommended by economists who study these matters. The organization of land use activities is likely, in the good society, to fall heavily inside the walls of government and regulatory authorities; but there seems reason to believe part of the problem can be effectively franchised out to enterprisers motivated by the hope of financial return. So far, in awarding television licenses or gasoline and restaurant franchises on public highways, governments have been disappointing in the efficiency with which they have worked out such arrangements. But this does not necessarily mean that turning over our landscape to the untender mercies of push-shove laissez-faire is better, or more feasible, than improving the efficiency with which the public sector organizes these activities.

Earlier I accepted the denial that externality problems which crop up in fisheries are equally applicable to forest economics. But that was in connection with the forest merely as a producer of cellulose. Ecologists know that soil erosion and atmospheric quality at one spot on the globe may be importantly affected by whether or not trees are being grown at places some distance away. To the degree this is so, the simple Faustmann calculus and the bouncings of the futures contracts for plywood on the organized exchanges need to be altered in the interests of the public (i.e., the interests of both Pareto-optimality and interpersonal-equity). Again, when the implied optimal sustained yield pattern comes to be estimated, it might well involve numerous clusters of trees planted hexagonally over much of the nation's terrain, rather than huge isolated forest reserves.

The Claims of Posterity

My time is almost up. Yet I've only been able to scratch the surface of what needs to be explored in depth by catholic men of good will. At the least I must conclude by touching on an issue that goes to the heart of the controversy. Suppose that the competitive interest rates which will guide commercial forestry practices turn out to be very far from zero – say, 10 percent or even more. Must one necessarily accept this penalty on the use of time as the untouchable correct rate of discount a good society will want to recognize in its capital and intergenerational decision-making? This is not an easy question to answer. My earlier equation systems (7) and (8) show there are indeed theoretical models from which market solutions emerge which *also agree* with a technocrat's computation of a society's welfare optimum. So perhaps there is some presumption in favor of the market solution, at least in the sense that a vague burden of proof can be put against those who argue for interferences. At least many of today's mainstream economists would so argue.

I personally think the issue is more open. But I do not wish to pronounce on a matter that time does not permit us to do full justice to. Let me simply conclude therefore with some overly brief comments.

(1) Economists like Cambridge's Pigou and Ramsey, or such Rawlsian writers as Phelps and Riley (1974), have asserted that we ordinary citizens in our day-to-day and lifetime decision-making about spending, consuming, and saving actually act in *too myopic* a way. If we display time-preference rate of 6 or 10 percent per annum, those rates are not the law of Moses and the Prophets. When we gather together periodically to form social compacts, set down constitutions, and elect representative legislators, a democracy may well decide that government coercion (involving taxing, fiscal changes in the public debt, and control by the central bank of the money supply) ought to alter the trends of capital formation and the amounts of capital bequeathed by each generation to subsequent generations. This is an argument for having lower interest rates at some future date when the policies described have become effective. It is not necessarily an argument for programming the use of publicly-owned forests now with a hypothetical interest rate much lower than interest rates that prevail elsewhere. The latter rates may very well be needed to ration optimally the supply of capital in its actual limited state.

(2) There is still some debate among economists as to whether the interest rates appropriate for a government to use should be at all lower than those of private enterprise, and in particular, of the smaller private enterprises and corporations. Marglin (1963) has argued in this fashion, and so in a sense Arrow and Lind (1970) seem to have argued. Hirshleifer (1966) has given arguments against such a dichotomy; Diamond and Mirrlees (1971) have applied the powerful techniques of Ramseyian second-best analysis to analyze the problem. Pending the ultimate verdict of the informed jury in this matter, it seems safe to guess that no simple historical notion of "maximum sustained yield" will be likely to be recommended as optimal.

Whatever else my analysis today may have accomplished, I daresay it will provide corroboration to the old theorem that, when economists and forecasters meet to reason together, economists are likely stubbornly to act like economists. This is an indictment to which I would have to plead guilty, and throw myself on the mercy of your indulgent sentence. Let the penalty fit the crime!

Bibliographical Notes

Rather than burden my text with footnotes, I include here some sketchy comments on previous writings. The notion is ancient that wood is so important and the time periods of forestry are so long that the state cannot leave the matter to commercial laissez-faire. See, for example, the Roman and German background as discussed in Fernow (1902, 1913); Fernow takes for granted that the ideas of Adam Smith are pernicious when applied to long-lived forests.

The foresters' notion of "sustained yield," with allowable cut to be regulated by how much the average tree age is above or below the optimal age that maximizes steady-state lumber yield per acre is already present in the 1788 "Austrian Cameral Valuation Method." With a little charity, we might interpret this as an attempt to reduce cut of trees below the age T_g at which $f'(T_g) = f(T_g)/T_g$ (as in my Equation (2)), and to encourage cut at older ages.

In the early nineteenth century discounting future receipts at compound interest had reared its head. A momentary 1820 flash of insight by Pfeil, which he later regretted, called for "a rotation based on maximum soil rent" (Fernow 1913, p. 139), as in my Equation (6). Von Thunen (1826, 1966, Hall English edition, p. 121) seems to anticipate the (incorrect!) Jevons-Fisher relation $f'(T_1)/f(T_1) = r$ (of my Equation (4)) in his statement: "When the right methods are adopted, only trees of the same age will stand together; and they will be felled (just?) before the relative increment in their value sinks to (r =) 5 percent – the rate of interest I have assumed to prevail throughout the Isolated State."

The highwater mark comes in 1849 when Martin Faustmann corrects an attempt by E. F. von Gehren to use present discounted values to put a fair price on (1) forest land taken by eminent domain for alternative agricultural uses, and (2) existing forest stands on that land. Because von Gehren uses too long a rotation age for his postulated interest rate, applies bad approximations to true compound interest, and mistakenly values unripe trees at their then-current wood value rather than at their best future value properly discounted, he arrives at wrong and inconsistent results. He concluded, for example, that land value is negative when he subtracted too high a stand value from total land-cum-stand value.

Faustmann corrects all this, applying the infinite cycle formula – maximum $[\Pr(T)e^{-rT} - WL][1 + e^{-rT} + \ldots]$ for our idealized case – as in my Equation (6b). He shows that evaluating each tree or age-cohort, or evaluating a synchronized forest, must always lead to the *same* result, a truth denied as late as 1951 by Lutz and Lutz (1951, p. 33). I rely on the excellent translation of Faustmann and von Gehren given in Gane (1968). In my quick reading, I judge Faustmann to know how to calculate the correct optimal rotation age; but I cannot recall exactly where he has done so, if he has indeed done so.

By this century, Irving Fisher (1906, 1907, 1930) has made present discounted value calculations standard in the economics literature. However, Fisher (1930, p. 161–165) still incorrectly calculates over one cycle rather than over an infinity of repeated cycles, deducing in effect as mentioned the relation for T_1 of my Equation (2), rather than the right Faustmann-Ohlin-Preinrich-Bellman-Samuelson relation for T_∞ of Equation (6c). Hotelling (1925) also concentrates on one cycle of a machine; and Goundrey (1960) claims the economist writers on forestry like Scott (1955) are still concentrating on one cycle. Lutz and Lutz (1951) give numerous alternatives including the correct infinite-cycle, but they fail to deduce just *when* this correct method is mandatory (and, as noted, they become confused on the synchronized-forest case). Preinrich (1938), Alchian (1952), Bellman (1957) provide more accurate discussion of the infinite-cycle case: but until this present paper, I have not seen an adequate elaboration of the maximum-land-rent aspect of the forestry problem. Hirshleifer (1970, p. 88–90) has the correct Faustmann solution and refers in his work to Gaffney (1957). I have to agree with Gaffney that Fisher is wrong, even though Hirshleifer is right in thinking that his principle of maximizing a *proper* PDV is not wrong. Ohlin (1921), I belatedly discover, gives an exactly correct analysis.

The "internal rate of return," r_i, today quite properly associated with Boulding (1935, 1941 and 3 later editions), was already explicitly or implicitly in Bohm-Bawerk (1889),

Fisher (1907), Keynes (1936). Samuelson (1937) and Hirshleifer (1958) have debunked "maximizing" this r_i as a proper goal for decision-making by either a perfect or an imperfect competitor, but the corpse will not stay buried. Under free-entry and perfect competition, maximizing proper PDV *happens when PDV is zero also* to make r_i, by tautology at a maximum. The only other possible defense for maximum-r_i is farfetched in any application, but has to my knowledge independently been glimpsed or proved by Boulding, Samuelson, Solow, Gale, and Chipman. If there is available to you a time-phased vector of net algebraic cash receipts, which you can initiate at *any* intensity *with no diminishing returns* (as you force down lumber prices, force up wage rates, run out of free forest lands, and bid up the land rent you must pay!), then any dollars that you initially have can ultimately be made, by investment and reinvestment into the postulated golden goose, to grow proportionally to $e^{r_i t}$; hence, having a higher r_i will ultimately come to dominate any lower r_i. However, under these unrealistic assumptions, r_i will come to form r, the market interest rate, itself; for if one could borrow at $r < r_i$, infinite scale would be optimal for this activity, a "meaningless" situation in a finite world; or, in the present application, the fact that trees grow on finite land will require positive rent payments that undermine any excess of r_i over r.

I found Goundrey (1960) a valuable survey, even if in the end he mistakenly comes out in favor of maximum internal rate of return. For the forestry literature on sustained yield, see items like Shepard (1925) and Waggener (1969).

On the proper discount rate to be used for governmental welfare decisions, see Ramsey (1928), Marglin (1963), Arrow and Lind (1970), Hirshleifer (1966), and Diamond and Mirlees (1971).

References

Alchian, A. A., 1952, *Economic Replacement Policy*. The Rand Corporation, Santa Monica, Calif.

Arrow, K. J. & Lind, R. C., 1970, "Uncertainty and the evaluation of public investments," *American Economic Review*, 60, pp. 354–378.

Austrian Government, 1965, "The Austrian command valuation method." *The Forestry Chronicle*. 41, 84–92. English translation of the 1896 republication.

Bellman, R., 1957, *Dynamic Programming*. Princeton University Press, Princeton.

Boulding, K. E., 1935, "The theory of a single investment," *Quarterly journal of Economics*, 49, 475–494.

———, 1941, 1948, 1955, 1966. *Economic Analysis*, Harper & Bros., New York.

Brock, W. & L. Mirman, 1972. "The stochastic modified golden rule in a one sector model of economic growth with uncertain technology," *Journal of Economic Theory* (June).

Chipman, J. A., 1972, "A renewal model of economic growth," *SIAM* (January). Also p. 43–83 in Day R. H. and Robinson, S. M., eds. *Mathematical Topics in Economic Theory and Computation*, Society fur Industrial and Applied Mathematics. Philadelphia, 1972.

Crutchfield, J. A. & Zellner, A., 1962. "Economic aspects of the Pacific halibut fishery," *Fishery Industrial Research* I., U.S. Dept. of the Inferior, Washington, D.C.

Diamond, P. A. & Mirrlees, J., 1971, "Optimal taxation and public production I-II," *American Economic Review*, 61, 8–27, 261–278.

Faustmann, M., 1849, "On the Determination of the Value Which Forest Land and Immature Stands Possess for Forestry," English edition edited by M. Gane, *Oxford Institute Paper* 42, 1968, entitled "Martin Faustmann and the Evolution of Discounted Cash Flow," which also contains the prior 1849 paper by E. F. von Gehren.

Fernow, B. E., 1902, *Economics of Forestry*, Thomas Y. Crowell & Co., New York.

———, 1913, *A Brief History of Forestry*, 3rd Edition, University Press Toronto, Toronto.

Fisher, I., 1906, *The Nature of Capital and Income*, Macmillan, New York.

———, 1907, *The Rate of Interest*, Macmillan, New York.

———, 1930, *The Theory of Interest*, Macmillan. New York, particularly p. 161–165.

Gaffney, M., 1957, "Concepts of financial maturity of timber and other assets," *Agricultural Economics Information Series* 62, North Carolina State College, Raleigh, N.C., September.

Gordon, H. S., 1954, "The economic theory of a common-property resource: The fishery," *Journal of Political Economy*, 62, 124–142.

Goundrey, G. K., 1960, "Forest management and the theory of capital," *Canadian Journal of Economics*, 26, 439–451.

Hirshleifer, J., 1958, "On the theory of optimal investment decision," *Journal of Political Economy*, 66, 198–209.

———, 1966, "Investment decision under uncertainty: Applications of the state-preference approach," *Quarterly Journal of Economics*, 80.

———, 1970, *Investment, Interest and Capital*, Prentice-Hall, Inc., Englewood Cliffs.

Hotelling, H., 1925, "A general mathematical theory of depreciation," *Journal of the American Statistical Association.*" 20, 340–353.

Koopmans, T. C., 1967, "Intertemporal distribution and optimal aggregate economic growth," pp. 95–126 in *Ten Economic Studies in the Tradition of Irving Fisher*, John Wiley & Sons, New York.

Lutz, F. and Lutz, V., 1951, *The Theory of Investment of the Firm* (particularly Chs. 2 & 8). Princeton University Press, Princeton.

Marglin, S. A., 1963, "The social rate of discount and the optimal rate of investment," *Quarterly Journal of Economics*, 77, 95–111.

Merton, R. C., 1975. "An asymptotic theory of growth under uncertainty," *Review of Economic Studies*, 42, 375–394.

Mirrlees, J. A., "Optimum accumulation under uncertainty," Unpublished MS, December 1965.

Nordhaus, W. D., 1974, "The falling share of profits," *Brookings Papers on Economic Activity*, Okun, A. M. and Perry, G. L., eds., pp. 167–217. The Brookings Institution, Washington, D.C.

Ohlin, B., 1921, "Till fragen om skogarnas omloppstid," *Ekonomisk Tidskrift*, "Festschrift to Knut Wicksell."

Phelps, E. S., & Riley, J. G., "Rawlsian growth: Dynamic programming of capital and wealth for intergenerational maxi-min justice," Columbia University and UCLA. (Paper for private circulation, early 1974).

Preinrich, G. A. D., 1938, "Annual survey of economic theory: The theory of depreciation," *Econometrica*, 6, 219–241.

Ramsey, F. P., 1928, "A mathematical theory of saving," *Economic Journal*, 38, 543–559.

Samuelson, P. A., 1937, "Some aspects of the pure theory of capital," *Quarterly Journal of Economics*, 51, 469–496. Also reproduced in Stiglitz, J. E., ed., *Collected Scientific Papers of Paul A. Samuelson, 1*, pp. 161–188, M.I.T. Press, Cambridge, Mass. 1966.

———, 1964, "Tax deductibility of economic depreciation to insure invariant valuations," *Journal of Political Economy* (December) 604–606. Also pp. 571–573 in Merton, R. C., ed., *Collected Scientific Papers of Paul A. Samuelson, 3*, M.I.T. Press, Cambridge, Mass.

———, 1971, "Stochastic speculative price," *Proceedings of the National Academy of Sciences*, U.S.A., 68, 335–337. Also pp. 894–896 in Merton, R. C., ed., *Collected Scientific Papers of Paul A. Samuelson*, M.I.T. Press, Cambridge, Mass. 1972.

———, 1973, "Reply on Marxian matters," *Journal of Economic Theory*, 11, 64–67.

———, 1973, "Optimality of Profit-Including Prices Under Ideal Planning," *Proc. Nat. Acad. Sci. USA*, 70, 2109–2111.

Scott, A., 1955, "The fishery: The objectives of sole ownership," *Journal of Political Economy*, 63, 116–124.

———, 1955, *Natural Resources, The Economics of Conservation*, University of Toronto Press, Toronto.

Shepard, W., 1925, "The bogey of compound interest," *Journal of Forestry*, 23.

Smith, V. L., 1968, "Economics of production from natural resources," *American Economic Review*, 58, 409–431.

Thunen, J. H. von, 1826, *Isolated State*, English edition edited by Peter Hall, 1966. Pergamon Press, London.

Waggener, T. R., 1969, "Some economic implications of sustained yield as a forest regulation model," University of Washington, Contemporary Forestry Paper 6.

Samuelson's *Economics of Forestry in an Evolving Society*: Still an Important and Relevant Article Thirty Six Years Later

GREGORY S. AMACHER

Department of Forest Resources and Environmental Conservation, Virginia Tech, Blacksburg, VA, USA

Not since Faustmann's ground breaking 1849 treatise on the optimal forest rotation has an article been more influential to the field of forest economics than Samuelson's 1976 article, "Economics of Forestry in an Evolving Society". At the time Samuelson wrote that piece, a debate stirred among foresters and forest economists concerning the best time for a private, industrial, or public forest owner to harvest a stand of trees, or in its simplest sense, a tree. The arguments developed in the 1976 article clarified points of debate that had existed since Faustmann was an accountant in Germany searching for ways to levy forest property taxes more fairly. To this day Samuelson's derivations and discussion have without doubt shaped the field of forest economics and effectively framed how economists look at forest policy questions and solutions. Largely, his purpose was to abolish the singular focus foresters of the time (particularly in connection with the National Forest Management Act of 1976) had on achieving the maximum sustained yield (MSY) of an (even aged) forest, a focus that ignores land rent. Even today, the concept of land rent as an opportunity cost of delaying harvesting is what essentially distinguishes how resource economists and non-economists think differently about the management of forest resources (e.g., see Amacher *et al.*, 2009).

Samuelson's main objective was to compare maximum sustained yield interpretations of rotation age with other solutions. He dispelled MSY as a valid economic solution by showing and arguing the importance of including land rents in any economic rotation decision involving forests, when the objective is to maximize the returns that can be captured from land devoted to forest production. To this end, he made clear an important equivalence, under perfect capital markets of course, between three rotation age solutions: the rent maximizing rotation age for multiple rotations that Martin Faustmann correctly solved for in 1849, under conditions of constant prices, forest growth patterns, costs, and interest rates; a single rotation age solution under similar conditions that incorporates annual opportunity costs to holding land (given by foregone returns in the next best use of land); and a single rotation solution where a land sale in a competitive market occurs at harvest time that, again with perfect capital markets, guarantees a land price equal to the Faustmann net present value of all future rotations, assuming there are no other future pressures on the land such as development. These derivations frame the long lived debate over rotation age choices by examining the positions that both foresters and economists had aligned with: the single rotation solution that maximizes only financial returns and ignores rents to land where trees are cut when growth rates equal the market rate of interest, a related approach that maximizes internal rate of return or compares this rate to a hurdle rate, the maximum sustained yield solution that ignores discounting and other opportunity costs such as occupying the site and delaying future rotations but maximizes forest productivity over time, and the Faustmann solution and its equivalent single rotation approaches.

The principles that Samuelson called for in rotation age analysis have underpinned every economic analysis of the problem since then. His idea that land rent is a market phenomenon, and that scarcity of forests is revealed or capitalized in land rent if markets are working "perfectly" has been referred to countless times in articles concerning the forest rotation. This said, to the deliberate reader there is much more to Samuelson's paper than his comparison of rotation solutions and his statements about which ones are correct. Samuelson's thoughts remain a treasure trove of topics that have occupied and still occupy forest and resource economists. Without providing a detailing survey, I will discuss briefly citing classic articles how some subtle points made by Samuelson have shaped our field. Indeed, 36 years on we are still engaged in research encouraged by the comments Samuelson made in his one defining foray into forestry and forest economics.

The first point of interest is Samuelson's mention of the problem of externalities. It has been my experience that many foresters and non-economists often think of economics as a purely financial approach and that economists blindly seek to solve forestry problems in order to maximize only profit from growing trees, rather than, as we actually do, solve such problems to allocate scarce resources for the social good or maximize social welfare however it is defined. The early arguments for maximum sustained yield were that the financial approach would lead to forests that were not as productive in providing ecosystem services or that were cut too soon. Yet Samuelson is very clear in pointing out the debate inherent in social costs and externalities associated with owners and non-owners of forests, and the need to make these part of the rotation solution. Interestingly, in the same issue of Economic Inquiry that published Samuelson's article, Hartman published his famous article (Hartman, 1976) describing how the optimal forest rotation changes if there are non-timber benefits that evolve in a certain way over time and that the landowner values. Hartman derived the first example of Samuelson's externality argument, showing under certain conditions that optimal rotations could in fact be longer than the Faustmann model predicts. This result has held in recent and more dynamic models (Tahvonen & Salo, 1999; Snyder & Bhattacharyya, 1990).

Not surprisingly, the importance of social costs and externalities has been a prolific focus in forestry. Samuelson predicted the types of results that would later be shown when externalities, such as fire risk, have a spatial pattern over a landscape. At first externalities by forest economists were studied in Faustmann or single rotation/land rent models under the limiting assumption of a single forest stand, where a basic external cost arose because a private forest owner did not value non-timber or nonmarket goods produced from his/her forest in the way that these are valued as public goods by society as a whole. Predictably, whether the rotation age is too short or too long at the private solution depends on the nature of these amenities and how they change over time and space (Strang, 1983). However, forest economists have gone much further. We know there can be generational externalities over time in that bequest intentions of forest landowners affect their harvesting decisions and land sale decisions (Tahvonen, 1998; Amacher *et al.*, 1999). We also know much more about spatial externalities and how they can be critical to social costs of private management decisions and even deforestation in tropical countries (Albers, 1996). How amenities and risk mitigation such as fire fuel reduction depend on adjacent land parcels and other landowners (private and public) has also been an important focus of economics research aimed at constructing policy instruments that can provide sustainable market forest goods and ecosystem services over time (Swallow & Wear, 1993).

Underlying all of this work is the issue of understanding the mechanism, complexities and uncertainties that drive the incentives of forest owners and users to make decisions which may not coincide with social decision makers. Samuelson speaks essentially of first best policy instrument problems, where an externality involving forests is corrected by internalizing social costs to those private forest owners or users who ignore them. However, for the past two decades at least there has been an active area of forest policy analysis aimed at examining the second best policy case, where externalities may be present but there are other distortions, such as government revenue constraints, that make it difficult for a social decision maker or government to implement first best policy instruments. In this context there are also government failures, or difficulties, government decision makers face (either due to budget constraints, corruption, or other influences) in designing policies to minimize the social costs from forest-based externalities. And we understand more about how altruism-based externalities, specifically noted as an important issue by Samuelson, result in changes in the long run steady state forest stock in an economy—the work here is still ongoing and far from complete.

Interestingly, and perhaps alarmingly, the modelling of externalities remains fairly simple in policy theoretic models since 1976, even in stochastic models (e.g., Reed, 1993; Conrad, 1997; Alvarez & Koskela, 2007). These are nearly always assumed to be basic functions of time or forest stocking levels which change in a predictable way through time. As economists we need to spend much more effort determining how to model realistic public goods from forests and characterizing how they evolve over time as forests and markets change. Indeed, what is especially needed is empirical validation of how amenities depend on temporal, site, and adjacency factors, along with better understanding of the uncertainties that surely underpin them.

Since Samuelson's words were printed, another large and almost singular focus within forest economics has been, and will probably always be, solving forest rotation solutions under various conditions, and then showing how these solutions are related to Faustmann's solution, the single rotation financial solution, and Samuelson's single rotation/land rent based solution. We know the effects of risk of natural disasters that cause reductions in rents on these optimal rotation ages (first modelled by Reed [1984]), and the impact of unknown future market conditions that may either increase or decrease rents during a rotation; these models often find a shorter optimal rotation age unless costly protection effort can be implemented. In other cases where there is high variability of rent-based market parameters such as prices, optimal rotations can be longer than Faustmann and Samuelson predicted. Interestingly, this basic result derived in Brazee and Mendelsohn (1988) has been found to hold in much more complex models where market risk and volatility are assumed part of a stochastic process that evolves over time (Chang, 2005; Insley, 2002; Willassen, 1998). Rotation decisions in more complex forest level cases have also been examined. This includes understanding the optimal rotation age for multiple age class/forest parcels under both certain and uncertain future market parameters (Haight, 1987; Tahvonen, 2004). We also have examined the issue of a short lived landowner, assumed away in Samuelson under the perfect market assumption, but who in reality may seek to cost minimize during a rotation rather than rent maximize, altruism externalities aside—the results from this cost minimization show that an equivalent rotation solution to Samuelson's single rotation/land rent model does in fact hold under certain conditions involving constraints on volume produced (Brazee & Amacher, 2000).

Despite all of this scholarly work on the optimal rotation solution, and the many extensions that have followed, for which the reader is referred to Amacher et al. (2009) if interested, we have yet to untangle the basic premise Samuelson noted in thinking about the importance of forests in a long run economy. This is the fact that forests are long term investments managed under a complex web of multiple uncertainties. Certainly some risks are correlated or do not fit into the typical Markov assumption of time independence (e.g., Meilby et al., 2001). Further, while all of the articles on forest rotations since Reed (1984) consider parameters that have an unknown realization but known distribution, the fact is that pure uncertainty can exist. In other words, forest landowners and policy makers may not even know the distribution of future market and natural parameters. This is without doubt the case when talking about amenities and non-timber public goods such as ecosystem services that may be spatially and temporally dependent. There are also still very few studies of examining interest rate risk, despite that this parameter is extremely important and discussed specifically in Samuelson's paper (e.g., see Alvarez & Koskela, 2003). And, finally, we have barely if at all begun to study how policies should be chosen when it is difficult to predict how landowner targets of these instruments will change behaviour. But we know governments do not have perfect information given the limitations of current landowner decision models, and there is a growing literature about enforcement difficulties and incentives to cheat that undermine policy implementation.

There remain opportunities for future work we can glean from reading Samuelson's paper. First, the relevance of the perfect market assumption so vital to Samuelson's results should continue to be questioned. It is unclear empirically what types of forest values are actually capitalized into real estate market prices for land. If markets are perfect, all future discounted net rents are reflected in the land price. But we know this is a difficult assumption, because not only are there uncertainties inherent in trees being a long term investment, but we also know there are cases around the world where capital markets do not function perfectly. For landowners in developed countries, work on this topic, largely originating from Scandinavian forest economists and in two period utility-theoretic models, has found varying results concerning effects of policy instruments and the decision to harvest in the short and long run when landowners are credit constrained and cannot borrow and lend freely at market interest rates (Koskela, 1989). In the US, insurance of forest holdings against various risks is generally not available, and this can be an important factor in the decision to establish forests among competing land uses. Samuelson also discusses another issue that has been shown important in these models, and that is the fact that under certain cases a landowner's preferences will not separate from his/her rent maximization decisions. This is true especially when the landowner is credit constrained and values amenities from un-harvested forests.

Unbelievably, much more can be written about the influence of Samuelson's article, such as the issue of common and private property raised in Samuelson when calling neither to abolish public or private ownership, and some of the parallels between fisheries and forests that were not being studied in 1976 but that are today critical for tropical forest policy design. As Samuelson noted, local rather than central control of forests is desired, and in fact this has driven developing country policies from Non-Governmental Organizations (NGOs) like the World Bank for the past several decades. I am fairly confident that upon my next reading of "Forestry in an Evolving Society" I will notice something else Samuelson conjectured which has turned out true.

References

Albers, H. (1996) Modeling ecological constraints on tropical forest management: Spatial interdependence, irreversibility, and uncertainty, *Journal of Environmental Economics and Management*, 30, pp. 73–94.

Alvarez, L., & Koskela, E. (2003) On the forest rotation under interest rate variability, *International Tax and Public Finance*, 10, pp. 489–503.

Alvarez, L., & Koskela, E. (2007) The forest rotation problem with stochastic harvest and amenity value, *Natural Resource Modeling*, 20, pp. 477–509.

Amacher, G., Brazee, R., Ollikainen, M., & Koskela, E. (1999) Optimal forest taxation in an overlapping generations economy with timber bequests, *Environmental and Resource Economics*, 13, pp. 269–288.

Amacher, G., Ollikainen, M., & Koskela, E. (2009) *Economics of Forest Resources* (Cambridge, MA: MIT Press).

Brazee, R., & Amacher, G. (2000) Duality and Faustmann: Implications for evaluation of landowner behavior, *Forest Science*, 46, pp. 132–138.

Brazee, R., & Mendelsohn, R. (1988) Timber harvesting with fluctuating timber prices, *Forest Science*, 34, pp. 359–372.

Chang, F. (2005) On the elasticities of harvesting rules, *Journal of Economic Dynamics and Control*, 29, pp. 469–485.

Conrad, J. (1997) On the option value of old growth forest, *Ecological Economics*, 22, pp. 97–102.

Faustmann, M. (1849) Berechnung des Werthes, welchen Waldboden sowie noch nicht haubare Holzbestände für die Waldwirtschaft besitzen, *Allgemeine Forst und Jagd-Zeitung*, 25, pp. 441–455.

Haight, R. (1987) Evaluating the efficiency of even- and uneven-aged management, *Forest Science*, 31, pp. 957–974.

Hartman, R. (1976) The harvesting decision when a forest stand has value, *Economic Inquiry*, 14, pp. 52–55.

Insley, M. (2002) A real options approach to the valuation of forestry investment, *Journal of Environmental Economics and Management*, 44, pp. 471–492.

Koskela, E. (1989) Forest taxation and timber supply under price uncertainty: Credit rationing in capital markets, *Forest Science*, 35, pp. 160–172.

Meilby, H., Strange, N., & Thorsen, B. (2001) Optimal spatial harvest planning under risk of windthrow, *Forest Ecology and Management*, 149, pp. 15–31.

Reed, W. (1984) The effects of risk of fire on the optimal rotation of a forest, *Journal of Environmental Economics and Management*, 11, pp. 180–190.

Reed, W. (1993) The decision to conserve or harvest old growth forest, *Ecological Economics*, 8, pp. 45–69.

Samuelson, P. (1976) Economics of forestry in an evolving society, *Economic Inquiry*, 14, pp. 466–492.

Snyder, D., & Bhattacharyya, R. (1990) A more general economic model of the optimal rotation of multiple-use forests, *Journal of Environmental Economics and Management*, 18, pp. 168–175.

Strang, W. (1983) On the optimal forest harvesting decision, *Economic Inquiry*, 21, pp. 575–583.

Swallow, S., & Wear, D. (1993) Spatial interactions in multiple-use forestry and substitution and wealth effects for the single stand, *Journal of Environmental Economics and Management*, 25, pp. 103–120.

Tahvonen, O. (1998) Bequests, credit rationing, and in situ values in the Faustmann-Pressler-Ohlin forestry model, *Scandinavian Journal of Economics*, 100, pp. 781–800.

Tahvonen, O. (2004) Optimal harvesting of forest age classes: A survey of some recent results, *Mathematical Population Studies*, 11, pp. 205–232.

Tahvonen, O., & Salo, S. (1999) Optimal forest rotation with in situ preferences, *Journal of Environmental Economics and Management*, 37, pp. 106–138.

Willassen, Y. (1998) The stochastic rotation problem: A generalization of Faustmann's formula to stochastic forest growth, *Journal of Economic Dynamics and Control*, 22, pp. 573–596.

Reflections on Samuelson's *Economics of Forestry in an Evolving Society*

PETER BERCK* & LUNYU XIE**

*Department of Agricultural and Resource Economics, University of California, Berkeley, USA;
**University of California at Berkeley, Berkeley, CA, USA

Paul A. Samuelson called me (Peter) into his office in the fall of 1974 because he thought I knew something about the Faustmann problem, the question of present value maximizing rotation length in a stationary forest setting. While I did know the technical answer to the optimization problem, I was soon to learn that its solution had originally been found by Gustav Faustmann in 1849. More amazingly, its solution had evaded a long list of brilliant analysts.

Samuelson asked me to find him textbooks that treated the rotation problem and we quickly discovered that most got it wrong. It was this wrong headedness that got Barney Dowdle, at the University of Washington, to interest Samuelson in the rotation problem in the first place.

While the technically oriented will certainly take from Samuelson's article (1976) the correct formula in his equation 6, there is much more there.

First, there is a relentless assault on the use of internal rate of return as a proper criterion for anything. As Samuelson (1937) and others have persuasively argued, internal rate of return is not reasonable. Today that is simply accepted. In 1974 it was still "a corpse that will not stay buried".

Second, Samuelson explicitly linked the land rent to the Faustmann problem. Thinking in terms of land rent meant that one could increase the scope of inquiry from just how to manage a forest stand to which forest stands one should manage. American public forest planning revolves as much around the question of which stands are commercial, have a land rent less externality cost that is positive, as it does around how old these stands should be when they are cut. Land rent, of course, determines the allocation of land to forestry versus agriculture or even homes.

Third, there is an exploration of externalities, which are simply rampant in the world of forestry. Samuelson discusses flood control and more generally irreversible changes in the environment. In Samuelsonian fashion, the choice between wood and environment is just like the trade-off made by our electorate "by that same pluralistic process which determines how much shall be spent on defence and other social goods . . ." Yes the famous guns and butter have now reappeared as owls or dimension lumber. Hartman (1976) provides a rigorous and justly famous generalization of the Faustmann problem to the case where there is a positive externality from standing timber. Berck and Bible (1984) spell out the model with standing timber valued, in terms of the standard linear programming model of forestry.

Fourth, there is talk of what the proper interest rate is. The market rate clearly leads to smaller trees than does a lower social discount rate. Here Samuelson is unsure what is right, but with hindsight he gives good guidance. He distinguishes a general need for more capital, including forest capital, to be left to succeeding generations, from leaving just more forest capital. Presumably, if his talk were a bit longer, he would have said that leaving just forest capital is an externality problem and should be dealt with as other externalities by specifically subsidizing the positive external effect. A more general problem of myopia, however, would need to be dealt with by an even-handed subsidy of all capital, letting the market decide which type of capital is best left to our descendants. These few paragraphs in Samuelson's talk make us think that Samuelson might have been more amenable to the arguments for using low interest rates in valuing climate change, the position of Nicholas Stern (2007), than are our American contemporaries, like Bill Nordhaus (2007), who are fundamentally convinced that a time preference rate of "6 or 10 percent per annum" *is* the "law of Moses and the Prophets".

Fifth, there is a long bibliographic note about who worked on this problem, when, and what results they got. The most interesting of these papers is by the trade theorist, Bertil Ohlin. Ohlin (1921) not only gets the formula right, he gives a real forestry example so that managers can see what is at stake.

The Faustmann-Hartman-Ohlin-Hartman et al.-Samuelson problem can be quickly reduced to a calculus problem and then a comparative statics problem. By simplifying notation a little bit we also get a nice condition for an increase in external values to increase the rotation length.

Define $G(L)$ as the net benefits to a harvest at age L for a single rotation. It includes benefits from timber sales $F(L)$ and the environmental benefits $E(L)$. We let α be a shift variable, taking the value of zero for an agent who does not value environmental services and one for an agent that fully values environmental services. This differs from Hartman in $E(L)$, which is the future value of all environmental benefits taken at end of rotation. Hartman builds this up from an integral. Benefits from timber sales are the revenue (price p times volume $V(L)$) minus costs for harvest and replanting c. Here we assume c is a constant. Now we have

$$G(L) = F(L) + \alpha E(L) = pV(L) - c + \alpha E(L)$$

We assume that $V'(L) > 0, E'(L) > 0$ and $V''(L) < 0, E''(L) < 0$. So we have as usual $G'(L) > 0$ and $G'(L) < 0$. We define $G(L)$ as the future value at time L relative to the beginning of the rotation. $G(L)e^{-rL}$ is then the value of that harvest at the beginning of the rotation, where r is the interest rate. There are an infinite number of identical rotations, so the value of these, called the soil expectation value, or *SEV*, is

$$SEV = \max_L \sum_{i=1...\infty} G(L)e^{-riL} = \max_L \frac{G(L)e^{-rL}}{1 - e^{-rL}}$$

The first order condition (after cancelling common terms) is

$$G' - rG\left(1 - e^{-rL}\right)^{-1} = 0$$

It can be rewritten as:

$$(F + \alpha E)' - r(F + \alpha E)\left(1 - e^{-rL}\right)^{-1} = 0$$

or

$$pV' + \alpha E' - r(pV - c + \alpha E)\left(1 - e^{-rL}\right)^{-1} = 0$$

Now that we have reproduced several versions of the well-known Faustmann first order conditions we will show how the rotation age changes with (1) the interest rate r, (2) the price p, (3) the cost c, and finally (4) the shift variable α.

We start by seeing how the FOC vary with the rotation age L:

$$\frac{dFOC}{dL} = G'' - rG'\left(1 - e^{-rL}\right)^{-1} + r^2 G\left(1 - e^{-rL}\right)^{-2} e^{-rL}$$

and substituting from the FOC,

$$\frac{dFOC}{dL} = G'' - rG'\left(1 - e^{-rL}\right)^{-1} + rG'\left(1 - e^{-rL}\right)^{-1} e^{-rL} = G'' - rG' < 0$$

(1) We show the sign of $\frac{dL}{dr}$

$$\frac{dFOC}{dr} = -G\left(1 - e^{-rL}\right)^{-1} + rLG\left(1 - e^{-rL}\right)^{-2} e^{-rL}$$

$$= G\left(1 - e^{-rL}\right)^{-1}\left(-1 + rL\left(1 - e^{-rL}\right)^{-1} e^{-rL}\right)$$

the sign depends on the sign of

$$-1 + rL\left(1 - e^{-rL}\right)^{-1} e^{-rL} = -1 + \frac{rL}{e^{rL} - 1}$$

$$= -1 + \frac{rL}{\sum_{n=0}^{\infty}\frac{(rL)^n}{n!} - 1} = -1 + \frac{rL}{rL + \sum_{n=2}^{\infty}\frac{(rL)^n}{n!}} < 0$$

Putting $\frac{dFOC}{dL} < 0$ and $\frac{dFOC}{dr} < 0$ together gives $\frac{dL}{dr} < 0$, since $\frac{dL}{dr} = -\frac{\frac{dFOC}{dr}}{\frac{dFOC}{dL}}$. Rotation does increase in interest rate.

(2) We show the sign of $\frac{dL}{dp}$

$$\frac{dFOC}{dp} = V' - rV\left(1 - e^{-rL}\right)^{-1}$$

substituting from the *FOC*

$$\frac{dFOC}{dp} = -\frac{\alpha E'}{p} + r\left(V - \frac{c}{p} + \frac{\alpha E}{p}\right)\left(1 - e^{-rL}\right)^{-1} - rV\left(1 - e^{-rL}\right)^{-1}$$

$$= -\frac{\alpha E'}{p} + \frac{r}{p}\left(\alpha E - c\right)\left(1 - e^{-rL}\right)^{-1}$$

$$\text{If} \quad \alpha = 0, \frac{dFOC}{dp} = -\frac{rc\left(1 - e^{-rL}\right)^{-1}}{p} < 0$$

$$\text{If} \quad \alpha = 0,$$

$$\frac{dFOC}{dp} = -\frac{rc}{p}\left(1 - e^{-rL}\right)^{-1} + \frac{\alpha}{p}\left(rE\left(1 - e^{-rL}\right)^{-1} - E'\right) < 0 \, when \, \frac{E'}{E} > r\left(1 - e^{-rL}\right)^{-1}$$

Putting it together with $\frac{dFOC}{dL} < 0$ gives us $\frac{dL}{dp} < 0$, when $\alpha = 0$ or $\alpha > 0$ and $\frac{E'}{E} > r\left(1 - e^{-rL}\right)^{-1}$ So when there is no weight given to environment services, $\alpha = 0$, rotation age decreases as price increases. When environment services are weighted, a sufficient condition for increasing price to decrease rotation age is that the percent increase in environmental benefit exceeds the modified interest rate at the original optimal.

(3) We show the sign of $\frac{dL}{dc}$

$$\frac{dFOC}{dc} = r\left(1 - e^{-rL}\right)^{-1} > 0$$

Putting it together with $\frac{dFOC}{dF} < 0$ gives us $\frac{dL}{dc} > 0$. So increasing cost implies increased rotation age.

(4) We show the sign of $\frac{dL}{d\alpha}$

$$\frac{dFOC}{d\alpha} = E' - rE\left(1 - e^{-rL}\right)^{-1} > 0 \, when \, \frac{E'}{E} > r\left(1 - e^{-rL}\right)^{-1}$$

So $\frac{dL}{d\alpha} > 0$, under the condition $\frac{E'}{E} > r(1 - e^{-rL})^{-1}$.

Therefore, if we have an initial optimal rotation, considering both internal and external benefits, timber and environment, and we weight the environment a little more heavily, the optimal rotation age increases whenever the rate of increase in environmental benefit exceeds the modified interest rate at the original optimum.

In summary, we have shown that so long as the environmental benefits grow at a faster rate than the modified interest rate, increasing cost, decreasing price, decreasing interest rate, and increasing environmental weight all lead to longer rotation ages. In Samuelsonian fashion we should now rename the problem with our names at the end, but instead we will simply note that just as the mantle of Keynes had descended on Samuelson, so did the mantle of Faustmann.

References

Berck, P., & Bible, T. (1984) Solving and interpreting large-scale harvest scheduling problems by duality and decomposition, *Forest Science*, 30(1), pp. 173–182.

Faustmann, M. (1849) On the determination of the value which forest land and immature stands possess for forestry, in M. Cane (Ed) *Martin Faustmann and the Evolution of Discounted Cash Flow*, Paper 42 (Oxford: Oxford Institute).

Hartman, R. (1976) The harvesting decision when a standing forest has value, *Economic Inquiry*, 14, pp. 52–58.

Nordhaus, W. (2007) A review of the "Stern Review on the Economics of Climate Change", *Journal of Economic Literature*, 45(3), pp. 686–702.

Ohlin, B. (1921) Till fragen om skogarnas omloppstid, *Ekonomisk Tidskrift, Festschrift to Knut Wicksell*. [Concerning the Question of the Rotation Period in Forestry], *Journal of Forest Economics*, 1(2), pp. 89–114.

Samuelson, P. A. (1937) Some aspects of the pure theory of capital, *Quarterly Journal of Economics*, 51(3), pp. 469–496.

Samuelson, P. A. (1976) Economics of forestry in an evolving society, *Economic Inquiry*, 14, pp. 466–492.

Stern, N. (2007) *The Economics of Climate Change: The Stern Review* (Cambridge & New York: Cambridge University Press).

Samuelson and 21st Century Tropical Forest Economics

ELIZABETH J. Z. ROBINSON* & HEIDI J. ALBERS**

*School of Agriculture, Policy, and Development, University of Reading, UK; Environment for Development Tanzania; University of Gothenburg; **Environment for Development Tanzania; Oregon State University, USA

1. Introduction

Much of Samuelson's seminal paper on forestry (Samuelson, 1976) implicitly or explicitly addresses rich country settings where market and governance institutions function well and where forests are managed for timber through rotations. Yet, we argue, the central international forestry issue of the last two decades concerns the widespread and rapid deforestation and forest degradation observed throughout much of the tropics in low and middle income countries (that we will refer to as less-economically developed countries, LEDCs, from here on) in the Americas, Africa, and Asia (Laurance, 1999).

A central contribution of Samuelson's paper is an analysis of the optimal rotation period for a forest, and so the focus of his paper is naturally timber, and by implication planted forests. Although private and government owned forest plantations exist in the tropics, most tropical forest land is primary or secondary forest subject to clear cutting, selective harvest, shifting cultivation, and conversion to other uses, leaving the concept of an optimal rotation of little relevance.

But one of the central ideas found in Samuelson's paper, that economists are generally likely to recommend cutting earlier than ecologists and forest managers who typically focus on "maximum sustainable yield" rather than maximum economic yield, resonates with the debate over how and by how much to reduce the relatively high levels of deforestation and forest degradation observed in many LEDCs (Achard *et al.*, 2002). Such countries may, for example, have deforestation rates higher than deemed appropriate by wealthier countries variously due to a perceived need to convert raw resources into income in the near term; higher social discount rates due to poverty; and a lack of ability to capture as cash various benefits from standing forests.

In this brief paper we build off several comments or tacit assumptions in Samuelson's article to address issues of forest economics in those LEDCs that face forest degradation and rapid deforestation. Several stylized characteristics inform the application of forest economics in such countries, relating to markets and subsistence, property rights enforcement, and externalities (Larson & Bromley, 1990). We therefore argue that Samuelson's paper remains relevant to debates over forest use, particularly whether to cut or conserve, but that it has a very different relevance from when it was first published, and arguably one with far wider ranging consequences in an era of climate change and continuing loss of tropical forests.

2. Institutions: Markets and Property Rights

> ... if I own yonder acre or have leased it from a public or private owner, and if I desist in chopping down a tree that is not yet ripe, I expect to find it still there when I do come to chop it down. In return for this exclusive use of my own area of cultivation, I expect to pay a land rent. If I own the land outright, I pay it to myself at an opportunity cost rate that is perfectly well determined in a freely competitive market (p. 119, paragraph 1).

This quote from Samuelson contains a tacit assumption that property rights function well in the forest setting considered, whether the forest landowner is public or private. Yet, property rights in many LEDCs can be ill-defined; defined only through removing trees; or inadequately enforced (Heltberg, 2002). Economic analysis of forest use and land cover in this context must, then, explicitly examine how incomplete property rights influence forest management by landowners and influence illegal timber harvest, forest conversion, and forest degradation by other people (Clarke *et al.*, 1993). If the incentives of timber values or cleared-land values outweigh the disincentives associated with being caught and punished for undertaking illegal forest activities—often a reality in LEDCs where forest managers rarely have sufficient budgets to deter all illegal activities—even public forest landowners cannot "expect to find [the timber] there when [s/he] comes to chop it down." As in the case of fire risk, the risk of illegal harvest/clearing induces owners and managers to harvest earlier or more than in a context of well-defined and enforced property rights. With lack of funds for enforcement of property rights, illegal timber production causes deforestation at higher rates than preferred by those countries.

Poverty and limited market access in rural forested areas in LEDCs can also lead rural people either to convert land to agriculture, which leads to permanent deforestation, or to harvest fuelwood and non-timber forest products from forests, which leads to forest degradation. Villagers may convert forest to farmland because it is more cost effective than farming more intensively on existing farmland, especially with poorly enforced property rights for the forest land. In some contexts, clearing land is tantamount to establishing ownership. In addition, villagers may clear more land because, with limited enforcement, someone else may clear the forest for agricultural land for themselves or simply to harvest timber, which causes everyone to lose access to that forest. Where markets for products and labour are thin, villagers have little cash and are likely to meet most or all of their fuel needs by extracting from nearby forests that they do not own (Robinson *et al.*, 2002). Products extracted from forests can represent very large fractions of rural households' effective livelihoods (Cavendish, 2002). Rural people critically depend on forest resources but that extraction often occurs illegally in response to low levels of enforcement of forest property rights. Although that extraction provides important benefits to rural people, it causes forest degradation. That extraction, paired with other extractive activities for timber and charcoal by extractors from afar, occurs due to the lack of property rights enforcement in many countries and contributes to widespread forest degradation (Albers & Robinson, 2012).

3. Externalities

Indeed, if the externalities involved [in forestry] could be shown to be sufficiently important, I am naïve enough to believe that all economists would be found on the side of the angels, sitting thigh next to thigh with the foresters (p. 117, paragraph 3).

Ecologists know that soil erosion and atmospheric quality at one spot on the globe may be importantly affected by whether or not trees are being grown at some distance away (p. 141, paragraph 2).

Economists and ecologists alike now recognize the role of tropical forests in generating positive externalities such as biodiversity and climate control. Because a large proportion of the benefits of these externalities may accrue to people outside of the tropics, even national government decisions may cause too much deforestation from an international social perspective.

Increasingly, particularly in LEDCs, economists are identifying, valuing, and creating markets for non-extractive use values of forests and therefore situations in which forests are more valuable maintained rather than cut down. These non-use values help to align the "economist's" verdict on the value of a tree remaining in the forest versus being cut down with the ecologist's supposed preference for keeping a tree uncut for longer periods. Payments for Environmental Services (PES) is one such approach that rewards communities for protecting forests, or for reforestation, that provide services valued at some distance from the forest. Examples include China's sloping land conversion programme that compensates rural households for reducing deforestation and converting farm land to forest to reduce flood risk in the Yangtze and Yellow rivers (Bennett, 2008).

REDD (Reduced Emissions from Deforestation and Degradation) is currently perhaps the most high profile PES opportunity for tropical forests (Albers & Robinson, forthcoming). The recognition that loss of forest biomass is estimated to account for between 12 and 17 percent of annual greenhouse gas emissions has focused yet further attention on the non-realized value of tropical forests. REDD is a mechanism for providing financial rewards to countries that reduce carbon emissions caused by the loss and degradation of their forests. As such, REDD resembles other PES programmes adopted to reward communities for not cutting down nearby forests.

In Samuelson's world, over three decades ago, economists are painted as likely enemies of the natural environment, with suggestions that it might not be optimal to keep fish stocks at their maximum sustained level, or that optimal agricultural policy includes growing crops in the arid plain states until the top soil has all blown away. Therefore, through REDD, economists are closer to Samuelson's angels because mechanisms such as REDD rely on and encourage the development of markets, and the economic valuation of previously non-economically valued aspects of forests. If someone is willing to pay land owners and land users for the carbon stored in a forest due to the positive externality that it creates, then the chances that the forest remains standing rather than being cut and degraded increase because the externality is internalized through the PES programme.

Implementing REDD is highly complex and controversial despite being premised on a fairly straightforward concept—that carbon stored by trees has value for which governments and high-polluting industries in richer countries will pay. In many low-income situations, rural households depend critically on forests for timber, fuel, and other non-timber forest products. Where households in LEDCs rely heavily on forests (albeit often illegally) for their key cooking fuels in rural (fuelwood) and urban (charcoal) areas, unless these households are able to switch to alternative fuels, reducing access to these forests is likely to harm livelihoods or simply displace the extraction and production of these biomass fuels to other less protected, non-REDD-designated forests (referred to as "leakage"). Also, in the rush to embrace REDD, there are increasing reports of forest-dependent people being evicted from forested areas. For example, the Worldwide Fund for Nature has recently been criticized for supporting a process that shifted resource control and management from local to regional and global actors and evicted traditional mangrove rice farming households in the Rufiji Delta North in Tanzania, who use a system of natural mangrove regeneration (Beymer-Farris & Bassett, 2012). Unless programmes and markets to pay for positive externalities of forests address this impact of reduced forest use on the rural poor, the solution to the forest externality problem creates other social welfare concerns.

The trend towards creating and using markets to solve forest externality issues moves economists towards alignment with ecologists' aims and Samuelson's angels. But that trend may also lead to the perception of economists in low-income countries as enemies of rural communities. To avoid burdening the rural poor, markets and policies that commodify standing forests need to provide benefits and incentives to the resource-dependent communities, which may imply more sustainable resource use by locals rather than pure forest preservation.

4. Final Thoughts

Samuelson's paper focuses on optimal timber rotations, which have little relevance to managing natural forests in tropical low and middle income countries. Yet Samuelson's paper remains relevant to tropical settings because of its discussion of externalities and the appropriate rate of forest clearing. Further, using incomplete markets and poverty as a lens to reading Samuelson's paper allows us to identify places where an economist's market emphasis can inform policy in rural settings. We hope in this short paper that we have motivated people to read Samuelson's paper in a slightly different light, recognizing that many of his insights address some of the central issues for managing natural forests today.

References

Achard, F., Eva, H. D., Stibig, H.-J., Mayaux, P., Gallego, J., Richards, T., & Malingreau, J.-P. (2002) Determination of deforestation rates of the world's humid tropical forests, New Series *Science*, 297(5583, August 9), pp. 999–1002.

Albers, H. J., & Robinson, E. J. Z. (2012) A review of the spatial economics of non-timber forest product extraction: Implications for policy, *Ecological Economics*, doi:10.1016/j.ecolecon.2012.01.021 (forthcoming).

Albers, Heidi J., & Robinson, Elizabeth J. Z. (forthcoming) REDD, entry for the *Encyclopaedia of Environmental and Resource Economics*.

Bennett, Michael T. (2008) China's sloping land conversion program: Institutional innovation or business as usual? *Ecological Economics*, 65(4), pp. 699–711.

Beymer-Farris, B. A., & Bassett, T. J. (2012) The REDD menace: Resurgent protectionism in Tanzania's mangrove forests, *Global Environmental Change*, 22, pp. 332–341.

Cavendish, W. (2002) Empirical regularities in the poverty-environment relationship of rural households: Evidence from Zimbabwe, *World Development*, 28, pp. 1979–2003.

Clarke, H. R., Reed, W. J., & Shrestha, R. M. (1993) Optimal enforcement of property rights on developing country forests subject to illegal logging, *Resource and Energy Economics*, 15(3), pp. 271–293.

Heltberg, R. (2002) Property rights and natural resource management in developing countries, *Journal of Economic Surveys*, 16(2), pp. 189–214.

Larson, B. A., & Bromley, D. W. (1990) Property rights, externalities, and resource degradation. Locating the tragedy, *Journal of Development Economics*, 33(2), pp. 235–262.

Laurance, W. F. (1999) Reflections on the tropical deforestation crisis, *Biological Conservation*, 91, pp. 109–117.

Robinson, E. J. Z., Williams, J. C., & Albers, H. J. (2002) The influence of markets and policy on spatial patterns of non-timber forest product extraction, *Land Economics*, 78(2), pp. 260–271.

Samuelson, P. A. (1976) Economics of forestry in an evolving society, *Economic Inquiry*, 14, pp. 466–492.

Putting Samuelson's *Economics of Forestry* into Context: The Limits of Forest Economics in Policy Debates

DAVID H. NEWMAN & JOHN E. WAGNER

Department of Forest and Natural Resources Management, SUNY College of Environmental Science and Forestry, Syracuse, NY, USA

Paul Samuelson's 1976 paper, "Economics of Forestry in an Evolving Society (EFES)", is justifiably hailed as one of the most important articles in the field of forest economics. A relatively recent review of the optimal rotation literature found the article to be the second most cited article (Newman, 2002), following only Faustmann's (1849) original study. It pointed the field in a number of important directions and heralded a very rapid expansion in the literature as more individuals began to examine a host of economic questions related to forests and forest management.

However, it is important to consider the context in which Samuelson's work was written. The paper was a keynote presentation at the Economics of Sustained Yield Forestry Symposium held at the University of Washington on 23 November 1974. Professor Barney Dowdle organized the symposium and the speakers, who were not forest economists, came from more mainstream economic disciplines. The symposium was attended by over 150 people and reflected a broad diversity of forestry experience from throughout North America. For years after the symposium, the presentations were copied and passed on to students and practitioners as only two of the papers were actually published (Samuelson's and John Ledyard and Leon Moses') and only Samuelson's was easily accessible.

There were five papers presented at the symposium touching on a variety of issues associated with the topic of sustained yield. In addition to Samuelson, Jack Hirshleifer of UCLA discussed the trade-off between sustained yield and capital theory; John Ledyard and Leon Moses of Northwestern University discussed economic dynamics and land use change in relation to forestry; Marc Roberts of Harvard discussed sustained yield and economic growth; Anthony Downs, then Chairman of the Real Estate Research Corporation in Chicago, discussed sustained yield and American social goals. Together, these papers made a strong argument that worshipping at the altar of sustainability (specifically sustained yield) was not necessarily beneficial, especially when the measure of sustainability was placed only in physical terms.

While sustainability is a commonly used buzzword for a variety of natural resource issues now, the sustainable harvest question in forestry has had a particularly tortured history. The concept of sustained yield, or managing a forest to produce a continued and constant level of timber harvests over time (i.e., harvest less than or equal to growth) is a central concept in forest management. It is generally accomplished by organizing a collection of forest holdings in such a way as to provide constant harvest levels by harvesting a constant area or volume each year. However, when transitioning to this organized state of constancy, there is a significant transition period in which old growth timber is removed and replaced by younger trees.

Since the volume per acre of old growth is so much higher than a second growth forest, a manager is faced with a dilemma in trying to maintain constant harvest levels over time. Because an over-mature forest has a lower growth rate than a second growth managed forest, any management actions that increase future growth allow an immediate increase in the amount of over-mature timber that could be harvested today. This "allowable cut effect" could lead to some highly questionable conclusions: An investment in management actions that would increase future timber yields could generate immediate returns by increasing harvest levels today—thus the return from investing in management always appeared positive. The problem is that investing in management should be tied to the future revenues these actions may generate, not to any change in current harvest levels.

At the time of the symposium, public policy with respect to the management of the public lands in the United States was fully caught up in this dilemma. Traditional forestry was under fire for perceived mismanagement of the nation's forests. In addition, laws affecting forest management, including the Multiple Use – Sustained Yield Act of 1960, the National Environmental Policy Act of 1969, and the Endangered Species Act of 1973 had been passed. There was also the need to reform the law guiding the Forest Service as a result of court ordered prohibitions of clearcutting (The Monongahela Decision). Thus, inserting a discussion of economic efficiency into this milieu was particularly appropriate and appealing. After all, who could argue with trying to provide the greatest net benefits to society from the management of our natural resources?

It was in this setting that Samuelson's discussion threw down a gauntlet regarding what should be our objectives with respect to forest management; namely, providing the greatest economic net benefit as opposed to just physical benefits. Rotation lengths that did not maximize land rents implied potentially large opportunity costs to society. More importantly, reliance on the biological criteria by which foresters based their decision would lead to large social losses. These were the main outcomes from their paper. Virtually all of the analytical outcomes described in the paper had been derived by others (which Samuelson freely admits), but the clarity with which he presents his results and his explanation of the power of them was important. Key results that supported his main outcomes were that land was in fact not a free resource and needed to be included in the determination of harvest timing and that rotation lengths must vary due to economic factors. Thus, "sustainability" should not be the overall policy objective, but rather maximizing social welfare from the forest.

The major problem with physical sustainability as a goal, as portrayed by the participants at the symposium, was the fact that significant opportunity costs were ignored. Hirshleifer compared foresters at that time to modern Druids, who, though they were willing to harvest trees, still worshiped at the altar of sustained yield as their higher calling. Higher economic returns were foregone in order to allow trees to grow older and, because of the allowable cut effect, irrational investments were made to look beneficial. By questioning these outcomes, Samuelson and the others were able to make a strong case for challenging the status quo.

While the economic logic presented by EFES and others at the symposium was strong, the argument for greater focus on economic efficiency was ultimately unsuccessful in affecting actual public forest policy. The National Forest Management Act, passed in 1976, codified maximum sustained yield and non-declining even flow into law and the National Forests were expressly prohibited from managing the public forest estate for maximum economic values. While timber harvests on public lands did increase through the 1980s, they ultimately crashed as a result of environmental litigation, endangered species, and changing management emphases. As a result, the concerns that all the speakers addressed at the symposium, that of increasing inefficiency and loss of public values, have in fact occurred. The National Forests contribute little to the treasury and concerns of forest health and wildfires have led many to question their value.

While the symposium's focus was pointed at managing National Forests, Samuelson's paper helped usher in a renaissance in the economic analysis of the traditional concept of managing forests for commodity outputs but also the more recent concept of managing forest-based ecosystems to produce various goods and services demanded by society. Newman's (2002) study showed a dramatic increase in optimal rotation articles following the publication of EFES and the extensions that authors have developed have only served to highlight Samuelson's insights. Probably the most important extension of EFES was Hartman's (1976) evaluation of the impact of nonmarket values on optimal rotation. Although this paper was actually published before Samuelson's, it is clear that Hartman had read the 1974 draft EFES and utilized it in his discussion. This paper's results, although empirically shown to have a rather small effect on optimal rotations (e.g., Calish *et al.*, 1978), has had a profound effect on our understanding of forest management decision-making. The fact that nonmarket values could increase the value of timberland was clearly understood, but the fact that they also impacted rotation lengths was an important extension of EFES.

Samuelson's mathematical analytics and approach provided a rational voice in the debate concerning, primarily, the management of publicly owned forestlands. Using this approach, he came to a conclusion which was ultimately against the concept of a biologically derived sustained yield rotation. In addition, he tied his analysis to the larger social implications of a public forest management decision—primarily the choice of a rotation age. Furthermore, his analysis touched on aspects of environmental (e.g., externalities and property rights), micro- (e.g., production systems, capital theory, and marginal conditions for maximization) and macro- (e.g., inflation, taxes, general equilibrium, and Pareto optimality) economics. Samuelson's ability to bring all these seemingly wide-ranging concepts to bear on this debate was a significant contribution to the field of forest resource economics. While the focus of this retrospective is on Samuelson's paper, this is not meant to diminish the stature of the other speakers (for example, Dr. Hirshleifer is often described as deserving of a Nobel Prize for his contributions to the field of economics) nor the contributions of the other four papers presented that day.

The legacy of EFES—a revitalization of analysing forest resource management decisions from an economic perspective—was in part due to the breadth and nature of Samuelson's analytics and its accessibility. This enticed researchers from outside the sub-discipline of forest resources economics to examine questions related to managing this resource as well as researchers from within the sub-discipline to broaden their work beyond a narrowly focused optimal rotation question. Finally, the papers from this symposium—Samuelson's in particular—were some of the foundational articles upon which many graduate students of that time developed their research approach and agenda. This inspiration then spread to their graduate students in often very unique and interesting directions. And the process still continues today.

References

Calish, S., Fight, R. D., & Teeguarden, D. E. (1978) How do non-timber values affect Douglas-fir rotations? *Journal of Forestry*, 76(4), pp. 217–222.

Faustmann, M. (1849) On the determination of the value which forest land and immature stands pose for forestry, in M. Gane & W. Linnard (Eds) *Martin Faustmann and the Evolution of Discounted Cash Flow*, pp. 27–55 (Oxford: Oxford Institute).

Hartman, R. (1976) The harvesting decision when the standing forest has value, *Economic Inquiry*, 14(1), pp. 52–58.

Newman, D. H. (2002) Forestry's golden rule and the development of the optimal rotation literature, *Journal of Forest Economics*, 8, pp. 5–27.

Samuelson, P. (1976) Economics of forestry in an evolving society, *Economic Inquiry*, 14(Dec), pp. 466–492.

Samuelson on Forest Economics: An Inadvertent Tribute to Faustmann, and a Few Others

COLIN PRICE

90 Farrar Road, Bangor, Gwynedd, UK

1. Introduction

Paul Samuelson's 1976 paper is one of the most cited in the whole literature of forest economics. Google Scholar listed 472 citations. Hartman's paper on optimal rotation, appearing in the same journal in the same year, also claims 472. But an earlier discussion of the same subject by Bentley and Teeguarden (1965) had 72 citations, and a later review by Newman (2002), 42. This intensity of citation seems strange for a work whose main innovative feature was, on the face of it, the name on the author line.

When the article first circulated among us, the general response of the small group of young forest economists to which I belonged was "so what?" There seemed to be nothing significant in here that had not been part of our day-to-day discourse, whether on the conflict between maximum sustained yield in biological and economic senses, or on precise economic criteria, or on externalities, or on common property resources. The correct solution to the valuation of forest stands had been derived a century and a quarter earlier by the Hessian forester Martin Faustmann (1849/1968). One senses that Samuelson was taken aback by the sophistication of this early work: "In at least one case, the remarkable 1849 German article by Martin Faustmann, the analysis does come close to an essentially correct solution" (p. 469). Samuelson actually identifies no shortcoming at all, except that the condition for optimal rotation—often called "the Faustmann condition"—is not explicitly stated (though it was implicit in that famous work).

At that time, the matter of who had made the first correct statement of the Faustmann condition was under discussion, and Samuelson himself did not resolve the issue. Both Pressler (1860) and Ohlin (1921) had given algebraic statements of the condition, but subsequent scholarship established that descriptive treatment had been given much earlier by Marshall (1808), according to Scorgie and Kennedy (1996). And *that* was based on yet earlier work, as reviewed by Viitala (2012). In fact Faustmann himself, writing anonymously as "F"

(1849), had stated the condition mathematically in the same year as that in which his more famous paper appeared (Viitala, 2006).

In the late 1970s, then, we were familiar with the various concepts of optimal rotation discussed by Samuelson. We knew which ones would give the longer and which the shorter rotations. Textbooks then current (Petrini, 1951; Hiley, 1956; Gregory, 1972) were familiar with Faustmann's work, and tended to favour the Faustmann criterion for optimal rotation. (Johnston et al. [1967], however, used a strange hybrid, maximizing the net present value (NPV) of a single rotation, but including the opportunity cost of *one* successor rotation.) But above all Faustmann's paper, recently translated, was in front of us, and that sufficed to provide us a definitive answer to what was the most valuable rotation.

2. Innovation?

"So what?" . . . So what had Samuelson added to this already-centuries-old discussion, and what had he brought to the fore, that was not already known by those debating the issues? What might one note, in retrospect, that deserves a particular attention within the paper?

- In the central part of the paper, he dwells on algebra-intensive renditions of the problem that would have dissuaded most foresters from reading further. The marginal (first-order) condition for optimality—the Faustmann condition—makes its re-appearance: that the increment in value over the next period should have fallen to the interest on the value of both timber and the land on which it grew (Pressler, 1860; Ohlin, 1921). This is an approach to optimizing rotation that I have subsequently found of practical use, only under circumstances of change between rotations (Price, 1989, chapter 13). And these are precisely the circumstances in which the classical algebraic account is invalid, because the first derivative of one function has to reach equality with a function to which it need not be algebraically related. In any other circumstances, a straightforward numerical calculation of net present value of a perpetual sequence of rotations should be performed, for a number of alternative rotation lengths. Selection of the rotation yielding the highest value is the swifter, even if less elegant, solution than the algebraic one.
- He links the micro-economy of the forest to some general equilibrium equations for the macro-economy. The equations might have represented a new synthesis of interest to theoreticians, but it has not, I dare to surmise, ever been used by a practising forest economist in determining the felling age of a single stand, nor been advanced by any theoretician as a critique of that determined age.
- He takes particular issue with the rotation of maximum internal rate of return (IRR), as proposed by Boulding (1935) and which has since then been sometimes advocated; he notes the improbable condition for the correctness of that criterion—unbounded possibilities for reinvestment in facsimile rotations. He states that "Anyone who misguidedly adopts this foolish [IRR-maximizing] rotation will find that he either goes broke or is permanently sacrificing return on original capital that could be his." But it is not clear that this is true in some sense different from what is true of any other non-Faustmann rotation.
- He does acknowledge that, with environmental externalities, issues other than those determining the Faustmann optimum will affect the rotation length. Other writers (e.g., Hiley, 1956) had earlier noted the effect descriptively, and Samuelson does no more than that. It was left to Hartman (1976), in the same year and the same journal, to introduce a quantitative statement.

- He expresses surprise at the low interest rates used by Faustmann and others (4–5%), and is rather contemptuous about them, "showing"—as though it was not already known to foresters—the severe effect of higher rates over customary rotation periods. He does mention the social time preference rate: it might be lower than commercial interest rates. All this too was familiar territory for our discussion group: I went through the argument that he puts, as an enthusiastic young forest economist in the late 1960s, and thinking myself such a fine fellow, before beginning to question whether all the proceeds of investment really were reinvested at compound interest, and whether even the *social* time preference rate gave due regard to sustainability (Price, 1993).

In the years since the paper was published—well within one temperate forest rotation—the discount rate used by individuals and institutions, many of whom are fully acquainted with the arguments Samuelson deploys, has dropped to and even below the levels of which he was so contemptuous.

3. Missing From the Analysis?

Over several pages Samuelson gives an ordering by length of the various proposed optimal rotations: in rising order, the rotation of maximum IRR, the Faustmann rotation, and the single rotation of maximum NPV. But this is only correct if IRR exceeds the interest rate, which is most unlikely for temperate forests, under the high interest rates he favoured. If this condition is *not* fulfilled, the ordering is reversed: the single rotation is the shortest (because its ending does not bring an obligation to initiate further unprofitable rotations); and IRR longest (because its internally generated interest rate is lower than that externally given).

Moreover, he makes no mention of the "second increment"—the improvement of quality and hence of price with age, which had much occupied Pressler (1860). With this factor included, it is technically possible for the Faustmann rotation to exceed the rotation of maximum sustainable [biological] yield, and indeed it is even quite likely that it will do so at the modest discount rates of which he was so improperly contemptuous.

4. Samuelson and the Watershed Year

Newman (2002) considers the year of publication, 1976, as a watershed year, perhaps because thereafter the "correct" solution for the base case optimum was mostly agreed among forest (and other) economists. Perhaps Samuelson gave a definitive verdict on alternative theories that were still being bandied about in North America at that time, and for all I know may still be today: those who still adhere to such alternatives will probably still not be persuaded.

The year 1976, then, was the time when an eminent mainstream economist, whose name was known to millions of students, put his authoritative seal on what had in essence been discovered 170 years before or even earlier; when he gave support to what most competent forest economics postgraduates of the time could have said, concerning the relationship of maximum sustainable yield and various economic rotations. Thereafter an adaptive radiation into refinements and variants of optimal rotation theory could begin. Newman charts the progress of thinking over the subsequent quarter-century.

I look at all the insights and sophisticated developments in the theory and application of optimal forest rotation determination that have occurred since that time. And I ask: did Samuelson's paper inspire or make possible any of them, and I conclude that it did not. The sense is that it was written by a famous mainstream economist to show forest economists how things should be done, and the fact that it is still often quoted suggests that some authors believe that that was indeed what he achieved. In fact the paper comes to acknowledge that a forest economist not only found the correct solution to a forest economics problem, but that he formalized the technique of discounted cash flow appraisal more than half a century before Irving Fisher (1907) published his work on the subject.

So in this case, Samuelson, who had plenty of innovations of his own to be proud of, simply drew the historical innovations of others to a wider attention. His paper seemed to us then, as it remains to this day, a review, offering nothing that was not already known in a practical sense; and—as a matter of interest only, not of application—connecting capital theory in forestry to that in general equilibrium. Perhaps he was able to persuade mainstream economists that some forest economists were not just lumberjacks with calculators. If so, it could be said that he performed, for both professions, a valuable service.

References

Bentley, W. R., & Teeguarden, D. E. (1965) Financial maturity: A theoretical review, *Forest Science*, 11, pp. 76–87.

Boulding, K. E. (1935) The theory of a single investment, *Quarterly Journal of Economics*, 49, pp. 475–494.

"F". (1849) Anlösung einer Aufgabe der Waldwertrechnung [A solution to an exercise on forest valuation], *Allgemeine Forst- und Jagd-Zeitung*, 15, pp. 285–299.

Faustmann, M. (1849/1968) On the determination of the value which forest land and immature stands possess for forestry (Translated by W. Linnard), *Oxford Forestry Institute Paper*, 42.

Fisher, I. (1907) *The Rate of Interest* (London: Macmillan).

Gregory, G. R. (1972) *Forest Resource Economics* (New York, NY: Ronald Press).

Hartman, R. (1976) The harvesting decision when a standing forest has value, *Economic Inquiry*, 14, pp. 52–58.

Hiley, W. E. (1956) *The Economics of Plantations* (London: Faber).

Johnston, D. R., Grayson, A. J., & Bradley, R. T. (1967) *Forest Planning* (London: Faber & Faber).

Marshall, W. (1808) *A Review of the Reports to the Board of Agriculture: From the Northern Department of England, etc.* (London: Longman, Hurst, Rees & Orme).

Newman, D. H. (2002) Forestry's golden rule and the development of the optimal forest rotation literature, *Journal of Forest Economics*, 8, pp. 5–27.

Ohlin, B. (1921) [translated as] Concerning the question of the rotation period in forestry, *Journal of Forest Economics*, 1, pp. 89–114.

Petrini, S. (1951) *Elements of Forest Economics* (Translated by M. Anderson) (Edinburgh: Oliver & Boyd).

Pressler, M. R. (1860) [translated as] For the comprehension of net revenue silviculture and the management objectives derived thereof, *Journal of Forest Economics*, 1, pp. 45–87.

Price, C. (1989) *The Theory and Application of Forest Economics* (Oxford: Blackwell).

Price, C. (1993) *Time, Discounting and Value* (Oxford: Blackwell).

Samuelson, P. A. (1976) Economics of forestry in an evolving society, *Economic Inquiry*, 14, pp. 466–492.

Scorgie, M., & Kennedy, J. (1996) Who discovered the Faustmann condition? *History of Political Economy*, 28, pp. 77–80.

Viitala, E.-J. (2006) An early contribution of Martin Faustmann to natural resource economics, *Journal of Forest Economics*, 12, pp. 131–144.

Viitala, E.-J. (2012) Discovery of the Faustmann formula in natural resource economics, *History of Political Economy* (forthcoming).

Thoughts on Paul Samuelson's Classic, *Economics of Forestry in an Evolving Society*

ROGER A. SEDJO

Resources for the Future, 1616 P. Street NW, Washington, DC 20036-1434, USA

Paul Samuelson's classic, "Economics of Forestry in an Evolving Society", was originally published in *Economic Inquiry* in 1976. It addressed an issue that has persisted in forestry for well over a century—the issue of the length of the optimal timber harvest rotation. As Samuelson notes, "there has been a tradition in forest management which claims that the goal of good policy is to have 'sustained forest yield' or even 'maximum sustained yield' somehow defined" (p. 466).

Part of the problem, I am convinced, relates to the "somehow defined" notion. Indeed, much of the difficulty is related to the different perspectives of sustainability between economists and biologists. Foresters are typically more fully trained in biology than in finance and economics and so the biological perspective has established a strong foothold in the profession. Furthermore, in many cases there is limited understanding that the differences are tied closely to two different perspectives, and indeed to two different definitions. These definitions are generating two different methodologies and implicit objectives and hence different outcomes.

The financial or economic problem of the optimal harvest rotation was first solved in 1849 by Martin Faustmann in his paper "Calculation of the Value which Forest land and Immature Stands Possess for Forestry". He correctly identified the conditions that lead to the correct solution of the optimal rotation for timber value. For a fixed market price, a homogeneous timber product, and a declining rate of timber growth, he correctly determined the rotation beginning with the establishment of a forest on base ground. He noted that the value of the forest asset increased as long as the incremental timber growth rate exceeded the opportunity costs of the harvested timber, which was equal to the discount rate. However, when the biological growth rate equalled or fell below the externally determined discount rate, the value of the harvested asset exceeded that of the forest asset and a harvest was called for. Thus, the optimal financial harvest should take place when the biological growth rate was equal to the discount rate. The Faustmann results were repeated and refined by analysts including Ohlin (1921) and Bentley and Teegarden (1965) and became widely accepted in economic and financial circles.

However, this view had a competitor among biologists and many biologically oriented foresters. As Samuelson (1976) noted, there has been a tradition in forestry to maximize the sustained yield. It is this tradition that has been in competition with the Faustmann optimal value rotation approach. In this case it is said that maximum sustainability requires that harvests should not occur until growth achieves the "culmination of mean annual increment". In effect, the opportunity cost is viewed as zero, or, stated differently, the discount rate is treated as equal to zero. This approach will generate a forest with a larger stock and a greater harvest but with less than optimal present value, since there is an adjustment for opportunity costs and the delayed harvest.

Samuelson's piece was initially presented as a lecture at a symposium at the University of Washington, at the invitation of Professor Barney Dowdle. Professor Dowdle, my former professor, was well known for initiating controversy and was well aware of the differences between the view of economists and that of most foresters and much of the general public. Thus, he convinced Samuelson, one of the world's most renowned economists, to add his weight to the debates. It was one thing for the policy process to ignore Faustmann's century old treatise or even the current writings of ordinary economists. It was quite another to dismiss the views of the world famous Paul Samuelson.

Samuelson entered the discussion with a host of questions that may not always be viewed as part of the major issue to be addressed. He raises issues such as externalities, appropriate discount rates, the relevant time horizon, inflation and income taxes. Additionally, he discusses an important theoretical question of that period, which related to the efficacy of the internal rate of return criterion versus the discounted present value criterion. These two approaches were vying for acceptance as the more relevant investment criterion. Subsequently, the discounted present value criterion has prevailed, which was fortunate for Faustmann, who essentially used that approach for the harvest question, and was supported by Samuelson. Ultimately, Samuelson's piece added to the weight of science in favour of a present value approach to the determination of the harvest rotation. Also, those involved in these issues increasingly came to realize that the economic criterion and the biologically driven notion of maximum sustainable yield were really two separate ways of looking at the forest harvest issues and these approaches would, by definition, give different results.

In the intervening period much of the debate has abated. Timber production has become more specialized even as the other values of forests are increasingly appreciated. Planted forests are gradually becoming increasingly dominant as sources of industrial wood (Bael & Sedjo, 2007). Commercial forests, particularly, planted forests, are usually driven by concerns of profitability and utilize an economic harvest rotation perspective as faster growth of newer utilized species has often resulted in the rotations in these forests becoming quite short.

At the same time management of many other forests often has become driven by objectives other than wood production. The US Forest Service current harvest levels, for example, have been roughly 16% of what they had been in the 1987–88 period. Non-timber objectives are now driving Forest Service management. In the US this change has occurred largely, but not exclusively, on public forest lands. But private forestlands are also sometimes affected as their management may now be associated with conservation reserve programmes where optimal financial rotations may no longer be entirely appropriate for their new objectives. For these forests the harvest rotation lengths have ceased to be as important as formally. Indeed, in many cases rotation and harvest decisions have given way to issues of sustainable natural forests where commercial logging and harvest rotation issues play, if any, only a minor role.

References

Bael, D., & Sedjo, R. (2007) *Toward Globalization of the Forest Products Industry: Some Trends* RFF Discussion Paper 06-35, August 2007. Available at http://www.rff.org/rff/Documents/RFF-DP-06-35.pdf (accessed 9 July 2012).

Bentley, W., & Teegarden, D. (1965) Financial maturity, a theoretical view, *Forest Science*, 11, pp. 76–87.

Faustmann, Martin (1849) Calculation of the value which forest land and immature stands possess for forestry, *Journal of Forest Economics*, 1, pp. 7–44.

Ohlin, B. (1921) In Ekonomisk Tidskrift, vol 22. (Reprinted in English) Concerning the Question of Rotation Period In Forestry, *Journal of Forest Economics 1*, (1995) pp. 89–114.

Samuelson, Paul (1976) Economics of forestry in an evolving society, *Economic Inquiry*, 14, pp. 466–492.

Index

For Product Safety Concerns and Information please contact our EU
representative GPSR@taylorandfrancis.com Taylor & Francis Verlag GmbH,
Kaufingerstraße 24, 80331 München, Germany

Printed and bound by CPI Group (UK) Ltd, Croydon, CR0 4YY

08/05/2025

01864520-0002